I0085631

UFOs and ALIENS
'THE Good Old Days'

Ufos and Aliens in the Early Twentieth Century

MOIRA McGHEE

UFOs and Aliens – The 'Good Old Days'

Reports of UFOs and Aliens in the early twentieth century.

Copyright 2023 by Moira McGhee . All rights reserved.
Printed in Australia. No part of this book may be reproduced in any manner whatseoever without written permission

INUFOR books may be purchased for business, educational or sales promotional use. For information address: INUFOR. P.O. Box 169, Katoomba N.S.W. 2280 Australia.

INUFOR Web Sites; www.independentnetuforesearchers.com.au. www.facebook.com/inufor.
Email: ind.net.ufo.res@bigpond.com

First INUFOR Paperback Edition published in July 2023

ISBN-978-0-9587-045-1-9

CONTENTS

CONTENTS

INTRODUCTION

During the 'Good Old Days', which were probably the most important in ufology, and ended in the 1970s, I was still a very young researcher/investigator. Reports of strange craft and beings flooded in from all levels of the public, military and academia. Before officialdom clamped down on public reporting and discussion, the entire subject was exciting, and full of the promise of the new discovery of other life in the Universe.

Researchers studied ancient documents and manuscripts, and the legends of indigenous peoples, with accounts of what appeared to be UFOs and alien visitors. Old newspapers, many from libraries using microfilm and magazines, were meticulously checked. Despite often being ridiculed, we all ploughed on with what we considered to be possibly one of the most important issues of the day. Armed with Geiger counters and specimen containers, we visited sites and witnesses to thoroughly investigate all reports.

A few years ago, I decided to record the information I had researched, investigated and amassed in several books which have taken me a lot of hard work and time to write. Hopefully, all this data, lodged with several government libraries in hardcopy format, will still be available for many years after I have 'shuffled off' this Earth.

In 2002, researcher Barry Greenwood, documented some problems which have become apparent in recent years; *'As of this writing, the modern era of the UFO controversy is 54 years old. If one counts earlier manifestations of odd aerial phenomena, then the controversy is much older still. A vast majority of the record of UFOs exists on paper, with the remainder contained on audio and videotape, photographic film, electronic storage, (computers), and in the memories of living witnesses and participants.'*

He noted that the most fragile of these records were the memories of the people involved, and unless recorded and documented at the time, lost when witnesses and others reached old age and subsequently died. It is also a fact that photographic film, as well as audio and videotapes, deteriorate over time. Greenwood advocated the need for researchers to take steps to transfer the information to 'a more stable containment'.

He could see a problem when so much information is now stored electronically or on the internet, and expressed his dismay that many libraries have replaced their 'hardcopy' holdings, especially of newspapers and periodicals, with computers, deeming this practice to be 'space saving and ease of use'; *'However, unless the information on the internet is backed-up in duplicate, the information can be removed forever in a blink of an eye, or in this case a 'click' of a mouse. Computer viruses can destroy records easily.'*

Greenwood also commented on how the lifetime records of investigators and even 'groups', can be lost, maybe forever. I was also aware of cases when investigators either died, or went into aged care, and uninterested relatives threw everything into the trash. One colleague, upon learning he had a terminal illness, gave me all his research. In another case, I managed to rescue a van full of records and valuable material before it reached the local waste disposal facility.

Greenwood said; *'In other cases, records are sold to dealers where they can, and have, disappeared into private collections. One such example are the records of Robert Giglio, a UFO investigator from New Hampshire, whose records, primarily tape recordings of witnesses, were turned over to a private individual who has yet to make any of the tapes available after more than a decade. Only a tiny percentage of donated UFO files go to a public institute or relevant organisation.'*

In 1978, New Zealand investigators, Fred and Phyllis Dickeson, both retired wartime N.Z. Air Force officers, summed up the early impressions and situation;

'In the early 1950s, pioneers in the field were mostly quite gullible, believing that the UFO visitors were friendly, coming from outerspace to help mankind. It was idealistic, all 'brotherly love, peace and harmony'. The thought of rebuilding a grand new world for humanity, with their guidance and knowledge, was a beautiful concept, especially after the chaos of World War II.

'It was also the period of satellites and space probes, first venturing into space, going to the Moon and ushering in the Space Age – all very exciting and an era of great hope and promise. During this time, the rivalry between the two super-powers, America and Russia, increased in the space-race, each making claims

as they advanced....the race was on. So too, was the 'Cold War' between the big powers, when atomic tests were carried out, all too frequently on a gigantic scale.'

Even though some people were having contact with friendly humanoid beings, there were already some disturbing incidents in our skies, and then came the more evil 'Greys' and accounts of people being injured, or abducted from their homes and subjected to unpleasant medical procedures.

By the end of the 1960s, the benevolent aspect was fast fading, and entering a more sinister stage, as hostile reports accelerated. The 'Good Old Days' of trust and innocence were coming to an end.

The Dickesons also had some more wise words to say; *'Another point to be considered also was, that man's historic Epic of the Moon landing in July 1969, closed the decade, and brought new dimensions to the Space Age and the Sixties to a dramatic conclusion, paving the way for further probes into space.*

'It also proved that our Solar System planets were not inhabited by beings like ourselves. This was a great blow to many who once thought or were told we were being visited by Venusians, Martians etc. There are, however, quite a number still clinging to this concept, who cannot accept scientific findings that these planets are not inhabited by beings like ourselves.'

Like the Dickesons, I moved on to a new era of research, however I could not dismiss the thought that these visitors may have bases on other planets within our Solar System.

As time went by, all competent investigators had to seriously consider whether the strange objects being seen in the sky were in fact our own advanced craft. During the 1950s and 1960s, many major American defence contractors, including Lockheed, Convair and Boeing, were secretly working on the design and manufacture of different types of aircraft, including some with 'saucer' shapes. It is not known how many, at the time, progressed beyond the drawing board to 'black project' prototypes. If they were in fact 'our own', it seems unlikely that they would be flown in full public view.

Many of the reports I have included in this book may well have been our own prototypes. It is up to the reader to decide for themselves.

UFOs have been around for many centuries, however, most researchers consider that the birth of modern ufology commenced with the sighting by American pilot Kenneth Arnold in 1947. Not only is this not essentially accurate, I have discovered that few, in the 21st Century, are aware of the full details reported at the time.

It all began three days earlier, on 21st June 1947, when harbour patrolman Harold Dahl, along with his fifteen year old son and two patrolmen, were on harbour patrol near Maury Island in Puget Sound, off Tacoma, Washington.

They saw, 2,000ft above their boat, six hovering objects, which resembled 'inflated inner tubes'. Five were circling around the sixth as it descended to a height of about 500ft. They later said that they could now determine that it appeared to be metallic, circular, 100ft in diameter and had no jets, rockets, wings or propellers. It had an 'observatory window' on the underside, and symmetrically placed portholes around the perimeter. (But was this true?)

Before ascending to join the others, it discharged a cloud of aluminium type particles, some of which the witnesses collected, into the water. The strange craft then all sped off, at high speed, towards the Canadian border.

These are essentially all the details that most people, interested in the UFO phenomenon, are aware of. Investigator, John Keel, dug a little deeper, and in his article, *'The Maury Island Caper'*, published his findings;

'The truth is fundamentally simple. In 1947, the Atomic Energy Commission's, (AEC), huge metallurgical plant at Hanford, Washington, was processing plutonium and creating vast quantities of radioactive waste. Getting rid of this material was already a major problem, and one method was to load it into cargo planes and dump it unceremoniously into various large bodies of water....such as Puget Sound and Tacoma harbour. Dahl happened to be an unwitting witness to one of these dumping operations.'

The pilots had seen the harbour men photographing them, and apparently Dahl was 'persuaded' to change his description of the craft they had sighted. Keel wrote; *'The 'Man-in-Black' who visited Dahl was actually an agent for the AEC, intent on covering up what was even then an illegal dumping of dangerous atomic waste.'*

On 24th June 1947, Kenneth Arnold, a respected Idaho businessman, was flying, in his personal single-engine Callier plane, from Chehalis to Yacoma,

Washington. He was returning from a trip to install fire-fighting apparatus in Chehalis, and whilst at the airport, learned that there was a $5,000 reward for anyone who could locate a Marine aircraft which had gone down in the mountains. For an hour he had diverted from his planned route to help search for the large military Marine Corps C-46 transport plane, which had reportedly disappeared near Mt. Ranier the previous night.

Suddenly, as he proceeded back to his previous course, he observed nine peculiar looking objects, of a 'wing' or 'boomerang' shape, flying in a diagonal, five mile long chain-like line, from north to south at an altitude of about 9,000ft. He estimated their speed as being about 1,600 or more miles per hour.

After arriving at his final destination, Pendleton, Oregon, Arnold went to report the incident to the local FBI. Their door was shut, so instead, he went to see Nolan Skiff, the editor of the *'End of the Week'* column in the *'East Oregon'* newspaper.

Much to Arnold's dismay, the subsequent article, published on the 25th June, created a media frenzy; *"I could have gone to sleep that night if the reporters, newsmen, and press agencies of every conceivable description had left me alone. I didn't share the general excitement. I can't begin to estimate the number of people, letters, telegrams and phone calls I tried to answer.*

"After three days of this hubbub, I came to the conclusion that I was the only sane one in the bunch. In order to stop what I thought was a lot of foolishness, and since I couldn't get any work done, I went out to the airport, cranked up my airplane, and went home to Boise."

Even there, journalists and TV crews besieged the home of Arnold and his wife.

Arnold's report had also created some humorous accounts in a disbelieving media, who had been sceptical about Harold Dahl and the other witnesses. Arnold had heard about the Maury Island incident, and not only contacted the witnesses Harold Dahl and Fred Crisman, but also rang a contact in 'intelligence'. They subsequently gave a sample of the strange metallic type substance to two agents, from army intelligence, Brown and Davidson, but they never actually loaded the 'slag' sample onto the aircraft, as intended. Although the pilot and another crew member parachuted to safety, the two agents were unfortunately killed when that same plane crashed on the way back to Hamilton Air Force Base. Later, when being interrogated by Air Force intelligence, it was claimed that Crisman and Dahl said the whole incident was a hoax. One wonders?

In his book, *'The UFO Controversy in America'*, David Jacobs wrote; *'An Air Force investigator privately noted in mid-July that Arnold was "practically a moron in the eyes of the majority of the population of the United States."'* Even though he developed a life-long interest in the subject, Arnold himself was not happy, and stated; *"If I saw a ten storey building flying through the air, I would never say a word about it!"*

The military, however, despite their efforts to impugn the witnesses, were privately concerned, as there had been sightings of unidentified 'bright lights' over Maxwell Air Force Base, Alabama on 28th June. On the same day, an Air Force pilot in a F-51 saw a formation of five or six 'circular objects' off his right wing. Unidentified craft were also seen at Almagordo, New Mexico, over the White Sands Proving Ground, on 29th June.

On the 4th July several excited Portland, Oregon residents, including policemen, former pilots and harbour patrolmen, reported unusual craft in the sky. They were variously described as being 'large, disc-shaped objects, flying at a high rate of speed, and oscillating about their lateral axis', and 'shaped like chrome hubcaps' that oscillated as they flew overhead. That night a United Airlines crew, flying near Emmett, Idaho, saw five craft which were 'thin and smooth on the bottom and rough appearing on the top'. Two days later the crew of an Air Force B-25 saw a bright disc-shaped object flying below them.

The military really started becoming alarmed when, on 8th July, a white, aluminium looking, unidentified craft flew over Muroc, (later Edwards), Air Base, one of their super secret test bases in the Mojave Desert, California. And so commenced the alleged 'secrecy' and 'cover-ups'.

NICAP investigator, Ted Bloecher, later reported in the *'UFO Investigator'* that; *'Well over a hundred papers, representing most of the major cities of the United States, refer to more than 700 specific sightings for the period of June and July 1947, most of which, following their appearance in the local dailies, have never been referred to in any books on the subject.*

'Reports of sightings were found for all but two of the fifty states – Mississippi and Rhode Island – and from many points in Canada. These new reports contain enough data to demonstrate that the unknown, high speed and

6

manoeuvring devices were being reported in unprecedented numbers for a period of several weeks that summer – often by persons of known competence and character, such as police officers, pilots, physicians, meteorologists and, in several cases, astronomers. The wave built up gradually in June and reports crested on the four days between July 4 and 7; on July 7 alone there were more than 150 sightings.'

Then there were the alleged UFO crashes in New Mexico, which I discuss later in this book. No wonder the military were, behind closed doors, extremely concerned.

Sometimes, as investigators, we received tantalizing inconclusive photographic evidence. In October 1967, Ellis Matthews and his wife noticed some strange circular lights suspended in the sky above Alberton, South Australia.

Ellis took some footage with Ilford super-8 colour film, which he didn't get developed until some months later. Realising it was something unusual, he contacted some investigators who sent it, for analysis, to Major Colman Von Keviczky at ICUFON in the U.S.A.

The subsequent report of this circular pattern of lights, obviously around the rim of an object, indicated that it was 'unidentifiable as any earthly commercial or military vehicle', and further that – 'The object is consistent in form and type with what is popularly termed UFO.'

It appeared to be circular, with no protrusions, and self illuminated in a striking blue colour. In some frames, there appeared to be an intelligently controlled light beam scanning the night sky and its surroundings, Further, in what appeared to be a back-lighted cupola or cockpit underneath, a dark silhouette of some kind of possible 'vaguely humanoid' figure could be seen.

Twelve years later, on October 27th 1979, at Motunau, New Zealand, Norman and June Neilson were taking photographs of their newly acquired fishing boat, and it was only after they were developed that the noticed, on one slide, a cluster of blue-white lights in the sky above. They took it to a local newspaper, who kindly showed the colour slide to investigators Fred and Phyllis Dickeson, who were, themselves, photographic experts, and gave them a black and white copy negative.

They said; *"After careful scrutiny, we regard the colour slide as genuine. The authenticity of the photograph is unquestionable. It is a genuine photo taken of a UFO under existing cloud formation, when the sun had risen to a few degrees above the horizon.'*

The object appeared to have eight lights on top, and six underneath, with perhaps five more in between. All, except two were blue-white in colour.

The resemblance between the Alberton and Motunau photographs is striking, and yet all these years later, we still know nothing more about these craft and their possible occupants.

There were many other occasions when valuable photographic evidence was either confiscated by the authorities, or just mysteriously 'went missing'. Journalist and researcher, John Pinkney, told of how a colleague, Bruce Postle, an award winning 'Melbourne Age' photographer, was in a taxi when, by chance, the driver showed him some excellent colour photographs, along with the negatives, of a flying saucer.

He had been at a picnic ground in Ingham, Queensland, and took some photos when an immense, domed, silver disc moved slowly, about 250 feet overhead. Bruce immediately took the photos, along with the driver, to his newspaper offices, where everybody became very excited – they had a 'scoop'!

They were assessed, by all the photographic experts present, as being genuine, and the newspaper offered to buy them on the spot. The driver refused to sell the photos, as he had promised to show them to an investigator, from the 'U.S. Flying Saucer Bureau' who was coming to see them the next day.

He was obviously a trusting fellow, because the investigator, from the alleged 'Flying Saucer Bureau', disappeared, along with the photographs, never to be seen or heard from again.

THE HYDROGEN BOMB

We detonated our first atom bomb in 1945, and between 1946 and 1958, the United States conducted 66 nuclear bomb tests on the Marshall Islands alone. Most of the initial reported contacts with friendly 'off planet' aliens, who warned against our new weapons, commenced in about 1952. Could this be because our first hydrogen bomb test was conducted, over the Pacific Ocean, by the United States in November 1952? It was said that it yielded a blast equivalent to 10.4 million tons of TNT, greater than all of the ordinance detonated in World Wars I and II combined. The Eniwetok Atoll completely disappeared, and was replaced by a crater, one mile across and 175ft deep.

The H-bomb was unpredictable, and not the same as its atomic predecessor. The 'Bravo' blast in 1954, was 2.5 times bigger than scientists had expected. Later tests, in the atmosphere above Johnson Island, resulted in auroras, and highly coloured sunsets, over large parts of the world. It was said these bombs released highly charged particles into our upper radiation belts and atmosphere. Many scientists were seriously concerned that these experiments could seriously harm our environment. One contactee was told by his extraterrestrial 'visitors' that the Tectonic Plates on our Earth's surface could be irreparably damaged.

In 1962, the New Zealand newspapers, the *'Christchurch Star'* and the *'Timaru Herald'* were already sounding the alarm. Two 'Thor' intermediate missiles, used to rocket the nuclear package aloft, had exploded before their payload was detonated. It is not known if extraterrestrials were 'sending a message', however U.S. officials assured everyone that there was nothing to worry about, and that they destroyed the missiles themselves, due to a 'malfunction in the system'.

Atomic Energy Commission scientists tried to justify these latest tests with the following explanation; *'A one-megaton weapon, bursting at a fifty mile altitude, will disrupt high frequency radio waves, (the most useful kind for long distance communication), for 600 miles around. The most serious military effect probably concerned radar – particularly the powerful radars that were being developed to spot ballistic missiles plunging down from space.*

'High altitude nuclear explosions acted like an enormous radar blinding smoke screen. Radar beams, that searched the sky for invading warheads, may be absorbed or totally reflected by bomb-ionised air.'

Scientists also claimed that nuclear explosions in our thin upper atmosphere, or the vacuum of space, do not behave as they do in the dense air near sea level. The military were anxious to learn their effect on satellites, missiles or even aircraft. Other scientists were expressing their concern that these tests could permanently damage the Van Allen belt, and the lines of force in the Earth's magnetic field.

The Soviet Union, having conducted their first atomic test in 1949, acquired their own H-bomb soon after the U.S. The media were quick to point out that the Russians had detonated 25 bombs, with the equivalent of 58 megatons the previous year.

In New Zealand, it wasn't just the newspapers expressing concern. Many experts were also ringing the alarm bells. Henk Henfelaar, from 'NZ Space Scientific Research', along with Bruce Cathie, made their thoughts known in the group's August 1962 Newsletter; *'We do not longer swallow the tale that radiation has not increased. From very recent information, ('Auckland Star' 20th August), it is clear that the 9th July high-altitude test has formed a huge new radiation belt which is scaring the scientists considerably.*

They discussed the analysis of the latest findings, between August to December 1961, of the 'Explorer-X11 Energetic Particles Satellite'; *'It appeared that instead of there being two Van Allen Belts, centring 1,200 miles and 800 miles above the Earth, 'Explorer-X11' made a pattern emerge of at least four belts, each with distinctive characteristics and different particle populations.*

'The average distances of the four new belts are 4,000 miles, (high-energy protons), 8,000 miles, (low-energy protons), 12,000 miles, (high energy electrons and protons), and 20,000 miles, (low energy electrons). As Dr. Brian O'Brien, one of the ray experts involved, puts it: "What we have is one big mess out there!"

'Dr. James Warwick, of the high altitude observatory at Boulder, Colorado, states that the new radiation belt is 600 miles high, or even higher. It consists of high-energy H-bomb electrons – invisible atomic particles – and follows the path of the Earth's magnetic equator. Although Dr. Warwick believes it to be 'temporary', (meaning a period from months to five years), it is obvious that this radiation has to come down sooner or later.

'This explosion created a disturbance of the Earth's magnetic field, resulting in an artificial aurora that was clearly seen over the whole of New Zealand. Even if this disturbance was only 1%, it will still cause upsets in nature that will eventuate in new changes in the weather or even volcanic eruptions.'

Further some of our own experts had suggested that these weapons could create an unstoppable 'chain reaction'. Soon, in the late 1960s, commonsense, or extraterrestrial influence, prevailed. Only very rare, illicit hydrogen bomb tests have been conducted since then.

Luckily, the 'danger period' did not last too long. In 1945/46 there were the atomic bombs over Hiroshima and Nagasaki, and the Bikini Atoll tests. Further tests in 1947 were quickly followed by a wave of UFO sightings, and in 1952 the first American H-bomb was detonated.

1954 saw an H-bomb test over Bikini Atoll, during which some Japanese fisherman were injured by the radioactive fallout. Another wave of UFO sightings followed soon after. The British performed experiments on Australian soil, and in May 1957, they conducted a test at Christmas Island. By the end of that year there was a major UFO wave, primarily over the south and mid-west of the U.S.A.

Were the aliens trying to tell us something? Between October 1958 and September 1961, there was a moratorium on further nuclear testing by the major powers. In the fall of 1963 a nuclear test ban treaty was signed, however the next year the Chinese went ahead and exploded their first nuclear bomb. In 1968 the French, not wanting to be excluded from the exclusive 'club', also went ahead with a test of their own!

Some scientists had totally 'hair-brained' ideas, which were fortunately not adopted. In 1958, after the Russians had launched their first satellites into space, Professor Freeman Dyson encouraged the U.S. to build a spacecraft powered by nuclear explosions, in particular the hydrogen bomb. Concern from both his contemporaries and the public prevented him from ever testing his dangerous theories.

Regardless of the inherent dangers of the hydrogen bomb, researcher John Keel reported in 1995 that countless contactees repeated the phrase – "We are One". *"You are endangering the balance of the Universe," is their warning. They are apoplectic over our atomic experiments, (over 1,000 nuclear bombs have been exploded in the earth's atmosphere since 1945), crying that we are not only threatening our world, but are also affecting 'many other worlds'.*

In the 1940s, it would be another ten years before we launched our first satellite, Sputnik-1, into orbit. By the time 1960 rolled around, identifying UFOs had become increasingly difficult. Our own technology was much more sophisticated. We had developed missiles and satellites, and by 1969 would land men on the Moon. Gone were the days when researchers could enthusiastically declare it was most probably 'alien'. They had to examine each sighting and ask themselves if the upsurge in reports was due to our own technology and prototypes, or a growing interest and concern by extraterrestrials?

'Strange Times', a little known British periodical, produced by researchers Gloria Dixon, Bill Rose and Dave Newton, published an interesting article in 2001.

In 1967, Jack Pickett, a World War II combat veteran, was employed as the editor of several official USAF news publications. He worked out of the massive MacDill Air Force Base, near Tampa, Florida. By chance, his assistant had, through an unprotected section of security fencing, caught a glimpse of several unusual 'planes' in the MacGill Salvage Yard.

Jack made his way up the chain of command, and was eventually told that there were four highly classified prototypes waiting to be broken up in the Salvage Yard. He sought permission, which was eventually approved, to write about these unknown craft. He and a colleague were given an escorted tour of the Salvage Yard.

'...There were four saucers, which all had design similarities, in a closed area of the Salvage Yard. The craft ranged in size from about 20 to 100 feet in diameter, and Jack described the largest craft as taking up roughly the same amount of space as a B-47 bomber.

'Each aircraft had an upper cockpit, which tapered backwards to a single vertical tail fin, and there were contoured air intakes visible on each side of the cockpit, with exhaust outlets at the lower end of the vehicle. The small discs appeared to be powered by two turbojets, while Jack thought the large vehicles were probably equipped with four engines.

'Ailerons and flaps were apparent in some areas, and a tricycle undercarriage, which became more substantial as the size of the craft increased, supported each vehicle. This seemed to suggest that the discs were not designed for *vertical takeoff and landing, but might have had excellent short runway performance.'*

Jack prepared a substantial article for the USAF Club magazines, but needed some photographs to complete the publication. The craft awaiting destruction were in a very sad, dilapidated state, with panels hanging open, components falling out, and other pieces partly detached. The Air Force decided that they would prefer more suitable photos of their prototypes to accompany the article, and he was accompanied by a senior officer and two armed USAF police officers when shown excellent official photographs of some prototypes.

'Most photographs showed the prototypes in flight, and they were often escorted by conventional USAF jet fighters, which Jack recalled were mainly P-80 Shooting Stars and F-86 Sabres. He thought these particular pictures were taken in the 1950s.

'Jack said there were pictures of several different designs that were more advanced than the Salvage Yard prototypes, and these were equipped with engines described as the next stage on from normal turbojets. The contractors who built the flying discs were never mentioned during the meeting, nor were the development histories or technical specifications...which he was assured were already on file at the Base.

'Jack distinctly remembered being told that early test flights had been primarily responsible for creating the 'saucer flap', and some UFO crashes had been caused by experimental prototypes similar to those in the Salvage Yard.'

The next day, when Jack and his team were preparing to include the photos with the article in their latest edition, a senior officer arrived and confiscated their notes, the photos, and preliminary draft article. All the craft in the Salvage Yard disappeared, and everybody was ordered to 'say nothing about the affair'.

Following the seizure of wartime technology and scientists from Nazi Germany, much of the covert experimental work was relegated to secret bases and establishments in the remote Canadian areas of Alberta and British Columbia.

The British also had joint military ventures with the Australians, and it would be logical to assume that in any joint projects involving secret craft, they would find the vast outback of Australia an ideal area and quite useful.

The same applies to U.S. covert prototypes and their testing grounds. It is known that several Lockheed U-2A spy-planes were based in Britain at Lakenheath in 1956, and later the Mach 3+ SR-71 Blackbird at the adjoining RAF Mildenhall.

In the 1990s the *'New York Times'* published an article by William Broad. He quoted a CIA study, which noted that in the 1950s and 60s, during the Cold War, the military lied to the American public about the true nature of many UFOs in order to hide its own growing fleet of spy planes. First there was the U-2 spy-plane, later replaced by the Lockheed A-12, which was designed to carry air-to-air missiles. Then came the SR-71 Blackbird. All were capable of flying between 60,000 to 80,000ft, while commercial airliners only reached altitudes of 30,000ft.

For those who subscribe to an alien presence and motives, there are so many varying and contradictory theories. Some of their contacts give a clue, but we can never know for sure. Certainly, many experiencers have reported messages that we are developing dangerous weapons and new discoveries. We could endanger other parts of the Galaxy, and certainly destroy ourselves and planet Earth. They reiterate the same pleas for peace, love and harmony.

No advanced alien intelligence would give us the equivalent of its own technology, but may provide sufficient knowledge to help us progress and mitigate the damage we are creating to the environment. I have considered the possibility that they have imparted enough knowledge to enable us to discontinue our reliance on fossil fuels, and nuclear power. Other forms of less detrimental and free easily-accessible sources and technology would assist our recovery if disaster struck.

Despite any good intentions of the aliens, whoever 'They' are, UFO technologies are dangerous in the wrong hands. One witness reported that; "They don't like the clandestine operations that only benefit a handful of people trying to commandeer the knowledge for their own selfish purposes."

Even 'Simple Simon' knows that 'brotherly love' over the globe is not going to happen! Vicious conflicts are occurring ad infinitum, and we see the rise of radical religious societies, intent on dominating the globe. Innovations such as the League of Nations have failed, the United Nations and mutual co-operation among various countries remain fragile – the USSR collapsed and the E.U. is not so united anymore.

Many academics postulate that a society must first live in peace in order to successfully develop the technology to venture into outer space and other planetary systems. Otherwise, they will have destroyed themselves with that very same technology. If a society had one only government, albeit a harsh, dictatorial authority, this would also curtail the possibility of self-annihilation. Is this a solution attempted by the 'Visitors'?

In 1956, despite the subject of UFOs only attracting a passing interest for him at that time, over the next ten years, radio commentator Frank Edwards commenced serious research into the subject. In 1967 he published his book, *'Flying Saucers - Serious Business'*, which, in my opinion, was one of the best reviews of UFO cases and the current situation. The authorities were not pleased.

Edwards was not happy about the government's 'press censorship' and quoted one case where it was taken to extremes; *'At 4.30pm January 11 1965, a group of twelve Army communication specialists who were meeting in the Munitions Building at Nineteenth St. and Constitution Ave. N.W., rushed to the windows to watch an interesting spectacle to which they had been alerted by friends in the radar section.'*

Edwards went on to name some of these specialists who watched as two delta-wing jets were being outmanoeuvred as they pursued twelve to fifteen white, egg-shaped objects, moving erratically across the sky at altitudes from 12,000 to 15,000 feet.

'The Washington Star' was quick to interview the witnesses, but when they contacted the Defence Department they were told that the twelve communications specialist – *'...had seen nothing at all. There was no such incident. It just did not happen!'*

A TV crew had already made their way to the centre, to interview the witnesses. As they were setting up their equipment, a Pentagon 'spokesman' rushed in, and put an end to the proposed broadcast;

'The specialists were taken into another room and informed that they could not discuss the incident for public consumption. When some of the civilian specialists wanted to know in what manner the Pentagon could force THEM to maintain silence, the flustered officer told them that since they had observed the

objects through a government window, they came under the government regulations on the subject!'

Edwards was openly critical of the governments suppression of the evidence, and quoted from a January 1958 edition of *'Life Magazine ; - 'During the coming year there will be authenticated sightings of roughly 200 Unidentified Flying Objects, of which the Pentagon will be able to disprove 210.'*

Edwards noted that by 1965, many of the media and foremost news reporters had grave doubts about the official statements in regards to these strange craft.

In the 21st century, UFOs and aliens continue to be reported, however, unlike the 'Good Old Days', many are lost on the internet, and certainly not thoroughly investigated, if at all!

CHAPTER ONE

THE AUTHORITIES

PART ONE

The Americans had several official inquiries into UFOs – Projects 'Sign' and 'Grudge' – 'Project Blue Book' – the 'Robertson Panel' and the 'Condon Committee'. They all had one thing basically in common – to convince the general public that there were no such things as UFOs.

There were several reasons for governments to maintain a strict policy of secrecy where UFOs were concerned. There was the fear of public panic and social disruption, plus security issues surrounding the possible military and other applications of extraterrestrial technology.

In addition, there was uncertainty and mistrust regarding the ultimate intentions of extraterrestrials, and the authorities were not happy that normal members of the public were secretly interacting with them. Finally, there was embarrassment and consternation over the military's inability to secure world air space from repeated penetrations by extraterrestrial spacecraft.

In December 1947, the U.S. government established 'Project Sign', (nicknamed 'Project Saucer',) its first full-time investigation into the UFO phenomena. In 1948, it published a report on 243 of the best known sightings, and concluded that 'simple and understandable causes' had been responsible for most of the incidents. It soon became apparent that there was a credibility gap between what was being witnessed to what was actually in their reports. Many of the project staff became disillusioned, and some resigned. Apparently they had forwarded an initial top secret 'Estimate of the Situation' to Hoyt Vandenberg, Head of the Air Force, in which they argued that 'UFOs were real and extraterrestrial'. Vandenberg sent it back saying that he required physical proof.

British investigator Jenny Randles, later wrote that in 1952, following the 'Washington Flap', which provoked some concern in Britain, Ralph Noyes, then a secretary with the Air Ministry, recalled at a Cabinet level discussion, Air Chief Marshall Cochrane complaining; "I thought Vandenberg put an end to this in '48."

The media and the public wanted answers. In February 1949, 'Sign' was renamed 'Project Grudge', and the 2A security rating removed, with UFO reports to be handled like any other routine intelligence matter.

The initial 'Grudge' report documented 244 reports, and came to the conclusion that; 'The phenomena present no threat to the security of the United States and the vast majority of sightings are misrepresentations of conventional objects'. The 23 percent of cases they could not explain were dismissed as probably attributable to psychological factors.

Obviously, President Harry Truman thought somewhat differently. In a press conference in Washington D.C., on 4th April 1950, he was reported as saying: "I can assure you, the flying saucers, given that they exist, are not constructed by any power on earth."

By 1952, the public's interest in UFOs had grown to the extent that there was another 'change in plans', and the project was renamed 'Blue Book'. Its senior officer Capt. Edward Ruppelt, and consultant Dr. Allen Hynek, were underfunded and understaffed, and were only supposed to publicly comment on cases they could explain away.

Ruppelt must have felt very frustrated, and in 1954, made his views known in a letter to Major Donald Keyhoe; *'If the reported speeds and manoeuvres of the reported objects are correct, I also agree that they must be from another planet, as our level of technical 'know-how' is not high enough to build such craft. Many people in high military circles agree on this point; the only question was, were the reports correct in their descriptions of speed and manoeuvres. The Air Force did not believe they were.'*

In 1953, the CIA set up the 'Robertson Panel' to review some of the 'Blue Book' cases, and although they officially recommended 'Blue Book' be given more support, this never eventuated. Later evidence, uncovered by 'Freedom of Information' applications, revealed that their main recommendations were to debunk as many sightings as possible and to defuse all interest.

This attitude extended to the later 'Condon Committee' set up, under the auspices of the University of Colorado, to study the UFO phenomena. Despite assurances of 'impartiality', in a memo, dated 9th August 1966, project co-ordinator Robert Low, wrote the following in a memo to officials at the University; *'....Our study would be conducted almost exclusively by non-*

believers who, although they couldn't prove a negative result, could and probably would add an impressive body of evidence that there is no reality to the observations.

'The trick would be, I think, to describe the project so that, to the public, it would appear as a totally objective study, but to the scientific community, would present the image of a group of non-believers trying their best to be objective, but having almost zero expectations of finding a saucer.

'One way to do this would be to stress investigation, not of the physical phenomena, but rather the people who do the observing – the psychology and sociology of the persons and groups who report seeing UFOs.

'......If the emphasis were put here, rather than on the old question of the physical reality of the saucer, I think the scientific community would quickly get the message...I'm inclined to feel, at this early stage that, if we set things up right, and take pains to get the proper people involved, and have success in presenting the image we want to present to the scientific community, we could carry the job off to our benefit....'

Two disenchanted members of the committee, David Saunders and Norman Levine, who had 'leaked' a copy of this memo, were promptly fired!

In 1975, Victor Marchetti, a veteran of fourteen years with the CIA, co-wrote the book, *'The CIA and the Cult of Intelligence'*, in which he claimed multiple cases of deception where UFOs were concerned. Marchetti claimed that the 'Condon Committee' was deeply entrenched with the CIA

One such case, on July 2nd 1952, involved Warrant Officer Delbert Newhouse, a Naval Aviation Photographer, who was driving to Tremonton, Utah. As soon as he spotted a group of fourteen UFOs manoeuvring at high speed in the sky, using a telephoto lens, he shot forty feet of film through his movie camera.

The Naval photo-lab spent over six hundred hour analysing the footage, and came to the conclusion that the objects were 'unknown objects under intelligent control.' In 1976, Arthur Lundahl, a top government photographic interpreter, had to wait for his retirement before he could confirm that he had also analysed the film, and it 'could not have been faked'.

On January 12th 1953, at a specially convened conference, CIA agents denied the facts surrounding the Newhouse film. Maj. Donald Kehoe, in his book,

'*Aliens from Space*', wrote that an Intelligence Colonel told him; *"We were double-crossed. The CIA doesn't want to prepare the public....they're trying to bury the subject. Those agents ran the whole show and the scientists followed their lead. They threw out the Utah film – said the Navy analysts were incompetent.....I know those CIA agents were only following orders.'*

Kehoe also quoted '*Project Blue Book's*', Capt. Edward Ruppelt as saying; *"We're ordered to hide sightings when possible, but if a strong report does get out we have to publish a fast explanation – something to kill the report in a hurry, and also ridicule the witnesses, especially if we can't figure a sensible answer. It's a raw deal, but we can't buck the CIA. The whole thing makes me sick."*

By the end of 1965, very few had faith in the government's 'investigations'. The '*Richmond (Virginia) News-Leader*' newspaper said; *'Attempts to dismiss the reported sightings under the rationale as explained by 'Project Blue Book' won't solve the mystery, however, and serves only to heighten the suspicion that there's something out there the government doesn't want us to know about. If 'Project Blue Book' officials want the problem to go away, they'd be well advised to wish on another star!"*

'Project Blue Book' investigators, Ruppelt and Hynek, were both disillusioned, and went on to continue their studies in a private capacity.

After eighteen years, Hynek said; *"I have finally been bowed down by the sheer weight of competent evidence."* Perhaps, in an effort to justify his original negative stance, he also explained some of the difficulties with previous investigations; *"The crux of the UFO reporter problem is simply that perfectly incredible accounts of events are given by seemingly credible persons – often by several such persons. Of course, what the UFO reporter says really happened is so difficult to accept, so very difficult a pill to swallow, that any scientist who has not deeply studied the UFO problem will, by the very nature of his training and temperament, be almost irresistibly inclined to reject the testimony of the witnesses outright."*

When it came to UFOs, the concern of the authorities, certainly in the U.S.A., started just after World War II, and probably even before.

In *'The Alien Gene'*, I detailed the amazing 'air battle' over Los Angeles in February 1942. For hours, ground based ordinance fired multiple rounds at as many as fifteen unidentified craft which appeared over the city.

In 2010, MUFON published the text of some very revealing documents, which throw a lot more light on the incident.

On the 26th February 1942, General George Marshall, America's Army Chief of Staff, sent an initial memorandum to the President, detailing the Los Angeles incident.

The next day 'FDR' sent a return memorandum to Marshall. This was very different! It mentions 'the disposition of the material in possession of the Army that may be of great significance toward the development of a super weapon of war.' He talks about 'the study of celestial devices', and precludes any sharing of information with the Soviet Union.

On March 5th 1942, Gen. Marshall sent another memo to the President. This time it mentions an 'Interplanetary Phenomenon Unit', and makes specific reference to the **Navy** salvaging one unidentified airplane off the coast of California – *'it had no bearing on conventional explanation. The **Army Air Corps also recovered a similar object** in the San Bernadino Mountains, east of Los Angeles, which cannot be identified as conventional aircraft.*

'This Headquarters has come to a determination that the mystery airplanes are in fact not earthly, and according to secret intelligence sources, they are in all probability of interplanetary origin.'

(This correspondence probably alludes to two different crashes. Investigator, Dr Michael Wolf, may have provided the answer when he claimed that the first UFO came down in 1941, into the ocean west of San Diego, and was retrieved by the Navy. He explained that was why the U.S. Navy claimed a prominent role in UFO matters.)

Going back to a more popular theory, an interesting comment, allegedly made by Edgar Hoover, in a letter to Clyde Tolson, dated 15th July 1947, throws some light on the mystery: "I would do it, (study UFOs), but before agreeing, we must insist on full access to **discs** recovered. For instance, in the L.A. case, the Army grabbed it and would not let us have it for cursory examination."

Behind the scenes, the U.S. government was not letting the war hinder their investigations into what could be learned from these strange craft, and a top secret memo from Franklin Roosevelt, dated 24th February 1944, was addressed to 'The Special Committee on Non-Terrestrial Science and Technology'.

In 1947, as soon as the U.S. Air Force became an independent service, Brigadier-General George Schulgen asked Lt.-General Nathan Twining to assess 'the so-called Flying Discs'.

In his reports Twining noted that the craft were 'real', circular or elliptical in shape, flat on the bottom and domed on top. They had a metallic or light reflecting surface, and were as large as a man-made aircraft.

He added; *'The reported operating characteristics such as extreme rates of climb, manoeuvrability, (particularly in roll), and action which must be considered evasive when sighted or contacted by friendly aircraft and radar, lend belief to the possibility that some of the objects are controlled manually, automatically or remotely.'*

Twining's findings did not say that the UFOs were of interplanetary origin, and suggested that they may be some secret, high security project being conducted by their own or a foreign country, and regretted the absence of any crash recovery exhibits.` (Was this actually true?) He noted; *'The possibility that some foreign nation has a form of propulsion possibly nuclear, which is outside of our domestic knowledge.'*

He also admitted that due to secrecy and 'compartmentalisation' he did not know if these craft were "of domestic origin....the product of some high security project, not known to this command or General Schulgen."

Twining went on to recommend; *'Headquarters, Army Air Forces, issue a directive assigning a priority, security classification and code name, for a detailed study of this matter to include the preparation of complete sets of all available and pertinent data which will then be made available to the Army, Navy, Atomic Energy Commission, JRDB, the Air Force Scientific Advisory Group, NACA and the Rand and NEPA projects for comments and recommendations.....A completed exchange of data should be effected.'*

Researcher, George Filer, conducted some in-depth investigations into General Twining and his activities, and it wasn't until 2015 that he claimed access to Twining's flight logs.

Filer wrote; *'On 8 July 1947, General Eisenhower ordered Lt. General Nathan Twining, the commander of the Air Material Command to go to White Sands to make an appraisal of the reported unidentified objects being kept there. With a team of experts, technicians and scientists, Twining was directed to not only appraise the unidentified flying object, but also to deal with the military, political and psychological situation surrounding its existence.*

'Lt. General Twining flight logs of 1947 have recently been released, so his location between July 7 and July 9th 1947 has been confirmed. This trip to New Mexico was Twining's only trip, during the summer of 1947, to inspect two crashed UFOs. IPU Summary Page 4 states the following – 7th July 1947 – Twining went to Alamagordo AAF for a secret meeting with Army Air Force Chief Of Staff General Spaatz and to view recovered remains of craft from crash landing site 20 miles northwest of Socorro.

'8th July 1947 – Twining went to Kirtland AAF to inspect parts recovered from power plant. 9th July 1947 – Twining went to White Sands Proving Ground to inspect pieces of craft being stored there. – 10th July 1947 – Twining made inspection of R&D facilities at Alamagordo and then returned to Wright Field.'

On 30th December 1947, Twining's recommendations resulted in a full time UFO research team – 'Project Sign' – being established.

Another interesting comment was contained in Twining's correspondence; *'It is possible, within the present U.S. knowledge – provided extensive detailed development is undertaken – to construct a piloted aircraft which has the general description of the object described – which would be capable of an approximate range of 7,000 miles at subsonic speeds.*

'Any development in this country along the lines indicated would be extremely expensive, time consuming and at the expense of current projects and therefore, if directed, should be set up independently of existing projects.'

As most people are aware, our own developments of prototype aircraft and space vehicles, possibly involving the back engineering of captured craft, were compartmentalised within many private corporations.

Whilst officials in the U.S. were loath to admit anything to the public, behind the scenes they were very concerned. In 1950, Wilbur Smith, a senior radio engineer at Canada's Dept. of Transport, and head of the secretive 'Project Magnet', was more forthcoming. In a Memoradum on 'Geo-magnetics' he wrote;

'The matter is the most highly classified subject in the United States Government, rating higher even than the H-bomb. Flying saucers exist. Their modus operandi is unknown, but concentrated effort is being made by a small group headed by Dr. Vannevar Bush. The entire matter is considered by the United States authorities to be of tremendous significance. '

In 1979, Gordon Creighton, one of the most esteemed consultants to the *'Flying Saucer Review'*, wrote of how in 1951, one of their correspondents, Derek Dempster, interviewed General George Marshall, who subsequently became Secretary of State and instigator of the 'Marshall Plan'.

Gordon asked Derek Dempster, then *'FSR's'* editor, of what Marshall had said, that couldn't be published until after his death? Derek said his interview followed an earlier sighting of three saucers, hovering over the airport at Mexico City, where any photographs taken were confiscated by the authorities.

Derek said that the General had try to shrug off the Mexico airport incident as 'mass hysteria', but Derek pointed out that a camera does not become hysterical, and dozens of pictures were taken that day;

"Having got that far, he revealed that it had been established that these were visitors from another planet. That they were completely friendly – their hovering over defence establishments and airports being taken to mean; 'We could blow you all to bits at our leisure, if we had any evil intent'. That they were undoubtedly trying to work out a method of remaining alive in our atmosphere before landing and establishing friendly communications, and that the United States authorities were completely convinced that Earth had nothing to fear from them. That the U.S. Air Force had been ordered to take no action against their craft.'

General Marshall had gone on to explain that reports had been censored, and the aliens' existence denied, because the Orson Wells' 'War of the Worlds' broadcast, some time earlier, had demonstrated what reaction could be expected were the true facts generally known: a welter of hysterical nonsense, and a complete disorientation from the tasks in hand. Rumours and speculation would create an atmosphere that the skilled propagandists of the Kremlin would be sure to make the most of. The U.S.A. wanted her people to concentrate on the real menace - Communism; and not to be distracted by the visitors from outer space.

Derek went on to question him about reported landings, and Marshall then admitted there had actually been contact with the men in the saucers - that on three occasions there had been landings which proved disastrous for the occupants. On each of these occasions, breathing the heavily oxygenated atmosphere of this Earth had literally incinerated the visitors from within, and burnt them to a crisp.

Derek remained fairly sceptical until later that year, when he was talking to a group of Mexican engineers. One of them had been engaged in a highway construction, in an uninhabited valley in the Sierra Madre. One day he was called upon to help load a flying saucer and its dead crew into an American 'Flying Box-Car' aeroplane.

The engineer continued; *"Ah, Señor,"* he said, *"they were handsome, those little men, with fine features and beautifully formed hands. But there must have been an explosion in their craft, for they were burnt black, and when I touched the face of one of them, the skin came off under my finger as though it had been cooked!"*

By 1952, senior intelligence officers were already making their thoughts known. CIA Director, General Walter Smith, wrote in a Memorandum to the National Security Council; *'The Central Intelligence Agency has reviewed the current situation concerning unidentified flying objects which have created extensive speculation in the press and have been the subject of concern to government organisations...Since 1947, approximately 2,000 official reports of sightings have been received, and, of these, about 20% are as yet unexplained.*

'It is my view that this situation has possible implications for our national security which transcend the interests of a single service. A broader, co-ordinated effort should be initiated to develop a firm understanding of the several phenomena which are apparently involved in these reports.'

Slightly different statistics were sent to him the same year in a Memorandum from the Agency's Assistant Director of Scientific Intelligence, Marshall Chadwell; *'Since 1947, ATIC has received approximately 1,500 official reports of sightings, plus an enormous volume of letters, phone calls, and press reports.*

During July 1952 alone, official reports totalled 250. Of the 1,500 reports, Air Force carries 20% as unexplained, and of those received from January through July 1952 it carries 28% unexplained.'

Chadwell emphasised that although he did not anticipate an imminent invasion from outer space, the situation did have 'national security implications' for the United States. There was the potential for the Soviet Union to wage psychological warfare by using the UFO phenomenon to create unrest in the U.S. Also there was the possibility that UFO sightings might interfere with America's air defence against Soviet bomber attack.

In a later memorandum, he stated; *'The reports of incidents convince us that there is something going on that must have immediate attention....Sightings of unexplained objects at great altitudes and travelling at high speeds in the vicinity of major U.S. defence installations are of such nature that they are not attributable to natural phenomena or known types of aerial vehicles.'*

Chadwell and his office went on to establish the 'Robertson Panel' which aimed to remove the 'aura of mystery' surrounding the UFO phenomenon.

One of the first scientists to speak out was Professor Herman Oberth, the German rocket expert, and founding father of the space age. He certainly was in a position to know if the strange craft in our skies had originated from Nazi innovations, were our own prototypes, or had even been, as some speculated, back engineered from captured extraterrestrial vehicles.

In a 1954 article in the *'American Weekly'*, he said; *"It is my thesis that flying saucers are real, and that they are space ships from another solar system. I think they are possibly manned by intelligent observers who are members of a race that may have been investigating our earth for centuries. I think that they possibly have been sent out to conduct systematic, long-range investigations, first of men, animals, vegetation, and more recently of atomic centres, armaments and centres of armament production."*

Worried about the ongoing public interest in the subject, and an increasing need for secrecy, the authorities started to clamp down on any military or civilian personnel 'leaking' any details.

In 1957, the *'Holloman Daily Bulletin'*, (mandatory reading for all civilian and military Base personnel), contained the following item in the official section;

'Unidentified Flying Objects'. On November 7, six airmen claimed they sighted an unidentified flying object and did not report this to the proper base authorities. They did, however, give the information to the local press. Request that each member of the military and civilian, employed at this centre, refrain from any public statement on political, diplomatic, legislative or scientific matters or any controversial subjects such as UFOs, without first contacting the Centre Information Services Officer. This request is in accordance with AFR 190-6. Disciplinary action may be taken against offender.

Signed: Lt. Col. McCurdy, HDN.

In 1957, when the 'National Investigations Committee on Aerial Phenomena', (NICAP), was established in the U.S., their Chairman, Retired Admiral Delmer Fahrney told a press conference; *"There are objects coming into our atmosphere at very high speeds....no agency in this country or Russia is able to duplicate, at this time, the speeds and acceleration which radar and observers indicate these objects are able to achieve."*

He told reporters that he had no preconceived ideas as to whether the unidentified flying objects were from outer space, but believed they involved 'a tremendous amount of technology of which we had no knowledge', and that their development, must have taken a long period of time.

By that time, other high ranking personnel were beginning to speak out. On February 28th 1960, *'The New York Sunday Times'* quoted Vice-Admiral Roscoe Hillenkoetter, former Director of the CIA, as saying; *"It is now time for the truth to be brought out in open congressional hearings. Behind the scenes, high-ranking Air Force officers are soberly concerned about the UFOs. But, through secrecy and ridicule, many citizens are led to believe that unknown flying objects are nonsense....to hide the facts, the Air Force has silenced its personnel."*

He later added; *'It is imperative that we learn where UFOs come from, and what is their purpose."*

In 1964, Frank Salisbury, Professor of Plant Physiology at Utah State University, presented a paper to the U.S. Air Force Academy in Colorado. In it he mentioned the problem scientists have when it comes to commenting on UFOs; *"I must admit that any favourable mention of flying saucers by a scientist amounts to extreme heresy, and places the one making the statement in danger of excommunication by the scientific theocracy. Nevertheless, in recent years I have investigated the story of the unidentified flying object, and I am no longer able to dismiss the idea lightly."*

A decade later, these views were still prevalent. Whilst at a Royal Society function, a couple of scientists sidled up to me and whispered; "I'm very interested in what you are researching – let me know if I can help, but don't tell the others!"

Years later, when analysing the infamous 'Condon Report', another scientist, Professor Peter Sturrock, Deputy Director of the Centre for Space Sciences and Astrophysics at Stanford University, had this to say; *"The definitive resolution of the UFO enigma will not come about unless and until the problem is subjected to open and extensive scientific study by the normal procedures of established science and administrators in universities.*

"Although...the scientific community has tended to minimise the significance of the UFO phenomenon, certain individual scientists have argued that the phenomenon is both real and significant....To a scientist, the main source of hard information, (other than his own experiments and observations), is provided by the scientific journals. With rare exceptions, scientific journals do not publish reports of UFO observations.

"The decision not to publish is made by the editor, acting on the advice of reviewers. This process is self-reinforcing; the apparent lack of data confirms the view that there is nothing to the UFO phenomenon, and this view works against the presentation of relevant data."

Yale University's *'Scientific Magazine'*, of April 1963, was cautious, but outspoken; *'Based upon unreliable and unscientific surmises as data, the Air Force develops elaborate statistical findings which seem impressive to the uninitiated public, unschooled in the fallacies of the statistical method. One must conclude that the highly publicised periodic Air Force pronouncements, based on unsound statistics, serve to misinterpret the true character of the UFO phenomena.'*

Most scientists were a little reticent to comment on the possibility of extraterrestrial life or visitations, however nobody was going to ridicule Einstein or Oppenheimer. In my book, *'UFOs Now and Then'*, I detail their joint paper, *'Relationships with Inhabitants of Celestial Bodies'*, drafted in 1947, a few weeks **before** the famed Roswell incident.

They, along with other scientists, were concerned about our development and deployment of nuclear weapons, and suggested that the recent intense UFO activity was related. They discussed, among other things, the possible nature of extraterrestrials, and the issues presented if they wished to settle on Earth.

It was quite a lengthy, detailed thesis, and was intended to be forwarded to the President, however, it was never signed and submitted, as the real controlling 'powers' did not want these two eminent scientists discussing this with the President. What was very significant was that either the authorities thought these two prominent scientists were losing their minds, or much more likely – were telling the truth!

Even as early as the 1950s, some other scientists were brave enough to make some cautious comments. Professor Hermann Oberth, one of the great pioneers of rocketry, could, due to his fame and prestige, evade criticism when he was quite outspoken in his beliefs, and said that he believed some UFOs were extraterrestrial. Other academics had to be more cautious.

In the 1957 'Trend' publication, *"Flying Saucers – Fact or Fiction'*, Max Miller had this to say; *'Frank Edwards, former Mutual Broadcasting System news commentator for the American Federation of Labor, announced one night; "Top scientists, whose identity I am not at liberty to reveal, have been investigating the phenomena of unidentified flying objects since 1947, analysing samples of various types, inspecting every bit of evidence for whatever could be learned from it. With their permission, I can read this one significant paragraph, from their statement to me, dated September 8, 1953;*

"Our research in this matter leads us to believe that these unidentified flying objects are observation vehicles from another planet, and further, that this information is being kept from the people. A statistical analysis of the evidence collected thus far, proves without doubt that we are dealing with extra-terrestrial influences from an unknown source."

Miller then quoted from an article by Arthur Joquel, a noted authority on rocketry and space travel, and author of the book *'The Challenge of Space'*;

'For hundreds, or even thousands of years, observations and reports have been made regarding these objects. Accurate, well-trained impartial witnesses have described them, using almost the same terms in all ages and times. There have been sufficient reports concerning these objects made by scientists, military personnel and trained civilians, to have removed any doubts as to their existence.

'No country on Earth could have built such vehicles hundreds of years ago. It would strain the ability of any country today to develop such flying objects, and to construct, test, and launch them, and furthermore keep their place of origin a secret. It seems much more logical, under the circumstances, that flying discs have their origin somewhere in space, and visit the earth for some reason or purpose.'

The authorities, especially in the U.S.A., were well aware of the presence of these strange craft. On 3rd August 1952, several huge silver discs, each sixty to one hundred feet in diameter, were tracked by radar on Hamilton Air Force Base, California. Numerous eye witnesses watched as two of the discs circled the base at different altitudes, executing strange manoeuvres. Six more came into sight and joined the other two. The objects then took up a diamond-shape formation and headed west.

On 3rd May 1957, an unidentified object hovered, close to the ground, over the practice range at Edwards Air Force Base, California. It was a luminous, gold colour, shaped like an inverted plate, with a dome, surrounded by portholes or panels, on top, and a halo around the rim. Many photographs, all of which were later confiscated by 'intelligence', were taken by the witnesses.

In his book, *'Let's Face the Facts About Flying Saucers'*, Gabrielle Green wrote of how the NASA tracking station at Wallops Island, Virginia, was visited by UFOs on several occasions;

'In October 1964, several technicians and a NASA engineer observed a triangle-shaped object as it sped over the base, executed a sharp ninety degree turn, and then disappeared over the horizon;

"The device was travelling too fast to be an airplane," said one witness. "Besides, an airplane, as we know them today, cannot execute an abrupt change of direction."

'Dempsey Burton, chief of the Wallops Island base, was the next NASA official to see a strange object in the sky. On January 6th 1965, Burton was standing near his home and searching the sky for an artificial satellite.

'A flying object appeared on the southeast horizon, moving at fantastic speed. The UFO glowed with a brilliant yellow-orange intensity, and other residents witnessed the amazing flight: "I was a sceptic before, but there really is something up there," said one observer.

'This same NASA tracking station was visited a third time, by a glowing UFO, that acted in a hostile manner. Similar to the glowing object seen by Dempsey Burton, this UFO shot down out of the sky on January 12th 1965, and darted directly toward a NASA public relations staff member and her husband. The two sighters ran from the speeding object and escaped serious injury.'

Sometimes there would be an unexpected events and landings at U.S. airfields. Major Donald Keyhoe mentioned a couple in his book, *'Aliens from Space'*.

'In July 1962, a strange flying object descended toward the Camba Punta Airport in Argentina. Airport Director, Luis Harvey, immediately ordered the landing strip cleared. In a few moments, a UFO described as a 'perfectly round flying object' approached at high speed. Then it stopped and hovered for three minutes.

'Though the Argentine Air Force had been alerted, no interception was attempted. But, unfortunately, some excited witnesses ran out for a closer inspection, and the flying disc hurriedly took off.'

Another case occurred on December 22nd that same year, at the Ezeiza International Airport near Buenos Aires, when a disc-shaped object landed at the end of the runway. A DC-8 jetliner, was forced to maintain a holding pattern, wondering what was going to happen next. Fortunately, after a short time, the strange craft slowly lifted off and climbed out of sight.

One wonders if these were alien craft, or one of our own prototypes a little 'off course'?

Sometimes these objects were definitely extraterrestrial, and these events didn't always go well. Raymond Fowler wrote of one such incident, which was documented by Len Stringfield, at the Nevada Nellis Air Force Base in 1968:

For three days a strange craft had been hovering overhead, and at one stage three small alien craft were seen separating from the parent craft; *'One landed on the air base grounds. Sent to greet the landed craft was a Colonel with a security detachment properly armed. There was no mention of attempts to assault the craft.*

'While waiting for a sign of intent, a humanoid, who was described as 'short and stocky', was observed to disembark from the craft. Then a beam of light was directed at the Colonel. The Colonel was instantly paralysed, according to the report.

'Orders then came from the officer next in command for the troops of the security detachment to fire, but their weapons were mysteriously jammed. The Colonel was recovered and hospitalised....The UFO was observed to retreat to its parent craft and then departed.'

'Len checked out the existence of General T., and his secret assignments at Wright Patterson AFB, through an Intelligence source, and obtained additional corroborative information concerning the Nellis AFB incident.'

Although seldom discussed at the time, of much more concern to the authorities, was the interest and interference by UFOs into our missiles and their bases.

U.S. researcher, Linda Moulton Howe, wrote that, on 14th May 1947, there was a classified test launch, from the White Sands Proving Ground, of a V-2 rocket, complete with warhead . A group of highly ranked general staff officers and civilian scientists watched in amazement, as an object instantly appeared beside the ascending missile, which immediately changed course to a north-easterly trajectory. It crashed about two minutes later.

'New Mexico's State Representative, Andrew Kissner, wrote after his personal interview with an Army officer at White Sands Proving Ground: 'Whatever had

mysteriously appeared and vanished after observing a V-2 in close proximity to the rocket, it apparently affected the rocket's trajectory....

'The 'peculiar phenomenon' object was defined as hostile....and was by every definition an 'advanced foreign weapons system'. Effort would be expended to guard against further intrusions and high priority was assigned to collect a specimen of the technology for further analysis, covertly if possible.'

On September 29th 1958, Private Jerome Scanlon was on guard duty at the Maryland Nuclear Missile Base. When he was walking back from his sentry box to the barracks, he heard a humming noise overhead. He looked up to see this 'thing', similar to a 'jet', moving very slowly, about 300ft overhead.

He, and several colleagues, including their sergeant, watched as it 'skittered' over the tree tops, breaking branches before it landed, sending up a shower of sparks and casting an eerie glow over the whole area.

He later stated; "By the time we got to the landing spot, the craft had gone, but broken branches were strewn around, and there was a scorched strip on the ground for half a mile."

At the time, the media reported that the Defence Department in Washington were making further inquiries. Later, authorities tried to downplay the incident by claiming it was a light from a power company's welder torch during a power tower repair, however the electricity providers said there was no power line even in need of repair at the time. The Air Force then claimed it was floodlights from a farmer's barn. The only structure anywhere near the base was not even wired for electricity!

In June 2001, the *'Florida Today'* newspaper columnist, Billy Cox, published an article, *'UFOs Haunt Missile Crew – Walker AFB, NM. 1961-3'*.

He reported that 1st Lt. Jerry Nelson, a former Atlas ICBM launch officer, told him that – *'on several occasions, while on alert in the underground launch capsule on Atlas Site 9, missile guards at ground level had frantically reported a silent, very bright UFO hovering over the site; "The guards were scared.*

These objects would hover over the silo and shine lights down on them without making any noise."

Nelson said he had personally been involved in several incidents, 'probably more than three but less than ten', over a period of about a month or so.

Another former officer from the Walker AFB, Lt. Col. Philip Moore, spoke of an incident in the fall of 1964. One night, whilst on alert in the launch capsule at Atlas Site 7, the commander of the neighbouring Site reported an extremely bright light hovering directly overhead, racing away and then returning to hover again.

Some of Site 7's own enlisted men were ordered up to the 'silo cap' to monitor the situation; *"They reported the UFO zooming from the direction of Site 6 to the direction of Site 8, and hovering for a while at the end of the movement.*

"They all described it as a silent light that moved extremely rapidly – instant go and instant stop – no getting up to speed or slowing down. The common comment I remember was that everyone thought it was a UFO, and that it was hovering directly over Sites 6 and 8, and nowhere else. Thus it was specifically interested in those Sites.'

Maybe, due to an oversight by the authorities, Moore and his crew at Site 7 were never debriefed or warned not to discuss the incident.

Not long after, one evening in 1964/5, Airman 1st Class Thomas Kaminsky was on duty at the same base, when his senior officer, a Captain and the missile commander, directed him to go topside and report on some unidentified lights which had been reported.

After he confirmed two distant lights, moving in unison, he was told that they were already being tracked on radar, and two intercept jet fighters had been scrambled. He said as soon as the jets appeared the lights put on a burst of speed and outran them.

During a later debrief, their senior officers denied entire event.

Other more disturbing incidents were occurring during the 1960s. Staff Sergeant Albert Spodnik, this time at Ellsworth AFB, in South Dakota, told of how, in 1966, he and an offsider had been called out to a Launch Facility (Silo), 'Juliette-3', to correct an 'electrical malfunction'.

Both the commercial power system to the site, plus its own emergency power system, had inexplicably failed, making the Minute-Man-1 missile temporarily inoperable. Just as they were topside, taking a break, under the supervision of a Security Guard, they could hear excited chatter over the vehicle's crew cab radio.

A security alarm had been triggered at 'Juliette–5', and as with 'Juliette-3' the power systems had failed, making the missile inoperable. When the Security Team arrived, a strange object was sitting on the ground inside the security fence that surrounded the missile silo. It was apparently round, metallic and resting on a 'tripod landing gear'.

Spodnik and his companions, whilst still monitoring the radio chatter, climbed on top of the crew cabin to get a better view. They could see a very intense glow which seemed to be enveloping the entire launch facility. Despite being ordered to do so, the Security Team were reluctant to approach the object and requested permission, which was refused, to open fire.

After a while a military helicopter approached the area, but when it was about five minutes away, a brilliant white light was seen, ascending vertically, and at great speed, over the facility.

Later, after they had finished their work at 'Juliette-3', they were met by the Missile Maintenance Commander, who wanted to know if they had seen or heard anything unusual. The Security Guard admitted to eavesdropping on the radio, but Spodnik and his colleague 'knew nothing' and claimed that they had been underground the whole time.

The next day they were called into the Commander's office, where they were interrogated by an individual dressed in civilian clothing. They stuck to their story that they had heard and seen nothing, and were eventually returned to duty. Neither he nor his partner ever saw the Security Guard again.

In March 1967, UFOs visited the Echo Flight facility and all its missiles 'went down'. A week later, thirty-five miles away, at the Malmstrom, Oscar Flight Launch, AFB in Montana, ten Minuteman ICBMs inexplicably 'shut down' immediately after a UFO was sighted in the vicinity. In total, twenty missiles were disabled in a period of a few days.

Two weeks after that, another four or five U.S. missiles suffered the same fate in similar circumstances. No wonder the Americans were concerned!

Investigator Raymond Fowler related even more disturbing incidents which occurred in about 1966. He was told of how the strike team at Pease Air Force Base got a signal from one of the silos that 'something was there'. They arrived to find the exceptionally heavy cover opened, and all three combination locks compromised. A nuclear warhead was gone!

In Russia, the situation was even more dire. A UFO was seen hovering over a missile base and the adjoining village. When the missile commander was interviewed he said that – *'a countdown had been started, when this huge disc-shaped object was seen standing on end over the base. The countdown only lasted a few seconds, but it was as if Moscow had sent the correct code and the two launch facility officers had turned the key and sent this missile on its way to the United States.*

'The object left, and the countdown stopped. Electronics people came in and took all the equipment and examined it, and there was nothing wrong with it.

"So you have enough of these incidents," Fowler concluded, *"to indicate that someone is interested in preserving posterity as far as atomic weapons are concerned. Someone who is saying; "We can do this", and is maybe giving us a warning."*

Disturbing events were not just occurring on the ground. In later years, Air Force Lt. Robert Jacobs and Major Florenz Mansmann, spoke of an incident on the 15th September 1964, when a missile was launched from Vandenberg AFB.

Jacobs was filming the event with a telescopic lens. When it was sixty miles over the Pacific, and the final booster stage had dropped off, a small spherical, saucer-shaped UFO circled the missile nose-cone, or dummy warhead. It emitted flashes of 'strobe-like' light before flying off. Seconds later, the warhead fell to earth, missing its target by hundreds of miles.

Jacobs said; *"It was like a warning from someone with vastly superior technological skills."* Mansmann, who studied the film before it was confiscated by the CIA, commented; *"I have never, ever seen anything like that before or since."*

'Omni' magazine, who later published the details of this incident, were told by an Air Force spokesman; *"We have no documentation of a UFO incident. The dummy warhead hit the target!"*

In 1975, there was an event of considerable more concern than any of the previous incidents. Researcher Susan Michaels, who wrote the book, *'Sightings',* and helped produce the subsequent TV series, liaised with investigator Barry Greenwood who had interviewed aircraft mechanic, Rick Eberhardt, regarding disturbing occurrences at Wurtsmith and Malmstrom Air Force Bases.

"Then, on November 7th 1975, the unthinkable happened. At the Malmstrom nuclear missile silo, code-named K-7, an unseen force tampered with the nation's infallible missile launch system. Some time that evening, the electronic security sensors around K-7 were triggered.

'Malmstrom's Sabotage Alert Team was called in and reportedly observed an enormous, orange glowing object, (later described as a bright orange disc, the size of a football field), over the silo. The UFO was also tracked on radar by NORAD, and two F-106 jets were scrambled and reached the UFO within minutes. As soon as the interceptors came into view, the UFO rose quickly to 200,000 feet, hovered briefly, then disappeared.

'Inside the Launch Control Facility, military personnel made a startling discovery. During the over-flight, the computer on the nuclear warhead had somehow changed its own launch code.

'Greenwood explained; 'Somehow the object managed to change the tracking numbers on the missile. According to one witness, the missile had to be removed and retooled to make it operational again.'

Apparently, this was not the only base where this occurred.

Of even greater concern, was the UFO activity over or near our nuclear reactors. U.S. investigator Walt Andrus, told of an incident in about mid-July 1945, when

Navy test fighter pilot, Rolan Powell, was stationed at NAS Pasco, sixty miles away from the Hanford nuclear plant. This was a large plutonium production facility, which produced the material used for atomic bombs.

One day, at about noon, after radar detected a fast moving object, the alarms went off, and he and his colleagues were scrambled for an immediate response. By the time they got into the air, the object was in a holding pattern, directly above the Hanford plant.

It was a bright, pinkish colour, saucer-type craft, estimated to be the size of 'three aircraft carriers side-by-side', and was extremely bright. It was very high, much higher than their F6F 'Hellcats' ceiling, and discharging a 'cloud-like vapour' from ports or vents around the outside.

One by one, as the pursuit planes ran low on fuel and returned to base, the UFO, which had been hovering for well over twenty minutes, disappeared as quickly as it came.

The governments of countries all around the world were taking a quiet interest in these unauthorised appearances in our skies.

In Australia, in the early days, the Air Force were rather circumspect and non-committal. On January 7th 1954, the *'Melbourne Sun'* quoted a spokesman as saying; *"We would be foolish if we were not interested. People are definitely seeing something and we hope to find out what it is. The RAAF has an open mind on saucers. We haven't rejected them as impossible or accepted them as fact yet.*

"There is s high ranking opinion in the Force that saucers do exist, and you can't shake it. The RAAF has been receiving saucer reports and investigating them since the war."

The next day, the *'Melbourne Herald'* added to this statement; *"We are serious to get to the bottom of the reports. We have an open mind, but who are we to say the public is just seeing things. We don't know if we are the only planet with life on it, or if there are better brains in the Universe than ours.*

"We should be flying into space ourselves within 100 years. Our investigations show that 10% of the people making the reports should know what they are talking about, especially pilots.'

UFOs must have been a hot topic in Victoria that week. On Tuesday 9th January, the *'Melbourne Age'* quoted a 'high ranking officer' of requesting that members of the public, who are sure they have seen something to notify the RAAF who were; *"...charged with the defence of Australia. It was its duty to investigate reports of flying objects. No one in the department could say definitely what the objects were."*

The same day, the *'Melbourne Argus'* quoted another officer as commenting; *"The RAAF are keeping an open mind on the objects. But I, personally, am convinced they have an interplanetary source. People on this Earth should be able to fly into outer space within about forty years – why shouldn't people from other planets already have reached this stage?"*

The Soviets, whilst they had many UFO events of their own, were much more reticent to make any details known, let alone be discussed publicly.

It wasn't until decades later that Ukrainian researcher, Anton Anfalov, told the world of an incident which occurred in 1920. He quoted from the book, *'UFO Liaisons of the Universe', Lugansk'*;

'A mobile Red Army group was moving along a local road in the rugged mountains of the Crimean Peninsula. There was a total of five soldiers, including one woman. They were moving in a cart wagon, and were armed with rifles and 'Maksim' machine guns.

'Suddenly they noticed a lighted area on the side of the road, and then stopped near the road, prepared their weapons and began to check the area. They soon came upon a strange, dome-shaped object on the ground, and several tall figures walking near the object. The figures were described as dressed in a kind of armoured suit, resembling chainmail. The figures were about two metres in height, or taller.

'Thinking that these were foreign enemies, the group prepared to fire upon the strangers with their Maksim machine guns, but were suddenly blinded by a bright flash of light, and knocked down, losing consciousness. When they

returned to their senses again, the object and the strange figures had disappeared.'

U.S. investigator, Dr. Mcdonald, told of an ex-German scientist, then employed by an American Army research lab, who related an experience in the spring of 1945, when he and about twenty other German scientists and technicians were waiting, in a harbour in North Germany, for a ship to escape the Russians.

Suddenly, a luminous, spherical object, at high angular elevation, took about twenty minutes to traverse eastward across the sky through a thirty degree arc. None of the scientists had any idea of what it could be.

Dr. Clifford Wilson reported on another incident, which had escaped the veil of secrecy: *'In the spring of 1959, UFOs brought near panic to Soviet radar and air force personnel by hovering and circling, for more than twenty-four hours, above Sverdlovak, headquarters of tactical missile command. The Red fighter pilot sent aloft to chase the UFOs away reported that the alien objects easily outmanoeuvred their jets and zigzagged to avoid their machine-gun fire.*

'Dozens of nervous candidates for Soviet civilian flying licences have complained about UFOs sweeping at them and even following their planes back to airfields.'

In the August of that year the civilian radar post at Vnukovo Airport at Moscow, reported a sighting of these 'disc-shaped flying objects' over the outskirts of the city. They were approximately a minimum eighty metres in diameter, and at an altitude of 16,800 metres.

The Soviet Air Force sent up jet interceptors, which failed to come in contact with them, as the intruders had disappeared at a height well over thirty kilometres. The possibility of an optical illusion or natural explanation was apparently out of the question.

The Czech aviation magazine, *'Kridla Vlasti'* reported that in November 1959, Air Force Commander Duchon, along with fellow officer Bezac, were ten kilometres away from the airfield when their car suddenly stalled, and they saw a strange bright, sapphire coloured light moving quickly across the sky.

After the car started again, they arrived at the aerodrome to find that no planes had landed there at that time. Pilots and ground staff said the 'thing' had moved over the airport, at an altitude of about 1,000 metres. It made a ninety degree angle turn and had flown back over the tarmac. Minutes later, it returned, and hung motionless over the aerodrome before speeding off after a couple of minutes.

The size of the silent, rotating disc, surrounded by a glowing band, was estimated to be about 500ft in diameter, or twice that of the largest known bomber. Witnesses said that it was impossible for any earthly plane to have performed its manoeuvres.

Investigators Philip Mantle and Paul Stonehill unearthed another major incident, about which we knew very little until many years later; In August of 1961, when a test flight of the then most modern Soviet military jet fighter was to take place, a film crew, headed by Victor Dudinsh was on the ready to record the event.

Over a hundred military officers were there to witness the momentous occasion, and everybody was mystified when, despite being checked and rechecked the night before, the jet engines of their new prized possession refused to start up.

'While the pilot tried in vain to once again start the jet's engine, a sinister sound pierced the air and a very strange object appeared in the sky above....It seemed to come out of nowhere....Fear seemed to grip the assembled military officers, and it is alleged that they began to panic and run off in all directions.'

Dudinsh focused his camera at the object, and left it running before also taking shelter nearby.

'After the UFO had disappeared, the nervous Soviet military slowly emerged from their various hiding places to discuss what they had just witnessed. There was apparently no doubt in their minds that they had seen something that was not of this world.

'Dudinsh ran back to his camera, which was still working. The film had run out, and he wanted to take it to the lab. nearby to have it processed. The base commander had a different idea, however, and he confiscated the entire film....Some time later the KGB turned up and took the film away with them.'

The pilot was sure the strange craft was responsible for the malfunctioning of his test plane, however all the witnesses were told never to talk of this incident again. At the time, it was conveniently explained as being a 'meteorological probe' or balloon.

Many years later, a number of former Soviet military officers, including air force Colonel Mordvin-Schedro, confirmed that a UFO had also appeared over the Baltic that day.

After the advent of 'glasnost', the Dudinsh film was shown to an audience which comprised mainly of UFO debunkers. Investigator Eduard Mirov said that this created enormous debate and controversy, and a resultant opinion that 'this strange object in Riga's skies was no meteorological balloon, but instead something not of this earth.'

It wasn't until many years later that the Soviet Union was more forthcoming regarding unidentified craft, however, researchers Frank Edwards and Gabriel Green reported that in the summer 1965, there was some concern in Russia about a plethora of sightings being reported from Kazakstan.

The government controlled media reported very little, but the people congregated in taverns to discuss the strange phenomena, and speculate as to whether they may be kidnapped by ugly space aliens. Residents brought out their bibles, and encouraged their children to get baptised.

One old man insisted everybody should attend church, and ran around shouting; "The end of the world is near! The angels have warned us!"

This had resulted in a widespread religious revival and return to God, something the authorities did not want to encourage. Brezhnev himself, went to the capital, Alma-Ata, and spoke to their leaders regarding the possibility of the situation causing a 'breakdown in Communist morale'.

Despite the Soviets conducting fruitless intensive investigations of their own, in order to prevent the villagers believing the 'end days' were nigh, high level officials left Moscow to conduct public 'reassurance' meetings, and the Kazakstan newspapers published reports suggesting that these flying saucers were actually secret devices with which the U.S. were experimenting.

The crew and passengers of Soviet commercial planes were also not exempt from the occasional sighting of these 'non-existent' UFOs. In 1970, the crew and passengers of a Tu-104 Soviet airliner were on a flight between Moscow and Leningrad. They were nearing the city of Bolgoye when a massive, glowing disc suddenly appeared out of a bank of clouds and shot under the plane.

The metallic looking device then made an abrupt turn, and moved away from the plane, still maintaining a parallel course. A witness reported that a bulging core, which resembled a cabin of some sort, could be seen at the heart of the disc. After flying alongside the airliner for a minute or so, the disc swerved suddenly and disappeared.

It didn't help when Dr Mitrovan Zverev, a Soviet scientist who was on special assignment to the Chilean Observatory, Serro Galam, slightly undermined his leaders' efforts when he said; "There are unknown objects, which we do not understand, which are moving freely around the earth." At the same time, the Observatory Director stated in the Chilean newspaper, *'La Tercera de la Hora'*, *"... that we have scientific proof that mysterious objects are visiting our planet and we are not alone in this world."*

Despite the Soviet clampdown on any publicity regarding UFOs, a couple of other astronomers were able to make their sightings known to the rest of the world.

Dr Zigel, who was more outspoken than most, told of reports from the Mountain Astronomical Station in Kazan during July, September and October in 1967, where crescent shaped objects, along with a bright disc were seen. They were estimated as being between 500 and 600 metres in diameter, and travelling at a speed of five kilometres per second, or 11,160 mph.

U.S. research group, 'NICAP', wrote; *'Earlier sightings listed by Zigel include these 1965 and 1966 cases;*

'At 9.35 pm, July 26, 1965, Latvian astronomers Jan Melderis and Esmeralda Vitolniek observed a large bright disc from an observation station at Ogra, Latvia. Viewed through a telescope, the lens-shaped disc was estimated at 100 metres in diameter. Three rotating balls were seen around the disc. After 15-20 minutes, the balls and large disc departed in different directions.

'A daytime sighting, on October 20, 1966, was reported by V. Duginov, Director of the Kherson Hydrometeorological School, who along with some 50

other observers, saw a disc-shaped object, 'about one third the sun's diameter', moving eastward.

'Radar confirmation of UFO reality was revealed by the head of a Latvian space tracking system, Robert Vitolniek. In the newspaper 'Sovetskaya Latvia', the tracking station chief reportedly said that UFOs are solid bodies which "generally appeared on radar screens as perfect circles and could not be artificial satellites or meteorological equipment."

Zigel also mentioned an incident which occurred in Kazakhstan on August 8th 1960. Scientists, from a Leningrad Research Institute's geophysical expedition, were at their field camp one night, when they suddenly spotted a strange, luminous object moving over the mountains on the eastern slope of the valley.

It was bright and lens shaped, with the edges a little less bright than the centre, and a visible diameter about one and a half times longer than the moon. It was moving, at constant speed and altitude, from north to south in an arc. At one stage, it went behind a mountain, then reappeared and headed out of sight in a south-easterly direction.

In later years, at the 1994 MUFON Symposium, investigator George Knapp told of an interview he had with Russian Dr. Avremenko, who never spoke publicly, and often used an alias.

Knapp said; *'According to Dr. Avramenko, the reality of UFOs is beyond question. In his opinion and the opinion of unnamed colleagues, UFOs are the emissaries of an advanced intelligence, probably extraterrestrial. He says both the Russians and the Americans have known this for decades, and that information from UFO studies has been incorporated into Russian SDI research.'*

Dr. Avramenko had said; *"The first time I saw UFOs was in 1959. I saw it with radar, and it was orbiting Earth......We also saw vehicles whose characteristics we can't match, even now...We saw tens of these in 1959, entering and leaving the Earth's atmosphere...Surely the existence of these UFOs caused problems for the U.S. defence systems. You were faced with the problem of separating aggressive vehicles from the unknowns.*

"Are aliens and UFOs real? For me and my colleagues, this isn't even a question. I know this government has many programs on this...The information on UFOs helps us manufacture plasma beams for use in our Star Wars. 'The weapons of the aliens' we call them.

Troubling words!

In the 1960's, reports and comments were coming from all over the world. South America and the Caribbean had experienced more than their fair share of 'visitations', and some of their most respected military personnel and scientists spoke out in August and September, 1965.

Lt. Commander O. Pagini, special assistant to the Sec. Of the Argentine Navy, wrote in a letter to 'NICAP'; *'The case of UFO interference with our naval transport, the 'Punta Mendota', was but one of fifteen such cases which the Argentine Navy has reported since 1963.'*

Professor Gabriel Alvial, from the Cerro Calan Observatory, stated that; *"There is scientific evidence that strange objects are circling our planet. It is lamentable that governments have drawn a veil of secrecy around this matter."*

He was backed up by his Director, Professor Claudio Anguila, who added; *"We are not alone in the Universe!"*

CHAPTER TWO

THE AUTHORITIES

PART TWO

All over Europe, there was a growing interest in the appearance of mostly disc-shaped objects, both in the air and on the ground. In 1971, the newspaper, '*L'Aurore*', reported that French policemen had been tasked with investigating and registering all UFO reports. A specialised questionnaire, which comprehensively covered every aspect of the incident, was devised, and the officers of the law had to include descriptions of the craft, its occupants, and even the behaviour of the animals in the area. They were instructed to be mindful of any possible radiation, and further; – 'Possible landing sites were to be photographed with infra-red film, at a height of thirty feet, by means of a helicopter!'

In 1978, Dr. Claude Pober, who headed 'GEPAN', the French government's investigative body, wrote in his report to the National Centre for Space Sciences; *'Taking into account the facts that we have gathered from the location of their observations, we concluded that there generally be said to be a material phenomenon behind the observations. In 60% of the cases reported here, the description of this phenomenon is apparently one of a flying machine whose origin, modes of lifting and/or propulsion are totally outside our knowledge.'*

As early as 1958, French Air Force General Lionel Chassin, told author Aime Michel; *"The number of thoughtful, intelligent, educated people, in full possession of their faculties, who have 'seen something', and described it, grows every day....We can...say categorically that mysterious objects have indeed appeared and continue to appear in the sky that surrounds us."*

In February 1974, French Defence Minister, Robert Galley, opened up to an astonished audience during an interview on Radio *'France Inter'*, when he tackled the subject of UFOs; *"....in 1954, a department for collecting and studying reports about unidentified objects was established under the defence ministry. I have read a number of these eyewitness reports over a long period of time. I think over thirty reports up to 1970, the earliest comes from November 20th 1953, the observation of a Lt. Jean Demerry of the Air Force Base 107, near Villa Coublay.*

"There were also reports from the police. Further, there are sighting reports made by pilots and commanding personnel of various Air Force bases, with a long list of details which all tally with one another in a completely, rather disquieting fashion, all of them during the year 1954.

"I am therefore of the opinion that one should have an open mind about these phenomena. That is, our stand should not be disbelief or automatic dismissal. I want to go as far as saying it is an undeniable fact that today, there are things which cannot be explained."

Certainly, for many years, the French military had been aware of these unidentified intruders. One afternoon in September 1967, General Paul Stehlin, a top-level pilot in the French Air Force, had been flying over Villa Coublay, a military airfield near Paris. A silvery cigar-shaped object flew parallel to his plane for several minutes before rapidly accelerating out of sight.

Incidents were also occurring in Asia. In 1967, Air Marshall Roesmin Nurjadin, Commander-in-Chief of the Indonesian Air Force, said; "UFOs sighted in Indonesia are identical with those sighted in other countries. Sometimes they pose a problem for our air defense and once we were obliged to open fire on them."

Indonesian Air Commodore J. Salutun, confirmed his statement, and added that; "The study of UFOs is a necessity for the sake of world security in the event we have to prepare for the worst in the space age, irrespective of whether we become the Columbus or the Indians."

The same year, Japanese Chief of Air Staff, General Kanshi Ishikawa, was reported as saying; *"If UFOs are flying objects, hovering in the sky, they should be caught by radar. Much evidence tells us they have been tracked by radar, so UFOs are real and they may come from outer space....I can imagine there are two types of UFOs, small ones for scouting and large ships for interstellar travel, utilising electro-magnetic fields.*

"The dream of our pilots is to acquire the technique of gravity-control, capable of perfectly free manoeuvrability. I believe the saucer-shape is the best design,

and various materials show scientifically that there are more advanced people piloting the saucers and mother ships."

There had been incidents much earlier, and this was nothing new to the Japanese. At 7.30pm on 29th December 1952, the radar at a U.S. Base in northern Japan, tracked an unidentified object and launched its own intercept planes.

The crew of a B-26, the pilot of a F-95, and Col. Low, piloting a F-84 jet fighter, all reported on the unusual craft. It was a 'saucer', at an altitude of 35,000ft. with lights rotating in a counter-clockwise direction – a steady rotation between eight and twelve times per minute. One part of the machine was rotating, and it would undergo colour changes from red to green to white. There were also three beams of white light, which remained constant, shining outwards.

Col. Low chased the object, which always pulled away when he got too close. Eventually, it turned, speeded up and flew off very swiftly.

The Chinese were always reticent to divulge anything. Investigator Timothy Good, in his book, *'Above Top Secret'*, unearthed three events from the 1960s. Were these extraterrestrial craft, or Western spy missions?

'On an unspecified day in October 1963, a Li-2 airliner, (a Soviet-built version of the Douglas DC-3), on the Kuangtun to Wuhan air route, was chased by three luminous unidentified flying objects for fifteen minutes. The pilots gave a minute-by-minute report by radio to the Chinese Civil Aeronautics Administration, and on landing the crew was debriefed by Air Traffic Control. The passengers were interviewed by the authorities and were ordered not to discuss the incident with anyone.'

On 1st January 1964, a huge cigar-shaped aerial object flew slowly over Shanghai. MIG fighters failed to force the object down, and citizens were told it was an American missile.

'In early 1968, four coastguard artillery men, of the Naval garrison at Luda, Liaoning Province, North China, saw a gold, luminous, oval-shaped object, which flew alongside, leaving a thin trail in the air. It then climbed steeply, at an incredible speed, and disappeared.

'At the moment when the object began to climb, all communications and radar systems failed, almost causing an accident in the fleet. The Naval patrol went on the alert, and the Fleet Commander ordered his men to prepare for combat. Half an hour later, communications and radar returned to normal. A two-man coastguard patrol reportedly saw the UFO land on the south coast and fired at it with automatic rifles and machine guns, but soldiers sent to investigate found no trace of the object.'

The Spanish authorities were a little more reticent in divulging their investigations into UFO phenomena. In September 1968, their hand was forced when thousands of Madrid residents watched a large object flying above the city. Immediately, an F-104 plane took off in pursuit, however, the strange craft accelerated into the sky, eventually reaching an altitude of 75,000ft, and beyond reach. The incident was headlined the next day in most of the newspapers, who queried the army's role in such events.

Maybe, even in Spain, there was some inter-service rivalry, because on 5th December, the press department of the Spanish Air Force called upon all citizens to report all sightings to their nearest Air Force installation. The Air Force was under the command of General Mariana Cuadra, the Vice Chief of Staff, and it was obvious the common practice of denial and debunking was in full force. In January 1975, when several soldiers witnessed two typical 'saucers' landing on their exercise grounds, before taking off again, the Air Force told the press that the men had been suffering from 'optical illusions'.

This didn't stop Air Force General Carlos, Cavero telling J. Benetiz, in an interview for *'La Gaceta del Norte'*, (27 June 1976); *'I believe that UFOs are spaceships or extraterrestrial craft.....The nations of the world are currently working together in the investigation of the UFO phenomenon. There is an international exchange of data. Maybe, when this group of nations acquires more precise and definite information, it will be possible to release the news to the world.'*

Eventually, control of any information was taken away from the Air Force, and put directly under the General Staff, who decided; *'to keep secret anything that affected national security....and therefore to treat UFO files as secret matters.'*

In Greece, there was also a hesitancy for public officials to speak openly. Investigator, Michael Hesemann, stated that Staff Sgt. William Baker, who was attached to the American NATO unit in Greece, said; *"I could name high ranking Greek officers who had UFO sightings and who described them as very threatening, but the official policy in this matter compels them to silence."*

Hesemann also wrote about the government's attitude to the problem; *'In 1978, the Greek Defence Minister, E. Avaroff Tositas, declared before the NATO General Staff in Brussels, that the UFO operations represented a potential for the European continent; "I recommend an immediate investigation into the origin and identity of these unknown phenomena in the air."* At a press conference held after at an exclusive hotel in Athens, he told the reporters: *"I once had my doubts whether there were UFOs, but now I don't have any!"*

At first, NATO was hesitant about publicly commenting on the subject. In late 1955, *'Neues Europa'* published an account of Vice-Consul Dr. Alberto Perego's sighting over Rome on November 6th 1954.

He, along with many other witnesses, saw about a hundred flying saucers, approximately six or seven miles overhead. They were travelling at seven to eight hundred miles per hour, and suddenly arranged themselves into a 'V' formation. Immediately afterwards, he saw another group, coming from the opposite direction. 'They approached each other at terrific speed, and combined at both points of their 'V'.'

'By order of the authorities this sensational incident was not mentioned in the press. However, for a report which Dr. Perego forwarded to the commander of the NATO powers, a letter of thanks was received. The letter closed with the words; 'Your letter is considered very interesting, but at the moment it is not desirable to reveal more details about the matter to the public.'

'According to Dr. Perego, mankind is pretty close to the revelation of the secret of the flying saucers. He emphasised the fact that these objects are of extraterrestrial origin. The world would be in a panic if this secret is brought to the public's notice without warning.'

Already, as early as 1961, NATO was more forthcoming in expressing its concern. General L. Chassin, the NATO Air Defence co-ordinator at the time, said; *"....flying saucers are of great importance to us. I have demanded that the governments take initiatives, and instead of ridiculing those who believe in saucers, to start investigation commissions and that, in as many civilized countries as possible. We must seriously make sure that the conspiracy of silence does not suppress news about phenomena of great importance, for that would have consequences which are incalculable for the whole human race."*

In 1962, Peter Norrris, editor of *'The Australian Flying Saucer Review'*, noted that some of the world's leaders had already expressed tentative opinions about the possibility of extraterrestrials coming to our planet. He published some of their comments; *'Canada's former Foreign Minister, Lester Pearson, said in Ottawa on Jan.9.1958, the best hope for world peace might be the discovery that another planet was sending spaceships against the earth.*

'President Eisenhower stated in Washington on February 24, 1955, that the philosophy of government must be kept in step with the problems of the times, alluding to the possibility of Martians visiting the United States within four centuries.

'Soviet Deputy Premier Kozlov agreed with a Detroit reporter, in mid-1959, that a U.S.S.R-U.S.A alliance might be needed against the Martians, but smilingly added that the people of Mars might be a peaceful race; "Then we should not make warlike alliances against them but would try to live in peace with them."

'Chairman of the 'Provincial Institute of Space Law', (UK), C. Shawcross, Q.C., wrote to the Russian top scientist, Leonid Sedov, in 1959, about 'the possibility of exploration, if not invasion, by the inhabitants of another solar system.'

It was not long before the subject of extraterrestrials and 'visitors' from outer space, had already come to the attention of the United Nations.

George Tararin reported that in October 1959, the General Assembly was discussing world disarmament; *'Portugal's delegate, Dr. Vasco Garin, remarked that the concept of total disarmament raised many 'delicate questions'. He warned that a disarmed world would cut a very poor figure against an invasion from outer space. Dr. Garin stated that it was certainly farfetched, but 'not absurd', in view of the way things were moving, to imagine a sudden invasion of earth by aggressive warriors from another celestial body.'*

In 1966 'NICAP' published a comprehensive analysis of their Resolution;

'Space Civilizations'

'U Thant has been aware that UFOs might emanate from outer space civilizations, since June 30th 1965. This warning of the significance of the subject was issued to the United Nations by a member of its Secretariat Office, Coleman von Kevicsky, holder of a Master of Military Science and Engineering Degree from Budapest, and a scientific investigator into the UFO phenomena for fourteen years. Von Kevicsky is an expert in the subject.

'It was on the basis of his strategic and tactical study of UFO operations, that the '1967 Mainz (West Germany) Resolution' was presented and signed by twenty-four nations. Among the declarations of the 'Resolution' was the following; "UFOs are identified as alien space-vehicles originating from celestial bodies".

The *'Resolution' was forwarded to U Thant, first in a draft copy, then for official filing in February 1966. Five of the main points listed were as follows;*

'1. The fundamental premise of the scientific outer space exploration must involve the security of the Earthly nations as well as extraterrestrial beings, and not our preparedness of the war potential. This article demands that all nations launching outer-space missions, must do so in a spirit of goodwill, and peaceful activities, and that all Earthly nations should be prohibited from initiating, conducting or participating in, any war, war action, or mission in outer space against extraterrestrial people.

'2. Only the United Nations, as the assembly and representation of the nations is authorised to represent Earth-man in interplanetary relations.

'3. Peaceful extraterrestrial human beings, their space ships and properties within our ionospherical region, until they land, are under permanent protection and jurisdiction of the Assembly of the United Nations. In case of landing, the protection and jurisdiction belong to the authorised territorial government of the landing site, but the protection and jurisdiction have to be carried out in accordance with the 'Constitution of the United Nations' and to the satisfaction of the General Assembly.

'4. The General Assembly of the United Nations is authorised to stop immediately any exploratory mission or operations in progress by the nations,

in the case of offensive danger – forced or armed action to be expected or started at any time, anywhere on or around the Earth by known or unknown extraterrestrials against the life, property or existence of human colonies, nations and Earthmen.

'5. To enforce the above four articles, the U.N. Secretariat, in co-operation with the member nations, should be authorised to establish and organise a research and analytic group to keep surveillance and file on UFOs, Unidentified space-beings, its super and sub-human creatures, Unidentified Outer-Forces, and Earthly exploratory activities in outer space.'

'The United Nations' 'International Space Security Pact', approved and adopted by 67 nations, incorporated several other ideas of Von Keviczsky. In addition, the United Nations, alerted by Keviczsky's determination, set up two committees of study, also to advise the members of Unidentified Flying Objects' activities. One committee, the 'Outer Space Affairs Group', is headed by A.H. Abdel, Ghana's Ambassador to the United Nations. The second group is headed by Kurt Waldheim, Ambassador of Austria.'

Before his campaign was successful, Colman von Keviczky, from his New York office, issued several press releases, which included copies of his correspondence to the Secretary General of the United Nations. I was fortunate enough to obtain one of his original, personally signed, 'Press Release No. 2.', dated 27th June 1966.

It is quite voluminous, and includes detailed suggestions for in-depth research, and a proposed 'Project UN-UFO' analytical group, with mention of '124 + 11 filed documents'.

In one letter he says; *'A long line of highly honoured statesmen, scientists, military experts all over the world have been issuing official statements about the inhabited universe and the evidence of the UFOs. Recently, on May 23, Knut Hammarskjold, director general of the Internl. Air Transport Asscn., as a first hand authority – addressed to the Aviation Convention about the 'prospective of mentally and technically highly civilized extraterrestrials', and they will cause a political, technical and legal chaos amongst our misinformed people.'*

In a later enclosure he commented; *'Only the intelligence and confidential defence services, all over the world, know that they are real, because they investigated the cases and sightings, and they silenced a most important strategical and tactical fact – that we have no earthly defence and weapons against these interplanetary space vehicles.'*

He disputed any rumours that these craft were advanced American or Soviet prototypes, and referred to the hundreds of authentic photographs of these objects, - *'but ONLY ONE of the hundreds accepted as GENUINE is quite enough to support the fact, that EXTRATERRESTRIAL AND SUPERIOR HUMAN BEINGS ARE AROUND and ON THE EARTH, WITH UNKNOWN ASSIGNMENT, FROM UNKNOWN PLANET/S/, AND THEREFORE WE HAVE TO PROTECT OUR PEOPLE.'*

He went on to query why should the statements of leading scientists and military leaders not be considered truthful? He also cautioned against any misunderstandings or conflict between us and any extraterrestrial 'visitors'.

He finalised by saying; *'In presenting this draft of the "International Space Security Pact', it is with sincere expectation that this acute international problem relative to the UFOs, will be seriously studied and considered by the Trusteeship of the United Nations, and will culminate in becoming the world recognised authority for conducting UFO matters.'*

Whilst his proposed 'Pact' was adopted, the United Nations remained silent on the matter of 'UFO Research'. However, in 1970, during the 'International Conference on World Federation' in Ottawa, a journalist approached Secretary U. Thant and asked him if the U.N. would take up the problem of UFOs. He said; *"There are things about which I neither can, nor am permitted to speak....Yes, it is certainly possible. As soon as one of the governments represented at the U.N. officially presents a motion to investigate these things, we shall set up a department to deal with the study."*

The next year, Grace Inbingira, the Ugandan ambassador unsuccessfully lobbied the U.N., and later said that it seemed to him – *"that a strong presence is being exercised within the U.N. which prevents this matter from receiving the attention it deserves."*

Two months later, the Canadian Foreign Department had something to say on the subject; *'The Canadian Government does not underestimate the seriousness of the question of UFO's, and this matter is being considered and studied in a number of departments and agencies. Canada's representatives at the U.N. have maintained a close liaison with the Secretariat and other missions in New York on this subject. But we do not consider that the prospects for the adoption of a resolution by the General Assembly at the present time are encouraging.'*

Let us consider for a moment, that all these discussions were being held at the same time the general public were being told that they were either hallucinating or seeing weather balloons or swamp gas!

As time went by, our legal considerations expanded. In 2010, Australian astronomer and researcher Dave Reneke, who was writing mainly about the geographical and other conditions on nearby planets, mentioned a recent conference in Vienna, Austria. Scholars and space scientists were discussing the U.N. 'Outer Space Treaty of 1967', which was still currently in force. The Treaty was similar to maritime law, where countries or states have jurisdiction within their own spacecraft, and they noted that in over forty years, what with jointly owned space stations and other activities, the situation had changed somewhat.

There were criminal and civil laws to consider; *'What if one astronaut, from one country, punches another while in an international space station, or pulls out a weapon? If astronaut damages part of an international module – where do you send the cheque? There are also patent law problems, where should an invention be patented?'*

He also alluded to another, currently unlikely possibility; *'Since the 1967 Treaty defines the Moon for the good of all humanity, it can never be considered the territory of any country back on Earth. So what nationality would a child have being born there?'*

In 1994, my colleague, Irish investigator Ann Griffin, wrote about a Symposium on 'Extraterrestrial Intelligence and Human Future', which was held on October 2nd 1992, at the U.N. in New York.

It was not an official event, and was sponsored by the United Nations' Staff Recreational Council and their in-house Parapsychology Society. Regardless, it attracted a number of high profile speakers, who signed an 'Open Letter' to the

Secretary General, requesting him to reopen a long, since forgotten General Assembly Decision of December 18th 1978, which called for 'the establishment of an Agency or Department of the U.N. for undertaking, co-ordinating and disseminating the results of Research into Unidentified Flying Objects and related Phenomena'.

In it they said; *'We now have the data to prove, beyond a shadow of a doubt, that unidentified objects are operating in our skies on a regular and uninterrupted basis. The technology demonstrated by the UFOs is futuristic, beyond present capability of human technology.*

'Without warning, UFOs appear and confuse the lives of humans throughout the world. We, as world citizens, should no longer stand idly by, and allow this to continue without a serious and united effort to address the problem.'

Ann Griffin commented; *'The only way that the U.N. will ever become interested in UFOs seriously, is for a spaceship to land on the Plaza of the U.N. building and abduct the Secretary General. It is not now a very serious problem, but has become a National Security issue, and only then will it be discussed by the U.N.'*

In America, robust debate was still continuing. In 1966, Major General LeBailly, (Director of Information, Office of the Secretary of the Air Force), elaborated on the officially 'unidentified' reports. (This was a far cry from the statistics and 'swamp gas', among other explanations, fobbed on the public.)

On April 5th, he told a House of Representatives' Committee on Armed Services hearing; *'....many of the reports that cannot be explained have come from intelligent and technically well qualified individuals whose integrity cannot be doubted. In addition, the reports received officially by the Air Force include only a fraction of the spectacular reports which are publicised by many private UFO organisations.'*

Dr Allen Hynek, former Chairman of the Department of Astronomy at Northwestern University, was probably the most qualified of all to comment, having been the Scientific Consultant to the Air Force's 'Project Blue Book', which sought to 'explain away' all reports.

In a 1966 interview with the *'Chicago Times'*, he said; *'Each wave of sightings adds to the accumulation of reports which deny analysis by present methods...An investigative process in depth is necessary here if, after twenty years of confusion, we want some answers.*

'When the long awaited solution to the UFO problem comes, I believe that it will prove to be not merely the next small step in the march of science, but a mighty, and totally unexpected, quantum jump.'

Later, in 1992, John Scheussler quoted Hynek as also saying; *"I have begun to feel that there is a tendency in the 20th-century science to forget that there will be a 21st-century science, and indeed a 30th-century science, from which vantage point our knowledge of the universe may appear quite different. We suffer, perhaps, from temporal provincialism, a form of arrogance that has always irritated posterity."* He made that statement in 1966, and it is as important today than it was then.'

In 1964, my friend and colleague, investigator Paul Norman, had something to say about the authorities continuing attempts to debunk sightings and discredit the witnesses.

He wrote; *'The crew of a Canadian destroyer reported two such objects. The Navy report revealed the objects to be two miles high and seven miles away. These strange machines were sighted visually and recorded on radar. The explanation; "The Planet Jupiter"! The fact that Jupiter doesn't come in pairs, and was several million miles out of radar range, seemed to be beside the point.*

'Missile men at a base in Maryland, N.J., reported a brief landing and take-off of a UFO. To kill interest in the subject, the American Air Force rushed out an official explanation; "Lights from a welder's torch...the power company crew repairing power-line tower." A check with the power company revealed – "No power lines even in need of repair!" The Air Force then rushed out a substitute explanation; "Flood lights on a farmer's barn." A search was then made of the area by people desiring to know the facts, and the only structure found was not even wired for electricity!

'A manoeuvring object was investigated by the police patrol near Red Buff, California. As the patrol reached the vicinity, their radio faded as their description of the object was being radioed to headquarters. The object was

500 feet high, and sweeping the ground with a search light. As the patrol car drew near, the mysterious craft flew away. The official explanation; "The planet Mars". An astronomical check revealed the planet Mars, at the time of the sighting, was still below the horizon.

'Thus officialdom leaps great gulfs of logic to increase the percentage of explained sightings!'

By 1966, even the media were sick and tired of being fobbed off with ridiculous explanations for UFO reports and sightings. They published a long series of 'B.C.' cartoons, depicting characters pretending not to see UFOs for fear of ridicule. One showed little green men, armed with ray guns, disembarking from a flying saucer, and asking a passer-by to direct then to the professor who had called them 'swamp gas'.

Another showed a sky full of saucers, darting here and there, and a character commenting; "The swamp gas is restless tonight!"

The Hollywood motion picture industry were quick to capitalise on the public interest in UFOs, and the intelligence community realised that movies would be an ideal way, without any admissions, to educate the public into believing whatever they wanted them to in regards to the aliens' motivations and intent.

Some films depicted benign visitors, and others 'monsters', (perhaps to deter people from seeking closer contact.) In 1951 there was *'The Day the Earth Stood Still'*, followed by *'The Thing'* and *'The Man From Planet X'*. In 1952 we had *'The Red Planet Mars'*, and *'The War of the Worlds'* and *'It Came from Outer Space'*, in 1953. 1955 saw the showing of *'This Island Earth'* followed by *'Earth Versus the Flying Saucers'*, *'Invasion of the Body Snatchers'*, and *'Plan 9 From Outer Space'*, in 1956. *'Invasion of the Saucer Men'* reached the cinemas in 1957

After our first ventures to the Moon, most astronauts had to remain silent on the matter of extraterrestrial visitations. Astronaut and Senator, John Glenn, summed it up in an interview; *"Back in those glory days, I was very uncomfortable when they asked us to say things we didn't want to say, and deny other things. Some people asked, you know, were you alone out there? We never gave the real answer, and yet we see things out there, strange things, but we know what we saw out there, and we couldn't really say anything.*

"The bosses were really afraid of this – they were afraid of the 'War of the Worlds' type stuff, and about panic in the streets. So, we had to keep quiet, and now we only see these things in our nightmares or maybe in the movies, and some of them are pretty close to being the truth."

In 2001 the *'Washington Post'* published an article which demonstrated how our own ventures into space had totally altered our official policies.

During a breakfast interview, U.S. General Michael Ryan had endorsed the use of space-based weapons, saying that the United States had many critical assets in space – an estimated 100 military and 150 commercial satellites, which were becoming increasingly vulnerable;

"I would suggest that sometime in the future here, we're going to have to come to a policy decision on whether we are going to use space for defensive and offensive capabilities.'

A commission on space, headed by Donald Rumsfeld, before he became Defense Secretary, called for the development of anti-satellite weapons, as well as a doctrine for space combat, concluding that the weaponisation of space was inevitable.

At the time, many countries were in favour of an international convention or treaty preventing the weaponisation of space, however I consider that any agreements made would soon be disregarded in the event of serious hostilities.

Of course, as we were soon to discover, there were many different types of aliens visiting this planet, with varying appearances and reactions to our atmosphere. Some did not always have benevolent, agendas.

CRASHES

There has always been a lot of talk about extraterrestrials liaising with the U.S. government, and I honestly do not know the truth of the matter. In 1995,

William Hamilton told of how he had been contacted, through his local MUFON Branch, by Charlie, who had been in the Marines during the early Vietnam era.

Charlie claimed his father had been with President Eisenhower at Edwards Air Force Base in 1954 when an extraterrestrial spacecraft had landed. He said these beings were not 'little aliens' but apparently human types, with flaxen hair and pale blue eyes.

Charlie went on to describe how, in 1958, whilst he was aboard the aircraft carrier the *'U.S.S. Oriskany'*, he was assigned to load on board, a disc which had crashed in Vietnam;

'According to Charlie, this disc was ten metres in diameter, and lighter than a Volkswagen. It had a crew of two aliens. The recovery team transported the disc back to the 'Oriskany' where it was stored on the flight deck, between mattresses that were used to cushion the craft on deck.

'A tarpaulin was thrown over the disc, and when the 'Oriskany' put port in San Francisco, the cover story told by the Captain was that a special water tank was being brought in for maintenance, and the tarpaulin was used to protect it from storms at sea. Charlie referred to this disc as the 'IRC-10'. 'IRC' is an abbreviation for 'Interstellar Reconnaissance Craft'. Charlie also referred to this 'Sports Model' as an IRC-16 because it was 16 metres in diameter.'

Over the years, much has been written about UFOs crashing on Earth. The subject has received so much discussion and speculation - so many articles – it goes on ad infinitum. Whilst I have no doubt that these reports, of craft having unfortunate accidents, are correct – were they 'ours' or 'theirs'? Probably both, depending upon the incident.

The 'Roswell Incident' is probably the most discussed and contentious of all. I have no doubt that something, containing small bodies, crashed in the New Mexico desert in 1947, but what was it, and from where did it originate? So many investigators have written about this, I'm not about to regurgitate all the previously published information. Instead, I will concentrate on the lesser known reports.

There was one theory I heard, only whispered in private, often at various meetings and conferences. Nobody was game to say it out loud, until, in 1999, Colin Norris, formerly in the Air Force himself, included this article in his August edition of the *'Australian International UFO Flying Saucer Research'* publication.

I cannot attest to its authenticity, however, here it is for the reader's own consideration; *'The following account is as accurate a record of my father's statement to me in 1958 as I can recall. I still recall it as a child, because that is how I have always remembered it.*

'The conversation occurred in the lounge of our Oxford home in the early summer of 1958. I was ten years old – over the years my father had recounted stories of the War. (He was in the 8th Army Medical Corps at the battle of El Alamein, and spent several years in Africa, latterly in the Intelligence Corps.)

'On this day I had been reading my 'Eagle' comic, and we were admiring the artwork, in full colour, on the cover page, of 'Dan Dare', a futuristic space man. On this page was a small green man, with a large head, called 'The Mekon'. My father asked me if I thought aliens would be little green men? I said I didn't know. He then asked me if I knew why aliens were often depicted as little green men with oversize heads, and then he explained that a spacecraft had supposedly crashed in America carrying little green men. One had survived. This had caused panic in America, and the Government had discredited the story, saying it was put out to test public reaction, and that the whole occurrence was simply an exercise.

'However, what he told me next, he asked me not to tell anyone until I was very old, as he said what he was about to tell me was very secret and dangerous!! Why he chose to tell me at this tender age, I shall never know, but he did! And I have kept this information to myself for more than forty years.

'I shall now recount it for the first time: My father said a craft did crash land, and there were beings on board, but they were not aliens. My father told me that German scientists, working in America, were planning to launch a rocket into space with men on board, just like 'Dan Dare'. However, the main problem was not firing the rocket into space, but surviving the landing back on Earth.

'He told me that experiments had been, and were still being carried out on the best way to re-land on Earth – he said landing craft were being dropped from aircraft to test parachutes/balloons and retro-rockets to soften the landing impact to ensure that the spacemen were not injured.

'He told me landing craft were being dropped from large balloons – with various animals inside, such as dogs, monkeys and pigs, to see if a landing could be achieved without injuring the animals.

'What he told me next, chilled me then, and it still chills me now, and I have often wished he had not told me at all. He said while some of the tests were failures, some were successes, but no-one really knew if a human would survive as animals had. There was only one way to find out, and that was to land a craft carrying humans. However, as the danger was so great, there were no volunteers, so the scientists did the only thing they could think of – they obtained humans from a Government mental hospital. These humans had been bed-ridden and comatose – he said one was alive, but had no brain or eyes.

'Unfortunately, secrecy was compromised when the craft crash-landed when the balloon carrying it tore. The 'tiny green being' was allegedly seen by a member of the public. Knowledge of this, and a world-wide outcry, would have branded the U.S.A. as barbarians. The 'little green men's' story was seen as a more desirable cover story, and an easy one to discredit later.

'I accepted what my father told me as fact, but as I grew older I doubted it. However, recent documented accounts of people being intentionally radiated, even children – to study the effect of exposure to a nuclear bomb – now make me believe what my father recounted to me as fact.

'All the subsequent stories about what is now called 'The Roswell Incident' have been part of one huge cover-up. I tell this account now as I have a heart problem, a similar one to that which killed my father in 1976, and to his memory.'

There is no evidence that what Colin's father actually said was actually true, or where or when this particular 'crash' occurred. Whilst he mentions 'Roswell' as being the incident his father referred to, I think, given the publicity this event later received, it may have been an assumption on his part. There were many other, famous and lesser known events around the same time.

Investigator, Nick Redfern, referred to a similar type scenario when interviewed for an article in the *'Australian Ufologist'* in 2005.

After Nick had given a lecture to a MUFON group in Los Angeles, a lady, who had worked at Oak Ridge, in 1947, sought him out.

'She said that in a clear period in the summer of 1947, a number of strange bodies were taken to the Oak Ridge installation....and later transferred to Los Alamos....Some of the bodies just looked like normal Japanese people. Some of them exhibited strange burns, evidence that some had been in severe air accident crashes – and some were just pulverised.

'She said that there were others that were obviously physically handicapped people with all sorts of syndromes like Progeria and Turners syndromes, which do, no disrespect intended, make people look unusual. With Progeria you get an average height of four to five feet, with a large bald head... and sometimes, polydactylism, which is an extra finger, which is a factor in a lot of these other syndromes.'

She was told that near the end of the war, when re-taking an island in the Pacific, the Americans came across a scientific medical laboratory allied to the Japanese government's notorious 'Unit 731', which performed appalling experiments on its helpless victims. A massive amount of documentation, along with the survivors, and possibly some of the scientists, were brought over from Japan to the United States, to continue the research.

'She was told that a number of experiments were undertaken from White Sands missile range in New Mexico....from May 1947 to possibly August 1947. Basically there were three or four different types of tests. There were high altitude balloon experiments, where people were put in gondola type devices and just lifted up. In some cases they would be afforded no protection or high altitude breathing apparatus, nothing at all, purely to see what the affects would be.

'There were other experiments used with prototype ejection capsules, ejecting people at high speed, if you like. Some of these, she said, were ground based ejection capsules that would just shoot somebody out – not like an ejection seat, but literally a capsule. Several of these living 'Unit 731' people were used in these experiments and tests, with several crashing off range, and having been seen by the general public.

'Roswell' itself has probably been the most discussed event in UFO history, and I am not going to indulge in any repetition here, however there are some less mentioned aspects to that incident, which attracted the interest of a few scientists, and provided some indication that the crashed disc did not originate in the U.S. Alien or not, perhaps we will never know the whole truth of the matter!

In later years, researcher John Keel suggested another theory, which many investigators did not accept. In 1945, the Japanese had been sending 'balloon bombs' over to the United States. In Oregon, Rev. Archie Mitchell had taken his wife and some local children on a summer picnic in the woods. While he was busy parking his car, one of the children saw a large balloon stuck in a tree. As they tried to get it down, the bomb went off killing the minister's wife and five of the children.

Keel claimed that the U.S. government decided that the deaths, and any other evidence of these weapons, be kept secret, so that there would be no public panic, and the enemy would not know that they had reached their target. Apparently, this strategy worked, and the Japanese thought their Fugo balloons had been lost before they reached America. However, it was possible for one to be trapped in the upper atmosphere, and to circulate for years before falling to earth.

It would be remiss of me not to include additional evidence that the vast majority of researchers are correct, when they consider that an extraterrestrial craft, containing alien beings, crashed both at Roswell and in the New Mexico desert in 1947.

Stanton Friedman and John Carpenter investigated a separate incident which occurred on 5th July 1947. Gerald Anderson, a former police chief and County Deputy Sheriff, was only a young lad when his uncle drove his family into the desert 150 miles east of Roswell. They were going to fossick for moss agate, but found far more than they expected when they rounded the corner of a dry creek bed.

Stuck on the side of a ridge was a silver disc, about fifty feet in diameter. It had a gash in the side, as if it had been crushed in. Anderson later thought that the contours of the vehicle would fit the gash perfectly. He speculated that maybe two of these discs had a mid-air collision, with one falling at Roswell, and the other crash landing where they found it. (In hindsight, this makes sense. Later reports state that a high powered government radar, which had been set-up nearby, interfered with the controlling mechanisms of the saucers.)

There were four bodies on the ground, shaded from the hot sun by the wreckage. They were about four feet tall, with almond-shaped black eyes, and, by human standards, heads disproportionately large in relation to their bodies. Two were lifeless, one apparently injured, and a fourth obviously terrified. The craft itself, although sitting in the hot sun, was cold to the touch.

A professor, Dr. Buskirk and his five college students arrived, curious to discover what they had seen crash from the sky the night before.

While Buskirk was trying, unsuccessfully, to communicate with the frightened alien, another witness, civil engineer Barney Barnett, arrived in his pick-up truck. Anderson had telepathically sensed the creature's terror, and felt great empathy. Just as it seemed to calm down, the alien 'went crazy' at the sight of a contingent of soldiers, armed with machine guns, which suddenly arrived.

The civilians were manhandled, told it was a secret military aircraft, and threatened if they ever divulged anything about it. After they had been ushered back up the hilltop, the witnesses saw more military arrive, including trucks and planes which landed on the blocked-off road. Whilst Anderson and the others were pressured into silence, they all knew what they saw was not a crashed weather balloon.

In 1994, Gordon Creighton published an interesting article detailing part of an initial *'Memorandum'* from Admiral Hillenkoetter to Eisenhower when he became US President in 1953.

'There then followed accounts of hundred of UFO sighting reports. On the basis of these, various military agencies, independently, have attempted, with national security in mind, to verify the nature and intentions of these objects. Eyewitnesses were interviewed and there were various attempts – unsuccessful – by our own aircraft, to pursue these objects. The reaction of the public, on some occasions, was well-nigh hysterical.

'Despite these efforts, we were unable to learn much about the objects until a rancher reported that one of them had exploded in a remote region of New Mexico.

'On July 7th 1947, a secret operation was commenced to recover the debris of this apparatus with a view to making a scientific study of it. During the course of this operation, aerial reconnaissance of the region revealed that four beings, resembling humans, had apparently been ejected from the machine moments before it exploded. They were lying on the ground, some two miles away to the east of the spot where the debris of the machine lay. The four beings were dead, and badly decomposed.

'An analytical study of the affair, arranged by General Twining and Dr. Vannevar Bush, under the direct orders of the President, resulted in a preliminary estimate (September19-1947) that the disc was probably a short-range reconnaissance craft. This conclusion was based upon the fact that the disc was of small dimensions and apparently carried no food. An analysis of the four corpses was made by Dr. Bronk'.

As advised, the four small bodies were analysed by Dr. Bronk and his U.S. team. The provisional assessment of this group, (November 30, 1947), was that although the creatures resembled humans, the evolutionary and biological factors resulting in their development were apparently very different from those of Homo Sapiens.

'As it is virtually certain that these craft come from no country on Earth, we have had much discussion as to their point of origin and as how they could reach us. Mars is a possibility, though some scientists, particularly Dr. Menzel, considers that they are beings coming from another solar system.'

(This part of the report is especially interesting, as publicly Dr. Menzel always debunked and ridiculed every UFO report.)

'Among the wreckage of the craft there were many items bearing writing. All attempts to decipher them have been fruitless. Equally fruitless have been the efforts made to ascertain the method of propulsion and the nature of their power source. This was even more difficult inasmuch the craft has – alas – no propellers, no propulsion tubes or exhaust or other conventional fittings for steering or driving the craft, and likewise there is total absence of metallic wiring, vacuum tubes or recognisable electronic components.

'Since the motives and intentions of these visitors are still unknown, National Security is still involved in the entire affair. Moreover, since the activity of these craft has increased greatly since last May, and throughout the whole

autumn of this year, it is believed that this indicates that there will soon be fresh happenings.

'For these reasons, as well as due to considerations of international and also a technical nature, and the need to avoid at all costs, a general panic, the Majestic-12 Group are of the unanimous opinion that the strictest security precautions (ie. absolute secrecy) must continue, without interruption, throughout the next Presidential administration. At the same time the 'Contingency Plan', (MJ-1949-04P78 Top Secret), must always be held in readiness for the case in which the necessity for issuing a communiqué to the public might arise.'

Several witnesses had mentioned handling a 'memory metal', which sprang back into its original shape after being crumpled or deformed. The military were interested in the potential of this new, previously unknown alloy, and Wright Patterson quietly contracted a study to the Battelle Memorial Institute in Columbus, Ohio. Dr. Howard Cross, expert in exotic metallurgy and Titanium alloy research, headed the project in the early 1950s.

Authors Tom Carey and Don Schmitt, with contributions from Anthony Bragalia, detailed Battelle's subsequent research and success in the book, *'Witness to Roswell':*

'The direct connection between the Roswell debris and the Battelle studies is revealed in a material known as Nitinol.

'Nitinol is as specially processed combination of Nickel and Titanium, or NiTi. It displays many of the very same properties and characteristics as some of the crash debris materials that were reported at Roswell. Both are memory metals that 'remember' their original shape, and both are extremely lightweight. The materials are reported to have similar colour, possess high fatigue strength and are able to withstand extreme high heat.'

It wasn't until a decade later that Nitinol made its public appearance, with the Naval Ordinance Laboratory taking credit. Carey, Schmitt and Bragalia had some difficulty in substantiating this sequence of events, however there were some obscure references in existence.

They interviewed the family of scientist Elroy Center, who specialised in this aspect of research, and worked at the Institute from 1939 to 1957. They said he had an intense interest in UFOs and the extraterrestrial. Later;... *'Researcher,*

'Dr. Irena Scott, of Columbus, Ohio, (herself a former Battelle scientist), interviewed a close professional associate of Elroy Center. Elroy had privately related to him... that while he was employed at Battelle, he had been involved in a strange laboratory project....He said that he had been tasked to assist on a highly-classified Battelle study that was contracted by the government.

'He said that the project involved work on a very unusual material. Center understood that this debris material was retrieved by the U.S. government from the earlier crash of a UFO. Center referred to the item he studied as a 'piece'. He explained that this 'piece' was not something with which anyone was familiar. He also said that the debris had been inscribed with strange symbols, which he called 'glyphs'. Similar markings have, of course, been reported by some of the witnesses to the Roswell crash. Center, who passed away in 1991, stopped short of providing any further details.'

Whilst there is little doubt that a craft crashed in the desert, nearly eighty years ago, there is still ongoing debate as to its origin and occupants. I am not qualified to determine the answers to those questions. Perhaps we shall never know the 'truth' about Roswell.

COLORADO

Jack Elliott, a country and blues musician, waited several decades before recounting what had happened when he was a young lad, about fifteen miles south of Ackron, Colorado.

In mid-September, 1947, he had been helping his uncle dig and erect fence poles on the family farm, when he saw an aeroplane, which he recognised as a P-51, approach at a very low altitude. He drew his uncle's attention to a bright silver ball which was above, and in front of the plane.

When silver ball moved downwards, and out of sight, the plane slowed down and started circling. They only seemed to be a mile away, however Jack's uncle insisted they keep building the fence. About an hour later, a Piper Cub aircraft, similar to those used as artillery spotters during the war, flew over then 'dropped down'.

When Jack told his uncle he was sure the plane had landed, or maybe even crashed, they jumped into the pick-up and headed towards the spot, where they noticed the P-51 was still circling. As they drove over a slight hill in that particular pasture, they saw two army personnel blocking the road which led to a small gully, where the Piper Cub was nosed over on its prop. Jack assumed it was obviously a bad landing, probably about thirty yards away from the round silver sphere, which had also come down there.

He and his uncle got out of the pick-up, but as they walked towards the site, the soldiers pulled their side-arms, ordered them away from the area, and remained in position, as if 'on guard'. They drove back to a cattle-crossing gate, from where they could see what was going on. They watched for quite some time, and several neighbours, who had also seen the planes and silver sphere, came by.

The original P-51 continued circling, and didn't leave until another one took its place. A second Piper Cub arrived and made a smooth landing, with three soldiers getting out. At the same time, four army trucks came down the sandy-gravel road, and ploughed straight through the fences, rather than stopping to open the gates. One truck was a long 'flatbed', another carried some heavy equipment and a tractor, and the other two were full of soldiers.

When they reached the site, some soldiers started dismantling the wrecked Piper Cub, which was still on its nose, while others circled around the silver sphere, which was quickly winched onto the 'flatbed' truck, and covered with tarps. It was at that stage that Jack realised it was a round, flat object, about a fifteen feet wide, and more the shape of a traditional 'flying saucer'. By that time, darkness was falling, and the soldiers turned on some floodlights.

The intact Piper Cub then took off, and the military contingent drove away, with the two MPs or guards leading the way, and motioning the onlookers to leave. Jack, his uncle and several neighbours followed them back to the highway, but soon gave up and retired to a truck stop for a coffee whilst they mulled over the incident.

Three days later some of the farmers in the area were questioned about the event. Those that admitted knowledge of what had happened were told that it would not be appreciated if they said anything at all about it. His Uncle Al was visited by an Air Force Colonel, who didn't speak to Jack, probably thinking he was too young.

Since this happened only a few weeks after the much discussed 'Roswell Crash', I guess we will never know if the 'silver sphere' was an extraterrestrial craft, or one of our own prototypes.

CHINA

It's only in recent years that we have learned of a similar crash in China at about the same time.

Researcher, George Filer, mentioned information leaking out that on the 18th July 1947, a farmer near Chengdu found some unusual 'remains' in the fields. News spread, and the police and military took over the gawking locals, declaring the object to be a 'weather balloon'.

Head of the Physics Department at the local university, Professor Zang Zanhan, who was analysing the debris, and thought it to be a 'UFO', was 'asked' to say it was a 'weather balloon' instead. It was said that the U.S. military were stationed in the area at the time, and they may have been responsible for the 'cover-up'.

ARGENTINA

Leonard Stringfield followed up an interesting account after the witness, Dr. Enrico Botha, wrote to him and the 'Aerial Phenomena Research Organisation', five years after the event. On 10th May 1950, Botha was driving through a remote part of the Pampas region of eastern Argentina, when he saw a metallic looking disc on the ground, not far from the side of the road.

It was about thirty-two feet in diameter, and had a six by seven feet circular tower section with a flashing light on top. The craft was lying in an inclined position, with no visible 'landing gear'. Botha went over and looked through a small open hatch on the side, but could see no signs of life or activity.

He crawled inside, and saw three small men sitting inside the tower area. They were about four feet tall and very 'human looking'. They had dark, bronze skin, bright eyes and short grey-chestnut coloured hair. Their clothing was identical – tight fitting grey overalls and boots. Once he realised, due to their rigid bodies, that they were all dead, he took the opportunity to look around.

There were screens, a large panel of bright instruments, a transparent rotating sphere and two levers in front of one being, who appeared to be the pilot. The other two 'men' were reclined on couches which curved along the circular walls. One couch was empty, and when Botha left after five minutes, he wondered if there was a fourth, missing crew member.

He drove seventy-five miles back to his hotel, and informed several friends, who decided to accompany him back to the spot the next morning. When they arrived there, the disc was gone, and in its place was a pile of warm grey ashes, which turned their hands green upon contact.

In the sky above was a large cigar-shaped object, with two smaller discs hovering nearby. The two discs moved towards the larger craft, and seemed to 'coalesce' with it. The 'cigar' then turned blood-red and quickly disappeared from sight. Botha took some photographs, which he later gave to Leonard Stringfield. This is reminiscent of other cases around the world, where other UFOs have appeared after a crash. Could they be on a 'retrieval mission' of their own?

Argentina has always hosted a plethora of UFO activity, and forty-five years later another crash occurred, but due to the passing of time, we have to query if this incident had an alien origin, or was caused by one of our own prototypes?

George Brownie compiled this report for the 'Ufologist Magazine': It happened in the rainforest area Anta, near the Sierras Colouradas. On 17th August 1995, Tony Galvano, along with 'thousands' of other witnesses, saw a huge, bright metallic 'flying saucer', about 250 metres in diameter, speeding across the clear sky from north to south. It was followed by two other objects, thought to be missiles, which impacted with it. The disc plummeted to earth, followed by a powerful explosion, which shook the ground around a three hundred kilometre radius. A thick column of black smoke rose into the air.

Tony ran to the airstrip, and took to the sky in his Ultra-light-Flystar. The thick smoke impeded visibility for miles around, and he could not locate the crash site. Two days later, he tried again, and this time saw what appeared to be a crash area on top of a plateau. There was impact damage and a furrow, cutting a trail, five kilometres long by six hundred metres wide. There was massive damage to the trees and vegetation.

Suddenly his own aircraft motor began to malfunction, and he was lucky to survive an emergency landing on the side of the mountain. He managed to gather up some strange white dust, which was all over the scene. Later analysis, by the University of La Plata, determined that it was a potassium compound, with a 98% purity, not found on this planet, and the remainder an unknown material.

About two weeks after the event, several men, dressed in black, arrived in four wheel drives and on terrain motorcycles. They took over the investigation. They said very little, but knowing Tony and his friends were planning excursions into the area, one of them said; "Forget it, Galvano, what's coming down is very heavy!"

The terrain at the crash site was mountainous, with impenetrable foliage and dangerous packs of wild boar. It is not known if Tony and his colleagues ever had any success.

SPITZBERGEN – NORWAY

In 1956, in his book, *'Flying Saucers come from Another World'*, investigator Jimmy Guieu wrote about this rather contentious incident, which had occurred in early July 1952.

A Norwegian airman had spotted the wreckage of a craft in a remote area near Spitzbergen. When the authorities arrived, they conducted a thorough investigation.

The saucer, which had a diameter of about 150 feet, was reportedly marked with Russian characters, however, in his book, *'Flying Saucers – Serious Business'*, researcher Frank Edwards claimed that a representative of the Norwegian Board of Enquiry said this was not the case, and that they had concluded that the craft was of extraterrestrial origin.

Its engine was composed of 'a disc carrying 46 automatic reactors on its periphery, which revolved around a central sphere, containing instruments for radio control.'

Dr. Norsel, one of their technicians, was said to have discovered a radio-navigation transmitter, with a plutonium element, transmitting on all wave lengths with Hertz 934, a measure hitherto unknown.

Guieu noted; *'In the light of what we now know – according to information given out by the British Royal Air Force, the Russians have admitted the building of Flying Saucers and cigars – this story does not seem incredible.*

'So far as we know, Flying Saucers, made on earth – of whatever nationality they may be – are by no means perfect. Once in the sky, it is quite possible that control over one is lost and that it crashes, but always in an area fairly near the launching base. This might be true in this instance, but the Russian 'Flying Saucers' are said to be launched from a base situated in Novaya Zemlya, at least 600 miles from Spitzbergen. Nothing but the Arctic Ocean separates those two territories, and it is therefore a most suitable area for experimental flights.

'It this be true, and it is highly possible, it is an added reason for us to believe that Flying Saucers, in the inhabited areas, far from the desert regions, where experimental bases are usually located, have extraterrestrial origin.'

We have to ask ourselves if this was correct, or just a 'cover story'? Investigator, Allen Erskine, also wrote about this incident in his book *'Why Are They Watching Us?'*

He quoted an article from the Norwegian newspaper *'The Stuttgarter Tageblatt'*; *'Oslo, Norway, September 4, 1955 – Only now a Board of Inquiry of the Norwegian General Staff is preparing publication of a report on the examination of remains of a UFO crashed near Spitzbergen, presumably early in 1952.*

'Chairman of the Board, Colonel Gernod Darnbyl, during an instruction for Air Force officers, stated; "The crashing of the Spitzbergen disc was highly important. Although our present scientific knowledge does not permit us to solve all the riddles, I am confident that these remains from Spitzbergen will be of utmost importance in this respect.

"Some time ago a misunderstanding was caused by saying that this disc was probably of Soviet origin. It has – this we wish to state emphatically – not been built by any country on earth. The materials used in its construction are completely unknown to all experts who participated in the investigation."

'According to Colonel Darnbyl, the Board of Inquiry is not going to publish an extensive report - "until some sensational facts have been discussed with U.S. and British experts. We should conceal what we found out, as misplaced secrecy might lead to panic."

'Contrary to information from American and other sources, Second Lieutenants Brobs and Tyllensen, who have been assigned as special observers of the Arctic regions since the event at Spitzbergen, report that flying discs have landed in the polar regions several times.

'Said Lieutenant Tyllensen; "I think that the Arctic is serving as a kind of base for the unknowns, especially during snowstorms when we are forced back to our bases. The flying discs, in my opinion, take this opportunity to land.

"Shortly after adverse weather conditions, I have seen them land and take off on three separate occasions. I notice that, after having landed, they execute a speedy rotation around their discs. A brilliant glow of light, the intensity of which is variable with regard to the speed of landing and at take off, prevents any view of the things behind this curtain of light and on or inside the disc itself."

GERMANY

There were other, lesser known reports of crashes. Brinsley le Poer Trench wrote of the January 1965 Italian publication *'Clypeus'*, describing a submerged flying saucer being found in the North Sea, close to the coast of Germany.

Aluminium in colour, the round disc, which was ninety feet in diameter and sixty-nine feet high, was found at low tide, with its dome protruding above the water. Dr. Hans Loberg, a Norwegian scientist, conducted investigations from the fortified German island of Heligoland.

The saucer, which had no signs of bolts or welding, could withstand temperatures of 15,000 degrees Fahrenheight, without showing any trace of melting.

'Dr. Loberg stated; "The cabin of the craft was closed hermetically. When we were finally able to enter, we noticed in one of the compartments there were beds similar to the portable beds in an ambulance. When we got to the next

room, (the sleeping quarters), an unbelievable sight met our eyes.....for at that very moment, we saw seven 'human beings' almost one on top of the other due to the inclination of the craft to one side at the time of impact. All the men were dead.

"Statements from other scientists, as well as myself, considered their age to be approximately twenty-five to thirty years. All were severely burnt, the height of those men was approximately one metre and eighty-five centimetres. Their teeth were of considerable perfection."

'The discovery, according to Dr. Loberg, has contributed to the clearing up of certain obscure facts concerning the mystery of the UFO, and most important of all, confirms the existence of extra-terrestrial beings.'

KECKSBERG - PENNSYLVANIA

On December 9th 1965, a 'fireball' followed by a flash of light was seen by multiple witnesses over Pennsylvania and Illinois. The local media became interested after they received numerous phone calls, and a young boy, and many other people in the district, reported seeing something, followed by a trail of smoke, falling out of the sky, and feeling the vibrations of what might have been a possible impact.

After the authorities claimed there was a subsequent forest fire, near Kecksburg, about forty miles from Pittsburgh, local firemen raced to the area, which was subsequently cordoned off by police. The military arrived, and armed soldiers prevented anyone entering, or getting close to the site. Whilst they were seen to place the strange object and debris onto a tarpaulin covered flatbed tractor-trailer and several trucks, the official story was that nothing had been found – it was only a meteorite!

Witnesses, who had been able to get to the site ahead of the authorities, described a large, shining, metallic 'acorn' shaped craft, partly buried in the ground. It was one solid object, about six feet high, twelve feet long by ten feet wide, bronze-gold in colour, with no visible seams, rivets or signs of a hatch or entrance. It was lying on its side, and one witness, volunteer fireman Jim Romansky, said that on the end he could see strange markings, similar to Egyptian hieroglyphs. He and his crew were soon ordered out of the area.

Many investigators thought that it seemed suspiciously similar to 'Die Glocke', ('The Bell'), an experimental aircraft developed by the Nazi's just before the end of World War II. Other researchers believe the object which crashed was not extraterrestrial, but rather a further development of this revolutionary invention.

Was this an extraterrestrial craft? I'm not sure. On that very same day the Russian spacecraft 'Kosmos-96' came crashing back down to earth. The Americans would have been anxious to analyse and investigate all the Soviet technology. To admit recovering it would have required them to give it back as soon as possible. However, the Soviet Embassy denied that 'Kosmos-96' had crashed at Kecksberg, and other investigators insisted that it had crashed in Canada thirteen hours before the Kecksberg incident.

Many years later, researcher Stan Gordon interviewed a security policeman who arrived at Lockbourne Air Force Base, near Columbus Ohio, on 10th December 1965. He said that both there and at Wright Patterson Air Force Base, extreme security measures were in force.

Another witness, whose family owned a cement factory, drove 6,500 double-glazed bricks to the Base. They had been ordered for building a double-walled shield around a 'recovered radio-active object'. He sneaked a look inside the hanger, but before he could get a 'good look' he was thrown out by a security guard.

As he was unloading the bricks, there were lots of men, wearing white overalls, helmets and rubber boots and gloves – 'Running around like frightened chickens'. One of them, whom he thought was a technician, said; "We're trying to get inside it – but even with diamond drills and acid, we can't crack the damn thing!"

There are times when we just didn't know whether wreckage, either salvaged or on the ground, comes from an alien craft, one of our own crashed prototypes, or is even just 'space junk'.

British researcher Jenny Randles, wrote of one such 1964 incident which occurred at the Fort Riley Army Base in Kansas.

At 2am on 10th December, 'David' was on guard duty when he and three other men were told to report to a remote corner of the base. When they arrived they saw a large helicopter with a searchlight that was illuminating a strange object on the ground. They were ordered to patrol around the craft and shoot anyone who tried to get near it.

David said it looked like a 'giant hamburger', about forty feet high and fifteen feet across, with a dark line along its rim, and a small tail-fin stabilizer. There was no sign of a door, or any life within it, but it appeared to be emanating 'warmth' into the surrounding cold night air.

David and his colleagues were relieved shortly before dawn, but just before breakfast, another witness, who had driven to that same part of the base, ignored a 'Restricted Access' sign, only to be met by armed guards who ordered him away.

'However, before he left, he noticed a large, flat-bed truck with a roundish object on top, completely covered in canvas so that its precise nature was not visible. Half a dozen men, wearing white suits and face masks, were standing beside the truck.'

Investigator Rufus Drake, who himself was a pilot and Air Force veteran, told of conflicting reports regarding a 'crashed' saucer, being held at their Nevada Base in 1953. The Air Force 'cover story' was that Franciszek Jarecki, a Polish pilot, had escaped and crashed landed a MIG-15 fighter on the Danish island of Bornholm. The Americans had supposedly brought it back to the States for careful examination. The only problem with this explanation was that, for political reasons, the Danes had quietly returned the MIG to Poland.

Rufus wrote; *'A member of the ATIC team at Nellis, assured of anonymity, gave me this description of what the 'Polish MIG' looked like when it arrived from the East Coast in 1953;*

"It was a perfect saucer, 30.3 feet in diameter, with thickness ranging from one foot around its circumference to nine feet at its centre. It had a raised cockpit similar to that of a fighter plane, and an enclosed area beneath, five by five by seven feet. Its propulsion system had been totally destroyed, and most of the instrumentation and wiring, although involving familiar materials, was almost incomprehensible.

'No one ever seriously believed this was an interstellar star ship. The feeling was, it was a small craft designed to operate from a mother ship in orbit around the Earth. Judging from its dimensions, and from the battered wreckage of acceleration couches, it was designed to carry two crew members, apparently with human-like limbs, but considerably smaller than human beings. It took months of work to redesign the thing so a human pilot could fit into it.

"There was exhaustive debate at Nellis over whether the thing could be flown. Metallurgy experts understood the composition of the machine, and actually identified new alloys that we had under development. But nobody could figure out what held it up."

Whilst the information officer at Nellis denied any knowledge of this craft, Rufus came across reference to a now missing photo in Pentagon records. The file number –'34920 A.C.' was of a *'UFO in Flight'* and bore the pencilled notation *'space saucer at Nellis'*. A friend, once posted to ATIC headquarters, told him that he had come across a Form 31F – *'Record of Destruction of Classified Material – Nellis Saucer, 1953-55'.*

In their book, *'The UFO Cover-Up'*, Lawrence Fawcett and Barry Greenwood detail an interesting case from 1973. A former member of Naval Intelligence was quite young when he was stationed at the Great Lakes Naval Base, in Chicago.

One night, when he was on guard duty, he was given a 'top secret' envelope, to be personally delivered to the officer-in-charge of one of the restricted buildings that he was guarding. Normally he would hand it to someone at the door, but this time he was required to get the Duty Officer to sign a receipt. When he went inside, the three burly special police who accompanied him, led him down a corridor to a large warehouse area where the Duty Officer was. He was told not to pay attention to anything going on around him – just to get his signed receipt and leave.

'As I went to the doorway where Duty Officer was, I saw a very highly unusual craft over to my left. The craft was possibly thirty to thirty-five feet long, about twelve to fifteen feet at its thickest part, then it tapered off in the front to a teardrop shape.

'I only caught it at an angular view. It looked like it did not have any seams to it. It had a bluish tint but that was only if you looked at it for a few seconds. If

you looked at it and turned your eyes away real quick, all you saw were white
lights, but as long as you stared at it took on a light bluish appearance.

'It was sitting on a pedestal or frame made out of four by four wooden blocks.
It was held up by crossbeams underneath it and was sitting a foot or two off the
floor......At this time I had a very good view about halfway from the craft to the
tail section. The whole craft tapered back to a very high edge. It looked as if it
had a razor sharp edge. The bottom went about three quarters the length of the
craft, then angled sharply upwards.'

As soon as he got the required receipt, he was escorted back out of the building,
and didn't think too much about it until two months later, when he was sent to
San Diego, and got talking to one of the crew from a destroyer.

The sailor said that they had shot down an unidentified craft, with a surface-to-
air missile, in the Pacific; *'They hit the craft but didn't destroy it. According to*
him, they didn't even dent it, but it sent up a concussion through the craft and
whatever was inside of it was destroyed or hurt or whatever. I don't know, he
didn't say. He did say that they were able to pull some sort of life form from out
of it.'

The sailor went on to tell him that the Global Explorer was used to extract the
strange, downed craft out of 350ft of water, from where it was taken by rail
from San Diego to Chicago. His confidant, who said it was like nothing he had
ever seen before, sketched the object. It was an exact copy of the craft he had
seen, hidden in the warehouse at the Great Lakes Naval Base.

SAN ANTONIO – NEW MEXICO

In the early years, there were other little known incidents occurring in the USA.
In 1945, only a few weeks after the first atomic bomb tests in New Mexico, two
young boys, Jose Padilla and Remigio Baca, watched, for several days as
soldiers, in army fatigues, loaded scraps of debris onto small vehicles, and what
appeared to be the shattered remains of a flying object onto a huge flatbed truck,
and hauled it away.

In later years, they recalled how they had been on horseback, searching for a
missing cow, when they had to shelter from a sudden storm. The storm had
already abated, when they saw another flash of bright light, and heard a

'crunching sound' which shook the earth around them. They found the cow and her calf, and sat down for a snack before returning to the ranch house.

It was whilst they were munching on their tortillas that they noticed smoke coming from a 'draw' near the local creek, and they went over to see what it was. There was a long wide gap in the earth, and an object lying askew, partially buried at one end, surrounded by a large field of debris. It was a circular, dull, metallic coloured object, and the grass around it was smouldering.

They made their way towards the main body of the object, and as they did, picked up strange pieces of what seemed to be thin, shiny material, which sprang back into shape when folded. They were sure, that inside the craft, they could see 'little guys' frantically moving backwards and forwards.

It was on the ranch of Faustino Padilla, Jose's father, and he and Remigio had raced home to tell Faustino of their discovery. Two days later, the two boys took Faustino and the local policeman to the site. The main body of the craft was now covered with dirt and debris, and harder to see from a distance. Further, the surrounding field of debris had been removed – but by whom?

It was then that the authorities were advised, and Jose could remember the military visiting and asking permission to remove the wreckage. They tried to claim that although the object was only a crashed weather balloon, nobody was to divulge any details of the crash or recovery operation, to anyone. Faustino and the two boys knew that there was no way this was a weather balloon, as several had crashed in the vicinity before.

PARADISE VALLEY – ARIZONA

Researcher, Rupert Matthews wrote of another event, which occurred in October 1947.

Selman Graves, along with some friends, was rabbit shooting at Caves Creek, in Paradise Valley. They came to a large area of ground, which had been sealed off, and were turned away by military guards. Selman was curious, so he climbed a nearby hill.

He could see men moving around on foot, and trucks traversing a dirt road, towards a strange object. It looked like it was a silvery coloured tent or dome structure, and it the time he assumed it was something military. In hindsight, he wondered if it had been a crashed saucer.

Given the much publicised 'crashes' of that year, and subsequent controversy, it is hard to determine the origin of this particular disc.

KINGMAN – ARIZONA

A few years later, in 1953, there was another 'crash' in Arizona. In 1973, MUFON investigator, Richard Hall, told of speaking to Arthur Stancil, who at the time, was a government employee and project engineer, working on highly classified projects.

On May 21st, 1953, he was seconded to a special assignment, which involved being taken, with other specialists, in a bus, with blacked-out windows to somewhere southeast of Kingman. They were met by an Air Force Colonel, who told them they were to investigate the crash of a super-secret test vehicle. Secrecy was to the extent that they were not even to discuss anything with each other, no matter what the circumstances, and on the way back they were all made to sign the 'Official Secrets Act'. Stancil was escorted to the site by military police, and his instructions were to determine the forward and vertical velocities of the vehicle when it impacted the earth.

He said the 'saucer', which was embedded in the sand, had a diameter of approximately thirty feet, and looked like two convex oval plates, inverted over each other. Although he determined that it had impacted at a velocity of about 100 knots, it had no dents, marks or scratches on its burnished, aluminium type surface.

Another specialist told him that a 1.5 x 3.5 feet hatch was open, and he had managed to get a look inside the craft. There was an oval interior cabin with two swivel seats and many instruments.

Stancil looked inside a small medical tent on the site, and was taken aback to see the body of a small, brown-skinned creature, about four feet tall, wearing a skull-cap and silver one-piece suit.

In 1977, investigator, Len Stringfield, received some supporting testimony from a man who, in 1953, had been in the National Guard at Wright Patterson AFB. He said that he witnessed a delivery of three bodies, shrouded in fabric and packed in dry ice. They were about four feet tall, with large heads and brownish skins, and he was told that they had been recovered from a crash site in Arizona.

Investigator Richard Hall received further second-hand evidence regarding a 1953 crash. A man who had been head of military security at Wright Patterson, made a death-bed confession to his son. In 1953, he had witnessed two disc shaped UFOs, one damaged, the other intact. He also saw the humanoid bodies, and gave a similar description, but added that that they looked totally human, except for their fingers, which were considerably longer than ours.

SYRACUSE – NEW YORK

Researcher, Raymond Fowler, wrote of one such incident, which occurred in Syracuse, New York, sometime between October 1953 and May 1954.

At about 3am one Sunday morning, Bill Marsden and his wife, both respectable university graduates, were returning from visiting friends and a father-son Cub Scout banquet. Upon reaching an intersection, not that far from the airport, they saw four or five police cars, and a lot of flashing red lights. Thinking there had been an accident, they slowed down, and after passing looked over their shoulders.

There was an object, about twenty feet in diameter and fifteen feet high at the centre. Phosphorescent lights of several colours, were spaced around the surface, illuminating several men, some in uniform, who seemed to be walking around the object and examining it.

Bill's wife commented that perhaps it was the 'Avro' disc which she had read about, and seeing nothing in Monday's newspapers, Bill rang the local Sheriff's office, to be told; *"Yes, we know about that, but it's a military secret and we cannot discuss it."*

One of Bill's colleagues, a city newspaper editor, rang the Air Force, only to be told that no such incident had occurred. In later years, when NICAP conducted their own investigation, they were given all kinds of explanations, from a 'dummy bomb' to a weather balloon and even a wing tank falling off a plane.

Marsden dismissed these theories; - *'they didn't explain why the object he and his wife had seen stood much higher than the men who encircled it. In addition, he stressed that the craft, carrying individual multicolour lights, was shaped like a bowl inverted upon a bowl, and there was a clearly defined edge where the rings of the bowl-like segments touched.'*

POLAND

In 1976, British researcher, Arthur Shuttlewood, wrote of an interesting case, which apparently happened in the 1960s. In those days the Soviet Union said little, if anything, about unidentified craft in, or over, their territory.

'Several years ago, an object was seen to fall into the harbour at Gydinia, Poland, one wintry day in January. Some while later, a man was found wandering along the seafront, in an extremely confused state. He was taken to a local medical clinic for observation, and apparently he had an abnormal number of fingers; whether more or less than usual is not clear. He was dressed in a one-piece suit that defied all efforts to remove it by the hospital staff. Eventually, it was removed with the aid of metal shears, and found to consist of exceptionally tough material.

'A bracelet on one of his wrists was removed, after which he died immediately. A post-mortem examination revealed significant differences in the arrangement of both of his internal organs and circulatory system, which was reported to follow a spiral path round his body.

'Suddenly, the hospital was sealed off by the authorities, who placed guards at the entrance. No-one was allowed in or out of the bay where the body lay. Some time afterwards a lorry arrived, complete with a refrigerated container, all heavily guarded. The lorry later left with its strange cargo – and, according to the report – the container was addressed to a research institute in Moscow.

'The hospital duly returned to normal, and Mr. Szachnowsky thought it was little more than a nice sensational story with a hush science fiction flavour. However, he subsequently chanced to meet in London a fellow-Pole who, during a conversation, confided that he was actually on the staff of the hospital at Gydinia when the rare incident took place. Moreover, this compatriot verified all the details as a true account. Szachnowsky said he had 'no reason to doubt his word'.

Sometimes a 'crash' can be explained as being one of our own craft. The British *'Awareness'* newsletter and *'BUFORA Bulletin'* contained articles which suggested that the strange object, which had crashed at Bicester in 1967, was not extraterrestrial.

Researcher Bill Foley, stated that *'the object had been identified as a USAF, D21 supersonic reconnaissance drone. The description of the 'UFO' fits the D-21 which entered service in 1966 as a replacement for the Lockheed U-2 spy plane – one of which had been shot down over Russia with the capture of the pilot Gary Powers.*

'The idea was to launch the drone from under a B-52 heavy bomber at high altitude; overfly Soviet airspace and then return to home base with information gathered. Clearly, to control a pilotless aircraft to land safely after a complex mission to Russia would be difficult, and some of the 31 built are known to have crashed. Hence the D-21 in question at Bicester would have been whisked away very quickly by USAF recovery teams to avoid the top secret drone being seen by too many people.'

There are many other cases where we will never know the truth. The *'Fortean Times'* published an interesting account from an area bordering England's Lake District; however some sceptical researchers were not convinced.

Apparently, during maintenance work on the St. Kentigern's Church in the small village of Caldbeck, some interesting documents were discovered. They were written accounts of interviews the previous vicar had conducted with several locals, who claimed that on 4th March 1954, they had seen a 'fire-ball' crash nearby.

'A farmer and his son saw a disc-shaped craft, marked with serpentine insignia, crash into the 'fell'. They were detained at Kirkbride Airfield for two weeks, by RAF personnel, while the wreckage was recovered, and were later being given a large cash sum and relocated to the south of England.

'Another local, a poacher named Dyker, stumbled across the crash site, and found two alien cadavers with 'the face of the devil'. Shortly after his discovery, he went mad and never recovered.'

In many of the 'crash' reports we can never be sure whether the craft were extraterrestrial or of earthly origin. We will probably never know!

CHAPTER THREE

THE RACE FOR SPACE

During those exciting, heady 'Good Old Days', we were determined to venture outside the confines of our own planet – exploring 'new worlds' and the possibility of meeting any of the 'new neighbours' who may have already been visiting us.

The possibility of aliens already being in our Solar System or on our Moon was very controversial, but popular in the 1950s. In his 1957 book, *'The Flying Saucer Conspiracy'*, Major Donald Keyhoe was convinced that there was an alien base beneath the rocky surface of the Moon. He also thought that there could be one on Mars.

Keyhoe found a quasi-confirmation when speaking to Paul Redell, an aeronautical engineer. When he asked if there was actually a saucer base on the Moon, Redell mentioned the observations and reports of astronomer Dr. H.P.Wilkins, and J. O'Neill, science editor of the *'Herald Tribune'*. Redell suggested that Keyhoe read their articles, and then added; "You won't find *all* the dope....after O'Neill and Wilkins let it out, they were put under pressure to stop talking. But you'll find enough."

While we discuss our ventures into space, and what has been discovered and seen out there, we must not forget our own astronomers, in powerful observatories, who are scanning the skies every night.

In his book, *'Flying Saucers – Where Do They Come From?'*, Richard Tambling, a former Air Force photographer, discusses a photograph of a strange object, taken by a member of the Ballarat Astronomical Society on 4th June 1969, forty-eight days before Armstrong set foot on the Moon.

It was five hundred kilometres long, with a metallic mirror-like hull, and cast an immense black shadow on the lunar surface. Another member of the Society independently took two further photos of it, surrounded by haze. The roll of film contained other local pictures, and when later developed, it was analysed and pronounced genuine by independent photographers and laboratories.

As our telescopes and exploratory probes venture further and further into space, our views of the galaxy, and indeed our own Solar System are constantly being reshaped. Minor planets, such as Makemake are being discovered, and the 'heliosphere', the Sun's zone of influence, is asymmetrical, not spherical as previously thought.

Many do not realise the vast distances covered to even reach the outer limits of our own Solar System. It takes years for our craft to travel the Solar System, and dozens of hours for commands, travelling at light speed to reach our far flung probes.

On 15th May 1954, the *'New York Herald Tribune'* published an article detailing how, in 1953, astronomer Clyde Tombaugh had confirmed the discovery of two unknown artificial satellites orbiting the Earth. Until then, the government had also kept the information secret.

Rumours had been circulating, since 1953, of these unidentified objects being discovered. Some researchers claimed that United States radar had detected at least ten objects, all around two to five thousand feet in diameter, and in 1954 *'Aviation Week Magazine'* also wrote about 'two mysterious satellites'.

In his book, *'Aliens from Space'*, Maj. Donald Kehoe stated; *'Since 1953 the Air Force had known that giant spaceships were operating near our planet.'* It was during that year that the military began experimenting with new long-range radar equipment; *'While making the initial tests, A.F. officers were astonished to pick up a gigantic object orbiting near the equator. Its speed was almost 18,000 miles an hour. Repeated checks showed that the tracking was correct. Some huge unknown object was circling the Earth, 600 miles out.'* Shortly after, radar tracked a second large object which came into orbit about four hundred miles out.

In his book, *'The Rainbow Conspiracy'*, author Brad Steiger confirmed this when he wrote; *'In late July, 1957, three months before the Soviet launching of Sputnik 1, Italian astronomers tracked a huge mystery satellite orbiting Earth. Other sources corroborated the astronomers' discovery, and there were even reports of a naked-eye large object – which was seen to move across the sky in a steady fashion, a pattern that the world would soon come to associate with an orbiting satellite. The satellite disappeared from its orbit of Earth just a few days before Sputnik-1 became our planet's first official satellite.'*

All these early reports, made before the launching of Sputnik-1, are important, because there is very little likelihood they were craft of our own making.

In late 1957, Dr. Luis Corrales, at a tracking station in Venezuela, who was photographing Sputniks-1 and 2, said that one of them, Sputnik-2, was being followed by an unknown object. The object, which had been maintaining a parallel course, suddenly deviated then returned, indicating some form of intelligent control.

On November 7th of that year, The *'London Times'* reported that four astronomers at the Commonwealth Observatory near Canberra, had tracked Sputniks-1 and 2, when suddenly a third object came into their telescopic view. It was a vivid pink in colour, and remained in view for two minutes, apparently trailing one of the Sputniks. Officially, the Americans didn't launch their first satellite until early 1958, so this sighting remained 'unknown'.

On 31st January 1958, the American 'Explorer-I' went aloft, carrying a small scientific payload which was instrumental in discovering the magnetic radiation belts around the Earth. On the 5th March of that year, the U.S. launched Explorer-II atop a Jupiter rocket. The 70ft rocket, trailing a wake of orange flames, roared quickly into air and disappeared into the overcast sky overhead. It was never heard from again!

Between July and September 1958, another 'mystery satellite' was observed in a southwest-northeast orbit. It had a brilliance fluctuation rate about twice that of Sputnik-3, and crossed from horizon to horizon in just over four minutes.

Professor Ettore Martin, from the Astronomy Observatory, Trieste, Italy, gave a detailed report of the object, noting that it did not emit any radio signals, and was blinking on and off at regular seven second intervals. Unlike our own satellites, it was on a polar orbit, at an altitude of about 300 miles above the earth's surface.

Later, Olave Fontes wrote an interesting article, titled *'Project Argus, and the 'Anonymous' Satellite'* for the *'Flying Saucer'* magazine. He suggested that three solid-propellant rockets, each tipped with a nuclear warhead, 'were aimed to go off precisely at the times when a certain artificial satellite orbiting the earth was in the proper position'. Within the three minute time zone, the rockets zoomed off into the sky. The strange intruder was not sighted after that!

This operation was conducted in August 1958 by US Navy Task Force 88, located in the Atlantic Ocean, off the Falkland Islands. After its return, two of its senior officers, Admiral Mustin and Captain Gralia, both received the Legion of Merit.

The U.S. instigated 'NASA', its 'National Aeronautics and Space Administration', and in October 1958, announced its program to explore space. Later, in 1959, Dr. W. Whitson, a scientist from the Advanced Research Projects Agency, stated at a ' California Institute of Technology' conference, that a network of observation posts, now established across the country, were able to detect satellites with 'unfriendly' objectives. In an article, investigator Olave Fontes stressed that Dr. Whitson was 'not talking about Russian satellites, but about objects not made by Earth-man'.

During October 1958, the tracking facility at Cape Canaveral began picking up unusual radio signals, and other stations were alerted. They also monitored the frequencies, and were initially unable to locate the source of these transmissions, despite using Doppler and other radio direction finding equipment. The source was an unidentified object 3,000 miles from Earth and moving towards the Moon at a speed of 9,000 miles per hour. Suddenly, it altered course and headed out into deep space.

On 4th January 1960, the US Navy had tracked an unknown object, weighing about fifteen tons, in a near Polar orbit, and dubbed it the 'Black Knight', noting that it did not emit any kind of radio signals.

At first the Americans, who considered it to be 'man-made', thought the object may be of Russian origin. This was soon disputed by Russian Professors Masevich and Boshich, who were responsible for the U.S.S.R. Sputnik tracking stations. They 'very much doubted' that the mystery object was a Russian satellite or any remains of a payload launch rocket. At that time, all Russian satellites were launched into orbits of 65 degrees to the equator, taking them well clear of the Poles.

Later, it was discovered it had a 'twin', approximately the same size, and also in Polar orbit. While the Americans were persistent in their belief that the mysterious objects were Russian, nobody mentioned that the safest place, at that time, for an alien intelligence to monitor Earth would be from over our Polar Regions.

It wasn't just high orbiting objects that astronomers, who were skilled observers, were reporting. At the end of September 1953, Dr. James Bartlett, a noted Baltimore astronomer, was observing a transit of the star Fomalhaut. At first four large lights were seen with the naked eye, and then monitored through 7-power binoculars.

Dr. Bartlett said; "The lights moved slowly, and came from the noses of two enormous craft which more than filled the binoculars. They were quite low, apparently at about 3,000 feet altitude. A cabin was observed in the nose, and ports in the sides of the hulls in each craft, which were either cylindrical or cigar-shaped. A sound like a piston engine at great height emanated from the craft, but these were not airliners, neither were they dirigibles.

"At the time I believed them to be a U.S. secret, and it was not until late in 1957 that I revealed the sighting to a group of Washington astronomers."

Before then, Dr. Bartlett had been a complete skeptic, often ridiculing anyone who believed in the reality of UFOs; "I believed these were secret developments because they were apparently unmolested in the vicinity of, and over, many of our highly sensitive installations. Later, I noticed an occurrence pattern that showed that these craft appeared on a world-wide basis – over Communist territory as well as over our own.

"During the Korean conflict both sides shot at one of these craft, and obviously each side thought them to be enemy machines. This clearly implied that they were of unknown origin."

After several more sightings of anomalous objects, Dr. Bartlett made the following statement; "My belief in UFOs is simply expressed. UFOs do exist. They are some type of mechanism controlled craft, their origin unknown. Beyond this, I have no definite conclusion. It has not been scientifically proven that they are interplanetary. At the same time, it has not been scientifically proven that they are not. Such an explanation for them should be fully explored."

He was not the only astronomer to entertain the extraterrestrial hypothesis. On 10th May, at a 1971 news conference in London, controversial astronomer Sir Fred Hoyle said; *"Human beings are simply pawns in a great game being played by alien minds which control mankind's every move. These alien minds come from another universe, one with five dimensions. Their laws of chemistry and physics are completely different from ours. They have learned to shatter the time barriers that restrict us.*

"These super-intelligent entities are so different from us that to comprehend them or describe them in human terms is literally impossible. These entities seem to be totally free from any physical restrictions as bodies, and they are more like pure intelligence; we know that some of them are like that.

"They are not all the same, but some of them seem to have the ability to be anywhere in the Universe in a matter of seconds. The Universe, as we understand it, with all of our so-called limitations, and all of this garbage about the limits on the speed of light, simply does not exist.

"The aliens are everywhere; they are in the sky, in the sea and on the Earth. They have been here for countless aeons, and they have probably controlled the evolution of 'Homo Sapiens'. All that man has built and become was accomplished because of the tinkering of these intelligent forces."

Apparently, it was not until the late 1970s that Professor Sergei Bozhich, of Moscow University, announced that in the early sixties the Soviets had spotted a 'startling space wreck', 1,240 miles above the Earth.

He believed the object was broken into ten pieces, the two largest being about 100 feet in diameter, and after using computers to track the orbits back in time; "We discovered that they all originated in the same spot, on the same day – December 18, 1955 – obviously the result of a powerful explosion. We are convinced that the objects are not from Earth." (The first man-made satellite – Sputnik-1 – was shot into space, by the Russians, two years later in October 1957.)

After years of study, Bozhich was convinced that it was an alien craft, an opinion shared by Dr. Vladimir Azhazha who said; "There is absolutely no doubt in my mind that we are dealing with the remains of a large alien craft. It must hold secrets we haven't even dreamed of."

Professor Aleksandr Kazantsev, a noted astrophysicist, added; "The size of the two big pieces would lead one to assume that the craft was at least 200 feet in length and up to 100 feet in width, with small domes housing telescopes, saucer antennae, for communications, and portholes for visual contact. Its size would suggest several floors, possibly five."

Whilst I think that Kazantsev was being very speculative, one must consider that these pronouncements were made over twenty years later, when the major countries had gained a better chance to 'get up there' for a closer look.

The Russian announcement was, in some part, verified by Western astronomers, Dr. Clyde Tombaugh and John Bagby. John Bagby had said, years before, that the Earth has; - "...at least ten close natural moonlets which broke from a parent body."

Clyde Tombaugh had detected huge 'blips' of spaceships orbiting Earth in 1953-4. On thirteen occasions they had tracked craft orbiting at altitudes from 100 to 500 miles, often in an equatorial pattern. As soon as they were discovered, an emergency tracking centre was set up at White Sands Proving Ground in New Mexico.

One cannot blame the aliens if they were concerned about our initial ventures into space. A couple of senior U.S. military had unsuccessfully proposed 'nuking' the Moon, as part of a scientific project, 'A119'. In the 1950s, the 'boffins' were also designing a craft with nuclear fuel, where their 'Orion Drive' would propel a craft through space with a series of nuclear explosions. Thankfully, this idea was also abandoned in 1964.

In 1959, the 'New Zealand Scientific Space Research Group', who referenced both the British *'Flight'* and American *'Aviation Week'* magazines, reported that on January of that year, a Soviet Lunar rocket, the last of a series of eleven or twelve, was fired towards the Moon. Some of the rockets carried thermonuclear warheads, and none reached their destination. The official reason given was that unexpected strong magnetic fields, prior to third stage cut-off, prevented the rockets from hitting the Moon.

Dr Steven Greer, interviewed retired U.S. Air Force Colonel Ross Dedrickson in September 2000. In his testimony, he confirmed that in the late 70s or early 80s, the Americans had also attempted to put a nuclear weapon on the Moon, and explode it 'for scientific measurements'. He claimed that the extraterrestrials destroyed it before it reached its destination, as they did any nuclear weapon we sent into space.

The first official artificial Earth satellite was Sputnik-1, a Soviet space vehicle launched into orbit on October 4th 1957. If that is correct, what were the objects detected orbiting our planet long before that? Were they alien, or were they our own secret vehicles our governments didn't want us to know about?

In 1949, 1951, 1953, 1954, 1955 and July 1957 there had been reports of anomalous objects circling high above us. They were often there for only a short time, before disappearing as mysteriously as they had first appeared.

Two incidents were reported by Donald Keyhoe in his book *'Flying Saucers from Outer Space'*. The first occurred in the late 1940s over White Sands Guided Missile Base. One large disc was tracked travelling at 18,000mph **56 miles** above the Earth. Another two smaller discs were tracked by five observation posts, and seen to pace a high altitude rocket. After circling it for a moment, the discs speeded up and rapidly out-climbed the Army projectile.

Again, in late February 1950, witnesses at Key West, Florida, saw two glowing saucers, and Naval radar screens tracked two objects **50 miles** above the Earth.

But, this was not the first time unidentified objects were detected orbiting the Earth. In 1859, Richard Carrington, at England's Redhill Observatory, caught sight of two bright objects, which were too slow to be meteors, sailing through the sky.

Nineteen years later, astronomers Dr. James Watson and Dr. Lewis Swift observed two unknown objects, approximately one-quarter and one-half a mile wide, circling at about 20,000 miles above the Earth.

My dear friend and colleague, Rosemary Decker, wrote that; *'On July 10th 1947,one of the United States' most prominent astronomers was driving from Clovis to Clines Corner, New Mexico, with his wife and two daughters. They were in sunlight, but the western half of the sky was clouded. As they headed west, they suddenly spotted a curious bright object hanging almost motionless among the clouds. The astronomer made calculations, determining that the object was between 65 and 100 feet thick, and 160 to 245 feet long. The elliptical body, whitish and apparently luminous, disappeared behind the clouds, reappeared then disappeared, not to emerge again. The sighting lasted about two and a half minutes. The astronomer, (who preferred anonymity), was baffled because, when the wobbling object arose, its vertical speed was between 600 and 900 miles per hour!'*

Rosemary also noted that in '*Mysteries of Time and Space*', astronomer H. P. Wilkins had reported a sighting of his own; '*While on a visit to the U.S. in 1954, he was flying from Charleston, West Virginia, to Atlanta, Georgia, when suddenly he spotted two brilliant oval objects hovering above lofty cumulus clouds about two miles away. They were bright gold, much brighter than the sunlit clouds.*

'*The objects began to move slowly northward, as the clouds drifted south. He wrote; "Suddenly, a third, precisely similar oval object was seen against the shadowed side of the cloud, but looked greyish in the shadow. The third one began to move with accelerated velocity, described in a curve, and vanished behind a nearer cloud mass....the whole display was visible nearly two minutes.'*

Apparently, Wilkins regretted not having a camera at the time, however some years later, he was able to photograph another close sighting of a disc. '*Unwilling to risk his professional reputation, he gave the photo to Desmond Leslie, with the remark that "a member of the family" had taken the picture. Long after Wilkins had passed on, Leslie brought the photo to Gordon Creighton, editor of 'Flying Saucer Review'. And it was published in the summer, 1998 issue.'*

Rosemary said that it was not unusual for astronomers to only come forward late in life, when they no longer felt that their careers would be threatened. These scientists were also not always happy about our ventures into space.

In 1975, at a Manchester University conference, leading astronomer Sir Bernard Lovell, when discussing Man's search to discover the nature of the universe, noted that the intercontinental ballistic missiles, that led to the launching of the first satellites, were in themselves designed to destroy mankind.

He said; "*Since Sputnik 1, eighteen years ago, the Soviet Union has launched 834 space missions, of which 516 have been for military activities.*"

It wasn't just astronomers who were noticing strange anomalies. During October 1958, the tracking facility at Cape Canaveral began picking up unusual radio signals. Other stations were alerted and also monitored the frequency. Technicians, using Doppler and radio direction finding equipment, tried to locate the source of the anomalous transmissions. The object sending the signals was 3,000 miles from Earth and moving at 9,000 miles per hour toward the moon. Moments later it altered course and headed into deep space. It was never identified.

Both Russia and the U.S. were anxious to venture further above the planet than they had previously gone. The main problem to overcome was a life support system needed for manned craft.

Between 1948 and 1952, the Americans flew a number of monkeys in captured German V-2 rockets, and from 1949 to 1956, the Russians launched similar flights using dogs. It is unlikely that scientists and astronomers were not aware of this activity, and probably followed it with interest.

Officially, the first Soviet satellite, Sputnik-1, went into orbit in October 1957, and burned up on re-entry on 4th January 1958, so there was no question as to the non-Earthly origin of satellites before that. The first official space casualty was a Russian dog called 'LAIKA', who was sent aloft, in Sputnik-2, on November 3rd 1957. She orbited the earth for seven days before she was finally euthanized.

One important factor of future space travel was the need for effective and reliable life-support systems. Since 1953, the American Board of Preventative Medicine has held a certified subspecialty of 'Aerospace Medicine', which encompasses research in both aviation and aerospace.

Between 1949 and 1956 the Russians had already sent dogs up in rockets, some reaching an altitude of 213km, and the U.S. sent monkeys aboard captured German V-2 rockets between 1948 and 1952.

It was said that then, between the end of 1957 and the beginning of 1959, the USSR sent some objects, containing dummies, aloft and then made four attempts to place a human in orbit. The Italian News Agency, *'Continentale'*, soon announced the sad results.

The first aspirant was Alexel Ledowsky who reached a height of 300 kilometres before his transmission failed, and no more was ever heard from him.

Serenty Schiborin went aloft in February 1958, and his fate is also a mystery. Andreij Mitcow, a leading test pilot, lost his life when twenty minutes into the mission the rocket exploded.

(Russian 'losses' continued during the following years. An unconfirmed report also detailed a Soviet man and woman exploration team, whose rocket was launched on May 17th 1961. It was tracked for a week by stations all over the world, until it mysteriously disappeared on the 24th May. Was this Mirija Gromov, the only female we know of who went aloft in a 'space aircraft'. All that we heard was that the mission 'ended tragically'.

In April 1967, Soviet cosmonaut Vladimir Komorov plunged to a fiery death when the parachute on Soyuz-1 failed to deploy, and he crashed to earth. In 1971, astronauts Dobrovolski, Volkov and Patsayev suffocated when the pressure capsules opened prematurely on their Soyuz ferry craft which was returning them from the Salyut-1 Space Station.)

Russia had certainly suffered more than its fair share of accidents during that period. The 'New Scientist' magazine quoted Dr. Zhores Medvedev who said that nuclear waste had been buried for many years near the Urals town of Blagevveshusk. In 1958 there was an enormous explosion, like a violent volcano. The nuclear reactions had led to overheating in the underground burial grounds.

"The explosion poured radioactive dust and materials high into the sky," Dr. Medvedev said. "Tens of thousands of people were affected, hundreds dying; though the real figures have never been made public."

In 1960, the elite of Soviet rocket technology were gathered around the Baikonurs cosmodrome launching area of a 'Moon Rocket' which failed to ignite. Rather than waiting for the fuel to be drained out, technicians positioned some ladders and platforms around the rocket, in an attempt to locate the fault.

The ignition on the rocket unexpectedly kicked in, and the ladders and platforms blocked it, causing the rocket to fall on the men and women below; "They were some of the best representatives of Soviet space technology," Medvedev sadly commented.

According to the 'Chicago Daily News', on 9th December 1960, another unsuccessful attempt to put a man in space, was made by Russia in the October of that year. The cosmonaut's capsule failed to separate from the rocket, and the entire space vehicle disintegrated. After his 'escape' to the 'West', this was later verified by Jaanimets, an Estonian sailor who, at the time, had been on board Krushev's yacht, the 'Baltika'. He said that everything was in ready for a big celebration, to coincide with Krushev's visit to the U.N.'s General Assembly, if that October mission, for the first man in space, had been successful.

In their December Newsletter, *'NZ Scientific Space Research'* published the translation of part of a speech made by Krushev at the General Assembly; "Now, just imagine that our little planet Earth would be attacked from space – how would people react? Would we still have two divisions, or would the mutual danger unite people in defence? We all want the same – we all want to reciprocate, and we have sufficient space on our little planet." (These words have great similarity to those later spoken by U.S. President Ronald Reagan.)

Not long after, on April 12th 1961, Yuri Gagarin, with his successful epic flight, was our first real 'astronaut'. In 25 hours, he orbited the Earth over seventeen times, and became a global hero. While his Russian contemporaries were usually silent on the matter, before his premature death in a plane crash, Gagarin was also reported as saying; "During my space flights, I saw something that is far beyond any fantasy. If I am ever permitted to tell this publically, I am sure that the world will be in shock."

The Americans also had their fair share of accidents. In 1961, Virgil Grissom nearly drowned after making a Mercury sub-orbital flight. When he landed in the ocean, the hatch on his capsule blew prematurely, causing it to sink. Nobody can forget the disastrous Challenger explosion, which killed seven NASA astronauts in January 1986.

America launched its first satellite, 'Explorer-1', into orbit on January 1st 1958, and by the 1960s, despite the fact that they must have had other accidents of their own, American technology appeared to be giving the U.S. an advantage in the race to the Moon.

On May 5th 1961, Alan Shepherd became the first American in space, making a fifteen minute sub-orbital flight aboard the 'Freedom-7' capsule. John Glenn became the first American to circle the Earth, orbiting three times on February 20th 1962. Edward Wood performed the first space-walk by an American in 1965 during a four day Gemini mission and Frank Borman, James Lovell and William Anders orbited the Moon at Christmas 1968.

On 4th July 1960, American *'Newsweek'* detailed the eleven U.S. satellites and one Russian object known to still be in orbit. The Air Force Space-Track program, at the National Space Surveillance Control Centre, also noted one U.S. and one Soviet probe circling the Sun, and Pioneer V heading towards Venus.

Many scientists considered that there was one other object, which was neither Russian nor American. Some speculated that the Russians had sent two men up in a capsule, and failed to bring them back. Were they still up there?

In the early 1960s, Western publications were rife with reports of secret Soviet satellites. In 1963, the *'Sunday Telegraph'* published an article by John Delin. It claimed that twelve Russian space efforts had failed, and speculated about the number of possible lost cosmonauts. Russia responded with public denials.

The Royal Aircraft Establishment produced an amazingly accurate *'Table of Artificial Satellites'* which noted a tentative identification of six 'Sputniks' launched between September 1st 1962 and January 7th 1963. They had unknown or uncertain orbital data, however neither the U.S.A. nor the Russians admitted to launching these craft. Just who or what were orbiting our planet?

Maj. Donald Keyhoe wrote; *'On April 8th 1964, NASA launched from Cape Kennedy the first two-man Gemini capsule, a crucial step in our effort to land an astronaut on the moon. This report was given to me confidentially by two scientists present at the test. The Gemini capsule was still in its first orbit when four spacecraft, of unknown origin flew up to it. While startled radar trackers watched their screens in open-mouthed amazement, the four took up positions around the capsule – two above it, one beneath and one aft.*

'Whoever was inside those strange craft appeared to be inspecting the capsule minutely and with care. They drew close to the capsule and paced it for a full orbit of the Earth. Then, apparently finished with their scrutiny, they pulled away and vanished into the unknown.'

In the following decades, several countries have launched numerous known and secret satellites, as well as Space Stations and ventures beyond our planet. Most are highly classified with military significance, and the true nature of the 'Black Knight' or the objects discovered by Boshich may never be known. Both the Russians and Americans have remained silent on the matter, and one can't help wondering if 'someone out there' was interfering with our off planet ventures.

Many of the early satellites went 'missing', including the Soviet 'Molniya' satellite. Of the thirty-four U.S. 'Explorer' satellites, not all could be considered a success. Five simply 'vanished' from our tracking systems, two failed to achieve orbit, and one, which was sent to the Moon, missed its target due to a velocity error. In 1965, a Soviet communications satellite also 'disappeared'.

Other satellites and probes, including 'ANNA', 'TELSTAR's 1 and 2, 'MARINER-2', and 'RANGER-3', inexplicably stopped transmitting, only to mysteriously start working again. In 1968, an Australian ground station turned off the transmitter on the American scientific satellite, 'PEGASUS'. Nine years later, in August 1977, it mysteriously resumed sending radio signals.

Years later, the much feted 'Mars Observer' inexplicably became 'deaf-mute', and all attempts to restore communications were futile. Experts were unsure as to where it was. Some sceptics claimed that it was engineered to prevent any discovery of alleged artificial artefacts on the planet's surface.

NASA launched a satellite for RCA, which was designed to relay telephone and television transmissions. It was working perfectly, when it suddenly vanished. Neither NASA, NORAD, nor the North American Defense Command, all of whom had excellent tracking equipment, could locate the satellite or explain its disappearance.

From the late 1950's onward, we sent exploratory, unmanned craft to the Moon and our nearest neighbours. Many, inexplicably, went 'missing'. From 1961 to 1964, the Russians 'lost' two 'Venera' and two 'Zond' missions to Venus and Mars. In November 1964, the U.S. launched Mariner-4, destined for Mars, where it was to take photographs and transmit them back to Earth. In July 1965, it reached its destination, and took 24 pictures. Once it passed behind the planet, it mysteriously took over twelve minutes longer than anticipated to reappear, when it commenced sending the photographs back to the Australian Tidbinbilla tracking station. There were other bothersome signals – termed 'anomalies' – interfering with the transmission, and at the same time a glowing, oval-shaped UFO was reported, by many witnesses, to be hovering only a few miles away, between the tracking station and Canberra Airport.

Paul Dodd, of the Meteorological Bureau, said it appeared to be a steel revolving disc, and Air Traffic Controller, Tony Frodsham, agreed that it was a metallic object, glinting in the sunlight. Scientists at the neighbouring Mount

Stromlo Observatory could not identify it, and the instruments at the nearby Goldstone tracking centre were recording strange irregularities in the messages from Mariner.

As long as it was there, the tracking station was plagued by anomalous signals. An Air Force jet was scrambled, but the pilot reported that as he neared the object, 'it flipped up' and left him, vanishing at a great altitude. At the same time, the anomalous signals ceased to interfere with Tidbinbilla's reception.

Other satellites and space probes, both American and Russian, either went missing or acted strangely. Both Voyager-1 and Telstar-2 suddenly stopped transmitting, and then inexplicibly resumed their activity days or even weeks later. Nobody could explain these anomalies, and in 1969, John Casani, a member of the Mariner-7 science team at the Californian Jet Propulsion Laboratory, invented, tongue in cheek. a 'Great Galactic Goul', who 'feasted' on any unsuspecting probes from Earth that wandered into his Martian domain.

Reports from Russian astronauts are rare. On 12th October 1964, 'Voskhod' brought its three cosmonauts back to Earth in Central Asia after only twenty-four hours and sixteen Earth orbits. Since Soviet officials had been predicting a 'long flight', there was speculation as to the reason for the early landing. Some suggested that there had been a defect in the craft's radio transmitter, and others noted a rise in the cabin's temperature, indicating a faulty orbit, too close to the Earth's atmosphere. The next day the astronauts commented that they regretted being brought down so soon as they "had seen many interesting things, and wanted to investigate them more fully."

At a later press conference, a Western journalist asked the 'Voskhod' Commander if they had encountered any UFOs during orbit. He and the other two crew members immediately got up and left the room, and the meeting was abruptly terminated.

Investigator, Major Donald Keyhoe later wrote; *"In Moscow there are, in fact, persistent rumours that the last manned satellite was repeatedly overtaken by extremely fast flying discs which struck the craft violent, shattering blows with their powerful magnetic fields."*

On 18th March 1965, Pavel Beljajev and Alexei Leonov, the crew of Voskhod-2 reported two strange cylinders which they could see in space. They were perfectly formed and had no apertures, and it was assumed that they were 'man-made satellites.' Leonov also became the first man to 'walk' in space, when for ten minutes he 'stood' in space, with a thick cable linking him to the cabin.

They were given instructions to land as they completed their seventeenth revolution, but they made an unexpected eighteenth, and descended manually to an equally unexpected spot in the Urals. It was nearly nine hundred miles away from the designated landing place in Kazakhstan. Newspaper reports claimed that the craft had come down in flames, and its radio antennae were burned off. The astronauts had apparently lost contact with their mission control for several hours before their crash landing in the snow.

On 27th March, at a press conference they said that their solar orientation system had failed, causing them to make an additional orbit and overshoot the nominated landing area. They also mentioned an 'unmanned mystery satellite' they had sighted only a few orbits before they landed.

Moscow suggested that this object may have been of American origin, designed to monitor Voshod, something which was strenuously denied by the USA.

One contemporary Western researcher commented; *"It sounds far more as though this were another UFO. And the big question is, did they come down in a hurry to get away from it, or did it 'assist' them to come down, and by driving them out of orbit down on to the edge of the Earth's atmosphere, and give them both a very narrow escape from death?"*

Over the years, the Russians also sent probes into the Solar System, including a series of at least ten to Venus. Some were successful, however on the 30th July 1967, Venus-4 unfortunately landed on top of an extremely high mountain. They developed and launched several space stations, including Cosmos-557, and seven of the Salyut series between 1971 and 1982.

In 1973, on April 3rd, the Russians launched their space-lab Salyut-2. It was planned to house three cosmonauts, who would be conducting tests for nearly a month. German space expert, Harro Zimmer, head of the Wilhelm Foerster Observatory in West Berlin, reported that, in between Salyut's 22nd and 24th orbits, it was joined by eighteen unidentified objects, which accompanied it along the way. On April 14th, it was badly damaged by an unexplained accident, and began to disintegrate. The cosmonauts were never sent aloft to board their space station, and the Russians never gave any explanation.

U.S. astronauts rarely made comments, however Gordon Cooper and Edgar Mitchell both stated that UFOs, alien visitations and technology are a very real occurrence. Gordon Cooper, who flew the Mercury-9 Mission, and was the commander of the eight-day Gemini-5 Mission, only admitted to a 1951 sighting when piloting a plane over Germany. He saw a group of 'double lenticular –shaped' objects, flying in formation, higher and faster than any plane of the day.

It was thought that Cooper, being one of the most experienced astronauts, would have been chosen for an Apollo Mission, however Maurice Chatelain, in his book, *'Our Ancestors Came From Outer Space,'* suggested that Cooper had already seen too much, and his nature was such that he would want to talk about it.

When the United Nations held a debate on UFOs Cooper wrote to them and stated the following; *'I believe UFOs exist and that the truly unexplainable ones and are from some other technically advanced civilization...I believe that these extraterrestrial vehicles and their crews are visiting this planet from other planets, which are obviously a little more advanced than we are here on Earth......I feel that we need to have a top-level, co-ordinated program to scientifically collect and analyse data, from all over the Earth, concerning any type of encounter, and to determine how best to interface with these visitors in a friendly fashion.'*

In 1969, America, in its Apollo craft, landed the first astronauts on the Moon, however the program lasted only a few short years. One astronaut sadly described their trips as being merely 'swoop and scoop' missions. Why?

In so far as the sightings by astronauts are concerned, I have an interesting 1976 letter, sent by arch-sceptic James Oberg to New Zealand's Fred and Phyllis Dickeson. He reminded them of his access to NASA's files, and engaged in his usual dismissal of all reports. He then unexpectedly noted; *'Have you heard of the Apollo12 'moon pigeons? Have you seen the Skylab-2 photo of the thousand foot UFO solid object (NOT a light in the Dark). How about the recently released X-15 photos from fifteen years ago?...I'm sorry your summary didn't include Gemini-4 and Gemini-11, two of the strongest astronaut UFO cases on record.'*

Apollo 14 astronaut Edgar Mitchell, who became quite spiritual after his Moon landing, did not testify as to any sightings, but made this cryptic comment to Richard Thieme; "If we could do what they can do, they wouldn't have sent me to the Moon in a 'tin-lizzie'."

In October 1998, when addressing the 'UFO Experience Conference' in North Haven, he called on Congress to grant immunity to officials who have taken an oath of secrecy so they can acknowledge the existence of UFOs and aliens. He was ninety percent sure that many of the UFOs observed over the years belonged to aliens, and added; "...this suggests that there are humanoids manning craft which have characteristics not in the arsenal of any nation on Earth."

That same year, in an interview with Steven Greer he said; *"Yes, there have been UFO visitations. There have been crashed craft. There have been material and bodies recovered. And there is some group of people somewhere that may or may not be associated with Government at this point, but certainly were at one time, that have this knowledge. They have been attempting to conceal this knowledge or nor permit it to be widely disseminated."*

Suddenly, despite three more craft having been built and ready to go, and an increase in Mars Probes, there were no more astronauts officially sent to the Moon.

In 2003, the late Stanton Friedman made this interesting observation; *"A question for which I have never had a satisfactory answer is why the USA didn't launch Apollo 18 and 19? The hardware was all built. The crews had been selected and trained. President Nixon said it was to save money. But almost all of the bills had already been paid. Yes, I am aware that some have suggested that the aliens secretly told us to stay off their moon......At best an idea in my grey basket.*

"So the big question is, do we Earthlings want to take dominion over the Solar System, or do we wish to continue to be a primitive society whose major activity

is tribal warfare? I am certain that the lost astronauts had greater vision than that."

Were there further secret Apollo missions to the Moon? According to William Rutledge, who claimed, in 2007, that in 1976, he worked at NASA on the two failed missions, Apollo 19 and 20, which were launched from Vandenberg Air Force Base. They were classified joint operations, between the U.S. and Soviet governments, to further investigate a large object which had been photographed by Apollo 15 on the far side of the Moon.

This report cannot be verified, but if Stanton Friedman was correct, we already had the craft built and ready to go. Further, investigator Richard Boylan said that the late USAF Colonel Steve Wilson told him military astronauts trained at a separate secret aerospace academy, and operated out of the Vandenberg Air Force Base, in Northern California. This information begs another question. Was there an Apollo 18, and if so did it also go to the Moon?

In Aldrin's book *'Return to Earth'* he mentions a strange occurrence at a 'pin party' held later for the astronauts from Apollo 10 and those from Apollo 11 who had landed on the Moon.

'The highlight of the evening was a film showing Fred Haise...stumbling around on the surface of the Moon until, in desperation, he retreated to the lunar ladder which, the moment he stepped on the ladder, tumbled into pieces around him.'

Wait a minute! Officially, Haise was only on Apollo 13, which never landed! So, when was this film taken? Could there have been an Apollo 18?

Also, if even one of the reported UFO/alien encounters is correct, it lends credence to another statement made by Dr. Richard Boylan in 1998. He said; *"The reality is that in the 60's, a space station was sent up and manned by US and USSR personnel, and has been operating ever since. Among its tasks is keeping tabs on incoming extraterrestrial traffic, and outgoing, and other matters."*

Dr. Clifford Wilson wrote about a 1969 report in the Calgary, Alberta *'Herald'*, which stated that Dr. G. Henderson, the Senior Space Research Scientist with the General Dynamics Corporation at Fort Worth, Texas, had said that American astronauts had not only sighted UFOs, but also taken photographs.

He claimed that the astronauts had been instructed to say nothing about the sightings, and their photographs had been locked up.

The authorities were quick to explain away nearly all reports made by American astronauts. Scott Carpenter, piloting Mercury-VII, is reported as having confirmed that while in orbit on 24th May 1962, he photographed a UFO, which authorities later claimed was a 'tracking balloon'. Carpenter said; "At no time when the astronauts were in space were they alone. There was constant surveillance by UFOs."

My colleague Rosemary Decker said an astronaut once admitted to her that he was not allowed to answer certain questions on what he saw and learned on the Moon. Despite reports of intercepted transmissions, or comments made by astronauts, when openly questioned, everything is denied.

What happened to our astronauts after their voyage to the Moon? They are the only humans who have officially gone there, and their experiences, although many and varied, affected them both spiritually and emotionally.

Rusty Schweickart, from Apollo 9 commented; "I am not the same man. None of us are. I completely lost my identity as an American Astronaut. I felt a part of everyone and everything sweeping past below."

Neil Armstrong, who became a little reclusive, did not seek publicity, and left NASA in 1971 to become a professor in aeronautical engineering at the University of Cincinnati. Buzz Aldrin found the attention too much to cope with, and also left NASA in 1971, returning to the Air Force as a commander of future astronauts. He still suffered psychological problems and sought professional help in 1975. He wrote two books, and eventually became the chairman of the National Association for Mental Health.

Pete Conrad, who was known for his sense of humour, coped well. He extended his contract with NASA, and in 1973 flew into space for the fourth time as commander of the first manned Skylab mission. He once said; "Nobody seems to remember what Skylab was. I do. For me it was the most beautiful thing in the space program. The moon was a great adventure, but that was it."

James Irwin of Apollo 15 said; "It's made me a warmer, more human person. We all came back with new understandings and new perceptions. We are keenly aware of the necessity for all men to work together on the planet so it may continue its travel through space peacefully, just as we travelled through space." He was a committed Christian, who admitted to praying to God for guidance, rather than contacting Houston, if any problems occurred during their Moon mission. After leaving NASA, his later evangelical preaching proved too onerous, and he suffered two heart attacks requiring surgery. After recovering, he wrote his autobiography, and continued his religious pursuits.

Alan Bean, from Apollo 12, flew Skylab-3, and then left NASA to pursue his favourite pastime – painting. Al Shepard, who commanded Apollo 14, and is remembered for hitting two golf balls into infinity, left NASA in 1974, to concentrate on his already thriving financial business.

Ed Mitchell, although a scientist who spent twenty years helping the U.S. conquer space, was very spiritual, and actually conducted private telepathy experiments whilst on Apollo 14. Mitchell said; "My whole view of myself, my role in life, my philosophy about myself and mankind has changed immensely – You develop an instant global consciousness, a people orientation, an intense dissatisfaction with the state of the world, and a compulsion to do something about it." He left NASA in 1972, wrote three books, and founded the 'Institute of Noetic Sciences' in Palo Alto, California.

Bill Anders, of Apollo 8, said; "Seeing the Earth from out there evoked feelings about humanity and human needs that I never had before", and Tom Stafford, of Gemini-6 and 9, and Apollo 10 commented; "You don't look down at the world as an American, but as a human being."

Apollo 15's Dave Scott resigned in 1975, and founded his own company, 'Scott Science and Technology'. John Young, commander of Apollo 16, and the ninth American to set foot on the Moon, was once asked if UFOs exist: "If you bet against it," he said, "you'd be betting against an almost sure thing..." He was also present on Gemini-3, Gemini-10 and Apollo 10. He considered going to the Moon – 'just a job' - and after being in charge of eighty astronauts, commanded two more shuttle missions before retiring.

Charlie Duke said his trip to the Moon on Apollo 16, led to the beginning of a deep religious conviction. He later said; "I was overwhelmed by the certainty of what I was witnessing was part of the universality of God". Duke left NASA in 1975, and after some difficult times, psychologically, travelled around the world giving lectures on the need for peace. Jack Schmitt, the only astronaut who was essentially a scientist, and not a pilot, later became a politician, and then a lecturer.

In 1973, Apollo 17 Commander Eugene Cerman, was the eleventh man to set foot on the Moon, and had also been on the Apollo 10 dress rehearsal for Apollo 11. He left NASA in 1976, and founded his own firm, the 'Cerman Corporation'. He was quoted in an article published by the *'Los Angeles Times',* as saying; "I've been asked about UFOs, and I've said publicly I thought they were somebody else, some other civilisation."

Considering that there was a 'space race' occurring at the time, I have often wondered why the Russians, who certainly had the technical expertise, didn't follow up their initial Sputnik program with their own planned Moon landing expedition?

In those days, speculation was also circulating about who or what may be on our Moon. While attending a meeting, over forty-five years ago, a young teenage girl approached me during a supper break. She showed me a letter she had received from her uncle, who was in the U.S.A., working for NASA. He said they were all very excited as they had received photographs from the far side of the moon showing the remains of massive, unnatural structures rising miles into the sky. I checked all kinds of clues on the correspondence, handwriting, stamp, postage marks, and stationery. It all seemed genuine, and certainly confirmed later reports.

In 1965, Airman Karl Wolfe worked for the Director of Intelligence at Langley Base, Virginia. There was a NASA installation on the base, but he did not possess the security clearance required to enter it. One day, when NASA's own technician was not available, he was called over to fix a problem with some malfunctioning equipment.

He saw, to his surprise, that there were several international scientists working in the facility, and noticed many photographs which had been downloaded from a lunar orbiter. He was told that they were working on a reconnaissance project to determine the best landing spot on the Moon for the forthcoming Apollo missions.

Karl asked why there was so much security, and was told that they had discovered a 'base' on the dark side of the Moon. It was then that he spotted the massive artificial structures, some with circular antennae, clearly depicted on the enlarged pictures. He later commented that they were all different shapes, some tall and thin, and others spherical and domed. They didn't compare with anything we have on Earth.

This was four years before our astronauts first landed on the Moon, and being too scared to ask any questions, he never found out if this 'base' was alien or our own.

We must wonder why the Russians never attempted their own manned landing to the Moon. There have been other Russian successes, despite some failures, with unmanned craft. Luna-21 landed there in 1973, and released the Lunokhod 'moon-buggy' which travelled across the surface for more than four months, sending information back to Earth. In 1974 Luna-22 orbited the Moon, relaying information back to the Soviet Union. Later that year Luna- 23 crash landed on the surface, damaging much of the equipment, however in 1976 Luna-24 made a successful landing.

NASA had also spent many years surveying the Moon, partly to discover who or what may be up there, and partly to designate the most suitable landing spots for future missions.

One of their projects, 'Operation Moon Blink', included a *'Chronological Catalogue of Reported Lunar Events'*, which listed the locations of mysterious lights and clouds observed by astronomers for more than a century. Later unmanned space probes were launched, and five Lunar Orbiters successfully photographed virtually all of the Moon's surface. The authorities were fully prepared to ensure that the public only ever got to see photographs of a bleak and desolate rocky outpost.

So why, in all the following decades have astronauts not officially gone back to the Moon? It has always been of utmost priority to the USA, Russia and probably China today, to not only to establish a manned, habitable Lunar Outpost, but also to mount a manned expedition to Mars. Some whistle-blowers claim that 'photos of UFOs on the edge of a crater' were genuine, and that aliens already there had warned us off.

According to some journalists, NASA has proffered several plausible, but questionable, explanations for the cessation of manned journeys beyond our own planet.

1. They were suddenly concerned about the biological effects of space radiation on astronauts.
2. There were problems with the 'take–off' of craft returning from the Moon and Mars – (despite several successful Apollo missions and the fact that both have a lower gravity than Earth).

3. There were multiple technical risks, including vibrations on the craft structure and the inability to recreate the material used for the Apollo Thermal Protection System, which provided a heat shield for craft re-entering our atmosphere at hypersonic speed.

(One must wonder why we cannot recreate something utilised fifty years ago? Also, if our probes travelled to the Moon and Mars and reduced speed to land or orbit, why could our craft not adopt the same procedure when returning to Earth?)

While there could be some truth in the conspiracy theories, it could be something so simple as the more recent realisation that solar flares are far more dangerous and unpredictable than previously thought. If the enormous cost of venturing into space is a factor, then perhaps George Adamski had a point when he noted that our economy is based upon spending enormous amounts of money on wars and armaments; money which could be better used for space exploration.

Today, besides thousands of pieces of 'space junk', there are countless military and commercial satellites orbiting our planet. Some are extremely scientifically advanced, with amazing capabilities. There are both known and secret Space Stations, with 'shuttle craft' ferrying personnel to and from.

Also the major powers are finalising plans to land an astronaut on Mars. The race is on! But the question still remains – how did we get this sophisticated technology, and is anyone else out there?

Of course, what goes up usually has to come down, and over the years, many satellites and other man-made objects have been mistaken for UFOs when re-entering our atmosphere.

In December 1977, Soviet spy satellite, Cosmos 954, malfunctioned and splattered its debris across northern Canada. It led to intensive searches, and accusations that it was carrying a dangerous payload of one hundred pounds of enriched uranium 235.

Was radioactive material, or worse still, nuclear weapons being shot into space? No wonder the extraterrestrials were concerned. The atomic bombs dropped over Hiroshima and Nagasaki, and subsequent testing, signalled that mankind was playing with some very dangerous toys.

The inevitable development of the hydrogen bomb would have created even more concern. In November 1952, the Pacific island test led to the complete disappearance of Eniwetok Atoll, and its replacement by a crater 175 ft deep and one mile across. More tests followed, culminating in the explosion in near space of a bomb over Johnson Island, which sent electrified particles into the upper atmosphere, and caused auroras over large parts of the world.

In 1998, a huge American Titan IV rocket, carrying a top-secret spy satellite, crashed off the coast of Cape Canaveral. It started to self-destruct at 6,000 metres, forty-two seconds after launch. Controllers blew up the rest of the rocket to prevent a serious accident, and officials warned the public not to handle the debris, as it may contain 'hazardous material'.

In 1979, the 'Home Office' circulated a restricted document which outlined the problems, and procedures to be followed, if a nuclear powered satellite crashed on British soil, and whether the public should, or should not, be advised of the danger.

In 2001 space station Mir crashed back to earth; however the most memorable was Skylab's fiery fall, when it landed in the West Australian desert in 1979. Another West Australian crash, at Marble Bar, in 1981, was possibly Cosmos 434, a Russian satellite which authorities feared was nuclear powered.

In 2004, NASA's Genesis space capsule, bringing back a container of solar wind particles, smashed into the Utah desert, after its parachute failed.

Both the Russians and Americans realised that whoever controlled the space around our planet, had the 'upper-hand' in any future war. The Russian technology was primitive, and any crashes or accidents were kept secret, even from their own people.

The U.S. was quick to respond to any perceived threats, be they Russian or alien. On 23rd November 1958, *'Aviation Week'* published a report that the first U.S. reconnaissance satellite the 'WS 1171 Sentry', was scheduled to be shot into orbit on 15th December from Vandenberg Air Force Base, California.

It would be carrying a telescopic camera and associated telemetry equipment, with provisions to orientate the satellite so that it would constantly view the globe. It was anticipated that up to ten passes around the Earth, on a north-south trajectory, would be made before it re-entered the Earth's atmosphere and burned up. Recovery procedures had already been established, and plans were already underway to launch even more sophisticated satellites.

Since the Russians had already announced their intentions to land a man on the Moon, the Americans realised this was of enormous strategic importance, and they would have to 'catch-up', and quickly!

In 1961, at a special joint session of Congress, President John Kennedy announced; "I believe this nation should commit itself to achieving the goal, before this decade is out, of landing a man on the Moon, and returning him safely to Earth." He went on to add; "No nation which expects to be the leader of other nations can expect to stay behind in the race for space."

What most people did not realise was that the U.S. had already made plans to go to the Moon several years before. In their book, *'Unsolved UFO Mysteries'*, William Birnes and Harold Birt wrote: *'Buried away in army records, so securely that not even former astronaut and retired United States Senator John Glenn knew of their existence, are a series of once classified documents belonging to an army program called 'Project Horizon'.*

'Originally conceived as early as 1956, 'Project Horizon' proposed the creation of an entirely new army command composed of elements from the Signal Corps, Artillery, the Medical Corps, the Army Corps of Engineers and other units assembled for one purpose: to place a United States Army military base on the Moon within the ensuing five or so years.

'Championed in 1959 by Lieutenant General Arthur Trudeau, the Director of Army Research and Development and former Commander of Army Research and Development, 'Project Horizon' argued the necessity of the army reaching the Moon before the Soviets or any other hostile foreign power could seize the ultimate high ground.'

'Project Horizon' was officially turned down by the Eisenhower administration when NASA took over the space administration and Moon launch program.

So what were the thoughts of the general population when it came to our efforts to 'land a man on the Moon'? Many people had heard of George Adamski and other contactees, who had spread messages of peace and love during the 1950s. They had suggested the money spent on wars would be better diverted to space exploration. (See my book, *'The Days of the Space Brothers'.*)

Some of the pilots, who were later to participate in our space program, were already aware, a decade earlier, of the existence of unidentified visitors above our planet.

Donald Slayton, later a Mercury astronaut, was flying over Minneapolis, testing a P-51 fighter in 1951. He said in an interview that he was at about ten thousand feet on a bright, sunny afternoon when he saw an object he first took to be a kite or maybe a balloon. When he got closer he realised it looked like a saucer – a disc, which quickly moved away.)

During these high altitude flights, other pilots, some to later become astronauts, also encountered inexplicable objects. In 1962, the U.S. was conducting very high altitude flights in the X-15. On 11th May, Pilot Joseph Walker claimed that one of his tasks was to detect UFOs. He was over fifty-five miles above the Earth, and during that time filmed five or six UFOs. During a later conference he declined to speculate on the objects.

A couple of months later, on 17th July, Major Robert White reached an altitude of fifty-eight miles, and spotted an object which was greyish in colour and thirty to forty feet away. He had no idea what it was and exclaimed over the radio; "There are things out there! There absolutely is!"

In 1962, through to the end of 1966, when Conrad and other high-flying pilots took 'snapshots', all photographs were dismissed by the officials as being 'flakes of ice' – 'lightning lit clouds' – 'other satellites' – 'booster rockets' or even 'air brushed fakes'.

(It wasn't just American astronauts who had witnessed strange objects in space. At a 1998 international UFO enthusiastic event, Romilyav Remenko, who had been part of the Russian space program, admitted that they knew that, from the very beginning, the UFOs were not terrestrial.

In 1961, Major German Titov saw UFOs in space, and filmed them, subsequently publishing the photos in a Russian magazine. Pilot/astronaut Alexandr Baledrin said that flying saucers had also been seen and filmed by the crew of the MIR space station.)

1965 and later were not good years for either American or Russian satellites. "Spacetrack' admitted losing track of several 'Explorers', and other satellites stopped transmitting only to suddenly 'come back to life' later. Two Russian 'Cosmos' craft unaccountably burst into dozens of fragments.

(Of course, as the years went by, we launched a multitude of satellites, space craft and stations of our own. By 2019, nine countries that we knew of could independently launch spacecraft. Besides the United States and European Space Agency these were China, India, Iran, Israel, Japan, North Korea, Russia and South Korea.)

In April 1970, China launched its first satellite, 'The East is Red-1', and by 2003, its first human into space. In 2019, it landed the first probe on the dark side of the Moon, and was well on the way to a space station of its own.

In 1967, eighteen countries signed up to the United Nations' five 'Treaties in Space'. Today, there are about seventy nations with satellites in space. They are an integral part of everyday life. They support military operations, surveillance, communications, meteorology and a multitude of social and industrial purposes.

Of course, what goes up, usually has to come down. As the years went on, the crashing remains of satellites and other 'space junk' were often mistaken for UFOs! Within forty years of the first Sputnik launch, over six million tons of our craft and technology had been launched into orbit, very little of which still comprised functioning craft. Our outer limits were scattered with dying satellites, nose cones, fragments of blown up booster stages, and many other smaller, but equally dangerous objects, orbiting at speeds of up to 28,000 miles per hour! Much of this debris will remain in orbit for hundreds of years, posing a long term hazard to our space activities.

There were already some incidents during those 'early years'. In 1962 a satellite fell in Southern Africa, setting fire to a farm. On April 24th 1964, a United States satellite, with isotopes on board, disintegrated over the island of Madagascar, releasing plutonium into the atmosphere.

In 1978, some authorities were becoming uneasy when nuclear powered satellites came crashing to Earth. Russian Cosmos 954 came down over northern Canada, spreading radioactive debris over the area, and 1402 into the ocean. In 1979, the 178 ton U.S. Skylab space station crashed into the Indian Ocean, with some charred remains landing in the West Australian desert and everybody scrambling to pick up souvenirs. The local Esperance Council responded by issuing the Americans a 'littering' fine for over $400, which they eventually paid. At the time I was involved in emergency services, and plans had been put in place to mitigate any damage should it hit an urban area, however, my primary instructions were to guard any remains until the authorities arrived!

Some years later, in 1991, Russia's Salyut space station came down, with some debris falling over Chile and Argentina, causing a fire in one area. In December 1995, their Cosmos 398, made a much safer descent into the South Atlantic Ocean. In 1981, their Cosmos 1275 broke up for no apparent reason, showering space with 275 satellite fragments, in a pattern suggesting a collision.

In March 1993, the Cosmos 2238 launch-rocket caused some consternation when it re-entered the earth's atmosphere. At the time, there were multiple reports of UFOs over Ireland, Wales and the west of England. Whilst many of these 'lights in the sky' could be attributed to Cosmos 2238, some could not.

The Ministry of Defence did 'investigate' some of the reports, and was very non-committal regarding the sighting of strange craft, helicopters, jet fighters and a twin-hulled aircraft flying in the late hours and early morning at the time of the launch-rocket re-entry.

It only stands to reason that we would be carefully monitoring all Russian activities, but perhaps the aliens were also watching. In his book, *'Alien Update'* Timothy Good stated; *'The Russian Authorities are fully aware that their space program has been subjected to some very intense scrutiny by UFOs.*

For the most part the UFOs appear disc-like, and are able to traverse Russian air space at will, and in some extraordinary ways!'

Even minute particles of debris can cause enormous damage. By the mid-nineties, objects as small as four inches across could be tracked from the ground by high powered radar and other devices.

Both Russia's 'Mir' and the U.S. 'Colombia' and 'Challenger' missions suffered damage to windows, doors and outside light-bulbs. In 1995 the crew of the 'Endeavour' had to manoeuvre their way past a derelict Air Force satellite. Since then, steps have been taken to better protect our spacecraft and minimise the debris orbiting our Earth.

In 2008, a missile from a U.S. Navy warship hit a defunct American spy satellite 247kms above the Earth. It was in its final orbits before re-entering the Earth's atmosphere. The Americans claimed it was an attempt to blow apart a tank of toxic fuel, however I suspect it was also to prevent valuable, secret equipment falling into the wrong hands! It also demonstrated our ability to target and destroy objects flying at more than 27,400 kms per hour above the planet, which must have been of some concern to any alien visitors!

The previous year, in January 2007, the Chinese had also used a ground-based missile to destroy an 'obsolete weather satellite'. There was some criticism regarding an estimated 25,000 bits of debris which were left floating in space.

In February 2009, the *'Sydney Morning Herald'* reported a collision, 800ks over Siberia, between an inactive Russian satellite, launched in 1993, and a communications satellite launched in 1997. The crash produced massive clouds of debris in the upper atmosphere. In March 2019, India successfully destroyed one of its own satellites, creating 400 pieces of space debris. Any criticism did not deter India, who planned to be the fourth nation to make a soft landing on the Moon with its Chandrayaan-2 mission.

The situation by 2020 was quite disturbing. Above our planet was a cosmic junkyard, cluttered with debris. By then over 8,000 objects had been launched into Earth orbit, and five hundred were still whizzing around. Some of our launches had been quite tiny, and others the size of a school bus, weighing a good eight tons. The risk of collisions, causing a possible chain reaction, grows by the day. Recently there was a near miss between 'Cosmos' and 'Iridium 33'.

Besides the 15,000 larger objects, even the estimated 100 million pieces of less than one centimetre micro-debris, travelling at 25,000 feet per second, can be deadly.

We are belatedly beginning to realise that space is fragile, a finite resource, and steps are being taken to devise a method to clean up the debris, which includes 8,000 ton of abandoned hardware still in orbit. Any serious incident could prove to be a global disaster, as our military, besides telecommunications, internet, financial transactions, GPS, and modern navigation systems for cars, ships and airliners, all depend upon the satellites orbiting overhead.

Even today, there is still much controversy and debate regarding our 'Moon Missions', which far surpassed any UFO reports, and were certainly the most exciting events of the 'good old days'. Every so often, more 'testimony' emerges, throwing light on matters which were kept secret at the time.

In all, nineteen Apollo Missions, that we know of, were destined to the Moon. Three orbited, and six landed. The missions were not without their problems and fatalities. On 27th January 1967, astronauts Grisson, Chaffee and White were incinerated when their Apollo 1 capsule caught fire and exploded during tests on Pad 34, at Cape Kennedy. A similar fate befell Soviet cosmonaut Valentin Bondarenko in 1960.

The first successful crewed flight occurred in 1968. However, one Apollo Mission was struck by lightning on the launch pad, and another suffered an explosion which demolished its power system, and nearly caused the flight to end in disaster.

(All of these flights were not just monitored by the authorities on Earth. Sometimes ordinary citizens were just, if not more successful. At the end of 1976, the 'Guardian' newspaper reported that Geoffrey Perry, a schoolmaster from Kettering Grammar School, in the English Midlands, had been awarded an MBE by the Queen, and a medal from the Royal Astronomical Society.

In 1962 Perry and a friend, both amateur radio operators, began regular tracking of the Soviet's 'Cosmos' satellites, which unlike the American and Chinese vehicles, broadcast on shortwave frequencies. At first he listened from a simple set in the corner of the school's physics lab. Soon his pupils became interested, and enthusiastically formed a small 'club', restricted to other physics students, and by invitation only.

As he listened in, Perry picked up a little Russian, and was delighted when the school added Russian to its curriculum. The boys became so proficient in the language, that they once broke the code of a Soviet satellite transmitting information to its ground station.

Over the years they tracked every one of the more than 800 Cosmos launches, and were very excited when they tracked Cosmos 246 passing over Cape Canaveral thirty minutes after Apollo 7 was launched.

The United States Senate's Aeronautical and Space Committee said, in its report, that data from Perry and his students was unmatched by any public release of information by the Soviet, United States or British Governments.

The *'Guardian'* said that in fact Perry and the school 'club' had *'tracked more accurately than the United States space centres; have discovered the location of the newest of the Soviet launching sites; reported on technological achievements and failures; and even followed the course of the 1973 Arab-Israel war, where the Soviets monitored the fighting by satellite. As the satellites shifted position, the boys were able to alert the British press that the fighting had shifted from the Golan Heights to Suez.'*

When the old original radio began giving trouble, and the boys had to thump it to keep it working, the *'Daily Express'* newspaper and other firms gave the class new equipment.)

Apollo 8's initial mission, was to fly around the Moon, without attempting to land. Although these three astronauts were the first to reach the Moon, because they didn't actually land, they never received the accolades they rightfully deserved. NASA had arranged this trip to occur at Christmas 1968, with astronauts Frank Borman, James Lovell and William Anders to send a Christmas Eve message back to Earth, however they were not told what to say, as long as it was 'appropriate'.

William Anders was the first to speak; *"In the beginning God created the heaven and earth, and the earth was without form and void; and darkness was on the face of the deep, and the spirit of God moved upon the waters. And God said 'Let there be light,' and there was light, and God saw the light that it was good, and God divided the light from the darkness."*

James Lovell then continued; *"And God called the light 'day', and the darkness he called 'night', and the evening and the morning were the first day. And God said 'Let there be a firmament in the midst of the waters and let it divide the waters from the waters.' And God made the firmament and divided the waters which were under the firmament from the waters which were above the firmament; and it was so, and God called the firmament 'Heaven', and the evening and the morning were the second day."*

Frank Borman finalised; *"And God said; 'Let the waters under the heavens be gathered together unto one place and let the dry land appear'; and it was so, and God called the dry land 'Earth'; and the gathering together of the waters he called 'Seas'; and God saw that it was good.*

"And from the crew of Apollo 8, we close with Good Night, Good Luck, a merry Christmas, and God bless all of you on the good Earth."

It is not known who composed this message, but it was not what some of the people back in the Control Centre had expected. There was some criticism that due to the varying beliefs of the population, it should have steered clear of any religious connotations.

Once their manoeuvres were successfully completed, Commander Lovell announced; "Please be informed, there is a Santa Claus!" NASA claimed it was never meant to refer to anything alien or extraterrestrial, however on November 24th 1977, the Novosty Press Agency was present when Vlagyimir Georgijevic, Assistant Head of the Oceanographic Department of the USSR National Academy of Sciences, gave a lecture regarding UFOs. In it he said; *"According to the orders of the Control Centre in Houston, the UFO's code name was 'Santa Claus'"*

After finishing their mission and taking many colour photos, Apollo 8 made a final orbit of the Moon. They had to 'burn' the engines to propel them out of orbit, and head for home. Any mistake would render them stranded, and there would be insufficient oxygen to last until any rescue attempt could reach them.

In May 1969, Apollo 10, with astronauts Thomas Stafford, John Young and Gene Cernan, also flew to the Moon. It was designed to examine the far side in more detail, and test the Lunar Module, close to the surface, without actually landing. Stafford reported hearing strange 'whistling' and modulated sounds, for which no definitive explanation has ever been given. During their trip, they also experienced some guidance system malfunctions.

Vlagyimir Georgijevic, also made the following claim during his lecture: *"The Apollo 10's American astronauts' scientific explosion on the Moon failed. Namely, they tried to induce a moon quake, but couldn't trigger it."* It is not known if this assertion was correct.

The third mission to orbit the Moon, without landing, was Apollo 13. In April 1970, Apollo 13, although it orbited and took photographs, was unable to land due to an explosion in one of the oxygen tanks. Astronauts Jim Lovell, Jack Swigert and Fred Haise were luckily returned safely to Earth.

In 1968 and 1969, astronauts on Apollo missions 8, 11 and 12 all allegedly reported unidentified objects.

Did the astronauts Armstrong, Aldrin and Collins on Apollo 11 see UFOs on the Moon? This is still a contentious issue.

Despite conspiracy theorists saying we never went there, I personally believe that, from 1969, we did make several successful Apollo missions to the Moon. In those days I was a very junior employee working with government engineers who were assisting NASA with the project.

Further, Armstrong and Aldrin had deployed an 'Early Apollo Scientific Experiment Package' on the Moon's surface. It was designed to transmit, back to Earth, data on temperature and seismic activity, which it did for about a month.

(Already there were signs of comradeship among astronauts, no matter what their nationality. Before Apollo II departed from the Moon, they left, on the surface, the medals of Yuri Gagarin and Vladimir Komarov, two dead Russian astronauts, and the insignia of Virgil Grissom, Roger Chaffee and Edward White, the three American astronauts who perished in a fire in an Apollo spacecraft during training on the ground.)

At the time, a copy of the original magnetic data tapes, from the 'Scientific Experiment Package', were sent to the Australian designer, physicist Brian O'Brien, who left them in the care of a colleague at West Australian Curtain

University. In 2006, after discovering that, in the 1980s, NASA admitted 'mislaying' the original video tapes of the historic Moon landing, O'Brien went in search of the data tapes. They had also apparently gone 'missing', but there was nothing suspicious about it this time. After being safely stored for 25 years, they were moved due to a change in premises. A thorough search finally located the boxes – some under the students' lecture room seats, and others under some outdated electronic equipment.

They were still in good condition, and O'Brien was happy, because he considered that they were further proof that we really had landed on the Moon.

Pilot-Cosmonaut Leonov has also confirmed that Soviet radars monitored everything, and were able to observe the Americans, with Leonov and his colleagues 'rooting for them.' Obviously they also monitored all the original, unedited transmissions which came from the Moon during that time, including the mention of UFOs.

The *'National Enquirer UFO Report'* quotes Soviet Dr. Valdamir Azhazha, in a telephone interview, as saying; *'According to our information, the encounter was reported immediately after the landing of the module. Neil Armstrong relayed the message to Mission Control that two large, mysterious objects were watching them after having landed near the moon module. But his message was never heard by the public – because NASA censored it.'*

Another Soviet scientist, Dr. Sergei Boshich said; *"It's my opinion that other civilizations learned of the proposed moon landing...and two spaceships probably were dispatched so there would be back-up in an emergency. Undoubtedly, their objective was to learn the extent of Earth's technological know-how. Having verified the landing, they departed without making contact."*

On November 24th 1977, the Novosty Press Agency was present when Vlagyimir Georgijevic, Assistant Head of the Oceanographic Department of the USSR National Academy of Sciences, gave a lecture regarding UFOs.

He said; *"The report of the American astronauts, (Armstrong, Collins, Aldrin), who landed on the Moon is extremely interesting. The Apollo11 crew noticed two UFOs shortly after their take-off, but considered this to be a part of the Saturn 5's stage rocket. But the object escorted them, then advanced on their craft. The size of the ship was about 1.5 km.*

"When Armstrong/Aldrin's landing manoeuvre was completed on the Moon, they observed a few saucer-like UFOs on the opposite side of the crater. Armstrong cries; "Damn, they are already here!"

"According to the orders of the Control Centre in Houston, the UFO's code name was 'Santa Claus', but Armstrong and the crew were so shocked at the sight, that without coding it, reported; 'straight ahead, on the opposite side of the crater, spacecraft of cosmic origin are pacing and watching us."

"Houston ordered them to stay in the Lunar Module. Five hours later, when convinced that the UFOs had no hostile intentions, they were permitted to step on the Moon. Aldrin filmed the UFOs, and the movie became Top Secret. This communication was released much later, and I hope the film will eventually be shown.

"The astronauts left a box on the Moon, which contained the Declaration of the United Nations in 72 languages, related to outer space and the celestial bodies. But, this action to contact extraterrestrial civilisations had no result at all. It was kept Top Secret for a long time, but the manufacturer of the box blundered out the secret.

"The encounter on the Moon with the UFOs bewildered the astronauts. Aldrin has had a nervous breakdown, and as of today, his health hasn't been totally restored. Collins has become a virtual monk.

"The Moon seems to be a permanent base of the UFOs, and all the Apollo crews to the Moon were under UFO examination. Also, the Apollo 10's American astronauts' scientific explosion on the Moon failed. Namely, they tried to induce a moon quake, but couldn't trigger it."

Timothy Good claimed that a university professor reported a conversation he supposedly had with Neil Armstrong during a NASA Symposium. Armstrong had said that they were warned off by the aliens, so there was never any question then of a permanent Moon space station. Their ships were big and menacing, and far superior to ours in both size and technology.

Armstrong has never confirmed this conversation, however in 1979, Maurice Chatelain, the former head of NASA Communications Systems, confirmed in an interview that Neil Armstrong had reported seeing two UFOs on the rim of a lunar crater.

Allen Hynek, in his book *'The Edge of Reality'*, also commented about this; *'The astronauts? Some of the NASA movie frames that I examined were most interesting – particularly those taken on the Apollo II flight, one of the few for which NASA has come up with some sort of explanation. And several astronauts have stated that they definitely saw things in space which they could not identify. Thus - it satisfies the definition of UFO! Unidentified!'*

It must be remembered that the television film footage from Apollo 11 and 12 were not 'live', and came 'second-hand' from NASA, who claimed the original was of poor quality, which had to be 'improved' by an 'optical system'.

(At the same time Apollo 11 was heading towards the Moon, Russia's unmanned Luna-15 was also in orbit, apparently in an effort to collect samples of lunar soil and rock and return to Earth before the U.S. mission. It was tracked by Jodrell Bank Observatory, who noted it crashed on the surface shortly before the Americans arrived.)

In November 1969, Conrad, Bean and Gordon made a successful landing in Apollo 12. In 1999, the British 'Contact International UFO Research' organisation published an alleged transcript of a conversation between the astronauts and Houston.

They claimed they were being followed, through space, by two shiny spinning objects, one in front, and one behind their craft. After seven hours, Houston came back with a couple of lame, possible explanations. Basically, nobody could identify what the objects were.

The astronauts could also hear strange noises, like static or a whistling sound in the background, both in the craft and on the lunar surface. On their way back to Earth, they saw a sharp, bright light, which has also never been identified.

In February 1971, Apollo 14, carrying Shepherd, Mitchell and Rossa had a successful mission, as did Scott, Irwin and Worden on Apollo 15 in August 1971. In his book *'Cosmic Top Secret'* Jon King quotes NASA's former data and photographic documentation supervisor, Ken Johnston, who claimed his superiors erased film footage taken by the Apollo 14 astronauts. It showed structures of unnatural origin on the Moon, and also five or six lights in a crater on the far side.

Apollo 16, with astronauts Young, Duke and Mattingly, landed in April 1972, with some more experiments being conducted on the Moon's surface. Young and Duke spent seven hours exploring the 'highlands' in their electric 'Moon Buggy', and planted the fifth American flag on the surface.

Apollo 17 followed soon after, in December 1972. This was, unexpectedly, the last landing mission. Schmitt, the only scientist/astronaut to walk on the Moon, was a geologist who conducted a survey of the minerals there, and before leaving set some explosives to test the Lunar crust. Cernan, Schmitt and Evans set-up a sixth measuring station, and were also engaged in intensive lunar back-side photography, with the King Crater area of specific interest.

THE MISSING MOON SLIDES

Before my dear friend and colleague, Australian researcher Paul Norman (U.S.A.) passed away, he sent me copies of some amazing correspondence, dated 1971, between NSW researcher Bill Moser (deceased) and a colleague in the U.S.A.

It related to three sets of slides showing some unexplained items on the Moon. They included: '*SLIDE Z 6/78 FW: Taken by Apollo 10 crew, showing crater I.A.U. No.302. A very bright blue object – height estimated at over 20 feet – showing clear against background and looks a bit thicker on top.*' and -

'*SLIDE Z 20/96 MD: Taken by Apollo 11 crew, showing South-West part of Mare Tranquillitatis with crater Maskelyne. Again a bluish looking globule was noticed, shaped like an orb.*'

Moser had shown the slides to an Australian radio-astronomer, a Government astronomer and a Deputy Director of the CSIRO, and all had considered '*a proper research investigation could be done much easier in the United States than anywhere else.*'

He requested a U.S. colleague forward the slides to Professors Hynek and McDonald, noting he could make more copies available for any other scientists, as required.

In 1995 Paul Norman wrote to Bill Moser's colleague in the States – who subsequently contacted seven different investigators in America trying to locate these slides and the final appraisal by the two professors. He replied to Paul in rather mysterious terms, asking how Moser had come by the slides – who had initiated his request to on-forward them to Hynek and McDonald, and why hadn't he sent them direct? He also wanted to know the involvement of the Australian scientists and went on to say he had enjoyed meeting and talking to Dr. Lindtner and *'his death was a most unfortunate thing.'* (Dr. Lindtner had been pushed under a train in Europe. Was this a hidden warning?)

Paul Norman wrote to me later in 1995, and asked me to follow-up the slides and publicise it at a later date, (after he, Paul, had 'passed-on'.) I wondered if Paul was scared, due to the reference to Dr. Lindtner's 'accident'. Paul was a little non-committal, but said that given the circumstances there was the distinct possibility this may have been considered a 'sensitive' matter. I did not pursue the missing slides, as obviously someone 'on-high', did not want them released or scrutinised.

I wondered if these slides had really existed, but then found confirmation in some old records from the UFOIC organisation, where Bill Moser had been Vice President and Hon. Gen. Secretary. Bill had indeed shown them slides of both Moon landings and Moon rocks in the April of 1971. The rocks were Lunar samples, collected by astronauts Shepherd, Mitchell and Rossa on Apollo 14, however no mention was made of which mission the 'landing' slides had come from, although in relation to the rocks, the name of Dr. Robin Brett, the vice-chairman of a preliminary investigation team, was mentioned.

CHAPTER FOUR

THE ARCTIC AND ANTARCTIC

In the past, many people believed in the 'Hollow Earth' theory, and that aliens lived in the interior of our planet, accessed via 'holes' in the North and South Poles. Many adherents of this belief belonged to secret, but powerful occult societies, who often influenced the politicians of the day.

In the 1950s, one fanatic was Reinhold Schmidt, who claimed to have seen a saucer land, and been invited on board by German speaking occupants, who took him on a flight which cruised over Alaska.

He was committed to an asylum for three days, and released when his insanity could not be proven. Investigators had second thoughts when his claim that the Russians had placed undersea devices in the Arctic, as markers to vital American cities, was proven correct by the American Navy.

Schmidt then claimed other trips in his alien friends' spacecraft, including over Russia, where he saw a devastated area caused by a nuclear disaster. He claimed it had been caused by an attempt by Russia to launch a nuclear missile at the USA.

This further claim by Schmidt also engendered some credibility, when later, the *'New Scientist'* magazine quoted Dr. Zhores Medvedev as saying that nuclear waste had been buried for many years near the Urals town of Blagevveshusk; - "The nuclear reactions had led to overheating in the underground burial grounds." The Russian government had kept it secret that in 1958 there was an enormous devastating explosion, like a violent volcano.

A lot of people believed Schmidt, who later wrote an article, *'An Amazing Story'*, as an anonymous author, for Australian Fred Stone's *'Australian Saucer Magazine'*. Fred had published it 'tongue in cheek', and didn't expect the strong supporting letters he received regarding Schmidt's claims. In light of our knowledge today, his claims are rather dubious, however, it is up to the reader to decide how much of Schmidt's *'Amazing Story'* is factual. In the 'good old days', it is of some importance that many people believed him.

'An Amazing Story'

'I should like to write for your magazine the following account telling of my experiences with the saucer people, trips aboard the space ships, and in particular my visit to a saucer base in Antarctica, located within a 140,000 square mile oasis beyond the South Pole in Queen Maude Land. Yes, I saw fabulous cities of an unknown, advanced civilization responsible for the flying saucers – a civilization whose ancestors belonged to the race that inhabited the lost continents of Atlantis and Lemuria.

'Conventional aircraft cannot reach the oasis due to the storms of hurricane force that act as a shield around it. The oasis itself is below sea level, has a mild climate, and forest covered. Also there is a huge lake within the oasis of rather warm water heated by underground volcanic heat supply. Warm air rises from the lake, giving the region a mild climate. The oasis is surrounded by a high wall of ice leading up to a plateau, causing storms of hurricane force. This is Antarctica's "Hell Hole'.

'The saucers are able to leave and enter the area because they nullify the effect of the atmosphere and hence storms do not affect them. This is why so much of the Queen Maude Land lies unexplored by the rest of the world, in that our planes cannot penetrate the storm area in order to reach the oasis.' (By 1961 Russia had commenced building a base near that very location.) 'There is however, another way to reach the oasis other than by air, and this is by submarine through an underground water passage that connects the lake within the oasis with the cold Southern Ocean.

'Yes, your government can confirm what I say by a submarine expedition. Tell your people to proceed to Weddell Sea, and under the ice staying near the bottom. The entrance to the passage lies at the Filchner Ice Shelf, where it connects to Vahsel Bay. The submarine can proceed along this underground-water-channel or passage and come to surface when it reaches the lake. Water near the bottom of the lake is very hot, and water from the lake, flowing into the passage to Weddell Sea is quite warm. The saucer people have a ship that can travel as an air-ship, even to outer space, as well as to act as a submarine and travel underwater. On my trip, we flew to the oasis, and left by the underground water passage.

'Within the oasis is an entrance to the Cavern World. Yes, it is possible to sail into the interior of the earth. Richard Shaver spoke of this region many times, and his 'DEROS' are very real, for this is the entrance to 'HELL'. I went a short distance into the cavern, which is not dark at all, but well illuminated. The rocks and walls within the underground channels give off light in many different colours. I am told that the network of channels leads to a great hollow area. Within this area is a 'Sun'.

'This 'Sun' gives off heat and light, and illuminated the whole of the great hollow area. It is located at the exact centre of the Earth....Most of land masses are floating on hot magma, which comes to the surface and we call lava. There are certain areas on Earth in which a break occurs in this hot layer of molten rock. Within these areas are entrances to the inner earth. One such area is within Antarctica.

'Before you get ready to laugh at what I am telling you of a hollow earth, inhabited within, and the entrance in the polar regions, let me tell you this; Dr. Edmund Halley, the discoverer of the comet that bears his name, believed in a hollow earth, as well as the Swiss mathematician Leonhardt Buder. John Cleves Symes, born in 1780, started a movement that led to Rep. J. Johnsen of Ohio introducing a Bill in the U.S. Congress for a government financed polar expedition for the purposes of establishing trade and commerce with the people living in the interior of the earth.

'The bill failed, but then a backer of Symes, J. N. Reynolds, was able to convince two of President John Quincey Adams' cabinet, Secretary of the Treasury and Secretary of the Navy, to sponsor a seaborn expedition to the Antarctica for the purposes of sailing into the earth's centre. Work was started on the project when President Adams was defeated in 1828. Andrew Jackson killed the plan.

'Later in 1830, Reynolds raised funds for an expedition under Capt. Nathaniel Palmer. Needless to say, they did not locate the entrance to the earth in the Antarctic region. (Ref, 'The Silent Continent' by Kearne and Britton Harper and brothers 1955). Then we have the experiences of Richard Shaver as described in his book, 'I Remember Lumeria', and Marshall Gardner, who in 1929 wrote 'A Journey to Earth's Interior'.

'If the idea of a hollow earth is so ridiculous, and with inhabitants, how then would a former President of the United States, and two of his Cabinet, become so convinced as to back a government-financed expedition to Antarctica? (Ed.

Note; It must be also remembered that Jules Verne wrote of this, and today this is the only forecast of his that has not been fulfilled – as yet.)

'Today, the U.S. Government, as well as many other nations, is sponsoring expeditions to the Antarctica – Why? Is this being done for scientific reasons, or are there definite military implications? When Rear Admiral Byrd went to Antarctica in 1946-47, censorship of information was the tightest it had been since World War II. This is confirmed by the 'New York Times' accounts in April 1947 to Washington D.C. Why the censorship if the expedition was for scientific purposes and not military? Would it not be military if the government recognised the threat of invasion of saucers from Antarctica?

'And why did the Air Force of the U.S. silence a saucer researcher and close down his UFO group in 1953 – a saucer researcher known to all of us as Albert Bender – for discovering the source of the saucers to be Antarctica? Yes, if you check one of the last letters written by Bender before he was silenced, he mentioned Antarctica as a saucer base, (Gray Barker's book, 'They Knew Too Much About Flying Saucers', page 212), and if you will check issue sixteen of 'Saucer News', Bender told editor Moseley, that he feared an attack of saucers from the polar regions by an unknown race.

'This is only half the story. The first **known** nation on earth to develop flying saucers was Nazi Germany. This was Hitler's wonder weapon that came too late to turn the tide of war. The first flew February 14th 1945, at Prague, and in three minutes reached over 40,000ft, and over 1,200 mph. This saucer was 138ft in diameter, and was built by three Germans, (Schriever, Habermohl and Miethe), and an Italian, (Bellonzo), and was built at Breslau. (See 'German Secret Weapon of World War II' by Rudolf Lusar, former wartime head of the Technical Arms Dept. German War Ministry, and published by Neville Spearman Ltd. of London).

'In the June 1957 issue of the British magazine 'Uranus', it reports that German engineer Victor Schauberger, of the Biological Institute of Bad Ischl, well known for his Golden Plogh, and his water purification system, built and flew, in 1940, a small model of a hat and bell-shaped saucer, using electro-magnetism.

'At the secret German laboratories at Lake Schramberg, the Germans developed a translucent metal harder than diamonds. When it became obvious that Germany could not win the war, (1943), plans were made to build *underground factories in Patagonia, Argentina. Much money was poured into this Nazi base, and many technicians from Germany went there, along with the plans to build the saucers, and stage a later comeback should Germany lose the war.*

*'Hence, Patagonia became a saucer base for the Germans, and Hitler escaped Germany before it fell, and went to this new base by submarine. He escaped Germany by plan, and made contact with the submarine off the coast of Norway. The December 1960 issue of the 'National Police Gazette' (New York), ran an article containing proof that Hitler is alive today. Yes, he is alive and I **met him.***

'In 1939 Hitler sent Alfred Ritscher to Antarctica to map out New Schwabenland, which lies beyond the South Pole in Queen Maude Land. The Germans did not have the mass facilities for production at Patagonia to produce saucers in large numbers, but produced experimental numbers. The first saucers that flew in 1945 used jets. Schauberger's ideas of using electro-magnetism worked fine for small models in 1940, but it wasn't until 1952 that the Germans had a full scale model using the electro-magnetic type of propulsion.

'The ship took off from the Argentina base to explore New Schwebenland. Since the atmospheric conditions of the oasis do not affect such craft, the Germans, in exploring the regions in and around the New Schwabenland, were able to penetrate the storm barrier and reach the 140,000 square mile oasis, and make contact with the advanced civilization living there. They landed at one of the cities, and since then the Germans have been allowed to have a base within the oasis and work closely with the people living within it.

*'Many of the so-called contactees like Adamski, Allingham and Schmidt, have not contacted those from outer space at all, but those living in this oasis beyond the South Pole. These people have travelled to the Moon and other planets, and these planets are **not capable of supporting human life.** On some there is plant and animal life, but **not humans**. These space people from the South Pole have told people they were from other planets in order to conceal their true origin. They no longer care if the truth is told since Ray Palmer has already given much publicity to the idea in his publications. Until he released the news, the information was being held back. Bender almost released it in 1953, but the government stopped him in time.*

'Bender made a mistake in sending his paper to a publisher who co-operated with the government. The government did not know of Palmer's plans to release the information, but as he pointed out since, he has had trouble distributing his magazine. His first article was in the December 1959 issue, and in his February 1960 issue Palmer complains of the loss of 5,000 copies, and that his printing plates were destroyed. Later he had to cancel issues of his magazine and mortgage his home because of the financial loss.

'Rienholdt Schmidt was singled out for severe persecution by the government, as you recall, because an all out attempt was made to discredit him. The one fact that scared the government, was his statement that the visitors spoke German, yet claimed they were from Saturn. Obviously, if Saturn was inhabited, the people wouldn't speak a language native to Earth. (Editor; We do not agree here, but will pass it on.) No, here was a clue to the secret German saucer base; and this was the thing which made Schmidt's story different from others in that here was our clue of space visitors deceiving people about coming from other planets when actually their origin is **Earth** .

'My own first contact took place near Renton, Washington, on the night of July 8th 1960. At that time, I too was deceived, and told by my visitors that they were from Neptune. Because of many years as a UFO researcher and investigator, I had an intellectual advantage over the rest and was eventually able to make out the fact that my visitors were Germans and not from Neptune. Since then I have been taken on rides to Venus, to prove to me that there is no life on that planet, but that Adamski was contacted by those of this earth. I was also given a trip to Antarctica and Patagonia saucer bases, where I met Hitler, who is now an old man, with white hair, but is in excellent health.

'The ships using electro-magnetism can travel very fast, and can reach Venus in seven hours of our travelling time at millions of m.p.h. It takes practically no time to travel from the U.S. to Antarctica – a matter of minutes.

'On Venus there is some vegetation and animal life – mostly marine creatures. Vegetation is giant and the land is swampy and steamy – humidity and temperature quite high. Evaporation of water is quite rapid, turning daytime and land covered with thick fog. Temperatures in some areas reach boiling point. We landed in the cooler polar region, where the temperature was about 112°F. Because of the high humidity and high temperatures, the decay of *vegetation is very rapid. The life-span on Venus is very short, and the rapid decay of vegetation causes an abundance of carbon dioxide.*

'The reason there is no human life on Venus is that a human being could only live a few days on that planet. Most animals are Marine. Everything grows very fast and dies fast. Most animals that do go on land are also able to live in the water too. The bottoms of the oceans, or near the bottoms of the lakes, contain cool water while the surface is very warm.

'What of the future? The major two conquerors of Nazi Germany were the U.S. and Russia. Hitler seeks revenge by bringing these two powers into a war to destroy each other. German scientists are working for both sides – supplying both sides with the needed weapons for such a destruction. World War III is scheduled for 1966, and will be caused by a Nazi underground.

'The Allies are now building up the West German Army, and by 1966 the Nazi underground will take control and surprise the Allies. The West German Army will attack East Germany to unify by force. This will bring the Russians in to save East Germany, and the U.S. the West. Hence, the third power causes World War III.

'Neither the U.S. nor Russia want war, but they will be led into war by the third power. The idea is that the U.S. and Russia will destroy each other, then the third power will move in, pick up the pieces, and rule the world.

'Hitler's plan was revealed many years ago. In September 1960, 'Los Angeles Herald and Express' Jack Moffatt says; "Hitler repeatedly stated that conflict between the East and West was inevitable, and that when it ripened, he would have his triumph."

'I don't want to give the impression that all saucers originate from Earth, some are coming from outer space...another solar system. This is Alpha Centauri. The Earth was originally seeded with life by this race from outer space. They are the Titans. They are now consulting with their brothers in Antarctica and making plans for the final takeover of Earth in 1967. These people are having again a problem of surplus population on their planet, and they are looking for a planet to send some of their people to alleviate this. World War III will reduce Earth's population and allow room.

'So you can see why the space people are willing to co-operate with Hitler and the Nazis, because World War fits into their plans also. They do not wish to

conquer us directly, because their weapons are such that if they used them, it would destroy the possibility of Earth supporting life. Furthermore, the U.S. and Russia will not use the atomic weapons anymore than Hitler would have used germ warfare to save Germany. Neither side would use the weapon because they don't want it used against them. Hence, such 'wonder' weapons will not be used by them but conventional weapons. Thus, World War III will not end civilisation as many people think. The Earth will still be capable of supporting Life.

'We have saucer flaps at five year intervals – 1947,1952,1957,1962 and 1967. These are the Titans coming from another solar system.   Note that Alpha Centauri is 4.3 light years from Earth. This compares favourably with saucer flaps at five year intervals. Note that World War III will start twenty years after World War II, just as that started twenty years after World War I. This means that 1966 and the saucer flap of 1967 follow one another and the war representing the moving in of the Third Power. Al Bender found this out in 1953 – **no wonder he was scared.**

'Alpha Centauri, is a multiple star, and the saucers are coming from the planet Zuna of the star Proxima Centauri.   There have been two squadrons in operation – one leaving Zuna as another arrives at Earth. For example, when one leaves Zuna in 1952, and due to arrive in 1957, another arrived at Earth in 1952. Sightings between flaps are of an earthly origin.

'The next saucer flap is 1962. The Titans are giants of 7 and 8ft tall, as those of Atlantis and Lemuria were giants. At this time, the polar regions were free of ice, and also inhabited by giants. An explosion of the Sun affected the Earth and caused a shift in its axis, and thereby changing climates, and certain land masses to sink, and others to rise. Soon after this the atmosphere was affected from the radiation of the Sun. Some left Earth for their home planet in this other solar system.

'At the time of Atlantis these people had space ships. Others chose to remain and went underground until the period of radiation cleared.   When they surfaced through entrances in the polar region, the atmosphere was such that they lived, but succeeding generations became of smaller size and no longer were giants – the size being the same as we are today.

'The succeeding generations forced their giant elders into the Inner Earth, and they were held prisoners in the centre of the earth. Also they refer to the lost cities of Antarctica as 'Shambalah', 'Agartha' and the 'Rainbow City'.

So what do we know about the Antarctic, and how many of Schmidt's claims ring true? (Of course, his predictions of World War III never came to pass.)

It is known that, during the 1950s, researchers Schmidt, Ray Palmer, Bender and Australia's Edgar Jarrold all subscribed to these theories, and they all claimed to have been intimidated, and that fear caused them to suddenly, and without notice, exit ufology .

Until recent times, and the advent of widespread satellite surveillance technology, this part of the world was safe from spying eyes. Even now, satellites do not cover the entire globe, although one which can do so was being proposed in 2017, and would now probably be in operation.

In 1513, Ottoman Admiral Piri Reis had a map compiled from twenty different documents, many very old (some dating back to 400BC or earlier), and sourced from several countries. It has, in some respects been verified, but details show it does not reflect a complete knowledge of modern Antarctica.

This famous 'Piri-Reis Map' was made before modern Europeans discovered Antarctica, yet details the sub-glacial geography of the continent, including coastline, and rivers and mountains in the interior. How and when this information was first obtained remains a mystery.

The continent seemed to be placed hundreds of kilometres to the north, with a warm climate. However, modern science indicates this situation hasn't existed for many millions of years. The detailed topography suggests that either some source maps were well over 6,000 years old (the last time this continent was possibly free of ice), or else it had been charted from above, using technology only available to our current society.

My personal belief is that Schmidt, Bender, Palmer and others were mislead when told about Atlantis, Lemuria, the Titans and others. Perhaps aliens have used the area from time to time, and maybe were there during the first half of the twentieth century. It is possible they were, in the past, the originators of these detailed maps.

Our first-known modern expedition to Antarctica was in 1821, when Mikhail Lazarev and Fabian Gottlieb von Bellinghausen landed there with Russian explorers. In 1839, Charles Wilkes sailed to the Antarctica looking for the 'Holes in the Poles', which the 'Hollow Earth Society' said were entrances to ancient civilizations now living inside the inner earth. (Of course, these days, although the 'Society' is rumoured to still exist, nobody else supports this early theory, and Wilkes never reached his goal due to lack of funding and suitable equipment.)

During the twentieth century other missions were undertaken, including two by Germany in 1910 and 1925. After an initial voyage by Captain Ruser-Larsen, in the early 1930s, the Norwegians began exploring and claiming territory in Queen Maud Land, between the Stancomb Wills and Shinnan Glaciers, which the Germans later 'annexed' in 1939.

From December 1938 to February 1939, during the summer months, under Admiral Ritscher, Nazi Germany began expeditions and plans for a base in Antarctica. Their stated reason for this was to make formal claims on a little-known part of the continent (the same Queen Maud Land, claimed by the Norwegians), and they renamed the area 'Neu Schwabenland.' They claimed their defeat of Norway, early in World War II, legitimised this claim in the name of the Third Reich.

In 1938, the German Thule Society invited Richard Byrd, the first man to fly over the South Pole, to lecture their personnel before they departed for Antarctica. (Others have claimed that Byrd did not make the flight, and merely reported on the flight of a Lt. Conrad Shinn. Shinn said he had flown over a 'strange, great ice-free valley, twenty miles long and eight miles wide, with a large number of black 'hillocks' about 15-30 feet high.)

A converted German aircraft carrier, the 'Neuschwabenland', left Hamburg in December 1938, arriving at the Antarctic in January 1939. Two planes onboard made numerous aerial mapping flights, dropping swastika flag/markers. The official reason for the 'German Society of Polar Research' – 'New Schwabia' expedition - was to establish a whaling station, as they needed whale oil, and did not want to continue to depend upon the Norwegians for their supplies. They also reported discovering a 300-square-mile, geothermally heated, ice-free region containing several lakes with a connection to the sea.

There have been many unsubstantiated reports about German machinery and technology being taken to the area over the next few years. Certainly, the Nazis had the requisite expertise and fleet of U-boats. It beggars belief that they also had a large enough Navy and sufficient man-power, manufacturing ability and raw materials to establish an enormous self-sufficient base while at the same time conducting a war across Europe and the north of Africa.

The British military and security agencies closely monitored this activity during and after World War II, with secret military bases of their own established on the Antarctic continent, as well as the nearby Deception and Wiencke Islands. The codename for their covert presence was 'Operation Taberlan', and in 1946, using their 'sovereignty' of the Falkland Island Dependency, declared themselves legitimate owners of some territory in the Antarctic, including parts which Chile and Argentina could have also claimed.

The British had sufficient intelligence reports to indicate that many Nazis may have fled there in submarines, and had a large underground base with advanced technology. We can only speculate that they already suspected they were more alien than human facilities. They wanted to retrieve this ahead of both the U.S. and Russia. The British already had a well-established base at Maudheim, 200 miles away from the suspected Nazi or alien position, and it was from there they launched an expedition in 1945. It was thought that the entire team had perished, but not before they sent radio messages about Nazis, strange men and tunnels.

The next summer Britain sent another expedition, which purportedly found a self-sufficient base, with a massive network of tunnels and caverns, which they partially demolished after considerable loss of life.

Not much was known about these expeditions, however in 2005, researcher James Robert wrote of how a former British SAS officer, then in his declining years, confided about his participation in the second incursion.

In October 1945, he had been serving with his unit in Palestine, when he was suddenly ordered to report to Gibraltar. When he arrived he was told he was being sent, along with several other specially selected elite British soldiers, to the Falkland Islands to be trained for a secret mission. He was ordered not to speculate or talk about why he had been selected, and all the soldiers on the plane from Gibraltar maintained complete silence;

"Upon reaching the desolate and forbidding Falkland Islands, we were introduced to the officer who was leading the expedition and a Norwegian who had served in the Norwegian Resistance, an expert in winter warfare, who was going to be training us for the mission that we had no inkling about."

He said their training was hard and arduous, and finalised with them being advised that if the military's suspicions proved correct, there would be little chance of them all returning; *"We were informed that we were to investigate 'anomalous' activities around the Mühlig-Hoffmann Mountains from the British base in Maudheim. Antarctica, so we were told, was 'Britain's Secret War".*

They were advised that, apparently, when the British realised that the Nazis had been to Antarctica in 1938 and 1939, they also began to set up secret bases around the Antarctica in response. Maudheim was one of the most clandestine.

At the end of the war, some U-boats surrendered, but many more were missing and could not be accounted for; *'British forces had captured three of the biggest names in the Nazi party – Hess, Himmler and Dönitz – and with their captures Britain was given information that was not going to be shared with Russia or the United States. That information compelled Britain to act alone, and we were spearheading the operation.'*

Before they were parachuted into the area, they were also given the details of the previous expedition, and the reasons for excluding Russia and the United States. Apparently both those countries had a technological advantage over the British due to the scientists, equipment and research they had already taken from the defeated Germans.

When they reached the base, it appeared to be deserted, however a trip wire activated an alarm siren, and a lone survivor from the previous expedition emerged from hiding. He directed them to 'Bunker One', where he said another survivor was in hiding, along with a 'Polar Man'. 'Bunker One' was opened, and a young member of their unit was selected to enter. They heard two shots being fired, and the 'Polar Man' fled so quickly, only a few token shots could be aimed at him. Inside, they found the bones of the other survivor from the first mission, and their own young soldier with his throat ripped out.

They demanded answers from the first survivor they had found, and he then detailed what had happened during the first expedition. When the entire complement of thirty personnel at Maudheim Base was ordered to investigate, they found the initial tunnel with considerable ease, as its entrance was located in one of Antarctica's unique dry valleys.

'They followed the tunnel for miles, and eventually came to a vast underground cavern that was abnormally warm; some of the scientists believed that it was warmed geothermally. In the huge cavern were underground lakes; however the mystery deepened, as the cavern was lit artificially. The cavern proved so extensive that they had to split up, and that was when the real discoveries were made. The Nazis had constructed a huge base into the caverns, and had even built docks for U-boats, and one was supposedly identified.'

As they travelled deeper, they had found 'hangers for strange planes and excavations galore'. After witnessing their comrades getting captured and executed, the two survivors fled. They were unable to block the tunnels, and instead separately hid in two bunkers at Maudheim Base.

The rescued soldier was not believed by the scientist in their party, who said the fellow was 'certifiable', however the Major in charge decided his claims must be investigated, especially as they included discovering 'an unknown energy source'.

They made their way to the dry valley, and while the men set up camp, the Major and the scientist went in to investigate. Upon their return, they said the walls were smooth granite, and it was not an ancient tunnel. That night, they lured the 'Polar Man' back to their camp and killed him. A post mortem showed he was human, but had more hair than normal.

The next day they prepared to enter the tunnel; *'We made sure that we took enough ammunition and explosives to wage a small war, and hopefully destroy the whole base in its entirety, for that was our mission; not to salvage, but to destroy.'*

The party of ten walked for five hours before arriving at the vast cavern which was artificially lit; *'As we looked over the entire cavern network, we were overwhelmed by the numbers of personnel scurrying about like ants, but what was impressive were the huge constructions that were being built. From what we were witnessing, the Nazis, it appeared, had been in Antarctica a long time.'*

For the next few days, without being caught, notes were made and photographs taken. Mines were laid in strategic positions, but as they made their way back to the tunnel, for a safe exit, they were spotted, and a troop of Nazis and another

'Polar Man' gave chase. They unsuccessfully placed more mines at the entrance.

'The mines did indeed close the tunnel, but for those Nazis and 'Polar Men' behind, the chase was still on. In a fighting retreat, only three out of the ten escaped the tunnel: the Norwegian, the scientist and myself. The rest had fallen gallantly in making sure that some of the party survived.'

The remaining men returned to Maudheim Base, where they were evacuated to South Georgia. They were issued with a directive that they were forbidden to reveal what they had heard, seen or encountered. The mission was totally whitewashed and never made public, with the tunnel being written off as a 'freak of nature'. The 'Polar Men' were described as 'unkempt soldiers who had gone crazy', and no mention was ever made of the Germans, although 'certain elements of the mission were to be leaked to the Russians and the Americans.' The witness rued the fact that the expedition, its casualties and survivors, were never given the recognition they deserved.

Most underground bases would be quite undetectable, and except for the odd conspiracy theory, very few people have considered the best location of all, beneath the ice and snow of the continent of Antarctica, the fifth largest continent, with a land mass of fourteen million square kilometres, larger even than Australia. While the surface of Antarctica is totally inhospitable for most of the year, this would not necessarily apply to subterranean areas. (From time to time there have been more reports of ice-free regions and lakes. In 1977 scientists from the Scott Polar Research Institute discovered seventeen lakes under the Antarctic Ice, and in 1995 Russian scientists actually found a 'warm' 250-kilometre-long lake under their Antarctic base.) Perhaps earlier claims of alien activity on this mostly-forgotten continent were not so far-fetched after all!

Later, in 1946-47 during the following Antarctic summer, U.S. Admiral Byrd conducted *'Operation High Jump'*, to supposedly investigate possible sites for bases, as huge mineral deposits had been found in this vast unexplored continent. The four participating military groups were collectively referred to as *'Task Force 68'* participating in 'The United States Navy Antarctic Developments Program'. (It has long been believed this was actually to eradicate any remaining Nazis or aliens, and if the reports are accurate, Admiral

Byrd spoke of well-documented German activity there before, during, and after, the War. I consider this was a 'cover story' and that after the British expeditions, he already suspected an alien presence, in addition to any remaining Nazis.)

At the time, it was commented that considering the several thousand U.S. military personnel and the ships and air-power involved, it looked more like an assault, invasion team than a survey mission. The expedition included flagship aircraft carrier 'USS Philippine Sea', with many planes, destroyers 'USS Brownson' and 'USS Henderson', submarine 'Sennet', two tankers (the 'Canisteo' and 'Capacon'), and the supply ships 'Merrick' and 'Yancey'. There were two icebreakers, the 'Burton Island' and 'Northwind', plus seaplanes and helicopters. (Hardly necessary for a few penguins, seals, and large fish!)

The 'expedition' built a headquarters and made numerous reconnaissance flights, recording over ten mountain ranges. 'Operation High-Jump', planned to last several months, ended prematurely after forty days in a strategic retreat. The U.S. contingent met stiff resistance, and engaged in several battles, suffering many casualties. There were reports of 'ray-type' weapons and Byrd described 'flying objects that could go from pole to pole at incredible speeds.' A Chilean newspaper reported, at the time, that Admiral Byrd had advised the U.S. to initiate immediate defence measures against hostile forces threatening from the Arctic or Antarctic! He is also quoted as saying this resulted from his personal knowledge gathered at both the North and South Poles! Of course, once he returned to the U.S., the matter was conveniently covered-up.

The British did not return to the Antarctic until 1948-49. It is rumoured that 'hostile forces' were later eliminated by several 'large explosions'! The truth of what happened will probably never be known.

In the 1950s, the post-war powers agreed to co-operate in their activities on this icy continent. In 1957, the Americans and scientific representatives from 67 countries, officially returned to the Antarctic as part of the International Geophysical Year. Many stations were established on the continent.

Did they find anything to substantiate Schmidt's claims? In 2015 Linda Moulton Howe published information from a retired U.S. Flight Engineer, who was stationed in Antarctica during the summer seasons, of 1983-87. On several occasions he saw silver aerial discs darting around over the Trans-Antarctic Mountains. One area was designated a 'no-fly' zone, which he was told was an 'air sampling' area. Once, when traversing it without permission, for a medical emergency, they saw a very large hole, like an entrance, going down into the ice. The debriefing they received indicated it was a lot more than an 'air sampling area'.

They were told 'they had never seen it', and never to talk about it. After their flights they would have a few beers at the bar, where they heard scientists talking about 'guys at the South Pole working with 'strange-looking men', and confirming a future trip to the 'air sampling area' (ie. big hole in the ice!) 'to meet-up with the ETs that were there.'

He also mentioned another occasion when 'a group of about a dozen scientists disappeared for about two weeks'. When they reappeared, he and his crew were sent to pick them up; "They would not talk, and looked scared."

On March 1st 1950, Commander Augusto Vars Orrego, the head of the Chilean Base in Antarctica, reported that several of the explorers under his command had seen and photographed several discs above the lonely station during the bright Antarctic night. He said they were wheeling and turning, one above the other, at tremendous speeds.

The Commander discounted the possibility of them being 'optical illusions' as the pictures corroborated what was observed. Commander Orrego also added that whether the photographs would be published or not depended on his superiors as they were the property of the Chilean Navy.

British researcher, Gordon Creighton, wrote about another group of Chilean scientists who, during the 2nd International Geophysical Year 1956-8, watched two UFOs over a two day period.

The Chilean Navy had taken a party of four men by helicopter to Robertson Island, where they were to spend a month studying flora, fauna and other features. The 500 square kilometre island, of volcanic origin, was situated in the Weddell Sea.

On 8th January 1956, 'Dr T.' was out of their 'shelter' observing any 'night-time' meteorological phenomena of interest. In the clear sky above, he saw two metallic cigar shaped objects, hanging vertically, still and silent, and vividly flashing the reflected rays of the Sun. He raced in and woke 'Dr. B', who peered at the objects through his binoculars. The craft seemed to be solid, with smooth, polished metallic surfaces.

At 7am, their medical officer came out of the hut, and immediately yelled; "Look Professor – flying saucers!" Their assistant then came rushing out and stared in amazement. By this time they all realised that what they were seeing was not a mirage or hallucination.

Two hours later, the first motionless object suddenly changed to a horizontal position, and shot away in a flash towards the west, its colour changing different colours from infra-red to ultra-violet. It silently traversed the sky, zigzagging around, sometimes overhead. Without slowing down it would make incredible changes of direction. Its manoeuvres included abrupt stops followed by sharp turns and instant acceleration. After about five minutes, it returned to its former position, close to the second object, which then took off towards the east, and for about three minutes, performed similar aerobatics before returning to its original position near its companion.

The scientists had two Geiger-Miller Counters with them, and they now showed that the radioactivity around them had increased by forty times the normal readings. This caused some anxiety, as their radio had broken down in a recent storm, and they weren't due to be picked up for another twelve days.

They felt that they were being confronted by a phenomenon from beyond the realms of any known earthly science, and tried, unsuccessfully, to adopt some form of normality, despite these unknown craft still hovering in the sky above. They managed to estimate the altitude of the two objects at about 8,000 metres, their length about 150 metres and diameter, at the thickest part, 25 metres.

When the objects executed a few more manoeuvres, 'Dr. B.' did some more calculations, which indicated that their speed was 40,000 kilometres per hour, 'not far short of terrestrial escape velocity'. He concluded that; *'Since the object would invariably start from zero speed, and attain 40,000 km.ph. instantaneously, then halting again abruptly, with no gradual deceleration whatsoever, the inertia inside the craft would clearly be fatal for any living creature unless it had its own gravitational field in accordance with the 'Plantier Theory of UFO Propulsion.'*

At the end of the second day, an Antarctic blizzard occurred, and by the next morning the strange objects were nowhere to be seen, and the radioactivity readings had returned to normal.

When they returned to base, they did not lodge an official report at first, preferring to tell a high ranking Chilean Army Officer, who had heard of other UFO reports, registered by nearly all of the expeditions to Antarctica. Later they were asked to complete questionnaires from the U.S. Air Technical Intelligence Centre.

Personally, I believe this was indicative of a covert, advanced alien presence. What type of alien, and if they were connected to the Third Reich, would be a matter of conjecture. The Nazis did not have the ability or technology, at the time, to construct a substantial, meaningful, permanent, underground base in such a hostile environment. If they had possessed the craft documented by these scientists, and earlier by Admiral Byrd, Germany would have won World War II.

Another interesting ability of the early UFOs seen over and near the Antarctica, was their ability to operate both in the skies and under the water.

Author-researcher John Keel wrote of an incident which occurred to the north, off the coast of Tasmania, the southernmost tip of the Australian Continent, in 1942. The witness, who had been an Australian Air Force officer, said *"At 5.50pm...we were flying some miles east of the Tasmanian peninsula when, all of a sudden, there came, out of a cloud bank, a singular airfoil of glistening bronze colour. I'd say it was around 150 feet long, and about 50 feet in diameter. It had a sort of 'beak' at its prow, and the surface seemed...rippled or fluted.*

"On its upper surface was a dome, or cupola, from which I seemed to see reflected flashes as the sun struck something which might, or might not, have been a helmet worn by someone inside. At the other end the airfoil finned out into a sort of fin. Every now and again there came from its keel greenish-blue flashes. It turned at a small angle toward us, and I was amazed to see, framed in a white circle in the front of the dome, a large grinning 'Cheshire cat'!

"The damn thing flew parallel to us for some minutes, and then it abruptly turned away and ...it went off at a hell of a pace, turned and dived straight down into the Pacific, and went under, throwing up a regular whirlpool of waves! Just as if it had been a submarine."

Also on the southernmost tip of Tasmania is Maatsuyker Island, the closest part of the Australian continent to Antarctica. Its lighthouse, erected in 1890, was still manned in 1965.

Investigator, Keith Roberts, from TUFOIC, unearthed some interesting sightings made from this remote location. One night, in early 1965, two of the lighthouse keepers saw a 12-15 ft diameter 'ball' shaped object travelling slowly from east to west across the sky. It had a solid looking red centre, with an outer white band, and lit up the island, 'like day', for thirty to forty seconds. The next day, the witnesses found an area of flattened or scorched vegetation, in its line of travel, on the highest point of the island. (An obstruction had blocked their view when the object went over that area.)

Later, in the August of that year, Head Keeper, F. Armstrong, wrote; *"I saw the same unidentified object appear as reported to you a few weeks ago.'* Again, in September, the object returned. This time there were multiple witnesses, including other 'Keepers' and their families. They noted it looked like 'a child's spinning top, with a 15ft tail'.

In October, the strange craft was seen on six different nights, once again in November, and several times during December. After February 1966, it was not seen again. Although some researchers wanted to explain the reports as a display of the 'Aurora Australia', the witnesses would have been familiar with this phenomenon, and dismissed this explanation. Nobody seemed to consider the proximity of the Antarctic, just across the ocean from this southernmost tip of Australia.

Colin McCarthy, reporting in the early days of Australian research, spoke of an incident possibly in the late 1950s, at the Australian Antarctic Base. The ground radar had picked up a stationary, unidentified blip at a range of fifty miles. It was a fine summer day, and the scientists got their binoculars and went outside to attempt visual contact.

They could see a classic, cigar-shaped object about fifty miles away, and estimated its length to be over 600 feet. Every few seconds, there would be a burst of colour, which shone brilliantly around the craft. They believed that this was due to highly ionised air, and as this colour built up, the proton precision magnetometers in their research station would soar off-scale, showing a very large, pulsating magnetic field.

They desensitised their equipment, and determined that this unknown craft had field strength of over 1,000,000 gaus; *'To have a magnetic flux density of these fantastic proportions, radiating from a craft 600 feet long, was literally "out of this world" – this was the only explanation that the scientists could give! Nothing manufactured on this planet could have produced such improbable readings on their instruments.'*

On 3 July 1965, a giant lens-shaped solid flying object was seen, at an altitude of about 5,000 metres. It was tracked and photographed over the Argentine Scientific Naval Base on Deception Island off the Antarctic coast. Commandant Daniel Perisse watched as, at a height of about 5,000 metres, it alternatively hovered for up to 20 minutes at a time, then accelerated and manoeuvred at tremendous speeds. Its colour changed from red-yellow to green and orange and caused strong interference with the variometers they used to measure the Earth's magnetic field. The object interfered with other electromagnetic instruments, and magnetograph tapes showed unusual registrations, for over an hour.

Similar reports came from the British Base and a Chilean naval transport ship, the *'Punta Mendanos'*, whose compass needles pointed directly to the object, over a mile away, indicating it emitted an unusually strong force. Altogether, the craft was sighted by 31 people, ruling out any hallucinations or collective psychosis. None of these many witnesses believed the object was of terrestrial manufacture.

Commander of the Chilean Antarctic Base, Air Force Commander Mario Barrera, was most definite; "It was not a star. Neither do I think it was an earth-built aircraft. No apparatus, constructed by man to date, has anything like this either in shape, speed, manoeuvrability or other characteristics."

(Recently, Russian scientists have theorised that electro-magnetically operated extraterrestrial vehicles would take advantage of the streams of magnetic energy, which is at its greatest at the North and South Poles.) Admiral Byrd was apparently tasked with recording such forces.

In 1976, it was reported that years previously, Brazilian scientist, Dr. Rubens Villela, saw a strange object which looked like a 'silver bullet', while on an icebreaker in Admiralty Bay. It came shooting out of 40-foot-thick sea ice, and flew off, high into the air. Huge chunks of ice 'came hurtling down'. In the large hole left in the ice, the water seemed to be boiling, with steam all around.

This was not the first time Brazil's scientists and military had encountered strange craft that may have originated to the south in the Antarctic. Trinidade Island, in the Atlantic Ocean, is situated about 1,200km off the coast of Brazil. During World War II this small, rocky isolated place was used by the United States as a submarine base.

Brazil, was preparing to establish a Naval meteorological and oceanographic station there during the International Geophysical Year. On 16th January 1958, the sailing vessel *'Almirante Saldanha',* of the Hydrographic and Navigation Division of the Brazilian Navy, was on a preliminary visit and anchored off shore.

Dr. Willy Smith investigated this case and reported that at 12.20pm, a fast moving, bright object was seen approaching the island. Almiro Barauna, a member of the expedition and a professional photographer, took several shots of the strange craft, and 48 excited eye witnesses were also on deck to attest to the event.

The object was like a flattened sphere, with a metallic appearance of an ashen colour, and encircled around the middle by a large ring or platform. They could not hear any noise coming from the craft, but it had what appeared to be some form of condensation of green vapour around the perimeter, especially in the advancing edge. It was not luminous, and some witnesses likened it to the planet Saturn.

The craft, whose estimated size was 350ft, and speed 600 to 700 mph, moved with an almost undulating motion – 'like the flight of a bat'. After approaching the island, at about three to four hundred feet above the water, it moved out of sight behind the central mountain, reappeared a few seconds later, and went in the opposite direction back towards the sea. Once it was over the water, it appeared to stop mid-air for about ten seconds before moving away and disappearing into the distance.

This was the fourth time that an unidentified aerial object had been seen over the island in the preceding forty days, and Captain Bacellar and the other officers insisted that, despite limited facilities, Barauna's photographs be immediately developed onboard.

They were given to the authorities upon their return to the Brazilian mainland. The Ministry of the Navy later said that the Navy could not venture an opinion on the nature of the object, and astronomy professor, and arch-sceptic, Donald Menzel, claimed they were 'faked'. A 1978 examination, by an independent laboratory, concluded that the photos seemed to be genuine, and it was unlikely that they were hoaxed.

By 1998, meteorologist Rubens Villela was a veteran of eleven expeditions to the Antarctic – two with the U.S. Navy, eight with the Brazilian Antarctic Programme, and another on the sailing ship *'Rapa Nui'*.

The one incident he never forgot occurred during his first trip, in March 1961. He was on board the U.S. Navy Icebreaker *'Glacier'*, when they encountered a severe storm, and retreated to safe haven in Admiralty Bay in the King George Isles.

After the storm and fog subsided, Rubens was on deck, admiring the beautiful scenery. Around him, marines were installing searchlights, to spot any 'ice blocks' which might come their way after dark.

A strange light suddenly crossed the sky, and everyone looked up and started to shout, each with his own idea of what it could be. The light, which had originated from behind the mountains on the other side of the island, moved horizontally and slowly, around 80kph, from northeast to southeast. It was oval-shaped, with a multi-coloured luminous body, and left a long, tube-like orange/red trail;

"Suddenly it split into two identical pieces, as if it had exploded. Each part shone more intensively, with white, red and blue colours projecting 'V' shape rays behind it. Quite quickly they moved away, and could be seen around 200 metres above the ground. Before the object had divided, I would estimate its size to that of a fist at arm's length. Throughout the sighting no noise was heard by any of the witnesses."

There was an abandoned British base nearby, and the Captain insisted that a search be carried out, in case there were any 'unknown explorers' requiring assistance. There was no-one there, and the strange lights officially explained away as *'a meteor or some other natural luminous phenomenon'*.

Rubens didn't agree; *'How could they mistake a meteor with an object carrying antennae, completely symmetrical, and followed by a tail without any sign of atmospheric turbulence? – I wasn't convinced at all, as a meteorologist, the evidence didn't support such a theory, even allowing for the fact that many strange optical and luminous phenomena, including mirages, auroras etc., can be seen on Antarctica.'*

He wrote in his diary; *'Positively the colours, the configuration and contours of the object, as a bodied light, with geometric forms, did not seem to be from this world, and I did not know what could possibly reproduce it.'*

Five years later, on 22nd May 1966, there was another incident. The British *'Northern UFO News'* reported on the testimony of two witnesses who were stationed, at the time, on Adelaide Island as part of the British Antarctica Survey.

Early one morning the meteorologists saw an unusual dense cloud rise vertically in the south, at a speed of about ten feet per second. By the time it reached an elevation of about five to eight hundred feet, its size was estimated to be about 100ft by 100ft.

This was no ordinary cloud. It alternately expanded and contracted, and emitted a low 'buzzing' sound. It was in view for a total of forty-five minutes, before 'dissolving', and at one time a thick black ray came out and struck the ground. A secondary ray was visible at the point of impact, where the snow was visibly disturbed. The event was reported to the authorities, but the witnesses were not provided with any follow-up, however BUFORA's photographic experts were given a colour slide, taken at the time, to examine.

In 1982, Queensland's *'UFO Encounter'* published an interesting report, sourced from the *'APRO Bulletin'*, after a former U.S. Coastguard helicopter pilot came forward.

On April 20th 1964, 'Mr. X' was on duty at the South Pole as part of 'Operation Deep Freeze'. At that time he was crew chief on a C-130 transport plane, and during the early morning hours, he and five other crew members were inward bound to the Naval Base at McMurdo Sound. Suddenly, the starboard watch called out that he had a series of UFOs approaching at about 400 knots. Unlike a Russian Transport plane, which was about five miles away, these objects were not showing up on radar.

There were nine glowing objects, flying in a 'V' formation, which closed in on the C-130, at first tailing the plane, and then moving over and to the left.

'At this point they attempted to send a 'Mayday' call, but discovered that their radio had gone dead, as had their radar. The aircraft then began to lose all electrical power. The pilot attempted to switch to auxiliary power, but found it was out also. 'X' said is was as if the plane's entire electrical system had shorted out. The turbo-props were still going at this time, but then they gradually began to grind to a halt. He theorised that because the engines were receiving no electrical power, the oil had begun to congeal in the cold temperature, causing the failure.

'At this point the big transport should have been falling like a rock, but, to the surprise of the crewmen, the aircraft was apparently maintaining a steady altitude and course. 'X' had no idea why the aircraft didn't go down, but it would seem that the UFO was somehow keeping it airborne. He said it was 'a hell of a feeling', flying along with no engines, in complete silence.'

It was if something was controlling their flight and flight-path, until they suddenly entered a strange haze, similar to a 'white-out', but full of dry, static electricity. They all felt very 'odd' whilst in this haze, and if they got close to any metal, they could receive an electric shock. After about twenty minutes, the haze vanished, and they could still see the UFOs for a short time before their electrical power came back on.

They restarted the engines, one by one, and as soon as all their systems were functioning normally, they continued on to McMurdo. When they arrived, they discovered that during that 45-50 minute encounter, they had covered 265 miles, much more than normally possible. Further, they had too much fuel left on board following a fight from Christchurch, N.Z. Even more unusual, some metal objects, especially ones made of iron and steel, seem to have 'lost' up to 50% of their original weight. One of the 'ground chiefs' insisted that there was something wrong with the tractors they unloaded, because they didn't weigh enough!

Crew members were interrogated by officers they thought were from 'Intelligence', and the photos they had taken from the plane were confiscated. They later learned that most of the photos were 'foggy', as if exposed to radiation, but regardless, they were all told, in very strong terms, to keep their mouths shut about what they had seen and photographed.

On January 3rd 1965, 'X' had a slightly less confronting experience. This time he was crew chief aboard a C-130C, only about 100 miles away from where the previous encounter had occurred. There were no other aircraft on their radar, but suddenly they lost all electrical power, including the radio and secondary generator.

He said; "The crew all stood ready to jump, when, out of nowhere, an elongated, glowing object passed the transport with 'a hell of a bang'!"

It was larger than the C-130C, and going fast enough to create a sonic boom. They slipped into the wash the object left behind, and were buffeted around for about three minutes before their power came back on, and they were able to contact two nearby bases, who had not detected anything on their radar.

The mysterious 12,500ft Mt. Erebus, is situated on Scott Island, on the shores of the Ross Sea, and 25 miles from New Zealand's Scott Base. It has an active volcano, 450ft below the summit, with a circular crater, over 1,500 ft in diameter at the top, and 'live' inner crater measuring over 600ft. In the summer of 1974/5, there was much publicity regarding an expedition from New Zealand which was conducted by a multi-national team, who determined that the northern half of the inner crater had high temperatures and lava activity.

Only five years later, in November 1979, the mountain was again in the news, but this time for all the wrong reasons. An Air New Zealand DC-10 scenic flight had failed to return, and the next day the burned-out wreckage of the plane was found scattered over the icy slopes of the mountain. Two-hundred-and-fifty-seven lives were lost.

Weeks before, experts had warned of the possible danger of such flights, noting the lack of special survival equipment, navigational aids and rescue facilities in the event of an emergency. The incident was subsequently categorised as an 'unfortunate accident', with suggestions of 'pilot error'.

In my book, 'Contact Down Under', I noted that not everybody agreed. John Pinkney, a Victorian investigator and journalist, rang me, and said he was determined to publish the real facts, as he believed them to be. In December 1979, his article appeared in the 'Melbourne Truth'.

In it he said that immediately after the crash, the Australian and New Zealand Air Forces were placed on 'full alert'. Quoting ham radio operators, and senior government and RAAF sources, he claimed that just before it crashed, the plane transmitted distress messages that it was being buzzed by a craft of unknown shape and origin.

He didn't accept my possible theory that, given the lack of navigational aids on the DC-10, perhaps the UFO was trying to warn the pilot he was heading for the side of the mountain. John insisted on making a tenuous link to the case of missing pilot, Frederick Valentich over the Bass Strait a year earlier.

In 2002 British investigator, the late Graham Birdsall, attempted to research current scientific activity in the Antarctic, and was met with a fear to speak by some who knew the details. Graham and Dr Richard Sauder wrote about this in '*UFO Magazine*', and it certainly appeared there was far more happening in the Antarctic than we were being told.

What of the Antarctic today? In another article, a new witness came forward. He preferred to remain anonymous due to the 'Official Secrets Act'.

His report was due to him reading about the British Antarctic Survey and the British National Space Centre setting up a new 'Exobiology Committee' to study extraterrestrial life.

From 1994 to 1996, he had served on the Royal Research Ship, '*Bransfield*', with the British Antarctic Survey. Just after Christmas, 1995, the ship, having unloaded its cargo, was tied up on an ice shelf at Halley Island.

"Rumours began to circulate – as they do in a closed community – about the Chief Officer, Graham Chapman. He had apparently seen a 'flying saucer', first on radar, then through binoculars, and had made a note in his log. He received some 'stick' from the crew. No-one, (not even me at the time), believed his story.

"The next day, the Russian icebreaker, 'Polar Stern', turned up, and deployed its helicopter."

Under orders from the Ministry of Defence B.A.S. Headquarters in Cambridge, the Captain of the '*Bransfield*' ordered them away. His crew were then refused permission to leave the ship, and soon after an American vessel arrived with some heavy lifting equipment and a pre-fabricated hanger. His ship and crew were subsequently told to leave, and escorted back to the Signy Islands by the Americans.

Later, three scientists told him that a joint British/American team had begun construction of a new base called 'Europa S8', with an **extremely short landing strip**.

"I asked the Captain whether the base existed, and was told the base that the Yanks are throwing together 'doesn't exist', and if I spoke of it again, I would be flown home without a reference or pay.

"This was in 1995-96, and in 1998 a committee is set up to study 'bio-molecules?"

We have to ask where did the unusual craft, seen over the last 60 years originate? Were they ours or 'Theirs'? More recently, there have been reports of secret visits to the Antarctic by some of the world's influential leaders. Why?

Up until his untimely death, British investigator Graham Birdsall pursued his interest in the Antarctic. In his 2003 *'UFO Magazine'* he mentioned a mysterious gigantic dome at the end of Lake Vostok, and of how two young Australian women, intent on ski-ing near the area, were picked up by U.S. Navy Seals, and dumped by helicopter in New Zealand, prompting the Australian government to lodge an official protest with the U.S.

Graham also mentioned that when Valerie Urarov, departmental head of Russia's Department of National Security Academy, was asked about Lake Vostok, he visibly paled, and said he was not allowed to talk about it.

In 1998, Graham also published, in his 1997/8 December issue, an article by Rubens Villela, with a photograph which showed a nuclear generator being unloaded from a U.S. supply vessel in Antarctica. Graham suggested that he had been warned about publishing this information, but personally, I do not consider this to be suspicious or unwarranted, as a reliable power supply would be needed for these remote bases.

It wasn't just the Antarctic experiencing strange craft. By 1960, and the height of the Cold War, military bases were established at the opposite end of the Earth in Alaska and the remote Arctic wilderness. The indigenous Eskimos already had myths and legends about visitors from the skies. They spoke of the 'tinmiukpuk', or 'thunderbird', an enormous eagle which would, with a sound like thunder, come from the sky.

Another story was of a ball of fire, like the moon, coming down, and a large creature, resembling a skeleton, arriving at the village and killing most of the inhabitants. Apparently, some of the 'Visitors' were more benign, seducing some of the women and producing children said to be conceived from the 'moon spirit'. Eskimos who chose to visit the 'Sky Land' were called 'pavungnartut', which may correspond to our definition of a contactee.

Many reports were being lodged by the scattered bases, however some suspiciously resembled rocket type vehicles coming from Siberia. Others were not so easy to dismiss.

It wasn't just the Americans and Canadians who were seeing unidentifiable craft in the Arctic. If the Americans and their allies were suspecting the Russians were responsible for these advanced craft, the Soviet Union thought exactly the same about their Cold War adversaries.

Soviet pilot V. Akkuchatov was the chief navigator for the Soviet Air Base at the North Pole. In 1956, one of their planes was flying over a strategic ice area near Greenland, when a large disc, resembling a lens with a pulsating edge, closed in from the port side and flew parallel to the plane.

Thinking it was American, the Russian pilot flew back into the clouds for forty minutes, only to find the disc still there. He ventured closer, and the UFO also altered course, and later shot off at tremendous speed to a higher altitude and accelerated out of view.

George Eberhart wrote that; '*in July 1947, two officers at Fort Richardson, near Anchorage, watched a spherical object fly through the sky at tremendous speed. It seemed to be ten feet in diameter, and left no vapour trail.*

'*Eight disc shaped UFOs were photographed by Mikel Konrad as they landed about fifty miles north of Juneau in April 1950. And that same year in September, George Peck took an apparent double-exposed photo of four lights in the sky at Adak.*'

At midnight on January 22nd 1952, a military outpost in northern Alaska tracked a strange object on radar, and three F-94 jets were immediately scrambled. When the intercept planes approached, the radar screen indicated that the intruder had slowed to a hover.

The F-94 pilots reported that they could see nothing, but after the fourth time they circled the designated area, the radar screen showed the object streaking away to the west.

On April 14th of that year, a huge disc passed over Anchorage, and several inexplicable vapour trails were seen over the area later that month, followed by other sightings of strange objects in 1953 and 1954.

On May 27th 1962, the Air Force was unable to explain two apparently controlled UFOs which manoeuvred above Palmer, Alaska. At the end of August 1965, a large disc hovered above Hyder for over eight hours. It then zoomed away in the late evening. On 15th November 1967, an airport weather observer at Fort Simpson in northern Canada, reported an object, with radical speed variations, making right angle turns.

Dan Willis, who in 1969 was stationed at a Naval communications base in Los Angeles, told of how a ship near Alaska reported a strange craft had emerged out of the ocean, near their port bow. It was a bright, glowing, reddish-orange elliptical object, approximately seventy feet in diameter, and as it shot out of the water, it was seen, and tracked on radar, as it raced upwards, travelling at about 7,000 miles per hour.

During the 1950s and 60s, many reports of strange craft and lights in the sky, as distinct from the 'Northern Lights', were received from Alaska, Greenland and Canada's Northern Territories. In later years, it seems as if the military and officialdom have placed a lid of secrecy over any happenings at either of our Earth's Poles.

CHAPTER FIVE

AUSTRALIA'S VAST INTERIOR

Australia is an enormous country, with huge, isolated, mainly uninhabited areas across the Northern Territory, Queensland, N.S.W. and both West and South Australia. The desert provides a vast region suitable for natural security, probably the biggest prohibitive locale in the world. Right in the centre, near Alice Springs, is the secret Australian/U.S. Pine Gap facility, and another base, at North West Cape, is on the West Australian Coast. The vast majority of this continent is also an ideal place to experiment with prototypes belonging to both us and our allies.

Researcher Keith Basterfield wrote in his 2004 *'Disclosure Australia Newsletter'*; *'Recently, while further researching the use of then 'black' aircraft in Australia, reference was found to the English Gloucester A-W Meteor PR19 aircraft. The PR19 was first flown in 1956, and like the U-2 made secret over flights of the USSR. Interestingly, it exceeded the U-2 in altitude performance. The RAF reportedly also flew these aircraft out of Butterworth in Malaya and from Laverton in Australia during the period 1960-1962. Flights were reportedly all made at night. As the U-2 seems to have generated some Australian UFO reports, the possibility exists that so did the English PR19.'*

Keith also noted an RAAF Report Form, which was subsequent to a report received following a sighting in Tasmania on 25th May 1961. It asked *'Location of any air traffic in the vicinity at the time of sighting.'* Typed in were the words; *'U-2 aircraft over Great Lake at approximately 8.15 am travelling in a northerly direction, leaving a distinct vapour trail.'*

It is not known if some of the later prototypes were 'manned' vehicles, but the possibility certainly exists. Brian Richards from 'UFORUM' reported on a 1966 case at Willagee in Western Australia;

'Mrs. Audrey W's children, aged 5 and 7, were playing on the front verge with their neighbour's children, more or less the same age. It was dusk, but not dark. Suddenly, their children created a great commotion, and their dog flew into frenzy, its hair on end.

'The children came running in, very excited, and declared they had seen 'priests' looking out of portholes at them, from a funny round thing, with a round thing on top. The children went on to describe the occupants of the craft as wearing dark 'shirts' with round, white collars. Apparently, this saucer-shaped object dipped downwards towards the children, before speeding off north towards Perth.'

Apparently, some overseas investigators knew more than the Australian public about the testing of new prototypes. In 1956, French researcher, Jimmy Guieu, wrote about an Avro disc-shaped craft called the 'Omega': *'It is not impossible that the Omega has been tried out in Australia. At any rate, one thing is certain; in September 1952, the British were experimenting in Australia with some form of pilotless aircraft. It is well known that since September 1952, the proving ground at Woomera, South Australia, has been the scene of very great activity.*

'Experiments are said to have been carried out there with 'miniature' supersonic aircraft, jet planes in the form of 'cigars', and super-rockets capable of carrying an atomic bomb.

'On November 26th 1952, the British announced that they were envisioning the construction of piloted rockets, launched from the ground, flying at 1,500 miles per hour, capable of reaching, in fifty seconds, an enemy bomber flying at an altitude of over 50,000 feet. It is believed that all these machines, both British and Australian, have been tested at the Woomera base.'

There is the 'Woomera Prohibited Area', and adjacent to that, the 'Maralinga Test Area'. (A third spot, where it is inadvisable to spend any amount of time visiting, is the 'Emu Atomic Area'.) This is where, in the 1950s, after World War II, the British reputedly tested twelve nuclear bombs.

To the south, a highway and train line runs across the Nullabor Plain from Adelaide to Perth, and, in the past, has given rise to several incidents. Some may well be our own experimental craft, and others lead us to consider alien activity.

In *'Contact Down Under'*, I discussed an incident in January 1985, when a goods train encountered a mysterious craft. Three years later, in January 1988, the Knowles family's car was lifted off the road, about 80kms from the W.A. -

South Australian border. In October of that year, a bright light paced a Pioneer Express Coach, near the same spot, terrifying the passengers and driver.

In '*Aspects of UFOs and Aliens*', I mentioned another case. In his thirty-six years of working on the highway, 53 year old Alan Stewart, a supervisor with the W.A. Main Roads Dept., has suffered more than his fair share of encounters.

He believed the strange craft were alien in origin. The UFOs he encountered were usually discs, but sometimes cigar-shaped, and more often than not a blue to pale green colour. Some were as large as a football field, and others so small he thought they may be 'scout craft'.

In 1977 he was alone in his caravan on the South Australian side of the border. He said that he could hear voices, and suddenly found himself away from the caravan, and clinging to the leg of a being, surrounded by a mist or cloud. Another time, when alone in a Main Roads Dept. camp at Mundrabilla, he woke to find all the pumps going full bore.

He said that twice these strange craft 'zapped' him, possibly as some form of warning. Both times he ended up in hospital, once for nine days. Doctors could not explain the subsequent dark marks on his shoulder or kidney area, nor the pain he had experienced.

Even in the 1950s, strange craft, which may have been our own prototypes, or indeed extraterrestrial, were being reported from South Australia, and further to the north in the Northern Territory.

In his '*Catalogue of More Interesting Australian Close Encounters*', Keith Basterfield mentions a case from Central Australia in February 1951; '*Members of the Unmatjera tribe of Aborigines reported seeing two shiny, circular objects, some 9-15m across, on the ground. A very small man-like creature, with a bulbous head, wearing a shiny suit, transferred from one object to the other. Both then took off, making a buzzing sound.*'

UFOR(QLD) documented a 1955/56 report from Darwin, in the Northern Territory. It was early one evening when the ship, the '*Wangara*', was at anchor in the harbour, and a lot of the population were 'out and about'.

An object, bigger than the moon, with a dark centre, surrounded by a glowing light, was seen rapidly, and at a high altitude, approaching the town. It stopped and slowly descended, silently hovering over the water. When it tilted sideways, and the front end was lower, witnesses could see that it was circular, quite large – 'bigger than a house' – with three levels, lighted by 'portholes'.

People on shore were panicking, and residents and sailors on the *'Wangara'* taking photos, which the local media were quick to publish. For more than an hour, the strange object seemed to 'drift' over to the land, and headed towards the RAAF Base and Qantas airfield, twelve miles out of town. Where it went from there is not known, as the military weren't commenting, however the local newspaper claimed that five Sabre Jet aircraft were sent up in hot pursuit.

Three days later some men arrived in town. They were all wearing black suits, ties, hats and dark sunglasses. As one witness said; *"No one up there wore clothes like this, so they stuck out like sore thumbs!"*

They only stayed for a day or so, but co-incidentally, the media 'clammed-up', and had no more to say on the matter.

A few years later, in July 1961, Darwin was again visited by an unknown craft. The *'Australian UFO Bulletin'* reported that between 7.55pm and 8.40pm, on 27th July, a saucer-shape, bluish, glowing object, came in from the north, and circled Darwin Harbour.

One witness said that she and other witnesses saw it from the wharf. She described it as 'coming in quite low and fast', and being very large with a long tail. A fellow witness, Mrs Hostelek, said; *"We watched it for probably thirty seconds. I believe it was manually controlled by the path it took.'*

It then moved southwards, and practically 'buzzed' a train travelling from Larrimah to Darwin. *'The driver, Douglas Clarke, stated that he saw a 'big ball of fire' coming towards the train from behind. Speaking for himself and his fireman, he said; "It gave us quite a turn. I've never seen anything like it. I don't believe it was a comet. I don't know what it was."* It was last seen ten minutes later over Tennant Creek.

This was not the first time when something strange was seen over Darwin. Certainly, during World War II, Japanese bombers arrived on surveillance and bombing missions, but there was a little consternation when in 1938, a mystery plane appeared in their skies.

Although it displayed all the signatures of a small plane, nobody could ever determine, in any of the sightings, where it came from or went to. Investigator, Jon Wyatt, said that many ufologists felt that a small percentage of mystery planes were ET craft in disguise. We will never know!

The April 1959 *'UFO Bulletin'* reported that on March 28th, residents of Purnong, 91 miles north-east of Adelaide, had been seeing, in recent weeks, multi-coloured objects in the sky.

A couple of weeks earlier, on 13th March, Carl Towill, the local postmaster at Claypans, and Percy Briggs, a carrier, saw a huge, dome-shaped object sitting on a nearby property, about two miles from Purnong. It was huge – 'bigger than an airliner' – and surrounded by brilliant lights, which kept changing from red to blue.

The two men watched for about thirty minutes, and decided to approach the field, to get a better look. When they were about 200 yards away, it rose from the ground, hovered silently for a moment, then gained altitude, and shot silently off, at immense speed, towards the south.

They both insisted that the craft was intelligently controlled, and later, Percy Briggs was questioned by investigators from Woomera Rocket Range.

We will probably never know how many of the strange craft, seen during the 'early years' in Australia's vast interior, were extraterrestrial or our own prototypes.

In his publication, *'Australian Saucer Record'*, Fred Stone wrote of Colin Norris's investigation of a landed object seen on the lower level of the Adelaide Hills. At 7.30pm on 28th October 1962, Ellen Sylvester, a high-school teacher, was driving back to Adelaide with her three children.

For forty minutes, they stopped and watched this unusual occurrence, which was certainly no optical illusion or hallucination. The object, which was resting on three legs, was oval, and possibly orange in colour, although this may have been to a reflection of the rays from the setting sun. There was a light around the outer rim, and it had round shaped windows. Her son remarked that he could see some people inside.

Eventually, an occupant, who was about six feet tall, got out. They noticed he was dressed in some form of uniform, and wore a type of helmet, similar to the gas masks which had been used during the war. There were lights on either side of the helmet, and some form of breathing apparatus coming from there down to his chest.

He seemed to be having trouble adjusting the object's 'legs', which eventually retracted. As soon as this was accomplished, he went back inside, and the craft took off, at first slowly, and then headed north at an incredible speed, faster than anything Ellen had ever seen before. She commented that she was positive it was not any known object normal to Earth.

'VUFORS', the Victorian UFO Research Society, investigated a 1965 report from Donnybrook in Western Australia.

At about midnight on 25/26 July, Glenys Keevins and a friend were driving on a little used road, about nine miles out of the town, when, upon rounding a corner, they came upon an object hovering just above some trees, a few hundred feet away from the road.

It was disc-shaped, about fifty feet in diameter, with a series of 'portholes' around the rim, and a bright white light emanating from the underside. After the witnesses slowed down to watch, the bright light went through a series of colour changes to a bright blue, and then shot up into the sky and was out of sight within a few seconds.

As more cases were reported, in '*UFOs Now and Then*', I mentioned how the aboriginals often witnessed strange craft in the skies. Abdul, along with a fettler friend, suddenly found that the engine on their vehicle had 'died'. When they got out to investigate, they were astounded to see a 'gargantuan' object hovering 200ft above.

There were many other cases of strange phenomena in the area, many of which were never reported. Colleagues received one letter from a Mrs. M. B., which detailed an intriguing incident from late October - early November 1970; *'My husband and I were travelling to Western Australia, with some friends, across the Nullabor.*

'We had stopped at Balladonia, refuelled, and started our further journey to Norseman. We were running short of water, so decided to stop off at a water hole to refill our water bottles. We found an inland road with signs giving directions to water. On the way to the water hole, we hit a tree stump, which made the panel-van jump, and the roof rack came adrift from the vehicle.

'We found the water, and then unloaded the roof rack, and my husband repaired the brackets which held it onto the roof. It took us some hours to get re-organised, and by then it was starting to get dark. We hit the main road again as the sun was down.

'We drove for some time, then changed drivers – me to drive and my husband to sleep for a while. I can't remember for how long I'd been driving, when there were very strong white lights above me. The panel-van seemed to be going at an indescribable rate of knots. I had no control over the steering or speed. I thought that I was dreaming about the situation. The speed woke my husband, and he kept screaming at me to slow down. I said that I couldn't, so we swapped positions. I slid out under him, and he held onto the steering wheel. (The vehicle was automatic).

'When my husband took the wheel, he found the same problem. All we could see was bright lights above the vehicle, and there seemed to be some form of force, like a 'G' force, pushing us back into the seats. It seemed like a magnetic force – very strange and frightening.

'We had thought that the lights were animals on the road, then suddenly realised that there was something very wrong, as our panel-van seemed to be getting faster and faster. We didn't hear any noise, but suddenly our vehicle seemed to be up in the air. The wheels were screaming, as if it were up on a hoist.

'This seemed to last for ages. All that we could then recall, was finding ourselves on the road, without any idea of where we were. We realised we were

going in the right direction, because of the position of the sun, and we came across some road signs indicating that we were headed towards Norseman.

'Apparently our friends had organised a search party with the town police, who kept telling them not to worry, as we would eventually turn up. When we arrived, they were with a group of people, who then dispersed. Our friends came over, and when they put their arms around us, they received a strange 'electric' type shock, as they did when they touched the car.

'They looked strangely at us, and kept asking if we were okay. We had felt that this all had happened in a short time, but we soon found out that there seemed to be hours missing from our lives. We thought it was about eight hours, but it was longer – about 32 hours – a day and a half! We felt very strange – disorientated.

'Our friends later told us that our eyes were in a stare, and we looked tired. Our watches had stopped. My husband's worked again, but mine never did. It took us days to get over the effect of what had happened. We really have no explanation to what it all was, and my husband will not talk about it.'

Woomera is also situated in the South Australian desert to the north of Port Augusta. The Woomera Base was once a top secret facility where the military tested rockets, missiles, bombs and all kinds of classified 'goodies.'

In 1947, following the end of World War II, Britain and Australia formed a Long Range Weapons Establishment, which fired its first missile launch from Woomera in 1949. The first 'Skylark' rocket launch was in 1957, followed by the first 'Black Knight' the next year, and a deep space tracking station in 1959. In 1964 the first 'Europa' rocket, (a modified 'Blue Streak'), took to the air, and Australia's first satellite was launched in 1967.

Originally, from 1950 to 1974, much of the facility came under the jurisdiction of the Department of Supply, who were, among other things, responsible for the operation and management of space tracking stations, and certain other facilities on behalf of the U.S.A., and participation in the firing of European Launcher Development Organisation, (ELDO), rockets.

There are many reports of 'bogies', (unauthorised air traffic), and it is intended to only mention a few here. Needless to say, the official explanations were nearly always conventional, no matter how improbable.

The RAAF Base Edinburgh, in South Australia, was a 'Weapons Research Establishment', (WRE), later renamed the 'Defence and Science Technology Organisation', (DSTO). Researcher, George Filer, reported that a journalist, working on a corporate video for DSTO, claimed that he once entered an off-limits hanger that contained a saucer-shaped craft. *'He was swiftly escorted out, and told not to talk about what he had seen. Others have stated that there is a top secret project named 'Project Apotheosis' that involves the transport of alien craft from the DSTO to another secret location.'*

In 1979, a teenager, who lived five miles away from the base, was walking home just after 9pm, when a huge, dark circular 'shape', with no lights, passed silently 100ft overhead. He was terrified, and hid in a bush, from where he watched until the object had moved to a distance of a few miles away. He ran home, as quick as possible, but noted that, during that decade, he and others had seen strange lights moving inexplicably in the sky.

On 9th January 1954, the Australian *'Melbourne Age'* quoted a high ranking RAAF officer as saying that, during the previous months, there was an increase in UFO reports coming from aircraft in flight.

Two days later, on 11th January 1954, the *'Adelaide Advertiser'* carried the following headlines on its front page; *'Plane Crew Sees Sky Object'.* Capt. Booth, the pilot of an ANA airliner, had left Broken Hill for Adelaide at 6.25pm the previous evening. His First Officer Furness and the rest of the crew also observed the strange phenomena, on and off, from 7.40pm, when they were flying at eight thousand feet, about fifteen miles north of Morgan.

At first Capt. Booth was not concerned, thinking it was a north-bound plane, due to pass at that time, but the strange object seemed to move back and forth across their line of flight, as if circling. They thought it was another aircraft...due to the manoeuvres... perhaps the RAAF, but Parafield control room advised that there were no other aircraft in the area. Although it was dead ahead of them, they never caught up with it.

They watched for ten minutes until it became too dark to see the object. Several times it disappeared into the haze and cloud layer while it was circling. Probably mindful of their careers, both men said it must have been an 'optical illusion of some sort'. Furness couldn't explain how it occurred, and Capt. Booth commented that he had been flying for fourteen years, and had never seen a similar sight before.

5th May 1954, at 4.45pm., a radar operator was watching trials through binoculars and spotted a dark-grey, circular object with a translucent appearance. It seemed to be travelling directly across the path of an approaching Canberra Bomber aircraft, then turned right and went in the opposite direction. It slowed above the Canberra, and appeared to be hovering over its flight-path.

Although he worked for Vickers-Armstrong, and was familiar with all makes of aircraft, he said; "...during this time, I found it very hard to believe what I was seeing, so I shut me eyes and looked again, and it was still stationary over the Canberra."

The object looked to be about the same size as the plane, but travelled three times as fast. (Further reports estimated its speed as approximately 3,600 miles per hour at an altitude of 60,000 feet.) Group Captain Plither, Superintendent of the LWRE Range, corroborated the report, and noted that a similar object was seen on 3rd May by two ladies at Henley Beach.

Five months later, on 6th October 1954, Gunner Willis was operating a cine-theodolite, (a camera device for collecting and recording trajectory data), when he observed and photographed an unauthorised aerial craft. He was tracking a Jindivik target drone plane, in a very clear sky, when he saw a half-moon-shaped, silver-white object at 40,000 feet, travelling at medium speed. The sighting only lasted a short time, and the Department of Air 'gave the film negative to the Director.'

Ken Llewelyn, (author of *'Flight into the Ages'*), detailed another disturbing event, just before the test firing of a Black Knight rocket, in the late 1950s. Group Captain Tom Dalton-Morgan, in charge of range operations, and his recovery officer saw an unusual bright, white-green light coming in from the north-west, about 85 miles away. It was at approximately 5,000 feet, and travelling very fast. It silently orbited the range buildings, about five miles to the south, and then climbed away to the north-east at a steep angle. The witnesses said they had the impression the light emanated from 'a cupola-like cabin raised slightly above the invisible fuselage', and estimated its speed to be well beyond the capability of any current aircraft.

Dalton-Morgan said; *"I am unable to conceive of any object, plane or missile, during my posting to Woomera, that was able to perform the manoeuvres seen by my team. Observers at the control tower and launch site all agreed on the brilliant white-greenish light; the high degree of manoeuvrability, including rate and angle of climb; complete lack of sound; the lack of positive identification of the vehicle fuselage because it was a dark moonless night, and the exceptionally high speed of which it was capable."*

Also in the late 1950s, (between mid-1957 to mid-1958), James Stern was Telemetry Chief for the Australian Branch of the English Electric Company's Guided Weapons Division. James told me; "I was sitting in my car in Salisbury South Australia, when I got an urgent message: the Red Shoe trial team had a fully guided round (a missile), on the launcher at Range E, near Koolymilka. The Jindivik target drone plane was on the back track, prior to coming round on the firing leg, when radar reported a bogey in the intercept area. On instructions from the Range E Controller, the nearest cine-theodolite made visual contact, and then filmed it.

"The object had appeared at 50,000 feet as a three-to-four-metre diameter disc. It remained stationary for several minutes, before ascending to 100,000 feet in four or five seconds. The 100,000 foot level is where our radar van lost it. I don't know how far the range theodolite and radar vans tracked it.

"When the film was developed, the official assessment was: 'Film blank – radar fault'! There was an outcry from several of the radar operators and the girls on the theodolite. The assessment was changed to: 'Clear turbulence, causing visual and radar effect, not shown on film'."

James said, "Comprehensive records of every minute and step of the trials were meticulously kept, and I would expect the Guidance team to mention a radar bogey in their section. After each firing the trials teams were given the opportunity to view a screening of all the films taken. This time the alleged blank film was not included.

"We all thought that Base Security was in a flap and had put a lid on it. The other side of the Iron Curtain might have got something we didn't know about, and I bet the theodolite film, if it still exists, is probably in some security file."

This information from James certainly confirmed my suspicions about the evasive answers and vague explanations officially given by Woomera with regards to UFO reports.

'AURA' investigator, Dominic McNamara, said that; *"There was one case at Woomera where a strange object was spotted flying alongside one of the rocket launches. It was seen by about ten different people positioned at different areas of the base. That launch was supposed to be filmed but a memo came out the next day saying; 'You may have heard that a UFO was sighted during yesterday's launch. Those reports are untrue. No footage of yesterday's launch was taken.' Later that day a second memo came out saying.... 'actually footage was taken....none of it was exposed!'*

Obviously, in the past, personnel and civilians associated with the Woomera Base were not satisfied with the government's whitewash. What was most significant was that a Woomera UFO Group had been formed in the 1960s called the *'Scientific, Technical and Astronomical Research Society'*, (STARS). The authorities were not happy when they received reports completed on STARS forms, rather than official documentation. Senior personnel actively discouraged the 'UFO Club', and its activities had gradually faded away altogether by 1974.

In late August 1957, an employee at the Port Elliott drive-in theatre, near the Murray River, was driving home to Goolwa, at about 11.30pm, when he saw an object on the ground, about half a mile from the sea. It was about fifteen feet long, oval in shape, with lights shining from eight or nine portholes. It took off quite rapidly, climbed at a forty-five degree angle towards Hindmarsh Island, and soon disappeared.

On 10th July 1963, the *'Adelaide Advertiser'* told about a Willaston resident who was driving to Gawler. When he rounded a corner, near the Sandy Creek hotel, he came upon a glowing, blood-red object, landed upon, and extending across the road. He slammed on his brakes, stopping about three metres away.

He described the craft as being about eight metres across and four metres high, with a concave top and flat base. After suddenly rising to a height of about one hundred metres, it turned on its side, changed to a light red-yellow colour, gathered speed, and flew off towards Two Wells.

Some researchers have reported, possibly with 'tongue in cheek', that visiting aliens have developed a liking for ice-cream! Perhaps this explains an incident on 8th June 1966, when two ice-cream truck drivers, J. Armstrong and G. Polomka were travelling between Kingston and Naracoorte in South Australia.

For twenty minutes they watched as a strange craft hovered over their vehicle, and zig-zagged across the sky. It would hover over one spot, then move at fantastic speed to another. The body of the craft was like a brilliant white spotlight, interlaced with smaller coloured lights, and there was a red light on the dome on top. Fortunately, it eventually departed, leaving the witnesses and their precious cargo intact!

Other residents in this vast outback area were also seeing unusual flying objects. Farm manager, Alan Pool, at Yericoyn, 99 miles north of Perth, reported an unusual occurrence to police in 1967.

At 6.30pm one evening, he was out in his land-rover, looking for stray sheep. Suddenly he heard a whine-like noise, similar to a high speed electric motor; *"I looked up and saw this thing coming straight at me. It was about 400 to 500 ft. up and about half a mile away when I first saw it, and it seemed to be coming in to land."*

It did indeed land in a paddock, right next to Alan's land-rover. He described the metal craft as being circular, with a diameter of about fifteen to twenty feet, and about the same height as his vehicle. The bottom was flat, and the top 'dome-shaped – just like an up-turned bowl or saucer'. It was a smoky-grey colour, and had no visible lights. He said that there were what appeared to be porthole-like windows around it, and something like a cabin in the front, although he couldn't see inside.

The craft was so close, Alan barely had room to open the door of his vehicle; *"I was near enough to touch it, before it took off in a flash!"*

There were other instances in the late sixties, which may or may not have been our own prototypes, out on a test run. South Australian investigator, Keith Basterfield, included these cases in his catalogue.

On 18th November 1968, two children at Hill River, saw a small, football shaped object, apparently only about 60cm long by 25cm thick, land in a paddock. Whilst their account may have been doubted, a flattened, two metre, oval swirling area was later found in the paddock.

Another case occurred three months later, at Flinders Park on 17th February, 1969; *'Awoken by a noise which sounded like a 'whirr', a lady looked out of a window to see an unusual object in an adjacent area. It appeared about 100m away, some 10m across.*

'A 'man' emerged from the shadows and walked around the object. This figure was about 1.8m tall, lean, had light hair and wore white overalls. He walked around the object several times before the lady ran to get her neighbours. When they returned, the object had gone.'

By 1966-1967, while some sightings by locals near Woomera could be linked to the test range itself, some were most definitely intruders. UFOR(SA) reported that one poor man was walking home when he saw 'three lots of objects' in the sky. There was no wind or dust, and one broke away from the rest and hovered low overhead. He said it was "as big as a football field", and he felt as if he were "standing on air, but his feet were on the ground." After a while, it took off at great speed. He couldn't remember much, and when he arrived home he was taken to hospital, suffering from shock.

In 1988, Peter Moyle, of Maylands W.A., reported that twenty years earlier, in 1968, he was working at a men's camp, four kilometres out of the town of Woomera. It was the night before a major missile launch, and he went into town for a meal. He was walking back to base along a straight stretch of road – 'with nothing but the stars for company'.

He said; "Suddenly, directly in front of me, a light, infinitely brighter than the stars, appeared on the horizon. It was directly above me in about seven seconds. It was a staggering sight, and looked bigger than a football field. It was shaped like two saucers, inverted towards each other, with a protrusion on the underside, bathed in yellow light.

"Around the edge, where the discs joined, there were apparent portholes, from which a dazzling bright light was pouring. Through the windows I could glimpse three or four misty shadows moving busily about.

"To my relief, the saucer didn't hang about for long. After a few seconds it accelerated, did a right angle turn, and vanished way below the horizon. I was stunned. To my knowledge, there was nothing on earth, then or now, capable of travelling that fast."

Keith Basterfield, also wrote an excellent review of a case which occurred on 22nd August 1968. Two pilots, Walter Gardin and Gordon Smith, were flying an empty Piper Navajo charter plane from Adelaide to Perth. At 09.40-GMT, (5.40pm WA), Walter, who was at the controls, woke Gordon, who was asleep in the cabin, and asked him to come to the cockpit to see a 'formation of aircraft'. There was one large craft in the middle, and four or five smaller ones to the right, left and above it.

The Navajo was 130-nm east of Kalgoorlie, cruising at 8,000ft, airspeed 190km and tracking 270 degrees magnetic. Gordon said; "These aircraft appeared to be maintaining station with us."

They contacted Kalgoorlie D.C.A. communications centre, and were told neither they nor the RAAF had any traffic in the area. For the next ten minutes they lost communications with Kalgoorlie - just harsh static on all frequencies.

During that time the larger 'ship' maintained the same altitude, but split into two then rejoined, in a sort of cycle. The smaller craft, actually about six in all, stayed at the same level but kept flying left and right, in and out, and then 'formatting' with the two halves of the larger object. There movements were not consistent with normal aircraft, and they did not turn like normal planes.

Gordon said; "The shape of the main ship seemed to have the ability to change, not dramatically, but change from say, spherical to a slightly elongated form, with the colour always remaining dark grey to black. The smaller craft had a constant cigar shape, and were of a very dark colour."

Walter and Gordon said the whole formation maintained the same distance and bearing from their aircraft during the whole sighting. They could not accurately estimate the size of the larger object, except to compare it to a Boeing 707 from about ten miles.

At 09.50-GMT, (5.50pm WA), the whole formation joined together, 'as if at a single command', then departed at tremendous speed. Within three or four seconds they had diminished in size until out of sight. The Navajo's radio communications were immediately restored, leaving two flabbergasted pilots.

They discussed the matter, and after dismissing all conventional explanations, reached the conclusion that 'the UFOs were in fact aircraft, with the solidarity of aircraft, except perhaps for the fact of the larger UFO's ability to split and change shape slightly'.

This incident occurred near Zanthus, a locality on the East-West transcontinental railway line. Twenty-one years later, on 9th September 1989, trains traversing this route towards, and including Zanthus, also experienced strange UFO sightings. (See my book, *'Contact Down Under'.*)

Another airline pilot told of an incident which occurred on 24th July 1969. It was just after sunset when, in clear weather conditions, he was flying from Mt. Magnet to Perth, and had been given permission to pass through Pearce Military Control Zone.

About six miles north-east of Pearce they noticed what appeared to be an aircraft taking off from RAAF Pearce. The co-pilot remarked that it was unusual for a civil aircraft to receive clearance for this route when Air Force activity was in progress. They watched as it climbed, and drew closer. Concerned that normal separation standards could not be maintained, they asked the Perth ATC controller as to the 'aircraft's' intentions, only to be told that there was no known traffic in the vicinity.

They were looking at a bright light, similar to an aircraft landing light, with several smaller yellow lights, which resembled cabin lights. They changed frequency to the radar controller and enquired as to traffic on radar, and received the same response that there was no known traffic. When the pilot disputed this he was backed up by another pilot who was flying from Lancelin Island to Perth, and could also see the UFO.

The object was so close, they took precautionary action and quickly turned to the right, intending to pass behind it. As they turned, they flicked their landing lights. The object accelerated with incredible rapidity and in less than five seconds disappeared from sight. The next day newspapers reported accounts of ground sightings from places as widely separated as Perth and Albany. Again, the pilot waited several years before reporting the event to VUFORS in 1978.

Keith Basterfield also wrote, in the AURA-based *'Disclosure Project'*, about information he obtained regarding the retrieval of downed fragments of space vehicles. Keith estimated at least nine such pieces were found over New South Wales, Queensland, South Australia and West Australia, between 1963 and 1988. His research unearthed several records of spheres being recovered. All were determined to be of American origin and returned to the United States.

Jerome Clark wrote in *'The UFO Encyclopaedia, Volume 3'*: *'In 1961 the United States Air Force established the classified 'Project Moon Dust' to 'locate, recover and deliver descended foreign space vehicles'.'* I personally consider this was a normal and reasonable reaction of any government who not only wants to know the technology of other-earthly or more alien powers, but also needs to retrieve its own satellites and spacecraft.

'Project Blue Fly', with similar objectives, was also established. In a paper delivered at the '1992 MUFON International Symposium', Clifford Stone discussed some classified documents, relating to 'Project Moon Dust', which were released and then reclassified by the U.S. State Department.

He said; *"According to the Air Force document, 'Project Moon Dust' represents a specialised aspect of the U.S. Air Force's overall material exploitation program to locate, recover and deliver descended foreign space vehicles. This same document also mentioned an 'Operation Blue Fly', established to facilitate expeditious delivery of "Moon Dust' and other items of great technical intelligence interest to the Foreign Technological Division.'*

He noted that most documents pertained to U.S. and Soviet debris recovery, although some revealed that objects of 'unknown origin' were recovered. He went on to mention an alleged satellite recovery, of unidentified origin, in Sudan in August 1967, and four objects, one of which was a nose-cone shape, from Nepal in 1968. The government of Nepal had sought American assistance in returning the debris to the country which had launched them into space, however there was no record of the U.S. ever advising Nepal of the nature or origin of the objects.

Strange objects, which may have been remotely controlled spy drones, rather than satellite or crash debris, were also being found in other parts of the world. In 1956, Irish researcher and author, Desmond Leslie visited John Hutchinson at his farm near Moneymore. On 7th September John and his wife saw an object rapidly descending into a field in a small valley about 250 yards away. It came to rest on the far side of a hedge and small stream.

It was spherical, red and rubbery in appearance, and 'three-and-a-half feet on its major diameter, and two feet on its minor diameter'. It had a small red knob or point on top, and four thin, white stripes around the middle.

When John kicked it over, it righted itself, and when he picked it up it spun a few times in an anti-clockwise direction, then reversed and spun the other way. As he tried to carry it through the hedge, John lost his grip on the strange object, which immediately took off up into the sky and disappeared.

Just a few months later, on 15th January 1957, a similar event occurred on the other side of the world, in New Zealand. The *'Grey River Argus'* reported that William West was on his property near Balfour, when he and his friend, Wallace Liddell saw an object, which looked to be oblong, and about twelve to eighteen inches long, fall from the sky, and land on the lawn.

When they rushed over to pick it up, they claimed it jumped away and changed shape; '*Instead of being oblong, it turned into a blue sphere about eighteen inches in diameter, still glowing with a bluish-white light, but appearing to have a dull red glow in the centre.*

'*They continued their attempt to catch it, but each time it moved a little further away. Finally, after they had observed it for about a minute, it floated up and over the eight foot corrugated iron fence, and disappeared slowly across a paddock.*

'*Mr. West made a special trip to Invercargill to tell his story to meteorological officers at the weather station at the city airport, but they could offer no explanation. Mr. West is convinced that the object they saw was not of this world, but came from another planet.'*

In the late 1950s there was some speculation regarding mysterious metal spheres found in the vast Australian desert. It is possible that they were of earthly design, however it is just as possible they originated elsewhere.

Australian researcher, Bill Chalker, wrote; *'The Joint Intelligence Organisation (the re-organised JIB) maintains a secret 'Bolide' file. It still seems to be anchored in the premise that 'UFOs' could involve the chance of retrieval of Soviet hardware, and therefore contribute to some useful intelligence. It appears JIO have a 'rapid intervention' capability, as they have been able to instigate prompt, widespread ground searches in suspected 'hardware' crashes. They do this through 'special access' channels. This operation may be similar to U.S. activity operating under the code name 'Project Moondust'.*

'Flying Saucer Review' reported another three objects were found in 1963, and Mr. Allan Fairhall, UK Minister of Supply, stated that inquiries to the relevant American and Russian space agencies had failed to determine the origin of these spheres, raising speculation in some quarters. There was some mention and discussion of this and the mysterious spheres in the Australian media at the time, but the issue was basically downplayed.

In later years, my own career involved the possible scenario of my being first on the scene if something crashed into my local area. I was given strict instructions that no matter whom or what it fell on, if it was any part of any space vehicle or satellite, my primary duty was to guard the wreckage until the appropriate authorities arrived.

One of INUFOR's researchers discussed in a recent article how Timothy Good, in his book *'Alien Liaison'*, interviewed a witness who was employed in a workshop in the Woomera facility.

An unusual object ended up in their possession after being found by a helicopter searching for a missing girl. The mid-grey, metallic sphere was about two feet nine inches in diameter, and somewhat darkened, perhaps by extreme heat. It was lightweight for its size, and a perfect sphere – no bumps, rivets, welds or signs of being polished.

They tried everything to cut into it –saws, drills, hammers, chisels and even an oxy-torch, which didn't even heat the surface. Nothing they tried could raise it to oxidising heat, and it did not register any radiation, not even the background level.

The witness initially assumed that it came from a '*Black Knight*', the only missile in existence that could have contained something that size, but they denied it had anything to do with the '*Black Knight*'. He also realised we didn't have the technology to produce that object. Before they could do further investigations, Range Security took the object for the United States Wright-Patterson Air Force Base, as 'space debris.'

Australian newspapers reported later finds in South Australia and Queensland, and our witness's work colleague suggested the safest approach was that this object "never existed."

Military personnel also reported seeing unauthorised craft in the sky. Often their senior officers actively attempted to dissuade or discredit their reports. I would never have known of the following incident had I not been at a government training college in the 1980s, and one of the witnesses, a fellow student, confided in me:

"I was with another army serviceman, on patrol duty at Woomera in the 1960s. As we drove along the perimeters, making a routine security check, we spotted a large cigar-shaped object, hovering over the electrical cables. It was making a strange noise, and I got the impression it was drawing power from the lines. My hair stood on end, as if there was a strange magnetism in the air. In fact, as I am talking to you, the hair on the back of my neck is standing on end, just like it did that day."

Upon return to base, they were subjected to three days of interrogation, and less than subtle intimidation; "At first they suggested we had been drinking, but once we proved our sobriety, they changed their tactics and said we must have been mistaken, and should withdraw our reports. We remained adamant in our testimony until eventually the base commander released us back to normal duty. He warned us never to discuss the matter with anyone again."

___

The Maralinga nuclear testing range is located in South Australia, half-way across the Nullarbor Plain, but further north. Much of this is still a

Commonwealth-controlled area with limited or no access, due subject to long-term nuclear contamination created during the 1950s and 1960s.

There is a report that a RAF corporal, stationed at Maralinga sighted an unidentified craft hovering over the airfield for 15 minutes, following a nuclear test detonation. It was a metallic silver-blue colour, with a line of windows or portholes along the edge. Given the tight security around such projects, I don't think we will ever know full details or official analysis of this event.

Another better documented event was researched by Jenny Randles following Derek Murray's return to Britain after serving at Maralinga in 1957. In the November of that year, he and some colleagues had been playing cards at about 4pm, when someone came running in to say that there was a UFO over the site. At first they laughed, but their colleague urged them to go outside and see for themselves.

There were other people already staring at the hovering object, which was tilted at a 45 degree angle. It was a silvery-blue metal, with a dome on top, and what appeared to be plates on the side. There were also several squarish windows or portholes across the side. After about fifteen minutes, the silent object shot upwards and away at a fantastic speed. Authorities in Alice Springs and Adelaide had no idea what the craft was.

Many people don't realise that Australia's vast interior extends to the narrow coastal regions of Queensland's east coast, where, whilst UFOs are encountered, it is possible some of our own prototypes may stray. Northern Queensland was better known for sugar cane and banana plantations, so 'flying saucers' were a novelty and big news.

Following a 1969 article, by Stan Seers and William Lasich, in the *'Flying Saucer Review'*, in his 1970 book, *'Passport to Magonia'*, researcher Jacques Vallee also wrote of this incident which occurred at Euramo, near Tully in northern Queensland. We may never know the origin of the object which landed.

He had also followed up on a front page article, *'More Flying Saucer Nests!'*, which had appeared in the *'Sydney Sun-Herald'* on 23rd January 1966. At 9am on January 19th, banana grower George Pedley was driving his tractor, across his neighbour Albert Pennisi's cane growing property, near a swamp called 'Horseshoe Lagoon', when he heard a loud 'hissing' sound. Suddenly, only a short distance ahead, he saw a large craft, 'convex on the top and bottom', rising from the swamp. It was spinning, blue-grey in colour, about twenty-five feet in diameter and nine feet thick at the centre. He could not see any portholes or antennae. It rose to an altitude of about sixty feet before shooting off at a tremendous speed.

It was then that George noticed a thirty feet diameter area where the swamp reeds, which normally rose two feet above the water, had been torn out by the roots from the muddy bottom, and were flattened and swirled in a clockwise direction. Pennisi, who had previously been a sergeant in the Army, joined him, and waded into the six feet deep lagoon. It appeared that the swirling leaves were all floating on the surface of the water.

In late January, George Pedley sent a very brief report to the Queensland Flying Saucer Research Bureau, and it took some days for investigators to learn the full details.

In the meantime, *'Sun-Herald'* reporter, Ben Davie, had been hastily dispatched to the area, and Pedley, told him; *"Had anyone asked me five days ago if I believed in flying saucers I'd have laughed and thought they were nuts. Now I know better!"*

Pedley then divulged something far more interesting, which has made researchers, in later years, wonder if there was an additional element, of which he was not fully aware, to his experience. He said that, for the previous week, he had been dreaming of a UFO landing on his property, and at 5.30 am on the morning of the sighting, 'the dog went mad and bounded off towards the lagoon.'

Regarding the dreams, he was quoted as saying; *"I'd get them almost every night, and they were beginning to worry me. I couldn't understand them – it was always the same. This thing, like a giant dish, would come out of nowhere and land nearby. And I would watch it in my dream and get real afraid before it went away. Then on Wednesday morning, my dog seemed to go out of its mind. It was howling like a mad thing, and raced off towards the lagoon."*

Investigators from the Queensland Bureau, doing 'due diligence', questioned Pedley's character and stability. Amongst other things, Pennisi told them; *"...in answer to your questions regarding George, (Pedley), I have known him all his life, and most of his family also. He is quiet spoken, honest and level-headed. I have always found him truthful. He does not wear spectacles, and his eyesight is good.'*

Any misgivings *'Sun Herald'* reporter Ben Davie may have had, were soon put to rest when he discovered that many other local residents had sighted similar 'saucer-like' objects before this incident, and there were five separate landing areas, nicknamed 'nests', in the area.

He published the following description; *'I saw clearings in the reeds where 'they' took off, and it was as everyone described it. In a circle, roughly thirty feet in diameter, reeds had been cut and flattened in a clockwise direction. One of the nests is a floating platform of clotted roots and weeds, apparently torn by tremendous force from the mud bottom beneath five feet of water.'*

The 'nests', ranged in diameter from eight to thirty feet. Two of them had been found about twenty-five yards from the first one, but were hidden by dense scrub, but in only one, the reeds, which were dead, were swirled in a counter-clockwise direction. Police and Air Force Intelligence turned up with Geiger counters and took vegetation samples for testing.

In order to divert attention from the 'extraterrestrial' and 'secret government vehicles' gossip, ridiculous suggestions of a 'large brolga bird', 'amorous crocodiles', a 'willy-willy vortex', or 'small isolated waterspouts' were proffered.

In an interesting addendum to this event, following a recent documentary on television, 'Laurie', a very elderly gentleman contacted me, and stated that in late 1965 – early 1966, at the time of the Tully event, he had been an officer in the Merchant Navy, aboard the bulk carrier, *'Mittagong'*, and just off the Queensland coast, adjacent to Tully.

It was after dinner, and since there was no T.V. reception, he and his shipmates were playing board games in the officers' saloon lounge. There was no alcohol available, and he offered to get a couple of bottles of beer from his cabin, two levels above. This required going back on deck, and climbing a ladder to the boat deck, under the funnel.

He was at the top of the ladder, when he paused to look out, over the calm sea, at the darkening sky, with the stars starting to appear, and the fading remnants of the sunset flickering on the mainland. He was reflecting upon the beauty and calmness around him, when he suddenly saw a bright white light flashing down, at a 45 degree angle, from the southern sky. At first he thought it was a 'shooting star' or meteorite, but unexpectedly it 'stopped dead' over the ocean.

It suddenly 'transformed' into a huge red/orange object, and even though it was some distance away, it was longer and thinner than any known airship. It then moved slowly towards the mainland, but strangely, did not reflect on the ocean below. 'Laurie's' ship was located near the Whitsunday Islands, and he noticed that this craft was so large that as it passed behind one peaked island, its front appeared whilst the 'tail' section was still visible on the other side. He said it was so large that its edges extended right across from one small off-shore island to another.

After the object was over the mainland, it instantly changed back to a white light again, and at tremendous speed arced up into the sky and disappeared from sight. 'Laurie' marvelled at this enormous craft's ability to instantly 'transform' and become invisible. His experience had only lasted a couple of minutes, and unfortunately, no one was in the wing-bridge or office when he looked up, and everyone laughed when he described what he had seen. Nonetheless, he rushed into the chartroom, where a colleague determined that the nearest town was Tully.

A few weeks later, 'Laurie' went on a couple of weeks leave, and drove from Port Kembla to his family home in Sydney. He scoured the recent newspapers for any information on what he had witnessed. He found a couple of headlines, then noticed the later 'debunking' of the Tully reports, and decided to say nothing.

'Laurie' seemed a very intelligent and thoughtful man, and when talking with me made a couple of very interesting comments. He said that whilst he was observing the strange craft, he got the overwhelming feeling that it 'knew' he was watching, and since then the experience has changed him in several ways.

This was not the first sighting of unusual craft in the area. Researcher Clare Noble reported on a 1959 incident when Max Menzel, who was also driving his tractor at the time, noticed a nearby house illuminated in a vivid red-orange light. Hovering over the top of the sugar cane was a 'brilliant, large, conical craft, approximately thirty feet long.'

The year after the 'Tully' incident, other strange craft were sighted in the area. In 1995, researcher, Collin Norris, published an in-depth account of the 1966 investigations, and noted that there were some quite dramatic sightings the following year.

At 4.30am on 27th January, ten miles to the north, a big bank of coloured lights hovered over a council worker's caravan, and the same day a vivid light was seen to descend over Pennisi's cane farm.

During February there were several reports of strange lights in the area, one of considerable interest; *'At 5am on the 22nd , Peter Palcie saw a big, silvery object pass over his bush hut, seven or eight miles south of Euramo, near the Murray River. When it swooped low, he estimated the round, silvery object to be about twenty-five or thirty feet in diameter. Later he told Mrs. Zonta, in Euramo, that it had flames coming from underneath. She said he laughed at the Pedley sighting, but is now convinced about the reality of such strange happenings.'*

In 1968, several investigators haunted the area, setting up electronic monitor stations and visiting other reported 'nests' in the area. There was quite a rumpus when they accused someone from the 'government' of stealing their film from the Kodak laboratory. Were these strange craft alien or one of our own prototypes being tested?

Many years later, investigator Lee Paqui noted that; *'Curiously, nine days after the camera was triggered on the Pennisi farm, on March 13th, and about the time that Kodak claimed to have received the 'empty' film canister in the mail, two Air Force helicopters were observed inspecting the lagoon for a significant length of time.'*

We will never know the origin of one disc, encountered by Tully district farmer, Louie Maule, on 1st October. He was heading north from South Johnstone, when he saw a huge object descending from the sky; "It was gigantic, and seemed to be slowing down," he said.

Louie described the craft as being circular, large and black, about sixty feet in diameter, with red lights around its perimeter. He looked again, and noted that it was at an altitude of about 500ft, and had speeded up to about 100 mph as it headed towards some cloud in the direction of South Johnstone.

CHAPTER SIX

PILOTS

Was there really a plethora of Ufos and flying saucers in our skies during the 1940s–50s and 60s? In 2000, Dr. Richard Haines, a senior research scientist at the NASA-Ames Research Centre, authored a report, *'Aviation Safety in America – A Previously Neglected Factor'*, in which he documented over one hundred pilot cases of potentially hazardous encounters with UAPs occurring over the last fifty years, including nearly 56 near misses. He said that from 3,000 reports in eighty years, from 1916 to 1996, 52% were made by military pilots, 40% by commercial pilots, 7% by private pilots and only 1% by test pilots.

His data base contained first hand sightings by the pilots, as well as from the Federal Aviation Administration, (FAA), National Transportation Safety Board, (NTSB), and NASA.

He said he focussed on pilot sightings due to their excellent training and risk of their professional reputations. Usually, they will have thought of all the possible answers, before making a report, and often have greater credibility if details are confirmed by ground control.

He noted; *'A 1952 FBI memorandum says that, according to Commander Raymond Boyd, of U.S. Air Intelligence, pilot sightings that include radar records or ground collaboration, are "the most credible reports and are difficult to explain."*

'Pilots are the world's most experienced observers of air traffic, with extensive, specialised training. Their reports in 'Aviation Safety in America' include descriptions of a range of geometric forms in varying colours, and lights which are inconsistent with known aircraft or natural phenomena.

'Pilots and crews report that objects approached and paced their aircraft at relatively near distances. Some encounters disabled the pilots' instrumentation, while others involved rapidly speeding objects which narrowly avoided a head-on collision by making a sudden, abrupt turn.'

Even before we launched our first satellite, in October 1957, there was a growing body of evidence from experienced pilots, air traffic controllers and radar operators as to the existence of UFOs. Declassified government documents reveal that they made reports, often on a daily basis. Misidentification...? maybe some were...but even the most hardened sceptics would have to agree that these people were the most expert and well-informed witnesses available. They, unlike the general public, were more qualified and aware of whether a strange craft may be the product of our own new technology.

Ralph Noyes, who was with the British Air Ministry from 1947 to 1952 said; "Anything received by an RAF pilot was examined with very great care. We're talking about very highly trained people whose job in life is to fly about the skies and not to be conned by optical illusions or clouds or whatever.

"The Air Ministry would not have been keen to let it be public knowledge that some of our pilots had seen flying saucers. We had no explanation – one could imagine the kind of tabloid headlines there would have been!"

In the latter years of World War II, many Air Force pilots over Europe were plagued by small, glowing balls – "Foo Fighters' – approaching their planes. Not all craft encountered conveniently fitted into this explanation.

On the night of a raid on Turin, Captain W/O Lever, and his crew from the 61 Sqdn., had just completed their bombing run, and were heading in a north-westerly direction. Suddenly, they encountered a strange craft travelling at 500mph towards the south-east, at about the same altitude or slightly lower.

It was between 200 to 300 feet in length and fifty to sixty feet wide, with four pairs of red lights spaced at equidistance along its body. No trace of any exhaust flames was seen. A few minutes later, they spotted the object for a second time, when it was travelling up a valley, below the level of the peaks, in the Alps. As it progressed up the valley, its lights appeared to go out, and it was lost from view.

During the 1940s there were many other instances of strange craft and objects over war zones. Not all of these sightings of unidentified objects occurred over the European theatre of war.

Another amazing incident, documented by Keith Flitcroft, occurred in Australia that year. Rick Royal was flying, in horrendous weather conditions, over the Bass Strait, performing, among other duties, submarine reconnaissance. Royal said they were pretty much lost, with one motor 'packing it in'. To reduce the load, they had thrown everything loose, including their parachutes, overboard. All they could do was pray for a safe landing from what was a nerve wracking flight. Every other plane in the area had either crashed or already landed, and he was the last in the sky.

'Suddenly, he saw a brilliant light below, showing through the hazy cloud in which he and his crew were flying. Abruptly the bright glow climbed to travel along with them, just off the starboard wing tip. Little could he see except the rear portion of what was evidently a solid object, lit up by a brilliant, flaming tail, perhaps ten or more metres long. Every manoeuvre to get away from or closer to the thing was exactly matched, so that their distance did not vary.

'Ricky noticed very definite signs of a strong static field; the radio hissed continually while the hair on the back of the necks of the crew stood up....only the gyro compass remaining unaffected. Suddenly the spurt of flame lengthened, and the object shot ahead leaving them rocking in its wake.

'In strict confidence, Ricky expressed the opinion that the almost miraculous return to base by his aircraft was somehow due to the presence of the strange object. He gave no indication of how they had been aided to stay airborne, but was sure that they would normally have first have crashed.'

On 5 April 1943, Gerry Casey, a respected aviation writer and former U.S. CAA/FAA inspector, was training pilots at the Air Corps Ferry Command Base, Long Beach, California. While on a flight instrument practice trip on a BT-13, a craft came in at a moderate dive towards them at a perfect intercept angle. Gerry prepared to take evasive action, but the object made a wobbly turn, and aligned itself off his left wing, in perfect formation. Its adjustment to their altitude and course was perfect and instantaneous.

It was a radiant orange and appeared to shimmer in the bright sunlight. After a short while its aft-end made a slight alteration and it shot away, turning white as it disappeared in a climbing turn toward the ocean. The airmen estimated its speed as being about 7,200 miles per hour.

They reported the craft was round to elliptical in shape, with a round-hump topside, a smaller duplicate bump underside, and no visible openings or glass indicating a cockpit. It did not have a propeller, or any other type of propulsion that they could determine. They could not accurately gauge the size of the craft as they were not sure how far off their wingtip it was, but estimated it was anything from 35 to 75 feet in diameter.

Gerry did not take a photograph, because he had heard that Lockheed were producing a new experimental craft. He later realised that Lockheed only had the P-38 pursuit, and didn't fly the first P-80 jet until January 1944. In later years, he considered the possibility of a more mundane explanation, but what they had seen defied any conventional object.

He said; "In my thoughts a clear statement evolved; I'd seen a flying machine that was light years in advance of anything on earth." He didn't, however, report it because; – "I had obtained a position with the CAA at Seattle's Boeing Field GADO, and it would have been folly to relate the experience."

Not all sightings were made from the air. On 26th February 1942, the crew of the vessel, the '*Tromp*', on the Timor Sea, near New Guinea, were scanning the sky for enemy aircraft. A Dutch sailor, William Methort, later told researcher Peter Norris that he and the others on the bridge saw a large illuminated disc approaching at speed. It was about four to five thousand feet above them, and for the next three or four hours it flew in circles before suddenly, with an unbelievable burst of speed, veered off and disappeared out of view.

Another anecdotal incident was reported, years later, by a man who had been a navigator on an Air Force supply aircraft, operating out of Northern Australia. It was shortly before Japan's capitulation, in 1945, and there was no risk of attack by enemy aircraft.

On one flight, they were joined by a 'large, brightly lit 'barn door', sideways on'. *'It flew alongside, about 200 yards away from them, and all the crew observed it. They were keen for a closer look, but when the captain altered course, it immediately veered away. It stayed with them until they were almost bored by its presence, and then suddenly shot off at terrific speed into the sky and out of sight.*

None of them had a camera, and so didn't report the incident, as the authorities frowned upon UFO sightings, and it could have meant being 'grounded'.

Many of the upper echelons of the world's military were beginning to realise that we were not alone in the universe. At the conclusion of World War II,

General Douglas MacArthur made a very cryptic statement; "The next major war will be an interplanetary one!"

The sightings of mysterious unidentified flying objects continued long after the cessation of wartime conflict. In August 1946, Capt. Puckett and his crew were flying across the Atlantic, when an object, flying horizontally, narrowly missed colliding with their plane.

It was a very bright, long cylindrical object, twice the size of a B-29 bomber, with luminous portholes and a fiery tail. The witnesses estimated its speed as being 'twice the speed of sound'.

At the end of 1946, beginning of 1947, the RAF's secretive 'Operation Charlie,' was an attempt to intercept a UFO over East Anglia. It had been tracked by radar, and detected travelling, faster than any plane, over the East Coast of England. 'Mosquitoes' were scrambled on several occasions, and one had managed to lock onto it with its airborne radar. In those days, before the later Kenneth Arnold incident in the USA, UFOs were referred to as 'ghost planes'.

All the sightings prior to and during the early 1950s are important. If the Allies had seconded advanced German technology, or the rumours of a crashed Roswell disc being back-engineered were correct, would the resultant craft have appeared this early? Even if there were a few prototypes, they would not have been as large as some of the unidentified craft being reported. Neither would they have matched their altitude and speed.

At the same time, there were other, lesser known cases being reported. Researcher, Brinsley le Poer Trench wondered if the discs seen, on 4th July 1944, by Captain E. Smith, his First Officer Ralph Stevens and stewardess Martie Morrow, were the same craft reported by Kenneth Arnold over the Cascade Mountains in 1947.

Eight minutes after their DC-3 took off from Boise, Idahio, 'five flat and circular discs appeared in formation.' Whilst he was on the radio to CAA in Oregon, Stevens told Smith that the strange craft had gone, but shortly after, four more came into view - three in a group together, and the other on its own. They were in view for over ten minutes.

'These objects then appeared to merge, disappear then reappear. Finally, they left, and in the words of Captain Smith, "and fast". He stated that the objects were circular, flat on the bottom and bigger than any aircraft that we had on earth.

Only four days later, on 8th July, multiple witnesses at the U.S. Muroc Air Force Base, watched two silver discs manoeuvring 8,000ft overhead, and executing tight circles at a speed of 300-4000 mph.

A similar event occurred, on 23rd November, near the U.S. Air Force Base at Furstenfeldbruck in Germany. An object was tracked on ground radar, and seen by the pilot of a F-80, and others, as it flew in circles at an altitude of 27,000ft.

It was flying at speeds of up to 500mph, and had a bright red light, but as the F-80 jet drew closer, for a better look, it climbed out of sight. Radar operators tracked it to a height of 40,000ft, and still circling.

Major Donald Kehoe wrote about an incident which happened in 1948. *'At about 1.45am on July 24th, a flaming object came hurtling through the night skies over Robbins Air Force Base, Macon, Georgia. Observers at the Base were astounded to see a huge projectile-like craft race overhead, trailing a varicoloured exhaust. It disappeared swiftly from sight.*

'About an hour later, an Eastern Airlines DC-3 was west of Montgomery, Alabama, en-route to Atlanta. At the controls were Capt. Clarence Chiles, a former Air Transport Command flier, and Pilot John Witted, who had flown B-29s during the war. It was a bright moonlit night, with scattered clouds overhead.

'Suddenly, a brilliant, fast-moving object appeared ahead of them. At first the two pilots took it to be an Air Force jet plane.

"We saw it at the same time." Chiles later told government 'Project Saucer' investigators. "Whatever it was, it flashed down toward us, and we veered to the left. It veered sharply too, and passed us about seven hundred feet to our right, and above us."

'Whitted described it. "The thing was about a hundred feet long, cigar-shaped, and wingless. It was about twice the diameter of a B-29, with no protruding fins."

'Chiles said the cabin appeared like a pilot compartment, except for its eerie brilliance. Both he and Whitted agreed it was as bright as a magnesium flare. They saw no occupants, but at their speed of passing, this was not surprising. It was later suggested that the strange glare could have come from a power plant of some unusual type.'

"An intense dark blue glow came from the side of the ship." Chiles reported. "It ran the entire length of the fuselage – like a blue fluorescent factory light. The exhaust was a red-orange flame, with a lighter colour predominant around the outer edges."

'(This description paralleled the reports of observers at Robbins Air Force Base.)

'Both pilots said the flame extended thirty to fifty feet behind the ship. As it passed, Chiles noted a snout like a radar pole. Both men glimpsed two rows of windows.

"Just as it went by," said Chiles, "the pilot pulled up, as if he had seen the DC-3 and wanted to avoid us. There was a tremendous burst of flame from the rear. It zoomed into the clouds, its jet or prop wash rocking our DC-3." Chiles' later estimate of its speed was between 500 to 700 miles an hour.

'As the object vanished, Chiles went back into the cabin to check with the passengers. Most had been asleep or were drowsing. But one man confirmed that they were in their right senses. This passenger, Clarence McKelvie, of Columbus, Ohio, told them (and later the Project Saucer team) that he had seen a brilliant streak of light flash past his window. It had gone too swiftly for him to catch any details.'

Later computations made by Air Force engineers determined that 'an aircraft, without wings, of the size described by the Eastern pilots, could fly and manoeuvre as reported, if propelled by sufficiently great force.'

This still left the question - if this craft was aerodynamically possible, from where did it originate?

Authorities under the control of the U.S.S.R., and behind the Iron Curtain, were also experiencing problems of their own.

Russian researcher, Dr. Zeigel, reported that on June 16th 1948; *'Arkadiy Apraksin was flying a jet at 31,000 feet over the Baskunchak area, north of the Caspian Sea, when he spotted a cucumber-shaped object, which was sending out beams of light. The pilot reported the sighting to the air base, and received confirmation that radar had picked up the object.*

'He was ordered to close in on the object, and force it to land – or else to open fire on it. When Apraksin got within six miles of the UFO, he said that the beams opened up in a fan, and momentarily blinded him. His plane's entire electrical system and engine went out, but he managed to crash land without major damage.'

He was later subjected to intense questioning by intelligence officers, and posted to far flung bases across the Soviet Union. After reporting another chance encounter in May 1949, this highly decorated Soviet pilot was detained in a mental hospital for over six months. After receiving psychotherapy and shock treatment, he was discharged from the service as 'Group One Disabled'.

Investigator Dan Farcas wrote about a witness from Romania. Captain Commander Mihai Bârbutiu had been a military pilot since 1951, and one evening in the summer of 1957, when an unidentified object was reported in the skies above, he and a colleague, fearing that it was possibly foreign 'armed enemy', hid under the wheels of their truck, behind the local railway station.

'But much to their surprise, nothing happened, and there wasn't any noise, and no gunfire. Looking up, they saw on the ground a circular light with a diameter of about fifty to one hundred metres. It was an unreal light, so powerful you could see every blade of grass. It was impossible to see the shape of the source of the light, only the light itself, as if you were looking at a projector.'

After about twenty seconds it departed to the east, and he and his sergeant crawled out from under the truck, and contacted their superiors, who told them not to make a formal report or discuss the matter with anyone else.

In 1958, he transferred to a fighter-inceptor regiment in Timisoara. In 1966-67, whilst on patrol, he saw an unusual object, which was not on radar, but definitely was not a plane. A few days later he was called to Bucharest, where he had to sign an undertaking that he would not disclose anything of what he saw.

The next incident was only a month or two later, when he was piloting an MIG-19 fighter jet on a routine exercise. There was a full moon, and a mass of dense cloud 6,500 to 10,000 metres below them. Some distance away he spotted a huge flying object.

Remembering the unpleasantness after reporting the previous object, when his colleague sitting next to him pointed out the strange craft, Mihai insisted there was nothing there. When his ground commander insisted on a report, Mihai complied, and was then told to force the object to land. He tried to avoid this action, by saying he had insufficient fuel, upon which he was ordered to fire a 'warning volley'.

Mihai moved closer, and as he flew under the huge craft, it took ten or fifteen seconds to traverse its under-shadow; *'He also felt an 'electric pressure', as when you are close to a very strong electric field. The jet's navigation devices went haywire. He declared that, "It was as huge as a football field. It was grey in colour, circular in shape, had no wings and no portholes. We were trained to recognise all existing jet aircraft of the Russians, Americans and other states, but we had not seen anything to resemble this thing. I said to myself that it must be an object from another planet."*

He dived out of the cloud, to an altitude of 6,500 metres, but by the time he had prepared the guns to approach the object a second time, he radioed his senior officers to say that the object had 'disappeared'. He thought his problems were gone, but when he looked back he was terrified to discover that the strange craft was now following him! Ground control told him to get behind the object, and try to force it to land, but this was not possible. *"I thought to myself that if this object had technology so advanced that if I was now to arm the cannon and shoot, then my projectile could explode in the pipe. So I decided to arm the cannon later perhaps, when I would be closer to the airport – just in case."*

Suddenly, to Mihai's relief, the strange object passed in front of him and climbed steeply towards Serbia. He climbed after it, and used the previous excuse, of being low on fuel, to return to base. The General, who inspected the plane, noted that the additional large fuel tank, usually under the belly of the plane, was missing, and suggested that Mihai had jettisoned it, something he disputed as not being possible.

Later, the chief engineer noted that the rocket launchers, made of steel and embedded on either side of their plane, were bent – one at a thirty degree angle and the other at fifteen degrees. It would have taken a large shock to bend them, probably the same shock that produced the release of the extra fuel tank, which was later found, undamaged, in a sunflower field. The two flight crew were never offered an explanation.

In 2015, Mihai Bârbutiu, who had certainly risen to a senior rank in his military career, commented that he understood why these encounters were kept secret; *"They don't want the world to know that we are not the only ones here in this Universe, that we are visited by extraterrestrial beings and that the alien ships come to Earth, and are controlling our airspace. There are also, certainly, actions from the authorities not to arouse fear and adverse behaviour by the general public. That is the main reason. You see, if people would obtain the proof that these visitors swarm among us, they would kill each other; but people are starting to get used to this idea."*

George Fawcett, of MUFON, told of his friend, J. Howell, who was a pilot, standing with his colleagues on the ramp of Richmond County's airport on December 28th 1949.

Suddenly they saw a long, silver object, which hovered and then took off at high speed to the south-west. Phil Gibbons was the most experienced pilot among them, and he jumped into his plane and gave chase. As he climbed up, the object soon out-paced him, and he lost it, however the newspapers reported that it was seen not only in North Carolina, but also in Georgia.

Howell said; "I seem to recall that some Air Force Colonel came by the airport a few days later, and interrogated us about the thing. None of us who were at the airport that day believed in UFOs, but we never did determine what it was."

A 1981 edition of the *'CUFOS Associate Newsletter'* told of another sighting, which occurred one day in 1949. The witness was a student pilot, flying a two-seat Taylor-craft over Los Angeles. He had previously been a Navy air traffic controller, and when he saw an object speeding across the sky, from north to south, he knew it was nothing conventional.

When the craft came to a sudden halt, curiosity overcame fear, and he headed closer, within a few hundred feet, to get a better look. It was very large, cylindrical in shape, with no seams, overlapping plates, rivet lines or any markings. It appeared to have been moulded in one piece.

When he started to descend, in order to get a better view from underneath, the strange craft emitted an intense white flash, and moved away from its stationary position at incredible speed, disappearing in less than a minute.

By the 1950s, slightly smaller discs were being observed by aircrew and passengers. Were they alien or our own prototypes, which the witnesses doubted?

Due to the commencement of the 'Cold War', there was already some concern over reports coming from Alaska, in the far north, and its proximity to the Soviet Union.

In late January 1950, a PV-2 Neptune, piloted by Lt. Smith, was on a routine patrol mission from the Kodiak Naval Air Station in Alaska. He and his co-pilot spotted an unidentified light which had just been reported by their radar operator, who advised that there should be no other air traffic in the area. It was ten miles away, travelling at a speed of about 1,800mph.

At the same time, a seaman standing watch on the *'USS Tillamock'*, anchored in the channel, saw a fast moving red light, like a ball of fire, moving in a clockwise circle around Kodiak. The next night, sixty-two miles to the south, Lts. Causer and Barco, piloting another PV-2 Neptune, reported a bright light, which was never identified, ahead of their plane. It climbed rapidly and disappeared after about ten minutes. There were no known aircraft or weather balloons in the air at that time.

UFO encounters could have a profound emotional effect on pilots. Investigator, Jenny Randles, wrote about a letter she received from Lieutenant Robert Bowker of the U.S. Air Force. He had first encountered alien technology in 1960 whilst flying from Wake Island to Honolulu;

"Red lights in a pattern came up on the port side and spun the medium-frequency ADF, (on-board electronic navigational equipment), so fast I thought it would be destroyed, and turned it off." Soon after, Bowker had to comfort a

pilot of a C-54, inbound from Wake to Hickam Air Force Base to the island of Oahu;

"He was so shook up I had to help him hold his whiskey glass."

'Eight objects had shot straight at him, closing at 1,000 mph. Just before impact, four had passed above, and four below his aircraft. Both the C-54 pilot and Bowker were warned by a NSA security officer to remain silent about this top-secret encounter.'

Other, less publicised encounters were also taking place in the early 1950s. One instance involved a Qantas Super Constellation flight out of Karachi. An unusual cigar-shaped object paced the plane for approximately forty-five minutes. It was travelling alongside – within one hundred feet – and was seen by all the crew and passengers, some of whom were taking photographs. This object also rapidly flew away. The pilot, who is now retired, did not publicise the event, and was later promoted to senior positions in the aviation industry.

At 8.25pm, on April 27th 1950, Trans World Airlines DC-3, Flight 117, was cruising at 2,000ft, when the two pilots and passengers spotted a strange red disc below and behind the plane. It moved swiftly as at climbed, overtook the plane and closed in.

Witnesses described it as resembling a round blob of hot metal – a spherical shape which glowed brightly on top. It paced the plane for a while before diving away and speeding off at about 400mph. They noted that its glow seemed to dim as it slowed down, and grow as it increased speed.

The pilot, Capt. Adickes, said it looked like an 'outsize wheel' in the sky, and he had tried several evasive tactics before it finally departed. He commented; "Whoever is building these things, I think they are dangerous flying around the airways. If one got out of control, it could cause an accident!"

Where commercial flights were concerned, not all passengers displayed a peaceful curiosity when a UFO suddenly appeared.

(Ret) Major Donald Keyhoe documented the following incident; *'It was the night of 21st November 1954, and a Brazilian airliner bound for Rio de Janeiro, was cruising along in the dark. Flying at 8,000 feet, the plane was over the Pariaba River when a strange glow appeared ahead.*

'In a moment the weird formation took shape – nineteen round machines, each more than 100ft in diameter. Glowing like hot metal, the mysterious craft approached at supersonic speed. Before the pilot could move his controls, the saucers were flashing past and beneath his wings.

'As several machines streaked by the cabin, the thirteen passengers stampeded. One woman, screaming, ran into the pilot's compartment. Another passenger, fighting a member of the crew, tried to reach the main exit. For two or three minutes the cabin was a madhouse. With the danger of a crash mounting, the crew had to use force. The passengers were finally subdued, and the plane landed safely.'

Sometimes commercial airline encounters with UFOs can result in injuries to the passengers.

In 1956, U.S. radio commentator, Frank Edwards, wrote his autobiography, *'My First 10,000,000 Sponsors'*. An interesting few pages were devoted to the UFO incidents which pilots were reporting with increasing frequency.

He quoted one 1953 occurrence, told to him by a well respected airline pilot. Capt. Kidd had been flying a late night DC-6 from Philadelphia to Washington, when a strange object moved out of the cloud, and flipped on edge. It stopped, in front of his plane, and the co-pilot immediately switched on the landing lights, to warn that they were approaching.

Edwards then recounted the incident as described by the pilot; *"A blinding white light reaches out from it...finds you...and the thing comes straight at you. You shove the wheel forward....the big passenger liner plunges....you miss the thing with the blinding white light by a split-second.*

"You know the twenty-seven passengers you are carrying are piled up in the aisles, but now your job is to bring the ship out of the dive. At five thousand feet, you manage to level off, but there's hell to pay back in the cabin: passengers, pillows and overcoats all in one scramble.

"You get on the horn and flash the report of your experience to the National Airport at Washington, as per instructions. 'No planes in the area' says the airport control, and they will have medical facilities ready when you bring in your passengers. Your story makes the early morning newspapers, and then it vanishes."

The next year, Edwards received an even more disturbing account; *'On November 24th 1954, a Brazilian National Airlines passenger plane, approaching the field at Buenos Aires radioed an emergency call for immediate aid. The pilot reported that his plane was being circled by at least fifteen shiny, disc-shaped objects and that his panic stricken passengers were being kept in their seats at gun point by the co-pilot and steward.'*

Edwards noted that the incident was front page news in South and Central America, but was met with a stony silence from the U.S. media. He was initially accepting of the government's assurances that these objects were our own prototypes or misidentifications, but soon realised that he was being misled; *'When a veteran jet fighter pilot's radar locks on a strange object, and he chases it at full speed for hundreds of miles before it eludes him, it hardly makes sense to tell that pilot, (and the public), that he was chasing a weather balloon!*

'When a naval officer makes movies of several disc-shaped objects, manoeuvring in formation at speeds that were officially estimated to be in excess of nine hundred miles per hour, it is hard to accept the Air Force statement that the objects were only seagulls. Nature has done some wonderful things, but she has yet to develop a nine-hundred-mile-an-hour bird of any kind!

On April 14th 1954, Capt. J. Schidel, piloting United Airlines Flight 193, over Long Beach, California, was forced to make a steep climb to avoid colliding with an unknown object. The stewardess fractured her ankle, and one passenger suffered a broken leg.

In early 1957, a Douglas DC6A Pan-American Flight, en-route from New York to San Juan, Puerto Rico, had deviated from its customary course to avoid a storm. At 3.30am it was 150 miles east of Jackson, Florida, when Capt. Matt Van Winkle was startled by a beam of white light under his plane.

Research group, NICAP, reported that realising the light was definitely coming from a solid object, Van Winkle immediately zoomed the plane upwards, in order to avoid a potential collision; *'Passengers, diaper bags, suitcases, magazines, and stale lunchboxes, along with the stewardesses and the co-pilot, (who was in the cabin at the time) – all mingled in mid-air as Van Winkle sought to bring the plane under control.'*

Several passengers were injured, and ambulances met the aircraft at San Juan airport. Despite the fact that other plane crews had also reported a UFO that morning, the 'official explanation' given to the news media, was that Van Winkle had only seen a meteorite or 'shooting star'.

A few months later, on 17th July, on a flight from Dallas to Los Angeles, Capt. Ed Bachnet had a near miss with an object 'at least the size of a B-47', which passed about fifty feet above his plane. Upon landing, two passengers were taken to hospital. As with the previous cases, there were no known other aircraft in the vicinity at the time.

Only five days after that, Capt. G. Schemel, piloting a Trans-World four-engine Constellation, was over the West Texas plains when a big red and green light bore down on him, in an apparent collision course. He went into a steep dive as the object passed overhead. Passengers were screaming, and those who were not wearing seatbelts were thrown up against the ceiling and into the aisles. The cabin was a shambles. One elderly woman, bleeding from a severe cut to her head, was lying in a litter of hats and parcels. Several passengers and crew had been injured and there was a great deal of panic and hysteria. He had to make an unscheduled stop at Amarillo, to seek medical aid and hospitalize one passenger who was seriously hurt during the violent manoeuvre.

This time, despite the fact that there were no known planes within fifty miles, the Air Force tried to explain the incident away by saying that they had encountered a normal aircraft, which Schemel and his first officer had not recognised.

Schemel disputed this, saying that the speed of the object made this impossible. Further, no experienced pilots would misidentify something so completely as to end up endangering their passengers and being forced to make an emergency landing.

One notable incident, which was reported to 'Project Blue Book' investigators, occurred at 11.30am on 10th September 1951. Lt. Wilbert Rogers and Major

Ezra Ballard, both experienced fighter pilots, were flying a T-33 at 20,000ft over New Jersey.

Pilot Rogers noticed an unusual object, on their port side, below them. It was descending, and at an altitude of between five to eight thousand feet. Rogers immediately made a descending turn to the left, but was unable to catch up with the object, which was always below and ahead of their plane. Eventually the strange craft moved out to sea, and the pilot resumed his original course, and landed at Mitchell AFB.

At the same time, a radar operator, at the Fort Monmouth Army Signal Corps radar centre, picked up an object moving fast over the base. It was travelling fast and erratically at speeds varying between 400 and 700mph.

'Project Blue Book' stated that the airmen must have seen a balloon, as two had been launched from Evans Signal Laboratory a short time before. This was hotly disputed by investigator Dr. McDonald, who said the object's trajectory was inconsistent with those balloons.

The authorities spent more time determining how the press had got hold of the sighting, rather than investigating the incident itself. It turned out that the driver of the van, who was transporting the airmen after they landed at Mitchell AFB, had overheard their conversation, and leaked it to others. One enterprising reporter persuaded Public Information Officer, Major John Barron, to confirm some of the information, and allow him to interview Rogers.

Barron found himself in official 'hot water'. His later statement appeared on file; *'At no time did I suggest that the pilots saw a flying saucer. I am fully aware of the Air Force attitude toward flying saucers and would, under no circumstances, suggest to any member of the press that an Air Force pilot saw an object fully identified as a flying saucer.'*

Researcher, Dr. Willy Smith, commented; *'The moral of the story is that the world learned about this case only because a driver had big ears. Otherwise, the incident would not have rated more than a few lines in the official files.'*

1952 was a memorable year, and it can be said that, whoever was controlling these unidentified craft was certainly trying to get our attention. It was the year when George Adamski met with the humanoid 'Orthon' in the desert, and several other incidents that also stand out in 'UFO History'.

On January 9th 1952, crew members of two B-29 bombers, reported sighting globe-shaped orange balls of light, which emitted occasional flashes of blue light. They had flown parallel to their planes over Wonsan on the east coast of Korea and over Sunchon in central west Korea.

Given that this was an active war arena, one cannot discount enemy surveillance craft, and when the Air Force was asked to comment they said; "To affirm or deny it would put us in the position of discussing it, and we cannot discuss it!"

In March 1952, Bertram Totten, a veteran private pilot, and one-time airplane inspector for the Air Force, was flying over Fairfax, Virginia, on the outskirts of Washington and near Air Force Headquarters. He was at an altitude of 5,000ft, when he saw an object 'whirling along' about 1,000ft below. It was an aluminium colour, about forty feet in diameter and ten feet thick. He dived to get a better look, but before he could get very close, 'it zoomed up into the overcast'.

At 9.12pm, on 14th July 1952, two Pan-American DC-4 pilots were flying at eight thousand feet near the Naval Base and Air Station at Norfolk Virginia. Suddenly six, one hundred feet diameter, disc-like 'machines', in an 'echelon' formation, flew about two thousand feet under their plane. They glowed a brilliant orange, like red hot metal, which dimmed when they flipped on edge to make a 150 degree course change and shot away. After a few seconds, two more discs followed.

Less than a week later, on 20th July, an alarming situation occurred over Washington. These events were confirmed by multiple reports from airline and Air Force pilots, control tower operators, and tracked simultaneously on radarscopes at Washington National Airport and Andrews Air Force Base.

At 12.40am seven 'craft' appeared in the sky and 'separated'. Two were over the White House, one near the Capitol Building, and some near the Air Force Base. They were alternatively described as 'huge fiery orange spheres' – 'five huge discs' and also as 'a large white light'. At first their speed was estimated at only being about 130mph, but then they accelerated at terrific speed and streaked off, making manoeuvres and turns that would be impossible for our conventional machines.

They circled Washington for about two hours until the arrival of F-94 interceptors, when they flew away at speeds up to 7,000mph. As soon as the jets had returned to base, the objects came back and didn't leave until dawn.

Donald Keyhoe reported that in April, earlier that year, there had been a disturbing event involving two Navy planes en-route to Hawaii. They were carrying Admiral Arthur Radford and the Secretary of the Navy, Dan Kimball. Two discs, moving at fantastic speeds, estimated to be between 1,500 and 2,000 mph, buzzed the first plane, and then the second one, some fifty miles behind. A Navy aviation photographer filmed the entire incident.

Kimball knew the objects were not built by any American company, and was not happy when later, Air Force investigators told him; "It's against policy to discuss any case with witnesses."

A dispute then arose as to the handling of the investigations. It was whilst the Navy and the Air Force were in hot disagreement that the CIA moved in, attempting to take control.

The entire subject was generating a great deal of interest with all the authorities. A 1952 FBI memorandum stated that according to Commander Randall Boyd of U.S. Air Intelligence, pilot sightings, especially those that are corroborated by radar records or ground visuals, were 'the most credible reports and are difficult to explain.'

There were many more disturbing incidents occurring in the USA in July/August 1952.

On 14th July 1952, Captain William Nash and Second Officer Bill Fontenberry, both highly respected veteran pilots, were flying a Pan American DC-4 airliner, at a height of 8,000ft, and approaching Norfolk, Virginia, en-route to Miami.

They suddenly spotted six large flying discs, each about thirty metres in diameter, but only, as best as they could see, only about five metres in depth. They were glowing like hot metal, and approaching at extremely high speed. They flew under the airliner, at a height of about 6,000 ft, then abruptly flipped on edge, (a violent change of at least 150 degrees), their glow diminishing, and made a sharp angle turn to the west. They then flipped back to their original flat position, after which they were joined by two more identical craft, and all eight accelerated to a tremendous speed, estimated at not much under 20,000 km/hr, and flew off.

Several extremely in-depth investigations were conducted by the Air Force and other intelligence officers, all of whom designated the strange objects as 'unknown'. Arch-sceptic Donald Menzel, tried to say that all the pilots had seen was an 'optical illusion'. In an angry letter of reply, Nash said; *'Tell me sir...do you ride in the airlines? If I held your opinion of us, I'd walk...!'*

Just before 11am, on the morning of 1st August, a 30ft, round, glowing saucer with a shiny metallic gleam, appeared to be observing the Wright Patterson Field. As in the previous cases, it was tracked on GCI radar and seen by civilians and Air Force pilots. The object was at an altitude of thirty thousand feet, but when two F86 jets, piloted by Major J. Smith and Lt. D. Hemer, were sent to intercept, it climbed and sped away, at an estimated speed of 480mph.

The U.S.A. and Europe weren't the only ones to receive a 'visit'. On 5th August, the officers at the control tower at Japan's Oneida Air Force Base, viewed and tracked, on GCI radar, a dark coloured saucer with a glowing white light in front and a smaller one underneath. It slowly approached the tower, hovered nearby, then suddenly turned away and accelerated at high speed. Radar returns indicated it then divided into three parts, which raced off, at a speed of 300 knots, 'keeping accurate intervals.'

(Another well documented Australian encounter (detailed in my book *'Contact Down Under'*) is that of Lt. J. O'Farrell on the night of 31st August 1954, when he was flying a Sea Fury aircraft over southern NSW. The two objects were not only sighted by the pilot, but were also tracked by radar at the Royal Australian Navy Air Station at Nowra. After pacing the plane for some time, the objects took off at an incredible speed. It was unlikely that there were even any secret experimental craft this advanced in 1954. Like Michael Swiney, O'Farrell continued his career in the Air Force, also rising to the rank of Commodore, before retiring after an appointment as Naval Attaché to Washington.)

It was also in 1952 when ANA Captain Bob Jackson was flying into Mascot Airport, Sydney, at about 11pm one night. When he was over the Woronora Dam area, south of Sydney, he saw a flash of light, and watched as an object, with an orange light at the tail, shot past towards the coast near Wollongong. Mascot Air Control advised there were no other planes in the vicinity or on radar. Two minutes later he saw the object again. This time it made a complete circle around his plane, and then sped back towards the coast at terrific speed.

On 5th January 1954, the *'Melbourne Sun'* quoted Captain Jackson as saying the experience was 'nerve-wrecking'. He, like many other senior pilots, had not made an official report at the time, for fear of ridicule.

Researcher, John Schuessler detailed a CIA report, sourced from their own investigations and an article from Vienna's *'Die Presse'* in March 1952; *'Recently, two fiery disks were sighted over the uranium mines located in the southern part of the Belgian Congo in the Elisabethville district, east of the Luapula river, which connects the Meru and Bangweolo Lakes.*

'The disks glided in elegant curves and changed their position many times, so that from below they sometimes appeared as shapes, ovals and simply lines. Suddenly, both disks hovered in one spot and then took off in a unique zigzag flight to the northeast. A penetrating hissing and buzzing sound was audible to the onlookers below. The whole performance lasted from ten to twelve minutes.

'Commander Pierre of the small Elisabethville airfield immediately set out in pursuit with a fighter plane. On his first approach he came within about 120 metres of one of the disks. According to his estimates, the 'saucer' had a diameter of from 12 to 15 metres and was 'discus' shaped. The inner core remained absolutely still, and a knob coming out from the centre, and several small openings could plainly be seen. The outer rim was completely veiled in fire, and must have had an enormous speed of rotation. The colour of the metal was that of aluminium.

'The disks travelled in precise and light manner, both vertically and horizontally. Changes in elevation from 800 to 1,000 metres could be accomplished in a few seconds, the disks often shot down to within twenty metres of the treetops. Pierre did not regard it possible that the disk could be manned, since the irregular speed, as well as the heat, would make it impossible for a person to stay inside the stable core.

'Pierre had to give up the pursuit after fifteen minutes since both disks, with a loud whistling sound, which he heard despite the noise from his own plane, disappeared in a straight line toward Lake Tanganyika. He estimated their speed at about 1,500 kilometres per hour'

(Obviously the Americans, especially the CIA, were taking careful note of UFO sightings in other parts of the world, especially where there were uranium deposits, possibly needed for their own expanding use of nuclear technologies. Their own comments noted Pierre to be a dependable officer and zealous flyer, and his report was consistent with those received from other pilots and from materials from other 'unnamed secret research installations'.)

The article finalised by commenting that *'the technology displayed in this report is far beyond our aerospace technology back in the year 1952'.*

Major Donald Keyhoe wrote, in the 1954 *'RAF Flying Review,'* about several unidentified incidents which had occurred in the previous few years.

One, on 29th October 1952, involved Lieutenants Burt Deane and Ralph Corbett, who were flying, early in the morning, over Hempstead Long Island.

Suddenly, a fast moving object, showing a bright white light, appeared ahead of their F-94s; *'When Deane tried to close in, he knew at once they had been spotted. Whipping into a tight circle, the UFO cut inside his pursuit curve. At full power, Deane tried to tighten the circle. 'G' in the turn was so high he almost blacked out. But the saucer still turned within his orbit.*

'For eight minutes Deane and Corbett vainly attempted to match the machine's amazing performance. Finally, tiring of the game, the UFO climbed away at supersonic speed.

'Lt. Deane told intelligence; "It is my opinion that the object was controlled *by something having visual contact with us."*

In 1965 the *'Australian Flying Saucer Review'* published an interview with former Air Marshall Sir George Jones. Like James O'Farrell, he also rose to a high rank, despite reporting a UFO early in his career. Sir George mentioned an incident in 1930, when he was a Squadron Leader, and was sent to Warnambool to investigate a formation of 'aircraft' seen flying over the coast.

"I went there but could not establish what they were. They were not aircraft belonging to us and, as far as I could find out, they were not aircraft belonging to any other powers. The possibility that they might have been a formation of swans or other birds was always there, but the thing was left open – I could not establish what it was."

Air Marshall Jones also mentioned seeing a brilliant white light, below a shadowy shape in 1957. It was at 1,500ft, and moved silently, in a purposeful way at about 400mph. He had no other witnesses, and said nothing at the time.

By the end of 1952, it was obvious that the military and security hierarchies were aware, often on a personal basis, of the presence of unidentified craft in their skies. In August 1953, the U.S. Air Force issued *'Regulation 200-2'*. It stated that it was forbidden to release UFO information to the public from Air Force Base Level. A little later, another instruction further added that Air Force, military and sometimes even commercial pilots, releasing 'UFO Information', would be charged under 'JANAP-16' which stated that to discuss UFO reports publicly would be 'a serious crime, punishable with fines up to $10,000 and imprisonment for up to ten years'. Were they protecting the secrecy of their own prototypes, or just unwilling to admit they didn't know who or what was invading their own airspace?

Of even greater interest was the 1954 U.S. Air Force document 'AFR 200-2', which was unearthed by (ret) Major Donald Keyhoe. In Paragraph 9, called 'Release of Facts', it stated that *'only hoaxes, practical jokes, and erroneous UFO reports can be given to the Press.'*

In 1999, investigator Tim Iahn, published his article *'The Interceptor Files'*, where he discussed some of the early 'pilot sightings'.

Following many reports from the public, on February 11th 1953, Lt. Edward Balocco took off in his F-9, from Edenton, North Carolina. The control tower had asked him to 'run black' (ie. without lights), to investigate a 'bogey'.

When Norfolk Naval Station took over, and directed him towards the unidentified craft, it suddenly disappeared off the radar. After about fifteen minutes of unsuccessful searching, Balocco turned on his lights, and headed back to Edenton.

He hadn't taken much notice of a light below him, but suddenly it rose to his altitude, and was hovering, motionless, about 2,000ft away. It was disc-shaped, with red blinking lights on the hull.

Having recently served in Korea, he followed his normal reaction, which was to head for the intruder and start firing, but when he squeezed the trigger, he realised his ammunition cans were empty. When he came within 350ft of the object, his cockpit was flooded with an intense white light, and he momentarily felt as if everything was 'motionless'. The saucer then 'broke away', and headed south in a flash.

As soon as he landed, he was flown to Cherry Point for debriefing. This took several hours of being quizzed by high ranking Marine and Naval Officers. Before he was taken back to Edenton, he was instructed to say absolutely nothing, to anyone, about the incident.

There are times when we cannot be sure if a 'UFO' was conveniently blamed for unfortunate accidents. May 2nd 1953, was a dark, rainy night. British Comet jet liner, with 43 people on board, took off from Dum Dum airport, Calcutta, India, for a normal, routine flight.

No distress call was received by the control tower, but six minutes later, it collided with an unknown object. After careful examination of all the wreckage, which was strewn across four square miles, the Air Ministry concluded that 'the plane had been hit by an unidentified object'.

Ground staff at RAF Bases, in other parts of the world, were also sighting strange craft. In 1953, Clive Thomas, a RAF airframe maintenance officer, was stationed at RAF Heaby, near Bulawayo, Southern Rhodesia, (now Zimbabwe).

He was watching the sky, from the control tower, for returning aircraft, when he saw something low in the west, a couple of miles away, but when it came closer, he soon realised it was not one of their planes.

A dull grey, disc-shaped object, with a central dome on top, approached the tower, and hovered at an altitude of about 200ft. It was about 30ft in diameter, with what looked like some sort of blackened window. He and two colleagues stared in amazement and uttered some unrepeatable words.

It hovered for about ten seconds, and started to 'wobble', like a spinning top, after which it suddenly climbed upwards, with fantastic acceleration, and disappeared at extreme altitude.

Clive said; *"I reported the incident to the first senior rank I came across, who just happened to be an obstinate sergeant who bluntly refused to listen. None of us pursued the matter any further, but plenty of others on the base saw the object, and as far as I'm concerned, this was a UFO!"*

By 1953, whoever or whatever was controlling these strange craft, was quite adept at anticipating and outwitting our own intercept planes.

Major Donald Kehoe told of an incident at Sequoia-Kings National Park in California. For three nights a large disc-shaped UFO had descended over the park, and on the 1st August, the Air Force was ready and waiting.

Just before midnight, the object was seen slanting down at a reduced speed. The pursuit craft matched its speed, and levelled out above it; *'To the pilots, it seemed impossible for the spacecraft to climb without hitting one of the two jets, and seriously damaging the ship. Rather than take this risk, it appeared likely that the aliens would give in and land at the first safe spot.*

'But suddenly, without even slowing down, the UFO stopped midair. The jets instantly overshot. Before the pilots could even begin to turn back, the disc soared steeply above them and was gone!'

The Scandinavian countries were also receiving their fair share of reports. Researcher Don Berliner reported that in December 1953, the pilots of a DC-3 airliner, travelling between Malmoe and Stockholm, reported that they had 'met' a flying saucer.

'Chief Pilot Ulf Christiernsson was quoted as saying; "It was glittering like silver, and looked like two saucers put on top of each other, with 'bottoms' out. It was metallic in appearance, and moved at enormous speed."

Of course, the authorities resorted to the usual mundane explanations, but by 1954, there was an occurrence which they were not able to explain away.

An aeroplane travelling from Oslo to Savanger, Norway, had among its passengers, General Jorgenson, Commander-in-Chief of the Royal Norwegian Air Force, and members of the Royal Norwegian Astronomical Society.

Two enormous silver, rotating metallic saucers, were seen to swoop above a cloud, and then speed along the horizon, keeping an even distance from one another, before vanishing into the distance. One of the passengers, who had originally been photographing an eclipse, took a movie film through the plane window. Lord Dowding, former Air Chief Marshall of Great Britain, later commented that the objects on the film 'looked like flying saucers'.

Dr. Irena Scott wrote about another occurrence in the late spring of 1957, when an unidentified craft hovered over the Ellsworth Air Force Base in South Dakota. It looked like a traditional 'saucer' – silver/metallic in colour, with a dome and portholes on top. Planes and pilots were scrambled, and the object seemed to be 'playing cat and mouse with them'. It would hover until the planes got close, then take off at incredible speed. The noise of a crash was heard, and later, although everyone was told not to discuss the incident, one of the pilots said a plane had gone missing, and the wreckage never found.

In the early post-war days, the U.S., in particular, made it very risky for pilots and air crew to say anything. Pilots were so annoyed at being accused of hallucinating, or 'having one drink too many', that in 1959 airline pilots held a meeting in Dayton, Ohio and issued the following statement; *'We report cases such as these, and when we land, we are interviewed for hours. We are tired, and want to get home to our families. We are threatened not to make statements, and told that the thing that paced our aircraft for fifteen minutes was a mirage or bolt of lightning....nuts to this 'big brother' attitude, who needs it.'*

Author, Otto Binder, told of a report from August 1957 when a Brazilian cargo plane, bound for Rio de Janeiro, encountered a domed disc performing incredible manoeuvres around their craft. The co-pilot, Edgar Onofre, along with the chief pilot, radio operator and two stewards, were all terrified when a close pass by the UFO caused the engines to cough and splutter, the cabin lights to dim, and their radio to malfunction. For a moment, they all had visions of their whole electrical system cutting out, and a possible crash. As soon as the UFO sped away, all their equipment returned to normal, and the engines resumed their smooth rhythm.

By the time the 1960s arrived, we can be sure that all the leading countries had various prototypes of their own, some of which may have been mistaken as extraterrestrial. Our own technology was much more sophisticated. We had developed missiles and satellites, and by 1969 would land men on the Moon. Gone were the days when researchers could enthusiastically declare it was most probably 'alien'. They had to examine each sighting and ask themselves if the upsurge in reports was due to our own technology and prototypes, or a growing interest and concern by extraterrestrials?

Colin Phillip, (ex-president of UFOR.QLD), investigated a case which happened over Bouganville Reef, just off Queensland, at 3.25am on 28th May 1963. The pilot, co-pilot and stewardess on a charter flight from Brisbane to Port Moresby, reported to Townsville Ground Control that they were being 'buzzed by a flying saucer'. They described the object, which paced the plane for ten minutes, as being a 'round ball with exhaust gases coming from it'. They also advised they had taken photos of the object.

When they arrived in New Guinea the pilot was told not to get the photographs developed. As soon as they returned to Australia he was met in Brisbane, and the film and flight tapes were flown to Canberra. The crew and DCA officials were told they would lose their jobs if they ever discussed the matter.

In his book, 'The Jarrold Listings', Phillip Frola has published copies of several contradictory official letters received in response to various enquiries by researchers at the time. While there was an official denial of the incident, confidential testimonies received tend to confirm the sighting and surrounding circumstances.

On 16th July 1965, just before 11am, staff at Canberra's Airport Control Tower saw a mysterious glowing object hovering in the sky. It was there for nearly forty minutes. They described it as being a shiny white 'spot' at an altitude of about five thousand feet in the north-east. Several pilots confirmed the sighting, and other people at the airport also saw the object. Several witnesses called Mt. Stromlo Observatory, who could offer no conventional explanation. One officer described it as a circular light, and the meteorologist said it looked like a steel disc revolving in the sunlight.

Reports at the time stated that the RAAF sent a plane to identify the object, but it accelerated away before the aircraft could reach it. It was later suggested that it may have been more than a coincidence that the craft was near Tidbinbilla Space Tracking Station at the time 'Mariner-4' was transmitting reports on Mars. The signals had been 'jammed' at the time of the sighting, and returned to normal when the UFO flew away.

After the air traffic controller had retired, he confirmed the incident, and also that the object definitely appeared to be some type of revolving disc.

On 18th October 1968, an Air Force Hercules aircraft took off from Darwin, and the crew saw a series of white lights they assumed to be from another plane. It did not appear to have any visible fuselage, structure or navigation or anti-collision beacons. Their radar indicated a target at fifteen miles range, travelling at two hundred knots, and at least the size of their own plane.

The unknown craft crossed in front of the Hercules' path, at an estimated altitude of about 2,500ft. Ground radar was not operating at the time, and whilst no unauthorised aircraft were reported in the area, the official report stated that 'a possible violation of our national airspace cannot be discounted'.

Over thirty years later, INUFOR researcher, Alan Craddock, a pilot and air traffic controller himself, wanted our fellow investigators to be aware that there could be conventional explanations for the various anomalies which may have been reported. He wrote an article; *'UFO or IFO' - 'What you see is not always what you get'*, (which is published in full in my book, *'UFOs Now and Then'*), addressing some of these problems both then and in the past.

He said, in part; *'As can be seen, any number of variations in temperature, lighting conditions, atmospheric ionisation, cloud formations, meteors, satellites and bolides can cause us to misinterpret what we are actually seeing. This fact alone makes UFOLOGY still to be perceived by the general public as a group of fringe dwellers, though not to the extent that it once was.*

'Ours has to be an exact science, one which provides absolute proof to get our message across, and very little margin for error in our estimations. We have to be able to provide countless possibilities before arriving at the truth, and this, as you know, is not always that easy, especially when confronted with confused and sometimes scared witnesses.

'With the new generation of aircraft flying higher and faster, in particular the fighter planes that now frequent most skies, we all have a hard time to keep up with the new shapes that the military tries out to keep an edge over its competitors.

'So, as you can see, aircraft recognition, in our particular field of interest, is of paramount importance to sift through the wood from the chaff. Not only can a very basic lack of understanding of aircraft and their systems cause confusion with lay people, it can lead to some pretty wild claims on behalf of the witness in question.

*'So who can we expect to know the answers, at least to some of the questions raised when a person or witness comes forward with a story about an unknown air vehicle? **Us** – trained ufologists – that's who, and we had better be pretty good at our craft so as not to malign any information, or damage a person's credibility through our own misinterpretation of the evidence provided.*

*'I recommend that **all** investigators practice aircraft recognition, and keep abreast of all the new developments going on in the aviation industry, in particular the military. With reports of large black triangles and sonic booms frequenting our skies, who knows just what is being tested at the moment? One thing is for sure, people are probably seeing the next generation of 'Star War's' toys, or if not, alien technology that is so fantastic it makes the stealth technology look like an 'Airfix' kit.*

This was very good advice, and although I published it for all to read, I feel many, often prominent investigators, have failed to take note of these guidelines.

During the 1950s, we would obviously have developed prototypes of our own, but how far advanced were they? Surely the Air Force would have been aware of them?

It stands to reason, that if we had developed advanced prototypes, the Russians, and other major powers, probably also had similar craft.

That did not stop the communists being mystified over an incident which occurred near Greenland in 1956.

Soviet pilot V. Akkuchatov, along with his colleague, who was the chief navigator for the Soviet Air Base at the North Pole, were flying, in clear visibility, over a strategic ice area, when they saw a strange object flying parallel to their plane, and closing in from the port side.

It was large, disc-shaped, and resembled a lens with wavy pulsating edges. It had no gas jet, vapour trails or traces of smoke that might have identified it as something conventional. Neither were there any wings, portholes, windows or antennae.

Thinking it may be the Americans, they flew into the cover of thick clouds for over forty minutes, only to find the object still there when they emerged. It remained on their port side, and maintained a speed consistent with their own. When Akkuchatov ventured closer, the object also altered course. After about fifteen to twenty minutes, it shot off at tremendous speed, to a higher altitude, and accelerated out of view.

Major Donald Keyhoe investigated the following report in 1959. The incident had happened three years earlier in 1956, when Commander George Benton and Lieutenant Graham Bethune were flying a Navy R7V-2 Super-Constellation transport plane, (not that far from Greenland), across the Atlantic from Iceland to Newfoundland. Their aircrew passengers were asleep in the cabin.

They were cruising at 19,000 feet, when a huge disc-shaped machine rushed up from below, tilted and angled past their port wing. It then drew abreast, and paced their plane at a distance of about one hundred yards. Some of the passengers crowded into the cockpit, and they all witnessed the amazing metallic craft, which was at least thirty feet thick and four hundred feet in diameter. It looked like 'a gigantic dish inverted on top of another.'

After the UFO pulled ahead, and then quickly accelerated away, Benton contacted Gander Airport, who advised their radar had also registered the huge object. When they landed at Gander, Air Force intelligence officers interrogated and debriefed everybody, and later, when they reached their final destination, they each had to complete a written report.

It seemed the authorities never doubted what they had seen, but could anything so immense be one of our own prototypes in 1956? Six days later Benton met with a scientist from a 'high government agency', who showed him several photographs. Benton pointed to one which was identical to the disc they had encountered; "Somebody must know the answers," he said, "if you've got photographs of the things."

The scientist locked the photographs back into his dispatch case. "I'm sorry, Commander," he said, and left.

Graham Bethune, the co-pilot, later rose to the rank of Commander, and shared a couple of other experiences with researcher Frank Chile. He claimed that on two separate occasions he flew General George Marshall, and other VIPs, to two saucer retrieval sites, one outside Reykjavik, Iceland, and the other possibly in Utah. In both cases, the slightly oval discs, which measured about 100ft in diameter, were retrieved and taken back to Wright Patterson Base.

Bethune said that some of his high ranking passengers had discussed UFOs with him, and knowledge of these incidents seem to be quite prevalent in the upper echelons. Bethune also claimed that Admiral Forney had shown him some astounding Navy photos taken of discs in the 1950s. (Bethune's interest in UFOs continued over the years, and in 1998 he produced, with the help of MUFON's George Filer, a small booklet titled, *'A Research Report on Alcyone Craft from the Pleiades.'*)

This was not the only instance of officials arriving with photos for a witness to identify. Dr, Richard Boylan later wrote of a similar case which occurred in 1955. George Gaines was a well-educated civilian when he spoke about what had happened when he was a twelve-year-old in 1955. Following his sighting of a UFO, he had written to the 'UFO Office, Eglin AFB'.

'A few days later, at 0900 on Saturday, he got a call, and was asked if he had reported the sighting. When he said yes, he was told to stay right there, rather than going to swim practice at the YMCA as he had planned. Five minutes later, a new white Cadillac arrived, with a Colonel and Captain in uniform.

'They spent three hours questioning him and showing him UFO film clips and albums full of UFO photos. His parents were asked to stay in the next room. There was one album they did not show him before they started to leave. He asked what was in it, and they asked if he had seen any aliens. He said no, and was told that they only show it to people who report seeing aliens. He insisted on seeing it, and they complied. George said it was full of alien photos. Some were dead, and some appeared to be alive.'

There were other lesser known instances of the authorities already holding photographic evidence of these strange craft. Researcher, Max Miller, told of an event on 6th November, 1954, when an enthusiastic team of young people, from the 'Texas Flying Saucer Research Group', had gone to Palm Island, sure that a UFO was going to make an appearance.

Surprisingly, at 10.55pm, after they had all concentrated their thoughts for some time, a white, luminous disc, with a dome and flat bottom, appeared in the sky. A police patrol car arrived, with officers John McCoy and David Piller wanting to know what the youngsters were up to. As they were quizzing the group, another police car arrived, and it was at that time the witnesses admitted the purpose of their expedition, and pointed out the strange object in the sky;

"They did not laugh. They did not even crack a smile. They were too startled at such an amazing sight. One of our group handed the patrolman a pair of binoculars. The officer walked over to the side of the car and leaned on it. He stared at the saucer for fifteen or twenty minutes. I have never seen anyone so amazed."

The gathered policemen continued to watch through binoculars, but would not answer any questions put by the UFO enthusiasts. Deputy Sheriff Hoyd, and his colleagues then tried signalling, using a powerful spotlight on the vehicle.

Hoyd then told one of the witnesses that he had once seen a similar object, travelling at a rapid rate of speed, before; *"You know, although I told you I would like to be here if it lands, I am not so sure that you would be so anxious for it to land if you had seen some of the....(**Army or Air Force he told us)..photographs of these things, that I have seen!"***

The authorities obviously knew more than they were saying. In his book, *'Above Top Secret',* Timothy Good wrote of a 1964 incident from Canada; *'A enormous circular object, spewing a flame-coloured exhaust, passed slowly over a car occupied by Grant Gammie and his mother and daughter.*

'After he telephoned the RCAF in Vancouver, Gammie was visited by a senior officer who carried a briefcase full of UFO photographs to make comparisons. The officer, whom Gammie knew, emphasised that despite their acquaintanceship, he would deny having been there if the visit received any publicity.'

George Fawcett investigated another similar case from 1973, where a UFO buzzed an American nuclear submarine. The witness, 'Ed Sims' was standing, with three other witnesses, on the conning tower of the 'Abraham Lincoln'. Suddenly, a crimson coloured, 100ft circular disc dropped from the sky and made a wide, sweeping arc around the ship. After circling three times, it then took off at high speed. Whilst it was there, all sonar and navigation systems temporarily failed.

One of their group had been in the process of filming night lights, from nearby Panama, and the algae on the water. He took several excellent photographs of the strange craft.

When the submarine docked in California, the witnesses were told that their leave had been cancelled. They were taken, by Naval Police, to a nearby base, where they were individually questioned by CIA officers, who tried to tell them they had seen and filmed nothing. They even told 'Ed' he was lying when he said he had already seen 'stills' of the photographs.

'Ed' said that this interrogation went on for several days; *"Then, one afternoon, the CIA men changed their tack completely. They came in with an attaché case, filled with glossy photographs of saucer-like objects. These ranged from cigar and football shapes to objects resembling ice-cream cones. Others looked like car headlights. I was able to find one photograph that resembled what I had seen.*

"The questioners then made me sign a secret document. It said that if I ever revealed anything about the sighting, or the photographs I was shown, I would be court-martialled and jailed in solitary confinement.

"Military policemen then escorted me back to the submarine, where the commanding officer told me I was to be transferred immediately to Hawaii. I later heard that the other three witnesses had been assigned to different duty stations around the world. We never saw each other again, and I never got over the fact that we were threatened and punished for having seen a UFO."

There was certainly, even in those days, a 'cover-up' by the authorities. In his book, *'Flying Saucers – Top Secret'*, Major Donald Keyhoe also noted that sometimes Air Force pilots had fired upon flying objects they could not identify, but were later identified as being conventional objects.

He mentioned a case which occurred on 8th April 1956, when an American Airlines flight took off from New York for Buffalo. Shortly after, the pilot noticed a glowing light to the right of the plane. It seemed to dim, and slow down, to match the Convair's speed. At that time the pilot switched on his plane's landing lights, and the object's glow simultaneously brightened.

Griffiths tower told him to extinguish his lights, and after that, although their radar was not operational, they could see the object visually from the ground. They ordered the pilot to follow the UFO, and said two jets were being sent up to investigate. He heard or saw nothing of the jets, but followed the object as far as Oswego, towards Canada, before turning back to his original course.

A reporter from the Buffalo *'Evening News'* interviewed the airline crew, and published details of the incident in their 10th of April edition. After Major Keyhoe became the director of 'NICAP', he decided to investigate further, and was met with a brick wall of silence. The pilots, Air Force, and Civil Aeronautics Board all denied the incident, and it was just fortunate that a few days after the event, Captain Ryan, First Officer Neff, and Flight Engineer Bruce Foster had been interviewed on TV station WBEN where they confirmed the occurrence.

In 2015, the *'Ufologist Magazine'*, published an account of the Central Intelligence Agency (CIA) admitting that it was responsible for at least half of the reported UFO sightings in the 1950s and 1960s. They said that these craft were in fact secret, high altitude reconnaissance flights.

In 1997 I spoke at the 'Australian International UFO Symposium' where I met Chinese Researcher, Professor Sun Shi Li. He confirmed that Chinese pilots have also reported UFO encounters to control towers. At the same Symposium, Graham Birdsall, editor of Britain's *'UFO Magazine'*, discussed the enormous 'black triangle' craft, seen over Europe during the last few years. He discounted the theory that they were advanced secret military aircraft for two main reasons.

First, he considered there was such a large number being reported, they would be beyond the stated defence budgets of governments to produce. Secondly, the 'triangles' were so brazen in publically hovering at such low levels, no pilot of a secret advanced aircraft would ever be allowed to do this.

An incident on 3rd May 1957, does beg the question as to whether or not we had developed our own 'flying saucer' prototype. An object, described as an inverted plate, with a dome on top, hovered close to the practise range at Edwards Air Force Base in the USA. It was a luminous golden colour, with portholes or panels around the dome. Many witnesses took photographs, which were all confiscated by 'Intelligence'.

Why then do pilots remain totally silent and non-committal when asked about unidentified phenomena? Pilots spoke of being interrogated, sometimes all night long, 'treated like incompetents, and then instructed to keep quiet'.

One friend, a commercial pilot, told me that if they discuss UFO sightings, it is most certainly going to damage their careers and promotion prospects. Although they would not necessarily lose their jobs, when it came time to renew their medical and endorsement qualifications, necessary for their licences, it would be made extremely 'difficult'. This is why reports are often made once the pilot has retired, decades after the event.

Whilst the military have always ensured that their personnel do not publicly admit to UFO sightings, information continues to flood in from the civil aviation sector. We still hear of reports from passengers and crew of many local and international flights. I suspect we only know about relatively few of these airborne encounters with unidentified objects.

In the British summer of 1967, Captain Graham Sheppard and his crew were cruising along the main flight path from Scotland to London. It was a routine commercial flight, at an altitude of 24,000ft, with good visibility, when they received an unexpected warning message from Preston Radar Control; "You have fast-moving, opposite direction traffic in the airway."

Captain Sheppard and his two co-pilots looked out to see a thirty-foot wide disc-shaped craft race into view, and speed within metres of their plane. It was disc-shaped, metallic, with a slightly raised centre section, and no visible marking;

"The senior captain we were flying with at the time, he advised us strongly that we shouldn't report it...and said quite clearly to us that it would compromise our careers if we talked about it."

Graham Shepherd and his crew had also witnessed another incident in March 1967, when there was a ten minute aerobatic display by two unidentified objects over the Bay of Biscay. In 1993, Graham appeared on a TV program, where he described the incidents. As a result, he was summoned to the British Airways

Public Relations office, and told that they would not tolerate 'any talk of UFOs'. He received a formal letter, banning him from any contact with the media.

Eighteen months later he took early retirement and became a freelance pilot. He estimated that about ten percent of commercial and military pilots have had some sort of experience, but are afraid to speak out.

LARGE CRAFT

There were times when the unidentified flying objects reported were far too large to be one of our own prototypes, and unlikely to be a misidentification of a weather balloon or similar object.

In his book, *'Aliens From Space'*, Major Donald Kehoe noted the Air Force's concern over the reports of these giant craft, which were not of this Earth; *'Since 1953 it had known that giant spaceships were operating near our planet. At least nine times, huge alien spacecraft had been seen or tracked in orbit, or as they descended nearer the Earth for brief periods. Each time it had been an ordeal for the A.F. censors, as they struggled to conceal the reports or explain them away when attempts at secrecy failed.'*

In another book, *'The Flying Saucer Conspiracy'*, Donald Kehoe noted that between 19th August 1949 and 10th March 1950, one of these large, disc-shaped craft had been seen hovering over the American city of Cincinnati on ten occasions. On three instances, the large ship was seen to launch smaller objects; in one case, anti-aircraft searchlights picked up two groups of five smaller saucers.

In mid-1953, a giant object was sighted over California four nights in a row. On 29th July, Park Superintendent E. Scoyen saw an enormous disc race past Moro Rock in Sequoia-Kings National Park, and then zoom into the sky. Its brilliant yellow glow lit up a nearby canyon. He, as had other witnesses, estimated its diameter as being at least 1,000ft. At the same time, Air Force jets were placed on patrol, and one report, not confirmed, said that when they were diving towards the low-flying giant object, it suddenly climbed and shot away, narrowly missing its pursuers.

In June 1954, a huge, glowing object, travelling at high speed, travelled in from the Atlantic Ocean, and hovered for an hour, at about 79,000ft, between Washington and Baltimore. There was much concern, as from this position, it could spy on both cities and all the nearby airfields, but, despite standing orders to pursue all UFOs, no interceptor jets could reach that altitude. Eventually, the strange craft climbed steeply, and disappeared into the night.

Kehoe wrote; *On the night of 20th June, the strange visitor returned...a huge object, glowing orange–red, hovering over Washington and Baltimore. Again the jets were scrambled, and Air Defence Commands alerted. This time, the giant saucer remained for two hours, flying between the two cities, while the jets circled helplessly far below.*

'Though there were Nike rockets bases, from which deadly defence missiles could have been launched, not even a Nike could have reached the hovering giant. As before, the huge craft ended its surveillance abruptly, disappearing from radarscopes before its speed could be measured.'

These large craft were also being seen across the world in Australia. Frank Walford, a Blue Mountains City Alderman, told my friend and fellow investigator Rex Gilroy, of an incident that happened in 1943. He said; "I don't talk of this much, particularly if I want to get re-elected to Council."

One bright winter's day, he and a mate were camped out, beside a creek, in rugged bushland, when they saw a strange craft hovering over the Newnes Valley to the north.

It was a 'huge, bronze-coloured, round, doughnut-shaped craft', 200 feet across, and 50 feet tall. Through binoculars, they could see 'many windows, both round and square, in two or three rows around the side'. They were scared enough to consider packing up and leaving, but the strange craft moved further up the valley and hovered again before rising high in the sky and taking off at great speed, vanished over the mountains to the north-east.

Rex Gilroy also interviewed Tony Look, an employee of the Blue Mountains City Council, in N.S.W.

About 6.30am, one winter morning in 1958, Tony arrived at the Blackheath depot, to find his workmates staring up into the sky. Overhead, at an altitude of at least 10,000ft, was a 'monstrous' elliptical object, with a blinding white light which shone a glow over the depot and surrounding township.

The radiance seemed to emanate from a row of lights around the periphery of the craft, which hovered for about ten minutes before suddenly rising upwards, at a phenomenal speed, and disappearing into the clouds. The following week, a similar giant craft was seen to descend from the sky towards the nearby Grose Valley.

In 1964-5, some of the residents of Warminster in England, were reporting a huge cigar-shaped object, nicknamed a 'Leviathan', which made a huge noise, frightening residents and ripping tiles off rooves as it moved over. On one occasion, witnessed by members of the military, a huge chimney was demolished, scattering masonry all over the ground.

At times it was seen hovering vertically and silently in the sky. One impeccable witness, the vicar's wife, described it as throwing off an orange-red glow. She said there seemed to be a distinct, dark, circular patch or aperture at the end. Other witnesses had seen it glowing from both ends.

Mrs. Kathleen Penton, and other members of the community, saw it moving horizontally across the sky, and likened it to a 'railway carriage', with rounded ends, and patches emitting a stronger light, which may, or may not have been windows.

On the night of February 15th 1965, a chartered Flying Tiger plane, carrying Air Force and Army personnel to Japan, was cruising over the Pacific, when three enormous discs were seen flying at the same altitude in a parallel course.

They were also tracked on radar, and calculated as each being nearly 2,000ft in length. Due to their enormous size, an Air Force officer on board advised against calling out intercept jets from Okinawa. Suddenly the formation of strange intruders angled upwards, and shot away and out of sight at a speed estimated to be 1,200 knots per hour.

One interesting case occurred much later, in about 1977. The details only became available some years later, and when the pilot 'Trevor' (a pseudonym) spoke to me, he said he had not wished to make any public comment at the time.

Trevor was a pilot for British Caledonian Airways, and was taking a 747 cargo plane from London to South America. Just off the coast of Africa, Trevor and the other four crew members noticed an enormous object on their radar screen. It appeared to be on the same altitude as the 747 and directly on their flight path. They couldn't believe the size the screen was displaying. They contacted Algiers for verification, and were told that Algiers' radar didn't extend that far. They were given permission to alter course, but Algiers noted that there shouldn't be anything else in that airspace.

As they approached the area, Trevor and the crew were dumbfounded to see an unbelievable object which corresponded to the readings on the radar screen. It was silver in colour, with no windows, and hovering like an airborne fortress. As it came closer it moved around to the side, enough to give the 747 room to pass. Trevor claimed it was like something out of 'Science Fiction'. It seemed to have doors along the side, as if it might have been some form of cargo vessel.

It remained stationary, and did not interfere or communicate with their plane as they flew along the full length – at least **twenty miles**. The crew maintained a stunned silence during the entire encounter. After they had passed the object, the pilot followed Standard Operations Procedures, which entailed opening a small safe box, and handing report forms to the witnesses. Once the reports were completed they were locked back into the box, and the crew instructed to say nothing about what they had seen.

As soon as they landed back in Britain, the crew and locked safe were escorted back to a RAF Base, or similar government establishment. They said they were treated well, but virtually 'imprisoned' none-the-less. The witnesses were separated, and then questioned individually. Each was told they had seen a 'weather balloon', and would have to 'sign this' before they could leave. After three days they wanted to 'get out' and complied with the request.

If the crew's estimate of the size of this object is correct, it is extremely unlikely it originated on Earth. One can only speculate as to its resemblance to the reported 'mother-ships', and it was conveniently over the ocean, out of range of our ground-based radar systems.

Although we didn't hear about it very often, giant craft were also seen over Russia, and the Soviet Air Force and pilots had also experienced their fair share of inexplicable interference.

In 1967 Soviet Astronomical facilities at Kazan and Kislovodsk reported 'flying crescents', between 500 and 600 metres long, and travelling at over 11,000 miles per hour.

In 1983 a retired Russian Air Force Colonel told of how he personally knew of forty cases where Soviet pilots had been ordered to follow the unknown craft, and several had crashed whilst in pursuit.

In later years, the Russians were a little more forthcoming about UFOs. In May 1990, Gorbachev was reported as saying; "The leaders of our armed services have long recognised UFOs as genuine phenomena, calling for sensitive response. We are alert, but have no reason to believe that these visitors are other than peaceful."

The same year Igor Maltsev, Soviet Air Defence Director, said; "We have scrambled our jets to observe the craft. Our pilots were ordered not to attack, on the grounds that the discs might possess formidable capacities for retaliation. We obtained many photographs of the UFO – and also registered it on thermal and optical sensors."

In 1992, General Yevgeniy, of the CIS Scientific and Technical Committee, stated; "Our air forces have been recording UFOs and scrambling in pursuit of them since the end of the war against Hitler. The reality of these objects is beyond doubt, but what they are and where they come from is unknown. I am not aware of any overt hostility by the UFOs – and our pilots are ordered always to treat them in a peace-loving manner."

By the 1970s, the highly experienced older pilots, who had gained their skills 'by the seat of their pants' during wartime, were still flying. The aviation industry had grown and expanded, and they had been joined by a new generation of young, well trained aviators.

I would submit that while many early cases may have been more worldly espionage or surveillance, we will never know. Perhaps there is a conventional explanation for a number of the events. We know that unknown prototypes of earthly origin are covertly tested, but at the time, the characteristics of some of these strange craft surpassed the most advanced secret experimental technology.

What has really been happening in our skies?

CHAPTER SEVEN

THE BRITISH MILITARY

During the early 1970s my interest in astronomy expanded to UFOs, and the possibility of life out there in the vast universe. Having spent the early years of my life in Britain, besides becoming involved in a couple of Australian research groups, I joined the 'British UFO Research Association', (BUFORA), remaining a member until it closed down several decades later.

When I returned to the U.K., to visit relatives, in 1976, I was able to meet and liaise with several of their researchers. In the following years, I developed an interest in their research involving military bases, especially the RAF, where my own father had served on military aircraft, for over six years.

THE WAR YEARS

My father was a flight-engineer, who flew many SAS missions over Europe during World War II, and while he, along with many other airmen, confirmed seeing the notorious 'Foo Fighters' during that time, he never elaborated on any details. Later reports indicated that the allies thought they were a German secret weapon. It appears that the Germans were just as mystified, concluding that they were some new American invention.

The Allies also conducted a secret investigation into the phenomenon in 1943, enlisting Professor Hugh Dryden, an aerodynamicist at the then National Bureau of Standards. It was headed by Lt. Gen. Massey, who later classified the project in 1944. Massey was inspired by a report from a spy, a double agent, who, operating under the orders of the Mayor of Cologne, was denounced and executed at the beginning of 1944.

Jacques Vallee, who had been an engineer with U.S. Intelligence in Germany, claimed that by 1943 the Allies were already aware that these 'foo-fighters' had a possible electrostatic effect, and were capable of interfering with internal-combustion engines.

After the war, it was suggested that these annoying and often feared objects, were the top secret anti-radar 'Feuerball', produced by an experimental centre at Oberammagau in Bavaria. Even if this was correct, not all of them were fast moving balls of light. It didn't explain all sightings during the conflict.

The Germans also had their own concerns. In 1944, the Wehrmacht asked Oberkommando of the Luftwaffe to set up a centre to also collect information on all the various sightings of these objects. This was known as 'Sonderburo No 13', and although it didn't come to any definite conclusions, it amassed an impressive amount of information during its short existence.

One of the first sightings they studied had occurred on March 14th 1942, when Hauptmann Fischer, an engineer in civil life, landed at a secret airbase at Banak, Norway. He was asked to go back up and investigate a luminous object which had just been picked up on radar.

At 10,000ft he caught sight of an enormous long streamlined craft, about 300 feet long and about fifty feet in diameter. It stayed horizontal for a long moment, before rising vertically and disappearing at great speed. In his report Fischer stated 'it was not a machine constructed by the hand of man.'

This concerned the authorities, because a month earlier they had launched a test rocket from Kummersdorf, and the film of the experiment had shown an unknown spherical body following and circling their rocket.

Another case had occurred at 10.45am on September 29th 1944. A test pilot was trying out a new Messerschmitt jet, ME-262, when he noticed two luminous points to his right. He immediately approached, at full speed, and came within 1,500 ft of, and face to face with, a large cylindrical object, more than 300 feet long, with some openings along the side. It was fitted with long antennae in front up to halfway along its length, and sped away at more than 1,200 mph.

In his book 'Strange Company', Keith Chester writes of an incident in June 1942, when Lt. Roman Sabinski and the crew of his Wellington bomber were returning from a night-time bombing mission over Germany. They had left the coast of Holland, and were returning to base when a round, copper-coloured object, about the size of the full moon, approached from behind.

His gunners opened fire, and directly hit the craft. The tracer rounds seemed to be absorbed by the object, as there was no sign of them exiting the other side. The intruder pulled away, and climbed upwards at phenomenal speed.

In November 1942, the crew of a Lancaster bomber over Turin, Italy, reported an object travelling at approximately five-hundred miles per hour. It was two to three hundred feet in length, with four pairs of red lights spaced equally along the length of its body.

In 1977, the *'BUFORA Journal'* published an in-depth investigation by my colleague, Omar Fowler, into an incident experienced during a Bomber Command operation, involving several hundred planes, over Essen in Germany on 26/27 May 1943. They were at about nineteen thousand feet, and ready to make their final 'run-in', on a Krupps Armament Works, when they saw an object, much bigger than their own plane, in front of them, and slightly to the port side.

Second pilot, G. Cockfort, described it as being long and cylindrical, silvery-gold in colour, with what appeared to be portholes evenly spaced along the side, and possibly a second row underneath. It was very sharply defined, hanging at about a forty-five degree angle in the sky. Within about twenty to thirty seconds, it suddenly began moving, and climbed away, accelerating rapidly to an incredible speed, until it vanished from sight. They then completed their bomb run, and returned to base.

The entire crew witnessed this strange craft, and were amazed at its speed, which they calculated to be thousands of miles per hour. When they returned to base, they reported the incident during debriefing, but didn't know how much importance it was given by their senior officers.

Cockfort later said; *"I have never seen anything of this nature, before or since, and have never seen any of the saucer-shaped objects, but in retrospect, I am quite convinced that this cigar-shaped UFO was of extraterrestrial origin."*

On 11th August 1944, a Lancaster bomber (one of the largest planes in existence at the time) was returning from a mission over southern France, when it encountered a disc shaped UFO which dwarfed their aircraft many times over.

The radio operator, Ron Claridge, who was later awarded the Distinguished Flying Cross, said that all eight members of the crew saw the enormous disc, much larger than their own aircraft, about three thousand feet away from their plane. It had circular lights, rather like portholes on a ship, and was bright yellow changing to intense white. There was no noise or turbulence, only the lights, and it was there for about three minutes before it silently accelerated away and out of view.

Claridge later commented that whilst the entire crew were alerted to the object, all were strangely transfixed by the experience; "We had no feelings of fear, but feelings of great calm. Even our gunners, who would normally open fire, were helpless.

"I have never forgotten these feelings, and they are unchanged today. This was beyond religion, wars and suspicions. That this was not part of this world was certain."

When they arrived back at base, they were all interviewed, told not to discuss it amongst themselves, say anything to anyone else, or to record it in their log books.

Perhaps the thoughts of some of our leaders, in those 'good old days', were best summed up by British Air Chief Marshall Lord Dowding, who commanded the RAF during the Battle of Britain. He was, however, probably the most controversial, and outspoken, of all the military hierarchy.

On 11th July 1954, he wrote in a *'Sunday Dispatch'* article; *'More than 10,000 sightings have been reported, the majority of which cannot be accounted for by any 'scientific' explanation. They have been tracked on radar screens....and the observed speeds have been as great as 9,000 miles per hour.*

In another article he wrote; *'I have never seen a 'flying saucer', and yet I believe that they exist. I have never seen Australia, and yet I believe Australia also exists. My belief in both cases is based upon cumulative evidence in such quality and quantity, that for me at any rate, it brings complete conviction.....*

'In a brief article I cannot deal at length with the suggestion that they are new types of aircraft under development by Russia or the U.S. They have been tracked on radar screens in America – on one occasion by three screens simultaneously – the observed speeds have been as great as 9,000 miles an hour.

'No earthly materials that we know of could be forced through the air at such a speed without getting too hot to allow human occupants to exist. The

accelerations which they develop in starting, changing course, and stopping would also make human life, as we know it, impossible.

'I say then that I am convinced that these objects do exist, and that they are not manufactured by any nation on Earth. I can, therefore, see no alternative to accepting the theory that they come from some extraterrestrial source. And why should this be considered such a ridiculous idea?

'In ten years' time we shall probably have shot a rocket to the moon. In five hundred years' time we may have reached the nearer planets. Are we so arrogant as to maintain that the inhabitants of no planet are as much as five hundred years ahead of us in scientific development?

Dowding, at the time, had no idea how quickly we would progress, but he then went on to discuss the possible motives extraterrestrials may have for visiting our planet. He did not know, but presented three speculative possibilities; *'I think that we must resist the tendency to assume that they all come from the same planet, or that they are all actuated by similar motives. It might be that the visitors from one planet wished to help us in our evolution from the basis of a higher level to which they had attained.*

'Another planet might send an expedition to ascertain what have been these terrible explosions which they have observed, and to prevent us from discommoding other people, besides ourselves, by the new toys with which we are so light-heartedly playing. Other visitors might have come bent solely on scientific discovery, and might regard us with dispassionate aloofness, with which we might regard insects beneath an upturned stone.

'But it is not on this note that I wish to finish. It seems possible that, for the first time in recorded history, intelligible communication on the physical level may become possible between the Earth and other planets in the Solar System. Such a prospect is epoch-making in the literal sense of the word, and we should be guilty of criminal folly if we would do anything to hinder a contact which may well bring untold blessings to a distraught humanity.'

Lord Dowding was not the only member of British aristocracy to have an interest in UFOs. In my book, *'The Days of the Space Brothers'*, I wrote of an incident at Broadlands, the estate of Earl Mountbatten, where his employee, Frederick Briggs, witnessed a strange craft hovering above and a 'being' momentarily descending to the ground.

Researcher, Emily Crewe, reported that when George Adamski visited Britain in the early 1960s, Dowding and Mountbatten met him in London, and subsequently took him to Broadlands to see the site of Frederick Brigg's 1956 UFO sighting.

Researchers, Georgina Bruni and Nick Pope, discussed the memoirs of Sir Peter Horsley; *'One 31 page chapter in his book, 'Sounds from Another Room', details his involvement with RAF investigations of UFO sightings and alludes to keeping HRH Prince Philip, (Duke of Edinburgh), updated with ongoing developments.*

"As always, his mind was open. He agreed I should do a study on the subject in my spare time as long as I kept it in perspective and didn't bring the Palace into disrepute. He didn't want to see headlines about him believing in 'little green men", said Sir Peter, who also claims to have held a two hour meeting with an apparent human-looking extraterrestrial in London.

"I would say they come from another planet, somewhere in the universe, but not our galaxy", said Sir Peter. "They are benign, not aggressive and, like us, explorers."

Desmond Leslie, the son of Sir Shane Leslie, co-authored George Adamski's book, *'Flying Saucers Have Landed'*, and Brinsley le Poer Trench, the Earl of Clancarty wrote several books on the subject.

In 1951, after World War II, Sir Henry Tizzard, who was best known for his pioneering work on the development of radar technology prior to World War II, wrote a secret report to Prime Minister Winston Churchill, suggesting that most unexplained sightings were natural events, such as the weather, or meteors or of normal aircraft. Behind the scenes Tizzard, who at that time was chief scientific advisor to the Ministry of Defence, considered that reports of flying saucers should not be dismissed without some investigation, and in 1950 had already been instrumental in setting up a highly secretive 'Flying Saucer Working Party'.

In 1952, after a flurry of sightings, Churchill ordered his staff to investigate the matter further, and uttered the now famous words; *"What does all the stuff about flying saucers amount to? What can it mean? What is the truth?"*

Within two weeks, the Air Ministry replied, still insisting that there was nothing to worry about, and most of the reports were misidentifications.

Researcher, Timothy Good, reported that back in the U.S.A., a FBI memorandum, dated 29th July 1952, from US Air Intelligence Officer Commander Boyd, stated; *'Intense research is being carried out by Air Intelligence. The Air Force is attempting, in each instance, to send up jet interceptor planes. The objects sighted may possibly be from another planet.'*

Good also noted that, despite the frantic investigations being conducted in the U.S., Churchill was still presented with mundane explanations for all the reported events; - *'Sir Winston Churchill was either deliberately or inadvertently mislead.'* Good concluded; *'We must therefore assume that the Air Staff had not been given these facts by their American colleagues, or that they chose to withhold the information from the Prime Minister.'*

On 16th December 1953, a restricted memo was sent to all senior air staff in southern England, stating that all UFO reports were to be sent directly to Air Command, and any public release would officially be controlled by them....... *'All reports are, therefore, to be classified 'restricted' and personnel are to be warned that they are not to communicate to anyone other than official persons any information about phenomena they have observed.'*

In April 1955 Britain's Air Ministry publicly stated that a report on a five year investigation into flying saucers, by the Royal Air Force, had been produced and marked for the attention of high-ranking officers only. For security reasons, the report would not be made available to Parliament, the media or general public.

Parliament was definitely misled when Under Secretary of State for Air, George Ward, was asked why the report was not to be published; - "Reports of flying saucers, as well as other abnormal objects in the sky, are investigated as they come in, but there has been no formal enquiry. About 90% of the reports have been found to relate to meteors, balloons, flares and many other objects. The fact that the other 10% are unexplained, needs to be attributed to nothing more sinister than lack of data."

In 1980, when researchers tried to investigate further, the MOD advised that all records prior to 1962 had been destroyed.

'*Flying Saucer Review*' received an interesting report from a former member of the RAF, who had waited for the expiry of any 'secrets' embargo, and now felt it was time to speak out.

In August 1949, he participated in the fifteen-day, 'Operation Bulldog', which was an exercise designed to test British radar and defence capabilities, which extended across the south coast, and up the east into Scotland. The witness, who didn't give his own name, identified all the other officers who were on duty with him that particular day at the RAF Sandwich Radar ACI in Kent.

They, and other radar stations, tracked an enormous object, which was over the English Channel before turning northwards towards the Thames Estuary. It was at an altitude of fifty thousand feet, travelling at 3,000mph, with a calculated size of close to twenty thousand tons, and an echo similar to that of a large passenger or freighter ship. When it approached Bampton Radar Station, in Yorkshire, it suddenly increased speed and headed upwards. It vanished from their screens after it reached an altitude of one hundred thousand feet.

In those days there were no known aircraft of that size, or capable of such speed. Everyone was summoned to a meeting with the Commanding Officer, who reminded them of the Official Secrets Act. They were to forget about the occurrence, and not mention it to anyone outside of the RAF.

The servicemen and officers on duty had meticulously recorded every detail, but the following evening they noticed that the incomplete Duty Watch Book had disappeared, and had been replaced with a brand new one.

In August 1950, British RAF pilot, Wing Commander Stan Hubbard, had an unusual sighting of his own. In a later interview with researcher David Clarke, he told of how, that day, he had just left the Farnborough Flying Control Building when he heard a very unusual sound, and turned to see a strange object, some distance away in the sky.

It looked like a light grey, pearl coloured 'discus', or 'rotating pan lid', about 100ft in diameter, and was rhythmically rocking very slightly, from side to side, as it moved very quickly in a straight approach and passed silently overhead.

He thought he was the only witness, but a young woman ran out of the Dispatcher's shack, screaming his name, and asking if he had seen 'that horrible thing'. She was hysterical for some time after.

Hubbard immediately reported the sighting to his senior officer, who asked him to make a written statement there and then. Within two hours, investigators from 'Scientific Intelligence', wearing civilian clothes, arrived and questioned him extensively about the strange craft.

They visited a second time, and at one stage told him; "You must not discuss this with anyone, not even your boss. You are not to ask questions, and you are not to call friends in the Ministry, or make inquiries."

They returned about a month later, in September 1950, after a similar craft was seen, performing complex manoeuvres in the sky, south of the airfield, whilst the chief test pilot was taking up a Hawker P-1801 for its inaugural flight.

In 2002, when Hubbard was asked if he thought they may have seen some kind of secret prototype, either our own or one of the enemy's, he said; *"I have thought a great deal about it, and have got no more opinions on it, except to say we still do not have anything near the technology, or airframe, stability and control and power sources that could possibly do what this object did."*

In July 1952, RAF pilot Ronald Hughes was returning to base after a training mission over West Germany. He reported seeing a flash of silver light, which rapidly descended towards his Havilland FB-9 Vampire plane. As it came closer he could see it was a 'gleaming, silver metallic disc', about one hundred feet in diameter, smooth and seamless, with a highly reflective surface. The strange craft flew alongside of him before disappearing at incredible speed. It was captured on RAF radars, and confirmed at travelling at speeds far greater than any current aircraft.

Hughes was later summoned by Ducan Sandys, the Aviation Minister, to personally recount the event. Sandys, who initially asked Hughes how many beers he had, found the report and radar evidence 'convincing'. He referred the incident to Lord Cherwell, the government's chief scientist, who had tended to be very sceptical.

Sandys who was later promoted to Defence Secretary, wrote; *'Until some satisfactory scientific explanation can be provided, it would be most unwise to accept, without further question, the view that 'flying saucers' can be dismissed* as *'a mild form of hysteria'.....There is ample evidence of some unfamiliar and unexplained phenomenon.'*

In later years, Hughes' son said; *"We knew about the sighting in the family when we were growing up, but my father didn't talk about it much. We learned about it more from prompting him.*

"He was very matter of fact about what he saw, just describing the details. He never did any research into UFOs or flying saucers, and didn't have any interest in the supernatural or science fiction. If it was someone other than my father, who told this story, I would be sceptical. He once said to me – "People think you're mad if you say you've seen a flying saucer – I've only ever seen one once; I've never seen one since."

In 1952, the British military, as part of NATO, and nine participating countries, were conducting 'Operation Mainbrace', in an undisclosed region of the North Sea, somewhere in the vicinity of Denmark and Norway. It commenced on 13th September, and lasted for twelve days involving 80,000 men, 1,000 planes and 200 ships. Several investigators, including Richard Hall, later wrote about the following incidents.

On the very first night, Commander Schmidt Jensen, and several members of his crew, on the Danish destroyer, *'Willemoes'*, north of Bornholm Island, saw an unidentified, triangular object, 'glowing bluish' and travelling in the sky, at speed, (more than 900mph), towards the southeast.

Edward Ruppelt reported that an American press photographer, Wallace Litwin, taking colour photos of jets taking off from the aircraft carrier *'USS Franklin Roosevelt'*, noticed some pilots and deck crew were watching a silver sphere, moving swiftly across the sky. As it passed over the Allied fleet, he quickly took some excellent snaps of the object. Later investigations ruled out a balloon, and could not determine what it was, or where it had come from.

This was not the only unidentified object seen on that memorable day, the 19th of the month. Three airmen and two officers from British Coastal Command at Dishforth Aerodrome, near the Topside Naval Base, Yorkshire, were watching as a Meteor plane was coming in to land. Lt. John Kilburn's official report to the British Air Ministry was included in Aimé Michel's book, *'The Truth About Flying Saucers'*;

'The Meteor was coming down from about 5,000ft. The sky was clear, the sun shining, visibility perfect. The Meteor was crossing the airport from east to west, when suddenly I noticed a white object in the sky. It was round, silvery and circular, and seemed to be following the Meteor at about two miles distance, at a speed less than that of the aircraft, but on the same course, though a little above it.

"What on earth is that?" I shouted. My friends looked up where I was pointing; one of them said it might be the metal cone-capping of the Meteor's engine, which had come off, while another thought it was just a parachute. But while we were still watching the disc, we saw it reduce speed for some seconds, and then begin to come down. As it lost height, it began to flutter like a leaf, or, if you prefer, oscillate like a pendulum.

'The Meteor swerved to circle the airfield before landing. The object began to follow it, but stopped dead after a few seconds. It seemed to remain suspended in the air, revolving like a top. Suddenly it took off, accelerated, and flew off westwards at a terrific speed, before changing course and disappearing southeast. The whole thing lasted for about twenty seconds.

'While still in sight, it seemed to change shape, and become elliptical. During the short time it was revolving while stationary, we could see it shining in the sun. It then seemed to be about the size of a pursuit plane at the same altitude.

'We are absolutely certain that there could be no question of a balloon, or an optical illusion, or an effect produced by the Meteor's jets. It was a solid object. I have never seen anything like that in the sky in all my life.'

Radar operators in Britain were also detecting anomalies on their screens. In later years, researcher Nick Redfern interviewed a radar operator, who, during 'Mainbrace' was stationed at RAF Langton, Lincolnshire; *"On the first day....something was speeding across the screen; and this was fast – very fast. It looked like there were actually two objects, and they were approaching from the North Sea and flew across Lincolnshire, Peterborough and then up the country at about 2,000mph.*

"....Our Commanding officer arrived and reminded us not to talk about this as we'd signed the 'Official Secrets Act'. But this happened over a couple of days, and the UFOs were tracked over several shifts – not just ours."

Nick Redfern located another serviceman who was on duty at RAF Ventnor on the Isle of White; *"I was on radar in 1952 at Ventnor and one afternoon I picked up six objects travelling from the Bay of Biscay up towards the Channel.*

"These UFOs were travelling at fifteen hundred miles per hour – far quicker than anything we were flying. Initially, we thought that these were false radar returns – really because of the speed. But the RAF was concerned and scrambled Meteor fighters from RAF Tangmere. Of course, the pilots couldn't match that speed, and I don't know if the pilots saw anything or not."

At 7.30pm on the night of 20th September, three Danish Air Force officers, at Karup airfield in Denmark, reported a shiny, metallic disc which passed overhead, and travelled in the direction of the 'Mainbrace' fleet. They lost sight of it when it passed into some cloud.

The next day, a group of six RAF jet interceptors saw a shiny, spherical unidentified object coming from the direction of the 'Mainbrace' fleet. They attempted to catch it, but it soon outdistanced them, only to return to follow another plane, before speeding off into the distance when pursuit craft approached.

On 27th/28th September, just after the conclusion of military operations, there were multiple reports of 'comet-like' UFOs, strange brightly luminous objects with tails, irregularly hovering for prolonged periods near Hamburg and Kiel. On one occasion, three satellite objects were seen moving around a larger craft. Other unidentified intruders were seen over Denmark and Southern Sweden, giving rise to speculation that they may be Russian spycraft.

Did these anonymous observers originate from a foreign country, or from somewhere out in space? If the military knew, they weren't about to tell us.

It wasn't until many years later that researcher Nick Redfern contacted William Maguire, who had been a National Serviceman in 1952. He agreed to speak out about the events which occurred during 'Mainbrace': *"I'm seventy years old. What are they going to do? Call me up? I don't feel tied by the Secrecy Act."*

When 'Mainbrace' occurred, he was a senior aircraftsman, and part of a mobile team of radar experts who were sent to various stations to ascertain the readings on their radar instruments were accurate. One day in September, they were driven, in vehicles with unusually blacked-out windows, to a location he believed was close to RAF Sandwich in Kent.

They were taken to what looked like a normal field, but which, in fact, housed the entry to an underground base; *"This was a huge complex – it was completely operational – there must have been a hundred people down there......What did surprise me, as an experienced radar operator, was the extent of the machines; they were able to see right across to Eastern Europe, parts of Russia and way over to Sweden, which, at the time, I hadn't realised we could do."*

William noticed that due to the radarscopes tracking a huge, unidentified aerial object high over the English Channel, the place was in chaos, with mechanics being accused of not calibrating the instruments correctly; *"On every single instrument on the base, was the fact that sitting up, at an unbelievable height, this enormous thing, with the equivalent mass of a warship, and it just stood there...and stood there....and stood there.*

"Whatever this thing was, it had sat stationary in a stratospheric wind of several hundred miles per hour, which was quite colossal for the time. I wasn't on the height finder, but I remember the mechanics said that it was higher than anything we knew about.

"Nobody really had anything in the book for dealing with something sitting umpteen miles over the English Channel! But, eventually it suddenly split into three and zoomed off at some phenomenal speed. One went north, one headed over France, and the other disappeared in the Eastern Balkan region.

"We didn't, of course, interpret this at the time as being an alien spaceship. There was talk of an escaped V-2 rocket – which was rubbish – and temperature inversions. But we knew damn well what an inversion was; we could tell an inverted seagull, never mind something as big as a warship – and it bloody wasn't a misinterpretation!"

Afterwards, his senior officer told them all – "This didn't happen". Soon after the members of his team were split up and sent to different locations, a common practice in the Western militaries after UFO related events.

———————————

A month later, on the afternoon of 21st October 1952, Flt. Lt. Michael Swiney, and his student pilot Royal Navy Lt. David Crofts, took off, in a Meteor trainer jet, from Little Rissington, Gloucestershire for a cross-country training flight.

As they punched through a layer of cloud, at around fifteen thousand feet, they were astounded to find three white circular objects in front of them. They were circular and stationary, and looked like the traditional 'flying saucers' which had been reported in previous years.

Initially, Swiney thought they were parachutes, and quickly took control of the plane from Crofts, climbed to thirty-five thousand feet and levelled out. The objects still remained visible. He looked carefully, and noted that there were no discernible signs of propulsion, portholes, turrets or other tale-tale evidence that may have identified them as conventional aircraft viewed at an unusual angle. He decided to advise Traffic Control and return back to base.

Traffic Control had different ideas, and told Swiney to approach the UFOs. He followed instructions, and turned his aircraft, at full power, towards them. As he closed in, one disc turned on its side, and climbed away, out of sight, 'at great speed'.

Meanwhile, authorities at Fighter Command had been advised. It was the height of the Cold War, and since other ground radars had detected the unidentified craft, two more Meteors were immediately sent up, but didn't make contact.

One of the radar operators later commented; "They had entered our airspace going at a fantastic speed, approximately three thousand miles per hour. We had nothing that went that fast, and neither had the Russians nor the Americans."

When the airmen got back to base, they were interrogated for a couple of days, and the episode designated as 'unexplained.'

Michael Swiney later rose to the rank of Air Commodore before his retirement from a long career in the RAF. When he was in his seventies, he spoke to British researchers David Clarke and Andy Roberts, who conducted an excellent in-depth investigation of the incident. They managed to unearth an entry in the Operations Record Book of CFS Little Rissington dated 21st October 1952. It read;

'Flt. Lt. M.J.E. Swiney, instructor, and Lt. D. Crofts RN, student, sighted three mysterious, 'saucer-shaped objects' travelling at high speed at about 35,000ft whilst on a high level navigation exercise, in a Meteor V11. Later, A.T.C.C.

Gloucester reported radar plots to confirm this, but Air Ministry discounted any possibility of 'extra terrestrial objects'.'

Except for the official Operations Record Book entry, investigators could not locate any official report of the incident, and authorities claimed that they had no record of the event, despite Swiney having seen the file in 1974.

Robert Chapman, in his book, *'Flying Saucers Over Britain'*, wrote about an incident which occurred near West Manning RAF Base, on 3rd November 1953.

At 10am, Flying Officers T. Johnson and G. Smythe were on a routine flight, at 2.000ft in a Vampire jet. They saw a circular, brilliant object, which was, at first, stationary in the sky. Suddenly, it shot into motion, and passed their plane at a phenomenal speed. A two hour interrogation of the pilots was marked 'confidential', with the details not revealed. A later explanation to Parliament stated that meteorological balloons may have been the cause, although investigators thought it was unlikely that the witnesses were mistaken.

Just like their American counterparts, the British themselves were quick to 'cover-up' any reports. George Filer told of an incident reported by John Cotton, nearly 50 years after the event.

In late 1954, John was working at RAF Bawdsey in the RT recording area, and after Meteor NF-11s were sent up to investigate an anomalous object, he started recording the intercept.

'As the interceptors approached and got visual contact with the target, they reported that it was a stationary object, (confirmed by radar), and 'saucer-like' in shape. On being ordered to approach closer, the target shot off at high speed and then hovered again.

'The second time the fighters neared, the target went straight up at a very high speed, until it disappeared off the Type13 height radar. I, like many others in the 'hole', had gone into the control cabin, which wasn't in use, to see these phenomena.

'The chief controller that night asked to hear the recording of the interception, but for the first time we could remember there was no recording. It was a

simple system of continuous loop of clear film on which the voices and time signal were 'scratched' and supposedly fool proof.'

The next morning, they were woken early, and reminded, by the C.O. of the 'Official Secrets Act' as it applied to the events of the previous night. When they tried to contact the pilots, they were told they had gone on leave.

The *'Daily Mirror'* reported on 23rd February 1955, that Air Ministry intelligence officers were investigating a report that on the previous Sunday Flight Lt. James Salandin, a RAF fighter pilot, claimed that his Meteor jet had been 'buzzed' by a flying saucer. He was flying at 10,000ft, in a clear sky, near Southend, when he saw a metal 'thing', like two ordinary saucers, laced together with a bun-shaped bubble on top, and another underneath.

At first he thought it was a meteor, but as it passed him, he estimated its speed at 1,200mph. Suddenly, there was a second one in front of his plane, completely filling the windscreen. He said that it flew straight at him before turning away to his port side.

There are some inconsistencies regarding the date of this event. In 1958, the matter of UFO secrecy was raised in the British House of Commons by Roy Mason MP, who quoted the date of the 'Saladin' incident as being 14th October 1954.

On 13/14th August 1956, at East Anglia's Lakenheath Airbase in Britain, USAF and RAF army radar detected over twelve white lights darting across the sky at incredible speeds of up to 4,000mph. They covered a distance of more than fifty miles, sometimes in formation, and executing sharp turns. One object was tracked for twenty-six miles before hovering for five minutes then flying away again.

Two RAF Venom fighters gave chase, and when one obtained a radar gunlock on the target, it circled the fighter's tail, and remained there despite all attempts to shake it off. Another aircraft captain and co-pilot reported seeing a round object 'tail-chasing' a fighter plane. When the fighters landed to refuel, the UFO headed north, and ground staff reported seeing one or more white rapidly moving objects.

It was officially 'unidentified' and the following observation made; - 'The apparently rational behaviour of the object suggests a mechanical device of unknown origin'. The same night Bentwaters Radar Station, some 35 miles to the northwest of Lakenheath, made three observations at 10pm, about the same time as the Lakenheath incident. They said one object raced across the screen at over 15,000km per hour. Next fifteen objects, led by three more in triangular formation, moved north-east at 160km per hour, followed soon after by another UFO travelling west at 20,000km per hour. Some of them made right-angle turns at incredible speeds and would stop and start with amazing rapidity.

A cable sent from U.S. Air Force Headquarters in Washington warned of their 'considerable interest and concern' at the sightings, and demanded an immediate inquiry. The cable asked if they were linked to a similar scare reported by a British radar station, a week later, on the Danish island of Bornholm in the Baltic Sea.

In a later 'Condon Committee Report', issued by the University of Colorado UFO Study Group, the 'Bentwaters-Lakenheath' case was characterised as *'the most puzzling and unusual case in the radar-visual files.....The apparently rational, intelligent behaviour of the UFO suggests a mechanical device of unknown origin as the most probable explanation of this sighting.'*

This incident was of more importance than most people realised, and the late Dr. James McDonald researched it at length, publishing a nine page analysis in the March/April 1970 issue of the *'Flying Saucer Review'*.

Allen Hynek, who was still contracted by the U.S. government, also considered it important enough to include in the U.S. 'Project Blue Book'. He concluded; *'It seems highly unlikely, for instance, that the Perseid meteors could have been the cause of the sightings, especially in view of the statement of observers that shooting stars were exceptionally numerous that evening, thus implying that they were able to distinguish the two phenomena. Further, if any credence can be given to the manoeuvres of the objects as sighted visually and by radar, the meteor hypothesis must be ruled out.'*

In later years, researcher David Clark, in collaboration with Graham Birdsall, considered that the incident was treated so seriously by the military that it sparked a Cold War security scare. Apparently, the Lakenheath Base played host to the new super-sensitive American U-2 spy planes, and also provided storage facilities for atomic bombs!

Clark said; "I am a UFO sceptic, but this incident has me baffled. It is just possible that some form of Soviet spy craft was responsible, but difficult to match any of their planes to what was observed at that time."

Graham Birdsall added; "I am absolutely convinced that there were breaches of out airspace by some extraordinary flying machines."

On 4th April 1957, Wing Commander Walter Whitworth was the Commanding Officer at RAF West Freugh. Five objects were detected on radar at both Balscalloch and Stranraer. They were very real, and one gave off an echo similar to a ship, rather than a plane. Four were in a line, while the other hovered at fifty thousand feet before ascending to sixty-seven thousand feet within a minute, then quickly descending to fifteen thousand feet, with a trajectory containing a forty-five degree turn and moving off. Whitworth said at the speed the object was going, no plane could turn that fast.

He had copies of letters and newspaper articles from the time, but when he tried to get further details in 1971, the MOD said they had no records prior to 1962.

A disconcerting situation occurred at a Royal Air Force base in Kent, England, a few weeks later, on 20th May 1957. An unidentified object had been detected in British airspace, and as it was suspected to be Russian, and possibly hostile, pilots were ordered to take off and investigate, with their weapons armed and ready to fire.

Lt. Milton Torres did not speak out for fifty years until the information was released by Britain's National Archives. Torres said that he climbed into his Sabre jet and headed east towards where the blip on his radar indicated an object about the size of a B-52 bomber, about 24km away. He set his course, with rockets at the ready, to catch it.

He was convinced that the object was alien, as it was travelling at speeds, and performing manoeuvres beyond the capability of any known aircraft at the time. Just after he asked for, and received, authentication of the order to fire the 24 rockets he was carrying, the 'blip' disappeared off all the radar screens.

Torres said that the next day he was visited by an American, in a trench coat, who waved a National Security Agency card, and warned him that if he ever revealed what had happened, he would never fly again.

In 1984, a MUFON investigator interviewed her co-worker, Valerie Wilcox's friend, who had been serving as a Lieutenant with the Royal Navy in 1963. In the late February of that year, he was on board a frigate, part of the Royal Navy's North Atlantic Fleet, during a three day exercise off the coast of Norway. Due to the 'Secrecy Act', he was breaking the law by speaking out, and his name had to be kept confidential.

When he was in charge of the early morning shift in the radar room, they registered a hard, solid object overhead, at an altitude of about 35,000 feet. They judged its size as being approximately that of somewhere between a jet fighter and a '707'. They could not see the object visually, but a sister ship's radar had also detected it.

The flotilla commenced extensive 'Z' evasive manoeuvres, but the strange object followed them, still remaining at its original altitude. Attempted radio contact was unsuccessful. Within minutes, jet fighters took to the sky, but they were unable to intercept the object, which performed, at an incredible speed, a steep descent, and crossed over their ship's bow, before vanishing below their radar horizon. They were unable to determine if the object had entered the water, but it was a possibility.

At about lunchtime, all of the radar personnel were woken up and interviewed by their senior officer and the Captain, who reminded them of the Official Secrets Act. They were instructed not to discuss the matter with anyone, and later that day their radar log had been replaced by a new book.

Many researchers, including Tony Dodd and Graham Birdsall, have documented the following incidents. By 1970, the Cold War had grown very frosty indeed, with Russian aircraft, ships and submarines making sorties into the North Atlantic to test the response by NATO forces. The Western Alliance were concerned about the incidence of unexplained craft and objects in the skies over the North Atlantic, and commenced a secret exercise, *'Operation Aeneid'*, to ascertain the extent, nature and origin of the mystery.

This involved the RAF, USAF, members of the Royal Observer Corps., and the establishment of secret observation centres around Great Britain, including at least four in Lincolnshire. These were manned throughout the Autumn, Winter and Spring, from September 1970 to March 1971.

There were several incidents recorded, including a huge object, about 180ft long, accompanied by numerous 'glass balls', seen in broad daylight, over the Lincolnshire coast. The objects spent several hours hovering over the bombing range at Donna Nook, in full view of several airmen, before vanishing at high speed over the North Sea. In another incident, two fighter planes, ordered to intercept a UFO over the North Sea, found themselves confronted by a strange, unknown craft.

At 8.17pm on the night of 8th September 1970, a radar operator at Saxa Vord picked up an unidentified object between the Shetland Islands and Norway. It was monitored for several minutes, heading south-west, at 630mph and an altitude of 37,000ft. Its speed then increased to 900mph as it made a thirty degree turn, and sped to the south, increasing in altitude to 44,000ft.

Two Lightning interceptors took off from RAF Leuchars, on the east coast of Scotland. *'What had hitherto been a normal 'scramble', a procedure familiar to all NATO pilots and crew in intercepting their Soviet counterparts, quite unexpectedly, took on a new dimension.*

'The contact, which had been travelling at speeds consistent with Soviet aircraft, to the amazement of radar operators at RAF Leuchars, suddenly turned through 180 degrees, and within seconds had disappeared from their screens. It was later calculated that this manoeuvre involved speeds of 17,400mph.

'Two U.S. Air Force F-4 Phantoms were scrambled from their base in Keflavic, Iceland, and before long had once again 'locked on' to the intruder. For the next hour, the contact came and left radar screens on the ground, and in the air.'

Four Lightning aircraft continued the pursuit and attempted to get close to the object, but every time they narrowed the distance, it would quickly disappear off their radar screens. Radar operators then detected it heading southwest, off the northern coast of Denmark, at an altitude of 18,000ft and a constant speed of 1,300mph. By this time, NATO commanders were so concerned that they issued an alert to all Ballistic Missile Early Warning System establishments, and facilities in the U.S. started monitoring the situation. Strategic Air Command HQ at Omaha, Nebraska, then ordered its B-52 bombers to take to the air.

RAF Binbrook, along with other east coast airfields, was designated a 'Quick Reaction Alert' facility, to provide cover in case any unknown craft appeared on radar. As a result, many U.S. airmen were stationed in Britain. One such officer was Capt. William Schaffner, who was an experienced pilot, having served in Vietnam, and was on his second tour of duty as an exchange pilot with the RAF. He was stationed, along with his wife, at RAF Binbrook, near Grimsby, in North Lincolnshire.

At 9.45pm, RAF Strike Command ordered him to join in the pursuit. By 10.06pm he was airborne in a Lightning plane – 'Foxtrot 94' – and quickly headed out-to-sea to join the four other Lightnings, three refuelling tankers, two Phantoms and an RAF Shackelton MK3– all in pursuit of the intruder.

By now, the object was just 90 miles east of Whitby, moving parallel to the English coastline, at a speed of 530mph and an altitude of 6,100ft. Soon Schaffner radioed visual contact, and that he was alongside a conical shape object, emitting an extremely bright bluish light.

When the radar controller at Staxton Wold asked how close he was to the craft, Schaffner replied; *"About 400ft...he's still in my three o'clock. Hey, wait....there's something else. It's like a large soccer ball....It's like it's made of glass."*

Later, after descending to keep the object in view, Staxton asked Schaffner if the 'ball' object was still there; *"Affirmative,"* he said. *"It's not actually connected...maybe a magnetic attraction to the conical shape. There's a haze of light...Ye'ow...it's within that haze. Wait a second...It's turning...coming straight for me...s**t...I'm taking evasive action...a few...I can hardly.."* At this point, the two blips that represented Capt. Schaffner's aircraft and the UFO merged into one on the radar screen.

'From 500mph, the blip suddenly became stationary, 6,000 feet above the North Sea. Two and a half minutes after the blip came to a sudden halt, it started to accelerate rapidly to 600mph, climbing to 9,000ft and headed towards Staxton. Shortly afterwards, the single blip separated into two. One maintained a southerly erratic heading, close to 600mph, and the other turned through 180 degrees, and headed out to the northwest – vanishing at a speed calculated to be around 20,400mph.'

Suddenly, the radio at Staxton crackled, and Schaffner re-established contact. He sounded confused and said he felt dizzy, and his compass and directional instruments were 'u/s'. When asked if he could ditch the aircraft, he said it was 'handling fine' and he could bring it in.

Then, for some unknown reason, on the instructions of Strike Command HQ at High Wycombe, Staxton replied; *"Negative 94. I repeat, can you ditch the aircraft – Over."* Schaffner's last words, before his craft plunged into the sea were; *"Yeah...I guess."*

Another pilot saw Schaffner's plane plunge into the water, and reported it had remained in one piece, and although there was no sign of Schaffner, nor of flares or distress beacons, they had seen the canopy open and then close, before 'Foxtrot 94' slowly sank to the ocean floor.

A short time later, lifeboats and fishing trawlers arrived, but there was no sign of the pilot, and the plane had clearly sunk. (This is where the case gets bizarre – and one must ask why Schaffner's commanding officers wanted him to ditch the plane rather than flying it back to base, as he had suggested.)

'On 7th October, Navy divers from HMS Kiddleston inspected the wreckage, and reported that Capt. Schaffner's body was still strapped in the cockpit. Yet when the aircraft was brought back, in some secrecy, to RAF Binbrook, there was no trace of Capt. Schaffner, and the cockpit was empty.

'Aircraft wreckage from previous disasters off the east coast had always been brought back ashore to Grimsby, and taken to the RAF investigation branch at Farnborough – but this did not happen. Instead, Farnborough's investigators

were dispatched to RAF Binbrook, where the wreckage was kept under 'shrouds' and armed guards mounted around it.

'They were amazed to discover that many of the cockpit's instruments were missing. These included the E2B compass, voltmeter, stand-by direction indicator, and the complete auxiliary warning panel from the starboard side of the cockpit, below the voltmeter. This was a serious breach of regulations, and although the investigation team were told the instruments would be returned shortly, they never were.'

'The ejector seat was 'wrong', and there was a suspicion among them that it was not the original one fitted to the aircraft when it had taken off for the last time with Capt. Schaffner strapped in. There were many contradictions, and when the Farnborough team were eventually allowed to examine the aircraft at length, they were constantly supervised by five civilians, two of whom were Americans.'

The Farnborough investigators were dismissed from Binbrook soon after, later claiming this was due to 'national security', and they were to discuss the incident with no-one, not even their own families.

In early 1992, after Pat Otter, the editor of the *'Grimsby Evening Telegraph'*, wrote a lengthy article about the incident, he was contacted by Mike Streten, who had been a Squadron Leader flying out of Leuchars on that night. He said; *"I remember the reports on the aircraft well. The aircraft was effectively in one piece. What was very unusual, however, was that the canopy was still attached to the aircraft, and all the ejector seat straps and the seat dinghy were still in the aircraft. There was no trace of the pilot whatsoever."*

Most people who were fully aware of all the facts surrounding this case, dismissed the Air Force explanation of 'pilot error'.

Even by 1967, along with their American counterparts, the British military had 'clamped-up' on any information regarding UFOs. Many years later, John Artie spoke out about some incidents which occurred over RAF Welford, a base in

Berkshire, which, at the time, was primarily used by joint U.K./American forces to store munitions.

During 1967, there were several occasions when unidentified lights were seen hovering or moving high in the sky above the base. On 6th December, an orange circular disc, with erratic blinking lights on top, was seen. It was hovering at tree-top level, and when security personnel approached in their vehicle, it rose straight up and rapidly gained altitude.

CHAPTER EIGHT

UFO OCCUPANTS

During the 'Good Old Days', UFO occupants were usually described as being 'human' in appearance. Whilst most were 'Caucasian looking', others had more Asiatic features, and a few were dark skinned.

Our fast developing aerospace industry and military, would have much preferred the public to regard their top secret prototypes as being some form of alien craft. One must remember that our own military was also composed of servicemen from several racial backgrounds, and we don't know if the crew of our experimental craft were told, due to the necessary secrecy of their mission, to pretend that they were extraterrestrials. I can only present the facts, and leave it up to the reader to form their own opinion.

The *'Italian ' Settimana Incom'* detailed a Bologna event from December 1962, when, at 8.15pm, Antonio Candau was walking near a park, when he heard a hissing sound and saw, beyond some railings, a saucer-shaped object, with multi-coloured lights rotating around its dome, hovering some metres above the ground. It was about nine metres in diameter, metallic-grey in colour, with no visible portholes or appendages.

Antonio hid behind a tree, and the disc dropped lower until it was only a metre above the ground, and about ten metres away. A door opened, a 'stairway' descended, and two beings came down to the ground.

They were human looking, 1.7 metres tall, had **dark complexions**, and short, dark hair. They were wearing close-fitting yellow overalls with a dark belt, and small rectangular box at their side. Just afterwards, Antonio moved, and the occupants noticed him. One pointed his stretched arm and fore-finger in his direction, and said something unintelligible.

The two beings looked at each other, then turned back to their craft and climbed the stairs, closing the door behind them. The disc made another hissing noise, and rose 50-100 metres into the air before moving horizontally towards the south-west and disappearing.

The 1965 'GEPA' bulletin, *'Phénomènes Spatiaux'* received a report from Richard Gooch of Lynchburg, Virginia, U.S.A.; *'About the middle of January*

1963, a witness, who does not wish his name to be revealed, was cutting timber, (in Virginia), when between 5.40pm to 6,15pm he saw two UFOs standing on the ground. There was no sound or light from either of them. One was about 250 feet in diameter, and the other about 65 feet in diameter.

*'From the smaller craft, which seemed to be of glass or some very brilliant metal, three beings emerged. They were **dark coloured**, but their clothing was the same colour as their craft. They approached to a point only about twelve yards from the witness. Their appearance was very human, although one of them had very long fingers. Their regard was penetrating, and they emitted unintelligible sounds.*

'After a moment or so, they turned to re-enter their craft. A door opened, and closed again after they entered, becoming quite invisible, and seemingly merging with the wall of the craft. The machine then took off and vanished, and as it rose from the ground, the interior became lit up.'

The letter, unfortunately, did not mention whether the larger disc left at the same time.

What about the events which may have been a sighting of one of our own prototypes? I don't know. It is up to the reader to exercise their own judgement.

On several occasions, during the 1950s and 1960s, 'Caucasian' appearing pilots were only seen inside the 'cockpits' of their unusual craft.

In the late Spring of 1954, in Norco, California, Mrs. J., along with her husband and daughter, were sitting down to lunch, when they heard an unusual noise outside. They went to the backdoor, to see a strange craft which passed overhead, and hovered above a tree, about fifteen feet away, in the backyard.

It was an aluminium colour, approximately twenty feet long and ten feet across, with no wings or appendages, but a transparent dome on the top. Mrs. J. could see five men, sitting inside the dome, in a semi-circular position, and facing outwards, in her direction. They were wearing neutral coloured uniforms and helmets, and had rather long faces, with dull, olive coloured skin, and dark hair and eyes.

The occupants leaned forward, and for at least a minute, stared directly at a flabbergasted Mrs. J. and her young daughter. They then leaned back, and the craft slowly took off and headed towards the north-east before being obscured in the hazy sky.

At no time did Mrs. J. think this was an alien encounter, and always believed that the strange craft was some form of earthly prototype.

On the afternoon of 24th October, 1954, in Renton, Shrewsbury, an isolated farming area on the Welsh/English border, Mrs. Jennie Roestenberg, was called outside by her two young sons. They were obviously scared, and shouting that there was a "flying saucer on the roof".

She didn't believe them, but at their insistence, went outside to see a strange disc-shaped craft hovering low over their home. The bottom half rotated, whilst through the transparent top, which remained motionless, they could see two men who were wearing turquoise – blue 'ski-suits'. They appeared to be Caucasian, had shoulder length 'flaxen' hair, and except for higher than normal foreheads, they both looked quite human.

As Jennie and the kids stared upwards, the two occupants looked back down on them, possibly concerned about their reaction. After a few seconds, as the disc spiralled upwards and away, Jennie and the kids fled inside and hid under the table.

Early one evening in October 1968, in Lakeland, Florida, Mr. and Mrs. W. McMullin, along with three other witnesses saw a strange object heading across the sky towards their home. It stopped, about 150 feet away from the house, and hovered seven feet above a palm tree.

The UFO was disc-shaped, approximately thirteen feet in diameter and eight feet high. Through the transparent dome, they could see two occupants, dressed in tight white outfits with 'headgear'.

A few minutes before the UFO was sighted, and whilst it was hovering, their TV experienced audio and visual interference, and when it was visible, their dog became very agitated, and knocked a hole in the screen porch, as if trying to get away. Everyone could smell something like ammonia, which burned their noses and eyes.

Only a few weeks later, on November 1st 1968, three separate reports were received from within the vicinity of the Philippines Communications Satellite ground station, inside a Rizal Province valley. All the witnesses reported a white, low-slung, saucer-shaped vehicle which had landed and then taken off. The two occupants – one about six feet tall - were said to be 'Caucasian-looking', and wearing white flying suits and glass-like or plastic headgear.

In Canada, at the Cowichan District Hospital, Nurse Kendall was looking out of the window one night in January 1970. She was startled to see a strange craft, hovering outside, and called her colleagues over. It was disc-shaped, with flashing lights around and a transparent dome on top.

The object tilted towards her, and through the dome she could see two 'very human looking creatures'. They both wore dark clothes, but their faces were concealed by some type of helmet. They seemed to be facing a kind of control panel, and when one of them moved what appeared to be a control stick, the craft tilted even more.

The sighting didn't last for long. After circling five or six times, the strange craft took off and quickly disappeared from sight.

There were other cases when the occupants emerged from their strange craft. Investigator Prof. A. Gerevard reported that on the morning of July 30th 1947, José Higgins was, along with several indigenous workers, measuring a piece of land at Colonia Goio-Bang in Brazil.

When a 'huge metallic basin' descended from the sky and landed nearby, the workers ran away and José hid behind a rock. Three very tall men, wearing 'aluminium-like' clothes, came out via some form of escalator. One appeared to be 'keeping watch' whilst the other two seemed to be amusing themselves by tossing some large rocks around.

When they noticed José they came closer, and started talking in a strange language, that sounded like 'barking'. They then drew circles on the ground, which somewhat resembled a solar system, and pointed to one of the concentric circles, as if to indicate that was where they had come from.

After that, they gestured to José, who thought that they were insisting he should go with them. In desperation, he pulled out his wallet, and showed them a photograph of his wife and children, indicating that he should also bring them. They seemed to agree signifying that they would wait whilst he went to collect them.

Of course, José had no intention of doing any such thing. He went a short distance before stopping at a hidden vantage point. After a while, the beings seemed to lose patience, and boarded their craft which took off back into the sky.

Another Brazilian incident, ten years later, in 1957, has me doubting that the 'visitors' were anything but human.

A Campinas newspaper reported that in the May of that year a farmer and two workers saw a saucer landing on his farm. The witnesses took cover in a trench, and watched. The craft was a silver-gold colour, and resting on three chromium, mirror-like landing balls. On its convex ring-formed mid-portion were three cupulas, that formed an 'S' shape.

Three men, each about 1.6 metres in height, and wearing 'tights', came out and jumped onto the ground. They took some form of instrument - 0.4m long and 0.3m wide – and disappeared into the forest. The farmer said that they seemed to 'glide' rather than walk.

They were gone for three hours, during which time the farmer sneaked over to the strange craft, and looked underneath it. Through an opening on the central part of the underside, he could see 'part of the machinery, which looked like a translucent disc with more than twenty openings in it'.

The farmer went back into hiding, and when the 'beings' returned to their craft, he was able to observe that they looked quite human. They were carrying their 'instrument', which now appeared to be much heavier than before. After they had taken off, it was discovered that several items, including a camera, shotgun and some canned food, were missing from the farmer's home.

At 10.45pm on September 21st 1954, at Santa Maria Airport in the Azores, civilian guard, Victorino Monteiro, heard a humming or whirring sound, and saw a strange object land approximately thirty feet away from his guard post. It was oblong, or 'pear-shaped', of a light metallic blue colour, and about ten feet in length and eight feet in height. There was an orange light at its nose, and a bit further back a plexiglass-type section, also blue in colour, which housed the pilot. There were four pole-like appendages, two at each end, which supported parallel aerials.

A blond-haired man, about 5'10" tall, got out, walked over to the bewildered guard, and said something in an unknown language. Monteiro tried, without success, to converse in French, which the visitor obviously could not understand.

Monteiro was a little too scared to think of arresting the intruder, and when the lights of an oncoming vehicle appeared down the road, the stranger patted him on the back of his shoulder, 'in a friendly fashion', and got back into his 'flying cigar'. After fastening on a safety belt and some shoulder straps, the pilot pushed a button, and the nose-cone tilted up, and travelled a few feet before the craft levelled off and shot straight up into the sky.

Investigators noted that other strange lights had been reported in the Santa Maria sky that night.

As the years went on, so did the possibilities. One interesting case from 'Project Blue Book' occurred near Temple, Oklahoma, on 23rd March 1966.

The witness was driving along the road when he encountered a strange object, landed in the middle of the road, and blocking his way. It was seventy-five feet long, twelve feet high and nearly eight feet from top to bottom, much like a conventional plane, except it had no wings, wheels or visible engine. It had a smooth surface, 'bubble' canopy, very bright lights fore and aft, and was resting on some form of support.

As the witness got out of his car, and walked towards the unusual vehicle, he saw a normal looking man, wearing a baseball cap, and coveralls or a two piece suit that looked like green–coloured fatigues. The 'man' then entered a lit open doorway in the object, via metal steps from underneath. There was an unusual noise, and the craft rose vertically from the ground, and once attaining altitude, sped away to the southeast at an incredible speed.

The witness, who was subjected to intensive questioning by the military, did not consider the craft to be extraterrestrial, and thought it may have been an Army or Air Force experimental aircraft – but what was it doing parked on a public road? The main question is whether we had any such similar craft of our own? 'Blue Book's' analysis indicates that we very possibly did!

*'Various organisations were contacted around the Temple area to identify a possible (new) experimental or conventional aircraft. All attempts at such an explanation proved fruitless, since there were no aircraft in the area at the time of the sighting. Although there are numerous helicopters and **other experimental aircraft** in the area, none could be put in the area of Temple at approximately 0500 23rd March 1966.'*

Where extraterrestrials were concerned, one would expect a sophisticated craft, designed by a superior, advanced technology, to be smooth and seamless, with no appendages, windows or exhaust and probably silent, like many of the objects reported over the years.

Something of local origin, although it may appear unusual, would more likely be slightly 'primitive', and certainly not as exceptionally large, by comparison. It may have appendages, individual panels or rivets, and perhaps windows and legs to rest upon when grounded. There would possibly be a type of exhaust flame or gasses, and some form of engine noise which could indicate a more advanced propulsion. Often, our own craft would leave physical traces and occasional residual radioactivity. Certainly, many of the objects reported displayed these characteristics.

Another particular case, which I think may have involved one of our own prototypes, occurred in 1965, near Buenos Aires in Argentina. Ramón Pereya was driving his van along the road, when he saw an object descend from the sky, and land behind some trees on a hillside.

When Pereya went over to see what it was, he discovered a chrome-coloured, egg-shaped craft, standing on metal legs in a clearing. The lower half was extremely smooth, with no apparent joints or seams, and its top part was transparent, through which he could see a man seated at an instrumental panel.

A second, young blond haired man, wearing a plastic diver's suit, and small boots, was standing beside the craft. A sort of briefcase was attached to his right leg, and he appeared to be studying a piece of paper. As soon as he noticed Pereya, who asked what was going on, the stranger developed and angry expression and stepped back into the craft, which immediately took off. Would a technically advanced alien have a briefcase, and be studying a piece of paper, possibly a map?

In so far as flying saucer occupants 'losing their way', another interesting case occurred, over ten years earlier, in Vosges, France, at 2.30am one morning in 1954.

Researcher, Jacques Vallee, wrote of when Lazlo Ujavri, a Czechoslovakian citizen living in France, was heading to work. He encountered a rather portly man, who was carrying a gun, wearing a grey jacket with some form of insignia, and had what appeared to be a motor-bike helmet on his head. He apparently appeared totally human, except for a strange high-pitched voice when he spoke.

At first, the stranger addressed Lazlo in an unknown language. When Lazlo responded in Russian, the fellow answered immediately – "Where am I? In Italy, or Spain?"

Next, he wanted to know what time it was, and how far was he from the German Border? When Lazlo said it was 2.30am, the man pulled out a watch and said; "You lie – it is four o'clock!" He then inquired about the direction of, and distance to, Marseilles.

As they walked together down the road, Lazlo didn't suspect anything unusual until they came across a grey saucer-shape craft on the road. It was about five feet wide and three feet high, with an antenna on top. When they were about thirty feet away, the man told Lazlo to move away before he and the object flew off.

Jaques Vallee also told of another French incident at Dordongne, on October 4th 1954. Monsieur Garreau was astounded when a cauldron-shaped object, about the size of a small truck, landed in his field.

A door opened, and two normal looking European men, in brown coveralls, got out. They politely shook hands with Garreau and asked; "Paris? North?" Garrau was so taken aback that he didn't even answer. He said the strangers stopped to pat his dog before getting back into their craft and flying off.

British researcher, Charles Bowen, discussed an Argentinean incident which was reported in the *'Diario de Córdoba'* newspaper on 1st May 1957, and translated by his colleague Gordon Creighton.

One day in April, a resident was riding his motorbike towards Rio Caballos, and at about 7.30 am, when he was about fifteen kilometres from the International Airport at Pajas Blancas, his engine stopped.   Upon dismounting, he immediately noticed a large, disc-shaped object hovering fifty feet above the road.   It was sixty feet in diameter and more than fifteen feet high, with an indistinct bluish-green metallic colour.   For a few moments it remained stationary, before descending to about only seven feet above the road, where it remained motionless.

The terrified witness ran and hid in a roadside ditch, and watched whilst a transparent 'stairway' descended from the craft, and a human-looking occupant emerged.   After briefly looking around, he made his way over towards the witness, who was frantically trying to dig a hole in the side of the ditch to better hide himself.

'The Space Man – if that is what he was – was about 5 ft. 8 ins. tall, and wore clothing like a divers suit, fitting the body closely, and appearing to be made of plastic rather than cloth.

'The Spaceman said nothing, but gracefully reached out his hand to help the fear-crazed human from the ditch.   Then, when they stood side-by-side on the road, the being pointed expressively towards the hovering craft, and tried to make the man understand by signs that he should follow him without fear.

'Encountering only resistance, he turned and very gently stroked the man's forehead to calm him, and again pointed to the machine. This action must have had the required affect, for the Córdoban overcame his panic, and entered the lift device. This rose slowly until it came to rest in a large cabin inside the craft.

'Around the wall of the cabin were five or six panels, each about six feet wide, and covered by an intricate mass of equipment, including screens, (like those on oscilloscopes?). At each of the panels, a being was seated. Everyone of them was dressed precisely like the Earthman's guide. They paid no attention whatsoever to their surprised visitor.'

Although he had seen no windows on the exterior of the craft, there was light coming through large square windows on the walls above the panels. In addition, although no source could be seen, a phosphorescent type of light also pervaded the cabin. At one stage, he asked, by sign language, how the craft remained suspended, and he didn't understand the being's reply, which was to pass the palm of one hand over the other.

His 'tour' ended when he was invited to enter the lift once more, and once he was back on the ground, his host returned with him to his motor-bike, and indicated that it would not start up until after they left.

'At last the visitor turned to the man, and placed his hand on his shoulder, presumably in a gesture of farewell, and re-entered the lift, which then slowly disappeared into the craft. There was a short delay before the craft rose swiftly to some 2,500 feet and sped off to the northwest.

'A UFO, presumably this same machine, was reported over Cordoba at 8.45 am, and over Pampa del Pocho at 8.47 am. At 9.30 there was a sighting at Pilar, and later came some reports from Calamuchita and San Francisco Chanar. The final report that morning came from Arguello at 10am.'

Although this event occurred in 1957, we must ask that, even in those early days, could this craft and its occupants have been one of our own prototypes?

In so far as clothing is concerned, there was plenty of opportunity to be deceptive, something both the 'visitors' and our own people were very capable of. Whilst 'aliens' wore strange uniforms, and our own aircraft maintenance and other personnel tended towards overalls, there was nothing to stop one of them dressing to impersonate the other, however one must remember that long hair on men was not the 'normal' in those days, especially not for those in the military!

Long before World War II there were cases of strange craft with human-type occupants. Some of these incidents I have described in Chapters about *'Encounters'* and *'Experiencers'*, and in more detail in my previous books.

One lesser known incident occurred in Munico, Spain in the summer of 1938. Researcher Scott Coralles discussed this in his article, *'The Saucers of*

Wartime'. (The original report was written up in J. Benitez's book *'La Punta del Iceberg'*.)

Mariano Meigar was just a boy at the time, and it was his responsibility to watch over the cows who roamed freely over a pasture on his family's property. He wandered over to a stream, and as he was sitting under the shade of a few trees, he saw a silver flash as a strange object descended from the sky and landed about 'thirty paces away'.

As Mariano hid behind the trees, he could see that the 'craft', which was resting on three or four legs, was 'round, surmounted by a dome, and measured some sixteen to nineteen feet in diameter.' Around it were coloured lights, constantly flashing on and off.

Suddenly, the buzzing and humming noise ceased, and a door, similar to one on a 'modern airplane', opened, and as three figures descended, he could see the interior was full of strange devices. Two of the 'crew' walked away, and appeared to be collecting soil and vegetation samples, whilst the third was seemingly standing guard at the craft's entrance.

Mariano was intensely curious, and he emerged from his 'cover' to creep closer. He had only managed to move a few metres forward, when the 'guard' spotted him and fired a 'bolt of light' in Mariano's direction, nearly knocking him down. The boy retreated back to the trees, only to be repelled again, by another volley of 'shots', when he made a second attempt to get closer.

After about fifteen minutes, the 'visitors' appeared to have completed their task, and returned to the craft. Before re-entering, the sentry waved at Mariano, as if saying 'goodbye', before the object lifted off, spinning on its axis, and headed, at an altitude of between fifty to one hundred metres, towards the village of Barco de Avila.

At the time, due to the Spanish Civil War, Mariano thought this must have been one of 'Generalissimo's Franco's aircraft', and it was only in later years he realised that this could not have been the case.

Scott Corrales detailed another incident, investigated by Manuel Carballal, which occurred the same summer, on 25th July 1938. It was just five months after the siege of Granada, when two Spanish officers were startled by a blinding light.

'As the light dimmed, the military men were surprised to see a disc-shaped object, measuring approximately eleven metres in diameter, at an estimated distance of sixty metres away. The object appeared to possess a sort of 'column' containing two humanoid figures that gradually descended from its underbelly.

'The unknown object then started to project a circle of blue light on the ground, which expanded its circumference until it reached the onlookers, who felt a sensation of intense cold. The light dimmed, and the column was fully retracted into the object, its two separate 'halves' rotating in opposite directions as the powerful white light appeared again, and the craft vanished into the sky at considerable speed.'

Obviously, the 'visitors' did not want any witnesses to their proposed actions or intentions!

Sven-Olof Fredrickson of the Swedish 'Göteborg Information Centre on UFOs' wrote of an interesting incident which occurred in Angelholm, southern Sweden, in May 1946, just after the end of World War II. (Two months before the first appearance of the famous 'ghost rockets' over Sweden and northern Europe.)

Gösta Carlsson, a respected industrialist and member of society, was out for his evening walk, where he was looking for pollen for his bees. When started back for his house, it was getting dark, and he turned on his forehead lamp.

He noticed that there was a light coming from behind the trees in a nearby forest, and worried that someone had started a fire, he went to investigate.

"When I reached the place, however, I saw that in the farthest end of the open ground there was a disc-shaped object with a cupola, which seemed to be a cabin with oval windows. Above it there was a mast, almost like the periscope of a submarine. Beneath the disc there was an oblong fin, which stretched from the centre to the edge of the underside. There were two metal landing legs. A small ladder reached to the ground from a door beside the fin.

"The object was approximately sixteen feet in diameter, and four metres from top to bottom at the middle....There were a lot of holes around the edge of the disc, like those of a turbine, and it was from these that jet-beams came which

burned the grass when the object departed. The light came from the mast, which was about five metres in height, and three antennae were suspended from its top. Lower down, something like a lampshade was hanging."

It was shining with a strange purple light, flowing and pulsating like water from a fountain, which covered not only the whole object, but also the ground a couple of metres beyond it, where it had a 'sparkling' effect.

Just beyond the light, as if 'standing guard', was a man, who raised his hand in a motion for Carlsson to halt, which he did. From a distance of ten metres, Carlsson could see the fellow was about the same height as he was, fairly slim, and wearing white, close-fitting overalls.

"There were others like him, but the strange thing was, nobody said a word. It seemed as if they had just finished repairing a window, because they put their tools away and looked at me. Everything was silent. The only thing I heard was the sound of the guard when he walked on the grass......It seemed as if the 'cheese-dish' cover of light stood like a wall between us. I think it was created to isolate them from our world and atmosphere.

"There were three men working at the window, and two more were standing alongside. There were three women as well, and one more came out of the object later. On the far side was another guard. In all, I saw eleven persons. They wore short black boots and gloves, a black belt around the waist, and a transparent helmet. The women had ashen coloured hair, but I could not see the hair of the men as they wore black caps. They were all brown-coloured, as if sunburned."

He went a few steps closer, and the guard raised his hand again, so Carlsson stood still. He noticed the guard had a chain holding a black box around his neck, which he pointed at him. After hearing a click from his forehead lamp, it didn't work anymore, and he later discovered that the brand new battery was now flat.

One of the women came out of the craft, went to the edge of the light, and after throwing something into the darkness, appeared to laugh. Carlsson was beginning to doubt his own sanity, so he walked back to the seashore, and set off to return to the forest clearing, via a different route, thirty minutes later.

'Before he had time to leave the shore, he suddenly saw a bright red light. With a whining sound, the object slowly rose above the treetops. It went up with a

corona of red lights from the 'turbine holes'. At 400-500 metres its ascent slowed, and it wobbled a little. Suddenly the red light became brighter and turned to purple: the object accelerated at a tremendous speed and disappeared.'

Because Carlsson didn't report the incident until many years later, investigators examined some aerial photos taken at the time. Aerial photos from 1947 showed two circles at the landing spot on the ground, which were not there in 1939.

This incident has me puzzled. If the craft had been one of our own military prototypes, there certainly wouldn't have been any female personnel on board in 1946! Perhaps alien tourists in a less modern craft? We will never know!

Ron Halliday, in his book *'UFO Scotland'*, wrote of an incident in July 1947, when an Edinburgh man, Andrew Cherry, was waiting for an early morning bus to work. Suddenly, he noticed a strange object, hovering about 300 feet up in the sky nearby. It was disc-shaped, of a rough metal texture, twelve to eighteen feet in length, with a huge glass dome, in the style of an observation window. Andrew got a clear view of the 'occupant', who appeared to be 'humanoid', and was wearing dark clothes. It seemed as if he was sitting at or standing beside some sort of control panel.

He could hear a humming noise, and noticed some flames escaping from the disc as it tilted and 'showed tremendous power' before spinning away and disappearing over the coast in a matter of seconds.

Back in the 'Good Old Days', these incidents were occurring all over the world. On March 18th 1950, in Lago Argentina, rancher Wilfredo Arevalo encountered two strange craft, one of which had landed on his property.

It appeared to be made of aluminium, with a transparent cabin, through which he could see several tall men, who were clothed in garments that looked like 'cellophane'. Wilfredo crept to within 450 metres of the object, which was emitting a 'benzene' smelling, blue-green vapour.

One of the crew, who had been 'attending to some instruments', spotted him, and directed a light in his direction. At the same time, a blue light illuminated the craft, the vapour increased, and red and green flames emanated from the underside. There was a humming noise as it rose and joined its companion. Both craft flew off towards Chile.

Later that year, in July 1950, at about 11pm, Claude Blondeau, an ex-pilot, with 1,500 flying hours, both Air Force and commercial, to his credit, was taking a stroll near Guyancourt airfield, about twelve miles from Paris. He suddenly heard a 'whistling' sound, and turned around to see, hovering four or five inches above the ground, about 300ft away; "two perfectly round machines, resembling two enormous reversed deep plates, one beside the other. They were about sixteen feet in diameter, and four-and-a-half feet high in the centre. All round their edges were little oblong windows;

"On each of these 'saucers' a very thick oval door opened, and one man came out of each of them. They were about five-and-a-half feet tall, their hair was definitely brown, and they wore flying suits of dark brown or dark blue."

Blondeau watched as the men ran towards one of the machines, and, with their bare hands, seemed to be adjusting or replacing one of several rods which came from the centre of the disc to the outer edge. Blondeau walked up and asked them if they had suffered a breakdown, and one replied in slow, but perfect French; "Yes, but it will soon be alright".

They then walked back to their respective craft, and Blondeau took the opportunity to peer into one of the open doorways of the circular, strangely lit cabin. He could see a red padded chair, similar to one you would find in a dentist's surgery, and several unusual pieces of equipment and technology. There was also a large metal wheel, covered with signs and switches. When he asked about their purpose, the only answer he got was – "Power".

Blondeau said; "Then the little holes in the edges lit up, and in one second the engine must have noiselessly started, because the two saucers at once stood up, vertically, and in this position disappeared at tremendous speed, like two shooting stars."

Researcher Ted Bloecher wrote of an incident, which occurred in 1952, at Prospect Heights, Illinois, and was later investigated by him, Robert Runser and Dr. Alan Hynek.

Just after 10pm one night, Mrs Ann Sohn, a housewife and former nurse, happened to look out of the window, and was startled to see a bright light shining from the vacant block of land next door. Her husband was at work, and her father and the children in bed, so she pressed her face against the pane to watch from the safety of the house.

Upon a closer look, she observed a round disc-shaped object, about thirty to forty feet in diameter, hovering motionless and silent about 100ft above the ground. There was a dome, which she described as being made of plastic or plexiglass, at the top. A row of about fifteen square windows were along the side, and below them a line or seam, where the top and bottom sections were connected.

Except for the dome, which was pale bluish, and all but three of the windows, which remained dark, the entire craft glowed with a bright white light. Ann thought the dome, which had two faint vertical objects, like 'poles', inside, was being illuminated by the reflected light from the rest of the craft.

There was some form of vapour, drifting slowly underneath, being emitted from one end of the object, however Ann could not see any pipes or openings to account for this.

Three of the windows, at the rear end, were lit from inside by an intense white light. Inside each, Ann could see the upper portions of three 'crewmen', one of whom appeared to be standing motionless, as if studying a panel of dials or instruments on the wall. They were dressed similarly in a kind of 'jumpsuit' or 'coverall' with hoods or headpieces which showed only their faces.

One 'person', visible from another window, *'made a sharp motion with his right hand, as if he were pushing forward some type of lever; as he did this the vapour underneath the UFO increased. Almost at the same moment, he pulled backward with another lever with his left hand, and the colour of the vapour changed from white to green, with flecks of orange, and then to orange, with a few remaining streaks of green.*

'Immediately, following this, the figure in the central window pushed a lever forward with his right hand, and the entire ship, except for the darkened

windows and the dome, turned a brilliant reddish-orange colour, and departed in a shallow climb to the north at an 'intense speed' with no apparent acceleration.'

The wooden painted 'trimming' on that side of Ann's house was blistered, and later, a 25ft diameter circle of dead weeds was found on the vacant lot, and her and the neighbours' plants and trees, on either side, died.

Ann's house was only a few miles away from the NIKE Base, to the west of Prospect Heights, and The Great Lakes Naval Station six miles to the east. In my point of view, even as early as 1952, this entire incident had all the hallmarks of being one of our own prototypes with a totally human crew. We just don't know, and may never know for sure.

Ted Bloecher did not suggest this possible explanation, but in a 1981 article, went one to compare it with two other sighting reports.

In the summer of 1952, Suzanne Knight heard a buzzing sound, and looked out of her kitchen window in Mt. Pleasant, Maryland, a Washington D.C. suburb. She could see an object hovering above a street lamp across the road.

'It was shaped like an airplane fuselage, dull silver in colour, with thin white smoke coming out of the rear end. On a small mast at the front was a small red light. Through a row of large square windows, brilliantly lighted, she could see something like a row of cabinets with slanted tops, and to the left, in the front, a helmeted man looking straight ahead. He never moved a muscle all the while he was in view. No controls or instruments were visible, and he was seen only from the upper chest and shoulders.'

Suzanne left the kitchen to call both her relatives and the local newspaper, and by the time she got back, the man was no longer visible, and the craft began to glow, as if 'red hot', before rocking from side to side. She went to the telephone again, and when she returned, the craft was gone.

Another event, at 5.30am on August 25th, occurred when William Squyres was driving to work at a radio station in Pittsburg, Kansas. Hovering 10ft over a field, at the side of the road, he could see a silver-grey object, similar to two deep platters, placed rim-to-rim.

He stopped and got out of the car to investigate. The object was about 75ft long, with several large windows in the mid-section, through which movement could be seen against a blue light. Through another square window, at the front, he could see the head and shoulders of a man who was staring straight ahead.

The craft then suddenly 'took off', making a strange noise and disappearing vertically in a matter of seconds, with a backlash of wind depressing the grass below. The Air Force determined this case to be 'unexplained' – understandable if this craft was, in fact, 'one of our own'!

Researcher Scott Corrales wrote of another incident; *'UFO-related activity in the Amazon Basin goes back to the early days of the contemporary UFO era. In November 1953, Pedro Serrate was walking along the banks of the Mamoré River in Bolivian Amazonia when he became aware of a discoidal object some hundred and fifty feet away from him. The thing's hull seemed to be made of a dark blue, glassy material.*

'Curious, Serrate got closer to the craft and was able to catch a glimpse of its human-looking crew. When the uniformed humanoids, who were caught off-guard, became aware of Serrate's presence, the whole vehicle rose silently into the air, disappearing in a matter of seconds.'

British expert, Gordon Creighton, told of an incident which occurred in Grande do Sul, Brazil, on November 10th 1954; *'A Porto Alegre agronomist, out for a car ride with his family, saw a landed disc, from which emerged two apparently normal-sized men with long hair and overall-like clothing.*

'They approached the car with their arms above their heads, but the agronomist, urged on by his wife and daughter, accelerated and left the strange men behind. They saw them re-enter the disc, which rose into the sky at a dizzying speed.'

The next month, on the evening of December 9th, Brazilian farmer, Olmiro da Costa e Rosa, was working in his bean and maize field. He heard a sound – 'like a sewing machine' – and noticed the animals in a nearby field were scattering and running away. He looked up to see an unusual object, hovering just over the ground. He said it looked like a cream-coloured 'explorer's hat', and was surrounded by a smoky haze.

He could see three 'men'. They were of medium height, broad-shouldered, with long blond hair, pale skin, and wearing light brown clothing. One was leaning out of the craft and another appeared to be examining a barbed wire fence. The third man approached Olmiro, who was so astonished he dropped his hoe. The being picked up the hoe, handed it back to Olmiro, then made his way back to the craft, uprooting a few plants as he went. When Olmiro took a couple of steps further, the fellow near the fence motioned him to step back. They all boarded their ship, which rose about thirty feet before accelerating and speeding off into the west.

At 5pm, only two days later, less than a mile away, Perdro Morais heard one of his chickens squawking, and raced outside, fearing a hawk was on the attack. Instead, he found a strange object hovering just above the ground. From underneath, the bottom looked like that of an enormous, polished brass kettle.

He could see two 'men' in an adjoining field, and suspecting them of being trespassers, he raced forward. Whilst one of the 'men' raised his arm, in a 'stop' gesture, the other hurried back to the craft, plucking a tobacco plant from the ground as he went.

Before Morais could reach them, all three had re-entered the object which quickly, within seconds, disappeared into the sky.

These events were occurring all over the world, and we can never be sure whether the craft and occupants that were observed were extraterrestrial or involved our own earthly prototypes with human crews. However, one can assume that the earlier a 'sighting' occurred, the less likely it was that the craft and occupants were 'ours'.

Argentinean Professor Oscar Uriondo wrote about this incident which occurred on Route #143 between San Rafael and Mendoza. Early in the morning of 28th December 1954, seven people, one of whom was a history professor and concert pianist, were travelling in a car, intent on reaching the Province's Capital, where they were due to appear on television later that day.

After one of the passengers saw a brilliant light at the side of the road, and thinking it may be a fire of some kind, they pulled up for a better look. In a field, 150-200 metres away, was an object, the size of a 'large omnibus'. It 'had the form of two superimposed deep dishes, united at the edge', and from the equatorial flange, a brilliant bluish light, (similar to that of a welding torch), was being emitted.

The witnesses got out of their car, and started walking through the vineyards towards the strange object. As they drew nearer, and saw two human figures, they hesitated, and then stopped. They appeared to be well-formed men, of medium stature – one standing and one squatting.

They were wearing what looked like 'one-piece divers' suits or overalls, of a dark colour, which had an extension covering the head with a kind of hood, 'like those used by workers in iron foundries.' The witnesses could not make out the men's facial features, as it seemed like they were covered by a 'transparent material'.

The 'man', who was squatting, got up and joined his companion, whereupon both entered the craft through a door, which looked like a dark rectangular opening set into the luminous background of the craft. After the door closed, the object started emitting some form of smoke or steam through its 'equatorial region', and silently, rose vertically about two metres above the ground. Two lights appeared, one above and one below the craft, and they flashed on and off alternatively.

Without taking their eyes off this unusual craft, which was making strange zig-zag movements and abrupt stops in the sky, the witnesses made their way back to their car. As they proceeded along the road, they were startled to realise the object appeared to be following them, first on one side of their vehicle and then on the other or overhead. It was not a hallucination or in their imaginations, as a number of other trucks and cars were stopping, with the occupants getting out to look at the unusual craft.

After safely arriving in Mendoza, the passengers decided, at the time, not to report the incident, for fear people would think it was just a 'publicity stunt'. However, one of the witnesses told a close relative, who eventually 'leaked' the details. When speaking to an investigator later, the witnesses insisted on anonymity, but were all in agreement as to the details of their experience.

'The unanimous opinion of the observers was that they were looking at an aerial machine, not a terrestrial or aquatic one. It gave the feeling of enormous power, with its incredible movements in defiance of gravity and of inertia. The

witnesses at first were not afraid, but only curious. They became alarmed only when the UFO began to follow them.'

In these 'early' days, many times it was just young children and teenagers who witnessed these unusual craft and their occupants.

In my book, *'UFOs Now and Then',* I wrote about a case my colleague, Welsh researcher, Margaret Fry, investigated. In 1955, nine year-old Rae Fountain, attended a boarding school near Leighton Buzzard in Bedfordshire. At about 3.55pm, on 30th June, he was going to play in a school football match. As he walked down the muddy country track, with bushes on either side, he noticed some footprints which were unusual and very close together.

He looked up and saw two odd men ahead. They had closely cropped dark brown hair, were dressed in one piece overalls, and walking with very small foot-strides. He said he started 'stalking them, the way children do, by hiding behind the bushes.' The men were stopping all the time, and seemed to be picking up pebbles and vegetation, which they placed into something in front of them.

Suddenly a 'thing' swished down across the path ahead, and hovered a few feet above the ground. It was roughly a flat 'bell-shape', with a protruding rim just before the rounded top. The nearest Rae could describe the exterior was that it seemed to be a bluish-tinged metallic grey. In fact he had never seen anything that exact colour before.

A door on the top half slid open, a concertina type ladder came down, and the two men climbed in. Rae was close enough to see inside the craft, and noted someone there at 'some sort of wheel or instrument'. The door closed, and the object went straight up and swept across the sky. As it left, the schoolboy could see it had a flat bottom with three 'ball-like' wheels.

Rae didn't remember anything else until he woke-up in the dark with the headmaster shaking him, and several other teachers and pupils looking down as he lay on the ground at the side of the muddy lane. The headmaster was angry, as everybody had been out searching.

They took Rae back to school, and put him to bed. The next morning the headmaster did not believe him, and said the child must have had a bad dream.

Rae knew he had not fallen asleep on the road, but could not account for the missing time.

In my chapter discussing *'Priests and Clergymen'*, I mention the events surrounding Father Gill and the people of New Guinea. However, there were other incidents occurring in the South Pacific.

On 8th October, 1957, two middle-aged Fijian couples were in a punt, with an outboard motor, travelling from Nabouwalu, in south-western Vanua Levu, to Nawaca, eight miles away. As they neared their destination, they spotted a round white object, descending vertically from the sky. Thinking it may be an aircraft in trouble, the witnesses moved towards the object, which was hovering about twenty feet above the sea, and appeared to be revolving over one spot.

'CSINZ' reported; *'As they came closer, they saw what they took to be the figure of a man standing on the outside of the object. The figure shone a very bright light on their boat – a light so bright they were dazzled and weak. When the boat was about five chains from the rotating object, the figure disappeared, and the object then rose in a rapid vertical movement and was soon out of sight.*

'The report emphasises that all four agree on the details. They live in a fairly isolated area, without access to comic books or other literature on flying saucers.'

Preston Dennett researched another 1957 event which was initially documented in Charles Bowen's book, *'The Humanoids'*.

At 5.40am on November 6th, Richard Keyhoe was driving along California's Pacific Coast Highway, at Playa del Ray, when his, and two other motorists', cars stalled. Richard, and the other two drivers, Ronald Burke and Joe Thomas, along with their passengers, all exited their vehicles to stare at a large, tan or cream coloured, 'egg-shaped' object, which had landed on a beach only a few yards away. The craft had two metal rings around it, upon which it appeared to be resting.

'As they watched, two human looking figures, with 'yellowish-green skin', and wearing 'black leather pants', white belts and coloured jerseys, exited the object and began asking questions of the stunned witnesses.

'Keyhoe and the others were unable to understand the occupants, who appeared to be speaking in a foreign language. After a few moments, the figures went back into the craft, which then took off and disappeared.'

Once their car engines had started up again, Joe Thomas reported the incident to local police, from where it was leaked to the media.

Preston Dennett unearthed additional corroborative sightings from that day. A few hours later, at 3.50pm, an Air Force weather detachment, of twelve airmen and their commanding officer, at Long Beach, about fifty miles to the south, saw six saucer-shape objects zoom across the sky.

Again, at 6.05pm and 7.23pm, numerous unidentified objects were seen 'zooming overhead' by personnel at the Los Alamitos Naval Air Station, and the Long Beach police stations were being flooded with calls from concerned citizens.

My friend and colleague, Rosemary Decker, wrote about her car mechanic, 'Gary', who experienced a close encounter in 1957.

One night, when he was motoring a long, open stretch of a Texas highway, a circular, luminous, domed craft, moved rapidly into his startled field of vision and settled down on the road ahead, blocking it completely from shoulder to shoulder.

'He braked; engine power and lights were gone; the car stopped only yards away from the craft. To his great relief, he was not alone more than moments; a police car stopped behind him, disgorging two police officers who came up to his door, asking if he had a working flashlight. None of their electric equipment was working, and of course, neither was Gary's.

'At this point in his report, my friend actually shed tears as he blurted out that there had been people in the craft; "They got out and actually walked around the thing! They saw us...and sort of talked...and we sat there, petrified, 'til they took off in the thing. Nothing's ever going to be the same again, and I haven't

been able to talk to anyone until now. Who would believe me? And who knows what's going on?"

Both he and Rosemary had wanted to compare notes with the two police officers, but two years later they were unable to locate them again. One important factor which Rosemary discovered was that although Gary felt his family had some ESP abilities, his own psychic aptitude had been 'very much augmented' since the night of the close encounter.

British expert, Gordon Creighton, translated an interesting 1957 case from Brazil; *'At 10.30am on November 13th, the peasant farmers, João Ernani and Pedro Zilli, heard a strange hum and then saw, from a distance of 100 metres, two circular, aluminium coloured discs and six medium-sized men, of slim build, and wearing 'dark-grey suits, glued to their bodies', returning to them.*

'The discs, hovering at about a metre or so above the ground, seemed to be about ten feet wide. They rose with a sharp whistling sound, and bent some coconut palm trees almost double. At the same time, three more discs, unseen until then, rose from behind the trees. All five craft headed over the South Atlantic.'

These sightings of strange craft and their occupants, were coming from all over the world. In *'Contact Down Under'*, I wrote about several from New Zealand.

Early in the morning of 13th July 1959, when Eileen Moreland was collecting the cows for milking, an unusual object descended from the sky and hovered above a group of peach trees.

Through a clear, glassy dome-like structure, filled with bright white light, she could see two figures, seated one behind the other. They appeared to be a little over five feet tall, and were dressed in almost skin-tight metallic outfits. She could not determine their facial features as they wore large silver helmets which covered them 'from shoulder to shoulder'.

Eileen thought they were both looking at something, which appeared to be a brightly flickering light source in the cockpit. After a few minutes, the craft tilted slightly, and rose vertically, vanishing into the clouds at tremendous speed.

The cows did not seem to have been affected by the incident, but the peach trees died, and a few days later Eileen's hands and fingers became painfully swollen and puffy. This gradually subsided, but she also developed brown pigmented areas on her face, some of which persisted considerably longer.

There were other incidents in New Zealand, many of which were not reported until many years later. Investigator, Suzane Hanson, related one which had occurred in 1956, on a stud farm near Waipukurau.

The witness, Ann Kebbell, was only eighteen at the time, and one night, in late June, she and her family saw a small silver-grey saucer-shaped object which hovered, about twenty feet up, over the land between their cowshed and a line of pine trees. It was similar to the length of a car in width, and emitted a very bright light, which illuminated the surrounding paddocks.

For the previous six weeks, there had been reports of UFOs in the Hawke's Bay area, but they hadn't expected anything like this. Ann said her family seemed transfixed whilst she was terrified, and jumped around behind her father.

Their grazing sheep seemed unperturbed, but the dogs went berserk, howling and straining on their chains, as if trying to get away. After a few minutes, the craft rose quickly back into the sky, stopped, changed direction, and disappeared in a flash.

Ann's family, although amazed by the incident, did not seem to be affected. Ann, however, shook uncontrollably for some hours after, and developed a severe headache which didn't go away until the next day.

"After this experience my Father swore us to secrecy and we were not to mention any of it to anyone for fear of being a laughing stock of the community. However, Dad did take me into his confidence, and told me that he had seen things in the sky before, and said that the next afternoon he would show me some of them in daylight.

"True to his word, they were sitting above the horizon of the hills that were part of my brother's farm. There were three that were sitting on their sides amidst the clouds. They looked like zinc coloured objects as opposed to the light fluffy clouds around them.

"I have often wondered what else Dad had experienced that he did not share with us."

I, and other researchers, also wonder. Whilst this time no occupants were actually sighted, the craft was obviously under intelligent control.

An interesting 1961 account from South Africa, was also translated from a Spanish publication by Gordon Creighton.

An engineer 'H.M.' was working for a Spanish firm specialising in the development of automatic pilots for aircraft. He was in his car, twenty miles out of Cape Town, when a stranger, who spoke English, but with an unidentifiable accent, waved him down. After 'H.M.' had taken him to a mountain stream, and they filled a can he had loaned him with water, he gave the man a lift back to a rock face about 100 metres off the road. In its shadow was a strange craft, some ten to fifteen metres in diameter and four metres high.

There were some steps, leading to a lighted entry, and the stranger invited him in. There were four other men inside, all between 4'11" and 5'1'' tall, and one was lying down. He had apparently been burned, and it was for him the clean water was needed. They were all perfectly human in appearance, of slim build and clean shaven, with slightly pronounced foreheads, and short chestnut coloured hair. Each wore beige-coloured laboratory type overalls, fastened with a belt.

Although he was not allowed to go any further, 'H.M.' could see into a circular room, which was lit by a bright white light, which 'seemed to be coming from everywhere, all at once'. A couch went all the way around the wall and in the centre, set in a rectangle, there were two rows of levers, each about one metre high. On the other side of the room was an instrument panel, which somewhat resembled a piano.

The stranger assured 'H.M.' they didn't need a doctor, and asked if he had any questions. H.M. wanted to know where the craft's 'engines' were, and he was told there were no engines and they *'nullified gravity by the use of a very heavy fluid which circulated in a tube, and with this system they created a magnet, something like electro-magnets, except that they, instead of using electricity, were using this fluid.*

'The fluid was subjected to the velocity of electricity, but 'H.M.' said this was impossible in the confines of a tube. He was told; "It is simple, when the fluid is leaving the tube, it is already entering at the other end, thus its relative speed is infinite." So 'H.M.' realised that on the basis of this system, plus a few magnets, not yet discovered in earth technology, these beings had achieved enormous velocities and were able to conquer gravity.'

When 'H.M.' asked where they came from, the man merely pointed to the sky, and requested he leave shortly after, as they were getting ready to depart.

In 1965, the Victorian 'Australian Flying Saucer Review' published the following report; 'One correspondent wrote that whilst holidaying in Sydney in a cliff-side house, she had been watching a beautiful pink cloud. It remained in the same position from 5.30pm to 6pm.

'When she looked again, at 7pm, she was amazed to seeing it moving slowly towards the rocks at the base of the cliff. As the 'cloud' came nearer, the observer was able to look down into the cloud, and was astounded to see a 'magnificent, snow-white flying saucer'. The cloud was formed by a grey-coloured steam, which soon turned a pink after issuing from vents around the outer edge of the circle. The witness appears to have had a very clear view of the object, and describes the bottom of the saucer as coming to a point about three feet wide.

'A noise, like that of a 'high powered, well cared for engine', was heard, and as she watched, a shining ladder was lowered from the hatchway beneath the surface, and a man came down and sat on a rung of the ladder. From this position, he shone a strong beam of light into the sea, as if looking for something.

'Shortly after this, 'a brilliant pink flare went up further out to sea', and almost immediately the ladder, with the man aboard, was retracted, and the machine sped off in the direction of the flare. In the moonlight, the woman could make out a long shape in the water, and when the 'saucer' had reached this, they both disappeared 'in a vivid pink flash, beneath the sea'.

There were other incidents where 'human-looking' occupants appeared to be repairing their landed craft. Investigator Ted Bloecher, reported on the following incident, which occurred near New Berlin, New York.

In the early hours of the morning of 25th November 1964, Mary Merryweather could not sleep, so she got up, watched television for a while, and after getting a ginger-ale, happened to look outside, wondering if the weather was favouring her male relatives who were away on a hunting trip.

Suddenly, she saw an unusually bright light coming down from the sky, and realised it couldn't be 'shooting star', as it changed direction, eventually coming to a halt, and hovering several hundred feet across the road from her house. Her mother-in-law came out, and was a little scared, as both of them could hear a low, constant humming noise. Their dog, who would normally join them, would not go out the door, and just lay inside, shaking and quivering.

After a few cars went by, the object moved to the side of a nearby hill. Mary went back inside, and watched, with her binoculars, through the dining room window. She could see the craft, either hovering or on legs, just above the ground. There was a light shining down, from underneath, and illuminating several 'men' who had 'tools' in their hands, and appeared to be 'working' on the object, some standing and some on their knees, similar to the way she remembered her father had on farm machinery. They took something out from underneath the centre of the craft, and 'appeared to be letting it down gently with their hands', until it was resting just below their 'vehicle'.

They were 'built like men', but slightly taller than average, perhaps well over six-and-a-half feet tall, with a muscular physique, and dressed in 'something like a dark, skin diver's wetsuit'. Their features were human, their hair short cropped, and the visible skin, on their hands and faces, was of a pale colour.

Soon after, another light appeared in the sky, and flew down to rest on the crest of the hill, just above the original craft. More 'men' got out, and joined the ones already working on the ground. She thought they appeared to be cutting some dark, heavy cable into exact lengths, and taking it over to the piece of machinery, or whatever it was, lying underneath the first object.

Mary's mother-in-law stayed up with her saying; *"I can't sleep till they leave or something else happens, and I wouldn't leave you here alone for anything in the world. The dog is scared to death; she's almost as frightened as I am!"*

They debated whether or not to call the authorities, but decided against it. Mary said; *"You know, if we call someone, they're going to come up here with guns and firearms and bother them – and they just want to get that thing fixed and get away."*

At about 4.30am, the 'men', about nine in all, made several unsuccessful attempts to fit the machinery resting on the ground, back into the underside of the craft. Eventually they managed to 'get it right', and she could see them all running around, collecting their tools, various 'boxes' and pieces of cable, before apparently re-entering their craft.

By this time, there was enough faint daylight for Mary, looking from below, to see that the craft seemed to be round, or cylindrical, and the bottom tapered up. The vehicle on top of the hill left first, going straight up and then shooting away into the south-west where it disappeared almost instantaneously.

A minute later, the craft the 'men' had been working on, rose straight up to the crest of the hill, rose a little further again, then shot off, at the same speed, in the same direction as the first.

The next day, and also when her husband returned, they searched the area where the craft had been. There were significant marks and holes, and they also found a piece of tubular 'wrapping' which she thought may have been around the cable the 'men' had been cutting up. There was also a small piece of what looked like aluminium.

"But it wasn't aluminium," Mary said. *"It didn't behave like aluminium. Aluminium will crumple, and this didn't crumple. You couldn't crease it! It was very light, and had practically no weight to it at all."*

As was the case in many other incidents, the witnesses did not report the event. It was only through close relatives that researchers heard about, and followed up on the details of what happened that morning.

―――――――

Another case, where 'occupants' appeared to be repairing or making adjustments to their craft, occurred in Ecuador one night during the summer of 1965.

Scott Corrales wrote of how civil engineer, Hector Crespo, his son Urgenio and labourer Francisco López, were approaching the town of Zullengo, when they saw, from behind a bend in the road, two shafts of light going up into the sky. Thinking there may have been an accident, they went to offer assistance, and were surprised to find a disc-type machine, with a transparent dome on top. A compartment to the interior appeared to be open, and within the crimson interior glow, they could see complex instrumentation.

Having never seen anything like this before, the three witnesses crawled behind a raised levee, and watched from about thirty metres away. The 'vehicle' itself rested on telescopic legs, with 'plate-like' landing pads. Three silent, humanoid figures were outside the craft, and one appeared to be adjusting the device which was projecting the beam of light into the sky. The other two were just standing by, and at one stage handed their compatriot some form of tool.

They were all dressed in 'resplendent silver overalls', with white belts at the waist. They were also wearing some form of helmet, which did not display any form of breathing apparatus. If they were aware of the witnesses' presence, they didn't show any concern.

After a while, Urgenio felt ill, and his father, concerned that an amber-hued light revolving around edge of the craft may be radioactive, made everyone return to their vehicle, from where they saw the strange craft, rise with a 'wobbly' movement, to a height, from where it 'took off in a flash'.

In 1969, the *'UFOIC Newsletter'* wrote of two incidents which had occurred the previous year.

At Lakeland, Florida, in October 1968, the McMullens, and three friends, saw a mysterious object heading towards their home from a nearby hill. It was disc-shaped, about thirteen feet in diameter, and eight feet high. It stopped about 150ft from their homestead, and hovered about seven feet above a palm tree.

Through the transparent dome, they could see two occupants, dressed in tight, white outfits and headgear. At the house there was 'interference' on the television set, a 'burning' smell, similar to ammonia, and their dog knocked a hole in the screen porch in an effort to get away.

By the time the police arrived, the strange craft and its occupants had departed and were nowhere to be seen.

The next month, in the early hours of November 1st, three Fillipino farmers reported multiple sightings from a valley in the Rizal Province, only 32 miles from Manilla, and close to the Philippines' Communications Satellite ground station.

Their descriptions of a strange craft were almost identical. It was a white, low-slung, saucer-shape craft which landed and took off nearby. There were two 'passengers', whom one farmer described as being 'Caucasian looking, with one about six feet tall, and wearing white flying suits, without identification, and glass-like or plastic headgear.'

There were many other cases of normal looking 'Nordic' type entities being reported from around the world, often from North and South America.

On November 28th 1953, at Peidras Negras, Brazil, several witnesses reported beings with blond hair and pale complexions. In 1956, on July 20th, witnesses in Panorama City, California, described the occupants of a craft as wearing tight green suits and being nearly six feet tall, with long blond hair down to their shoulders.

On July 25th, the next year, witnesses in Sao Sebastio, Brazil, described the 'visitors' as 'two normal looking men', wearing one piece suits. They were of youthful appearance, and also had long fair hair down to their shoulders.

Whilst it could be argued that these normal looking humans may well be from our own military, the same could not be said for the many incidents which involved humanoid beings of a shorter stature, who whilst sometimes alone, and in complete control of their faculties, often appeared to fill a subservient 'assistant' role to the more 'Caucasian' type 'visitors'.

In the 1950s they were being reported from France and other countries. Researcher Rupert Matthews told of French builder, Georges Gatay, who was working on a building site, near Marcilly-sur-Vienne, on 30th September 1954.

Suddenly, a dome-shaped object that gave off a bright light, came down to hover just above the ground a short distance away. Everybody stopped work and just stared, but Georges felt an inexplicable compulsion to walk closer. As he neared the strange craft, a short humanoid figure stepped out, as if it had come from behind.

A beam of light shot out from a belt around its waist. Afterwards, it climbed back into the craft, which took off and flew rapidly out of sight. The next day, most of the men suffered nausea and giddiness. They recovered within 48 hours, but Georges suffered for about two weeks.

Researcher, David Ritchie, also published an account of an incident, involving these 'little guys', just a few days later, on October 11th, 1954.

At about 7.30pm, three men were driving along the road near Taupignac, when they pulled up to investigate a red light which was hovering overhead. About 600ft away was another object, about eighteen feet in diameter, emitting a red-yellow light, and silently hovering thirty feet above the ground. When it moved in a horizontal direction, and landed, two of the witnesses went over to get a better look.

They were surprised to see four small 'beings', each about three feet tall, performing what seemed to be some form of maintenance work on the craft. When the two men came within 45 feet of the object, the little 'humanoids' spotted them, and hurriedly clambered back on board. Their craft emitted a dazzling, multicoloured display of light, then departed vertically, at great speed.

(Less than a fortnight later, on 23rd October, to the south in Libya, another craft landed, with more 'normal' type occupants. A farmer, near Tripoli, saw an 'ovoid' disc, about eighteen feet wide and nine feet wide, gently land with its long axis horizontal. The lower half looked metallic, and the upper portion was transparent, with a bright white light inside. He could see 'landing gear' comprising six wheels, and an external ladder.

None of the 'crew' seemed to come out, but inside the farmer could see six men in 'coveralls', wearing 'gas masks', and working at instrument panels. When one of the men removed his mask, and appeared to exhale into a tube, his face looked to be perfectly human.

When the farmer walked up to the craft, and put his hand on the ladder, he received a powerful shock, which knocked him to the ground. One of the crew gestured, as if warning him to keep his distance. After twenty minutes, the object silently rose about 150 feet, then sped away towards the east.)

British researcher, Gordon Creighton, translated the following 1957 report from Brazil; *'On the night of October 10th, Spanish naval officer, Miguel Espanõl and companion, travelling by truck to Ceres, encountered a tremendous UFO. At first, high in the sky, bathing the whole region in light, the craft descended and stalled the truck. They thought the craft at least 500 feet wide, and 130 feet deep, and oval or saucer-shaped, with a long 'aerial' projecting from its dome and topped by a red light.*

'The hovering monster now switched off all its dazzling lights, and the two men saw seven, completely human-looking small beings, the size of children, with long hair and clad in luminous suits, appear in an open hatch of the craft, and gaze down silently for about three minutes at them. The great machine then flew off, releasing a small disc as it did so. The small disc disappeared northwards, while the big one went south.'

'The Australian Flying Saucer Review' published an enlightening article about an incident which occurred in 1967.

On 24th August, Ron Hydes was on his motor bike, travelling along the Hume Highway near Wodonga in Victoria, when he was nearly blinded by a brilliant blue-white light coming from above. He stopped, took off his sunglasses, and wiped his eyes; *"When I opened them, there was a disc-shaped object about 100 feet away to my left, off the road. The object was silver on top, quite a highly polished silver, and either a very dark grey, or black, underneath. It was just like two inverted saucers."*

On top was a small dome, about two metres high, with a small flat ball, about twenty centimetres deep on top. He realised the craft was not resting on the ground, but actually hovering about four or five feet above. There were two figures, both about five feet tall, at the side. They were dressed in metallic looking overalls, with no obvious zippers or buttons, and helmets resembling opaque 'fish bowls'.

Ron was a little frightened, and when he took a step forward, one of the 'beings' did the same, raising his hand and beckoning, as if inviting Ron to come over. At this stage, Ron panicked and raced back to his motor bike, taking off down the road as fast as he could.

Without warning, he heard a humming noise, and looked up to see the craft about 100ft away at an altitude of about 150ft. Suddenly, it was in front of him – was it trying to 'cut him off'? He slowed his pace, wondering what to do next. To his relief, the craft then turned bright red, tilted at about a 45 degree angle and disappeared from sight within a few seconds.

Another interesting case came from Spain in October 1958. Senor Angelu was also riding his motorbike near Figueras, when an object flew overhead and plunged into nearby woodland. At first he thought that a small plane must have crashed, and ran to the trees. But, this was a round, disc-shaped object, resting lightly on the ground, not like any plane he had seen before, and it obviously hadn't crashed.

There were two short figures, with large heads, nearby. Angelu hid in the undergrowth, and watched as they seemed to be collecting leaves and twigs. After about ten minutes, they returned to their craft, which took off and flew out of sight.

These 'little guys' often seemed to be preoccupied with collecting soil and vegetation samples. In 1954, a farmer near Campo Grande, in Brazil, was fishing some 400 yards away from his home, when his dog began to howl. He looked around, and was surprised to see a strange object hovering six feet above the ground. It looked like two spheres, 'a tiny one rotating around a much larger one'.

Three small human looking creatures, with rapid and agile movements, descended from the large sphere. One had a roughly 'basket-shape' object in its arms, and another a metal tube, with a type of funnel at the end. Using this, the other two gathered material from the edge of the river which was sucked into the basket in a similar fashion to that of a vacuum cleaner. Once full, they took it into the craft, then reappeared to repeat the operation a second time.

Once their task was apparently completed, they returned to the large sphere, which took off at high speed, and accompanied by the smaller object, disappeared into the sky.

This category of cases was rarely reported in Australia; however Dale White detailed one from near Hobart, in Tasmania, on the evening of October 28th 1962.

High school teacher, Mrs. E. Sylvester, along with her three children, was driving home at 7.30pm one evening, when a strange object swooped across the road in front of them. Her excited offspring insisted it was a 'flying saucer', to which she retorted; "Nonsense!"

The craft had landed off the road, a bit further up, and at her children's insistence, they stopped the car, and walked over to get a better look. If she had wanted to prove this was something conventional, her hopes were dashed. She held the kids back once they spotted, there on the ground, an egg-shaped object, about fifteen feet long and five or six feet wide.

Beyond the craft was a little man, wearing a close fitting silver-coloured suit and translucent helmet, with a tube connected to something on his back. For forty minutes they watched him collecting samples of soil, which he put into a shiny box that he was carrying. He suddenly noticed the family watching him, and immediately re-entered the craft which promptly took off and sped away.

Several well-substantiated reports, one in particular, came from Mogi-Guaçu, Brazil in 1965. Researcher, Coral Lorenzen, told of some happenings in the November of that year. Mrs. Filho, a landowner's wife, saw a strange light in a nearby field. She and her grandson went out and observed an object, sitting on the ground, and two small, humanoid figures beside it. One walked along the furrows in the ground, picking up twigs and leaves, which he carried in his arms. He and his companion quickly scurried back into the craft when a truckload of loud revellers passed by, only to re-emerge a short time later.

Mrs. Filho and her grandson noticed two similar craft hovering in the sky above, and a short time later the landed craft and its occupants departed.

On 13th of that month Mrs Filho's husband and bank manager were also in the house when they were alerted to another object which had landed only 400 feet away, and was focussing a bright beam of light upwards. Prior to its landing, the local sheriff and a police clerk, had been travelling along the road when they witnessed the craft hovering above.

Filho and the other witnesses saw more 'little beings' from a distance of about seventy feet. They were small, about the size of a seven-year-old child, and 'glowing'. One wore overalls, another chocolate coloured pants, and the third, who had a 'squarish, flat head, was dressed in what appeared to be 'a surgeon's apron'.

By this time, the local parish priest, and scores of policemen were observing from the farm next door. The same night, several motorists encountered a similar craft which had landed on a nearby highway, before taking off again at great speed, and lighting up the entire area.

Investigator John Keel wrote an interesting article, *'The Little Man of Gaffney'*, for *'Flying Saucer Review'* in 1968.

At about 4am on 17th November 1966, in South Carolina, Gaffney Police Officers Charles Hutchins and A. Huskey were on their routine cruise down an isolated and unpopulated road on the outskirts of town.

As they neared a right-angle bend in the road, they suddenly saw a metallic object, directly in front of them. It was about twenty feet in the air, and descending toward the ground; *'Hutchins described it as being spherical, like a ball, with a wide, flat rim around it. There were no portholes or lights on it. It was completely dark, reflecting a dull gold colour in the headlights of the police car.'*

As the object hovered, just above the ground, the two amazed officers got out of their patrol car. At that time, Hutchins was able to estimate the craft's diameter as being about twenty feet.

A small door opened, and white light poured out, although they couldn't distinguish what was in the interior. A short ladder descended to the ground, and a small being came down, and walked slowly towards Hutchins and Huskey, stopping in tall grass about fifteen to twenty feet away.

Except for his short height, maybe about four feet tall, he looked and moved like any other human. His face was *'rather ordinary and human-like, although neither man could tell if his complexion was light or dark.'* He wore no helmet or head-gear, and was dressed in a shiny, gold, metallic-like suit, with no buttons or zippers.

Hutchins said the little man started talking to them. He didn't have an accent, and spoke very precisely, more like a 'college graduate'. In fact; *"He did most of the talking. When we asked him questions, he wouldn't answer us, but just went right on talking."*

A year later, when he agreed to speak to John Keel, Hutchins couldn't remember everything that had been said, but he recalled the little being asking why he and Huskey were dressed the same, and also that their 'visitor' had a 'kind of funny' laugh.

After about two or three minutes, the little guy said he would be back in two days. He then slowly walked back to the ladder, and entered his craft which took off with a soft 'whirr', rose slowly into the sky, and vanished into the darkness.

Both witnesses regretted reporting the incident, and the subsequent ridicule and media attention, and ensured that Keel was 'not from the government' before they agreed to speak with him.

Researcher Jader Pereira wrote in the 1971 *'Flying Saucer Review'* about one such incident which occurred the far southern Brazilian State of Rio Grande du Sul in early January 1968.

At about 9pm, a strange round object, about ten metres wide and three metres high, was seen hovering, approximately two metres above the ground, nearly 400 metres away from the main homestead of the Lagoa Negra Plantation. Five witnesses, including the Fazenda's manager, owner and his family, were startled when a powerful red light, emanating from the metallic craft, penetrated through the chinks in the windows and doors of the house, illuminating the inside rooms.

As they watched, they saw two 'beings' appear beside the craft. They were quite tall, at least six feet, Caucasian, with 'full' faces, long, shoulder-length hair, and bare feet. They were wearing white 'overalls', with a broad white band at the waist.

Three much smaller 'beings' followed. They were no more than four-and-a-half feet tall, also Caucasian, with long shoulder-length hair. Their 'overalls' were a chestnut-brown colour, with a matching waist band, and they appeared to have small boots on their feet. They seemed to be able to walk quite rapidly, but never left the area below the disc.

The two larger 'visitors' walked towards a ditch, next to a wire fence, and followed this until they were halfway between their craft and a gate, then retraced their steps. A second venture, by a different route, took them to a small wooden bridge leading to the gate. After they returned to the disc again, they came back, crossed the bridge, opened and closed the gate, and approached the house.

The five guard dogs, who could be quite vicious, and would normally have been barking, had remained surprisingly quiet, and by this time, the Fazenda owner and manager were hidden under two palm trees and keeping watch. As the strangers neared the house, the manager, who was armed, wanted to challenge them, but the owner was quite frightened, he ordered him to keep quiet.

By this time, his wife was so scared, she opened the door and called out to her husband to come back inside. The 'beings' must have heard her because they halted, moved forward, hesitated, then returned to their craft, where all five entities went back in. The disc rose up vertically, with a slight rotary movement, and departed.

Later two kinds of footprints were found at the site – some were large, like bare feet, with angular heels and very long toes, and the others much smaller, with smooth heels. The forepart of the soles showed a mark, like a five-pointed star in the centre

---

There were many other incidents being reported in Brazil. Investigator Irene Granchi wrote of one which occurred at Pirassununga in the State of Sao Paulo.

On 7th February 1969, nineteen-year-old Tiago Machado, a vegetable pedlar, had run towards what he thought was a parachute landing nearby. Instead, he found a typical 'flying saucer', with a 'lid', out of which two small beings floated out.

'They were clad in metal, and their faces were protected by a transparent visor attached to a helmet. Through this visor he noticed a wrinkled yellowish skin, thin lips and large noses. Two more little men were visible inside the disc. They were growling and making guttural sounds which Tiago could not understand. He tried to communicate by gestures.

'Tiago was smoking, and seeing that they were interested, he took the packet of cigarettes from his pocket, and tossed it over to them. He was surprised to see one of them put out his hand, his palm down, and draw the packet up, as if by a magnet. He pressed the hand holding the packet down his trouser leg, and the packet vanished.

'At that moment, other people came running up and shouting for Tiago. When the beings heard this, they floated backwards into their vehicle, then upwards, and through the lid again. One of them bent down, brought up something like a blow-pipe, and aimed it at Tiago. A red and blue ray was aimed at the boy's leg. The pain was awful, and Tiago fell to the ground, motionless.'

The witnesses, who along with hundreds of people in the area, had seen the UFO take off, so there was no disputing what had happened. Further, Tiago still had a scar on his leg. Some time later, a local UFO research group arranged for him to appear on a TV show in Rio, however, some military officers were loath to believe his account.

Many years later, Irene was able to interview him. He had an addendum to his encounter, which it is more difficult to substantiate. He said that afterwards, a beautiful extraterrestrial lady came to visit him at his home, inviting him to go away with her. His family had been present, and his cousin had pursued the taxi she had arrived in, which had taken her back to the bus station. The taxi driver later had no recall of the woman or her trip to Tiago's home.

In later years, after the end of the 1970s, the more benign human-type visitors were replaced by the 'Greys' – beings who abducted people from their homes, and appeared cold and emotionless. In previous books I have discussed how some of the earlier contacts said that these entities were in fact advanced biological robots, who had revolted against their creators, and were instigating contacts and objectives of their own.

That is not to say that all the 'Greys' had revolted. Perhaps some had remained with their 'human', or other masters, serving their original purpose of being lower ranked 'assistants'.

In the well known case of Travis Walton, he was taken aboard a 'ship' after being stuck by a beam of light from a craft he and his colleagues saw near Snowflake, Arizona, in 1975.

Once inside, Walton initially encountered the traditional 'Greys' but was then startled by the sudden appearance of a 'man', who seemed to be in charge; *"He was a man, just like a human being....he was human enough, so if I was walking down the street in a crowd, he'd be an unusual looking person in passing...I thought he could be American just as far as I could tell..."*

Sometimes we can never 'get to the bottom' of a report, and just have to make up our own minds as to what really happened. Spanish investigator, Ignacio Darnaude, submitted the following account, which was translated by Gordon Creighton of *'Flying Saucer Review'*.

The incident occurred in September 1971, on a Spanish farm, near Aznacólar, owned by Lt. General Gabriel Buiza and two colleagues. They had an 82 year-old worker, Juan Dominguez, who had been in their employ for many years, and whom they considered to be totally reliable. He was relatively simple, and had little if no knowledge of flying saucers or aliens. He later admitted that he always thought of the following incident as being; "...some secret military operation that was being hatched up, some ambush, or some political plot against the government."

One evening old Juan appeared in a very excited and distressed state, saying that a great 'thing', like large bus, had landed in the field; "and people had started coming down out of it, and they shone a light on me, and I just came here, stumbling across the fields."

He had been in his watchman's hut, just before nightfall, when he saw the large craft landing near an artesian well, and a lot of people descending from it. He described them as looking 'normal', with no distinguishing features, and wearing 'blue uniforms'. He said he lost sight of them as they went down into a depression in the field, however five or six of their 'chiefs' had remained behind, and were looking towards him.

One of them got out something that looked like a 'lamp' and shone it into his eyes. He hid behind a well, but when he ventured out, the 'chiefs' shone the lantern on him once more, after which he fled, and went to find his employers.

Nobody believed him, and thought he was mad. Not thinking that their melon crop was in danger, they didn't even go back in the next days to see the marks the old man claimed were there following the 'landing'. From then on, he always kept a shotgun close at hand.

Robots can be large or small, as they are not confined to human physiology. Sometimes it can be hard to distinguish between a sentient being and a robotic entity. Researcher John Keel investigated this case, later reporting his findings in the *'Flying Saucer Review'*.

On 21st July 1967, fourteen-year-old Ronnie Hill was working in the garden behind his family's home in North Carolina. Suddenly, he noticed that the birds and local dogs had fallen silent, and there was a strange odour, like gas, in the air, which made his eyes water. The silence continued for about fifteen minutes, and the unpleasant smell only got worse.

A buzzing sound caught his attention, and he looked around to see something which resembled a large 'black hat' in the sky, and then a smaller 'white ball', about nine feet in diameter, which was 'moving by itself'; *"I fell to the ground....all sorts of things dashing through my mind....I knew no-one would believe me of what I saw, and I would have to have some proof, so I ran to the house to get my camera."*

When he came back outside, he heard a slight 'hissing' sound, and the 'white ball' was on the ground. A few seconds later, Ronnie heard a loud noise, and a 'little man', nearly four feet tall, came from behind the landed 'ball'. He was wearing a skin-tight, silvery metallic suit, with a dark blue belt around the waist. On its head, which seemed to be a bluish-green colour, there was a silver helmet, and the face had high cheekbones, with 'puffy' or 'fleshy' cheeks, and eyes which were 'tilting' or 'slanting'.

The 'little man' was moving 'slow and wobbly', and carrying a funnel-shaped black object in his right hand. He put it near the ground, then quickly pulled it back up to his hip, before turning and going behind the landed 'ball'. Ronnie noticed the 'little man' seemed to have trouble controlling his legs, swinging them stiffly when he turned.

There was another loud noise, then a bright blue flare came from beneath the 'ball', which slowly took off into the air. The larger, black craft reappeared, and with a 'rod' pulled the 'ball' back inside, through a 'hole', before zooming off at tremendous speed, and disappearing over the treetops.

Ronnie had managed to take a few quick photographs of the 'being', when it was only about fifteen feet away, but only one turned out. John Keel had experts examine the photo, which appeared to be genuine, and corroborated Ronnie's report. Further, whilst anonymity was requested all round, both his parents and school teachers testified as to the young man's excellent character, and the fact that he had little, if any, prior knowledge of UFOs.

Sometimes a craft's occupants appear to be robots, no matter how advanced and sophisticated. Researcher Gordon Creighton documented the following event.

At 3.30am on October 12th 1963, Argentinean truck driver, Eugenio Douglas was driving a load of coal along the road between Monte Maiz and Isla Verde. He was heading towards his home town of Venado Tuerto in the Province of Santa Fé, when his journey was hindered by a violent storm.

A brilliant white light suddenly shone through his windscreen. Its heat made his face burn and prickle, and the insides of his eyeballs felt as if they were ablaze. He tried to shield his face with his poncho, but collapsed over the wheel, and lost control of his truck, which went into a ditch.

He recovered, and upon scrambling out into the pouring rain, saw a huge oval or round object, at least thirty feet high, barring the road. Suddenly, a slightly lesser intent light appeared from a door opening at the side of the object. *Three enormous beings, in human form, whom he described as 'robots', emerged. Their height was tremendous. He told police later; "Perhaps four or five metres, or even more..."*

He found it difficult to describe their clothing, which seemed to be 'stuck to their bodies', but on their heads were glowing helmets, from which emerged short antennae, 'like those of a snail'. '(*Douglas had no recollection of the faces of the creatures, but felt that they could not have been too different from ours, for although he felt fear, he was emphatic that he felt no revulsion whatever.)*'

When the entities spotted him beside his truck, they shone beams of red light at him. They were powerful, burning and irradiating his skin. '*In his confusion and terror, Eugenio drew his revolver and fired three or four shots at them, then fled in panic back down the road to Monte Maiz, still feeling himself pursued by the burning red light.*'

Under the cover of his poncho, he looked back to see the creatures going back into the craft, which then took off and proceeded to make a series of dives at him as he ran along the road. Each time he felt the burning and prickling in his body again.

At the same time, the Ribas family, and some residents of Monte Maiz, were holding a vigil beside the body of a relative who had just died. The lights and candles in the room suddenly changed colour, and gave off an 'asphyxiating gas' which forced them to rush outside.

They could see a vivid red light in the sky, and the street lamps also seemed to be changing colour to red, and emanating the same unbreathable gas. Other people, some of whom were returning from a party, also witnessed this, and a number of residents rang the 'Electricity Plant' asking if there was a problem.

Suddenly everybody saw poor Eugenio, who was running toward them uttering piercing calls for help. His head was 'muffled up' in his poncho, and he was waving his revolver in the air. When he reached the first street lamp, they could see his face was covered with mud, and whilst still holding his poncho, he was wildly running around and around the lamp-post.

Everyone there came to his rescue, and took him down to the local Police Station, where he was questioned and examined. They called the doctor, Francisco Dabolis, who later testified that Eugenio was perfectly sane, and had burns, of an unknown cause, on his hands and face. His poncho had similar burn marks, and a later inspection of his truck determined that the wiring was burnt out.

A local businessman who was also driving down the road, reported noticing the change in the street lamps, and seeing Eugenio rushing toward him, his head muffled and brandishing a revolver. He said that he also had felt an indescribable sensation, followed by a temporary loss of memory.

Although the police report was sent up the line to the District's Administrative and Political Headquarters, no official report or explanation was ever offered.

Sometimes, a 'visitor', be they sentient or robotic, can come out of an encounter the 'worse for wear'. Jim and Coral Lorenzen recounted such a case that occurred at the end of July, 1967.

David Morris, from Ohio, was driving home in the early hours of the morning, after completing his evening shift at the Lamb Electric Company. He was using a little-used back road, and when he noticed a 'glow' through the fog, he slowed down, looking to see if someone's barn may have been on fire.

Instead, he spotted, hovering a couple of feet above a wheat field, twenty or thirty yards to his left, a glowing 'wedge' or cone-shaped object. It appeared to be about twenty-five feet high, and twenty feet wide at the base, with a ball-shaped object at the top.

He was so intrigued that he was not paying attention to the road, and when he looked ahead, there, in his headlights, were four or five small humanoid figures, each just under four feet tall, running backwards and forward, about fifty feet away on the road ahead. They also glowed an orange colour, and had a 'stocky' build with what looked like 'oversize' heads.

David slammed on his brakes, but he could not stop in time, and hit one of the little beings. He could hear the thump on the right, front portion of his car. At first, after he had brought his vehicle to a halt, he was going to get out and check, but realised these 'creatures' may not have been human, and the others would not have been happy that their companion had been injured or worse. Fear got the better of him, and he sped away.

The next day, he and a friend returned to the scene, but the only evidence of his unfortunate encounter was a set of skid-marks on the road where he had slammed on his brakes, and three dents and some scratches on the chrome trim of his car.

CHAPTER NINE

EARLY ENCOUNTERS AND CONTACTS

Many of the early researchers had sightings or experiences of their own, but rarely spoke of them.

In the 1980s I became acquainted with U.S. investigator Rosemary Decker. She soon became my mentor and firm friend, and stayed at my home when visiting Australia. What was of particular interest to me was that Rosemary was already acquainted with all witnesses to the first Adamski - Orthon meeting. She once let it slip that she was at Mt. Palomar that day, when the group all returned in a state of great excitement after their encounter with 'the man from outer space'. Over the next few weeks Rosemary spoke to each witness, individually and in private; they all confirmed the event and circumstances.

"Living within an hour's drive of Adamski all those years ago, he was the first contacted person I investigated. Yes, he was contacted, although his ego was inflated beyond a safe point, and he subsequently suffered the consequences. I have spent days, over several years of my life in the early to late 50s, in/at his open house weekends, where he had several good telescopes, donated by friends and admirers. Due to his hospitality, I met fascinating people from many States and countries, where we learned from each other and Adamski, each sharing their own experiences. It is a background I am grateful for."

Eventually, along with other supporters, including her good friend Millen le Poer Trench, Rosemary felt compelled to withdraw her support for Adamski, despite their long association: "He developed a great fear of undercover security agencies, and ignored the warnings and advice given by the 'Visitors'. We were all concerned about his well-being, and grew very worried about his later ego trips and false claims, but he was not reachable by reason."

This personality problem, which also discredited other early contactees, troubled Rosemary, who said; "I asked contactee Dan Fry (who maintained a stable course) if he understood the situation. He replied with one of the finest bit of counsel ever given me: 'You simply cannot know the intensity of the pressures, exerted from many sources, on the lives of contactees, unless you have walked in their shoes – as I have. Without condoning their blunders, be compassionate and be patient. We are in no position to judge them. Always keep in mind *their* Basic Purpose; to assist and enlighten – *and support them in that*."

Rosemary did say one thing in Adamski's defence; "My Uncle Bill owned a property near some acreage that Adamski and his colleagues had. He told me he had seen various original negatives of Adamski's spacecraft at the same time they had been photographed. He assured me that he considered them to be genuine, and that he had seen three craft himself, in silent triangular formation in the night sky while engineering in Saudi Arabia in 1949-50."

(Attempting to discredit Adamski, the '*London Evening News*' of 19th September 1975, claimed that his most-famous flying saucer photograph was that of a bottle cooler made by a Wigan, Lancashire firm. The next day a refrigeration engineer named Nicholson came forward on radio to state he had designed the cooler in 1959, six years <u>after</u> Adamski's photographs were first published. When challenged, Nicholson produced his patents, and noted that he had copied the design for the bottle cooler shade from the photograph in Adamski's book.)

Rosemary was good friends with Leonard Cramp, a U.K. engineer, and was very impressed with his fourth and final book '*The A.T. Factor*'. He confided in her that he had enjoyed a number of contacts with friendly human-looking extraterrestrials, who had visited his farm. He commented; "We must take into consideration the fact of thousands of years of earthly reports of the 'Visitors' human-like appearance, and the genetic kinship with homo sapiens (some are in the *Bible*, some worldwide.)" They apparently offered suggestions for his research into gravity.

In 1991, another expert, whose name I must withhold, also confided his personal meetings with the 'Visitors' to Rosemary; "They had occurred several years before, and were definitely friendly. He felt that most intelligences who are observing Earth's crisis are benign, and concerned not only for all our life-forms, (including Man), but also for our neighbouring planets."

Some of Rosemary's associates told of high-ranking military officers who liaised with the 'Visitors' on many occasions. They had learned, for their own safety and security, that people like Adamski were not the best of contacts. A couple of retired officers, mentioned that while the 'Visitors' could communicate telepathically, they spoke perfect English and were indistinguishable from humans.

While admitting her own long-term contact with the 'Visitors', Rosemary only confided a small portion to me; "If the audience ever ask, I only ever mention my close encounters of the first and second kind, which my daughter and I experienced together, some years ago. One happened in 1963-64 when we were driving one night, and our 'friends from above' saved us from falling over a cliff in the snow and ice. You wouldn't believe it, we had a second encounter the next morning in bright sunlight.

"Millen and I were neighbours in the U.S., and along with several other friends in California, watched saucers go overhead many times. Occasionally they stopped to hover, reverse, and do aerobatics. Once, after attending a lecture by George Hunt Williamson (one of the Adamski's 'desert witnesses'), at the Recreation Centre in Vista, California on 11th January 1958, we both saw, along with many other witnesses, what I can only describe as a gigantic mother ship hovering for over an hour. Man-made satellites were just making their first ventures above the Earth. And no, flying geese and the planet Venus do not have domes and portholes, but some of the craft we observed did!"

Rosemary noted that George Hunt Williamson, who was with Adamski during his initial desert meeting with Orthon, had done some excellent work on his trips to South America, but after he went public with his contactee experiences, he had a hard time adjusting to being treated as a charlatan, and eventually withdrew and became reclusive.

"Another time, when Millen and I were together, one afternoon in Ireland, we saw a classic flying saucer. It was glinting silvery in the sun, poised and hovering silently just off the peak of Errigal Mountain, and was widely reported in the local press the next day. I suddenly realised that the vicinity was heavily laden with quartz, as was our area back home, and wondered if there was an affinity between space-craft and quartz."

I asked about earlier years, but Rosemary was more reticent. She said that her first contact with a 'friend from a faraway place' was on 14th January 1953, but involved telepathic communication. She also commented; "I am so grateful that my experiences did not include seeing any of those little robot-type extraterrestrials. They seem to be manufactured rather than actual people. No wonder folks get frightened."

Another time she mentioned a 'Visitor' who left for 'Home' in 1960 – his last words to her and a friend were; "And do take care of your body." In 1995, in another correspondence to a colleague she wrote, 'Don't recall if I told you that the friend and mentor from 'Upstairs' suggested to me (on the phone, shortly before he left) that I might want to write a book on the Mars-Earth connection someday. He even offered a title – '*35 Minutes to Mars* ' - for the book! (That was over 30 years ago! Plainly my time scale and his were a bit different. No wonder he said; "Try to cultivate patience," to Millen and me, just as he was about to leave.")

Comments such as this confirmed my suspicions that Rosemary and Millen were liaising with the 'Visitors'. She once wrote; 'My contacts were such fine ETs, and our close cousins genetically.' As Rosemary was a friend and colleague of Dan Fry, (who admitted providing false identity documents for 'Visitors'), I wonder about Rosemary and Millen's involvement with helping 'Visitors' access human society.

Rosemary made some interesting observations about the 'Visitors'; "There is an order in their authority structure. Many of us who experience both human-like types and the small, large-headed humanoids, consider that the human-like people, although seen less often, seem to be in charge of the operations. In describing the human-like types, one has to keep in mind that they are more advanced than Earth-humans. Telepathy and ESP abilities in general are fully natural to them, and there are some physiological differences. Obviously, there is some genetic connection with *homo sapiens*, which is apparently a hybrid race, as our Bible and other early sacred books inform us."

Throughout her life, Rosemary embraced the study of space and maintained a strong interest in UFO research. She was, for many years, a historian for the 'Mutual UFO Research Network' (MUFON) and mentor and research assistant to many investigators, including myself. Her massive contribution to research on both Mars and ufology was quiet, and without the recognition she never sought, but richly deserved.

She rarely divulged her own experiences, and once commented; "I learned quite early in childhood to keep 'mum' about it, though I suspect my father had some experiences himself, and was equally quiet. He did recognise it, and in a kindly way warned me, when in my teens, against ever permitting myself to be exploited by the unscrupulous...Glad I heeded his counsel!"

The one aspect of 'contact' which Rosemary rarely discussed was the radio contacts, where, in the early 1950s, ham radio operators, all over the world claimed contact with extraterrestrials, either by coded or vocal communication. I wrote extensively about this in a chapter in my book, *'The Days of the Space Brothers'*.

It is well known that George Adamski met Orthon in the desert following a radio communication received by George Hunt Williamson and a ham radio operator in Arizona. Williamson later wrote amongst others, the books, *'The Saucers Speak'* and *'Other Voices'*. This intrigued 'Project Blue Book's' rather sceptical Edward Ruppelt, and he wrote about this new facet of extraterrestrial contact after attending the 'Second Annual Interplanetary Spacecraft Convention', in 1955, at 'Giant Rock' in California.

He later wrote; *'This year two young men had a new story with a new twist. Instead of communicating with the saucers by thought waves, or having the Martians appear from nowhere, they were downright sensible – they used radios.*

'The two men, Richard Miller of Detroit and George Williamson of Prescott, Arizona, who represent a nationwide net of interplanetary hams, told the crowd that they had made several dozen contacts with spacecraft. On occasions, they had also contacted other planets. A group in Michigan had made twelve contacts since September 1954. One of them was with a new type of equipment that transmits messages on a pulsating infrared beam. The design for this new equipment, they said, had been given to them by an electronics specialist of a flying saucer.

'The way that Miller and Williamson presented their facts and showed off their equipment, cut the smirks off the faces of the doubters down to practically zero.

'Communicating with flying saucers by radio or light beams was a new angle to me, and I thought I'd heard every angle. For two and a half years I had been in charge of the Air Force's Project Blue Book, the special project set up to investigate and analyse flying saucer reports. Every time one of the people who were guest speakers at the convention took a new series of photographs, or made a new contact, I soon heard all about it......

'I definitely wanted to talk to the two men because the more I thought about it, the more I was sure that I had heard similar stories while I was still in the Air

Force. Once a friend of mine, a ham radio operator, told me that he had overheard two other hams discussing this interplanetary radio business, and then, later on, a Military Amateur Radio System operator called me and told me a similar story. The MARS operator was very impressed by what he'd overheard.'

Certainly, ham radio operators, all over the world, were picking up unedited transmissions from our early space ventures, but they were much more covert about any extraterrestrial communications. I was fortunate to inherit, from a colleague, several private, secretive letters from ham operators in the 1950s and 60s, where they make mention of specialised equipment, and suggest that these radio transmissions were also occurring in Australia and New Zealand.

'Contact' a South African group, in their newsletter, '*Skywatch*', wrote about these radio contacts, and one of their participating members, Edwin, who in 1963 set up a 'Q. Base', where a handful of UFO enthusiasts met on Sunday mornings and received many messages via his specialised radio tuner. Later, when South African investigator Frank van Vloten visited Edwin, he was told that there were many such 'Q. Bases' all over the world. In some cases, the ham operators had been visited by government officials and their equipment confiscated.

Edwin indicated that the signal was coming from extraterrestrials just outside our atmosphere, and later, a Russian member of the U.S.S.R. Institute of Space Research also mentioned the transmissions, and said their source was from somewhere within our Solar System. He then qualified this finding with the following words; 'It is possible that they, (the signals), came from the upper layers of the atmosphere.'

Was this activity and communication continuing in later years? I don't know, but in the early 1980s, William Pearce, a ham operator from Colorado, noted that there were over 40,000 amateur radio operators in the United States alone. They communicated with each other, and many thousands of colleagues around the world.

He also said most were both professional and highly skilled, with a vast array of sophisticated equipment. Besides comprising normal everyday people, many operators were engineers, doctors and lawyers. He said that the U.S. fraternity had three amateur radio communications satellites circling the Earth, and the Russians had recently launched one of their own.

Many investigator/researchers started their interest in the subject of ufology due to a sighting or experience of their own. Some discuss this, and others remain silent. In 1999, one British colleague, due to some misinformation being spread about him, decided in his declining years to 'come clean' about incidents which went back to the 1930s. Up until then, I had always known him, personally, as a blunt speaking, no nonsense investigator. Because this article was mainly written for his close colleagues, and included in his 'group's' newsletter, I will only use his initials – 'E.S.'.

'Bringing Things Up To Date.'

'Based on the occasional talks I do, and the odd TV and radio broadcasts since 1960, I got interested in 'flying saucers', when they were called that, in 1947, while pursuing papers etc. in hospital with a broken skull. I was a cycle racer in those post RAF service days, and kept up the interest in the enigma while convalescing. On 'De-Mob' leave for three months, I joined Capt. Plunket's Bristol based 'Flying Saucer Bureau' and became a sort of reporter on a pedal cycle!

*'Via this, much of what I found was based on people, with scant knowledge, reporting night time objects which all turned out to be celestial. I bought books, read the papers etc., and pondered on what **was** the answer. That was until 1960, when I came across official cover-ups for the first time, after reporting to Thorney Island air base on the 'glowing cigar' I had just seen over Portsdown Hill, Portsmouth. At about 9.30am it seemingly hovered until two noisy Meteor jets scrambled over the rooftops. I watched in amazement as the two jets neared it, and the object turned slowly on end and vanished into a clear blue sky. My report was dismissed by the Thorney Island control tower officer, who told me twice that I hadn't seen anything!*

'His denial set me on a search for the truth. At that time, I could only think some sort of pre-invasion scan was going on, with technology beyond ours, and in the years that followed, I was to investigate all sorts of avenues in my search for the answer. I saw a couple more craft that defied gravity, and got another denial on one. In 1977 I saw a huge triangular object hovering and then speeding off over my then Southampton home. I found five other witnesses, in a car driving along the M27 at Bursledon, who stopped and watched the same object, at almost the same time, until it too vanished.

'In 1978, a slow moving huge craft passed over my Southampton home on three occasions in February, following a report in the local 'Echo' by a couple who'd seen a similar thing hovering and speeding off in the New Forest, on two consecutive nights. No official body would admit any knowledge of this. I read an 'Echo' cutting the night after my last sighting, saying that Southampton people had reported another huge, silent dark object passing over their homes at the same time. Officials knew nothing and had no explanation!

'During the last incident, with my then wife present, I had a kind of 'out of body' experience, which I thought weird! For some reason, we didn't have abductions etc. in those days. For some psychological reason our thoughts allowed craft with portholes and cabin windows – but crew – Oh no!'

In another article he mentioned that, in 1978, there were three, very close and almost consecutive occasions when huge, silent craft with 'funny lights passed over his home. The last incident had a profound effect on him; *"While watching it, until it was right overhead, I had the odd feeling that a 'ray' flashed from it to me. I laughed afterwards...ridiculous! But somehow I found myself in 'space', among a forest of brilliant stars, with a big light to my right that I couldn't quite get my head around to. Next second I was back on the ground, musing how wonderful nature was...I suddenly 'knew' everything was alive....even the stones beneath my feet, and the flowers and birds etc. At 53, quite a change!*

'This incident changed my entire life at once, and to this day. I discovered, (or IT discovered me), the gift of healing. Incidents, such as 'mediumship' etc. took place. I became interested in spiritualism and more incidents opened my eyes to the paranormal, not at once, but over a period of years. I appeared on TV and radio a few times. Twice weird incidents took place in the studios. I also became, at 53 years old, a sort of 'New Ager', concerned with the welfare of others and the planet, animals etc. etc. I had my eyes opened at last!

'Much more went on. Get my book when and if it ever gets published, to fill in the details, warts and all!' (I don't think it ever was.) *'Strange 'dreams' took place in my home and bedroom, while my wife lay beside me, unaware, since the 'dreams' were apparently physically real. Poltergeist incidents, electrical interference etc. took place in and around the home...much to my wife's terror. In the end, after ten years, it led to a divorce. I went down this new road alone, but was really never 'alone'. Sightings now totalled fourteen over the years.*

'Moving to Netley Abbey in 1982, brought me more in touch with nature, as well as 'ghosts', precognition, clairvoyance, meditation and my 'spirit guide', who had often been described by gifted mediums, but now I could see him on odd occasions. 'Communication' took place between us.

'So life went on. I got married again. Cancer struck me and also my wife. She died whilst I survived, and am clear of it.

'About three or four years ago, when I read about 'abductees' in books by Strieber, Jacobs and Mack, and an earlier one by Raymond Fowler, 'The Andreasson Affair', dim memories suddenly became clear, a couple going back to my schooldays in the 1930's – puzzling incidents that I have always recalled tiny bits of, but not the total. A mystery scar on my left wrist, still there after being acquired in about 1930-1938. Upon further thought, even ridiculous incidents in the seventies, and even stranger ones following the eclipse of the moon, a couple of years ago, when my 'memories' were jogged even more.

'Much was confirmed as being exactly the same as many abductees, Strieber's in particular – but dating from the 1930's!! - 'Aliens'? – Yes, but not necessarily those 'greys', but they came into it. Those strange 'dreams', were impossible to be such upon re-evaluation, and co-incidences that were far too co-incidental. I have met people who turn out to have hitherto unrecognised abduction memories. It is a fact that the mind shuts away disturbing memories until something awakens them, and they pour out.

'My ex-wife recently asked me how my book was going, but refuses to even remember those incidents in the 1970s. She was there on a number of occasions, but I can't recall what was happening to her, or even us!

'So we come up to the present day....more TV programs, articles etc. until in the last TV programs I have finally 'come out', as it were, on those personal encounters of the closest kind. Fortunately, so far, they have caused me very little trauma, possibly because they apparently began in childhood, and quite possibly because I have never been regressed so far....otherwise they may not be so un-disturbing. Who knows?

'My spiritual side, healing, meditation etc., I feel has enabled me to face up to the unseen world of the paranormal. Meditation itself has been a godsend in my somewhat precarious life, even since I found it in the late seventies. Currently, my life is very enjoyable. I don't worry about what the future might *hold as it may never happen. Philosophical? You could say that. My feelings are that the planet and its life are due for a big shake-up in the not too distant future – possibly when the Truth will appear – possibly causing upheaval in many areas as mankind may really come of age. A shock to many.*

'I see the recent and current public news stories, some involving the spiritual and paranormal, merely being a vindication of all that I and others have gone through, often traumatic episodes in our lives. Time, my friends, will tell. The Truth, so it is said, will set us free!'

Back in the 'Good Old Days' the use of regressive hypnosis, to retrieve encounter details, was rarely used, and investigators relied on witnesses' conscious memories.

British investigator, Phillip Mantle, documented a case which occurred on 14th May 1954, in Burnaston, Derbyshire.

Retired Royal Navy Commander, Horatio Penrose, was heading towards Birmingham on the Derby-Burton Road, and as he approached the Hilton Gravel Works, near Burnaston, he suddenly spotted a bright light ahead.

At first he thought it was a speeding, oncoming vehicle, and slowed down. As he braked, he realised it was an airborne object, which came to a sudden halt overhead. At the same time, it caused his own car to come to an abrupt halt, and he was thrown forward over the driving wheel, hitting his head on the windscreen.

He felt a sensation of movement, as if his car was rising into the air, and could see his Vauxhall's metal car roof, above his head, being distorted by the pull of 'whatever it was'. He peered out of the car window, to see the bright light still positioned overhead.

The next thing he recalled was lying in a hospital bed at the Royal Derbyshire Infirmary, where a nurse was telling him he had received several stitches for a cut on his forehead. As he lay there, the memories came flooding back. They were so confronting, he didn't confide them to anyone else for twenty-two years.

He recalled his car being lowered onto the other side of the road, and a man, in a one-piece suit, leaning through the window, pulling him out, and then, with very little effort, taking him up into the air to a large circular object which was hovering directly overhead, and into a brilliantly lit entrance on the underside.

He found himself in a well lit room, where he was placed on a type of examination table. Around the walls were some form of 'control mechanisms', being operated by about five men and women. They were only a little shorter than average, with white skin, short, dark hair, slightly almond-shaped eyes, and all dressed in blue one-piece suits.

One of the women, who was quite attractive, and appeared to be in her early twenties, came across and looked at his bumps and bruises and the cut on his forehead, before giving him an injection from a syringe containing what looked like green fluid.

They then had a conversation which was mainly telepathic. He asked about their craft, and was told it involved magnetic fields. She seemed unduly interested in his service in the Navy and his work with radar. He was wary of her interest, as the war was not long over, and whilst he tried to avoid giving direct answers, she also seemed to be asking questions to divert his curiosity about his surroundings.

He started to feel drowsy, and just before he drifted into unconsciousness, he was startled by the words she put into his mind; "We are not born in the same manner as you!"

He came-to sitting back in his car, where he was found by a RAC patrolman.

In later years there have been countless cases of people being abducted from their bedrooms and suddenly finding themselves aboard a strange craft. Several cases have made me consider that some form of physical teleportation may be involved.

In the December '*2010 MUFON Journal*', Steven White reported the following incident; '*In February of this year, Thomas awoke about 2am in his home in Knoxville, Tennessee. His body was in the air, with his legs pointed toward the ceiling. Thomas grabbed the headboard of his bed and held on. He said that he felt as though he were being returned from an abduction, but he doesn't recall any other details to support that he was abducted at the time.'*

Back in Australia, Ray and Donna Fairly (pseudonyms) contacted me over forty years after their experience. They were still searching for answers.

On 13th March 1973, Ray and Donna had just been to dinner with Ray's parents and were driving home to their apartment on the West Coast Highway in Perth, West Australia. When Donna commented on the beautiful full moon, over the ocean, ahead of them, they suddenly realised that the moon was actually behind them!

They pulled over and got out, staring in amazement at a big red/orange ball, larger than the moon, which appeared to be changing from a round shape to that of a disc. It was huge, and appeared to be near Rottnest Island, about twelve miles off the coast.

In a matter of seconds, the object came rapidly towards them, and stopped directly overhead. It now resembled an enormous disc, and was about as big as an aircraft carrier. Ray wasn't sure, from his angle of viewing, whether it was tilting up or down.

Around that time, a white car pulled up behind them on the highway. The driver wound down his window, rubbed his eyes or face, and then rapidly accelerated away. Ray and Donna were unsure how long they stood staring, but suddenly the object moved rapidly away, backwards towards the island, where it disappeared as a red/orange glow over the horizon. Then it suddenly repeated its original manoeuvre, and hovered once again over Ray and Donna.

Ray said; *'The object appeared to have a clearly defined disc type shape, and a bright orange/red light source appeared to emanate from inside the object and shine through the skin of the object into the surrounding air. It also had a black panel, in the centre, at the front. I could see what I took to be the 'skin' of the object, and it entered my mind that I would like to fire a rifle, to see if the bullets would bounce off what could have even have been a very thin metallic object. Although this was unlikely, due to the strange appearance of the object, and at the same time this was going through my head, I felt as though I was in communication with something. At the same time, Donna was excited, and said she would like to go on it!"*

It is not clear whether or not there was more to this experience than they recall, as their memories of the timing and sequence of events don't exactly 'tally'. Ray didn't remember consciously getting out of the car... '*Yet I found myself in front!*'

Ray commented; *"It was interesting that Donna was excited by the object, and yet my reaction at the time was one of fear. Strange, when we were both experiencing the same event. In the presence of the object I felt that I was being scanned or observed by something. Towards the end of the experience, I felt that I had been rejected. Time seemed distorted somehow for me, and I have great difficulty, even today, working out the timings of this event. I am unsure as to whether the object just disappeared instantly from our view, or retreated gradually back towards the island and moved upwards at a high rate of speed and disappeared. We were considerably shocked and excited by the event, went home, drew sketches and discussed whether to report it. We decided not to, owing to public ridicule etc."*

They did nothing for the next twenty-nine years, when in 2002, after moving to Queensland, Ray came across a photograph of a UFO on a website. It was identical in shape, colour and appearance to the one seen by him and Donna all those years ago. He discovered that it had been taken in 1981/2 by Carlos Diaz in Mexico. He tried contacting, to no avail, people and authorities in that country for further information. Further research indicated that several other credible people had also witnessed similar UFOs during the 'Diaz' investigations later in the 1990s.

At 3.45pm on 3rd December 2003, Ray and Donna noticed an orange ball-shaped object, which appeared to be disc-shaped when viewed through binoculars. It hovered in the northern sky for about fifteen minutes, and disappeared at the same time several 'fighter aircraft' flew over their roof.

In February 2004, a whole series of strange electrical phenomena took place around their home. Light bulbs exploded, the TV turned itself on and off, and there were sudden temperature changes. On the 24th of that month, Ray had a very disturbing experience.

'*At about 1am I had a dream? I was awakened by two little people, who were on each side of me, trying to lift and steady me up from the bed. I strongly resisted and struggled against them. They spoke to me telepathically and said; "It's no use. You are not going to get away this time."*'

'They were then escorting me down what appeared to be a corridor, with one on each side of me. As we reached the end of the corridor or tunnel, I was facing a wall or door that was slowly being bricked up. It may have been a ramp or door that was being closed from the bottom up, with a strong light shining through the narrowing gap at the top.

'At this point I panicked and fought to stop the hole being sealed. I succeeded in stopping the hole from sealing by trying to tear down the wall, ramp or door. While this whole scene was happening, I felt as though I was an observer of the scene. Even though I felt it was also happening to me personally, there appeared to be a strange detachment, almost anaesthesia, or even paralysis during the whole episode. As I was tearing at the closing gap, I realised that I was alternating between two realities in that I was both an observer and participant in the scene, whilst realising that I was also living out the scene in this present reality – in my bedroom?'

Donna said that she had awoken at about 1am, and upon hearing noises coming from Ray's room, had walked down the passage to find Ray protruding half way through the gyprock partition which separated his bedroom from the adjoining bedroom. He was tearing pieces of plasterboard from a large hole that was completely through both sides of the wall.

She said Ray's eyes were open, and when she asked him what he was doing, Ray replied that he was 'trying to get out'. She said that his room was in complete disarray, with furniture overturned and some destroyed. Clothes were strewn about the room, and framed photos, that had been hanging, completely demolished on the floor. Ray himself, seemed to be conscious, but completely non-responsive. He was coated with white plaster dust, and she suggested he took a shower. Donna then replaced the overturned bed, and persuaded him to go back and try to settle down.

The next morning Ray found that his television was broken, and many things in his room destroyed. The metal cabinet of the room air conditioner, mounted through the masonry block wall, appeared to have been bent and moved, and he had a large bruise on the inside of his right thigh. He photographed the bruise, along with the damage. Was this a case of a physical teleportation 'gone wrong'?

Donna said that Ray had been behaving irrationally for a few hours before going to bed, and subsequently he sought the help of a private psychologist. In late 2004, without identifying Ray, the psychologist attended a UFO conference, and after speaking to other contactees, wrote a paper to his local 'College Section Chairs', suggesting that Ray and others were suffering from 'Post Traumatic Stress Disorder', and more attention should be given to these particular cases, which had impressed him with their sincerity.

Ray was left desperate for answers, and even more determined to contact people involved with the Carlos Diaz events. In May 2008, he flew from Townsville to Los Angeles, and then on to Mexico City. A couple of days later he met with Mexican researcher Jamie Maussan, who arranged for some of his group to take him into the country to meet with Carlos Diaz.

Diaz was in Italy, and Ray stayed in the local town until his return five days later, where they met in a restaurant and then later returned to talk at Diaz's home. Ray was really reassured by Diaz's philosophy and insight into the reality of the whole phenomena. He set out on his way home the next day.

There has been a lot of criticism of George Adamski, and his claims of being taken out to planets in the Solar System. In *'The Alien Gene'* I wrote at length about 'Patty' a New Zealand contactee, who although she had conscious memory of her interactions with aliens on Waikeke Island, needed regressive hypnosis to 'fill in the gaps' when taken, by her 'Friend', on board the visitors' larger spaceship.

She talked about 'screens' along one side of a room on the craft. When turned on they showed lots of stars – *'somewhere else – not here'*. This only happened on one occasion, but she felt as if she were being taken away – as if she was being 'drawn in' and 'moving through'. *'There are stars going by – it feels like a window.'* When they arrived at their destination, on another planet, possibly outside our Solar System, Patty felt as if she was there – she could feel it and see it, but couldn't actually touch it.

Is that similar to what really happened to Adamski, who really believed he had physically been taken to other planets?

One controversial witness/contactee was the celebrity 'CBS Evening News' Anchor, Walter Cronkite.

In the 1950s he was part of a pool of news reporters who were taken to a small South Pacific island to witness the test of a new U.S. Air Force missile. Security was tight, and they had gathered some distance from the launch area, which was patrolled by security guards and their dogs.

Just as the missile was fired-up, ready for launch, a large, grey, disc-type UFO, about fifty to sixty feet in diameter, with no visible signs of propulsion, appeared and hovered about thirty feet off the ground.

As the guards and dogs rushed forward, the intruder sent out a beam of blue light which engulfed both the missile, which had just lifted off, and one guard and his dog. They seemed to be 'frozen in time'. After the missile, seventy feet up, exploded mid-air, the disc vanished, and the guard and his dog groggily staggered to their feet, to be taken away by medical personnel.

Cronkite and his fellow reporters, who had been ushered into a concrete bunker, were told that the incident was 'all part of the test', and that they should tell the public that UFOs were not extraterrestrial, and rather part of our own new technology!

Cronkite did not really swallow this explanation, but he was not happy, when many years later, colleagues told the U.S. *'Confidential Reporter'*, that he had recounted a much more personal experience of his own. They commented that he had wanted to keep the experience secret for fear of damage to his credibility.

'Walter told close friends that he was seated on his veranda with an aperitif, waiting for dinner. Suddenly the house and grounds were severely shaken. Cronkite felt himself passing out, and thought he was having a heart attack.

'Here's how the veteran newsman described the event to a close friend.; "I came to, stretched out on something like an examination table, in a round metallic room, perhaps twenty feet across. I tried to move, but was unable to.

"Several beings surrounded me – humanoid, I would say, but fuzzy – indistinct. They seemed to be fading in and out. I couldn't see them clearly. It wasn't my vision, because everything else was clear. I was mainly conscious of large, searching eyes. "

'For the next couple of hours, he said his mind was filled with events from his own past, and from many of the major news events he had covered over the years; "I think they were conjuring it all up and recording it in some way."*

Cronkite then told his friend; *"Every so often I get a powerful urge to go on the air with statements to the effect that the aliens are peaceful, law-abiding beings, who only mean us well, and can be very beneficial to us. But I don't KNOW anything, and am resisting every effort to become an apologist or propagandist for them.*

"I'm in therapy. In the first place I want to know that I am sane, and didn't hallucinate all this. In the second place, if it DID really happen, I want to know if I'm the victim of post-hypnotic suggestion to 'prepare the way' for these, whatever they are. I have never believed in UFOs, but now I have a great deal of indecision on the matter.

"I may be a great disappointment to them, but I am not going before the camera to tell the world they are our loving friends. Leave out the 'r' and they could be fiends."

Was his experience real? His housekeeper said that afternoon he was missing for four hours. Anxious calls were made to the police, and the grounds searched. She later found him sleeping peacefully in the chair on the veranda; *"I swear he wasn't there before. That was one of the first places I looked.*

It can take some time to unravel a strange series of events and memories. Many experiencers suddenly find themselves possessed with extra wanted and unwanted psychic and paranormal abilities. In *'UFOs Now and Then'* I wrote about Jocelyn Frazer, and her ongoing experiences which started, during the 'good old days', when she was a young child. In the book, I documented her conscious memories of the strange events in both her life, and the lives of her biological family, especially her father, but said little about the effect on her physically and personally, which is just as important.

Jocelyn, who is highly intelligent, and a medical professional, was concerned about her daughter, Sonia, and questioned the strange anomalies may also be affecting her. She spoke of what she remembered from previous years, and realised that there was also 'missing time', for which she has declined any regressive hypnosis, at least for the moment. She had also presented with 'needle' and other marks, (possible implants) also evident on her family.

She said; "I have been a vegetarian since the age of fifteen, have a concern with animal welfare and with peace and justice issues as well as concern for our natural environment. I am not a dietary fanatic, but am health conscious. I also attempt to keep myself fit, doing mainly yoga and Pilates, and meditate regularly. I have a general aversion to attending the doctor for any reason, but will go in instances of dire need...My daughter shares this aversion, but fortunately we are both disgustingly healthy." (One of Jocelyn's encounters, whilst still a child, involved being taken to a strange doctor, and involved a more 'intimate' examination.)

"I never had reproductive difficulties as such, and have menstruated as regularly as clockwork. One unusual thing I have experienced, from my early twenties at least, is persistent lactation, despite not giving birth until the age of forty. Embarrassingly, I remember, on a few occasions, 'letting down' in crowded shopping centres upon hearing a baby cry. I had this investigated, but no health abnormalities were found, as was no explanation for this occurrence;

"I also had a sense of profound loss at times with my period, as if I had lost a baby, although, clearly, I did not have signs of pregnancy, such as missed periods. (It is possible this merely reflected some frustrated desire for a child, as my husband did not really want further children, and had a vasectomy early in our relationship.)

"Now, I will attempt to explain how I got to deciding something strange has happened over the course of my life, as well as relating some recent experiences. This will sound quite bizarre, but I had never really given much thought to ETs, UFOs or anything else paranormal for that matter, until suddenly, in about 2015, this all started to enter my consciousness.

"Several things happened. Firstly, since 2010, I have heard a low drumming frequency, and I noticed that, although it does not bother me, it was becoming more intrusive, persistent and louder. At times, I was also hearing some higher frequency noises, and was convinced, and remain convinced, that these are from outside, not a problem related to the health of my ears."

In order to better understand the condition, she went on the internet, and; – "discovered the information on what people called the 'world hum'. This was nothing conclusive, and up until then, the only thing I knew about UFOs and aliens was the 'X-Files'. It led me to reflecting on past events in a new light, basically re-examining things which had been filed under NQR and stuffed somewhere in the back of my brain. I developed an interest, which persists, in the inconsistencies in many aspects of human history, from our evolution, to buildings we should not have been able to build, (and still cannot reproduce), and other historical anomalies and inconsistencies, and the whole issue of 'ancient aliens'.

"I started having some accurate premonitions, and started to develop an enormous level of anxiety about some impending cataclysmic event. In fact, it is with some sense of relief that I read other people have experienced this panic, as I began to feel that I may be losing my sanity for a while. I had never been into a philosophy of waiting for the end of the world, and looked on, with amused disdain, at people who spend their life preparing for disaster.

"I had this strong feeling that I had to get to a location at least 600m, best to be more, above sea level, and a place I had to go actually came to mind. It felt as if this fear had descended on me from somewhere outside of myself, surrounding me like a cloud....I swung into action, buying up non perishable foods, protein bars, vitamins, seeds for growing food etc.

"I also ensured our trailer had some needed repairs, and that the new car we had was fitted with a tow bar. Eventually, my panic ran its course, probably helped by knowing I have the means to pack and remove supplies in the event of a disaster. I have again started contemplating ways of moving us to higher ground, and looking at how well placed we are to sell this house. However, I no longer feel that sickening level of anxiety with which I was previously afflicted."

(Jocelyn was not aware of the fact that most contactees I have known, have experienced this same fear of disaster, and have been prompted to move to higher ground, sometimes even articulating the identical 600 metres above sea level!)

"I also recalled that in our Melbourne home, when I was in my thirties, we would frequently be woken by our stereo switching on to the radio, (thankfully ABC classic), in the dead of night. The volume would magnify to ear splitting levels, and would sometimes then fall in volume again, or fluctuate up and down. Once or twice, I got up to switch it off, although often, strangely, I would drift off to sleep again with this going on, despite always being a very light sleeper. I put this down as being a neighbour owning a piece of equipment which was interfering with the stereo. This may have been the case, but perhaps I was just 'in denial'.

"In later years, when my daughter was born, one of my husband's adult children gave us a regrettable pile of electronic type toys, which had belonged to their now older son. These too would activate at odd hours, suddenly springing to life at some ungodly hour. I put this down to the vibration of traffic, (although logically, I guess, you would really expect this to happen during the day, if this were the case.) I scraped them all into a bag, and donated them at a local op shop.

"Another oddity is an apparent life time inability to wear a watch. Every watch I have owned and worn, (as one usually does, of course), regardless of the quality, has stopped. I am talking here about dozens of watches. Some of these have included very good watches, including nursing watches, usually gifted to me by my mother, as well as piles of cheap watches. I eventually reached the point of refusing to invest in the pricier and higher quality watches.

"My mother gave me a lovely watch in my twenties, very expensive I think, which stopped suddenly. I concluded the battery must have died, and took it to a jeweller, which one did back then. He informed me that the problem was not the battery, and there was nothing wrong with the watch. He could see no reason why it was not functioning. I never wear a time piece now, and have not done so for years. I buy cheap watches, (as I do not own a mobile phone), which I keep in my bag, rather than on my body, and replace them when the battery dies.

"Another issue occurred at some time around my mid to late thirties, when I was experiencing the periods of lost time. Basically, overnight, I developed a significant phobia of heights. It seemed as if one week I was happily doing indoor rock climbing, and the next experienced profound and overwhelming fear when I was even under a metre from the ground. I cannot be sure that this is rooted in anything out of the ordinary, but thought I'd throw it in."

(What Jocelyn didn't know was that a couple of other experiencers had reported they suddenly developed an inexplicable fear of heights!)

Jocelyn also mentioned having a couple of very vivid and strange lucid dreams. Being a very sane and sensible professional, she had just categorized them as 'dreams', but eventually I persuaded her to tell me about them.

"I awoke to find myself floating in the bottom of a fairly large tank of clear fluid, which had a viscosity similar to amniotic fluid. Five people, including me, were in the tank, and it contained us comfortably. The fluid was a comfortable temperature, neither warm nor cold – body temperature. Obviously I was not breathing in any conventional sense in the fluid, but I was able to receive oxygen, I think somehow through my skin. I was also able to see in the fluid, without a blurring effect or any stinging to the eyes.

"The other tank occupants all appeared to be human males, possibly in the 20s to 30s age grouping. One man remained asleep on the bottom next to me. At the top of the tank, two men appeared to be trying to surface, but each time they bobbed their heads out above the liquid, it appeared they were pushed down again, as if by some invisible force. They continued in their attempts.

"Another man floated in a foetal position just below the surface, and gave the appearance of having given up with attempts to leave the tank. I then made the decision to get out, swam to the top, and hauled myself out. I found myself standing on a dull, silver metal ramp, and noted a small slope to the floor. Like the men in the tank, I was naked, and I watched my soggy feet paddling over the metal floor. Again, the temperature was comfortable, neither very warm nor cool, (luckily). Before very long at all, two beings appeared before me.

"They were probably what has become the stereotypical alien. One was taller by about a head, (I am around 157cm tall), and the other just slightly taller. They both had creamy-grey skin, and dark eyes, narrow chins, largish craniums, thin builds with arms proportionally longer in relation to their body than is generally the case for human beings. They were dressed in body suits of a darker shade of grey, (than they were), and I think there was an insignia on the breast, but I cannot remember what this looked like.

"The taller one communicated with me telepathically, saying you must get back in the tank. I replied in like manner with - 'no' - I will not get back in the tank!' After a brief hesitation, the same being repeated that I must return to the tank. I remember thinking they are artificial beings, and as such have difficulty thinking out of the square. I then replied, "I am not getting back in the tank, space boy! Furthermore, while I am here, I might take a bit more of a look around this place."

"The taller one then instructed the shorter being to stay and watch me while he went to get the 'in-charge' ones. After a short while, the grey being returned, followed by no less than four hugely tall, and rather muscular men, all with fair complexions and blond hair, which sat a bit past their shoulders in length. All were clean shaven, (assuming they have any need to shave), and dressed in identical blue body suits, which covered the whole body, including feet, and again I think there was an insignia of some sort on the breasts, but again I cannot recall the design. They also all wore dull red capes. (Again we have a case involving 'Nordic' visitors – with the 'Greys' filling a subservient 'assistant' role.)

"One man made a point of communicating, (nothing was verbal), to his companions – 'don't even try to convince me that this, (referring in some way to me), is any kind of improvement.' They then looked to one of their members, and I have the feeling that this man may have dealt with me in an ongoing way. He had a kind manner, and appeared mildly amused by the development, but I also had the sense of being communicated with as if I were a misbehaving child.

"He approached me and said; "Jocelyn, I know you want to see a better future for your planet, and that you are committed to this idea. I know this isn't always easy, but some personal sacrifices must be made in order to realise this vision. We would appreciate your co-operation." I must point out here that telepathic communication did not strictly mean language, but a sort of communication of concepts, which, as we think in terms of language, I then translated to language.

"I then, as was communicated, co-operated, climbing onto a nearby metallic table and lying back. I felt somewhat frustrated and defeated, but also resigned to what was about to take place. At this point the dream ended."

There was one more incident which was also vivid in Jocelyn's mind.

"The next experience I had in 2017, consisted of what seemed to have been an out-of-body type experience. I had dozed off on the couch, but think I was in the state somewhere between wakefulness and complete sleep. Suddenly, I had a strong sense of an electric current running through my body. This was not painful, but was unpleasant. I then had a sensation as if someone had grabbed my ankles and jerked me down the couch, quickly followed by a sensation of moving upwards.

"I do think this was some sort of out-of-body event, but strangely, I could feel the cord of my dressing-gown digging up uncomfortably under my rib cage. Initially, I had no vision, but then my vision cleared as I moved through a doorway and found myself in a round room with some sort of what looked to be a round control panel at the centre.

"Before me stood one of the other previously mentioned grey men, and he communicated to follow him. As I followed I was thinking these are not ones to exchange pleasantries, as they are artificial beings. I followed the man into a corridor which curved round, and was led to an arched entrance, which had no door. Inside was a group of children who appeared ten or eleven years of age, all dressed in short cream tunics. They all had longish hair, but otherwise did not look physically unusual in any way I can recall.

"They grey being gave me an 'information download', instructing me that the children wished to learn about human emotions, especially negative human emotions, and most especially about the concept of revenge. I proceeded to deliver a lesson to a very attentive young audience, and I will not lay out everything I communicated here. Suffice to say, I was thinking this is going quite well, and had reached a point where I probably did not have much more to add, and at that point found myself waking up on the couch. No more than a couple of hours had elapsed since first dozing off."

I wondered if this was merely a memory or a dream Jocelyn had – or an 'inter-dimensional' experience similar to those reported by contactees in later years.

Jocelyn also mentioned a couple of events which occurred in 2011. She did not know that a very similar report was made by 'Leesa', one of the contactees I wrote about in *'The Alien Gene'*. Jocelyn was at the local Coles, when a strange man walked up to her when she was at the check-out. Suddenly he put his arm around her and said; "How are you going? It's been ages." As she attempted to look around, he stepped back and stated; "My mistake. I mistook you for someone else."

The next week, she was back at Coles with Sonia, and as they were walking across the car park to do their shopping, she noticed another unusual man.

When they finished buying their groceries, and were heading back to the car, he was still there. He passed behind them, and she heard him say; "Come on Mum. Hold it together for her sake!" She knew he was referring to her daughter, and after initial feelings of anger and embarrassment, she realised she had been under a lot of stress in both her business and personal life, and decided to make changes and spend more time with Sonia.

Both these men were middle aged, had longish hair, rumpled clothes, and a slightly hippy appearance. (Identical in description to the one contactee 'Leesa' had encountered in a Nowra shopping centre car park). Just as 'Leesa' had described, there was something unusual about the interactions. Jocelyn sensed an inexplicable 'energy field' surrounding them, and an amazingly strong presence.

Jocelyn finalised by saying; "I have presented this information honestly, attempting to highlight areas of my experiences which may potentially pertain to this general area of ufology. I am interested in engaging in a process which may help with recollection, mainly in relation to the lost time that I have experienced in my 20s and 30s.

"I am fully aware that there is a distinct possibility that I may gain no further information about, or insights into what I may have experienced during this time. I am also aware that if I do manage to open a door to some genuine memories, that these may be potentially traumatising and confronting in nature.

"As you are aware, I am motivated to find out more, largely because the intergenerational nature of this phenomenon is clear to me. I am all too aware that this phenomenon may have already impacted, in some way, upon my daughter's life, and if my own experience is any guidance, may continue to do so, but more heavily in the near future. I have no fixed idea about what happened during the 'missing times', and am prepared to entertain the possibility something may have occurred which involved aliens, (of whatever type), an earth based military organisation or something else I have as, as yet, not considered."

The interference with electrical and electronic appliances seems to be quite common with contactees.

311

In *'The Alien Gene'*, I wrote about Elizabeth, who as a child in Britain, in the 1950s, had seen a large white saucer outside their farmhouse, and possibly had contact from an early age. She had been visited by the 'Men from the Ministry' whilst at school in Britain, and after migrating to Australia, at the age of nine, was visited again by 'men in suits'. They immediately transferred her to the headmaster's class, and then on to a 'selective' government primary school.

Elizabeth was also fairly psychic, and after a 1976 'contact' experience in a remote wilderness valley in the Blue Mountains, not only were her 'abilities' greatly enhanced, she experienced strange 'compulsions', which radically altered her life.

There were other 'side-effects' following her experience. Whenever she stood near computers they would 'go mad', and she was banned from the 'Photostat Room' at her office. The head typist could not understand why the copying machines and other equipment would malfunction when Elizabeth had not even touched them. When she was in supermarkets and banks, their equipment would suddenly 'freeze' until she walked away.

One Thursday night, when she was flustered and in a hurry, the fire alarms were activated as soon as she entered the local shopping centre. Everyone evacuated and the fire brigade arrived, but there was no fire. The next week she returned to the centre, and concentrated this time. Sure enough, the fire sirens rang loudly, but again there was no fire.

Whilst she could live with these unwanted 'abilities', there was one that greatly concerned her. Whenever she became really angry with someone who had mistreated another person or animal, something terrible would happen to them. Was she inadvertently causing harm?

Friends recommended a 'psychic', who was well known and respected. One afternoon she visited his office, and he taught her how to lower the electromagnetic frequencies emanating from her body. During the consultation, she brought up distressing instances when dire things happened to people who angered her because they had hurt others.

She said he went 'white in the face', and grabbed a picture of his Indian 'Guide' off the desk, and clutched it to his chest. He said it was not Elizabeth doing this but 'the powers around her'. He refused to answer her questions, and ushered her out of the door, saying if he spoke about it he would lose his abilities. The next week, to everyone's amazement, he vacated the office where he had practised for many years, and no-one knew where he had gone.

This report left me thinking that although contactees' affect on electronics may come from within, as a result of heightened frequencies following their experience, other events were being influenced by the 'visitors' themselves.

Miranda Vella, although profoundly deaf since birth, was highly intelligent and could speak and lip-read. Although she was fitted with a Cochlear implant when she was six or seven, any regressive hypnosis, regarding previous experiences, was not a practical option.

Like Elizabeth, as a child, Miranda had been visited at school by 'some people' who gave her IQ tests and transferred to a government, 'selective' primary school. She later went on to gain a Bachelor's Degree at University.

Originally she lived in Sydney, and in 1996, when she was going to bed, she saw a flash of red, and then a 'ghost train' going past her window. Two months later her mother said there had been 'something on the roof', flashing red lights.

In about 2006, her whole family, like many other 'experiencers', felt the need to get out of Sydney and onto 'higher ground'. They moved to a property bordering the forest/bushland at Springwood, in the Blue Mountains to the west.

By that time, Miranda was twenty-one, but the strange occurrences followed them. Inexplicable events continued even after they moved to the mountains, and it seems that some phenomena are associated with the people themselves, rather than the area where they are living.

On five different occasions, over a period of time, her mother, who often experienced accurate psychic premonitions, had seen 'blue flashes' which lit up the backyard. Miranda hinted that there were more possible similar experiences, but didn't elaborate.

When the TV was turned off at the power point, it would suddenly turn itself on and take the volume up to the highest level. The doorbell, which had no batteries in it, would ring in the middle of the night. This happened a few times, but they were too scared to go down to the door at 3am. It seemed as if Miranda possesses some form of kinetic ability – when she sits under a LED light, it starts to flicker. She also affected technology, causing static, and got mild to medium electric shocks when she touched door handles or the top of the car.

The paranormal activity increased in 2016. One night, early in the year, when Miranda was on the Gold Coast, her mother and sister were home at Springwood. They thought they heard a knocking on the window, and someone simultaneously walking outside the door. They both 'froze'. Was it a 'break-in? They could see nothing, and huddled together, listening to a sound of thumping – like heavy footsteps in the hall – not normal – then a 'scratching' on the walls – silence – then a loud sound like something shaking!

Later that year, in September, they looked out the back to see what appeared to be a fire in the bush behind their property. Miranda said there were three lights, in a triangular formation, flashing orange and red. If they were on an object, it would have been fairly large. Due to the darkness and terrain, she couldn't tell if it were on the ground or in the air. By the time the Fire Brigade arrived it was gone.

There were other indicators that this may have been a case of generational abduction. Miranda has 'female problems' consistent with other abductees, and she and her mother's sister and daughter all have, as do many others, ovarian cysts on the RHS.

There were also some instances of inter-dimensional travel, where Miranda was seen in two places at the same time, and as intriguing as this case was, the family didn't want any publicity, merely someone to talk to. It was only Miranda who wanted answers, and it would have been inappropriate to arrange any regressive hypnosis.

(In 1983, Argentinean Dr. Virgilio Ojeco, wrote a paper about his work with contactee Filberto Cardenas, who was both deaf and dumb, but could clearly hear the voices of the visitors 'in his head'.)

The contactees' effect on electrical and electronic equipment seems to be a common anomaly. Don Worley, an investigator from Indiana, noted that 'Sandra', a U.S. abduction case he had investigated, also had a strange effect on street lights, which would turn off from as far away as 50-100 feet.

'Alice', from Maryland, also affected street lights and turnpike signs. Shop and store signs would go dark - TV sets would malfunction, computers lose power and radios hiss and crackle!

This phenomenon was still prevalent in later years, when some witnesses reported similar events.

In June 1981, Steve Robbins was a plant operator at a petroleum plant on Teeside. Just before midnight, he was on his bicycle, returning to the control room, when he was startled by a silent, cigar-shaped object travelling slowly overhead. It was a dull bluish-steel colour, with a luminescence like a neon light. It shone, particularly around the perimeter, and was pulsating a bright yellow-white light.

He rushed into the control room, however the object had disappeared by the time his colleagues came out to look. A security guard, over a mile away also saw the object, and their supervisor was concerned. Teeside Airport said there were no aircraft flying at the time, and only four weeks earlier, another employee had reported an 'object' trying to land on the main road at the plant.

A few days later, Steve started experiencing 'problems'. His three-year-old television burst into flames, and he and his wife had to throw it out of the window. For the next few days, whenever Steve was home, many other electrical appliances failed. A vacuum cleaner, toaster, hairdryer, iron and mains alarm clock – all failed – and even a battery powered radio and electric drill failed. The electricity board was contacted, and they installed a mains voltage recorder, but they reported nothing was wrong.

The problems continued when Steve was at work. When he was there, computer terminals would 'go out of sync', as his colleagues referred to the malfunctions which happened whenever Steve was around. In 1983, he went to work offshore, and the problems with all electrical equipment continued to occur until 1988, when they subsided.

Investigator Louis Proud's, recent 2015 article in the *'NEXUS'* magazine, discussed the 'Electric People Phenomenon' in certain people, although they were not necessarily UFO contactees.

Although he claimed they were suffering from 'High Voltage Syndrome', (HVS), he could not state a definitive cause. He thought it could be the person's body generating it internally – but why and how? In some cases it followed an illness, in others after an electric shock, and in several there was just no explanation. He wondered if it was a case of psycho-kinesis, and mentioned how some of the affected people said the problem was more prevalent when they were stressed or upset.

I asked Elizabeth further about this. She agreed that her interference with 'electrics' had only started after her 1976 experience, and did tend to occur when she was stressed or upset, but in later years, she had learned to control it.

The use of hypnotic regression, to recover a witness's memories, is still a most controversial practice. In fact, some British groups banned it many years ago. I am not about to enter into the 'for and against' argument, except to say that in my investigations I have only utilised it occasionally, to 'fill in the gaps' in an otherwise recalled experience, and have always directed the contactee to the services of a known and trusted practitioner.

In 1980, after the 'Greys' had come onto the scene, Jerome Eden, an investigator from Idaho in the U.S., wrote, in confidence, to his colleagues, Fred and Phyllis Dickeson in New Zealand. He made some astounding claims, including an assertion that he had it on reliable authority that certain aliens, which ones he wasn't certain, had been actively interfering with UFO researchers who hypnotise and regress contactees;

'It may be that my long-standing impression of disinformation being given us via certain prominent contactees, throughout the years, vis-a-vis the 'benevolence' of certain was, and is, right on target.....

'The interference has been detected in the form of electromagnetic 'beaming', along with ultrasonics aimed at the contactee, to muddle and confuse the contactee during hypnotic-regression sessions. Further, the Report, which I have seen, indicates strong and continuous electronic 'harassment', amounting to physical torment, which plagued the contactee round the clock! This Report further indicates that these aliens are disguising their true intent towards us by programming the contactees with ideas and feelings that the Spacemen are very friendly towards us, when the truth is exactly the opposite.

'The information received suggests that hypnotic-regression sessions with contactees take place under the following conditions:

'Several hypnotherapists should be present, including if possible, a qualified physician. – The sessions be undertaken in a thoroughly shielded enclosure, e.g. a Faraday-cage-type structure, or X-ray room which is lined, walls ceiling and floor with lead – to inhibit electronic beaming.'

Even by this stage, he must have realised this was not possible for the average researcher to achieve, so he continued: *'If the above is not feasible, the contactee should be interrogated in a multi-storey hotel or motel, preferably in an inside room, (which the contactee should not be told the number of), off a central corridor above the first floor, or in a garaged automobile whose windows have been covered with at least 3 layers of heavy aluminium foil – the foil grounded by contact with the metal window frames, but the automobile itself not grounded.'*

As a final precaution, in addition to the contactee being monitored for physiological changes, both the contactee and the enclosure had to be continuously monitored by instruments capable of detecting electromagnetic and ultrasonic radiation!

I don't know if any government investigations employed these safety measures, but it was certainly beyond the capabilities of any investigator I knew!

Before World War II, nobody had really heard about flying saucers and strange craft in the sky, so most witnesses, especially children and younger people, were hesitant to say anything. Often decades passed, and these youngsters were entering their final years, before they finally 'spoke out' to someone who would believe them.

In 1931, Don Jennings was the foreman at wheat ranch in Oregon. One morning, when he was weeding around the boundary, and leading a team of six mules pulling a cultivator, he could suddenly hear beautiful music coming from the wire fence.

The mules could apparently hear it also, and they stopped, with pointed ears and white, fearful eyes. Their heads were turned towards the fence, but their bodies were pulling in the other direction. The music was 'pleasing to the ear', but like nothing Don had heard before, and definitely not coming from any known instrument. He managed to get the skittish animals moving again, but every time they reached that section of fence, both he and the mules would stop. The music was still audible.

At the end of the day, he took the mules back to the farm, and tied them to a post while he fastened the gate. When he turned around, they were all standing like statues, looking up at the spot where the 'music' was heard. Suddenly a large, silver coloured 'flying object' appeared from the other side of the hill, possibly from where the 'singing fence' was located. It was oblong, fifty to one hundred feet in diameter, and travelling very fast as it sped off to the northeast.

That night, when, over the dinner table, he recounted the event to his fellow workers, they suggested he had been out in the sun too long, and one colleague even mentioned a possible trip to the State Mental Hospital at Pendleton.

The next day, there was no more 'music' coming from the fence, however he felt vindicated when a neighbour reported seeing the same craft, and other witnesses had contacted the local Walla Walla newspaper, who wrote about the sightings.

John Schuessler from 'MUFON' in the United States, received the following report from an elderly man in Gibonsburg; *'I was ten years old in 1933, and returning from school. One block from my home at 424 W. Stevenson Street, I heard a whining sound and looked up. Passing from south to north I saw two discs, connected by a thin shaft, moving slowly through the air. I could not guess the height or size of the discs.*

'At the time, I was deeply in the hobby of building model airplanes, the balsam and tissue paper variety, with rubber band motors. I ran home and told my mother I had seen a different model airplane. She dismissed my story as imagination.

'I have searched through libraries to see if I could see a picture in books, like the discs I had seen, to no avail. I am now nearly 78 years-old, and have never forgotten this. I am a retired FBI agent, and was not dreaming when I saw what I saw!'

In Spring 1955, *'Flying Saucer Review'* printed a letter from Buck Nelson of Ozark Mountains, Missouri, about a 'flying saucer' which had 'landed' on his ranch on July 30th 1954. After the *'FSR'* requested further details, he sent a second letter, which they published in their May/June edition.

Buck said that he was watching his TV one afternoon, when a high pitched noise, and what appeared to be a foreign language, cut across the program. He turned down the volume, and tried to tune the set to no avail. At the same time his dog was barking and scratching at the door, and his pony appeared to have been disturbed.

'A huge disc-like object, at least fifty feet in diameter, was hovering over the house about 100 or 200 feet up. Then it moved off, and dropped below the trees, 800 to 1,000 feet from the house, and landed. I am pretty sure of that because the grass, which I examined later, showed where it had touched down.'

Buck went into the house and got his camera, but by the time he returned outside, the craft had climbed back into low cloud, where there were two other similar objects, which were alternatively hovering, turning left and right, and rising and descending sharply.

'I had a close enough view to see why they were able to make such sharp turns. The ships, which were of a dark aluminium colour, were built with a revolving central core which seemed to swivel so that one part always pointed in the direction of travel. The discs themselves never turned.'

When Buck tried to signal the one which had come closest to him, a beam of light, 'brighter and hotter than the sun', struck him. It had a powerful current which jolted him and threw him to the ground. He was afraid to get up, because he suffered from lumbago and neuritis, and just watched the discs until they disappeared.

It was unlikely that he could find any witnesses to the event, as his ranch was heavily timbered, a 25 mile round trip to the nearest town, and a long way from his nearest neighbour. However, all his joint pains had mysteriously disappeared, and hadn't bothered him since. His photographs were sent to the United States Air Force, and returned without comment three months later. Nothing else happened until the next year, when at midday on February 1st, the three discs returned.

'One of them circled low over the house, and someone spoke to me in plain English over some kind of public address system. I was asked to hold my arm up high to answer 'yes' to any of their questions, and to ask any questions by concentrating and thinking clearly anything I wished to ask.'

He raised his arm when they asked if he was friendly, and, if necessary, could they land, from time to time, on his property. Both times, when he asked if they would land and talk with him, and if they would take him to their home on another planet, their answers were a vague – "Yes, sometime".

In reply to other questions, especially where they came from, they said; – *'There are many others from here on Venus. The Moon is not inhabited, but many planets have a colony of their people living on and exploiting it. They are living underground and in bubble houses.'*

Buck went on to report that – *'As the ship flew around the house, it keeled over enough for me to be able to see through the transparent dome into the cabin. One man was at a control desk lit up with flickering coloured lights, while two others stood up to a circular rail. They were of normal height, but very big-boned, heavily built and muscular.'*

Buck had previously been digging a spring, near where the space ship had previously landed, and had piled a lot of soft, yellow slate-like rock, or shale, near the hole. Suddenly it had all disappeared, and he could only surmise that these 'visitors' had taken it with them, although he had no idea why.

'On March 5th, I had them visit me personally in my house. When they arrived they were wearing nothing, but carried their clothing over their arms. After shaking hands, they dressed in purplish-blue one-piece overalls, with low necks and short sleeves.

'Between this visit and the next, on March 22nd, two UFO investigators from Chicago called and spent three days with me. During that time, on two nights, without success, they set up three flares in a triangle, and a light beam with which they hoped to attract the attention of the Saucers. The investigators told me the reason why the Saucer crew had arrived in the nude was to show friendship and to prove to me that I was talking to real men.'

During their brief appearance on 22nd March, the 'visitors' told Buck that they had been considering approaching the flares and light beam, but there was a jet in the area. Although Buck was hoping to travel in space with these beings, there is no indication that this ever happened.

The instances of UFOs regularly landing on remote properties are not all that frequent, however, there have been a couple of similar reports, although they did not involve the occupants actually visiting the land owners.

Canadian Gene Duplantier reported a case from the Island of Allumettes, Chapeau, Quebec. On May 24th 1969, the *'Montreal Journal'* reported that Leo-Paul Chaput said that for sometime strange flying machines had used one of his fields as a landing strip.

At 2am, one morning three weeks earlier, he, along with his wife and two of his children, saw an intense light coming from one of their fields, 400 feet away. They went outside to be confronted by four objects, each about thirty feet in diameter and sixteen feet high. The light was so intense they had to shut their eyes. They were quite terrified, but after about five minutes, they heard a 'motor noise', and the lights went out as the objects departed.

The next day they found their field had four circles burned into the ground, each 27 feet in diameter with almost a two foot ring around the circumference. Since then they had seen these strange craft return over their fields on several occasions.

In my book, *'UFOs Now and Then'*, I wrote about contactee, 'Leonard', who was living at an isolated property thirty-five kilometres north-west of Tamworth in New South Wales.

One night he saw some yellow-orange lights approaching in the sky above, and thinking it might be a plane in trouble, he put on all his lights so that it would be able to land.

He soon realised that it wasn't a plane. He saw two craft, which came overhead and slowly moved from side-to-side. He sensed an immense feeling of peace and love, and after he mentally communicated that they were welcome, they landed.

Although he never went to the craft, or sought out the occupants, he said he seemed to have a telepathic communication with them. Leonard said that before he moved back to Sydney, for several years after many craft, of varying sizes, came, sometimes four or five at a time. Most had a clear dome, and were a dark, smooth, seamless aluminium on the underside.

The case of Betty and Barney Hill is probably one of the best-known and researched cases in UFO history. Betty and Barney, who appeared to be genuine, intelligent and credible witnesses, have been subjected to so much unwarranted ridicule and disbelief, despite a great amount of evidence substantiating their claims.

Betty and Barney Hill were driving home through the White Mountains in New Hampshire at 10 p.m. on 9th September 1961. They had noticed an unusual light for some time during their journey, when they had stopped a couple of times for their dog, Delsey. The last time they pulled up it was much closer, a large, eighty-feet, glowing white disc hovering very low over a nearby field. Barney, taking his binoculars with him, walked a short way towards it. Betty lost sight of him in the dark, and was trying to call him back.

As Barney ventured closer, he could see about six figures, wearing black uniforms, through the windows, which were curved around the disc. He realised he had been seen, but found himself unable to move. The craft slowly descended, extending its 'fins' and a ladder-like structure from underneath. Barney forced himself to race back to the car, and they sped off down the road.

They then noticed an irregular beeping noise and vibration from the boot, and both felt dazed, with a tingling sensation. Barney who was still driving, didn't know why he made a left-hand turn, and was eventually lost. After a while their 'awareness' returned, and they could still hear the beeping noise, but it was regular. They were now some 35 or more miles away, and didn't reach home until 5 a.m., two hours later than expected.

There were several anomalies on the car, Barney had some odd physical marks, and Betty suffered ongoing nightmares. They notified the police about the unusual craft and occupants, and were later interviewed by an Air Force officer who noted all details, and told them there had been similar reports. They were interviewed at length by a NICAP investigator, who although sceptical of any reports which included beings, concluded they were telling the truth.

By mid-1962 Barney had problems around his groin. His health had deteriorated to the extent he was referred to an eminent psychiatrist who used hypnosis to treat psychological disorders. The doctor was sceptical, but individual sessions with both Barney and Betty indicated they were taken from the car by several 'men' who carried them into the craft. Their captors were humanoid in appearance, with large eyes that stretched slightly around the side of the head. They did not notice any nose, and only a 'slit' for a mouth. They were all dressed alike, in something like military uniforms, similar to those worn by the Nazis in World War II.

Barney had been taken into what looked like a pale blue hospital operating room, put on a table, and a 'cup' put over his groin. He got off the table, feeling happy and relieved, and was guided back to the car.

Betty recalled being taken from the car and calling out to Barney, who didn't pay any attention. One of the men spoke to her, in what seemed like a foreign accent, saying: "Don't be afraid, we are not going to hurt you." She recalled walking to the craft and two of the men taking her by the arms when she didn't want to go in. They were taken up a corridor, and then separated, the man explaining: "No, we only have equipment enough in one room to do one person at a time. If we took you both in the same room it would take too long."

Another man came up, pushed up the sleeve of her dress, and using what looked like a big microscope and 'letter opener', scraped flakes of skin off her arm, and put them on a piece of plastic. He also took a sample from inside her ear, plus a sliver of her fingernail and a couple of strands of hair. (This suggests either a health or DNA check, or both).

The 'doctor' then examined her eyes, teeth, throat and ear, then touched her all over with needles attached to wires. Afterwards they got her to remove her dress and lie on a table. She became concerned when they inserted a long needle into her navel, which was quite painful, and didn't believe them when they told her it was a pregnancy test. It seems that at all times they conversed in English, however some communications were apparently telepathic. As in many other cases, the leader put his hands over her eyes when she became distressed at the needle. The pain went away, but she was sore later.

She was told she had to wait for Barney before returning to the car, and in the meantime asked if she could take something to prove the event. On a shelf she spotted a large book, with strange text which ran up and down in rows, rather than across the page. It was 'different', and contained unusual writing, like something she had never seen before. There were dots, and straight and curved lines, some faint, some medium and some heavy. She asked the leader if she could have it, as some form of proof of their experience, and he agreed, only to change his mind before she left, as his colleagues had objected. They felt it best if Betty didn't remember anything, but added that the Hills could find them again if they wanted to.

Betty was taken to another room where she was shown a map of the cosmos, and talked with the other beings who showed her various trade routes, but avoided pinpointing their own home planet. She thought the map had been rolled-up, and was an oblong two-dimensional depiction of star systems. After hypnosis Betty recalled a three-dimensional hologram, which she was able to draw. It contained sixteen precisely drawn dots of varying size, connected by solid, dotted or dashed lines.

The Hills were taken back to the car separately. It is unclear who was returned first but they found their dog, Delsey, frightened but unharmed, and still in the vehicle.

It was all a bit too much for Dr. Benjamin Simon, the psychiatrist who performed the hypnotic regressions. Perhaps he was thinking of his professional reputation when he concluded that the witnesses had undergone an imaginary experience, brought about by fear of the actual approach of the UFO. Barney must have certainly 'seen something and that it had been a very frightening experience.'

Barney died only eight years later, at the relatively young age of forty-six. The doctors said it was a cerebral haemorrhage, but I wonder if their experience contributed in any way.

There were aspects of the Hill's claims which gained a certain amount of circumstantial confirmation: One would wonder if extraterrestrials would have any 'books', but only six years later, in 1967, Betty Andreasson and her family were in their home in Ashburnham, Massachusetts, when a UFO landed in the backyard. Andreasson said before being taken onboard the craft, she gave one of the aliens her precious bible, and they gave her a thin blue book in return.

She was told it was a 'book of initiation', hers for just a short time, and only meant for those 'worthy' of understanding it.

Her experience was long and complex, much of which the 'visitors' wiped from her mind, but a few days later she opened the book, which had about forty extremely thin pages: *'One side of the pages had strange printing and symbols. The other side was glowing white...There were all sorts of symbols.'* Although the text was not the same as seen by Betty Hill, Andreasson also described dots and straight and curved lines. After about a week, the book was suddenly missing, and she assumed the aliens must have taken it back. Obviously they did not wish contactees being able to provide any proof of their experience.

Then there was the view of the cosmos, which Betty had been shown, and recalled under hypnosis. In 1966 an Ohio school teacher, Marjorie Fish, was fascinated with the concept of the star map and wanted to see if she could match it with known cosmology. She persisted, making a total of 26 three-dimensional models of nearby star systems, but she only found an exact match to Betty's map after a new 'Catalogue of Nearby Stars' was published in 1969, and she was able to conclude the map had used Zeta Reticuli as the base-star start point. Betty's map had been drawn years before these additional stars had been documented!

Marjorie's conclusions were verified by the astronomy department of Ohio State University. Whilst more recently, others have disputed Marjorie's results, they still believe in the validity of Betty's map, but due to later discoveries in astronomy, consider it relates to a different part of the galaxy.

Marjorie Fish, who had done the majority of the analysis on Betty's recalled 'star map', was always convinced it was genuine and accurate, even though it contained astronomical bodies which we had not yet documented. Respected scientist and ufologist, Stanton Friedman, wrote an in- depth review supporting Marjorie Fish's analysis. His extensive article can be found in the *'MUFON UFO Journal'* Oct/Nov 2009. A later study and astronomical commentary was also contained in *'The Zeta Reticuli Incident'*, by Terence Dickinson.

Nearly thirty years later, another case, halfway across the world, in Russia, lent some validity to Betty's claim of a 'star map'. In *'Aspects of UFOs and Aliens'* I discussed how Dr Valery Uvarov, of the National Security Academy, St.

Petersburg, wrote of an interesting event which occurred on 2nd November 1989.

Truck driver Oleg Kirzhakov, and his offsider Nikolai Baranchikov, were driving from Arkhangelsk to Moscow, when they found the road near Emtza railway station was undergoing repairs. They had to detour down a dirt road in order to reach their destination on time.

After rounding a bend in the road, they noticed a huge 'structure' on the right-hand side. The truck's motor stalled, and they coasted to a halt around the next bend. Nikolai remained in the cabin to keep watch and observe, and Oleg got out to investigate. Every time he tried to approach the object, Oleg felt some invisible resistance in the air around him, making it difficult to walk. After some persistence he came to within thirty feet of a huge disc, about 130 feet in diameter, with a dome-shaped top.

Along the perimeter were some dark holes, and underneath he saw two structures, which he thought were supporting the craft. The far edge of the disc was slightly elevated, and resting on some birch trees, two of which were broken. Oleg could see no signs of life, or any doors or windows on the object, and thought something must have gone wrong. Was some assistance required?

As if an unseen intelligence had read his mind, a glimmering red dotted line appeared in front of him. It morphed into a small transparent screen, upon which several words were written in red. Oleg thought it was asking for 'burning fire', and returned to Nikolai in the truck to get some matches and a bottle of laboratory alcohol, which they used as an anti-freeze in the braking system.

(Although the 'screen' and messages were in front of Oleg at all times, apparently Nikolai couldn't see it. I have spoken to witnesses in Australia, who have also experienced the same type of 'message screen'. It may be inter-dimensional or telepathic.)

Oleg told Nikolai to remain in the truck, and he returned to the shoulder of the road where he gathered some dry leaves and set them on fire. Suddenly the 'resistance' in the air was gone. A passage appeared on the surface of the object. It extended into the interior, forming a corridor, at the end of which was a glimmering, bluish light.

A 'shaft' extended down from the object to the ground, and a black 'mass', which looked like a 'bag or sack', came out of the corridor, slid down the shaft, and took the box of matches. By this time Oleg had fallen into a ditch with terror, and Nikolai's frightened face was pressed against the windshield of the truck.

The 'thing' had returned to the craft by the time Oleg had climbed out of the ditch. He stood there in disbelief, trying to recover his senses, and decided to wait and see what would happen next.

There must have been some form of telepathy in play, because as soon as Oleg thought he would like to observe the disc more closely, the screen reappeared with an invitation for him to enter. He tentatively approached, and noticed several round openings, which he thought may be portholes. A narrow metallic tube came out, just above his head, and when he grabbed hold of it, he suddenly found himself just inside an opening above.

He walked down a corridor, which had oval shaped walls and ceiling. There were no doors, just a shimmering light about twenty feet along at the end. Upon reaching it, he found himself in a large hall, with a domed ceiling and a diameter of about sixty feet. It had a diffused light, and panels of flashing lights along some of the walls. There was a long, straight divan, and a circular crack around the central part of the hall. He thought it may be to allow it rotate, giving access to various controls.

He saw two motionless black 'masses', like the one he had seen outside. They began to move towards him, and he stood still, his mind full of questions. The screen was still in front of him, but the answers appeared in his head before he could read them on the screen.

He was very curious about everything around him, including an oval control panel, and geometric symbols on the upper surface of some lamps. Eventually he got around to asking who they were, and where were they from?

The dome in the hall started to dim, and like a planetarium, a three dimensional star map appeared on the ceiling. One star began to pulsate and slowly descend, and he was told it was in his galaxy.

After a while he understood it was time for him to leave. He left the same way as he had come in, and returned to the road. The outer rim and dome had started to silently rotate in opposite directions, and a luminescence surrounded the craft until it resembled a 'ball of light'. It slowly began to rise, then accelerated and shot out of sight to the north east. Oleg was so overcome and trembling that Nikolai had to drive the rest of the way.

This case is interesting because it does seem possible that Oleg was interacting with alien artificial intelligence during his experience. The 'dark masses' he encountered never seemed to equate to a 'live being'. By 1989 we were more adept at detecting any intrusions into our atmosphere by extraterrestrial craft, and the 'visitors' would certainly have the advanced technology to access our citizens this way.

The second factor in Oleg's testimony is his reference to the 'star map'. In the Betty and Barney Hill case, Betty was also shown a 'star map' which depicted trade routes and other information. She recalled a three-dimensional hologram, which, despite being disputed by some experts, was later verified by the astronomy department of the Ohio State University.

.Sometimes it is hard to determine whether a report is genuine or not. This was the challenge which faced Charles Bowen, one Britain's most respected researchers in 1968. The two witnesses, Juan Peccinetti and Fernando Villegas, suddenly retracted their report, but only after they said that they were scared of losing their jobs, and the local authorities had made it a criminal offence to report flying saucers.

Bowen already had received reports from the Mendoza Province in Argentina, and tended to believe the two witnesses whose testimony had originally been published in their local newspapers.

In the *'Flying Saucer Review'*, November/December 1968, he documented the events which apparently occurred on September 1st 1968.

'Around about 4am that morning, the soldiers on duty in the guard-room at the General Espejo Military College were surprised by the sudden appearance of two young men, casino workers, obviously in a state of shock, and babbling that their car had suddenly stopped, and that when they got out to investigate the cause, they had seen a flying saucer close to the ground. Five small beings, who communicated with them in a strange manner, took blood samples from their fingers, left inscriptions all over the car, and disappeared up a beam of light into the object, which accelerated away vertically.

'The startled guardsmen, no doubt feeling singularly unqualified to deal with people who saw things like that, suggested the men should go at once to the Lagomagiore Hospital.'

The two men went to the police, and then onto the hospital. Unbeknown to them, the staff at the Mendoza railway station had a sudden and total blackout of the lighting system at the same time the witnesses reported their car had stopped. Also, at 3.45am, three minutes later, Senora Maria Spinelli telephoned police from Dorrego, 6km from the scene of the encounter, to say that a strange, luminous object was flying around, very low overhead. One of the soldiers on duty at the College, also said that he had heard an explosion and seen a glow in the distance. He later, also possibly fearing repercussions, denied the statement.

Further details were elucidated in subsequent interviews with the two casino workers. That morning, Juan and Fernando had finished their shift at 3.30am at the Mendoza casino. They set off for home in their Villegas' vintage 1929 Chevrolet, number plate 2999. When their car stopped, it was in quite a dark area. Juan thought that might have happened at 3.42am, as his watch stopped at that particular time.

When he got out of the vehicle, to see what was wrong, they both found themselves 'paralysed', unable to move, and face to face with three 'humanoid' beings. Charles Bowen said in his report; *'Two more of the creatures, so we are told, were standing near an enormous circular or oval-shaped 'machine', some 4 metres across and 1.5 metres high. This object was 'floating' in the air, 1.2 metres above a piece of wasteland. A powerful beam of light was directed from the object, towards the ground, at an angle of about 45 degrees.*

'The beings, about 1.5 metres in height, appeared to be of human height, except that their heads, which were hairless, were strikingly larger than normal. The creatures wore overalls like those of attendants at a petrol filling station. Their movements were 'gentle and quiet', and as they approached the witnesses, they crossed a ditch – 'as though by a bridge'.

Both men reported that when the entities came close, they could hear a quiet, foreign sounding voice repeatedly saying; "Do not fear, do not fear." Fernando said they received the following message: *'We have just made three journeys around the Sun, studying customs and languages of the inhabitants of the system. The Sun benignly nurtures the system; were it not so then the Solar system would not exist.....Mathematics is the universal language.'*

329

While they were listening to what the being had to say, another little humanoid was busily using a small device to trace inscriptions on the doors, windscreens and running boards of their car.

'Then there next appeared, close to the hovering object, a circular screen, not unlike that of a television set. On this there appeared a series of images. The first was the scene of a waterfall in lush country; the second a mushroom-shaped cloud; the third the waterfall scene again – but no water!' Clearly this was a warning about our use of atomic weapons.

Juan and Fernando said that after this the entities took hold of their left hands, and pricked their fingers three times. They noticed that the creatures' hands felt no different from those of fellow humans.

'Then they turned towards the hovering 'machine' and ascended to it along the light beam. Swiftly there followed an explosive effect, and the object is said to have risen into the sky, surrounded by a vast radiance, and then to have disappeared into 'space'.'

The hospital examined both men, and reported that three small identical puncture wounds were found on the fleshy parts of their index and middle fingers of their left hands. Blood tests proved negative, and for two days the witnesses were kept apart, but their testimony remained consistent.

At that stage, the Police Commissioner impounded the witness's abandoned car, however radiation tests proved negative, as did those made at the actual landing site.

Unsuccessful attempts were made to decipher the inscriptions on the car, and the Mendoza Centre for Space Research proposed this hypothesis to reporters from the *'Gente y a Actualidad'* newspaper; *'The sketch done by the humanoids represents two solar systems – the Earth's system, consisting of Mercury, Venus and Earth, and the Jupiter system, containing the planets Io, Europa and Ganymede. Between Ganymede and Earth there are two parallel lines, as though to indicate a two-way trip, and establishing that the source of these beings is Ganymede, a sphere that is 776 million kilometres from Earth.'*

Charles Bowen, naturally, did not agree with this interpretation. Investigators in Argentina considered that the witnesses were not 'fanciful' or publicity seekers, and were telling the truth as they knew it. This report was still being speculated upon some twenty years later.

British expert, Gordon Creighton, investigated in depth, and wrote of another unusual incident which occurred on October 28th 1973, in the Bahia Blanca region of Argentina.

Dionisio Llanco, a lorry driver, with a load of building materials, was embarking on a two day trip to Rio Gallegos in southern Patagonia. It was still very early in the morning when he soon realised one of his tyres was faulty, and stopped at the side of a deserted road to change it. As he was kneeling down, about to replace the wheel, an intense yellow light appeared behind him.

At first he thought it was another approaching vehicle, but when the light turned bluish, similar to a welding arc, he tried to stand up to look, but found his legs would not respond.

'Still kneeling, however, he managed to turn partly around and saw, near a grove of trees, a great luminous, plate-shaped object hanging motionless about six or seven metres from the ground. He also saw, close behind him, three strange people, who were eyeing him fixedly. Once again, he tried to stand up, but he could not, and he realised that he was also unable even to speak.'

They were two men, just over five-and-a-half feet tall, with blond hair, combed back, and a woman, approximately the same height, with long fair hair which reached half-way down her back. Their faces looked totally human, except for wide foreheads and elongated eyes, giving them a slightly 'Asian' appearance. They were all dressed alike, in tight-fitting grey one-piece suits, three-quarter length yellow boots, and long gloves of the same colour.

As they were speaking, in squeaky, sharp tones, in a language Dionisio had never heard before, one of them grabbed him by the collar, and pulled him upright. The other 'man' put a small object, with a 'nozzle' at the end, onto Dionisio's index finger for a few seconds, leaving two drops of blood when he took it away. Although Dionisio felt no pain, he must have fainted.

He remembered nothing else until he 'came to' nearly ten kilometres away. When he regained consciousness he was lying between some wagons at the 'Sociedad Rural de Bahia Blanca'. He had no memory, but feeling cold and nauseas, staggered towards the main road, where he must have fainted again.

The next he knew he was in a bed in the Municipal Hospital, where his clothes were neatly folded at the bottom of the bed, but whilst his watch, cigarettes and lighter were missing, his money was still intact in his trouser pocket.

When his memory returned, and his first concern was for his truck, which the police found where he had left it, jacked-up, ready for the wheel change. His documents, in the dashboard compartment, were still intact.

He spent the next ten weeks in hospital, initially suffering from total retrograde amnesia. He didn't know who he was or anything about his past or what had happened to him. Doctors thought he may have been hit by a car, but there were no signs of external injuries, and there was no evidence of a fractured skull.

Eventually, an entire expert medical team was called in, and after specialists tried Penthotal and hypnosis, his memory started to return, and he recalled some additional details, which were always consistent during his treatment.; *'He said that he had been changing the wheel on his truck ....and that a few minutes later he found himself inside a space-craft, the interior of which 'resembled the inside of a ship, and had a leaden-coloured metallic floor.*

'Seen from the outside, he said, the machine was of a vivid yellow colour on its upper part, and a purplish colour on the under part. He said that while inside the machine, he had spoken telepathically with three beings in tight-fitting clothing and yellowish-orange boots. They told him they had been visiting earth since 1950 in order to study our behaviour and make a record for posterity.'

'It seems that, according to the information that Dionisio says was given to him, during the ten years up to 1960, these extra-galactic beings had been taking back samples of terrestrial materials to their worlds. From that date, however, they have been concentrating on the establishment of contacts with us in order to determine the degree of adaptability capacity in human beings, and the possibility of moving them out onto their planet in inter-stellar space should the need arise;

"Those people said that our planet is bound to suffer very great catastrophes if our behaviour continues as it is at present."

He also noted seeing a cable stretched between the space-craft and a nearby high-tension wire, and later investigations disclosed a rise of power consumption that night. Other strange facts were that he was a very simple, uneducated man, unlikely to invent such a complex story, and once he emerged from the Penthotal and hypnosis, Dionisio still remembered nothing from when the beings seized him by the collar and he awoke in hospital.

One of the doctors later stated; *"He is speaking his truth....At the beginning I was most sceptical, and at the moment there is only one thing I can say to you; when subjected to tests by methods which in normal practice are acceptably sure, such as hypnosis and Penthotal, Dionisio told what he thinks he experienced."*

'The doctor also revealed that Dionisio had been given an exhaustive psychiatric examination, and that there was no evidence that he had been lying, even though his statement may not be sufficiently valid for his claim of having made contact with extra-terrestrial beings in a space-craft to be taken as the established truth.'

CHAPTER TEN

ALIENS AMONGST US

There have been, and still are, reported cases of extraterrestrials living, incognito, in society. There are many, often whispered accounts, of aliens, indistinguishable from ordinary humans, here amongst us.

THE EARLY YEARS

Many of the cases, which occurred before World War II, involved children or young teenagers, and were not reported until many years later, when the witnesses had reached adulthood. Often, there were only brief sightings and not much imparted to the youngsters regarding the 'visitors' activity on our planet.

There are some unanswered questions regarding the origin of some of the craft seen by witnesses in the early part of the twentieth century. It seems unlikely, in those years, that they were built on Earth.

British researcher, Jenny Randles, received an interesting letter from eighty-seven-year-old 'Frank', who was ten years-old in the summer of 1901. In a later interview, he detailed that at the time he was living in an end terrace house, at Bournbrook, near Birmingham.

One warm evening, when he was walking down a path behind his rear garden, he saw what looked like a 'strange hut' sitting on the grass. It was possibly about four feet high and six feet long, and had a bluey/green metallic sheen with a small turret on top with and a tiny door in the centre.

'As he approached the object, Frank saw two small beings, (less than four feet tall), come from the door, which opened outwards. One stayed by the door, but the other moved slowly towards him, arms outstretched, waving in what seemed to be a 'stay away' gesture. Frank obeyed and took a few steps backward.

'These two beings looked human, with normal features. They were clean-shaven, (at a time when many men were not), and wore closely fitted, military style uniforms of a grey-green colour but with no markings to suggest their origin. By far the oddest feature of this uniform was the helmet – a dark cap that covered the ears without means of support. From the top came two wiry extensions, either side of the head, each about nine inches high.'

As soon as Frank moved back, both beings re-entered the craft, and it emitted a blue, glowing arc before taking off with a 'whoosh', and speedily disappearing over the rooftops.

The 'Airship Scare' of the early twentieth century, may well just have been that – dirigible 'airships'. Researcher, John Pinkney, published a 1915 *'Bulletin'* cartoon which showed a cigar-shaped craft shining a brilliant search beam across a rural Australian sky. A bloke was standing in the foreground saying; "Well, I've seen some meteors in my time, but never one going backwards before!"

Gordon Newly, the gentleman who sent it to him, wrote: *'There was no other information at all. The reason may be that the war precautions act may have censored the papers, to avoid panic about an invasion.'*

By the end of World War I, the 'dirigible' type craft seemed to have faded into oblivion. Maybe most of them had an earthly origin after all. In their place came much more interesting and 'less worldly' reports.

In my book, *'The Alien Gene'*, I wrote about several of these early cases:

In June 1923, ten-year-old Norman Massie, from the United States, encountered a strange domed craft which had landed in one of his parent's pastures. Before it took back to the air, he could see five human looking occupants, who were at least four feet tall, with blond hair.

The next year, Ian Rogers, who was only a boy when he lived in the Australian outback town of Coolamon, was checking rabbit traps when he saw a strange craft land in a clearing in the Lysterfield State Forest. It was cylindrical, about thirty feet wide, with four square windows along the side. He also recalled seeing lights of some kind. Some 'people' got out, but went in a different direction to where Ian was hiding. After about an hour the craft took back up into the sky, leaving a burnt area on the ground, and singed trees and dead birds all around. At the time he souvenired a piece of 'magic metal' left behind. Unfortunately, by the time he made this report, many years later, he had mislaid his 'piece of metal', but apparently if he rubbed it with his hands, it would 'move off' of its own accord.

My colleague Bryan Dickeson received this interesting report, which dates back to 1920, in the cotton fields of Bethel, North Carolina.

Fourteen year-old Nicora and her family were day labourers during harvest time, when they saw 'something large' flying over the farm. It was silver, bigger than a car, and 'like two pie pans, placed together, lip to lip'. It zigzagged across the sky, and landed in the field in front of them.

Two little bald, white men got out, and pointed short 'sticks' at them. Nicora said they were the size of little boys, but their faces looked older. One began digging in the dirt, and then put the soil and a small plant into a bag. Still pointing the 'stick' they backed up and entered their strange craft, which then took off and zigzagged back in the direction from whence it came.

A 1963 edition of *'Flying Saucer Review'* published an interesting article by Alberto Albanesi, who was initially a very sceptical Italian investigator. During his research, he interviewed an elderly man, who in 1924, was managing director of the Reggio Emilia Gas Company.

One August night, just after midnight, he went back to his office; *"I noticed an enormous disc, with a diameter equal to the apparent diameter of the moon. The disc was at the far end of the furnace-yard, and at the side of the road leading to the steam-boiler. And it had the same reddish colour that the moon has when it is seen rising through mist.*

"The disc was slowly descending. It did not leave behind it the luminous tail that meteors have. I stood there, amazed, unable to utter a sound. I wanted to call the firemen, who were busy feeding the furnaces, but I couldn't. Meanwhile, the disc, still moving slowly, vanished behind the boiler-house."

French researchers, Joel Mesnard and Michel Seythoux, briefly reported a 1926 French incident, where a woodcutter saw a brightly lit sphere hovering at treetop level. Whilst the occupants ignored him, he could see several human-like figures inside.

Many years after the event, schoolteacher Richard Sweed told APRO of an experience from October 18th 1927, when he was driving from Bakersfield,

California to Yuma Arizona, and saw a strange bluish-grey metallic craft taking off from the ground nearby.

It had a diameter of about sixty feet, with holes or round windows, partly covered by protruding ceramic or metal 'lenses'. It made a 'whining, humming, wheezing, swooshing' sound as smoothly ascended into the sky at a 45 degree angle. On the spot, where it had been, there were 'fused-like glass crystals'.

Italian researcher, Paoio Fiorino, documented another 1927 incident from Corbola, when a twelve-year-old girl was collecting drinking water from the river 'Po'. A shiny red object, about three metres in diameter, and making a hissing sound, descended from the sky, later crashing into the water.

After a couple of minutes, there was a large 'bubble' in the water, and the craft resurfaced and flew off. During that time, she noticed what appeared to be a 'little man' sitting inside. She could only see his neck and face, but he was not wearing a helmet, and he had 'human features'.

The next year, across the world in America, Henry Dillon was driving along an unpaved country road near Yakima, Washington. Jacques Vallee described how, when Henry reached the top of a slight rise, he saw an object slowly coming into view; '....it was described as resembling a metallic hexagon, with a dome on top and olive-drab in colour. The witness could see rivets along a vertical section and a two by three foot window set in a metallic frame.

'In the window he could see the upper torso of a man dressed in a dark blue uniform. The man had a dark complexion and was totally human-like. He looked intently in the direction of the witness's car, and then the object rotated, flew across the road, and shot away at terrific speed.'

Was this one of ours as early as 1928?

'NUFORIC' unearthed another case near Burns, in Oregon in July, 1929: 'The witnesses were travelling east of town, climbing up through a cut in the rim rocks, when an object, very slowly flew over the top of the car, about 50ft over the top of the rim rock.

'The object stopped, and through a transparent window, the witnesses could see two completely human-like figures that appeared to be pointing down at them, using their arms and hands.

'One of the witnesses stepped out of the car, but his mother demanded that he get back in. He stood on the running board, observing the craft, which was two tones of brown. The craft, which had windows in the middle section, hovered for about forty seconds, emitting a slight hum.

'One of the figures then moved to another window, and the craft suddenly accelerated and was gone in a blink of an eye.'

In Australia, Ken Dyer, a retired school principal, recounted an event from 1929, when he was just a lad in Mathoura, a small town between Echuca and Deniliquin in New South Wales.

He and some other pupils from the local school had stayed behind after classes to play tennis. They were standing around, deciding who would play the next set, when they saw an object passing across the sky;

'It appeared from behind a big fleecy white cloud. It was travelling very fast, and in a few moments traversed the clear part of the blue sky, before passing out of sight behind another fleecy white cloud. We moved to see it reappear, but it didn't show up again. One friend must have seen it sooner than I, for I remember him saying; "Gee, did you see that?"

'It made no sound, was the shape of a bullet or cigar, silver in colour, and there were no flashing lights. We must appreciate the fact that in 1929 there were no aeroplanes or dirigibles that we could have mistaken it for. It had no wings nor tail piece.'

'In his 1990s letter, the now elderly man mused upon the possibilities; *'Since then, our scientists have sent probes into space to photograph other celestial bodies. Many of these, after having served their purpose, continue in space never to return.*

'I repeatedly ask myself if what we saw in 1929 was a probe launched from some other inhabited planet of perhaps another solar system. If so, was it sent to investigate 'Earth', or had it sent back information on some other planet, and having completed its mission, it had no alternative but to continue wandering about space and by chance just happened to pass within sight of our planet.'

In June 1931, Sir Francis Chichester was piloting a small plane from New Zealand to Australia. In his book, *'The Lonely Sea and the Sky'*, he wrote about many of his adventures, including that day, when he encountered a strange craft sharing his air space. Many years later, he was reported as saying; *"It looked like a strange kind of airship, but unlike any I've ever seen. Its colour was a dull greyish-white and it was ringed with brilliantly flashing lights. The thing followed me for several miles across the Tasman Sea, before accelerating from sight.*

"I hadn't a clue what I was sighting until the 1950s, with the spate of flying saucer sightings. Only then did I deduce that I might have been followed by a UFO."

Only a few days before he was found murdered in 1995, Russian UFO researcher and former cosmonaut, Aleksei Zolotov, was interviewed by Valery and Roman Uvarov. He revealed an experience which happened in 1933, when he was only seven-years-old.

He claimed he encountered an alien who was five or six feet tall, and of medium build. His head was one-and-a-half times bigger than that of a normal man, with prominent features. His face so wrinkled, that he appeared to be about eighty years old.

What surprised Aleksei was that he didn't seem to be wearing any clothes; *"His body, which was the same colour as a man's, didn't have a single wrinkle. A lot later, when I started to research the phenomenon of UFOs, I discovered that the aliens wear overalls, made from a fabric without wrinkles, which fully cover the entire body."*

The entity, which was humanoid in appearance, stood right in front of Aleksei, and had an 'impressive and penetrating gaze'. When their eyes met, Aleksei realised he wasn't a man, and after a few seconds he ran away. When he returned the 'man' was no longer there. He felt some kind of 'message' was silently imparted, and that was why he had a lifetime interest in the subject.

Certainly, he entertained the same thoughts as other contactees during the mid twentieth century. The extraterrestrials will not interfere in our affairs, or give us new technology, unless we are on the brink of destruction; *"But we have already discussed the fact that today it might be out of the question that they will contact us, in view of mankind's aggression and the low standards of its moral level.*

Looking at the history of the development of our civilisation, it's almost possible to say, with confidence, that we must find our own way out of our problem."

British colleague and researcher, Omar Fowler, interviewed retired Major F. Turner-Bridger in 1978. He had been a flying-pilot with the Royal Flying Corp in 1916, and spoke of some of his wartime memories, before mentioning an incident which occurred between the Wars in 1937.

He and his wife were driving along a lonely spot on the road between Sussex to Surrey, when they noticed a mysterious object hovering in the sky. They pulled up in a side lane, next to an unused field, and another car also pulled up behind them.

They all watched this baffling craft which was surrounded by orange flame, and had a hump in the centre. Suddenly the object flew out of sight over Blackdown Hill, but after about five minutes, reappeared further down the ridge. He *'watched in wonderment before it eventually disappeared at terrific speed.'*

"My thoughts then began to wonder, and as Farnborough, (Royal Aircraft Establishment), was not many miles away, I imagined that it was a very scientific object being tested out."

In 1968, the U.S. 'NICAP' organisation wrote about this following report, which it received many years later.

'One summer evening in 1933, Frank van Keuren, an electronic assembler and former Air Force veteran, was fishing with his father in the inland waterway complex between Tuckerton and Beach Haven, New Jersey;

"All of a sudden we were illuminated by a very brilliant floodlight from an object which couldn't have been more than a thousand feet...in the air. It didn't have any running lights or make a sound."

'The disc shaped object was travelling slowly through the dark sky, and after playing the bright light on the witnesses for several minutes, it crossed over and illuminated some radio towers in the distance.'

Night-time fishermen often unexpectedly witness strange craft in the sky. In 1968, the Sydney based group, 'UFOIC', of which I was a member, was contacted by Patrick Terry, who had always wondered about an experience he had in 1935, and a photograph he took at the time.

Between the wars, he had been stationed with the military at Newcastle, and enjoyed spending any spare time fishing from nearby Nobby's Head. That particular night, he noticed a flash over the ocean, and then a steady light appeared. It was brighter than a full moon, and hovering about a mile away, perhaps 10,000 feet above the water.

'It was yellow-bright on the lower part, gradually diminishing through three dark bands into grey. The whole complex appeared actually as a tremendously large mushroom-shaped object, consisting of three floors, smaller supporting the larger one, and the light from the bottom floor illuminating all three upper sections.'

The object then descended to a height of about 5,000 feet and remained stationary for a few seconds before quickly returning to its original position. Patrick's surprise and curiosity was such that he took some photos with a camera he happened to have with him at the time. After hovering for another ten minutes, the object began revolving at increased speed, and moved away, disappearing towards the north, and out of sight, within three seconds.

'UFOIC' analysed the photos, which they considered to be genuine. They showed a definite circular object with details seen well on enlargements.

In 1975, the *'Official UFO'* magazine carried an article from a North Carolina investigator, who mentioned a case which dated back to the 1930s.

Dr Katherine Rankin and Mary Rankin, now a retired school teacher, were both youngsters when, on a clear May day, a dark coloured, top-shaped UFO, about forty feet wide, landed in their back garden. They and their parents remained in the safety of the house, and stared in amazement as the object sat on the ground for five to ten minutes.

It appeared to be hollow, and was wide at the centre, and tapered at the edges. There was a 'window', through which they were startled to see the head and shoulders of an 'occupant' inside. They thought that this 'person', who was wearing a dark tight-fitting outfit and some form of helmet, or tight-fitting head gear, was responsible for the operations of the strange craft.

Finally the UFO lifted silently up, travelling smoothly away. It seemed to have the ability to both hover and move perpendicularly and horizontally. They could not detect any exhaust fumes, and one of the witnesses felt that it was 'propelled by some kind of electric power at varied speeds'.

British researcher, Jenny Randles also wrote of an incident which although it occurred in 1942, wasn't reported by 'Elsie', the witness, until she was fairly elderly.

During World War II, the young Elsie, who lived during the blackouts in Halifax, was bedridden with severe jaundice. Her bedroom was illuminated only by the dim embers of the coal fire. Suddenly, a huge electric blue sphere appeared outside her bedroom window, and three figures emerged, and then 'floated' to the foot of her bed.

The room was incredibly silent as they seemed to be 'busying' themselves at her side. They were about five feet tall, wearing silver overalls, and had something which looked like a 'goldfish bowl' on their heads. After a while, her nocturnal 'visitors' floated back through the bedroom wall, and as they disappeared, so did the blue glow.

Most people thought that, due to her illness, Elsie had merely been hallucinating. The next day, the doctor and her family were amazed to discover her jaundice had disappeared. She kept her silence for a long time, only to 'open-up' after seeing pictures of our own astronauts wearing the same 'goldfish bowls' she had witnessed all those years ago.

In 1976, the *'Irish UFO News'* told of a disturbing incident which happened over thirty years ago at Christmas 1945.

'NUFON' summarised the witness's account: *'It concerns a now older man, who went to visit a dying uncle on a small island off the West coast of Ireland. Unfortunately he had already died, and he consequently walked through the deserted fields towards the shore to wait for the boat to return him to the mainland. (He did so despite claiming there was a blizzard and a gale.)*

'Suddenly a flash was sighted out at sea. It flashed a second time, but stayed lit for two minutes. Then an object with a square underside and a silvery dome, surrounded by purple lights, shot from the sky onto the sea. It rested there, making a whirring like a drill, and then rose before descending slowly into the fields. (It had crushed two cattle underneath, who apparently had not run away.)

'The dome slid upwards, and two figures with squarish legs and out of proportion bodies, wearing grey-black rubber suits, got out. One walked to the nearby shore and out onto the water, and placed a 'phial like object' there.

'A farmer's dog then came onto the scene, barking. Thinking it was one of the cattle, a red ray was fired at it, and it burnt right through. Then the dog arrived, and a box with lights and antennae was pointed at it. Hypnotised, apparently, it walked right into the box and was put on board.

'Then they directed a huge scanner at the sky, and five or six objects flew by overhead, and disappeared. A beam of light was directed around the area of the landed craft. One of the beings head swivelled round, without the body moving 360 degrees to follow it! Then a gas enveloped the craft and the beings returned to it. They floated upwards into it – 'magically'. One being saw the crouched form of the witness, raised his hands to the sky and waved.

'The witness ran away and reported the incident to the farmer, who told him never to mention it, as he would have his life ruined. Apparently, he often found his field yellow in a morning, and his animals mutilated. Hundreds of dead fish turned up in the sea, and the water was discoloured. He saw lights often too.'

In other cases, even in those early years, the 'visitors' were more forthcoming regarding their presence amongst us. In my book, '*The Alien Gene*', I discuss the 1920 contact made by teenage Albert Coe, who was paddling down a remote Ontario river, in Canada, when he happened upon a blond-haired young man, who had fallen down a cliff. His torn bandana had blood on it, indicating a physiology similar to our own.

He helped him back to his 'aircraft', which was a twenty-feet round silver disc, parked downstream, and resting on a tripod. In later meetings, extending over five decades, the young man claimed that a natural disaster on their own planet had resulted in them migrating to our Solar System, where they later interbred with humans.

Some details, such as colonies on Mars and Venus, were a little suspect, however Coe was told that some of the 'visitors' race, the 'Norcans', had infiltrated human society since 1904, in order to observe and evaluate our progress, as humanity was on the verge of discovering nuclear power, which could have disastrous consequences for our planet.

Another meaningful 1932 contact was made by twelve-year-old Leo Dworshak and his young brother, who lived on a farm in North Dakota, U.S.A.

On several occasions they encountered a large, blue 'spacecraft', with inner and outer bands rotating in opposite directions, which would land in a nearby valley. After visiting the site a few times, they got to know the occupants, who looked like normal men, between five to six feet tall, with light beige complexions, short light brown hair, and blue eyes with dark pupils.

The two boys were allowed to see the inside of the craft, which had living quarters, and a 'movie screen' showing pictures of 'a place or process we could not fathom'. They told the lads that they were from another galaxy, and had been visiting Earth for thousands of years. At that time, up to 48 of their group were living here to monitor human activity.

Leo had spasmodic contact with his 'space friends', the last time being in 1963, when they told him that due to our own technological advancements we had become a threat to their ships.

In later years, another contactee, Udo Wartena, received similar information. In May 1940, he encountered a hundred feet wide, thirty-five feet wide, disc shaped craft in Montana, U.S.A. It had been hovering above the ground, apparently to take on water. A young 'man', with white hair, descended from the hull. He had clear, almost translucent skin, and wore a grey cover-all.

He engaged in conversation with Udo, and explained that he, and his older colleague, who was still inside the craft, were from a distant planet which had been monitoring our civilization for some time, including living with us incognito; "As you have noticed, we look pretty much as you do, so we mingle with your people, gather information, leave instructions or give help when needed." However, they were not allowed to interfere in any way.

Udo later regretted declining their offer to go away with them.

Australian researcher, Warren Aston, who was interested in this particular aspect of the subject, noted that the 'visitors' may have been with us longer than we think.

He wrote about a Spanish case from between the 15th and 16th centuries, which was originally publicised by researcher Salvador Freixedo; *'A famous medical figure, Dr. Eugene Torralba, was joined by an energetic young man, with very pale skin and blond hair named Zequiel, who offered to assist the doctor for the rest of his life. 'El Rubio', ('the blond'), as he came to be known, taught Torralba the use of herbs and various advanced practices as well as honesty in his dealings. 'Zequiel taught the doctor advanced theology, how to win at gambling and how to predict future events. The good doctor's wealth and influence grew over the years.*

'The culmination came with Torralba's 1527 claim that with Zequiel's help he had travelled from Spain to Rome and back, by air, in a single morning, carrying important news that only reached Spain more than a week later. Unsurprisingly, this drew the attention of the Spanish Inquisition, who charged Torralba with witchcraft; under torture, he was unable to deny what happened. His young assistant, of course, was no longer to be found.

Warren also discussed the much more recent case of Prof. Hernandez, a tenured professor in nuclear physics at the University of Mexico, and a member of his country's Atomic Energy Commission;

*'Hernandez received telepathic information that brought him recognition in another field, immunology. In 1972 he met the source of this information, an attractive young woman calling herself Elyense. Eventually confiding her origin, she took him aboard a space-craft on four occasions, and disclosed that her race was but one of many alien groups **visiting and living on Earth**. Their meetings continued over several years, but for his disclosures, the professor was placed in an insane asylum. Not long after his release, he vanished without trace in 1984.'*

In the 1950's, one well known, but sometimes doubted, contactee. Howard Menger, said he was told; *"A lot of our people are amongst you, mingling with your kind, observing and helping where they can. They are in all walks of life – working in factories, offices, banks. Some of them hold responsible positions in communities, in government. Some of them may even be cleaning women or garbage collectors."*

This belief was shared by Truman Bethurum, who claimed to have also been contacted by aliens, the 'Clarionites', who woke him whilst he was sleeping next to his asphalt laying rig in the Californian desert. Amongst them was a beautiful woman, Aura Rhanes, who told him that they had been coming to Earth for many years, and were able to walk around unnoticed.

She said that they were here to reaffirm the values of marriage, family and fidelity, as there was a 'dreadful Paganism' at work, and they did not want us to destroy ourselves with our new weaponry.

Bethurum claimed that he met with them, on eleven occasions in cafes, and saw them many other times, when they ignored him because they did not wish to reveal their identities.

Contactee, Dan Fry, admitted to obtaining false identity documents for his extraterrestrial friends, and Orfeo Angelucci, from Los Angeles, said he once met with his 'spaceman' contact in a Greyhound bus terminal.

All these contactees had one thing in common, they were told to spread the extraterrestrials' message of peace, love and harmony.

One interesting case from that era was related by Van Horn, a southern California park ranger. He was talking to an investigator who was waiting for the Head Ranger, who apparently had a new case to report to him. The investigator himself had witnessed a strange occurrence some years earlier, when he had been prospecting in a desolate part of the area. One day, after rounding a hillside, he saw a large 'spacecraft' in the distance.

There were people with several large machines, which appeared to be digging, or shifting rocks, moving around it. As he watched, several limousines were uncovered from an underground cave or vault. He noticed the 'people' looked similar to us, except for a larger than normal forehead, which most had covered with a 'cowboy hat'.

A similar report was documented by Gabrielle Green in his book, *'Let's Face the Facts about Flying Saucers'*. On the night of 6th March 1961, a resident of South Miami, Florida, saw a large, dirigible-shaped object, larger than any Navy blimp he had ever seen, hovering over a nearby tomato field.

A large door opened in the centre of the craft, and three small, saucer-shaped objects sped off into the night sky. Then, 'three shiny new Ford Galaxy automobiles' appeared in the doorway, and were lowered to the ground by a hydraulic-like elevator. After that, a large oblong-shaped capsule came down, and a group of normally dressed people stepped out.

They got into the vehicles, and drove across the tomato field, before turning onto a South Miami street and speeding away. The craft rose rapidly from the field, and disappeared into the night sky. The media ridiculed the witness's report, but one can but wonder.

At the turn of the century, Steven Greer hosted a famous 'Disclosure Project', where 'previously silent' witnesses came forward. Many more contacted him soon after, including Jim Oglesby, who wrote of incidents which occurred in 1967/68 when he was working at the 'Cape' during the Apollo Program.

He lived in a remote area, west of the St. John's River, and from 31st December 1967, until 15th September 1968, he kept a diary of all the UFO sightings that he observed, and that were witnessed by numerous other people.

'Many nights, choppers and jets, including one of those huge Air Force jets, equipped with night-time cameras, were active in and around the area where I lived....

'On 31 occasions I watched a UFO land near the shoreline of a specific lake. Less than a hundred feet from the craft was a black sedan. On three occasions between March and September of 1968, I observed beings move back and forth between the sedan and the craft. Because of the dark, I wasn't able to get a good look at the figures.

In 1992, the *'Sunday Telegraph'* published an interesting account of an interview they had with Glenn Steckling, an airline pilot who had recently attended a conference in Brisbane. His father, who had recently died, was Fred Steckling, a prominent U.S. investigator.

Glenn said the extraterrestrials, who look just like us, - *"walk among us, gathering information. They do not reveal themselves most of the time for fear of causing panic and leaving themselves open to danger."* 'He said he had seen several beings from other planets in his time;

"I saw them as a child with my parents, and I've seen them mingling with crowds at talks and conventions. Occasionally they will speak up during a debate and inject some thought or information to send us in the right direction – a little bit like tutelage. I have seen demonstrations which prove they're from another planet. For example, they have a small mechanical device they use to bend light rays, effectively making them, or other objects, invisible."

'He also had advice on what to do if an extraterrestrial makes itself known to you; - "I would be very respectful, and very aware – I would not want to give away that type of confidence to put them in danger."

Steckling's comments were of great interest to me, as I have written about similar circumstances from New Zealand in my book *'The Days of the Space Brothers'*, where extraterrestrials, incognito, accompanied George Adamski on his 1959 world tour.

There were many incidents in Italy in late 1962, early 1963, and the following years. The 'Amicizia', (Friendship), was the name used for a very secretive forty year interaction between normal citizens and humanoid and other friendly aliens. To the best of investigators' knowledge, it began in 1956, however some evidence indicates that it might have been occurring much earlier. There is evidence of similar groups in Switzerland and other neighbouring areas, where the same terminology was used; 'Amitie' in France and 'Freundschaft' in Germany and Austria.

In Australia, we have many migrants from Europe, who arrived in the decades after World War II. Colleagues and acquaintances who came from Northern Italy, Switzerland, Austria, Germany, France and Northern Siberia told me of some of their parents and older relatives who had been involved with the 'Friendship Groups'.

Umberto Visani investigated and documented the 'Amicizia', saying that their interaction did not just involve a small group of individuals, but specifically chosen people of varying walks in life, from professionals to students and housewives. Politicians, university professors, company presidents, military officers, engineers, journalists and many others, were all reputed to be part of this clandestine interaction. Further, there was ample evidence at the time, including recordings, photos and videos. The level of contact went from single encounters to deep participation lasting over forty years.

In 2009 Professor Stefano Breccia, a retired expert in artificial intelligence and computer sciences, who was apparently also involved, wrote a book, '*Mass Contacts'*, which detailed the accounts of Bruno Sammaciccia, a Catholic scholar, and the leader of the Italian group. Sammaciccia was a prominent Italian theologian and psychologist, and he entrusted his notes to Breccia, to be published after his death in 2003. Other books and articles have also surfaced, but usually not until after the supposed 'departure' of the visitors and the demise of the witnesses.

Breccia said that the Italians had nicknamed the 'Amicizia' visitors the 'W56' due to their first contact in 1956. Some of these beings were much shorter or taller than their human counterparts, and far different in physical appearance. Others were essentially the same as us. Together, they comprised a 'joint task force', collectively known as the 'Akrij'.

Sammaciccia had several meetings with his mentors, who reiterated their message, alluding to us ignoring their previous missionaries; *'A highly evolved humanity send you astronauts and missionaries from a distance of several light years to enlighten you on the nature of your existence, but instead of being thankful for their efforts, you ignore them and mock all the teachings they bring you; know that an evolution that has failed is a planetary catastrophe, and this will be the consequences of your acts!*

'In a past life, every one of you has worked towards the establishment of the civilisation which exists today; you have all collaborated in participating in the development of humanity.

'Understand that you are preparing yourselves today! As tutors of your kind, we can do nothing else but condemn your acts; know this, you are rigorously supervised by a superior race, who will never permit you to come to the disaster of a 'nuclear war'.'

New Zealand *'Xenolog'*, Number 107, details a 1952 report from near Mt. Etna, in Sicily, Italy. The witness, Eugenio Siragusa, was waiting for a bus, early one morning in Martyr's Square, Catania, when a white, mercury-coloured, luminous object appeared in the sky. As it zig-zagged and rapidly descended towards him, he could see it resembled a spinning-top.

When it hovered overhead, a brilliant 'ray' left the object, and "completely pierced me!" At that moment, his fears turned to 'indescribable serenity'. The 'ray' shrank back into the craft, which then moved left and right in an arc across the sky before disappearing. For the next ten years, his personality changed and he developed extrasensory perceptions, and telepathy;

'When I pulled myself together, I rapidly discovered, more and more, that something extraordinary had happened to me...Ever since then an inner voice began to instruct me on geology and cosmology. It opened my mind to the mysteries of Creation and of my former lives. This re-dimension of my existence was possible thanks to continued ESP contacts which were established between certain extraterrestrials and myself. This extra-sensory perception was continually developing within me. It lasted eleven long years before I could actually physically meet my extraterrestrial instructors.'

One night, in April 1962, he felt compelled to go back to nearby Mount Etna. As he was driving up towards Mount Manfre, it felt as if his car was being guided up the mountain by some superior force. He stopped his car at the side of the road, and as he walked along the path he saw two silhouettes on top of the isolated hill. They were two, well-built men, about 5'4", with long blonde hair and 'soft' features. They wore silver space-suits, with gold armlets around their wrists and ankles, a luminous belt and a strange metallic chest-plate.

At first, he was terrified, but one directed a green beam toward him, from an object he had in his hand. Immediately he felt a sense of calm, and the men spoke to him in Italian, saying: "We have been waiting for you. Record in your memory what we are going to tell you."

He was given a message to pass on to our leaders, similar to what other contactees of the day had been told: We must stop our warlike tendencies, and nuclear weapons, (especially the Hydrogen Bomb), and practice justice, freedom, love and fraternity to all. They mentioned being part of an 'Intergalactic Confederation', and said the 'Cosmic Counsel' condemns the people of Earth for their inhuman behaviour.

Siragusa heeded the message and dedicated the rest of his life to furthering their aims. His mission was to quietly spread their message by recruiting other contactees. They avoided the publicity of lectures or public meetings, and carried out their task quietly and effectively.

One of the W56 told Stefano Breccia that there was another group of entities interested in Earth, they called the 'CTRs'; "The 'CTRs' are the result of a 'W56' experiment that has run out of control. They are robots, in the full sense of the word, even if centuries ago they began as a biological reproduction with no soul or emotions."

He added that it would be difficult for us to discriminate between a natural being and a biological robot, and these entities are trying to understand how to bridge the difference between them and us. This certainly would explain the behaviour of the 'greys', and makes sense of their interest in genetics, and human and animal reproductive and biological material.

Bruno Ghibaudi, another long term contactee, had said that there are other reasons for the Space Brothers visiting and sometimes revealing themselves, but he was forbidden to speak of them. (The alleged conflict with, and attempted intrusion by the 'CTRs' undoubtedly being one, I would assume).

Umberto Visani also reported that in 1978 the 'CTRs' attacked and destroyed most of the 'W56' bases, including ones under the Adriatic. The largest, which was the scene of a heated battle, was at a depth of twelve miles from the surface, and extended from the centre of the Adriatic to the centre of Italy. At the time, massive explosions, of unknown origin, were reported from off the Italian coast.

(Obviously, there were extraterrestrial bases under the sea, sometimes deep beneath our oceans, however it was not common practice for the visitors to divulge their actual locations, or to take anyone there. In recent years, the Earth's major powers would be more capable of detecting any suspicious underwater activity.)

After losing the battle with the 'CTRs', many of the Akrij fled, and most had departed Earth by 1986. They promised that they would return, but we don't really know when. Some have remained integrated in our society, and maintain smaller bases elsewhere on the planet. Since then, reports of flying saucers with beautiful blond haired emissaries have been almost non-existent.

Gone were the days of innocence, where mankind met 'aliens' who were very similar in appearance to us. Some had white skin, blue eyes and blonde hair, and others were more Asiatic in appearance, but all were peaceful with messages of love and co-operation. Then, from the seventies onwards, the 'Greys', whom I believe to be the previously mentioned advanced biological robots, appeared with nightmarish abductions and inter-dimensional experiences.

The Akrij's references to the 'CTRs' also became much more meaningful in later years, when hapless victims reported unpleasant abductions by the 'greys' with skinny bodies, large heads, black wrap-around eyes, and no visible reproductive organs.

In *'The Days of the Space Brothers'* I wrote that as early as 1963, half way across the world, 'Mr. X', a New Zealand contactee, received the following message from his extraterrestrial humanoid 'friends'; *'We are sorely troubled at the trend of events in our sphere of influence. Rebellion has been threatening among certain cosmic entities which are even now moving in the direction of your location.*

'We are doing our best to divert their direction of travel, because if they come too close to your place in space, their influence will be tragic for your present uneasy peace, as past wars will be nothing to what this will cause if they succeed. We have been too busy with this cosmic trouble to communicate with you, but give this as a kindly warning, that trouble may come your way. We hope to be strong enough to stop it. May the good Lord help us.'

'God bless you and all who look for truth.'

They sent 'Mr. X' another note in June 1964; *'We have been long in writing to you, but we have been fighting a terrible battle, only partly successful. Many evil ones have broken through and are now at work on your Earth. We cannot foretell the results as we ourselves do not know yet. But you may expect trouble at any time. If so, we shall be in your skies in greater numbers, as we shall be there to help. If the following sign is seen it will be a warning of trouble, watch your skies for this 'Z', and know that we are not far away. These evil ones have already influenced one we trusted. They will spoil those in higher places.'* - *'Your Two Friends.'*

(I wonder if it related to the less than pleasant aliens, of different appearance, who later abducted and mistreated innocent victims? Were they also referring to the 'Greys', or 'CTRs' which the 'Amicizia' spoke about?)

What about these 'Greys' often reported in later years? In 2017 the *'New Dawn'* magazine published the thoughts of Britain's Royal Astronomer, Sir Martin Rees who considered it more likely that aliens would be some form of advanced electronic intelligence.

They followed up by mentioning some of journalist Nigel Kerner's opinion; *'Grey aliens are sophisticated self-aware machines created by a long vanished extraterrestrial civilisation. These artificially intelligent robotic entities seek to master death by obtaining something humans possess that they do not – souls. Through the manipulation of human DNA, these aliens hope to create their own souls, and thereby escape the entropic grip of the material universe in favour of the timeless realm of spirit.'*

I am not sure, given that the Akrj spoke of these entities as if they had originated from a vanished extraterrestrial civilisation. In addition to the reports of these beings abducting and mistreating human victims, there were other instances where contactees told of them working peacefully alongside human

353

type supervisors. Perhaps it was only one particular group of 'CTRs' who had rebelled, and were working against their original creators.

One wonders what our own authorities were doing about this? Surely they must have heard about these extraterrestrials, who looked just like humans, living and operating in our society.

In 2008, investigator Michael Salla wrote an interesting article, *'The Secret War on ET Contactees'*, for *'Nexus'* magazine. In it he wrote; *'Contactees described the extraterrestrials as benign, very respectful of human free will, and ancestrally linked to humanity, (thus dubbed the 'Space Brothers ').*

'Further revealed by the contactees was that extraterrestrials, who in many cases were indistinguishable from humans, had secretly integrated into human society. Their apparent goals were to acquaint themselves better with different national cultures and/or to participate in an educational uplift program to prepare humanity for galactic status. Contactees began to disseminate to the general public the nature of their experiences and knowledge, gained through interaction with extraterrestrials.

'Information revealed by contactees presented an unrivalled national security crisis for policy makers in the United States and other major nations. Two main elements comprised this crisis. First, the advanced space vehicles and technologies possessed by extraterrestrial civilisations were far more sophisticated than the most developed aircraft, weapons and communication systems possessed by national governments. This presented an urgent technological problem that required vast national resources to bridge the technological gap with extraterrestrials.....The evidence of extraterrestrial visitors and technologies would be kept secret from the general public, the media and most elected political representatives.

'Second, extraterrestrial civilisations were contacting private individuals and even having some of their representatives integrate into human society. This was encouraging growing numbers of individuals to participate in a covert extraterrestrial effort to prepare humanity for 'galactic status' – where the existence of ETs would be officially acknowledged and open interaction would occur. Also included was the issue of nuclear disarmament. Tens of thousands of individuals supported the contactees who distributed newsletters, spoke at

conferences and travelled widely, spreading their information for peacefully transforming the planet and calling for an immediate end to the development of nuclear weapons. Nuclear weapons threatened more than humanity's future, according to the extraterrestrials. Every detonation disrupted the fabric of space, which could also seriously affect their own worlds in destructive ways.'

Of course, these messages were not welcome by a world, involved in a 'Cold War', and intent on nuclear armament. *'Consequently, a highly secret and ruthless counterintelligence program was finally implemented that directly targeted contactees and their supporters.'*

Intelligence agencies monitored and attempted to discredit and debunk the activities of contactees and their supporters. UFO organisations and meetings were infiltrated by disruptive elements, in an effort to neutralise the growing contactee movement. This I can personally attest to, having witnessed some of these agents 'in action'.

Contactees themselves, were often subjected to intimidation by the mysterious 'Men in Black'. Michael Salla wrote that a leaked document from the reputed *'Majestic-12 Group Special Operations Manual'* (SOMI-01), of April 1954, stated; *'If at all possible, witnesses will be held incommunicado until the state of their knowledge and involvement can be determined. Witnesses will be discouraged from talking about what they have seen, and intimidation may be necessary to ensure their co-operation.'*

Perhaps this is why many people did not speak out until much later in life. Many others kept their interactions with extraterrestrials very secretive. Salla considers that operation 'COINTELPRO' is still in existence today, however, since the 1980s, the extraterrestrials themselves have been much more covert in their activities.

Not much is known about the 'early days', but according to investigator Steve Hammons, Victor Martinez, a former federal employee, said that a DIA contact revealed that beside the more general issue of extraterrestrials visiting Earth, who may blend in with the human population, there was a 1980 operation – 'Tango-Sierra' – which involved the 'finding, tracking and eventual capture of an extraterrestrial entity', who was living among us and had abducted one of their trusted female government employees.

Martinez's source also revealed that; *"In early 1980, the 7602 Air Intelligence Wing, Section III, began a detailed investigation involving the presence of extraterrestrial creatures having infiltrated the highest levels of the United States government."*

Not much more information has been forthcoming, and I guess we may never know the truth about some of our own security activities, except to say that there is evidence that the extraterrestrials are still living amongst us.

CHAPTER ELEVEN

THE DARK SIDE

PART ONE

Not all UFO experiences are friendly or benign, and often, as an after effect, witnesses can suffer severe injury or trauma.

Nuclear type radiation, whether if be from a UFO or one of our own prototype craft, can have a serious effect on the witnesses. Researcher, Leonard Stringfield, detailed an Ohio case from November 1957. Farmer James Allen and his wife were mystified when their TV suddenly showed signs of 'interference', with the picture and sound 'going in waves' and then blacking out. Seconds later an 'eerie light' shone through the window, and they could see a 'large, squat object, about twenty feet in diameter', hovering over their backyard.

When James went outside to investigate, he was frozen in disbelief as the object moved directly over him. He fled inside, and soon began to feel ill and feverish.

Stringfield wrote; *'Within 48 hours, James Allen was dead, his insides fried as though by the head of a microwave oven. Medical examination showed intense radiation.'*

As early as 1959, the authorities were also aware of the radiation danger. The *'Flying Saucer Review'* told of a former World War II Navy pilot whose Cessna plane had been approached and circled by three oval shaped craft on 13th August 1959.

He had been flying from Hobbs to Albuquerque, New Mexico, when both his standard and electrical compasses went 'haywire'. Moments later, three grey, identical craft, at least eight feet in diameter, passed directly in front of his plane. They looked like 'two bowls face-to-face', (one inverted on the other), but with the bottoms rounded instead of flat. They were in 'echelon' formation, and circled the plane, several times, at about 250 mph before zooming off behind him.

He said that, upon landing he was hustled into an office, and interrogated for two hours by an Air Force Major, who then told him that if 'anything unusual happened', or he got any unusual illness in the next six months he was to get to a government hospital straight away, and the Air Force would take care of him.

He was advised the whole matter was subjected to strict secrecy, except for his wife, who had to be prepared if he were suddenly stricken. He was ordered not to tell anyone about the encounter or radiation hazard.

The article went on to say; *'Some years ago, Capt. E. Ruppelt, former Chief of 'Project Blue Book', confirmed that Air Force instrumentation had recorded high radio-activity when UFOs passed over the test area. Also, several apparently genuine cases of illness from UFO radiation are on record.'*

The question has to be asked as to whether this radiation was coming from unknown objects or our own prototypes?

In *'Aspects of UFOs and Aliens',* I wrote about the case of Betty Cash, Vicky Landrum and her grandson Colby, who encountered a brightly lit craft, hovering above a road they were driving along, in Dayton Texas, just before 9pm on 29th December, 1980. They brought their car to a halt, and felt such an intense heat that both women got out of the vehicle, Betty for a longer period than Vicki.

As the object moved away, they noticed several helicopters, some later identified as Boeing CH-47 Chinooks, flying near it. Several other people in the area also reported seeing the helicopters, as well as the object, in the sky that night. At no time did they ever say it was a flying saucer with little green men. Along with the other witnesses, who also saw and heard the helicopters that evening, they believed it was a government sponsored operation of some kind.

Some hours later, after they returned home, thinking they had safely survived the event, Betty started to fall ill. Her skin turned red and developed blisters, and by the next morning she couldn't get out of bed. She was hospitalised, until 19th January, where doctors treated her as a burns patient, but she was re-admitted on 25th January, by which time she had lost most of her hair, and suffered from vomiting and diarrhoea, classic symptoms of radiation poisoning. Her eyes were permanently damaged, as were those of Vicky.

Other than a severe degradation of her eyesight, Vicky's symptoms of radiation poisoning were less severe, and soon subsided. They included some loss of hair, appetite loss, severe fatigue, and increased susceptibility to infections.

She was more concerned about her son, Colby, than herself. He had also experienced visual degradation, loss of appetite and weight loss. Vicky worried about the long-term effects, and the possibility of him contracting leukemia.

Betty went back to Birmingham, Alabama, where her mother cared for her. She received good medical treatment there, but her health deteriorated and she passed away exactly eighteen years later. All that time, with the aid of MUFON lawyers, she tried to hold the U.S. government to account. They were never going to admit that the craft may have been one of their own, and preferred the incident went down as a sighting of a UFO. Perhaps, one day, we will learn the truth.

The reports of ill-effects on witnesses, had been surfacing for many years. In 1956, at Santa Cruz, California, Muriel McDowell watched a UFO that looked like 'two giant silver plates cupped together', that had a whirling centre ring, with portholes, and gave off rainbow colours and intense heat.

As the UFO left the area, making a 'high-pitched whine', her dogs started to howl. Later, Muriel's face, hands and arms became 'lobster red', and she died four years later from leukemia, which the doctors suggested might have been caused by 'an overdose of radiation'.

In 1967, the Canadian Newsletter, *'Saucers, Space and Science'* told of an incident from the previous year, in April 1966.

Bob Howard had been visiting a friend who lived between Cassadaga and Sinclairville, New York. At about 8.30pm, his friend's son, who was frightened, called him outside to see a strange, humming disc, gliding over the woods at tree-top level. It was grey, about fifteen feet in diameter and seven feet thick, with three 'pipe-like' landing gear legs protruding from the bottom. It was rounded on top, like an inverted salad bowl, with a further rounded 'cabin' above this. He couldn't see any windows, but it emanated a narrow, powerful light beam, and around the rim there was a row of glowing lights, gradually changing, back and forth, from white to amber.

It passed over the chicken shed, and then rose to a height of no more than twenty feet as it proceeded over Bob's head towards the farm across the road, and hovered behind their barn. In order to get a better look, Bob ran across the road, then behind the barn. As soon as he got within ten feet of the strange craft, it moved away. At the same time, he felt an intense heat, which burned his scalp. Later he lost some of his hair, some of his teeth became loose, and he had trouble with his left eye ever since. The next morning, the rubber soles fell off the canvas shoes he had been wearing at the time.

The police arrived, and stared in astonishment. Later, they denied ever seeing it, and soon after, when a photographer from the *'Jamestown Post Journal'* turned up, they prevented him taking any pictures of the strange craft, which eventually wobbled about another twenty feet upwards and streaked away, back into the cover of the woods. The next day the same photographer was nearly prevented from photographing the area of scorched grass where the object had hovered for over twenty minutes the previous night.

In May 1992, I received a telephone call from an excited witness, 'F.D.', who was a reporter for a major news paper. She had at long last sighted a UFO, one of those elusive objects she was often called upon to write about, but, until now, had never seen herself.

She and a colleague were driving along the Pacific Highway, north of Sydney, when near Lake MacQuarie, they spotted something in the sky; "It was a large, dazzling, bright white flashing light, with red and green lights below, much larger than those on a normal plane. It was hovering very low, no more than 300 metres in altitude, to our right. Suddenly, it moved over us, hovering on our left, before flying away at an incredible speed.

"We were still debating what it could have been, when it suddenly returned and hovered again. We stopped the car, and I got out to get a better look. I watched for some time until it sped away to the south."

When she did 'due diligence' and initially contacted the Air Force, they told her it was an F-18 plane. She disputed that, saying that there was no way that this object was a plane or helicopter.

A couple of years later, 'F.D.' contacted me again. She had developed a brain tumour, on the side of her head which was turned towards that strange object she had got out of the car to observe. Did I think there could be a connection? I didn't know, but it was certainly a possibility.

Even in the early years some doctors suspected a connection between a UFO sighting, and the later illness of a witness. Researcher Nick Redfern, in his book, *'The FBI Files'*, discussed an incident from 1949, when a doctor from Decatur, Indiana, raised his suspicions with the authorities. On the 1st July that year the doctor, along with an FBI agent from Omaha, had seen a saucer in the vicinity of Lake of the Woods, Canada.

Shocked by what he had seen, in September, the doctor confided in an Air Force Office of Special Investigations officer, that he was convinced that a recent polio epidemic, was somehow connected with a spate of UFO sightings in the general area over the previous year.

'He further confided that he was not at all convinced that the sufferers had in fact contracted polio; rather, he suspected uranium poisoning at the hands of the saucers, and made additional checks to try to determine if the outbreak of contagious diseases throughout the U.S.A. was in any way connected with UFO encounters.'

Interesting!

This apparent 'radiation', or similar damage, was nothing new. There were many previous incidents in the 'early years'.

At 2 am on November 4th 1957, two Brazilian soldiers on guard at Itaipu Fort were startled to see a bright star suddenly appear on the horizon, and suddenly grow in size and brightness. As it quickly moved towards them, they realised it was a luminous flying object.

It was disc-shaped, with an eerie orange glow, and hovered, motionless and humming, about 120 to 180ft over the highest turret. As they stared in surprise, they felt a wave of intense heat. One sentry tried to stagger away, but lost consciousness and collapsed on the ground. The other guard stumbled around, his screams waking the entire garrison, where the power had temporarily failed.

As the UFO left, the power was restored, and everybody rushed out. The other soldiers found their comrades suffering severe shock and bad burns.

Another witness was not so lucky. The *'Brazilia Herald'* newspaper later reported that in August 1967, Inácio de Souza and his wife, were returning to a property, near Brazilia, where he had worked for six years.

They saw three people on the property's airstrip. Just after these 'strangers' started to move towards them, Inácio noticed an unusual 'aircraft' at the end of the landing strip. It looked like an 'inverted washbasin', and was touching, or almost touching the ground. Inácio, who was carrying a 0.44 carbine at the time, took aim and fired at the nearest 'person'.

Almost immediately the strange 'aircraft' emitted a beam of green light, which hit Inácio on the head and shoulder. He fell unconscious, and his wife watched as the three intruders entered the object, which then took off vertically, at high speed, making a noise 'like the humming of bees'.

Within the next three days, Inácio suffered headaches, nausea, tremors, and numbness and tingling in his body. Fearing that his symptoms may have been caused by a toxic plant, the 'Fazenda' owner took him to hospital.

The doctors did not believe his story about a 'flying saucer', and after doing blood, faeces and urine tests, prescribed an ointment for several burn marks on his trunk and head, which they still considered had been caused by contact with some poisonous plant.

Inácio's boss stayed with him whilst he was in hospital for the next four days, when the prognosis of 'leukaemia' was given, with only about sixty days left to live. He wasted away, and died three months later, in October 1967.

The doctors did not want to entertain the idea of a UFO causing Inácio's fatal condition, and suggested it should not be mentioned, saying that he and his wife must have been hallucinating. This did not prevent another report of a UFO 'ray attack' coming to light in Brazil, three years later. This time there were too many witnesses for authorities to dismiss the incident as 'hallucinations'.

The February 1977 edition of *'UFO News'* included a very detailed report of another event which occurred at Pinetree Villa, on the outskirts of the small Brazilian town of Pirrasununga, near Sao Paulo.

It was early morning when Maria dos Santos first saw the object hovering over a forest, about 500 yards from her house. She ran across the street, and after alerting her neighbour, Carlos Mertzner, they both went out and watched it, with Mertzner calling out to his stepson, Tiago Machado.

Machado said; *"It was 7am when the shouting and confusion woke me up. I heard my stepfather call me, and after I got dressed, I saw some people running for shelter, and others were kneeling in prayer.*

"Then I saw it. The ship was like two large plates stuck together, with the top plate upside down. It gave off a white-blue light, and was gliding over the fields. Then it slowly set down in the fields beyond town."

He grabbed a pair of binoculars, and met another neighbour, Francisco Hanse, outside; *"Then the two of us ran over to the Zoological Institute, which is a couple of doors away. One of the police officers there, Benedito Joana, said he had seen the saucer too, and the three of us decided to find where it had landed. Hundreds of people, including my mother, ran to the hill to watch it land.*

"We went through a wooded area, and I became separated from the others. In a short time I came upon a clearing where the saucer was resting on a large tripod. It sat upon a slight rise, and was giving off a bright light. It seemed made of a material, similar to aluminium, but it was luminous.

"The saucer's rim was spinning around the centre. It never stopped whirling. The centre section was stationary, and appeared to be made of a transparent substance. I could see what seemed to be shadowy figures in the cabin, gathered around what looked like an instrument panel.

"I stopped about 30ft away from it, as I was too scared to go closer. I put down my binoculars, and stood there, looking at the saucer, for about fifteen minutes. Then I heard the others shouting for me, and that's when I got hit by the ray! Suddenly, what seemed like a tongue of flame, had flashed from the machine, and hit me in the legs, from the knees to the feet. Then the spacecraft took off on a flight between the trees and into the heavens at an amazing speed."

Michado fell to the ground, paralysed but 'still in possession of his senses'. He was in a lot of pain as his stepfather and other friends raced to his aid. Other witnesses had also seen the craft take off, and commented on its rapid departure.

Michado was taken to hospital, where doctors examined his bright red, swollen legs, which looked similar to 'electric shock burns'. Air Force and other investigators found the long grass, in the area where the disc had landed, was beaten down in a perfect circle, about six yards in diameter. There were three holes in the ground, which matched Michado's description of the landing gear.

The Air Force collected signed statements from over fifty witnesses, and despite attempts to 'put a lid of secrecy' on the event, it was only a few days before the Brazilian press got wind of the story.

Researcher Gordon Creighton reported on another South American case, which occurred in 1968 or 1969, when Marcilo Ferraz and his wife were driving southward from the city of Sao Paulo in Brazil.

'Somewhere near the frontier of Brazil and Uruguay, they encountered the usual 'white cloud' on the road, and 'woke up again', in due course, in Mexico. Both suffered severe traumatic shock, and the husband began to feel so ill, that after a few weeks he consulted a doctor and was found to have a tumour on the brain. 'Shortly after that...he shot himself.'

Gordon had always tried to determine what the governments really knew, not only about the radiation damage suffered by many witnesses around the world, but also the less frequent teleportation cases.

'The Colonel, in charge of security matters in the Brazilian Air Force, is reported by our informant to have admitted that he knows of these teleportation cases, and that they are authentic, but that they cannot be discussed or even mentioned in the press as they have been classified as top secret, and fall within the scope of 'National Security'.

In October 1973, at Cape Girardeau, Missouri, a large tractor-trailer was travelling along the road when the driver noticed they were being followed by a bright glowing object. He woke his wife, who was sleeping beside him, and as the craft neared, they could see a strange, large metallic, 'turnip-shaped' object, which lit up the back of the truck.

As he stuck his head out of the window, to get a better view, a 'flash' came from it, striking him in the face. It blinded him, and felt as if he was being hit by 'a ball of fire'. His eyeglasses melted, and it was nearly six months before he regained most of his eyesight.

Another incident occurred in 1977, three years before the Cash/Landrum event; *'A dairy farmer near Salto, Uruguay, saw a large, brilliant object near the grain storage bin, just as the generator failed and the barnyard lights went out. The animals went wild. The dog ran under the disc-shaped object, sat on a mound of dirt and howled pitifully. Nearby trees began to burn.*

'The sparks that hit the farmer produced strong electrical shocks, heat and unbearable itching all over his body. Later his doctor said the burns on his arms were caused by ultraviolet radiation. The dog died three days later from an internal haemorrhage along the entire length of the vertebral column, and his organs were discoloured.'

Experts often debate and argue about how long extraterrestrials have been visiting us, and 'UFOIC' the research group I belonged to in the 1970s, dug up this interesting letter, printed in the *'Scientific American'*. It was written to the editor in November **1886** by Warner Cowgill from the U.S. Consulate in Venezuela.

'During the night of October 24st last, which was rainy and tempestuous, a family of nine persons, sleeping in a hut a few leagues from Maracaibo, were awakened by a loud humming noise and a vivid dazzling light, which brilliantly illuminated the interior of the house.

'The occupants, completely terror stricken, and believing, as they relate, that the end of the world had come, threw themselves down on their knees, and commenced to pray, but their devotions were almost immediately interrupted by violent vomiting, and extensive swellings commenced to appear in the upper part of their bodies, this being particularly noticeable about the face and lips.

'It is to be noted that the brilliant light was not accompanied by a sensation of heat, although there was a smoky appearance and a peculiar smell.

'The next morning the swellings had subsided, leaving upon the face and body large black areas. No special pain was felt until the ninth day, when the skin peeled off, and these patches were transformed into virulent raw sores. The hair of the head fell off the side which happened to be underneath when the

phenomenon occurred, the same side of the body being, in all nine cases, the more seriously injured.

'The remarkable part of the occurrence is that the house was uninjured, all doors and windows being closed at the time. No trace of lightning could afterward be observed in any part of the building, and all the sufferers unite in saying that there was no detonation, but only the loud humming already mentioned.

'Another curious attendant circumstance is that the trees around the house showed no sign of injury until the ninth day, when they suddenly withered, almost simultaneously with the development of the sores on the bodies of the occupants of the house.'

Warner had visited the victims, whom it is assumed must have been Americans, in hospital. He was at a loss to explain the cause of this incident, which, in the light of today's knowledge, seems to indicate some form of radiation exposure. I know of nothing earthly that could do that nearly 140 years ago!

Even the 'Soviet Bloc' countries did not escape these unfortunate events in the 'early days', and like their counterparts in the West, were sometimes victims of an 'unknown weapon', which aliens would use to disable a curious witness.

Russian investigator, Dr. Azhazha, reported that on January 7th 1960, two forest rangers, 'Ari Sarvi' and 'Mauno Erkko', (later called 'Esko Viljo' and 'Aarno Heinonen' by researcher Brad Steiger), were skiing over the snowy slopes of Kestenga near the Finnish border in north-western Russia. They spotted a round, twenty feet diameter, metallic sphere, which hovered in the air, and subsequently landed nearby, on cylindrical landing gear.

A strange creature emerged. It was about three feet tall, with a 'waxen' face and spindly arms and legs. It had a sharp, hooked nose, pointy ears, narrow sloping shoulders, and hands that were almost 'childlike'. It was dressed in tight-fitting green clothing and boots.

Apparently, neither men had ever heard or read about UFOs, and because they didn't quite understand what was happening, one pointed his ski pole in the direction of the unusual 'being', which immediately aimed a 'stubby barrel', around its neck, at them. A blinding, pulsating beam of light shot out, temporarily dazing and blinding them. By the time they recovered, the 'creature' had vanished, and its craft disappeared upwards into a red mist.

Savri became sick immediately, weak, cold, paralysed down his entire right side, and hallucinating before he eventually 'passed out'. When he regained consciousness, he began to vomit, and complained of feeling feverish with aches and pains all over his body. Four weeks later, he still suffered from nightmares, headaches and poor appetite.

Erkko complained of arm and chest pains, swollen eyes and a lack of sense of balance. The local doctor, who treated them, said their symptoms could have been caused by shock – however, since both had passed black urine, it could have been radiation poisoning!

LOOK - BUT DON''T TOUCH

John Fuller, in his book *'Interrupted Journey'* wrote of a case which occurred on 12th October 1954. Thirteen-year-old Gilbert Lelay was walking near his parents' home at Sainte-Marie d'Herblay in France, when he saw an unusual, phosphorus, cigar-shaped machine in a nearby field.

Gilbert went closer, and encountered a friendly man who was wearing a grey suit, hat and boots, and had a strange sphere, emitting purple rays, in one hand. Before he could come any closer, the man placed his other hand on Gilbert's shoulder and said, in French; "Look, but don't touch!"

Gilbert took his advice, but this didn't stop him from peering into something which looked like a control console with numerous coloured lights. Soon his new acquaintance climbed aboard the machine. The door closed with a 'clapping sound', and the craft rose vertically, throwing light in all directions as it made a couple of loops before vanishing.

It is apparently not wise to get too close to a strange, unknown craft. In August 1952, American Scoutmaster, Sonny Desvergers learned this lesson the hard way.

He was driving three scouts home after a meeting in their hall, near' a military area in West Palm Beach in Florida, when they saw six lights in the sky, which suddenly plunged down into the nearby woods. Thinking it might be a plane crash, they proceeded towards the area to see if they could be of any assistance.

Once they saw some immobile lights amongst the trees, Desvergers ordered the boys to stay in the car, and to contact the Sheriff if he had not returned within ten minutes. He turned on his torch, and used a machete to cut his way through the undergrowth, eventually reaching a clearing.

When he realised he could no longer see the stars, he pointed his torch overhead, and was startled to see a grey, metallic surface directly above him. He later said; "I could have touched it with my long knife if I held my arm straight out. I was scared!"

He cautiously moved towards the edge of the machine, which was disc-shaped, about thirty feet in diameter, with a 'kind of half-sphere top' outlined against the sky. He admitted to feeling a sudden rage, and inclination to strike out at this intruder. He didn't know why these hostile thoughts crossed his mind. Perhaps the crew of this strange craft detected his feelings, because. as he stood there, wondering if he should make a strategic retreat, the object shifted gently, and he could see an opening in the dome on the upper side.

"As soon as the dome opened," he later recounted, "a sort of ball of fire shot out towards me. It seemed to float in the air and surround me. There was a disgusting smell around me, which stung my throat. I raised my arm, and instinctively covered my face. It was then that I staggered, everything went dark, and I lost consciousness."

When he came to, the strange craft had gone, and it took him some time, dazed and in pain from a burnt arm and scorched throat, to stagger back to his young charges.

In the meantime, when Desvergers hadn't returned, his three Scouts ran to a nearby farmhouse, from where the owner contacted the Sheriff's office. The Sheriff was out on the road, but his staff contacted him by radio. After about half an hour, the Sheriff and a constable met the boys at the farmhouse, and drove them back to the car and the spot where Desvergers had left them. As they were explaining what had happened, the Scout Master suddenly appeared on a nearby bank. He was pale and trembling, his left arm bloodstained and badly burned. There were three holes in his shirt, and his hair was also burnt.

Some researchers have suggested that this was a hoax, but it seems unlikely. Desvergers was reported to be a respected married, family man, and known for his honesty. It was unlikely that he and the three boys would have concocted the story, and further, his severe burns were additional indisputable evidence.

This is where the suspicion of government involvement creeps in. Edward Ruppelt, from 'Project Blue Book', was contacted by an intelligence officer from an air base in Florida. This incident was considered of such importance, that he was offered a lift in an Air Force plane to Florida, so that he could interview the witnesses as soon as possible. It seemed that the Sheriff's office, not the witnesses, had leaked the story, and they were having problems stalling the newspapers.

The boys' testimony was consistent with their original reports, and it appears that they saw Desvergers' torchlight as he made his way through the trees. They said that they also saw the big red ball of light engulf him, and that was when they took off for the farmhouse down the road.

Ruppelt then arranged for a 'flight surgeon' to examine Desvergers, and his report suggested that the burns, which included the inside of his nostrils, were only minor. Ruppelt went to the site with his crew from ATIC, and an unusually large contingent of three intelligence officers and two law officers. Their Geiger counters apparently detected no radiation, but the roots of the grass in the area were inexplicably charred, and they did locate the scoutmaster's singed cap.

Ruppelt admitted his negative approach; *"To be very honest, we were trying to prove this was a hoax, but were having absolutely no success. Every new lead we dug up pointed to the same thing, a true story."*

The only reason that could be given for the charred grass roots, which were sitting in wet sand, was 'induction heating', which certainly could not be hoaxed. It would also explain the unusual odour, possibly ozone gas, which Desvergers encountered, and could have caused his loss of consciousness.

When Ruppelt consulted a scientist from Rand, he was slightly perturbed at his response; *"What do you want? Does a UFO have to come in and land on your desk at ATIC?"*

Ruppelt was not to be deterred, and one must ask why he was so desperate to write this incident off as a 'hoax', especially when he discovered that

Desvergers had been interviewed by the media, and had reputedly even hired a press agent. Ruppelt than contacted Major Dewey Fournet in the Pentagon, and asked him to check into Desvergers' past.

In his youth, the poor scoutmaster had spent some time in a reformatory for stealing a car, and had later been 'booted out' of the marines for being AWOL. This was enough for Ruppelt to make further unsubstantiated allegations about Desvergers' character, and write the whole incident off as a 'hoax'.

Some very interesting cases also occurred in the late 1960s, and no definitive answers have ever been given.

The first was on 20th May 1967, at Falcon Lake, eighty miles east of Winnipeg, in Canada. Fifty-one year old Stephen Michalak was preparing to prospect at a quartz vein, near a marshy area and small stream. Just after midday there was a great commotion from some nearby geese, as if something had disturbed them. He looked up to see two strange objects descending from the sky.

They were oval disc-shapes, at a forty-five degree angle, with 'bumps' on them. They glowed red as they silently approached, and one suddenly stopped and hovered about fifteen feet above the ground, while the other landed on a large, flat rock, about 160 feet away. The disc in the air hovered for a short while longer, then rose and quickly flew back into the west where it disappeared behind some clouds. Michalak noticed, as it rose, its colour changed from red, to orange, and then grey, only reverting back to orange as it reached the clouds.

He turned his attention to the craft on the ground nearby. It was also changing colour from red to grey, eventually resembling 'hot stainless steel' surrounded by a golden-hued glow. There were no rivets or seams of any kind visible. A brilliant purple light flooded out of the openings on the upper part of the object. It was so dazzling, he was glad he was wearing his welding goggles, which were part of his prospecting equipment.

He kept his distance for a while, content to make some sketches of what he was observing. After about half an hour there was a smell of sulphur, and he noticed waves of warm air radiating from the craft, accompanied by a hissing, whirring sound, similar to a fast electric motor.

A door opened on the side, and Michalak could see some lights inside. He walked over and hesitated until he heard two human sounding voices, one higher pitched than the other. By this time he was convinced this was some new experimental American craft, and walked closer.

He called out in several languages, asking if he could be of any help, but got no response. Eventually he looked through the opening, and saw a 'maze' of lights, running in horizontal and diagonal patterns on a 'panel', and another group of lights flashing in random sequence.

He stepped back outside, and suddenly three panels slid back over the opening, sealing it from further entry. He walked around, touching the highly polished smooth surface with his gloved hand, only to discover that his glove had burned and melted, as had his hat which brushed the side.

The craft suddenly shifted position, and Michalak found himself facing a grid-like exhaust vent which suddenly sprang to life, sending a blast of hot air onto his chest. His shirt and undergarment caught fire, and the pain caused him to tear them off before he felt a rush of air and looked up to see the object departing the same way as the first had.

He was in pain, nauseous and vomiting, and eventually made his way home, where his son took him to hospital. Three weeks later he developed blisters and a rash, and swelling on his chest. For quite some time after that, he could not keep any food down, and suffered from nausea, vomiting, diarrhoea, a drop in his lymphocyte count, and a weight loss of twenty-two pounds. After a while his health returned to normal, but he suffered several recurring episodes.

Some officials and researchers tried to label this incident a hoax, however clear ground traces of where the craft had landed were found. Canada's Chris Rutkowski conducted one of the most thorough and professional investigations I have ever read. He was convinced Michalak was telling the truth, and I tend to agree.

Only three months later, there was another incident in Texas Creek, Colorado. Some of the finer details were similar to the Michalak event. Kenneth Flack was driving home at about 11.20pm. He started to overtake two cars ahead, when his engine and headlights failed. The other vehicles were experiencing the same problem.

Everybody got out, and they all could see an unusual object between them and the Arkansas River. Flack, a sceptic until then, decided to investigate and walked closer. He could see it was 'egg-shaped', with three 'legs' supporting it on the ground. Unlike Michalak, he did not get too close, and was still approaching the craft when it rotated about a quarter of a turn. The back end raised up and there was a bright flash.

Flack came to a dead halt. He felt paralysed and unable to move, and could only stand and watch as the legs retracted and the object slowly and silently rose from the ground and headed north. Flack lost consciousness, and the other witnesses carried him back to the road, where they eventually revived him and took him home.

It seemed one did not have to actually touch a UFO to be 'attacked'. Researcher George Fawcett reported on a case which occurred in 1958 at Nakatocis, Mississippi.

Haskell Raper was driving home from work in his 1956 Ford, when he was surprised to see a strange craft, about fifteen feet away on the ground. It was a greenish colour, fifteen feet long, nine feet high, and flashing a beam of light.

Suddenly, Haskell's car started heating up, and when the engine burst into flame, he jumped clear; *'The UFO cranked up, 'sounding like a diesel engine', and lifted off the ground at rapid speed before disappearing. As it did, the car gas tank exploded and the car was a total wreck. Marshalls, state police, sheriff deputies and Air Force intelligence officers from Fort Polk, Louisiana, investigated the case, but found no rational explanation for the case.'*

It must be noted that, hypothetically, if this was one of our own experimental craft, no-body would claim responsibility, thereby having to pay Haskell a sizable amount in damages.

Ten years later, at 8.30pm, on March 19th 1968, when he was returning home from his grandmother's house next door, young Gregory Wells saw a strange object hovering over some trees.

Investigative group NICAP reported on the incident; *'The large red object was so bright that it illuminated the road', according to Mrs. James Wells, the boy's mother. It had a band of dimmer red lights flashing around its centre.*

"I stopped," Gregory recalled. *"I wanted to run or scream, but suddenly a big tube came out of the bottom, which moved from side to side until it came to me and a beam of light shot out."*

'Gregory turned away as the light beam hit the upper part of his arm, knocking him to the ground. His jacket caught fire and the boy rolled around on the ground screaming with fright. Both his mother and grandmother responded, and also reported seeing the UFO .which 'just faded away'.

Gregory was taken to Beallsville Hospital, where he was treated for second degree burns. Investigators later discovered that, at the time, neighbours had also seen a long, cylindrical object moving, very low, in the vicinity of the Wells property, and there had been unexplained interference on television sets, besides a large street light ceasing to function.

,_____

ELECTROMAGNETIC RADIATION

Electromagnetic propulsion is often suggested as the technique used by those UFOs that seem to produce electromagnetic interference with our own engines, radios and lights. In 1967, university students at Santa Barbara, California, proved this theory, in part, when they designed and built a small unmanned submarine that propelled itself by creating an electromagnetic field which acted against the water.

In addition to reports from human witnesses, there are often reactions displayed by animals, from cowering and fear, to wild barking, howling and aggression in dogs - bellowing and stampede by cattle - and whinnying and kicking at their stalls by horses. This reaction did not occur when normal aircraft flew overhead, and happened many times when the animals did not even see the UFO.

In the 1960s, scientists started to seriously investigate this, and discovered that whilst radar 'rays' can sometimes sound like a mild, high frequency 'buzzing', electromagnetic rays do not use our normal auditory channels, and instead enter the recipient by direct stimulation of the nervous system of the brain, thereby bypassing the ears and normal auditory system.

By 1978, we cannot be sure of whether our own craft were using some form of electromagnetic propulsion. Iddabel Epperson, from MUFON, California, investigated a case which occurred on February 4th. At about 4am, when Claire Semaza, her two children and a neighbour, were woken by a very loud humming sound, they looked out of the window, and saw an oval object, hovering just above the trees, not far away. It had bright red lights, at either end, which sent shafts of light towards the ground. Between the two lights were several bluish-white lights, 'strung between'. The object later rose, flashed a brilliant white light on and off for approximately three seconds, and quickly flew off, leaving a smoke haze behind.

It was the behaviour of their pet dog, Susie, who had just given birth to her first litter of puppies, which had them mystified. At no time had she seen the strange craft, but she started whimpering, which soon developed into loud howls and barks. Periodically, she would stop for a few seconds, and just stare at the wall.

Iddabel wrote; *'Susie made her anguish known clear and loud. It seems apparent that when Susie realised that her humans were not going to solve her problem, that she had better do it herself. There she was with seven puppies to protect, and she must have felt that extreme danger threatened. The cosy box that she and her puppies occupied was on the ground floor.*

'She carried a puppy upstairs, and tried to hide it in a couple of places – the last place she tried was under the bed – but that didn't satisfy her. She took the puppy out from under the bed and hid it behind the drapes. This was the right place she thought, so she carried the rest of the puppies, one by one, upstairs and hid them all behind the drapes.'

Obviously, the 'visitors' were aware of the effect their craft had on some animals, especially dogs. Timo Phyälä, of the 'Finnish Interplanetarians Society', had an interesting discussion with a Helsinki man, who claimed contact with beings who spoke to him, in October 1969, through a bright, colourless light which descended from the ceiling to half a metre above the floor.

They started by telling him; *'We have arrived here on a big craft, and at the moment it is behind the planet Mars. For the present, we cannot bring it nearer to Earth, for we know that the Earth's scientists would observe it with their telescopes, and this would create fear among the people here. At the moment, we are in the Earth's atmosphere, having come here in a smaller device.'*

When the witness asked why they were contacting him, they replied that although he had not realised it, they had followed him for some time, and found him to be suitable; - *'Do not be surprised, for you are not the only one; by now we have many acquaintances among the men of Earth. – All we ask is that as soon as you have the opportunity, you spread information about us. Tell them about us this way; we exist and we wish the people well, and we wish that they would stick to the facts regarding us, making neither religions and legends, nor campaigns of fear about us. Do not force them to 'believe' in us.'*

He wanted these beings to come into the courtyard, or to the local sports oval, so he could meet with them in person. After a while, when they would not come, they eventually said there were too many dogs in the area, and proffered an explanation.

'The device with which we are moving can be made soundless, and if need be, invisible also, but it is emitting such a high pitch noise that it can be heard by animals, especially dogs, and we cannot eliminate the sound. Dogs become furious on hearing it. They can become dangerous, and attack men.'

At 7am on February 15th 1963, Charles Brew and his son Trevor were milking their cows, out in their dairy, at Moe, Victoria. Gordon Creighton reported on how a thick, 'battleship-grey' disc, about 25ft in diameter, with a dome and protrusions on top, came shooting down out of the rainy sky. It slowed, then stopped and hovered briefly about 75ft - 100ft overhead, revolving and making a whistling sound, similar to a turbine, before speeding away, and disappearing into a cloud.

It threw all the animals into a panic, with the horses rearing up, and the cows 'turning somersaults'. Many of the cattle 'broke out', and had to be rounded up. For several days afterwards, they refused to enter the paddock which the strange craft had hovered over.

An investigator from VUFORS, travelled ninety miles to interview Charles and Trevor, only to discover that an 'official', accompanied by a CSIRO officer had already been, and after questioning them, had taken rock samples for analysis. Creighton wondered if they were checking for radiation residue.

The U.S. research group, NICAP, received an interesting report from Somerset, England. James Sharman, a British coal merchant, was on a night time fishing trip, with three colleagues, in October 1964.

An object appeared in the sky, and hovered overhead, spreading a red glow over the area, illuminating a stream and surrounding fields. Pandemonium erupted in what had been a placid herd of about fifty cows, who started making a lot of noise and charging around the field. The men narrowly escaped being trampled, and hid behind a car until the object accelerated and departed and the cows settled down.

In response to the sceptics, NICAP's director commented; *"Perhaps now and then a cow may have a startling delusion, though usually cows are rather placid creatures. But for fifty cows to have terrifying delusions all at once would be peculiar, to say the least.*

"Probably they had often seen the moon and Venus, as well as cars and planes, without being alarmed. And even Dr. Menzel, the most determined UFO killer, would think twice about saying that...the English cows were cultists hypnotised by some weird religion."

Reports of strange craft 'spooking' horses are not new. Frank Edwards wrote in *'Stranger than Science'* about two disconcerting events which happened in the U.S.A. in 1873.

At Bonham, Texas, a shiny, silver object came streaking out of the sky, and swung around, diving time and time again at workers in a cotton field. A team of horses ran away, and the driver was thrown under the wheels of a wagon and killed.

Only an hour or so later, a similar object swept down upon some army troops on the cavalry parade ground at Fort Riley, Texas. The poor horses were so terrorised that the cavalry drill ended in tumult.

'NICAP' documented the following incident, from New Haven, West Virginia. On the evening of April 17th 1967, a small boy's father did not believe him when he staggered in the door, slightly injured and his glasses broken, saying that it was all the fault of a UFO. Where was the family's wagon and pony? The young lad said that a UFO, with two large searchlights on the underside, had flown overhead, and terrified the pony, which wrecked the wagon and threw the boy to the ground, thereby breaking his glasses. It wasn't until the father went to the scene, that he believed his son. He found the wrecked wagon, and the pony 'was lying on his back, with his feet straight up'.

British researcher, Gordon Creighton, translated a report from Argentina, which was published on 7th September 1965; *'The Buenos Aires publication, 'Asi', contained a report about a spot some sixty kilometres southwest of Córdoba, where some fifty farm workers, three lawyers, a hotel keeper, a rancher, members of the Rosario Meteorological Service, and even a Captain of the Navy, have been witness to the flights of many flying saucers which seem to have taken the Valley of Loretani as the centre for their operations, and a nearby ravine as their special base and hiding place.'*

On one such occasion, Rubén Busquets, along with his family, and fifty workers, lived on a tree plantation in the valley. At 8pm on July 15th of that year, Rubén and his family were returning home when they saw huge, luminous, bluish, circular object, ten to fifteen feet in diameter, with a convex base, and a beam of light going upwards, into the sky, from the top.

It was then that it shone the light directly on their car, before descending behind a nearby hill, where they could still see the glow for a short time after. Rubén said; *"We went on up to the house, but before we reached it, we met one of our 'peones' who was lying on the ground, having been thrown by his horse.*

"He was pretty dazed, and covered with mud and dried grass. As a 'mestizo' can never accept that a horse has thrown him, he told us that the horse had "thrown itself belly-up in order to see them better."

These were not the only cases where an affected animal had been found in this position. The next year, on July 2nd 1968, brothers Fred and Wayne Coulthard saw a bright red light which descended from the sky, and eventually disappeared behind the Murray Hills in Ontario, Canada. The horses nearby, were in a state of panic, running around their field in circles.

When they went back into the house, they found one of their three cats lying on its back, with all four legs straight up in the air. They could neither rouse the cat nor bend its legs. Later, it seemed to recover from its 'trance-like' condition, and ran out of the house, never to be seen again.

Their second cat also vanished, and the third run over by a car, when normally a very alert animal, it didn't move from its position on the road when the vehicle, a police car, started its motor and slowly reversed.

Just before noon, on February 19th 1968, Martha Heggs was in her kitchen in Bengough, Saskatchewn, Canada, when she heard a high pitch whine which penetrated her to the extent of feeling like a mild electric shock. She looked out the window, and saw an object, about 100 yards away, circling around a 29ft transformer pole. Their dog was cowering in the snow outside, and frantically trying to cover its ears with its paws.

The craft then moved right around the farm and homestead, before disappearing from her view some twenty minutes later. Sixteen of their cattle had bolted into their shed, and refused to come out for the next thirty minutes.

UFO effects, sometimes deadly, to farm animals, are well known. Jenny Randles wrote about two British incidents investigated in 1978 by Bill Gibbons.

At about 4.30am, in the Scottish district of Drummore, dairyman Tommy Gibson, was collecting his herd of cows, ready for milking. Suddenly, two grey/silver, oval shape craft, each about thirty feet in diameter, approached from the southern sky. They silently moved low and fast overhead, and out over the nearby sea.

About two minutes later, they returned, this time making a whirring/humming sound, like a 'threshing machine'. Although the cows took no notice of practising RAF jets, from West Freugh Air Base, screaming overhead, this time the cattle stampeded – Tommy had never seen them so spooked before. To make matters worse, they wouldn't give any milk for the next few days.

That same night, 6,000 racing pigeons had been released from Preston, and were expected to fly back to Ayr, (which would have taken them over the Drummore area). Not one arrived, or was ever seen again. Jenny Randles commented; *'Surely some alien biologist did not need 6,000 of the things to study? If he did, we wonder what the flight home was like!"*

The affect on milking cows, after a UFO event was quite common. Several UFO investigators wrote about this event on the night of 19th August 1969.

Howard Butcher was operating a dairy-machine on his father's farm at Cherry Creek, New York State, U.S.A., when his radio became very static, and the engine of the tractor, which was driving the milking machine, suddenly stopped.

All the dogs were barking, a bull outside the barn was bellowing, and the cows seemed terrified. Howard rushed out, and could see, about a quarter of a mile away, a strange object hovering above the ground. In his distraught state, the bull had bent the quarter-inch iron bar, to which he was tethered, to an angle of almost 45°. APRO investigators later discovered that sixteen cows, who normally produced 3-4 cans of milk daily, only yielded one and a half cans for the next week.

PARALYSIS

There have been many reports of alien beings, usually of small stature, temporarily paralysing witnesses, often by use of a 'torch like' or 'pencil-shaped' weapon which they fire at their victim.

In most cases, there was no evidence that the paralysis was inflicted as an act of hostility. Walter Webb, who did an in-depth analysis of the phenomenon, wrote; *'In the majority of the cases, the witness was in the process of walking, running, bicycling or driving toward the UFO or its occupants – sometimes intentionally and sometimes unsuspectingly – and at some point, to prevent the observer from coming any closer, a directed beam, or possibly an immobilising field surrounding the object stopped the individual in his tracks.*

'With the terrestrial observer at a safe distance, and unable to move, the UFO occupants, if outside, usually re-entered their craft with dispatch, and took off at fantastic speed. Immediately, normal bodily movement was restored to the affected individual.'

The Evening Times - October 28 1954, carried an article titled – *'Man from Mars Paralysed Me with a Blue-Ray Lamp.'* (These were the days of shock and wonder headlines!)

The case itself is quite interesting, and involved Aime Boussard, a 47 year old farmer from Aubusson, Central France, who described encountering a creature about five feet tall, wearing something like a diving suit, with a green light on either side of its head. It was shining two powerful pale blue lights at him;

"Suddenly I was blown from one side of the road to the other, and stayed there for about ten minutes without being able to shout or call for help. At last the blue lights went out, and the being crossed the road and vanished. I felt pains in my legs and right hand – I can still feel them."

Police who went to the spot found freshly disturbed earth and turf torn up, but no trace of footprints. In the meantime a lorry driver reported seeing a 'flying cauldron' – as big as a five ton lorry – taking off from a meadow by the road to Angouleme, south-west France. He said it left a white trail as it vanished noiselessly into the clouds.

The U.S. research group 'NICAP' reported on a March 14th, 1965, case from Fort Myers, where one night dog trainer James Flynn was camping out in the Everglades. Early in the morning he saw a bright, oscillating light, and drove his swamp buggy closer to investigate.

He then went further on foot, and soon came across a large, 100 ft diameter, 25 to 30ft high, machine, with an inverted top, which had landed nearby. It was shiny and metallic, with a bank – four rows – of lighted ports or windows.

He didn't get a chance to see if there were any occupants, because as he moved closer, he felt what seemed to be a 'sledgehammer blow', which knocked him unconscious. When he came to, the craft had gone, and he was half blinded from a wound on his head.

The local Indians took him to hospital, and later, a round 75ft burned area was found at the spot. The tops of 25ft trees, surrounding the landing site, were also singed.

Boczor Iosif reported on a strange occurrence in the Romanian Carpathian Mountains on 23rd September 1978. These were the days of the Communist regime, and a group of soldiers were working at a Youth Hostel building site.

Around midnight, Private Johann Durr was walking around the barracks, unaware that at Niemtzewt, near Bilea Lake, a mysterious light had been seen hovering above the ground for a few minutes before disappearing. Johann suddenly spotted a 'dark being' standing six to eight metres away, but when he went inside to tell his comrades, they merely laughed at him.

The next night, when Johann and his comrade Vulpe were going out to check some animal traps, Sergeant Radu Ioan met them at the door, pointing out a dark humanoid form on the hilltop. Johann remembered the incident the previous night, and they all went back into their barracks.

After a while, Sgt. Ioan gained some courage, and took two soldiers to go with him and investigate. When they were about two metres from the intruder, Ioan tried to strike it with a club he had been carrying. To everyone's amazement, he was unable to hit it, and suddenly fell backwards,

The 'being' bent down and examined him for a few minutes, then after making a weird noise, the soldiers saw something flash in its hand. They could do nothing to help, as they suddenly found themselves paralysed, and unable to move. After the being finally disappeared, they recovered, and were able to carry Ioan back to the barracks.

'From the head to the waist his body was soft, but from the waist to the toes it was very hard. His face, feet and hands were redder than the other parts of his body. He still held the club in his hands. It took him ten minutes to regain consciousness.'

Another soldier and two other witnesses went out, and looked up the hill, where they could see a 'shining halo with four egg-shaped forms dancing inside it'. That night they barricaded the doors of the barracks, but didn't get much sleep. The following morning they discovered strange lines on the outer part of the window blinds.

The Romanian government prevented any investigations, and it wasn't until 1990, after the fall of the Communist regime, that the details were made public.

In 2002, Australian researcher, Keith Basterfield, published in the *'Australasian Ufologist'*. a very comprehensive catalogue of *'UFO Cases which Involve Paralysis'*.

In the early days, witnesses experienced temporary paralysis when they came close to a UFO, or sometimes when they approached the alien occupants, who pointed some form of strange device at them. Different ufologists had varying view points as to the alien technology and mechanism which produced this effect.

French researcher, Aime Michelle, considered that there might be a *'paralysis distance'* between the witness and the craft; *"Moreover, this paralysis effect, is not, so to speak automatic...one of the witnesses, Dewilde, stated definitely that the paralysis came on him when he was already standing quite near the craft, but not moving towards it – just as if a defensive device had suddenly been turned on."*

(In September 1954, Marius Dewilde, was investigating a 'dark mass' and two 'beings' on a nearby railway line, when he was temporarily paralysed by a bright beam of light. - See my book *'Aspects of UFOs and Aliens'*)

U.S. investigator, Raymond Fowler, also supported this theory when he wrote; *'Observational evidence in such cases seems to indicate that the paralysis and electrical interference associated with UFO events are directed rather than just being a non volitional by-product of UFOs.'*

In 1979, Dr Niemtzow, a member of the Houston-based UFO study group 'VISIT', reported on investigating many of these cases.

"Scores of people who have had close encounters with UFOs have suffered a very selective paralysis that soon wears off, without ill effects. It is a very selective and a very calculated paralysis, which is well defined throughout the history of UFOs.

"Their legs are completely immobilised – but they do not fall down. The mouth and throat are paralysed and they cannot speak – but they can breathe. It seems to affect any nerve that is not vital to the person staying alive. We don't understand how it is done.

"There are other signs of this paralysis. When a person is paralysed, animals and insects in the area fall silent – leaving one to consider whether the paralysis also affects them."

(This was apparent in a 1951 case from Sonderborg, Denmark. On June 19th, after he heard a whistling noise, and a UFO landed in a field, the witness,

Joseph Matiszewski, approached and was paralysed. Cows also seemed to be unable to move, and the birds stopped singing. Four 'handsome, brown skinned, male figures', dressed in shiny clothing, and eight hovering objects emerged from the craft. Other figures seemed to be making repairs. After all the objects flew away, everything returned to normal.)

"As a medical doctor, I can say without contradiction, that earthly medical science cannot do this. Only a very advanced civilisation or an advanced technology beyond our present knowledge could do something like this."

One interesting factor emerged from the countless investigations conducted into this phenomenon. In several cases the 'victims' were able to free themselves from the paralysis.

In October 1954, an Italian witness, in Parravicino d'Erba, had just locked his car up in the garage, when he saw someone standing by a nearby tree. Suddenly he was paralysed by a beam of light, directed at him this by 'being', who was about four feet tall, and wearing a luminous suit. He inadvertently regained movement by clenching his fist around the garage keys.

He rushed to accost the stranger, who immediately rose from the ground, and fled with a soft whirring sound. The Italian police, who investigated the case, said that after he went into the house, in a state of shock, he later developed a high fever.

In 1955, another witness in California, woke on several occasions to a high pitch sound, and only being able to move her eyes. She found that by concentrating on moving a toe and finger, the paralysis and sound 'broke'.

A similar case was reported from California, the next year, by Ann Druffel and Scott Rogo. *'Emily Cronin and Jan Whitley stopped to sleep after driving for some time. Then they saw a light, a high pitched sound and felt paralysed by it.*

'Emily recalled a mental message saying someone would take her away, and felt a man looked in the car's back window. Under hypnosis, Emily told of three entities. Emily focussed on moving one finger, and the paralysis broke, with the light and beings also going.'

Whilst I don't know the answers, these cases make me wonder if these 'paralysis' beams do not target our muscles or physical abilities. In light of Dr.

Niemtzow's comments, perhaps these 'beams' affect just our brains, making us believe we cannot move?

Strangely enough, the use of a similar weapon in the days before the World Wars, was not so benign. Australian researcher, Keith Basterfield, unearthed the following two cases, both of which involved normal 'human-looking' occupants, from the archives.

In 1893, in Central N.S.W., a farmer found a saucer-shaped object had landed in one of his paddocks. A 'man' in odd clothing emerged, and as the farmer approached, he shone 'some kind of torch' at him.

The farmer was 'stunned', and fell to the ground. When he recovered, the 'man' and his unusual craft had gone, but the hand, where the 'torch beam' had struck him, was paralysed for life.

The second case, also in Central N.S.W., occurred in 1919. The witness was travelling down a country road when he came across an unusual object resting beside the roadside. A 'man' appeared to be working on it, and thinking that he may be able to help, the witness stopped and went over to offer his assistance.

The stranger turned, and as if surprised, and pointed something at the witness, who was 'knocked senseless'. When he 'came-to' the craft and its occupant were no longer there, and he subsequently discovered that his memory was never the same again.

GIVE IT BACK!

There have been a few cases where witnesses had retrieved a strange object or piece of debris from a UFO landing area. Not long after, a stranger would come to their door, demanding the souvenir be handed over.

Investigators, Jim and Coral Lorenzen, told of a disturbing incident from 13th July 1967. Robert Richardson, from Toledo, Ohio, was driving one night with his friend, Jerry Quay, to Whitehouse Quarry, a swimming and camping spot. As he rounded a corner, a brilliant blue light partially blinded him, and he felt a bump as his vehicle hit something. When they looked back, the road was empty. Later they called the police, and after the site was examined, and nothing found, they were not taken seriously.

Because there were some dents and scratches on the hood and bumper bar of the car, the next day, Richardson returned to the scene. He found two small lumps of metal, which he took home, and later gave to 'APRO' for analysis.

At 11pm on 16th July, two unidentified young men called at his home, requesting details about the accident and its location. He did not mention the lump of metal. Later, when he checked the license plate number on their car, he was told that particular plate number had not yet been issued.

One week later, when Richardson was alone, two more men arrived at his home. At first they tried to tell him he hadn't hit anything, but then contradicted themselves by demanding they be given to two artefacts Richardson had souvenired. How did they know about this? When they learned he had given them to APRO, and was not prepared to demand them back, they became quite nasty.

Just before they left, one of them said; "If you want your wife to stay as pretty as she is, then you'd better get the metal back!"

In 1968, in Säo Paulo, Brazil, the aliens apparently took matters into their own hands.

Investigators Dr. Max Berezowski and Dr. Methodius Kalkasieff reported that at 5am on 18th May, night watchman Dos Santos returned to his home to find a strange object in his courtyard. It was metallic and cylinder-shaped, about the same size as a two pound coffee can, with glass or plastic-encased dials at either ends. On the dials were marks which he thought resembled Arabic figures.

Over the objections of his wife, who thought it might be a bomb, he brought it into the house, and let his young son play with it before putting it on the bathroom window sill. The next night, at about 12.45 am, his wife was woken by a tremendous noise, which seemed to be accompanied by a strange blue light coming from the bathroom. She and her son fled in terror to their neighbour's home.

Because his wife was pregnant, when Dos Santos dropped by to check on her, he found his house ablaze with lights, and the neighbours congregated outside. They suddenly heard a sound like tiles shattering, after which the noise and light ceased. He tentatively entered his home, and found broken tiles scattered about the bathroom floor. There was a gaping hole in the roof, just above where the strange object, which had now disappeared, had been resting on the window sill.

CHAPTER TWELVE

THE DARK SIDE

PART TWO

DELIBERATE ATTACKS

Not all human – extraterrestrial interactions are peaceful and benign. Author and researcher, Trevor Constable, wrote of a case from 1943, when Pierre Perry, a pilot and president of an Arizona copper mining corporation, and Isador Montoya, a Mexican miner, reported seeing an American military plane being attacked by two brilliant, luminous UFOs, which were casting strong rays, or beams of light at their unfortunate target.

Before the plane exploded and crashed, somewhere near Prescott, Arizona, the pilot and co-pilot bailed out. The same beams of light hit their parachutes, sending them to a fiery death. Parts of their stricken aircraft were scattered all over the mountainside.

The witnesses, who were on horseback, were terrified, with Montoya convinced it was *'El Diablo'* – the Devil. He told Perry; *"I have seen the same thing many times, senor!"*

A third craft joined the two other UFOs, and they all vanished south, towards Mexico at breathtaking speed.

Sometimes we cannot be sure if the injuries to a witness were deliberate or inadvertent. In *'UFOs – Now and Then'*, I wrote about the 1956 case of sixteen-year-old Shayne Hura from New Zealand.

Early one morning he was cycling to his part-time job at a bakery in the Waiomo Valley. He was suddenly enveloped by a strange fog, and when it lifted, he saw a bright green, cigar-shaped object, with a fiery exhaust, climbing vertically into the sky.

Two days later, whilst traversing the same route, he was cycling past Sharpe's Quarry when he noticed a bright ball of solid light, about sixty centimetres in diameter, up beside the cliff face. He watched for a short time before continuing on his way, and he suddenly noticed that the strange object had risen out of the quarry, and was keeping pace with him.

That was the last he remembered, and said that he must have blacked out. The baker arrived to find Shayne collapsed at the bakery door, covered in blood and crying for help. Some of his teeth were missing, his nose was pierced, and his lip was torn away. His boss took him to hospital, and later found Shayne's bicycle in a creek seven kilometres away. The frame was bent, and the front wheel buckled, but police could find no evidence of any collision with a car.

Whilst Shayne recovered, he surprisingly felt the experience had changed his life for the better. Although he had no memory of the time he was 'blacked-out', he developed certain 'psychic' abilities, and once recovered in a Darwin hospital after 'dying' from a venomous snake bite.

In 1949, Major Jermiah Boggs, an Air Force intelligence officer, admitted that some pilots had fired on UFOs, in order to bring them down for 'closer observation'. He said these incidents had occurred at a time when Air Force orders clearly stated that pilots should not fire at UFOs, unless they made hostile moves towards their planes.

(Of course, this directive may not have indicated friendly intentions on our part at all. Perhaps overly zealous pilots had been destroying our own secret prototypes! Further, alien craft, who often showed restraint and flew off when attacked, sometimes retaliated, with deadly results for our own pilots.)

In 1993, investigator George Knapp interviewed Russian General Maltzsev, who conceded that his forces had also been given standing orders not to fire on UFOs, because, as he stated; "They may have tremendous capacity for retaliation!"

Sometimes the cockpits of attacking aircraft were filled with waves of heat, causing pilots to black-out, and instruments and engines to fail, often resulting in a fatal crash. In July 1954, after approaching a UFO, the pilot of a F-94 Starfire, sent up to investigate a radar report from Griffiths AFB, reported a wave of heat, 'like a furnace blast', engulfing his cockpit. As the pilot jettisoned his canopy, and seized the ejection lever, he got a glimpse of the unknown craft as it passed overhead.

Although he and his navigator bailed out to safety, the plane crashed into a house in Walesville, New York, and five civilians were killed.

Researcher, William Spaulding, told of an incident in Cuba in March 1967. After the Boca Chica Naval Air Station reported radar reports of an unauthorised craft approaching from the north-east, two MIG-21 interceptors were scrambled when the object entered their air space.

It was travelling at near 'Mach' speed, at an altitude of approximately 10,000 metres. As the Cuban planes came within five kilometres of the object, the wing leader told Cuban Ground Control Intercept that it was a bright metallic sphere, with no visible markings or appendages.

After futile attempts to identify or contact the object, Cuban Air Defence Headquarters ordered the wing leader to arm his weapons and destroy the intruder. As soon as his missiles were armed, and radar locked on, the wing leader's plane exploded. The pilot of the second plane said that there was no smoke or flame - the other MIG-21 had literally disintegrated.

Cuban radar reported that the object had quickly accelerated, climbed beyond 30,000 metres, and headed southeast towards South America. The loss of the wing leader and his aircraft was officially listed as 'equipment malfunction'

Some other reports were hard to confirm, due to the reticence of authorities to make any comment.

Investigator Raymond Fowler told of speaking to retired Air Force Master Sergeant 'C.D.' who had been the chief investigator in a bizarre incident in June 1953, when an F-94C, a two seater fighter plane, with some kind of 'secret gear on board', attempted to intercept unknown objects near Otis AFB, Massachusetts, when they failed to respond to radio identification.

'According to the pilot's sworn testimony......at an altitude of 1,500 feet over the Base Rifle Range, the engine quit functioning, and the entire electrical system failed.....The pilot yelled to the radar operator, (over the battery-operated intercom), to bail out, (and), jettisoned the canopy because the aircraft...was seconds from impact...He landed...The crippled plane should have crashed.....but it wasn't there....The radar operator could not be found.'

Sgt. 'C.D.' also stated that; *"This incident caused one of the most extensive and intensive searches I have ever seen....For three months...The aircraft and the radar operator were never found."* To add to the mystery, the jettisoned canopy was found within the confines of the rifle range.

Later that year, on November 23rd, Lt. Felix Moncla Jnr., a pilot, and radio officer, Lt. Robert Wilson, and their F-89C plane, were being tracked on radar near Kinross Air Force Base in Michigan, while in pursuit of a UFO over Lake Superior. Without any distress signal being received, the two objects merged on the screen, 70 miles off Keweenaw Point. The early edition of the Chicago *'Tribune'* carried the headlines *'Jet, Two Aboard, Vanishes Over Lake Superior'*, but this was deleted from all later editions. Despite immediate search and rescue planes being dispatched, the plane, and its pilot and radio officer never returned from their mission, and to date, no trace has been found of the craft, crew, or UFO.

After the Canadian newspapers learned of the event, the Air Force went into damage control, saying the radar operator had misread his readings, and the 'UFO' was an off course Canadian airliner, something the Canadian government disputed. They then suggested that Moncla must have suffered an episode of vertigo and plunged into the lake.

We will probably never know the truth!

Researcher, Otto Binder, also reported a similar incident; *'Without any details, information leaked out that in 1955, a military transport plane, with 26 troops on board, was approaching its airbase from ten miles off shore. The base radar operator suddenly radioed a warning that an 'unknown' was streaking up fast at 2,500 miles per hour.*

'The next instant the two 'blips' collided, and the transport never landed. A general's briefcase was later found floating on the water, but the transport plane had sunk to a watery grave, after being struck – or deliberately rammed – by the UFO, whose 'blip' streaked away after the collision.'

Scott Corrales recounted a 1953 incident, which was purportedly reported by physicist Raymond Harvey. A new secret prototype interceptor craft, armed with atomic cannon, was being test flown out of Wright Patterson AFB.

Suddenly, the control tower ordered Steinbeck, the pilot, to return and land immediately, as there were eight 'unidentified machines' closing in on him from his right. Steinbeck panicked, and opened fire. Two blasts were heard coming from his atomic weaponry, before he crashed into the desert at high speed.

In 1975, Major Donald Keyhoe told of an incident which had occurred about five years earlier. He said that the Air Force had standing, although secret, orders that every radar sighting of a suspicious nature should be checked out.

That particular night, when a UFO was circling an Air Force base in the southeastern U.S., three jets were sent up to investigate. Although they approached the strange object gradually and carefully, they suddenly disappeared, and the UFO climbed straight up and also vanished. No trace of the planes or pilots was ever found.

Keyhoe said; *'The Air Force lied to the families of the pilots. Relatives were told each airman was lost in a separate accident, unrelated to UFOs. One was supposedly lost over the ocean, another in the Everglades, and the third I'm not sure about.'*

(In a similar incident in 1988, two F-14 Navy Tomcat jets suffered a similar fate to their predecessors when they were seen to merge with a large UFO over Puerto Rico. The episode was viewed by about a hundred witnesses on the ground. They said that the normal roar of the jet engines ceased abruptly when the aircraft merged with the UFO. There were no explosions, just a sudden silence and disappearance of the aircraft into the UFO, which then quickly zipped off to an unknown destination.)

Similar events were occurring in other parts of the world. In 1959 military pilot, C. L. Hawke, was serving as a specialised meteorologist and stationed at the Fifth Air Force Headquarters at Fuchu, Japan. In the spring of that year he was in the Combat Operations Centre, monitoring the weather conditions, when suddenly, 'all hell broke loose'. One operator was yelling; "They're back again."

He asked a colleague what was happening, and was told; *"There is an unidentified object here...We have seen them quite frequently. They travel at 2,000 miles per hour, and for some strange reason, they stop and hover frequently, sometimes for two or three hours."* Then they would go towards the Sea of Japan, and disappear.

The order was given to 'scramble'. One plane couldn't take off because his navigational aids were not working. Their Commander complained; "Damn! There it goes again! We've had this happen every time we tried to scramble!"

The other pilot took off, in his F-106, despite the fact that two of his navigational aids were defunct. He soon closed in on the strange craft, and described it as being a circular, metallic craft with a cockpit on top. After a few minutes he received permission to fire, but his rockets had detonated without hitting the object.

Suddenly, the pilot's voice came across in a falsetto tone, and he started screaming; "Oh, my God, they've turned on some kind of beam and they're turning. They're coming after me....It's coming closer!"

Radar then noted that there was no separation between the two blips on the screen, and suddenly the movements stopped, and there was only one blip on the screen. The military searched for four days, but found nothing.

At the Australian International UFO Symposium, held in Brisbane - October 1997, one of the guest speakers was James Courant. He had been a pilot, flying DC8, 727 and 747 airliners. He was also an instructor for multi-engine aircraft, helicopters, gyrocopters, gliders, seaplanes and balloons!

He had researched UFOs since 1962, and had three sightings himself within a three year period. He was also in contact with many witnesses in government departments, airlines, astronauts, scientists and the media. As a result, he was convinced that there is a global cover-up of UFO reality.

He recounted two startling cases I had not been aware of before. The first occurred in November, 1962, at an airbase in Greenland. A UFO had been visually sighted and tracked on radar. A jet fighter was scrambled to investigate. The pilot confirmed a visual, and suddenly his plane and the object merged on the radar scope. The plane and its pilot had completely disappeared.

A DC-3 search plane took off, sighted the UFO and also vanished off the face of the earth. A rescue helicopter was dispatched to investigate, and the crew reported seeing strange lights before radio contact was lost. The chopper and crew were not found, despite a major search the next day. Some months later the helicopter was found in the same area, but there was no trace of the crew. Their bodies were never found.

James Courant went on to liken this case to one that occurred over 25 years later, in 1989, over Puerto Rico, more than one hundred witnesses on the ground saw a F-14 Tomcat jet fighter disappear into a UFO.

He commented that it was no wonder that the U.S. Army concluded that aliens were hostile, and developed high energy lasers and particle beam weapons to shoot them down. He said that Col, Philip Corso (Ret) claimed these weapons have had some success, and they are much more powerful than those depicted in the movie *'Independence Day'*.

In 1997, researcher Wendy Wolfe wrote about another incident which occurred in 1965 in the Florida area.

Her informant was Samuel David, who was a U.S. Naval Officer, in the Investigation Section of the Military Police. His duties included 'writing up' incidents, and on this particular day, also collecting and confiscating all cameras, and swearing witnesses to silence.

A UFO had been detected on Naval radar. *'Military as well as civilian witnesses and civilian pilots had all reported sighting the UFO. A military aircraft was deployed to intercept the unidentified object, but in full view of many witnesses, it was struck by a beam from the UFO and disappeared.*

'Two more aircraft were then sent up to 'seek and destroy' the UFO. They took up positions to the rear of the delta-shaped object and radioed back that they were firing at it, but their ammunition was exploding before reaching the craft.

'In response to their offensive, one of these two aircraft was destroyed, probably by a beam from the UFO, or perhaps by their own ammunition being deflected back against them. Instruction was then given for the third pilot to fall back and return to base. The pilot was detained there for three weeks, being grilled for every small detail of the event, and not being permitted, during this time, to speak to any outsider.'

David said the report he prepared was 'the size of a telephone directory', and his superiors were not happy, asking him to amend it to 'something more appropriate'. When he refused to alter his 'accurate' findings, he lost his position, and was transferred, as an ordinary seaman, to a ship at sea.

Two years later, *'SIGAP'* newsletter and the British *'Spacelink'* magazine spoke of an incident which occurred in 1967. On Saturday, 4th November, Mr M. Chadd and his girlfriend were driving past Cutmill in Surrey. They stopped to watch a glowing disc-shaped object, which was hovering some ten feet away over some bushes and trees. After about fifteen minutes, the glow diminished, and the object disappeared.

'About fifteen to thirty minutes later, the Iberian Airlines Caravelle crash occurred at Haslemere, Surrey, only eight miles away. Thirty-seven people died in this crash, but yesterday, the Board of Trade said there would be no public enquiry, which presumably means they have found the cause. (This weekend also saw a tragic train crash near Hither Green, in which 53 people died!)'

In 1980 retired Major Colman Von Keviczky addressed the House of Lords. In his presentation, he quoted U.S. General Benjamin Chidlaw as testifying, in 1952, that *"We have stacks of reports about flying saucers, we take them seriously when you consider **we have lost many men and planes trying to intercept them!**"*

We have researchers Irena Scott and William Jones to thank for this report, again made nearly forty years after the event.

In 1957, Wallace Fowler was a young enlisted airman stationed at Ellsworth A.F.B., Rapid City, South Dakota. It was early evening, and as he was sitting on the steps of his barracks, he noticed a strange craft hovering overhead. It was saucer shaped, about the size of a house, metallic and silver in colour. There was a dome on top, which appeared to have portholes, through which he could see 'shadows' moving around.

Instantly realising this was no conventional plane, he jumped up to get a better look. As soon as he mentally challenged the object to land, it shot straight up, at incredible speed, into the sky. As he made his way over to the hangers and base control tower, he could see a number of pilots running towards their planes. Once inside the tower, he was ignored, but he could hear telephones ringing and radio communications from the pilots.

One said; *"This thing acts as if it's playing games with us, and when we get close it takes off and leaves us like we are standing still. Such speed!"*

After the control tower asked one pilot to try and get closer, there was the sound of a 'crash', and no further communications. Wallace was told not to talk about what he had seen and heard, and ordered to leave the tower. Later, on the base, very little was discussed about the incident, however one of the pilots said that the plane which had been chasing the object had gone missing, and no wreckage was ever found.

Investigator George Fawcett wrote of an incident in April 1959, about which we had few details; *"The Air Force at Seattle, Washington, acknowledged a 'frantic radio report', that 'we have hit something', or 'something has hit us', which preceded a mysterious crash of a C-118. No survivors. Many eyewitnesses on the ground reported the sighting of three or four parachute-like glowing UFOs that were following the plane prior to its crash.'*

Researcher, David Ritchie, published more details about this occurrence, which apparently involved a C-118 cargo plane, belonging to the Air Force's 1075th Air Transport Wing, flying out of McChord Air Force Base near Tacoma in western Washington State.

After the crash, witnesses stated that the plane, apparently with its engines stopped, and tail section missing, was being pursued by three shiny discs. They were darting close to the plane and disappeared after several loud explosions were heard. An investigation of the crash site indicated that the wreckage consisted of a great number of small, charred fragments scattered over a wide area. The tail assembly was reportedly located north of Mt. Rainier, miles away from the rest of the wreckage. Only three bodies, of the four crew members, were found.

On 28th March 1980, the Australian *'Mirror'* newspaper published an interesting article detailing a fatal encounter between an RAAF fighter plane and a UFO.

A retired RAAF technician, who was on duty at Laverton Air Force Base, in the early 1970s, got a message from a transport plane, flying at normal altitude. The pilot reported seeing a cigar-shaped object travelling at the same altitude and speed as his own plane. As Laverton confirmed the object on radar, the pilot radioed that a second object was on his left.

Radar readings then confirmed that several 'cigars' were clustering around the transport plane. The pilot was immediately given permission to land at Laverton, and a fighter plane was sent up to reconnoitre.

The *'Mirror'* quoted the technician; *"The fighter pilot radioed that the cigars were matching his greater speed. Then the objects moved really close to him, and he started to 'get the breeze up'. He told us he would break from his course and return to base, because he was getting nervous.*

"Then suddenly the fighter and the cigars disappeared from the radar screen. My friend later confirmed to me that he had been in the radar room all the time, and viewed the entire event. The plane was reported missing, and its wreckage was found a day or so later. "What staggered everybody was where it was found – more than four hundred miles from where it could have flown, even if it had been fully refuelled. The pilot's body was never found."

The *'Mirror'* did 'due diligence', and obtained supporting testimony from another ex-RAAF officer who was at the base when this happened.

Perhaps one airman considered himself, and his crew, lucky to escape a fiery death. Brad Steiger wrote of how, on the night of July 22nd 1956, U.S. Major Mervin Stenvers was flying in a C-131-D twin-engine fighter-bomber, when he radioed that he had been 'struck' by a flying saucer.

The mid-air collision knocked the crew off its feet and sent the plane into a downward spin towards the ground. He considered it a miracle that he was able to make an emergency landing at Bakersfield airport.

Lawrence Fawcett, in the book *'UFO Cover-Up'*, told of a 1969 incident, where we may never know the full details.

In the October of that year there had been reports of UFOs over an Atomic Energy Commission research facility in North Carolina. Eventually, when the radar showed two unidentified objects, stationary on the screen for over an hour, the Air Force scrambled two Phantom F-4 jets – one with wing cameras and the other with air-to-air missiles.

At first the strange objects took off, and after outdistancing their pursuers, came to a sudden halt. The F-4s were about three miles from their targets when first one plane, and then the other, disappeared off the radar screen.

The search parties located the plane wreckage scattered over a large area, and both pilots and co-pilots alive. We may never know what happened, because at the time of Fawcett writing his book in 1984, the survivors were confined in a military mental institution with 'little or no faculties'.

Many years later, on May 5th 1977, another pilot was seriously injured, however it may have not been intentional on the part of the UFO which he encountered.

Researcher Joseph Brill wrote of how a young and inexperienced Colombian pilot, Manuel Ojeda, was practising some landing exercises before attempting some more difficult flight manoeuvres. He was flying alone, in a Cessna 150 plane from the 'Aeroclub of Colombia Flying School.'

He later explained that it was when he was attempting slow, tight turns to the left and right that the plane began to vibrate 'with great intensity'; *"On coming out of the turn, the tachometer, air speed indicator and all the instruments on board were showing zero. The plane would not respond, and it was shaking with great force.*

"To the left side I saw an oval object the colour of a dark cloud. Surrounding it were yellowish and red phosphorescent lights which were shining with high intensity. It was somewhat disconcerting, the aircraft was not responding to my movement of the controls. It was at that moment I began to feel a strong pressure in my ears and head. My hands and body were itching. However, I was very conscious of what I was seeing and doing."

Manuel described the object as looking like an aluminium 'mass', about 15-20ft in diameter, and it moved down below the landing gear under his plane, without ever 'making contact'. Despite his inability to control the Cessna, the plane seemed to continue to fly in the same circle without losing altitude;

"Later, the UFO moved in front of the plane, and that was when I began to lose my sight. Everything looked cloudy. For just a moment it seemed I was recovering my visibility, but I was thinking to myself that this was the end for me....The strange object disappeared, and I was left blind!"

Once he regained radio contact with the control towers at Guaymaral and Eldorado, panic set in. (UFOs had been sighted in the past, but were rarely recorded on radar due to the hilly surrounds.) Emergency rescue plans went into action, all flight operations were suspended, and a fire engine placed next to the runway. Four aeroplanes, under the control of expert flight instructors, took to the air.

Communications with the young Manuel, who thought he was going to die, were difficult. Everything looked the same to him, like he was 'flying in circles over a desert', and his responses to the radio operators sounded as if he were 'in a drunken stupor'.

There were four unsuccessful attempts to guide him into the airport, and on two occasions it was feared he would crash into the control tower. The fifth time, a momentary recovery of sight, although far from perfect, enabled Manuel, with craft guiding him on both sides, to focus on the runway and make a nearly perfect landing. He was found, frozen at the controls, his body facing front, and his seatbelt still fastened.

He was taken to a nearby clinic, and given tranquilizers for his shattered nerves. After later treatment his sight was restored, and it was determined he was in a 'satisfactory physical condition'. No mention was made of his psychological state, or whether he ever continued with his ambition to be a fully fledged pilot.

Before we ascribe blame to any particular entities, one needs to look at the activities of unidentified craft in Colombia, before and after the event which affected Manuel Ojeda.

At 9pm on January 21st 1977, seven minutes after an Avianes Airlines aeroplane took off from Bogota's Eldorado Airport, Captain Gustavo Ferriera, co-pilot Pedro Tapias, the flight engineer and two stewardesses spotted a brilliant white light moving directly towards their plane. Radar operator, Jorge Jiminez, was detecting a radar reading of an object, supposedly three times the size of a normal plane, which was travelling at an incredible speed and following a zig-zag pattern of flight.

Bogota traffic control advised they had no craft in the area, and Capt. Ferriera, fearing a possible collision, turned on his landing lights so that the other craft could see him. The crew stared as the intense white light in front of them turned red. After Ferriera turned his landing lights on again, for a second time, the object responded with green lights, and with tremendous speed, flew away to the south at an angle of ninety degrees.

Other UFOs were sighted from the airport during the first two months of 1977, and air traffic controller Octavio Lemos commented that he wouldn't be surprised if one landed. On the night of 7th February, tower chief, Jaime Olarte saw a brilliant object hovering over Bogota for three hours.

Joseph Brill commented that; *'Among air traffic personnel, no-one denies believing in the flying object, from who knows where, because they have been sighted so frequently. One commented; "The only bad aspect of all this is that we humans should be so backward, and that we know so little about any other beings out there, that might be operators of these craft."*

However, given our own technological advances by this time, and the details of the next case, I can't help wondering if these craft that the Colombians were witnessing were in fact prototypes from one of their more advanced neighbours to the north?

On Saturday July 30th, two months after Manuel Ojeda's temporary loss of vision, Colombian pilot, Camilo Barrios, was in command of an Aerocondor cargo plane which was flying from Barranquilla, Colombia to Miami. At 3am, and nearing the end of his journey, between Jamaica and Miami, Camilo saw a circular object, 'like a flying saucer', giving off a light which was red, green, blue and finally white.

They were flying north, and the UFO appeared from the east, and flew parallel to their plane, at a distance of about 30 to 35 miles. Once Camilo and the crew realised what it was, they became quite excited, and tried to make contact.

He got on the radio, and identified himself, his crew, their plane and its route and destination. He asked the other craft that if they understood, could they please ascend. The UFO then ascended. Camilo then requested, that in order to be sure, could it please descend, and the strange craft obliged. It kept its distance, and flew parallel to them for the next hour, before taking off, and disappearing from sight.

These strange confrontations continued for many years into the future.

In 2000, an article, by Romeo Ferrao, titled *'An Alien Attack'*, in the *'Contact'* publication, told of an incident which occurred south of Moscow in the April of that year.

Captain Alexei Duryev was piloting a MIG-29 on a routine training mission when he was ordered to investigate an unknown object detected nearby. A second jet was scrambled a few seconds later.

Duryev managed to get within 1,000 metres of the strange craft, which was huge, with no identifying insignia, and pulsing a grey-green light. He saw a flash of light, coming from the belly of the ship, and 'felt a bump'; *"It was the most terrifying experience of my life....and I realised my plane was cracking up. I held my position as long as I could, and then I had to eject."*

The second pilot took photographs, which were later published in *'Pravda'* and *'Izvestia'*.

Air Force Major Dmitri Ivanov was quoted as saying; *"Our investigations were investigatory; we did nothing to provoke an attack. But, I can assure you we would have retaliated had we been able to.*

"Unfortunately, the UFO vanished after it eliminated the MIG-29. There was nothing left to shoot at. With a little luck, we will be able to learn something about the ray that downed the MIG by examining the wreckage. As in most UFO encounters, we have a mystery that cannot be solved."

CRUEL AND BARBARIC EVENTS

It does strike me as paradoxical that, every day, in fields and abattoirs, all over the world, humans slaughter and dismember tens of thousands of livestock for food, yet we get very upset when a relatively few number of cattle etc. are found mysteriously dead and dissected on our farms. Although I don't intend to write about the numerous cattle mutilations which have occurred over the years, humans seem to be exceptionally distressed when a horse is involved.

We have relatively few cases of animal mutilations reported in Australia, however in my book, *'The Gosford Files'*, I do mention one distressing case which occurred at Budgewoi, on the N.S.W. Central Coast.

An 'old timer' related how in 1982 the Smith family were away for the weekend, leaving their fourteen-year-old son, Ben, alone. His friend, Adam Watts, came over to keep him company on the Saturday night.

In the early hours of Sunday morning, they were startled to hear a whirring noise outside, and a strong white light flooded through the window. They looked out and all they could see were a mass of white lights. They were too scared to even venture out of the back door.

The next morning, when they looked around the paddock, they found Ben's pony lying dead. They called the local veterinarian who was quite mystified. There were no apparent injuries on the corpse, but the body had been totally drained of blood!

The U.S.A. case of 'Snippy', the horse, is well known in ufological circles. In May 1968, our own *'U.F.O.I.C. Newsletter'* contained some further details they had extracted from an article in the *'Daily Telegraph'* following Snippy's unfortunate demise, in the San Luis Valley area of Colorado, the previous September.

Harry King started to worry when one of his favourite horses, Snippy, did not return to his ranch for his usual evening drink, and two days later started searching for him. Snippy's body was found about a quarter of a mile from the house, which is in desolate mountain country.

All the flesh had been stripped from the horse's head and neck, and only bare bones remained. Harry called Snippy's owners, Burl Lewis and his wife, and together they investigated the vicinity where the horse had been killed, and found areas where the brush had been squashed to within ten inches of the ground, and fifteen circular marks were found 100 yards from the body. One investigating committee found another area with a circle 75ft in diameter. A forestry official checked the site with a Geiger counter, and high readings were found all around the area. Since many sightings and landings had been reported in the vicinity at that time, UFOs were blamed for this unfortunate death. (Researcher, Janet Bord, wrote, in the *'Flying Saucer Review'* - 1972, a detailed report of the various events reported.)

'An investigating committee returned to Denver with several samples taken from the horse, and an object, presumed to be a tool, found by Mrs Lewis on her second visit to the site on September 16th. It was covered with horse hair, but when she tried to wipe the hair off, her hand turned red and began to burn, and this persisted until she washed her hands later.'

Investigators noted that the carcass was neither unduly decomposed nor 'smelly', and it had not been touched by vultures or buzzards. *'An autopsy revealed that its abdominal, brain and spinal cavities were empty, and in addition to this, the pathologist who performed the autopsy said there were no signs of entrance into the horse's body....The pathologist said he was not surprised by the absence of all the abdominal organs and brain, as he had read of similar incidents in other countries.'*

In 1968, Gerald Duplantier wrote in his Canadian publication *'Saucers, Space & Science'* of another similar episode also involving horses in 1967.

About 8pm, one evening in late August, a doctor was riding his horse along a river trail on the Sarcee Indian Reserve west of Calgary. For no apparent reason, his mare became alert and stiff, and then extremely violent, and practically uncontrollable, twisting and turning.

As he was trying to control his horse, the doctor noticed a strange cloud, about seventy feet wide, out of which appeared a solid-looking object, about forty feet in diameter. It looked like fibreglass or plastic of a silvery blue, or bluish steel colour. He could only see the underpart, but it appeared to be oval, with two circular vent-like structures, slowly rotating in opposite directions, around a square central protrusion.

By this time his horse was violently thrashing her head about, but he was able to catch a glimpse of the object re-entering the cloud, and he could detect a slight vibration as the whole formation slowly moved off.

As he carefully proceeded to take his mare home, the doctor spotted something in the bush. It was another horse, on its side, and obviously dead. He noticed its exposed side was badly singed, although there was no sign of a fire having been there. Whatever had happened, it must have been recent. The body was still warm, with no sign of rigor mortis, and the smell of burned hair hung in the air.

The next day he took a neighbour to identify the dead animal. The imprint of where it had lain was quite visible, but the carcass had gone. There was no evidence of the tracks of any vehicle which would have been necessary to remove the body. It was as if it had been lifted up, directly from the spot, and hauled away by air!

For a couple of days the doctor's horse was very 'head-shy', as if her ears may have been affected by the incident. Several weeks later, the doctor noticed several sore-looking spots on her head and down her neck, as if caused by a burn. The vet was unable to diagnose the cause.

A DEADLY RETALIATION

In 1964, following a letter, regarding flying saucers and subsequent fires, from Gordon Creighton to the *'Watford and West-Herts. Post'*, a most interesting account of a 1922 Irish incident, in County Donegal, was received from a Mr Lawrence Bradley of Watford.

Bradley wrote that one night, in April 1922, he was fighting a scattered rear-guard action in Ireland, mostly in the mountains, in the army that he belonged to, during the civil war that was raging at the time.

'One evening, tired and dispirited, I laid down in the entrance to an old cave. In the fading twilight, I noticed that practically all the gorse bushes and grass that grew around the entrance to the cave were scorched and burnt.

'The only occupants of the cave were sick and wounded men who were unable to walk. The six able-bodied soldiers, who were looking after them, told me a strange story, which, at the time, seemed very far-fetched and unconvincing.

'It appeared that early that morning, they were awakened by a whirring noise from outside. Thinking that it was an enemy armoured car, they immediately opened fire. In the darkness before the dawn, it was hard to see the object they were shooting at, but after a brisk fusillade of shots, the object retaliated by firing jets of flame at the cave.

'The defenders had to withdraw in face of the fierce heat. All the undergrowth was now ablaze, and the smoke was billowing into the cave, so it was a case of facing the flame-throwers, or suffocating to death, which was a hard choice to make, as it meant death either way. The urgent need for fresh air made them choose the latter course.

'When they ran out of the entrance, they saw the flame-throwing object beginning to ascend into the sky. It was clearly visible in the first light of dawn – circular in shape and bright in appearance, as if made of aluminium. I daresay some of the men who saw this strange phenomenon are still alive today, and can vouch for this. For myself, I can only vouch for the scorched and burnt undergrowth.'

Jerome Clark wrote of a similar, inexplicable event, from Mt. Kenya in Africa in June 1954; – 'An 11-year-old African boy, named Laili Thindu, and several companions, watched odd lights flying over and landing on Mt. Kenya. The UFOs seemed to be involved in intense activity of some kind.

'One night, a short while later, a fleet of glowing objects swooped over a nearby village, beaming down bright rays of light. Laili Thindu witnessed the spectacle in astonishment, but not until the next day did he learn that the entire population of the village had been seared to death.'

Jerome continued; 'A brutal, serious attack, but not pointless. Whatever was being done on Mt. Kenya, was of sufficient importance to the UFO beings to cause them to destroy all the witnesses. The boy survived, however, and carried his story to the authorities in Nairobi.... As I have said, 'hostile' incidents do not in themselves prove that the overall plan of the UFOs is dangerous to us. But neither do they show that our visitors are the patient, all wise, god-like figures in whom some UFO students, (perhaps victims of the breakdown of traditional religion), insist on believing despite all the evidence to the contrary.'

THE PSYCHOLOGICAL EFFECTS

In this book, I have discussed the physical effects, both good and bad, which some witnesses experience during and after an encounter – but what about the continuing psychological damage they suffer?

Certainly, with some, an enhanced psychic ability is welcome, but their effect on electronic equipment can be disconcerting. There are often more troubling consequences. Many refuse to drive after nightfall. This fear of the dark is quite common, often extending to a reluctance to sleep alone, with some experiencers going to bed fully clothed, the light and radio on, and not falling asleep until daybreak. Beside insomnia and other sleep disorders, sexual and relationship problems often occur. After the initial anxiety, disorientation and confusion, experiencers can develop unexpected compulsions or even panic attacks. An irrational fear of doctors, hospitals or medical procedures often occurs.

Ron Halliday recounted one sad episode in his book *'UFO Scotland'*. During 1969, 'Bill', a Glasgow resident, worked as the mate on a ship in the North Sea fishing fleet. One warm summer morning, he was on deck, watching the sun rise. Suddenly he saw an object, too big to be a plane, hovering just over the water line. It looked just like the 'flying saucers' he'd seen portrayed on TV. A red band, gleaming brightly, was around the middle, and there were humped curvatures top and bottom.

He yelled to his shipmates, who raced up on deck. They arrived to watch the disc racing skywards and disappearing. The experience altered Bill, overtaking his mind until he could think of nothing else. He had nightmares of an enormous ship and its occupants, and later reflected that his obsession affected him so much it affected his relationship with his wife, causing his marriage to fail.

After leaving his seafaring life, and taking up a job with a Welsh radio station, he started fantasising about being imprisoned by aliens, who looked like us, and were living amongst us on our planet. They imparted secrets, which he began to accept as true, and believed that if he said anything about his experiences 'there would be retribution'.

He was mentally shattered, and eventually referred to a psychiatrist, who pronounced him to be mentally ill. Bill still believed his experiences to be genuine, but 'played along' with the doctors. After being put on medication, he returned to work, this time in a restaurant.

One night, he confided in the cook, which he later regretted when he noticed one of the waiters looking at him strangely. That night, when he got home, two men grabbed him as he entered his flat.

'They threatened him in blunt language, and told him that this time they would only warn him. But should he open his mouth again....Bill admitted that he didn't know what to make of it all, though the incident scared him badly. He was frightened not simply because he had been threatened. Even more terrifying was the possibility that he had imagined the whole thing, and his mind was going. But deep down he felt sure that it was fact and not fiction.'

The next day, Bill, who was only a casual employee, was sacked. Food he knew he had put in the freezer had been found on the storeroom floor. Despite getting other employment, similar events occurred, and Ron asked Bill why was this happening?

*'He had no doubt concerning who was responsible – aliens masquerading as humans; – "I have no idea why. All I know is that they do. They tell me to keep quiet. To say nothing to anyone....Maybe I've seen something they want me to forget. I know I'm not normal, but that's because of my experience with the aliens. I'm not lying. There **are** aliens on this earth. The government knows it, but are saying nothing."*

Ron knew of Bud Hopkins work, hypnotically regressing experiencers, and desperately wanted to get Bill to the 'Hopkins Center', however this wasn't to be. Before he could make suitable arrangements, Bill had moved on, and Ron lost track of him.

But, what about the unintentional harm caused by their fellow humans? My dear friend and colleague, U.S. investigator Rosemary Decker, wrote about the psychological problems encountered when a contactee or abductee has desperate need to communicate with someone who will listen empathetically, and without judgement.

'It is just at this crucial point that additional difficulties often arise, which will affect their personal life for years to come. Out of a sense of duty, they may take their story to the police or military. There, they may be shrugged off as either addled, hoaxing or lying, or they may be interrogated so exhaustingly or so frighteningly that they spend the rest of their life regretting tis action.

'They may confide instead in a trusted family member who fears they have gone 'round the bend', and they consequently suffer rejection in their home community. Sometimes, the witness may already be interested in, or

researching the subject, and feels that the logical and safe place to take their confidence is their local UFO study group.

'Unfortunately, this can be most traumatic – the entire group may exhibit suspicion and turn their backs. In order to save their job and status in the community, they then go 'mum', and years later may still hesitate to trust anyone, however much they would like to retrieve any possible 'lost time'.

Rosemary noted that; '*...among the encountered I have known in person, nine of the twenty-four were UFO researchers when their contacts occurred.'*

Sometimes the ridicule expressed by friends, relatives and work colleagues can do more harm than the experience itself, and harassment from the authorities and media only add to the problem.

Researcher Kevin Randle, in his book, '*Project Blue Book Exposed*', looked into the sad case of Dale Spaur, who was a Deputy in the Sherriff's department in Portage County, Ohio. He was very happy in his job until that fateful day on 17th April 1966.

It was early in the morning when Dale and Deputy Barney Neff were on patrol, driving along the road between the communities of Randolf and Attwater. They saw an empty car parked beside the road, and stopped to investigate. It was a rather strange red and white Ford sedan, with an unusual emblem painted on the side. It was a triangle, with a bolt of lightning inside, and the words 'Seven Steps to Hell'. Inside it was crammed with walkie-talkies and other radio equipment.

Suddenly the two officers heard a humming sound, and turned around to see a huge saucer-shaped craft, with a purplish-white light on its underside, rise out of the woods and cross the highway. Both of them felt paralysed as the strange object hovered over their patrol car, and surrounded them with the heat blazing from underneath.

Before the strange object moved slowly away, Dale heard a mysterious voice in his head, telling him not to run. As soon it was a short distance away, both officers raced for their car, and Dale radioed in to base, who flippantly told him to 'shoot it'.

The craft was still hovering nearby, and Dale noted down some details. It was about 40-50ft across, and 20ft high, with a large dome on top, and an antenna jutting out from its rear. A conical beam of blue-white light, from the underneath, hit the ground, rocking back and forth as the UFO tilted.

Their sergeant came on the radio, and when his officers said the object was slowly moving away, they were ordered to chase it. At the same time, switchboards all over Ohio were being flooded with calls from startled witnesses. The Police Chief at Mantus, Gerald Buchert, went outside his station, and tried to take a photograph. (Even though other police officers had also seen the strange craft, with military jets in hot pursuit, moving across the sky, the Air Force, who had attempted to explain the sighting away as an 'artificial earth satellite' and 'Venus', had no conscience about making Dale look a fool and even told Gerald Buchert not to release the photo he had taken of the strange craft.)

Dale and Barney chased after the object for some time, until it disappeared over a hill. They thought it had gone until they looked in their rear vision mirror to see that it was now behind them! They continued to follow the strange craft, which they nicknamed 'Floyd', until daybreak, and felt that, at times, it was almost waiting for them to catch up.

After over eighty miles of pursuit, their vehicle ran out of gas, and they had to give up. As they came to a halt, it was almost as if their quarry knew. The craft accelerated straight up and away at tremendous speed.

When they returned to the sheriff's department, there was a group of newspaper reporters waiting for them. Barney refused to talk, but Dale, in his innocence, spoke freely. His wife said that when he eventually arrived home, Dale was very pale and listless, just sitting around. She had 'never seen him so frightened before'.

Barney's wife said that, when he got home, he refused to talk about it; - "I hope I never see him like he was after the chase. He was real white, almost in a state of shock."

NICAP, who did a thorough investigation, were dismayed, to say the least, when Major Quintanilla, from 'Project Blue Book', issued his usual 'satellite – Venus' explanation after only a short telephone conversation.

From then on Dale was inundated with newspaper reporters, UFO researchers, crank telephone calls, government officials and Air Force personnel, all asking endless questions. He took on extra shifts, just to avoid them, and knowing their police network was being monitored by civilians, he made an agreement with the radio operators that if any other strange craft appeared, they would use the codeword 'Floyd'.

Then, sometime later, when he was alone in the patrol car, the same craft, or one similar, appeared again. He radioed the base, and told them that this time he was going to pull over, have a cigarette, and wait until it left, which it did shortly after. But, the persistent harassment continued with letters arriving and constant phone calls from cranks, the media, and researchers. Even well meaning friends played jokes on him. He stopped going home, and sometimes disappeared for days.

Inevitably, his marriage collapsed; *"Something had happened to him," his wife said. "Our marriage fell apart. All sorts of people came to the house. Investigators, reporters. They kept after him, hounding him. They hounded him right into the ground. And he changed.'*

Everything had become too much for Dale. He thought that he was an embarrassment to the sheriff's office, and felt he couldn't do his job as a law enforcement officer anymore. When he sought help from the church, the minister introduced him to the congregation as 'the man who chased the flying saucer'.

He literally ran away, getting a job as a painter, and finding a room in a motel. By the time he paid the rent, and sent money back for his wife and two children, there was little left to live on. His mental and physical health deteriorated. He lost forty pounds and grew a long unkempt beard.

One newsman, possibly with a guilty conscience, contacted Dale, and offered to help him get back on his feet, but later found he had left the motel, with no forwarding address.

Two other officers also regretted their reports of seeing the object. Patrolman Frank Panzanella of Conway, Pennsylvania ended up disconnecting his telephone, and Police Officer Wayne Huston, of East Palestine, Ohio, quit his job and went to Seattle, Washington, where he changed his name and found work as a bus driver.

(Daniel Harris noted that; *'In November, at Zanesville, Ohio, a barber named Ralph Ditter, took pictures of an object in the sky. In January, two teenage boys in Detroit, Michigan, also made a snapshot of a UFO. Both pictures made front pages across the nation.*

'Both pictures reveal a circular object, about 30-40ft in diameter, with a large dome on top, a blinding light on the underside, and an antenna at the rear. Both match perfectly Dale Spaur's description of the flying saucer named 'Floyd'.')

On 24th April 1964, policeman Lonnie Zamora was chasing a speeding motorist, in his patrol car, just south of Socorro, New Mexico, when he saw a bright bluish/orange flash, accompanied by a roaring sound. He turned off the highway, onto a side gravel road, to investigate.

In the distance, he saw what he thought was a small, overturned car in a gully, close to an abandoned dynamite shack. It seemed to be glowing white, and made of an aluminium type material, resting on four diagonal landing struts. with a strange red insignia on the side. As best he could make out, it was an upward pointing arrow, with a semi-circle above and a line underneath.

Beside the vehicle he noticed two indiscernible figures, which at the time he thought were only about four feet tall, in white overalls, and no head coverings, standing nearby. Before he reached the scene, his car engine and radio temporarily failed. By the time he got out of his patrol car, and walked towards them, the 'beings', who had spotted him, disappeared, and the craft rose about twenty feet into the air. It was oval, with a long horizontal axis, and sort of shiny white, with a bright blue flame on the underside. Zamora noted that it was smooth, with no visible windows or doors.

The strange object initially emanated the same blue flash and roaring noise as before. The light and noise then subsided, and it moved silently away, angled sharply upwards and only just missing the dynamite shack, disappeared into the distance, over an adjacent mountain range. Two tourists, Larry Kratzner and Paul Kies, had also seen the craft in the air.

Bushes around the landing site were smouldering, and due to the proximity of possible deteriorating explosives, Zamora called his police headquarters. Two other officers, Sgt. Chavez and patrolman Jordan, met him at the scene, and one immediately took photos of the imprints of four 'landing gear', where the craft had been on the ground. Military authorities, from the Air Force, arrived, and confiscated the film before it had been developed. Alan Hynek, who arrived a few days later, intimated that the film had been 'fogged', possibly by radiation. (Although Hynek considered Zamora and Chavez, (who both hoped the object was a conventional Air Force craft), to be genuine, apparently, this incident was later categorised as 'Unexplained' by 'Project Blue Book', with the comment that this was 'one of the best authenticated reports on record.)

Over the next couple of weeks, other interested people visited the site, and also witnessed the remnants of the charred brush and fading scorch marks. A large rock, which had been directly underneath the craft, had melted in two.

Due to the publicity at the time, Zamora and his family were subjected to a great deal of harassment and ridicule, and a multitude of unwelcome phone calls. He was a devout Catholic, but his priest was of little help. Unable to cope, he left the police force two years later, and ended up running a gas station.

It was only well over fifty years later, when classified government documents came into the possession of U.S. researchers, that more light was shined on this memorable event. Investigator, Dave Thomas, related how there were many military bases and facilities around Socorro, and on the same day, 24th April 1964, that Zamora encountered the strange craft and its occupants, the nearby White Sands Base was involved in the top secret testing out its 'Lunar Surveyor' craft, destined to be used in its Moon landings later that decade. Further, the 'Lunar Surveyor' was built for NASA by the Hughes Aircraft Company, whose 'logo' was similar to the one seen by Zamora on the side of the craft.

Three years later, life still didn't seem to be very positive for police officers who reported UFOs. In their book, *'Beyond Earth'*, Ralph and Judy Blum wrote extensively about patrolman Herbert Schirmer, a 22 year-old navy veteran, from the small town of Ashland, Nebraska.

At 2.30am on December 3rd 1967, he was out in his police cruiser when he could hear dogs howling, and saw an illuminated object, with flickering lights, on the highway. Thinking that it was a motorist in trouble, he focussed his high beam and spotlight on the object, and remembered it taking off into the sky.

When, upon later returning to base, he struggled to make out his report, as he was missing thirty minutes in his log. He was confused, with a red mark around his neck, a buzzing noise in his ears and a headache. Unsure of what had happened during that 'missing time', he was later besieged by the media and UFO investigators. Even then, he began to realise the less than pleasant side of such an event. One civilian researcher wanted Herb to change his story to confirm his own pet theory. When Herb refused, he turned in a bad report. Another veiled threat came from one of the investigators, who told him that one witness, from another case, was being held in an undesignated government mental facility.

Other researchers have told of how poor Herb was subjected to an enormous amount of scrutiny and in-depth questioning by the Condon Committee. Herb was then sent to a psychiatrist and afterwards to Dr. Leo Sprinkle, who placed him under hypnosis.

He regained some memory of the missing thirty minutes, during which time he had been 'paralysed' by a ray gun, preventing him from drawing his own weapon when he tried to approach the object, which had landed in a nearby field. It was shaped like a metallic 'football', 102 feet in diameter, with a silver glow underneath, and resting on tripod legs. When he got out of his car, he was grabbed around the neck by a 'being', who was short, no more than five feet tall, 'pasty-faced', and a thin head, slightly longer than that of a human. He was dressed in a close-fitting silver-grey uniform which went right up over his head, like a helmet, and on his chest was an emblem, of a serpent with wings.

His captor asked him a few questions before inviting him on board. After being given a brief tour, of what was apparently an 'observation ship', with a crew of four, he was advised they had used a reversible 'electro-magnetic' field to stop his vehicle motor, cut the lights, and silence his two-way radio.

Schirmer remembered the 'leader' showing him around the craft, which had two triangular-backed chairs facing some kind of control panel. He explained the guidance, controls, propulsion and equipment. Apparently, the craft operated against gravity, and they had only landed to drain a small amount of electricity from our power lines. It was used to help power the electromagnetic field that temporarily surrounded their craft when they had landed.

They were from another galaxy, but had a base on Venus. They also had underground and underwater facilities on our world. He recalled that while being told they meant him no harm, and as with all people they contacted, a 'screen memory' would be planted in his mind, so he would only remember the experience as an ordinary UFO sighting.

After it was all over, Schirmer returned to his duties as a patrolman. Shortly after, the police chief resigned, and Herb was appointed to the job, one of the youngest officers to hold the position. Two months later, he left the job.

"It wasn't because of pressure from around town or anything like that. There had been some joking about little green men from Mars, but you have to expect that. I resigned because I simply was not paying attention to my job. I kept wondering what had really happened that night. My headaches were getting pretty fierce. I was gobbling down aspirin like it was popcorn. You cannot be a policeman if you have personal problems. So I quit."

He later went on to work for a packing company, but his problems had not ended. Researcher and author, Warren Smith, who followed up Schirmer's case, reported; *'Things were going well in this new job, until some men, who appeared to be federal agents, showed up one day to speak with Schirmer's employer, advising him that the ex-policeman "saw flying saucers", and was considered "not very stable".*

'Such episodes cost Schirmer not only the packing job, but other employment as well.'

Life was not easy for any officer of the law who 'went public' about a UFO sighting or report. Investigators Ralph and Judy Blum told of Jeff Greenhaw the local 'police chief' at Falkville, Alabama. On November 16th 1973, the *'Decatur Daily'* published his sad story;

'FALKVILLE:- Jeff Greenhaw, the local police chief who made national news last month when he spotted a 'spaceman' on a deserted country road, resigned under fire Thursday night at the Falkville City Council meeting.

'Greenhaw, 26, and the only full-time policeman in Falkville, said the resignation came after he was asked to do so by Mayor Wade Tomlinson.....For Greenhaw, the loss of his job was only the latest of many blows he was suffered since spotting something that resembled a man wrapped in aluminium foil on a dirt road the night of October 17.

'Shortly after the widely published, and still officially unexplained sighting, Greenhaw was divorced from his wife, and had to replace the engine in his car after it 'blew up'. Then last week his mobile home burned while he was at a Falkville High School football game, and he suffered eye injuries from smoke when he tried to enter the mobile home.

"So now I've lost my car, my wife, my home and my job," Greenhaw said, "and I guess I'll have to go where ever I can find another job. I had planned to stay in Falkville in spite of all the problems I've been having, but now it doesn't look like I can."

At night, it was often the local police patrol car that was out on the road when UFOs were sighted or reported.

Ted Phillips from 'MUFON' told of an unfortunate incident which occurred on August 27th 1979. Early one morning, Deputy Sheriff, Val Johnson, was driving near the North Dakota border, when he saw a bright white light through his side window. He notified 'base', but before he could get closer, the object moved toward him, reaching his patrol car in a matter of seconds.

The light was so intense that Johnson was blinded. He heard glass breaking, and then lost consciousness. When he came to, possibly up to forty minutes later, he found that his vehicle had stalled, and apparently skidded across the highway. Within a short time, his colleagues arrived, and Johnson was taken to hospital, where doctors treated him for a state of shock, and irritated eyes – 'as if he had suffered mild welder's burns'.

Police investigators found that the car had travelled 950ft after the first impact. An inside headlight was damaged, the windshield was badly damaged, and there was a dent on the hood. Both roof and trunk antennae were bent, the dash clock was fourteen minutes slow, as was Johnson's mechanical wristwatch. He had set both accurately before starting his shift.

Obviously, something had impacted or affected his vehicle, but nobody could say, or was willing to say, exactly what it was.

Generally, it was not a good idea for policemen, or other County officials in America, to report UFO sightings, or even indicate an interest in the subject.

In 1989, in Puma County Arizona, ex-employee, and former Emergency Services co-ordinator, 62 year-old Robert Dean, sued the local authorities for discrimination when he was denied a promotion to the position of Emergency Services Director in the Puma County Sheriff's Department.

Dean was an ex-Army veteran, and in 1959, whilst on duty at a local base, he had witnessed a metallic disc, about thirty to forty feet in diameter, hovering silently in the air whilst they were launching an unmanned aircraft.

Later, between 1963 and 1967, he was attached to NATO headquarters in Paris, where he had top secret security clearance, and studied classified documents proving the existence of UFOs flying over Europe. After his retirement from the military in 1979, he joined the Sheriff's Dept., and having served for ten years as Emergency Services Co-ordinator, naturally applied for the 'Director's' position when it became available.

The first choice of the selection panel turned the job down, and Dean was the next on the list, however the Sheriff rejected their choice. He said it was not a matter of age, adding that he did not want anyone who believed in UFOs in charge of Emergency Services!

THE MEN IN BLACK

Reports of strange men, dressed in black suits and hats, coming unannounced to a witness's door, often demanding any photographs, were more common in later years. Sometimes they would just unexpectedly accost the witness, and demand their silence regarding a sighting or experience.

We didn't hear a lot about this in the 'Good Old Days', but there were some chilling experiences reported.

In his book, *'Flying Saucers Come From Another World'*, Jimmy Guieu wrote of a very disturbing event which happened to 'Carlo' near Florence, Italy.

It was one night in mid-1952 when 'Carlo', a well respected citizen of San Pietro, Vico, was fishing on the banks of the river Serchio. He stared in astonishment when he saw something moving silently across the water.

It was a large disc, about sixty feet in diameter, with five propellers on its tail, and a cupola on top, from where three rotors stuck out. It had a long tube, which was dragging through the water, hanging from the lower end, and a flood of orange light was coming from slits along the side of the object.

'Carlo' said; *"I was paralysed with amazement. Suddenly, a port-hole opened and a man's face appeared, protected by something which reminded me of a diver's helmet. He saw me! I flung myself backwards, but at the same moment a green ray shot through the dark and blinded me. I was shaken from head to foot. When I raised my head I saw the disc disappearing towards the east with the rapidity of lightning.*

"Six days later, I was fishing at the same spot, when a tall, slim man with grey eyes came up and spoke to me. He spoke Italian with a foreign accent, not American, but it seemed to me, with a Scandinavian inflexion. He asked me if I had ever seen any aeroplanes or other 'flying things' near the river.

"I said I had not, perhaps a little too quickly, because he remained silent, watching me, and then offered me a cigarette. It was a long cigarette, with a gold tip. I had only taken two puffs, when I thought I was going to die. My head began to swim. I quickly took the cigarette out of my mouth, extinguished it and was about to slip it into my pocket. But the man seized it brutally, broke it and threw it into the river, leaving me stretched out on the river bank almost dead."

CHAPTER THIRTEEN

SCHOOLS

In *'Aspects of Ufos and Aliens'*, I discuss many of the more memorable incidents that occurred at or near schools and children. The vast majority of these occurred in the 1960s and 1970s, although some were witnessed later, and even earlier.

The research organisation, 'APRO', received an interesting report from a witness who, in 1930, had been a student at Burton Hill School in Bristol, England.

In those days, even an airplane was not often seen, and when the headmaster saw something in the sky, he ran into the classroom shouting; "Stop everything – get the boys out into the playground quick."

About one hundred boys and teachers were gathered outside in time to watch a cigar-shaped, silvery-white object speed across the sky. The witness said; "It was extremely high, and most definitely metallic, going on a steady course across the sky. I do realise now that it could not possibly be an airship, because I knew what one looked like, and it was travelling too fast. Also it was too high up, and pressure cabins were not invented in those days."

Judith Crosier, who was later to join the 'UFO Investigation Centre', where I was also a member, first became interested in the subject in 1952/3 when she was a student at Sydney's Cremorne High School. A saucer appeared in broad daylight, in sight for about ten minutes. She said; "All the girls saw it. Our geography teacher couldn't tell us what it was. It shone with a brilliant white light."

More reports were received in 1954, when strange objects were sighted in South Australia around the Kapunda, Winkie and Lilburn areas. Between 8am and 9am on 9th April, witnesses, including a school teacher with all the children, spotted a round saucer, with lights all around, speeding silently across the sky, at about 1,000 mph., before it turned sharply on its side and disappeared. Some witnesses described a tremendous roar as it passed overhead.

'Jane Allison' told me that in January 1961 or 1962, she had just returned to the Mt. St. Joseph School, at Milperra in Sydney, after their summer break. It was the first period of the day, from 8.30 – 9.30am, and they were doing P.E. in the playground.

As they were just starting their exercises, a strange object moved slowly and smoothly overhead. It was a grey, rectangular craft, with a bulge on 'top centre'. It had silently moved out of sight after a minute or so.

Nearly thirty years later, when I was interviewing witnesses on the Central Coast, a quiet, well mannered man approached me, feeling that, at long last, someone would believe what had happened in 1963. When Alan was eight years old, his family suffered a difficult break-up, and for a couple of years, he was placed in a Boys' Home in North Parramatta, a suburb of Sydney.

It was the Friday night of a mid-year holiday weekend, and at about 8pm, Alan and his room-mate heard a humming sound outside their second floor room. At first they were frightened, and huddled together under the bed. After the strange noise had continued for about ten minutes, they gathered up enough courage to peek out of the window.

It was a clear night, and for thirty minutes they watched in awe as, some distance away, a strange object hovered about fifty metres above the ground. It was 'cigar-shaped', pink in colour, with a red light on the top. Suddenly, the humming sound became louder, and the object's brightness increased as it 'shot off like a bullet'. Just as quickly, it came to an abrupt halt behind the Boys' Home, and descended directly behind some nearby trees.

The next day, Alan and his mates made their way to the spot where they had seen the object descend. The trees had broken branches, as if something had 'pushed them down from above'. The grass below was flattened in a ten metre diameter circle, which was quite warm, despite the surrounding area being covered with frost.

A few days later, several reporters had congregated at the front gates, wanting to interview Alan and his mate about what they had seen on Friday night. While they were standing in the driveway watching, he and his friend were approached by the headmaster and a uniformed policeman, who told them that if they ever wanted to see their families again, they must not talk to the reporters or anyone about what they had seen. Why were they were pressured into silence?

In those years it was easy for children to be silenced, or even not believed. In 1988, researcher John Pinkney spoke to Carol MacKenzie, who in 1963, was a pupil in a school at Tokoroa in New Zealand.

She was only eleven at the time, and at lunchtime, was playing in a field behind the school. Five metallic, domed and 'leaden-coloured' UFOs, each about six metres in diameter, hovered overhead. She and her schoolmates watched as they came, in formation, closer in the sky. They stopped for a moment before flashing away over the hills.

That night, when she told her parents, all she got was condescending smiles, and despite there being other reports, and even photographs on the front page of the local newspaper the next day, countless so called 'experts' claimed that what they had seen was all in their imaginations!

It took over four decades for another witness to tell 'MUFON' of an incident which occurred in 1964; *'I was a student at a Catholic school in Melbourne, and on this day all 300 of us school kids were cleaning up the school yard in silence.*

'Before a bell sounded at 12.30 pm, I looked up and saw three discs, in tripod formation, stationary above us in a clear blue sky. Their estimated height was about 8,000 ft. The UFO in the front of the formation moved to a 45-degree angle, still stationary, and took off at such a speed you only saw it for a nanosecond.

'Twenty seconds later, it came back at a massive speed, and stopped in its original position. The back two UFOs manoeuvred the exact same manoeuvre, then took off and returned, pulling up at their original positions. The Sun was intensifying the metallic structure of these craft. Then they all moved into a single file, manoeuvring one on top of the other before returning back to their original positions – stationary.

'Then they all took off, north, south and west, and were gone. We were told to go to class, and our lunch period was cut short.'

During the 1960s, several unidentified craft were seen around Victoria, Australia. Did they account for what was being seen by local schoolchildren? Were they alien craft or merely prototypes from a nearby testing ground?

On 1st May 1966, a steady, circular object was seen glinting in the sun near Whittlesea airport. On 5th May, at 7.45am, the air traffic controller at Tullamarine Airport in Melbourne, followed an unidentified radar target, with good echo-signal strength. It travelled approximately eighty-five kilometres in twenty-nine minutes. On the same day the crew of the 'HMAS Anzac', despite no radar contact being reported, saw four closely grouped objects leaving trails of colour.

On 8th May, witnesses reported a silver coloured elliptical object with a dark core. They watched for ten minutes as it descended from eight thousand to four-and-a-half thousand feet before being lost from view behind a cloud. Three weeks later it was seen again, but had disappeared by the time an observer took off in an aircraft to investigate.

On 14th May an Ansett pilot saw lights ahead and below his plane. He was flying south of Wonthaggi in Victoria, and described three objects in an approximate 'V' formation. At first he thought he was overtaking them, but then they seemed to draw ahead of the plane. After about ten minutes he appeared to be overtaking them again, and realised there were two smaller objects in formation with a larger one, which looked like a large jet aircraft with swept back wings. He had been flying at some speed, and observing for fifteen minutes, but this experienced pilot, in order to evade an official inquisition, later said that he told the RAAF that what he had seen were in fact 'large metal buildings just south of Dandenong'!

In fact, during April 1966, UFOs seemed to have an abnormal interest in schools and school children. In his book, 'UFOs – Interplanetary Visitors', U.S. researcher, Raymond Fowler, said; 'During the month of April 1966, I received a total of twenty-two reports that were evaluated as being 'unknown' category. Six of these reports involved UFOs hovering over or around school buildings.'

On 6th April 1966, a disc was seen by pupils and teachers at Westall School, Melbourne, Victoria. I wrote about this event in 'Contact Down Under', and also received one unverifiable report that a couple of school children, who got too close to the landed craft, were later monitored by a government medical team. (Was there a risk of radiation exposure?)

One of the students later said; 'As I looked up I saw a dazzling, silvery object, flying around some pine trees which grew on a ridge about a quarter of a mile *directly behind the school. It then flew across some open paddocks, also behind the school, and returned to the pines. On the other side of the ridge there is a small field. The thing hovered over the pines and descended behind them, and must have been directly over the field. I then lost sight of it because of the pines.*

'As the thing was out of sight I began to notice many private aircraft, mainly Cessna, flying towards the pines. It was then the thing reappeared and rose to the level of the approaching aircraft. This enabled me to get a rough idea of its size. It was a silvery object, as long as one of the Cessnas, but very thin.

'As the aircraft approached, the thing tilted on about a 45-degree angle, and started to move into the distance, gradually gaining height. The planes increased their speed and began to follow it, but the object streaked away, leaving the planes far, far behind. The planes turned back, but we all stood, hoping it would return, but it didn't, so we all went into school, fifteen minutes late.'

Note the number of 'private aircraft' initially accompanying the disc. 'Authorities' arrived the same afternoon, much quicker than expected, the area was 'ploughed over' and cleared of any evidence. The same day children were pressured into not discussing the subject, with those who did speak to the press being punished with 'detention'. Another investigator who actually attended the scene soon after, believed this was one of our own experimental prototypes. I tend to agree, however, these are our personal opinions, not shared by many other researchers who also put a lot of time and effort into investigating this incident.

This case also has similarities to the U.S.A. – 'Cash and Landrum' case, which had several helicopters following a disc. I began to wonder if both the Australian 'school' incidents were due to our own prototypes either accidentally or deliberately landing near school children. Perhaps, just perhaps, it was an attempt to gauge public reaction? After all, children are not always believed, and easy to silence.

There were two other cases, involving schools, reported from Victoria in 1968. Unfortunately, they are not very detailed.

In July, thirteen schoolboys saw a silent object – 'twice the size of a house' – fly over their Banyal schoolyard. As it approached, it suddenly changed direction, and streaked upwards before disappearing into the distance. It was round and flat, a silvery-grey in colour, with a hole in the middle – 'like a life-saver'. The headmaster interviewed each of the witnesses, and asked them, individually, to draw his impression of what he had seen.

In 2004, an acquaintance reported an incident which had occurred forty-two years before, at Mornington High School, one afternoon in 1968. Although he did not see it himself, all his schoolmates claimed a strange craft had landed on the school oval. Later, some 'men' came to the school, and the kids had to draw, on the blackboard, what they had seen. All drew an oval shape craft with portholes on the side, and some claimed it had 'different colours coming from it'.

(We will never know if it were aliens favouring Victorian schools, or some of our early prototypes being tested from a nearby base. Many years later, Victorian investigator, George Simpson, told of how Darren had related an incident which had occurred in the early 1980s, when he was with his brother and some friends at Ringwood Primary School.

'The object he saw was quite awesome, about a kilometre in diameter, transparent and high tech to the max. He said; "Like something from the year 7,000, absolutely not man-made." The huge object reflected like a mirror yet was transparent; he estimated the location to be near the Ringwood Civic Centre. He and his brother and friends were not afraid, but gobsmacked by the object's design, size and rapid departure, which was silent.')

The *'Panorama'* newsletter reported that on 20th November 1968, an 18 year-old student teacher was arriving at the Glenelg School, in the neighbouring State of South Australia, at 9.10am one morning. He noticed about twenty children, standing in the school yard, talking excitedly and gazing at the sky above.

He joined them, and they pointed out six unusual objects, hovering in the sky, about six miles to the south over the oil refinery. They were all discoid in shape, with a 'dome' or 'hump' on the top, giving them a slightly 'belled' appearance. Two were bright white, and the other four a dull, metallic grey.

Five of the objects remained hovering, whilst one of the white ones went into a slow dive and appeared to land in front of some rolling hills in the distance.

At 12.30 pm, lunchtime recess, they all looked again. They could still see the white disc on the ground, which was in an area devoid of any trees or human habitation. Two of the darker discs had disappeared, whilst two remained hovering, accompanied by a solitary white object which seemed to be spinning on its axis.

By the end of lessons, all the strange craft had disappeared without a trace. The student teacher asserted that he could see red and blue lights on the objects, however, the investigator taking his report, doubted that this could be so, given the distance in broad daylight.

There were several other cases in Australia. Nearly twenty-five years after the event, 'Trevor Rogers' told me how, in 1969, he was in the scout hall, opposite his school in West Ryde, Sydney. He, and his friends, watched as a strange object descended from the early evening sky, and landed in their school grounds. It was an oval, metallic object, with orange/yellow flashing lights on the bottom, and a white light on the top.

In the early seventies, the students at the Silkstone State School in Booval, Queensland, were giving a dancing performance in the school hall. Suddenly, the audience of about sixty parents was distracted by three large lights, 'dancing' overhead in the sky.

After they had shot off, at great speed, in different directions, the sighting was important enough for the parents to hold a meeting, in one of the classrooms, to discuss the event. It was remembered by the witnesses for many years after.

In 1971, the *'Daily Mirror'* wrote about three schoolboys who were at the NSW Coonamble Rail post office at 8.30 am on 23rd April. This was a regular trip to pick up the mail, from a town that was so small at the time, the only other building was their one-room schoolhouse down the road.

What looked like a large ball of fire suddenly appeared in the sky, and shot towards them. When it came close, it came to an abrupt halt and the flames 'went out', revealing a 40ft wide egg-shaped object with large, square, sloping windows around its perimeter. It was a silver-coloured metal, with a reddish-yellow exhaust coming from the rear. (Surely, this was one of our own prototypes, and not a more sophisticated 'alien' model!)

As it passed low over their heads, four legs, with moon-shaped pads, were lowered from underneath, and it began oscillating from side-to-side. It banked to the left, and smoothly swooped over a nearby hill, where it descended out of view.

When he arrived just after, the headmaster found three 'ashen faced and terrified boys', who told him what they had seen, and separately drew similar sketches of the object. Three days earlier, the owner of a nearby property had reported 'circular burned patches' on his paddock.

After the mid to late 1960s, the reports from Australian schools diminished. Val James, who is now unfortunately deceased, was one of my colleagues in INUFOR. She related an event which occurred in the late 1970s, when, one day, she saw a dark, saucer-shaped object hovering over the eastern end of Casino High School. She watched it for ten to twenty minutes before it darted away.

She may have been the only witness, however at the same time, Neville Bienke, a flight instructor at the Casino Aerodrome, had also noticed the unusual craft. He jumped into his plane, and took off in order to get a better look. As he got closer, the object started moving away at a moderate speed, but was soon able to increase the distance between them, and Neville gave up the chase.

I searched my other friends' and colleagues' files and records, and discovered that there were several incidents involving schools, during the 1950s, 60s and 70s. Many were from Britain, Europe and the U.S.A.

On 10th July 1967, two schoolboys, lining up to go into class, reported seeing a strange object, about 37ft wide, flying low and then hovering about 500ft away from their school, at Whippingham on the Isle of Wight. At 10.45am, during their morning break, several boys spotted the object again, this time further to the west. Leonard Cramp later wrote of how investigators later found a twelve feet circle of barley, flattened in a continuous swathe, just below the spot where the UFO was seen to hover.

In 1976, on 15th July, ninety children and four teachers, from the Treleigh CP School, at Redruth, Cornwall in the UK, watched as a spherical object crossed high in the midday sky. At least, this one didn't land, but everybody in the school yard saw the white, saucer-shaped object, quietly and slowly, spinning overhead. Everyone said it resembled two dinner plates, face-to-face, and had silver and yellow flashes coming from it at a ninety degree angle.

The '*Northern UFO News*' reported that later in 1976, on 12th October, Mr Hughes, the caretaker of Mons Hill School, in Dudley, Worcestershire, was locking up at about 9.10 pm, when he saw his wife staring at a dazzling white, oval light in the sky.

They crossed the school yard, to get a better look, and were joined by two young football players who had been training in the school grounds. Later estimates placed the object quite low and close, about sixty feet above the ground. They all watched for several minutes while it made some complex manoeuvres back and forth, before shooting off to the east and disappearing from view. The police were notified, but the local airport had no explanation for the strange craft. Later, a man in Air Force uniform called, however Mr. Hughes and his wife were not in at the time, and he didn't return. One interesting addendum was that at the time of the sighting, Mr. Hughes was wearing a new quartz digital watch, which went 'berserk', giving off multiple readings, until he took it off his arm.

In 1977, British researcher, Norman Oliver, wrote an article for the '*BUFORA Journal*', detailing several incidents over the past few months, and asking if our schools were being 'singled out'.

On 4th February, at the Broad Haven County Primary School near Pembroke in Wales, fifteen children, most of whom were playing football, saw a silvery, metallic object on the ground within a quarter of a mile away. It was there between 1pm and 3.45pm, and the pupils described it as being a disc at the bottom and a sort of dome with a red light at the top. Some students said they saw three or four windows, and others heard a humming sound.

Several children claimed to have seen a silver-suited figure near the craft, before it 'moved behind some bushes and vanished.' A few of the boys were so scared they ran inside to tell the headmaster, who didn't believe them at the time.

After school, a couple of students crossed a stream on the school's boundary, and made their way to the field where the craft had last been seen. The area was very wet, muddy, and 'boggy', but they saw the object from about four hundred yards away. They said it was about the size of a 'coach', and looked like two saucers, stacked one against the other to form a dome.

It suddenly moved over the ground, becoming obscured by a hedge, and the frightened boys ran away. On the Monday morning, the headmaster was besieged by reporters. He took the kids more seriously, and got them to draw and relate what they had seen.

Two canteen workers said they had also seen the object, but were sure it was only a sewage truck. Later investigations proved this to be impossible – the field was a muddy bog, which no truck could enter.

Was this craft alien, or one of ours? To the north was a top secret rocket testing station at Aberporth, while at Brawdy, near St. David's, was a military base which trained pilots, and also housed both a Tactical Weapons Unit and a U.S. Navy underwater research station, which tracked Soviet submarines.

The following week there were two more reports from England. On 7th February, twenty children from the Herbrandston School at Hakin, Milford Haven, watched from their playground as a white, cigar-shaped object flew noiselessly overhead, at an altitude of about five hundred feet, and disappeared into a cloud.

The same day, another report came from Edenhurst School in Newcastle, when most of Prep II form watched a silent object for about ten minutes, before it also disappeared into a cloud, and then reappeared a couple of times later.

It was described as – *'a silvery-blue, cigar shaped object'* – *'a cigar shape of silvery-grey colour'* – and – *'a circular sausage-shape with a sort of a round dome on top, changing colours from brilliant white to orange, blue and red.'*

British researcher, Nigel Watson, reported that later that year, on 18th November, twenty, six and seven-year-old children saw a strange craft from the playground of Wawne Primary School in North Humberside. Wawne is a small, fairly secluded village, north of Hull.

The children described something which looked like a 'spinning top'. It resembled an upside-down dish, surmounted by a top 'cupola section', with windows. Mr. Michael Yates, their teacher, separated three of the children, and in isolation, they were told to make plasticine models of what they had seen.

When three remarkably similar models resulted, he could not deny that they must have seen a disc-shaped object in the sky, which was spinning on a vertical axis.

.On the afternoon of 16th February 1977, back in Wales, nine girls, and their teacher, were playing netball in the yard of the Anglesey Rhos-y-bol County Primary School, and stopped play for about four minutes to watch a strange craft up above.

Gwawr Jones said; *"Mrs Williams was showing us how to throw the ball in the net, when I saw an object high in the sky. I shouted to the others, and they all looked up and saw it. It had a black dome on the top, and a silver cigar-shaped base. It was travelling smoothly across the sky in a northerly direction...it went behind the only cloud in the sky, and reappeared again, then disappeared. Mrs Williams took us inside and without conferring, we got a piece of paper and drew what we saw....'*

Later that year, the *'BUFORA Journal'* received a letter from the librarian at Ashfield School, Kirkby-in-Ashfield, Notts; *'At approximately 11.30 am on Thursday 30th June, two cigar-shaped flying objects were observed by one of our P.E. teachers along with fifteen children. The objects were white or silver in colour, without wings or visible means of propulsion, and progressed roughly from N.E. to S.W. over the Nottinghamshire village of Huthwaite, which is two miles or so from the school.*

'They were flying in tandem, with one above the other, and hanging about a length behind. The teacher concerned estimates the air speed to be anything between 500-1,000 mph. - at a height of about 300 feet. Earlier in the day a 'Goodyear' Airship' had been sighted by the same teacher, and he is adamant that the UFOs in no way resembled airships.'

Ron Halliday, in *'UFO Scotland'*, also discussed a couple of similar cases: In the summer of 1952, Joan Torrence and several other students were leaving Elder Park Primary School, in Glasgow. It was 4pm, and due to the long daylight hours, they were planning what to do for the rest of their free time.

Suddenly a dark shadow blocked out the sun, and the pupils, along with a teacher and the school janitor, looked up. They could see a rotating, sombrero-shaped object hovering one hundred feet up, just above the school steeple. It was slightly tilted to one side, and after a short period of time, a distinct whining sound could be heard. The disc shot of across the city, where it was also reported by other witnesses.

In 1978, another incident occurred at Glasgow's St. Mark's Primary School in Muiryfauld. Again, it was a bright summer's day, and a group of schoolchildren, enjoying their playtime games, were startled to see a strange object hovering about twenty feet over the school fence. It was glistening in the sun, and was not very large, only a few feet across. It looked like 'two fedora hats joined together', was sharply defined, and silver-coloured, like shiny metal.

Witness, Euan Riley, didn't report the sighting until many years later. He said at the time they didn't think the teachers would believe them, and he couldn't remember how the saucer left – just that it 'vanished'.

The next year, across the Channel, another incident occurred in France. Jean Sider translated the following report for *'XENOLOG'* in New Zealand.

On 14th May, at Eyzin-Pinet, near Vienne, sixty school children, and their teachers, were coming out of the canteen after having lunch. They stared in awe as an oval disc, shining in the clear sky, came from the north, and passed directly over the school, at an altitude of about sixty metres.

The children rushed to the other side, in order to follow the object's path. They were all shouting; "The Martians are landing! They are Martians!"

M. Paul Viallet, the school director, said his nineteen-year-old son, Jacques, ran towards a field located above the Sallin Housing Estate. It was there that they had lost sight of the object, and he spotted it again as he reached a barbed wire fence.

The craft was in the field, about seventy metres away, and silently hovering five or six metres above the grass. It was an oval shape, not that large, at an incline, and changing in colour from 'black to brilliant'. The cows did not seem to be disturbed, but as Jacques tried to climb the barbed wire fence, the object slowly rose, accelerated in speed, and disappeared into the sky at an incredible rate.

Witnesses in the U.S.A. also reported incidents of strange objects over schools.

On December 11th 1965, the Waterville, Maine, Saturday *'Morning Sentinel'* reported on an incident which had occurred the previous morning at Fairfield Junior High.

At 9.30am, about fifteen of the grade 5 students, along with their teacher, Mrs. Marjorie Fernald, heard a strange 'bleep', and rushed to the window to watch a silvery object approach the school, at high speed, from the northwest, and then glide steeply out of sight behind some nearby houses.

In the afternoon, seven of the group were taken, individually, to a classroom where they described what they had seen, and drew a picture on the blackboard. They were consistent with an image of a silvery, metallic, egg-shaped craft, about ten feet long, which seemed to be illuminated from within, and had an 'antenna' on the end.

On March 21st 1966, seventeen girls in the women's dormitory of the Hillsdale College, Michigan, saw a brightly lit, football-shaped object swoop down and hover. (Apparently, over the previous two nights, other co-eds at the college also witnessed strange lights and objects in the sky, which they also described as 'looking like a squashed football.') Initially, it flew away to the south, and disappeared, only to return about half an hour later.

The Australian *'Panorama'* publication reported on the subsequent events; *'It flew over the garden behind the dormitory, and settled into a woody depression some 1,500ft away. William van Horn, the Civil Defence Director of Hillsdale County, alerted by telephone, rushed to the dormitory. Together with the girls and their housemother, they watched the object hover for several hours.*

'William van Horn could see two lights, which maintained a fixed distance apart as they 'rose and fell', reaching heights of 100ft to 150ft. Through his binoculars he perceived a 'light haze' forming what he assumed to be a structure connecting the lights. Silhouetted against this haze, he thought he saw a 'convex shape'.

Over a four day period, there had been numerous sightings in the area, and some photographs taken. Police Sergeant Nuel Schneider and Deputy David Fitzpatrick had also witnessed these strange craft themselves, and were not amused when the authorities, under the guidance of Dr. Allen Hynek, dismissed it all as 'swamp gas', and the photographs as 'astronomical anomalies'.

Schneider said; "I know what I saw – I think the Air Force is full of malarkey!" After that, they filed all UFO sighting reports without passing them on to other authorities.

'UFOIC' reported about a Florida incident, on 7th April 1967, just one year after the Australian 'Westall' event, when a similar incident occurred at Crestview Elementary School.

School teacher, Virginia Martin, was trying to line-up 200 children after morning recess, when a strange object landed in a field behind the school. Chaos broke out when the children broke ranks and ran yelling and pointing towards the fence. She called two other teachers, Marian Waters and Bob Apfal, who followed the children, and saw a silent, metallic, oval shaped object, hovering behind a pine tree in an open field. It momentarily moved forwards, and then back again, before rising and leaving at 'a terrific speed'.

Three Air Force officers from the Homestead Air Force Base arrived to interview some of the witnesses, as this was the second consecutive day when students had reported strange objects in the sky.

'The previous morning, Andy Cohen, and a company of schoolboys and girls saw two, metallic cigar-shaped objects flying north over the school grounds. Some of the girls became hysterical, and one of them ran back to the classroom, shouting for help.' The same day, another witness had seen, from her backyard, an oval shaped object, with red lights, hovering over the trees in the direction of Crestview School. It then shot off, and disappeared in a westerly direction.

(As with the earlier occurrences at other schools, including Broadhaven, in Wales, and those in Australia, at Westall and Parramatta, the discs seemed to make a calculated landing, near enough for the students to see, but not so close as to do them any harm.)

The *'Record American'* of Boston, Massachusetts, reported that only a few days later, on 12th April, a strange, unidentified flying object was seen over the Oliver Wendell Holmes Grammar School in Dorchester, at about 7.45pm.

About fifteen boys were practising basketball, after school had finished, and they, and several residents, saw a 'thing' as large as a helicopter, hover, circle and land on the four storey roof of the school building. Witnesses said it appeared to have two sections – an oval shape with a dome on the top – with a bunch of lights at the bottom which changed from red to white to green.

The students ran through the school yard to get a better look, and some thought that at one stage, the craft hovered for a while, then circled away, and sped out of sight before disappearing and then coming back. At one stage there was a bright white light shining down from the bottom of the centre section. By that time, most of the lads were so scared they ran home.

Two other boys, who'd been walking down the street, said that they had seen a second object, following the first. Both craft went behind the school, where they lost sight of them. At the same time, a mysterious power failure blacked out 2,000 homes in a nearby section of Roxbury.

Edward Garcia reported that on 17th February 1967, at 12.40pm, a round, white object was seen travelling fast over the Bell Haven School in Dayton, Ohio. Because it was most probably during their lunch break, it was seen by sixty students and three teachers. Later that day, thirty pupils reported seeing another three UFOs which 'formed a triangle'.

There was an incident in 1972, near Fort Stockton in Texas, USA, which was investigated by 'HBCC UFO Research', and unearthed by Jeff Rense.

It was one Saturday afternoon, and the witness was a 'sophomore' at the local high school. He was accompanying his father, who was making deliveries to one of the small stores in the main street.

'Just as my Dad parked the truck in front of the store, he reached across my brother, and slapped me on the chest. Then he said; "You boys ever seen a UFO?" I replied; "No, Sir". Then he said; "Well, there's ya one, right over there."

He pointed to the local elementary school, where 50ft overhead was a huge silver object, shaped like a boomerang, and 'about the size of a football field'. It seemed to be about ten to fifteen feet thick, but before the lads could get a really good look, their father insisted they get on with helping him unload the cases off their vehicle.

They kept quickly glancing over at the strange craft, but were surprised that although a couple of cars pulled up to stare and point at the unusual object, most people in the shop were taking no interest at all.

He was disappointed when his father drove them away from the scene, but soon noticed that it, or a similar craft, was hovering over the Junior High School. Later, as they continued their deliveries, he could still see the strange silvery object, which eventually appeared to be hovering over the local Gas Plant. His father looked terrified, and warned the boys, more than once, not to look at the UFO.

When he had finished his deliveries, they went back to the office to 'settle up'. *"All I wanted to do was get out of the truck and stare at the big silvery thing, but I feared my Dad more. So I asked my brother if he could see it. He replied; "Yeh! Why?" - "Well, don't you even care?" I asked him; "Daddy says it's a UFO, but everybody's acting as if it isn't even there". Then he replied; "Yeh, and Daddy told us not to be watching it, so I ain't watching it. If you want to watch it, that's your problem, but I ain't getting in trouble."*

Their father was gone for an unusual two hours, and when he came back to the vehicle, he still looked terrified, but never said a word. As they drove off, the witness noticed the strange object was gone, and they didn't see it again.

Although the media had reported other sightings and cattle mutilations in the area, this particular incident was not mentioned in the local press.

Investigator Raymond Fowler reported that 9pm on February 20th 1975, two students, Hope and Nancy, from Phillips Academy, Andover, were sitting on the wall of a quadrangle in the middle of their dormitory blocks.

A group of lights suddenly descended from the sky, and appeared to go straight down towards the far end of the campus soccer field. They abruptly stopped, just above tree level, then ascended up a short way, and hovered once again before moving towards the school infirmary.

The girls ran across the soccer field towards the infirmary, and stopped next to a large oak tree. They got a good view of the craft, which was, by then, only a short distance away. Suddenly, it moved towards them, and hovered again, now about 75 feet directly over their heads.

They described it as being an oval object, convex in shape, with a round bottom, and about ten to twelve feet in diameter. It was a dull gray colour, with a large blue light on top, and a circle of multiple red lights below. The girls alerted the other students, and thirteen of them raced out to see the object move off in a semi-circular track towards the bell tower, before disappearing behind some trees to the south.

They rang the police, and about half an hour later, an unmarked helicopter performed low-flying crisscross manoeuvres over the Academy campus.

Sometimes it is fortunate that very few children see a UFO hovering near their school. On April 29th 1964, ten-year-old Sharon Stull watched an egg-shaped object hovering near Lowell Elementary School in Albuquerque. For ten minutes she stared at the craft, which was on the opposite side of the sky to the sun. She said it had bounced up and down in the sky about three times before flying off.

When she got home, she was severely burned, and her parents and police questioned her further after she was treated for 'Infra-Red Burns'. Luckily, her eight-year-old sister, Robin, had refused to look at the object and ran off.

To the north in Canada, researchers were also discovering that sometimes strange craft are interested in our children.

In 1969, Canadian researcher, Gene Deplantier, had reported that at 8pm on September 21st 1968, a crowd of nearly fifty people gathered outside the Coaticook High School after several children panicked when two young girls said they had seen a Martian.

When the municipal police arrived, Constable Marcoux determined that all that scores of people had seen was just a reflection of a light from a nearby garage roof. Most witnesses disagreed, saying they had seen an object which emitted flashes of orange, red and green. Jacques Lessard had seen an orange, grey and green ball, surrounded by a 'blinking' ring, which made two turns before disappearing. He had also entered a nearby field, where he saw a 42 feet diameter circle burned in the grass.

One witness, Sharley Green, insisted that at 9.30pm she had seen 'a man who emitted sparks, and had a green face with no nose, mouth or hair'. Although one cannot rely on this single entity report, many sightings of a similar UFO were seen travelling swiftly in the sky that night.

Investigator, Nancy Usjack, reported that on 10th January 1979, a UFO landed, in full view of a teacher and three students, in the playground of the Queen Elizabeth Public School in Kitchener.

During later interviews, another teacher could only recall a lightning strike in the January, however all the witnesses drew detailed sketches of the craft they had seen.

An incident, at the Santa Leonor College in Callao, Peru, was probably not an intentional visit by an unidentified object, and more likely one of our own prototypes. At 10.10am on 25th August 1965, three hundred pupils, and several teachers, were startled when a strange noise was heard from the roof, and the desks and walls shook as if there was an earthquake.

They all raced outside to see what appeared to be a 'space-craft' on the roof. It was oval, shaped like a dish, terminating in a pointed top and emitting two red beams of light from the sides. Everyone stared in amazement as it took off, with a loud noise, and circled around as it gained height. There was fire and smoke coming through two vents on the side as it shot away and vanished towards the north-east.

Three years later, in early December 1968, across the Pacific in New Zealand, was another incident, reported in the Australian *'Panorama'* publication.

Students at the Te Mata School, Havelock North, were quite frightened when they saw a strange craft hovering over an orchard near the school. Some of the children, who were near the pool, where the teacher was giving swimming lessons, drew everyone's attention to the object, which they estimated to be half the size of the pool.

It was touching the top of a tree, about one hundred yards away from the playground, and making a 'clicking' noise, 'like a clock'. The craft was saucer-shaped, with lights around the bottom, and a 'diamond-shaped' light on the dome. It was white on the bottom with a black band around the side, where there appeared to be a hatch.

For about ten minutes it travelled backward and forward overhead before suddenly shooting upwards, and travelling towards Hastings, leaving a vapour trail in its wake. A teacher said it was too round to fit the description of any aircraft he knew, and the Bridge Pa aerodrome and Napier's Civil Aviation Department said that there were no aircraft in the area at 11.20am – the time of the sighting.

Twelve years earlier, at about 4pm on 20th September 1956, fifty schoolboys, along with their masters at Hamilton Boys' School, stared in awe at a brilliant white disc which hovered silently in the northern sky, at an altitude of 3,000 to 4,000 feet. After a short while, it sped rapidly to the north, and was lost from sight.

One teacher, Mr, Parry, made a report to the Hamilton Research Society. He said there were no clouds in that area of the sky. The brilliant disc was totally stationary, and he could see no markings, motion or spinning before it suddenly took off at a remarkable speed.

He was gratified when a second report came in, substantiating the observations made from the school. Fifty minutes later, Mrs Daphne Pick, had been hanging out the washing, when in the east, she spotted an extremely bright, white silvery object, with beams of light 'dashing from it'. It headed, at a moderate speed, in a northerly direction until it was lost from view.

Sightings were reported from New Zealand schools as late as 1970. The Napier 'Daily Telegraph' reported, on 8th May of that year, how the previous day, the Headmaster, Mr. W. Billing, along with teachers and more than 400 students at Richmond School, Maraenui, watched a strange object in the sky for over twenty minutes.

Mr. Billing was watching the children at 'playtime' in the school grounds, when he first spotted the object moving in from the south. When he realised it wasn't a conventional plane, he drew the teachers' attention to it, and the children stopped their activities to also watch.

A sudden, uncanny silence descended on the spectators as they watched a huge, round, wingless object hovering and moving in the sky. It seemed to be solid, and metallic, and glistened in the sunlight, in a clear blue sky. At one time, when it moved at right-angles, it seemed to have something round in the middle – like a transparent sheen.

Alan Coveny, the Supervisor of the Junior Classes, said he had read reports of people sighting unidentified objects, but he had been rather sceptical until that moment. He noted that it was totally silent, and appeared to be considerably larger than a jet plane. After alternatively moving slowly and hovering for some time, in an area between Wetshore and Tongoio, it then moved away at right angles, flattened out, and increased its speed, soon moving 'faster than a jet' as it sped away to the north-west.

Mr. Billing said the object was extremely brilliant, and concluded; "We thought half of Napier would have seen it. Here at the school, everyone was standing with their mouths open, trying to work out a logical answer to it." - A pupil had come up for an explanation; "He asked me if it was a flying saucer, and I said 'yes', because I couldn't give any other answer."

Perhaps some UFO sightings over schools are inadvertent, and not actually meant to be witnessed. At 9pm, on 22nd April 1966, only days after the Australian 'Westall' incident, in the U.S.A. at Beverly Massachusetts, ten people, including police officers, who had been called to the scene, watched for 45 minutes as an object, surrounded by a blurry light, hovered above the local school, before flying off. It was described as being round, with a bottom like a plate, a brightly lit 'mushroom top', and three flashing lights – red, green and white.

Researcher Ted Phillips reported several cases of 'levitation' to the *'MUFON Journal'* in 2006. One involved the students at the San Francisco de Chiu-Chiu School in Chile.

On 19th October 2000, a large craft, surrounded by multi-coloured lights and about three hundred feet in diameter, hovered close overhead. It was first seen by the school's custodian, Fresia Vega and student Valentina Espinoza, who saw a door open in the middle of the object.

Mrs. Vega said a bright, blinding light came out, and she experienced the sensation of being blinded and paralysed, and 'sucked in' through the door. There was a tingling sensation over her body, and people's voices seemed to be far away.

At the same time, a loud blast was heard, and beside the twenty other students, and their P.E. instructor who had been watching, other teachers and children ran out and also saw the object, which moved away. Valentina had been hiding behind, and clinging onto Mrs. Vega, who didn't seem to be able to speak. Both of them felt very cold, and had painful sore eyes, for some hours after.

At the same time, a meeting of the 'General Centre of Parents and Attorneys' was being held in the school building. Some of the thirty-five attendees saw the light outside the window, and heard the children calling out. It was only when the large 'explosion' occurred overhead – 'like an earthquake' – that they rushed out.

Following the 'blast' the village dogs started barking continuously. Some people fled on foot, and television signals were lost all over town. The State Police noted that the other children did not experience any side effects, however two residents also had eyesight damage due to the glare.

In April 1998, students from the Adikaran school in Bandarawela, Sri Lanka, reported seeing a strange object landed on the playground.

It was large, disc-shaped, about eight feet in diameter, and sitting on legs. It suddenly flashed bright red and yellow lights, and took off at a tremendous speed.

It was only 6.30 in the morning, and maybe it hadn't intended to be observed. Only two students, Indika Dissanayake and Harsha Ellawalagdera were present. Harsha was a promising child, who was entrusted with opening the classroom doors early each morning.

The headmaster believed them, as there had been previous reports of a similar object often flying overhead early in the morning. Other local residents, of good repute, had also recently seen unidentified craft both in the sky and on the ground. Was this an alien object, or a terrestrial craft, thinking it wouldn't be noticed, making a quick landing?

I have noticed that many of these 'school' events have been reported from 'Commonwealth' aligned countries, with political and military ties. South Africa is no exception.

One of the earliest reports occurred on October 16th 1967, when a very small, round disc, only twenty inches wide and six inches thick, touched down, only one hundred feet away from some students. It was metallic, like highly polished chromium, and made a scraping sound as it immediately took off again.

The school principal told NICAP investigators, who considered their report to be genuine, and that the students were sincere and reliable.

'Skywatch - South Africa' reported that on the evening of 12th November 1972, many residents of Middleburg, Eastern Cape, saw a strange craft move over the town. It changed its shape, and varied in colour from white to red and blue. Just after 9.30pm, it appeared to land near a tennis court at the Rosemead Primary School.

The next day the Commandant of Police, Colonel van Heerden, went out to investigate reports of damage to the tennis court. He found five huge holes in the all-weather surface, and pieces of tar up to fourteen metres away. The semi-circle holes had a large hole, four metres long and one metre wide, in the centre and two smaller holes on each side

There are instances when landings near schools are most likely extraterrestrial in origin. Only five days later, Colonel van Heerden was called out to another incident in Middleburg. This time several witnesses had seen a 'glowing ball', about the size of a full moon, which descended and hovered about three feet above the ground. It lit up the entire area.

One witness, Mr. Pretorious said that he saw two beings, resembling men, but only about a metre tall, alight from the ball. He said each carried a red, glowing torch-like object in their hands. After a minute or so the beings and the object 'just disappeared'. The Colonel and the postmaster climbed the hill where the object had been seen, but no traces could be found.

There are some other events, in later years, which cannot be explained as perhaps being our own prototypes.

On 14th September 1994, there had been multiple reports of bright lights and objects traversing the African night sky over Zimbabwe. Most were attributed to either a meteorite shower or the re-entry of one of the stages of a Russian satellite. Due to the massive discrepancies in the size, speed and altitude of the objects, investigator, Cynthia Hind, doubted both of these explanations.

The Ariel School was a private primary school, about twenty kilometres from Harare, and taught students from a variety of races and cultures. Two days later, on 16th September, all sixty-two pupils were on their morning break in the playing field.

They noticed three silver balls of light moving in the sky, and suddenly one came much closer, and appeared to land, or hover, about one hundred metres away, from where they were standing on the edge of the school grounds. This adjoining, unfenced area was very rough, and out of bounds, due to the thick vegetation, thorn bushes and snakes, spiders and other less than pleasant wildlife.

The older children were very curious, and described seeing a small man, about four feet tall, dressed in a shiny, tight fitting, black suit, appear on top of the object. He had a pale face, huge eyes, shoulder length black hair and a long scrawny neck. He walked a little way through the bush, and upon seeing the children, promptly disappeared. Either he, or someone similar, re-appeared on top of the object, which soon took off very rapidly and shot away into the sky.

The younger children, having been told legends of 'tokoloshies' eating them, ran back to the school building calling for help. All the teachers were at a meeting, and didn't come out. The mother in charge of the tuckshop didn't believe them, and later said she was not prepared to leave the food and money.

Cynthia took several investigators to the school four days later, and interviewed many of the students. In advance of her visit, Mr. Mackie, the headmaster, had over thirty drawings from the pupils. Some were better than others, but many depicted a typical flying saucer. Some mentioned three or four smaller objects in the sky above.

Despite an extensive search, the investigators could find no radiation or other traces on the 'landing site', and Cynthia wondered if the object had hovered just above ground level.

In early December, Dr. John Mack, along with colleague Dominique Callimanopulos, visited the school and interviewed the children, whom he believed. Many, who were standing at different vantage points in the playground, reported telepathic messages, or 'feelings', that mankind was not caring for the planet. Since the children have attained adulthood, their memories and evidence have remained consistent.

AN UNUSUAL SCIENCE PROJECT

Even in those early days, some U.K. teachers were more forward thinking than the old school establishment. In 1967, the Plymouth Secondary School raised quite a few eyebrows when their entry for the prestigious 'Schools Science Fair' project was entitled 'Aerial Phenomena and the UFO'.

'The British Association for the Advancement of Science' had instituted the competitive award to encourage an interest in scientific inquiry and structured projects. The two teachers involved, the science and art masters, didn't think their pupils would be inspired to much enthusiasm by topics such as 'Earthworms in Woodland and Grassland', 'Fungi in Birds' Nests' and 'Moths and the Weather', which had been some of the previous projects submitted for the competition.

They wanted to inspire imagination and wonder into their students, and their innovative topic certainly did that. The boys worked in pairs, investigating the history of the phenomenon, taking a poll of public opinions, and writing to Members of Parliament and authors. Two boys made a display of the Solar System, and others faked a photo of a UFO, and compared it with a genuine picture. Such was the interest among the pupils, that the teachers had to restrict the number of participants.

The youngsters' findings were in fact quite conservative;

1. That there is life in space.
2. That some form of life is more advanced than what we are.
3. That the odds of alien life-forms visiting Earth are small but the possibility must exist.
4. There is much bigotry about 'flying saucers'.
5. That the average person is unconcerned about UFOs.
6. That there is no sign of the phenomenon disappearing since first being investigated scientifically in 1947.

SCHOOLS' UFO CRASH DRILLS

Things have certainly changed from fifty or sixty years ago, leaving investigators in a position of not being able to take at 'face value' any reports made by school children.

In 2010 the UK *'Weston Mercury'* reported on a growing trend for schools to stage a UFO crash, with teachers showing the children how to react, and later properly 'investigate' and report on the incident;

'One teacher and organiser, Victoria Shepherd said; "PCSO Wright and PC Church were brilliant. They helped the children secure the scene, talked about

what to do in an emergency, how they gathered evidence, and how to interview witnesses etc.'

The newspaper commented that this seemed to be a more common event. *'A similar drill took place in February of 2009 when Lanchester Endowed Parochial Primary School, in County Durham, staged a surprise 'crash' behind the school..... In 2008, children from an Edgware school were made to believe, by teachers and police, that aliens had landed in their playground.*

'Again, each time, it was conducted by the school system and police – teaching children what to do in a UFO event. Afterwards, the kids are asked to write about their experience.'

In Britain, this practice seems to have continued. In 2013, parents and teachers, at the North Harringay Primary School, staged a UFO crash in the tarmac of the playground, in order to inspire students in their creative writing tasks.

One parent made a model craft, and on the day, dressed up as a forensic investigator to add credibility to the scene. The local constabulary co-operated by allowing P.C. Glyn Kelly to attend and rope off the area, demonstrating the security that would be provided in such an event.

Parents and children attended the event, and after some discussions about what may have happened, the pupils completed excellent creative writing essays.

I wonder if this was really about UFOs and aliens, or more about securing any foreign drones or craft that crash over British Territory? Regardless, it is probable that any later sightings, from pupils at these schools, would have been regarded as dubious.

I have often thought that often not enough attention is given to the possible psychological effects a UFO sighting or experience may have on impressionable children or teenagers.

'MUFON' in the U.S., spoke of a young fourteen year-old boy in Cambell County, who in 1974, had seen a 'UFO' with portholes, hovering, at tree top height, over his school yard. That night, he dreamed of a 'being', with an oval head, oval eyes, and a wrinkled head with no nose and a slit for a mouth. He was told he had been 'chosen', and although he shouldn't be frightened, he would soon be taken away.

On 26th October 1975, he was walking home, and startled by a cylindrical craft, silently hovering twenty-five feet overhead. It had a white light on top and rotating red lights underneath. After about twenty seconds, it shot off vertically. He was terrified that they had come back for him.

He told his parents, who were not interested, and then made a report to the police station, who merely gave him a number to ring. The next day, feeling that no-one cared, he withdrew all his money from the bank, and left a note for his parents, saying that the UFOs were out to get him. Luckily, he was later apprehended by airport security.

Some credence was given to his story when, the day before, a policeman had experienced a UFO pacing his car, and on November 4th, six witnesses saw a similar craft land in nearby woods.

CHAPTER FOURTEEN

THE WEIRD AND WACKY

PART ONE

Over the years, many weird and wacky reports have come over both my and colleagues' desks. Who is to say whether they are really true or not - some may well be! Often, the most improbable account turns out to be genuine, and the apparently authentic report a hoax or misidentification.

GOING AWAY WITH THE ALIENS

In *'Aspects of UFOs and Aliens'* I wrote about a 74-year-old vagrant, Charles Jevington, ('Old Charlie'), who in May 1955 suddenly went missing from the British Cumbrian village of Thursby. He was well known and liked by the locals, many of whom would buy him a pint of ale at one of the two pubs.

After a while, villagers became concerned, and determined that the last person to see him was Meg Crompton, the daughter of a local farmer. She said he had been wearing a haversack and hurrying across a field towards the woodland. An intensive police search failed to find him, and they could not locate any possible relatives.

Five years later, in August 1960, Charlie suddenly turned up, alive and well, in the local pub. He explained to the villagers that he had been on board 'one of those flying saucers' all that time. He told of how, five years ago, he met some aliens, who had been collecting plants in the woodland. They invited him to go on a 'long trip' with them, and even waited for him to collect some basic possessions.

He detailed some incredible voyages across the galaxy, and weird and wonderful worlds he had visited. One amateur astronomer scoffed at his tall tales, and when Charlie mentioned planets other than Saturn having 'rings', he disputed the whole account. This prompted disbelief in all the other drinkers, who laughed when Charlie stomped off and said he may go back with his alien friends in a fortnight.

Charlie did go permanently missing two weeks later, and around the same time, five discs were seen across the sky in Carlisle. In later years, NASA discovered that Charlie was correct, there are faint rings, not discernable by Earth's telescopes, around Jupiter, Uranus and Neptune.

Several years later, in 1975, musician Jim Sullivan also went 'missing'. Researcher Nick Faust wrote of how in one of his compositions, on his debut album, titled *'UFO'*, Sullivan sang about driving his car into the desert, his family left behind, and getting abducted by aliens.

He had a promising career, and left his wife and family in California while he pursued success in Nashville. Sometime later, his car was found abandoned 26 miles outside the town of Santa Rosa, New Mexico.

An inquiry was set-up, and a local police officer recalled that just before he had pulled Sullivan up for erratic driving. Once he had established that Sullivan was just tired from his long drive, he directed him to a nearby motel, where it was confirmed he had checked in.

No trace of Sullivan was ever found. What baffled police and his family was that all his belongings were still in his vehicle, including his 12-string guitar, which, as Faust noted, 'is usually a possession treasured more than family'.

THE SATELLITE MYSTERY

Astronomer, Andrew Pike, told of many hiccups in our fledgling space program, but this was his favourite of all time.

In April 1988, a Pan-Am jet liner, flying over Wales, picked up, and reported, what they thought was an 'SOS' signal. Authorities, who soon tracked it back to an orbiting Soviet satellite, immediately advised Moscow.

The Russians could not understand it. The satellite was controlled by signals transmitted from earth, and no commands had, as yet, been sent to their craft. Someone, or something, had activated it!

'Speculation then centred on a truly surprising scenario. It was seriously suggested that aliens were sending the signals from a ground transmitter somewhere in Wales.'

Eventually the source was traced to a site near the small Welsh town of St. Asaph. Having ensured there were no aliens or crashed Ufos in the vicinity, the local policeman, P.C. Jones, on his bicycle, went out to the reported 'transmission site' to investigate. He found an isolated cottage and elderly woman.

'Poor Mrs. Mathers hadn't a clue. Although deemed a prime suspect, P.C. Jones began to have serious reservations that Mrs. Mathers possessed the knowledge and means to signal a Soviet satellite, least of all that she was assisting in the alien invasion of Earth!'

After joining her for a cup of tea, the puzzled policeman began checking her home for something which may have triggered the satellite's command system. His eventual success came in the form of an electronic mouse trap, whose signal had been powerful enough to trigger the Russian satellite's transmitter.

Mrs Mathers was astounded; *"Well, it's not what I would have expected. The signal should only be heard by mice and rats!"*

SEX IN SPACE!

In 2000, the Russian newspaper, *'Pravda'* published a rather hilarious and thought provoking article.

Rositislav Beleda, who initiated the conversation, had worked for fourteen years, as the chief sexologist at the Central Aviation Hospital; *"Are astronauts' sexual needs taken into consideration during long-term flights? Certainly, in space, men exercise on treadmills. In addition, they can theoretically masturbate too. But they should not forget about condoms or other containers, otherwise drops of sperm will be flying chaotically about the cabin, and they will have to collect it....*

"Space flights affect adversely all life functions, especially the reproductive function. Astronauts get old very quickly. None of the U.S. female astronauts got pregnant after flights. Soviet cosmonaut Valentina Tereshkova was an exception."

After long term flights into space, astronauts suffered loss of muscle tone, low potency and other functional side effects – *"Scientists developed a special suit for cosmonauts, called 'Chibis'. The suit bears some resemblance to a metal barrel with a stool in it. The lower part of the astronaut is pressure-sealed, and the air is pumped out of the barrel to make blood rush to the legs. On the basis of 'Chibis', specialists later developed a device to treat ejaculation dysfunction.*

"Valery Polyakov, the world's flight endurance record breaker found Beleda's experiments immoral; "Astronauts' motivation and their attitudes to perform difficult tasks dominate certain relations between men and women during the flight." He doubted that NASA had ever conducted a 'sexual experiment' in space."

Beleda, however, was not deterred; *"While a lot of scientists, all over the world, are busy searching for extraterrestrial civilizations, astronauts plan a more earthly contact, that is conceiving a human baby at the orbital station. The biggest problem is how to conceive, because liquid cannot be spilt under the condition of weightlessness.*

"But they do not need a bed in space. They can love each other in the air....And what will come out of that? As soon as he touches her, she will fly away in the opposite direction. A bed, or at least some fastening device on a wall is more likely to be used."

The mind boggles, and how far Boleda's experiments went is not known. He admitted that; *"As a matter of fact, humans are not eager to make love in space!"*

Although this book is primarily about the earlier years, I felt I had to include this later occurrence. On 20th March 1999, the *'West Australian'* newspaper published the following intriguing article;

'UFO RESCUER HUNTS TWILIGHT ZONE SQUAD.'
'By Steve Pennells'

'The truth is out there....apparently somewhere between Kalgoorlie and the South Australian border. A $50,000 rescue mission has started for three stranded aliens and their 2km-wide spacecraft which allegedly crash landed on the edge of the Great Victoria Desert.

'Sydney woman Margie Parker flew to Kalgoorlie this week to organise a team of experts to find the stricken UFO. She claims that the extraterrestrials were off-planet engineers who experienced mechanical problems while flying over W.A. and had to make an emergency landing in the middle of the Nullarbor about 160km north of Haig.

'She will not say how she knows about the spacecraft, but says the aliens want help to repair it so they can leave the planet quickly. The extraterrestrials apparently need a welder, water and lifting gear. Ms Parker's plan is to get to the stricken spaceship and have her rescue team help the aliens carry out repair work. Offers of help have flooded in from interstate and overseas. One United States benefactor is offering $32,000.

'Ms Parker contacted the UFO National Hotline in Melbourne to set up the rescue. "We put her automatically in our 'fruit-cake' category, but she is very insistent;" the hot-lines' Ross Dowe said yesterday; "It is not usual for us to make an expedition like this. I don't think that we have ever been commissioned or paid to look for flying saucers before. No doubt, it will be a real eye-opener if something is really there.

"Ms Parker has commissioned a team of geologists, including a Perth expert. She was meant to meet him on her arrival at Perth airport on Wednesday night. She was booked on an evening flight, but did not make the meeting. She has reportedly begun setting up a rescue team in Kalgoorlie, and has approached air charter companies to fly her to the remote location. Kalgoorlie Police have also been asked to help. Kalgoorlie Police Sgt. John Hall said he had not received any report of stranded aliens."

The 'Journal of Alternative Realities' gave some mention to this, and asked the obvious question as to how Ms Parker knew of the crashed craft, and how had she made contact with the aliens, who surely had a contingency plan for such an event?

Their comments were very apt under the circumstances; 'The claim should be treated with suspicion, or at least healthy scepticism until more evidence is forthcoming......Surely NORAD, possibly Pine Gap, and/or the Exmouth Facility in W.A., and a number of high-tech 'monitoring agencies' would have detected the UFO entering our atmosphere and been aware of its demise. This would have created another 'Roswell', with the area being cordoned off, swarming with military and recovery teams, and a 'cover story' being issued.

'Whether this case turns out to be genuine, a hoax, or something else, I hope that the credibility of Ufology is not too damaged. Time will tell!'

Some crash victims may have not been so lucky. On 31st May 1969, the Nairobi *'Daily Nation'*, in Kenya, carried the following story; *'Star War – villagers hack UFO to pieces.'*

'Villagers near Lungalunga on the Tanzanian border, staged their own 'Star War' when they set out to track down a UFO. Armed with crossbows, axes and pangas, they staged the attack on the mysterious object from space.

'The object had landed in a small river and turned the water warm. Some villagers around the Kaseseni and Tindini areas had been so frightened that they abandoned their homes. But twenty brave ones had armed themselves and set out to retrieve the UFO which had caused so much panic in the villages.

'On reaching the spot, the villagers apparently tried to pull two pieces of wire which looked like aerials. But their mission was almost thwarted when strange noises emanated from inside the object. But bravery won the day as they returned and attacked the object with pangas, hacking it into pieces as they removed it from the water. Their mission satisfactorily accomplished, the villagers returned home.'

A member of the British research group, 'BUFORA' wrote to the newspaper, enclosing a copy of the article, and asking more questions about the incident. He noted the object may well have been space debris or a fallen satellite, but in the unlikely event that the object was extraterrestrial, the remains would be extremely valuable to science.

Obviously, by then, the veil of secrecy had already come down. His letter and copy of the article were returned without comment.

Nine years earlier, on 6th November 1960, the *'Sunday Express'* published the following amusing story; *'The 'Thing' from Space is Slapped in Jail.'*

'A 'Thing' from outer space is tonight locked up in a cell in the tiny, white-washed police station at Zoermerkaer, a village 120 miles from Pretoria. It is awaiting the inspection of scientists – American and South African – already embarrassed by earlier discoveries on Transvaal bush farmland.

'These were bits of metal said to be parts of the moon-probe rocket Pioneer VI, launched from Cape Canaveral, Florida, on September 25th. The metal is now being checked by launching men in Florida, but so far the Americans have not admitted they are from Pioneer VI. The metal, discovered two weeks ago, was thought to be part of the booster fuel tank of the moon rocket.

'But the 'Thing', now guarded by a burly constable, is a sphere of tough brown alloy. Its edges are seared by immense heat. Out of one side comes black fluid, which has blistered the face and hands of a villager.'

There were other occasions when our 'visitors' received a less then friendly welcome. Researcher Frank Edwards described an October 1954 incident from Milan in Italy.

A resident was cycling home, after attending an outdoor movie on the outskirts of the city. When he saw a bright light coming from inside a little used sporting field, he got off his bike, and peered through a crack in the fence.

Inside was a 'sizeable object', either on, or just above, the ground, and softly glowing with a dim fluorescent light. There was a dark figure moving around in front of it, and the witness, who felt a little scared, jumped back on his bicycle intending to pedal back to town.

He hadn't gone far, when he met a group of farmers, who returned to the scene with him. In total, thirty-one witnesses later affirmed to the police that they had seen the strange object, and 'creatures' moving around it. They described these 'little men' as being no more than four feet tall, wearing transparent helmets, and 'some sort of grey jackets'. They had 'backpacks' of bulky equipment, which was connected to the front and bottom of their helmets.

After several vehicles stopped, including a lorry of rotten fruit, some of the crowd forced the lock on the gate, and entered the area so as to get a better view. Not content with just 'looking', the crowd began throwing rotten oranges, some of which hit their targets. The unfortunate little beings, now under bombardment, started scurrying back to their craft, entering it from underneath. There was a humming sound, and the object rose up and shot away.

OOPS!

British researcher, John Spencer, wrote of one unusual incident; *'Probably the single most bizarre encounter case was reported from Austria in September 1955 by Joseph Wanderka. He was driving a moped along the road when, not paying proper attention, he accidentally drove straight up the ramp of a UFO and into the arms of tall aliens.*

'He apologised for doing so, and the aliens explained in German that they had arrived from Cassiopeia, and got him to explain how the moped engine worked. When Joseph apparently gave them an anti-Nazi lecture, they got bored, and threw him off the ship. However, they did make a suggestion that he could create a movement for world equality.'

ALIEN STUDENTS

Researcher, John Prytz, who conducted many in-depth investigations, later wrote a column for one of Australia's leading magazines. He had a good sense of humour, and in 1985, wrote a tongue-in-cheek article for the *'Journal of the Australian Centre for UFO Studies'.*

John couldn't help noticing a parallel between the hordes of school students, who came on excursions to Parliament House, where he worked, and the continuing alien visits.

'We've all noted that UFOs, given that they, (in part at least), are guided by non-human intelligence(s), appear to neither want to invade us nor establish diplomatic contact. Thus, the theory that, if 'they' are neither soldiers nor politicians/diplomats, then perhaps they are scientists studying us in a fairly cold and detached manner.

'One problem with that theory, frequently pointed out, is just how long, for crying out loud, does it take to study us already? Even discounting any UFO activity, before 1944/1945, that still leaves forty years of study they have done. How many abductions and 'medicals' are needed before you get to the point of diminishing returns? How many cars do you need to pace and stall before you are satisfied that your device works? How many grass/soil samples do our 'friends' really need? What about animal 'mutilations'? One would think that

after several dozen cases that would be enough – time to move on to something else!'

John noted the ritual associated with our school visits to Parliament House, and the varying assignments the children had to complete whilst they were there. Perhaps our visitors were alien 'students', also on an excursion to planet Earth! He envisioned them also having a series of questions to answer and tasks to perform in order to complete their 'assignments'.

'1. Navigation; Plot a course from Point A. to Point B. via Point C. (Note Points A., B. and C. are regions of high UFO activity.)

2. Physics: Select an isolated automobile in motion. Test out the QX-Beam machine on it. Confirm Qijn's theory of EM interference by stalling its primitive engine.

3. Geology; Obtain samples of the following for later chemical and physical analysis; a) Pond water b) Ocean water c) Ice d) Soil.

4. Botany; Obtain some samples of what Earthlings call grasses.

5. Cooking; Use the seeds from your grass samples to make up some of what Earthlings call 'pancakes'. You can use these as items of trade with the natives in obtaining more exotic items to study – (for more advanced students.)

6. Zoology; Find any one of several kinds of bovine ungulates. Perform minor surgery on this animal after putting it down. Take the established list of amputated organs back with you for detailed study in the laboratory.

7. Human Physiology; Abduct and study one, (at the most two together), human beings. To avoid unnecessary trauma to this person, reassure them with any one of a hundred varieties of mumbo-jumbo. (Notes; Religious messages are particularly useful in putting the human at ease.) Perform an elementary examination on this person. (Note; Advanced honours students doing an approved special project may implant a Gezt for long-term follow-up studies on this person.)

8. Piloting skills; Take over the controls of the excursion bus assigned to your small group. Call attention to yourself. When human military aircraft are scrambled in response to this action, engage in a mock dog-fight to test out your skills, agility and abilities in flight. At the end of the excursion, the best of all the raw pilots in their craft will engage in formation flying. (Note; Do not go beyond the echelon formation manoeuvre without prior permission.)'

'.......So there you go – the 'school excursion hypothesis'. Though not the be-all-and-end-all of UFO theories, it is, I suggest, a logical refinement of the ET (scientific expedition) hypothesis.'

A DANGEROUS SCIENCE PROJECT?

'The Weekday' newspaper, from West Palm Beach, Florida, contained an interesting article that recounted the fifty-year-old memories of a local resident;

'Mrs. Evelyn Wendt, beauty salon operator, recalls an incident fifty years earlier, in 1928, when she was a schoolgirl playing in the yard of the Holy Name Covent School; "The first thing I remember is that this egg-shaped thing was on the ground, and a bright light was shining in my eyes.".

'The light went out, a 'hatch' opened, and little robot people emerged; "They were smaller than I and resembled animated flowers with faces where the buds would be. Remember, I was just a bitty thing then, and kids don't fear flowers."

'They carried a weapon-like device to the school's science building; "I wanted to help them, but someone said – 'Stop'. I replied that they were so small I was going to assist. The creatures let me try, but I couldn't even budge the machine. I was told they were going to stop the work that was being done in the science building and they said if the work continued, they would destroy the place." Asked what the 'work' was, she said she didn't know – "All I know is later I heard the place was a shambles."

*'She said; "There seemed to be a **man** with the little people...everything looked real, even though I wasn't so sure. The conversation wasn't real talking", but she understood mentally what was being said.*

'As they were leaving; "They asked if I wanted to go. I said "No", but I could have gone." She added; "They promised to come back for me in about thirty-five years, but that time was up a long time ago and nothing happened that I know of." The 'saucer' then flew straight up, hovered a minute, and disappeared.'

One wonders what kind of experiments the kids had been doing in their science laboratory?

A CHANGE OF COLOUR

The *'Flying Saucer Review'* documented two weird and totally inexplicable cases which occurred in the 1950s.

Investigator Carl Olsen, from Norway, interviewed Trygve Jansen, who in October 1956, was driving back to his house in Ski. His neighbour Mrs. Buflot, whom he was giving a lift home, was also a passenger in the car.

As they travelled along the shore of Gjersjoen Lake, a saucer-shaped object came, at great speed, from behind a small hill, swung out over the water, then returned to the road, where it seemed to be following their car. It looked like a shining, rotating disc, with wings, and a kind of cockpit on the top. It emanated a strong greenish-white light, which at times lit up the whole forest.

Six or seven times the strange craft circled the car, occasionally making 'great side sweeps'. After the road left the side of the lake, the disc flew in front of their car, and stopped above the centre of the road. Carl came to a halt when the object started moving towards them. It halted just in front of their vehicle.

'Both witnesses had a distinct feeling of being scrutinised....and felt a prickly sensation to their faces, as if they were exposed to a strong beam of some kind. And most curious of all, Mr. Jansen's watch, which had kept perfect time for years, stopped at that moment.' (The watchmaker later stated it must have been exposed to a strong magnetic current.)

Suddenly, the object took off straight upwards, and disappeared at great speed behind the car. When he got home, he realised that his previously beige colour vehicle was now a shiny green colour. His wife, and many others, insisted he must have bought a new car.

That night, Jansen's arm was temporarily paralysed, and both he and Mrs Buflot felt decidedly unwell. It wasn't until the next day, when Jansen's car had mysteriously resumed its original beige colour, that his wife and neighbours believed the account of their strange encounter.

Just over a year later, in November 1957, the trawler the *'Ella Hewett'*, was just off the coast of the Isle of Man. In the early hours of the morning a massive, eerie glow surrounded the ship. The Bo'sun, Hugh Smith noted; *'There was no vibration, no explosion – in fact no sensation at all.'*

That night a truck driver had seen a huge, silent, red ball of light moving low and fast over the Brecon Beacons to the east in Wales. Five minutes later, a police patrol car saw a bright, greenish-blue delta-shaped object flying, at tremendous speed, over Glamorgan and the Rhondda Valley.

Soon after, to the west, it was spotted by more than one witness, four miles off Douglas on the Isle of Man. Coastguard James Harvey said; *"It travelled from west to east, blue-white with a red-orange glow behind. Snub-nosed, tapered like a carrot. It was miles high, and going at terrific speed.'*

The skipper of the *'Ella Hewitt'*, Fred Sutton, had been asleep during the incident. The next morning he radioed the owners, Hewett Fishing Co. – *'A funny thing happened to me last night. The white paint on the front of the bridge vanished. The paint was definitely there when I went to bed. This morning only the red lead undercoat was left. I have been scratching my head all day about it, and now you can scratch yours!'*

The following day, the perplexed trawler owners received the following update; *'Yesterday the bridge pink – today normal white!'* As with the Norwegian case, the original colour had mysteriously returned.

THE BEING IN THE BASKET

Researcher, Brad Steiger, wrote of an unusual case which occurred in Iowa City, U.S.A. in the summer of 1971. A nurse, in her early fifties, was driving to work at the hospital, at about dawn one morning, when she saw what appeared to be a cage, suspended by a line coming from the sky. The 'cage' was more egg-shaped than round, with bars running vertically.

As she came closer she could see that a man, who was gazing intently at the ground below, was inside. He was too high up for her to make out his features, but he was dressed in a shiny, form-fitting, one-piece suit. Although he didn't move, the woman felt he was looking down on her.

She possibly wasn't believed when she excitedly told the patients and other nurses at the hospital, but the police had received other reports of a UFO that morning, and the local airport had nothing in the air at that time.

A newspaper delivery boy and also a laundry delivery man had also seen the 'stranger in the sky', however the mystery was never officially solved.

AN ABDUCTION WITH A DIFFERENCE

Researcher Irene Granchi, although raised and educated in Britain, spent most of her life living and investigating in South America. She was very interested in a letter sent, in October 1967, by a prominent member of the community, to Brazilian journalist Jose Belern.

He, along with his four companions, two of whom were well known physicians, one a metallurgical engineer, and the other a local bank manager, had a disturbing experience, but all, understandably, wanted their identities withheld.

They were amateur fishermen, and one weekend in the June of that year, they were spending a weekend together at a beach resort near Fortaleza. At 3am on the Sunday morning, when they were at the water's edge, patiently waiting for the fish to take the bait, they heard a low humming sound, which was painful to their ears.

Before they could determine its cause and location, the noise suddenly stopped. One of the fishermen went off to see what was going on, whilst the others stayed put with their fishing lines. After about six minutes the noise started again, this time louder and more intense. They realised it was coming from behind a hill, about 500 metres from the shore, from where several beams of smoky-coloured light were spreading out into the sky, alternatively shining brightly and dimming.

They were all scared, and hurriedly hauled in their fishing lines, grabbed their gear, and rushed off to get back to their accommodation. They didn't get far. Their engineer friend reappeared, and came up behind them, shouting for them to stop; *"We did, and found him pointing his Taurus 38 revolver at us, ordering us to climb the hill above which the lights were shining. At first, we believed he was just joking, but as we started to laugh, he aimed his gun and started firing, warning us that he would kill all of us if we refused to obey him. We noticed that his eyes were wet and bleary, and they were shining strangely. Had he gone insane? We decided to obey."*

They started up the hill, in the direction from where the lights, now not evident, had originally appeared. As they stumbled along, the engineer kept urging them to hurry up. Every so often, they could hear some strange, unintelligible sounds, to which the engineer would shout "We're coming – we're coming!"

When they reached the top of the hill, they saw a huge, round object hovering about ten metres above the ground. It was about thirty metres wide and five metres high, a light green, phosphorescent colour, and had 'fins' jutting out from both sides. On top was a square, slatted 'hatchway', from which multi-coloured lights appeared. A metre-wide tube, with a 'kind of oval-shape door' at the end, was jutting out from the bottom;

'All of a sudden my memory failed me. My eyes went out of focus, and when I came to, I found myself lying on a kind of table, which seemed to be packed with something like foam rubber, for it was very soft. My companions were similarly placed. We were all lying there.'

The room, which was about two metres high, with no windows or doors, was milky-white in colour, with glass-like walls, which reflected the general light which was soft, and did not affect their eyes.

'I wanted to move and shout, but found myself incapable of it. A voice was heard, and I'm quite sure it came from a reddish-blue lamp in the ceiling, which tinkled and echoed within my head, telling us not to be afraid, and nothing would happen to us; to keep calm, for what was happening to us was for the good of the universe.'

They were asked many questions, many of which indicated their captors, whom I wonder may have been driven by an advanced form of artificial intelligence, had very little understanding of human beings or life on Earth. After a while they were all suffering from lack of air, and when the witness indicated this, a triangular-shaped window opened up and outwards, in one of the seemingly smooth, seamless walls, letting in the fresh air from the beach.

They were then asked if there was anything else they needed; *'This prompted one of the two doctors to demand to be told what this was all about, for he would not answer a single question more unless he were told. We all joined in, but the voice did its best to convince us that we would not be able to understand anything about it. However, it finally gave in. Now the questions rolled out of our mouths, all at the same time. There were so many of them, the voice could not grasp what was being said, so it asked us to speak one at a time, and diminish our 'frequency'.*

The information that was imparted was extremely interesting; *'We shall not appear to you for we are very different from you. There are six of us. We are from 'GOI', and have come to study 'TONK'. (our Earth). It is our first visit here, but other beings from our 'dwelling' have come here before to visit you. We are made from a substance similar to yours. Our life span corresponds to 300 of those things you call 'years'. We have used sound waves to bring you over and the light we used first reached your engineer friend.'*

The witnesses could hear noises that sounded as if someone were 'meddling with their belongings', and then they were asked about the gun. Having been told of its nature and purpose, their captor said that four of their companions had been killed by humans, but it was their own fault as they had been 'following something that flew in the air'.

They were also told that life like ours existed on other planets, but they were very much more advanced; *"It added that before what we called a 'year' had elapsed, they would manage to be here, and that some of those who dwell on 'GOI' are already among us.'*

After further questioning they got the impression that these 'visitors' were living in isolated, and possibly 'icy' areas. Their captors indicated it was time for them to leave, and that they would take 'one of each of their captives' things'.

The next thing they knew, the fishermen all woke up at 5.20am on the deserted beach. Hardly able to believe what had happened, they all walked back up the hill, but all they could find was a shallow windswept 'crater' where the craft had been. Each one of them found that something different was missing from their belongings, including the Taurus 38 gun, bullets and holster.

·————————————————————

SLIGHTLY UNUSUAL BEHAVIOUR

British researcher, Jenny Randles, wrote of two incidents where the behaviour of the aliens departed somewhat from the norm.

In 1914 at Georgian Bay, Ontario Canada, a group of people noticed what appeared to be a very unusual boat drifting off the shore. It had a grey spherical body and flat top, unlike anything they had seen before. On top were two smallish beings, about four feet tall, dressed in purplish-green uniforms. As they manoeuvred some form of tube in and out of the water, they were joined by three other similar 'beings' who were wearing khaki-coloured clothing.

After storing the tubing back into their craft, all bar one, who was standing on the rim, went back inside. The onlookers, who assumed they must be youngsters engaged in some form of escapade, were startled when the object suddenly shot off skywards, tilted, and flew away at speed. The stranded little entity was clinging to the side as if his life depended on it – which it probably did!

Another unusual incident, investigated by BUFORA's Phillip Taylor, was reported by 'Edwin', a retired military figure and scientist of some standing, who lived in a rural area near Hastings, Sussex.

In 1966/7 Edwin had found some mysterious flattened circles of grass in a nearby field, but on August 17th 1967, he discovered their cause. That day, whilst out walking his dogs, he met some unusual 'beings' who were very thin, just over five feet tall, with gray parchment-like skin, and were dressed in tight-fitting wetsuits with balaclava helmets. As was often the habit with country folk, he invited them into his home.

Between then and the 23rd September, they were guests in his house on nine separate occasions. He soon realised that they were 'not of this Earth'. Their facial features were different, they only had three fingers and a thumb, and spoke with whistle and twittering noises. They used gestures to communicate with Edward.

He had seen them emerge from a conical shape object, resting on three legs, but he never saw it land or take-off. Once, when he went to get a better look, his new friends physically carried him back to his house, indicating that they did not want him to watch them depart.

Their visits always occurred after midnight, usually arriving in pairs, and staying no longer than an hour. One night they even watched TV with him, and when he drew a map of the Solar System, they drew a dot outside of it, indicating they came from further away. They took samples of many things, showing a particular interest in fruit, and on their last visit stopped in the garden to souvenir bits of shrubs and bushes. They seemed to respect Edwin's refusal to allow them to also take his dog.

He gave them two china model dogs instead, which they took, and gave some bits of non-descript crystal and a plant, which died, in return.

NO PARKING HERE!

In 1967, the British *'Orbit'* publication documented an interesting report from earlier that year in Long Beach U.S.A.

Jack Hill, a 64 year old guard at the Consolidated Lumberyard, was on his bicycle, making rounds at 3.50am one morning, when he spotted a strange, silent, elongated craft hovering 100ft away and 50ft over the site. It was windowless, eighty to one hundred feet long, and about twenty or thirty feet deep, with a soft bluish-green light.

Jack decided that this intruder was there without permission, and possibly preparing to land. He watched for all of ten seconds, and deciding that 'it shouldn't be there', drew his gun and fired off six rounds in about thirty seconds;

"When I fired the first shot, its light went out, but it was light enough around here that I could still see it as a dark object up there. It started going almost straight up as I kept firing, and then it sped out of sight in a westerly direction toward San Pedro....It wasn't a plane or a helicopter, but I thought if I could shoot its engine out, there would be no question about UFOs."

After dawn broke, he collected four of the .38 calibre bullets he said had struck the object, and reported the matter to the Harbour Division Police, since it was against the law to discharge a firearm in the city. When they asked him why he had opened fire, he said; "I'm a guard here, and nobody is supposed to park without permission."

The police agreed that the isolated timberyard would have made an ideal landing spot for a UFO. Bill had always been sceptical, but not after that incident. He later said; "They're out there, and I know it now!"

WELFARE FRAUDS

A colleague sent me a handwritten copy of a 1993 article, written by a 'Rennie Mears', from an unknown publication. It was hilarious, and reported the views of purported UFO 'expert' Robert MacLaine – *who quotes highly placed Washington insiders as saying that extraterrestrials, masquerading as human beings are siphoning off as much as 15% of the national welfare budget each and every year.'*

MacLaine, who was president of a UFO research group called 'Stop Extraterrestrials Today', claimed that these intruders had robbed the American tax payer, in 1992 alone, of 172 billion dollars in food stamps, rent subsidies and medical costs;

"There are sceptics who say that space aliens can't possibly be ripping off our welfare system, but they couldn't be further off the mark. If you knew anything about federal bureaucracy, you know that anybody can pass himself off as being disadvantaged, and cash in, and from what I am told, there are hundreds and thousands of aliens on the welfare rolls!"

Naturally, Federal agencies declined to even comment on MacLaine's allegations, but he was not to be deterred, and produced an alleged copy of a secret White House memo, dated August 21st 1992, that he said; *'bluntly spoke of the 'space alien – welfare connection'. The memo called for the creation of a secret task force to 'assess the threat and propose an immediate course of action'.*

MacLaine said "Until they bring up the issue, the fraud is going to continue – and there is not a damn thing that people like you and me can do about it!"

I can understand the government's concern about illegal immigrants... but aliens? Yes, I've had reliable evidence of their presence among us, but certainly not in any significant numbers.

HUNTERS BEWARE

In *'Contact Down Under'* I wrote about a Tasmanian family, who in 1985/6, lived on a property 55 kilometres north of Hobart. George, and his sixteen year old son, Peter, were hunting wildlife on a neighbouring property, and were already carrying a couple of carcasses, destined for pet food, as they hunted even more game.

When they thought they heard someone coming, they turned off the spotlight, and noticed a bright blue object about five kilometres away in the sky. Within a few minutes it was hovering above the ground, and landed about 200 metres from where they were standing. It was bullet shaped, about 20 to 25 metres tall and six to seven metres wide, with a rounded top and straight base, and a ring or ledge halfway around.

Several blue lights were coming from the top of the craft, illuminating the whole area, around George and Peter, with a bright blue glow. George noticed his backpack, containing a twelve volt battery, was beginning to heat up and bubble, and as he and Peter started to run away, the craft began to make a noise. It sounded like a type of singing, possibly an unintelligible foreign language.

They dropped the dead possums, and had left behind the rifle and battery, (now cooled off), by the time they reached the car. They drove slowly home, without headlights. There was no sign of burning on George's skin, shirt or jumper, but his singlet underneath had a fifteen centimetre burn hole.

Perhaps the 'visitors' do not like us killing animals. Thirty years earlier, in 1956, teenage brothers, Bob and Tom Webb, were hunting rabbits one night in an Irish graveyard. They would sweep a spotlight around the headstones, and 'pick up a gleam from the rabbit's eyes'. Their dog would then rush forward and grab the poor animal for them.

They were walking back to the cemetery gates, and just like George and Peter, had two carcasses with them. In the pitch black silence, a pair of huge, bright red 'eyes' or 'coals' appeared, which lit up the headstones. Even when they turned the spotlight on, they could not make out the shape behind them.

The dog let out a whine and bolted, and as the two red lights glided towards the brothers, they did the same. Bob later said; "I can remember smelling hot metal, and feeling panic. I was sure we'd be attacked. We took off and didn't look back, but all the way to the gate the cemetery was filled with that strange red light."

'SWEET CHARITY'

Despite many horrendous accounts of animal abductions and mutilations, there have been stories of attempted dog-nappings by extraterrestrials. Perhaps some of them like our canine companions, despite their usual displays of fear or aggression when encountering an alien presence.

In 1995, *'Fate'* magazine published an account, the veracity of which I doubted, even though it tugged at the heart strings. However, since in ufology it is sometimes hard to separate fact from fiction, here is Mark Gaudio's account of his, and his dog, 'Charity's, interaction with beings from elsewhere.

'The evening was surprisingly warm and clear, even though most of the leaves had fallen from the trees and winter was about to begin. Charity, my gentle, female Border-Collie, and I were strolling in our immediate neighbourhood, as we did on a regular basis. I let Charity off her leash because she was never hostile, and the children we met on our walks loved to play with her and run their hands through her silky coat.'

As his dog pranced around, running, jumping and rolling in the fallen leaves, Mark thought to himself that, when they got home, it would take some time to get all of the leaves out of her tangled coat. Perhaps it was time to visit the dog grooming salon for a much needed 'clip' of her fur.

Suddenly Charity stood, 'on alert', in the one spot. She stared into the air, and began howling. Mark couldn't understand the change in her behaviour until he heard a 'propeller' noise, which sounded as it if was low to the ground, and coming closer. He then noticed a shadowy – blurry object approaching. It had a bright green and a bright white light at the front and back.

At first he thought it must be a plane, but it was far too low, and hovering. By that time, the unknown craft was overhead. The 'propeller' noise changed to a 'strange metallic hum', and a circle of bright blue light shone down on them.

Charity began howling again, and Mark called out; "What are you?"

The lights on the craft then changed to three equally spaced red rings, wrapped around its circumference, and descended to below to treetop level. Charity stopped howling, but remained alert and 'at attention'. The lights then changed once more to a 'blue strobes', which spun counter clockwise around the shadowy craft, still hovering overhead.

Mark desperately needed proof of what he was seeing. Nobody would ever believe him! *"Thinking the extraterrestrials might be able to read my thoughts, I said to myself, "Bring me aboard – Let me see you."*

'As if the E.T.'s were indeed reading my thoughts, a bluish white beam of light projected from the shadowy underbelly of the ship, but it didn't spotlight me. It shone directly on Charity. Seconds later she was gone.'

As Mark searched frantically for his dog, he turned to demand, if they had taken her, the aliens return his pet, but the strange craft had also disappeared. He called, and searched the area for some time, but Charity was nowhere to be found.

He ran home, and raced upstairs to his room, from where he was going to call the police. *'There, to my astonishment, lying on the bed, asleep and unharmed, was Charity. She was perfectly happy and perfectly groomed of leaves, clipped as if by a dog salon, and smelling of sweet perfume. No one had let her into the house, and we have no dog door!'*

FOR WHOM THE BELL TOLLS

Back in Tasmania, in 1976, on 28th February, the *'Hobart Mercury'* published a report about strange lights in the sky being seen over the logging town of Maydena.

They were first seen on 17th February – a pale yellow/orange light, followed by a second light, travelling at a slightly lower trajectory. They appeared at 10.55pm, and took twenty minutes to traverse the sky, travelling to the west, then swinging south or south-west and disappearing into the distance.

After that they continued to appear on subsequent evenings, between 10.15pm and 11.15pm. Constable W. Lowery, the local policeman, arranged for one man to ring the church bell as soon as the objects appeared. Crowds of thirty or forty people would gather in the side roads, with a bigger crowd watching from the main street.

The *'Mercury'* sent out a reporter on 26th February. That night, as soon as the bell rang at 10.55pm, everybody rushed out to get a look. The lights appeared to come from a valley in the northeast, towards the National Park, the first was followed within five to ten seconds by its companion, on a much lower trajectory. The initial object seemed to slow down, as if waiting for the other to catch-up, and then they continued in formation, on a flight path that took them almost over Maydena's main street. Again, after they passed the town, they altered their course, turning south or southwest as opposed to their original westward movement. Many witnesses had binoculars and telescopes, and some tried, unsuccessfully, to take clear photographs.

Tasmanian investigator, Keith Roberts, along with colleagues from 'TUFOIC', visited Maydena twice in March, but by that time, the 'lights' had ceased their regular appearance. They were able to interview many of the witnesses, who were mainly consistent in their reports, with some differing on the size of the objects, probably due to individual eyesight.

On the night of 10th March, the lights were seen again, this time travelling from the southwest to the northeast. At 9.50pm, the bell unexpectedly tolled, and everybody rushed out. Mr. T. Francombe, a Forest Operations Superintendent, and his neighbour, Mr. G. Sargison, neither of whom had witnessed the previous lights, were both at home when they saw the objects coming from the southwest, this time passing to the north of the town.

Whilst people in the town lost sight of the lights at 10pm, another witness, 18kms northeast of Maydena, also saw the strange lights, at 12.45am, in the northwest over Mt. Field East, which was 127mtrs in height, although all the observers agreed the objects were just below cloud level, and estimated their height at about 1,500 to 2,000 mtrs., and speed at about 150kph.

On 27th March, the bell rang again, however the sky was dull and misty, with light drizzle falling. Although the lights were in view for about ten minutes, and still very bright and distinct, it was hard for investigators to get definite details. The last report was on April 14th, from only one witness.

THE VISITORS' GARBAGE

In May 1967, Danish researcher, Willy Olsen from 'UFO-NYT', published an account from Sjellands Odde, in that country.

This incident, which had occurred sometime earlier, involved two boys who were playing in front of a large stack of hay near the waterfront. It was getting dark, and as they were preparing to go home, one noticed a dark grey object in the sky. One lad thought it may be a water-spout, which could be dangerous, and persuaded his friend to take shelter with him in a nearby ditch.

It was not a water-spout, and instead they saw an unusual object in the sky, which slowed down and descended. It was elliptical, with a window from which a light was coming. Three legs were lowered from underneath, and the boys thought it was going to land, but when only three feet above the ground, the legs were retracted. The strange craft then speeded up and continued on, at a low altitude, to Kattaget, (the sea). While it was over the shore, something which looked like 'boxes' was thrown out.

The craft turned around over the water, and another big 'box' was lowered on a rope or cable 'as thick as an arm'. Eight people came out from an opening in the bottom of the object, and climbed down the rope or cable. They were quite small in stature, one wearing a blue suit and the others a striped one. Apart from the being in blue, all had containers on their backs, from where a tube led to their mouths. They all had 'lights on both of their shoulders', which provided illumination at both ends, somewhat similar to an electric torch.

One boy said they looked friendly, and some of these 'people' smiled and waved at him, holding their palms vertical with quick horizontal movements. The object took off soon after, and the boys reported that all they could hear was a very soft 'humming', and they did not notice any 'breath of air' or heat radiation.

Investigators retrieved one of the heavy 'lumps' the boys had seen being thrown into the water. A piece was sent to a technological institute for examination, and their report said that they had never seen the way in which the elements, (some of which, lime and inorganic coal), were mixed.

LITTLE GREEN MEN

In fact, little green men are rarely reported. After 'Civilian Aerial Phenomena Research' in New Zealand, investigated an incident in 1971, Phil Ackman, a reporter from the local Hamilton newspaper published the following account; *'Oterchanga police are searching for a little green man carrying a 14-foot shovel and about half a ton of dirt. And if their suspect seems unbelievable, he's no more unbelievable than the fourteen-foot-deep hole which has mysteriously appeared in a local farm. Of course, the 'little green man' concept is only Oterchanga police humour. He could just as easily be a psychedelic purple or bright red, one police officer pointed out. But, whatever colour he is, he's certainly the only suspect, so far unearthed, for the sinister hole-digging crime.'*

This strange scenario had apparently occurred on more than one property. The first victims were a local farmer, Mr. Shields, and his share milker, Mr. Singh. On the night of the 3rd/4th September, they saw an orange object pass across the sky. It was smaller than the moon, but its bright halo was enough to obscure the moon and a bright planet nearby. They went to bed, and heard nothing that night. Further their dogs didn't appear to have been disturbed.

The next day, they noticed a hole, a foot wide and fourteen feet deep, about 100ft to 120ft away from a homestead, and mid-way between two fences on their 'cattle race' property. They were at a loss to explain it, as the ground was too muddy and inaccessible for a tractor or drilling apparatus. The green turf around the top had been clearly cut, and they pointed out that whoever dug the hole would have needed a very long shovel. Further, what had they done with the dirt, which it was estimated would have been 400 – 500lbs?

The police said they weren't even sure they wanted to catch the culprit, as besides other considerations, *'they couldn't be too sure what to charge him with'.*

Despite hilarity on the part of the press, the 'Otorohanga Hole' did exist, and experts from New Zealand's 'SACTU' were visiting the scene to investigate. They verified that the hole was in fact nine inches wide and fifteen feet deep, with a second hole only two feet away and one foot deep. They were located, within a three feet radius, in a muddy area, with no footprints to be seen. The area was inaccessible to tractors or drilling apparatus, and the 'holes' had smooth sides right down, as if made by a rotating tool. No machine in the area was capable of doing that.

Multiple soil samples were tested. One expert stated that; 'the mud had been originally heated – definitely over 400° C, and probably less than 800° C.' He suggested that there was 'something strange' or unusual about the one sample, however, the cause of this anomaly, or its perpetrators, was never discovered.

This was not the first mysterious 'hole' to be discovered. Several years earlier, in late 1963 - early 1964, a similar anomaly was found half-way across the world on the Isle of Wight.

The Bomb Disposal Squad was called to Puckwell Farm, at Niton, where in a field another mysterious hole, two feet wide and fifteen feet deep, had suddenly appeared. At first it was thought that maybe a bomb, from World War II, had landed there, fallen in a fissure, and somehow been covered and protected by a layer of rock. It was speculated that it could have been undiscovered, and ploughed over for years. No bomb was found, nor was any explanation for the 'hole'.

Its' similarity to the 'Otorohanga Hole' may be more than a co-incidence. British researcher, Leonard Cramp, visited the field, and noted that some connection with a space object could not be ruled out.

One of the earliest modern reports of 'little green men', came in 1947, from Italian artist Prof. Rapuzzi Johannis. On 14th August he was hiking in a mountainous region between Italy and Yugoslavia, when through the rocks, he saw a bright red, 'roundish' object, about ten feet in diameter.

Standing next to it were two small figures, which he first thought were 'boys' as they were no more than three feet tall. He walked towards them, but stopped in fright when he realised they were anything but normal.

Their skin was green, and they had huge yellow-green eyes on their outsize, hairless heads. Their mouths were wide and slit-like, and in some ways their faces reminded Johannis of a fish or frog. His later sketches of the beings indicated that they were covered by some kind of belted 'bodysuit' with separate footwear.

Johannis was an amateur rock collector, but when he waved his geologist's pick at the strange pair, they must have misunderstood. One of them touched his belt, and a strange ray or 'puff of smoke', with the force of an electric shock, knocked Johannis to the ground, temporarily stunning him.

As he lay there, unable to move, the two beings went back to their craft, which noiselessly took off and disappeared.

Only a year later, in 1948, investigators in Tasmania were a little unsure of whether to laugh, or take seriously, a report from two women who lived in Berriedale. Mrs Duffy and her sister were putting the dog out, when they became aware of a bright light hovering directly overhead. As it moved away, they could see three 'little green men' who were sitting on the rim of a disc-shaped object. They were singing, in unintelligible words to the tune of 'Three Blind Mice'! They watched for a few minutes until the craft moved away to the west.

In 1964, the *'Flying Saucer Review'* published the following account taken from the Newcastle-upon-Tyne *'Journal'*.

'Flashes....loud buzzes in the night.....little green men chasing each other around haystacks....egg-shaped flying saucers.....No, the leprechauns aren't loose, and it's no Irishman telling this tale....just the good people of Felling.'

The 'Tyneside Unidentified Flying Objects Society' were investigating several reports from witnesses at Leam Lane Estate, where a brightly glowing, egg-shaped object, accompanied by a buzzing noise, was seen in the sky, before flying off.

Fourteen-year-old David Wilson said; "I saw several small green creatures, about two feet high, running around a haystack on a farm near the estate." David's parents and friends described him as a truthful boy, who would not invent anything of this nature; *'But not everyone believes the stories. Last night, Mr. M. Coates, headmaster of Roman Road junior school, denied that he had called a special assembly of pupils to discuss the little green men, or that he had told the children to stay away from the farm. He said: "There is no truth at all in these silly rumours."*

In my book, *'Contact Down Under'*, I wrote about a 1944 case from Christchurch, New Zealand.

Mrs. Church had gone for a walk behind the Sanatorium where she worked, when she encountered an 'up-turned saucer', where she saw some 'little green men', each about four feet tall, in 'plastic cases'.

One was standing outside the craft, and another in a 'doorway window'. All of their heads were large, and out of proportion to their bodies, and she soon realised that they were not 'Japanese' or a similar Asian race, as she had first thought.

Once they saw her, the 'beings' went back inside the flat based craft, which had a dome on top. It was a dull aluminium colour, ten to twenty feet in diameter, and about nine feet high. On top was a 'mast', nearly two feet tall, which emitted a blue light before the object made a 'whirring noise' and took off, rising vertically into the sky, and disappearing into the clouds.

RUSSIAN DIPLOMACY

I can remember reading an article written by one of the scientists working in an early Antarctic research base. He said that one day they were invited over to the Russian settlement. As soon as they arrived, the jovial Russian senior officer produced a large bottle of vodka, and it was several hours before they staggered back to base.

In the March 1961, *'Flying Saucer Review'*, investigator Nikita Schnee wrote about the contact experience of a Red Army officer in the USSR. A lot of this article was taken directly from the officer's written statement, and does give us some idea as to how the memories of contactees are erased.

'The event took place at the end of May, or beginning of June, 1978. A high-ranking officer of the Soviet Army was walking away from Pyrogovskoye Lake. Suddenly he found himself being taken by the arms on both sides. When he looked around, he saw two men in dull-coloured, cellophane-like garments. One of them said; "We'd like to talk to you. It'll take just a few seconds. Everything we'll talk about will be erased, and you'll forget it".'

The officer considered for a moment, and said; "I've nothing against talking with representatives of another civilisation." The next thing he remembered was being at a table in a dome-like room. The walls were bright, and he wondered if the light was coming from within them. He saw two figures sitting there, but only has a hazy memory of their faces. Part of the room opposite him was dark, but he could make out more tables with buttons and a big screen similar to a TV set.

He was already wondering how to prevent them from erasing the memory from his brain. *'I had to try one of our old customs. I said; "It's a rule here to celebrate, (to wet), such important meetings with a drink."*

When they brought something which tasted like salty lemonade, he realised that would not 'do the trick', and suggested that such celebrations required a somewhat stronger liquor. *"They enquired with interest what kind of liquor we drank and requested an explanation of its character. I remembered the formula for alcohol, and asked for a pencil and paper."*

They told him that was not necessary, as he could write with his finger on a black misty wall, which felt like velvet to the touch. After he wrote the structure and formula for alcohol, one of them said; "We'll make it right away", and came back with a glass and gave it to him.

"How's this," I asked, "that such a highly developed civilisation does not use something like this?" One of them replied; "Maybe if we'd used it we would never have been so highly developed!"

"I went on to ask why they did not help Earth's people in their struggle against evil. "What evil?" they asked, to which I replied; "Against poverty, fascism, the rich and so on". Their answer to that was if they help the poor, then for the same reason they will have to give help after some time to the poor riches. So in the end, it will be difficult to know to whom to give help. They will either have to exterminate everybody, or let everybody be and let life on Earth go on the way it goes. They are not going to interfere, they are just watching us."

The conversation seemed to go on for about three hours, although he couldn't remember everything that was said. One of them indicated that they were now going to erase his memory, and went over to a switchboard, and started pressing some buttons. Obviously it was not going as planned. He was removing his hand and pressing again. There were 'pulses' jumping about on a small screen.

"I asked what was wrong, and was told that usually, after a conversation, the strongest pulses come from that part of the brain which has been affected by the conversation. It is these pulses that they erase, but now strong pulses are coming from many different parts, and he doesn't know which ones to erase. He could erase the wrong pulses by mistake, leaving untouched those that should be erased. In the end, he tells me not to let anyone know anything I am able to remember."

Next thing he recalled was standing back in the same place he was when the two men had taken hold of him, it was as though only seconds had passed, but thanks to the alcohol, he still retained some memory. He went home and told his wife. Although she begged him not to tell anybody, he mentioned it at work to be met with gales of loud laughter.

CATTLE ROUND-UP

Investigator John Pinkney published the following report in 1993, and I am still not sure whether this really happened, but I think he genuinely believed Les, the witness, who by that time was 70, and getting on in years.

In 1964/5 he was mustering at a property west of Bundaberg in Queensland. One evening, after dinner, he and ten colleagues were sitting on the property owner's veranda, when they heard a loud humming noise.

"We raced around the back, and saw a big blue ball with a shadowy figure inside, hovering over a gum tree. The ball was changing shape all the time, and seemed to be in trouble. As we watched, it sort of shivered – and settled to the ground. I was so scared, I fired my gun at the thing.

"The bullet set off a huge explosion that knocked us all flat, and set the tree on fire. There was a two-rail fence about 200 metres from where we stood – and even that caught alight. Then this brown oblong creature came out of the flames and ran at us. I pumped some more bullets into it. It grunted and ran off."

Les said that sometimes, when they were mustering, big silver discs would hover overhead. *"The cattle knew all about it. There was one road they refused to set foot on. An old bloke named George Madsen, who lived in a hut nearby, told me why. He said he'd watched a flying saucer hovering above the road, and unravelling a sort of green carpet stretching for about a kilometre.*

"George was so scared he locked himself in his hut. In the morning he heard birds screaming and calves bellowing. When he looked outside, he saw they were stuck to the 'grass stuff'. As he watched, the big disc came back and reeled the 'flypaper' material back in, with all the animals struggling to get off."

Les also said that on another occasion, a small domed disc came down and hovered over a fishing hole. Soon after a larger disc descended and sucked all the water out, leaving nothing but a few dead fish on the bottom.

He said that at the time, the local media were receiving many reports from out west, 'but the details were too weird for the newspapers to publish them.'

A WELCOME ABDUCTION

Following articles in Brazilian newspapers, including *'A Noite'*, on 18th September 1962, Gordon Creighton reported how, over the previous few weeks, flying saucers had carried off a total of 17 chickens, six pigs and two cows from the Barcelos district. Finally, on the night of 16th September, Senhor Telemaco Xavier, the local referee, was seen being abducted, by beings from a landed saucer, after a football match.

Gordon, who had a great sense of humour, added his own postscript; *'In view of Brazil's great prowess at football, it is regrettable to have to record that Senhor Xavier had apparently shown much bias in his refereeing, and had helped the visiting team to win, incurring thereby the wrath of the local populace. It would be nice to think that lurking UFO entities, observing the game, had been equally incensed by this display of poor sportsmanship. But the truth may well be that – like the cows, pigs and chickens – Senhor Xavier was wanted for the pot!'*

'A SONG FROM OUTER SPACE'

In July 1957, the Blue Mountains, west of Sydney, experienced several nights of UFO sightings, which I discussed in my book *'Contact Down Under'*. Despite multiple witnesses, having watched from Echo Point, near 'The Three Sisters', a local cliff formation, an Air Force Squadron Leader was dispatched to the area, making an official determination that all scores of people had been watching was 'the star Canopus'.

Local residents were disgusted, and a short time later, at the annual banquet of the local Apex Club, 120 members stood and sang the following song to the tune of 'Waltzing Matilda'.

'The Song from Outer Space'

Once a jolly Martian parked up in his spaceship,
Under the sky near the Sisters Three,
And he sang as he sat and waited till his vision cleared,
"You'll come a-flying , O Apex , with me."

Chorus: Spaceman to Apex, Spaceman to Apex,
You'll come a-flying, O Apex with me.
And you'll look and you'll watch and wait for me at Echo Point,
You'll come a-flying, O Apex with me.

Up came the papers, looking for a news flash,
Up came the Air Force – one, two, three,
Where's the Jolly Martian, Apex has in hiding,
You'll come a-flying, O Apex with me.

.Chorus: Spaceman to Apex....

Up jumped the Martian, and sprang into his spaceship.
You'll never take me alive, says he.
And his ghost may be heard if you listen in at Echo Point,
You'll come a-flying, O Apex with me.

Chorus: Spaceman to Apex....

CHAPTER FIFTEEN

THE WEIRD AND WACKY

PART TWO

THE ALIENS MADE US DO IT!

Fred Dickenson's *'Scientific Approach to Cosmic Understanding'* group in New Zealand published an interesting report in 1968.

Two Taradale youths had leapt out of their car, seconds before it crashed into a fruit shop window. Mr. Walker, one of the local residents, said that he ran outside as soon as he heard the crash, and saw the two boys who were hobbling from the scene, and trembling with fear.

It later transpired that after the lads had heard an explosion near the town dump, and seen a massive flashing object, rising from the ground, they reported the incident to local police, who laughed at them. After that, they set out on a regular 'UFO hunt', and the police laughed again when they made a second report.

Not to be deterred, they spotted another strange craft, and started following it around the town. Obviously, whatever intelligence that was operating the object, had enough of being trailed, and dive bombed the two youths in their car.

Mr. Walker, who employed one of the lads, said they told him that they were travelling at about 30 to 40 mph, when one called out; "Bail out, it's got us...." and they both jumped. He told researchers the boys didn't want to talk about it anymore.

Napier Police, however, were more forthcoming, and had decided to accept the boys' excuse. They admitted that at least two constables had confirmed seeing strange lights in the sky, and many residents, who would no longer travel alone after dark, were jittery about flashing lights in the night sky, and ominous rumblings around the hills.

When Dow, the 19 year-old driver, who was none-the-less charged with dangerous driving in the Napier Magistrate's Court, Mr. Monaghan, who appeared on the lad's behalf, noted that as his passenger leapt from the vehicle, he kicked Dow's feet, causing him to lose control of the car.

After hearing considerable evidence of the youngsters' hunt for UFOs, the Magistrate, Mr. W. Dougall, declined Mr. Monaghan's offer to provide independent witnesses to the sightings of unusual objects in the sky, and dismissed the charge.

OFFICER - ARREST THOSE ALIENS!!

On 3rd September, 1974, newspapers *'Diario Popular'* and *'Diario da Tarde'* in Curitiba, Brazil, reported that a local fisherman from Navegantes, had told police that his wife had been kidnapped by aliens from a UFO.

Apparently, the previous Saturday night, he and his wife were taking a stroll along the beach, when they saw a strange craft descending from the sky. It looked like two plates, with the rims stuck together, and gave off lights of various colours. Suddenly, it silently swooped down, and landed close by. Before Azevedo and his wife could get away, a brilliant light came from the object, and temporarily paralysed them.

They were helpless as three small beings emerged from the craft, and after examining both of their victims, seized Azevedo's wife and carried her into the craft, which took off and disappeared at great speed.

A distraught Azevedo raced to the police station, and described the kidnappers as wearing greenish overalls. He couldn't describe their faces, but said they 'reflected the colour of the clothes they wore'.

At first the police thought that Azevedo was mentally deranged, and didn't believe him, even suspecting some foul play on his part. Their attitude changed when they discovered another fisherman's wife had been 'taken', from the same beach, in a similar incident two months earlier.

Rio de Janeiro's newspaper *'O Dia'* of July 5th 1974, wrote of how Jose Uchoa wanted police to charge two entities with dangerous driving, and leaving the scene of an accident.

Jose, who had been found lying at the side of the road, was unconscious, and in a serious condition. He was taken to hospital, where he said his injuries were caused by 'a direct lack of skill by the pilots of a flying saucer!' The doctors suspected that a powerful blow – from a car – to his head, had affected his brain.

Eventually, after his continual insistence that he was telling the truth, they listened to his story. Apparently, the simple farmhand had met two strange men, dressed in reddish, luminous clothes, who asked him if he would like to see a flying saucer. After being a little startled, he said that he would. They told him to walk along the Brasilia Highway, a kilometre away, the next day, at a given time.

'The following day, Jose set out as instructed, and when he saw a light some distance ahead of him, he began to walk more briskly in eager anticipation, only to be struck down by a violent blow as the object passed by.

'And in his words; "They went off, fearing something had happened. And me, I want to lodge a complaint with the police!"

LITTLE NUDE MEN

On 8th July 1968, Canada's *'Ottawa Journal'* carried a report of a Quebec farmer, 73 year-old Emile Desbiens, who had seen a large burning object, which illuminated the sky, fall into his field. He was standing guard, with a loaded shotgun, over a hot, egg shaped piece of rock in the middle of a burned patch of grass, and was waiting for federal authorities to come and examine it. A few days earlier, hundreds of people in a nearby village had seen a 'strange tumbling ball of fire' falling from the sky. It had also been seen as far away as Vermont, Maryland and Ohio on the U.S. Atlantic coast.

Most people would think that this was probably meteorite activity, but another co-incidental event happened on Tuesday 2nd July, the same day the 'fireball' fell to earth. *'Montreal La Presse'* quoted Constable Michel Michaud, of the Quebec Provincial Police, who said that they had received several calls reporting a bunch of 'little nude men' running along a country road. Society usually frowns upon people running around without clothes. He and a fellow policeman arrived on the scene in time to see these 'little nude dwarves' jump into a ditch and flee, after which they mysteriously disappeared, and not one was ever caught. - The mind boggles!

AN UNWINNABLE LAW SUIT

Ever since 1947, there has been much evidence proffered that some extraterrestrial craft have crashed, and the aliens who survived taken prisoner. Researcher, Patrick Huyghe, wrote of how, after more than twenty-five years had passed, Larry Bryant, one of the administrators of 'Citizens Against UFO Secrecy' – 'CAUS', served a writ of Habeas Corpus on the Air Force, claiming that they had maintained custody over one or more occupants, dead or alive, of crashed flying saucers. They had been detained illegally, and denied the due process of law.

Bryant cited an authentic FBI memo, dated March 1950, which noted that the Air Force had recovered three flying saucers in New Mexico, each of which contained the bodies of three-foot-tall humanoids, dressed in fine metallic cloth. Even if deceased, they had the right to be claimed intact by their relatives.

Captain John Whittaker, appearing for the defence, denied that the Air Force had, nor ever had, any extraterrestrial beings or spacecraft. When the case was heard in the Washington District Court, Bryant stated that the evidence was 'a smoking gun'.

"Do you have anything else but smoke?" asked Oliver Gash, the sceptical judge, who was over 80, and although he thought the case to be imaginative, considered it was without merit.

Bryant explained that all the witnesses were sworn to an oath of secrecy, preventing them from giving evidence. The assistant U.S. attorney, Royce Lamberth, representing the Air Force, then won the case on a technicality; "The person bringing the writ, or his attorney, has to be authorised. Obviously, since the applicants have never talked to these extraterrestrials, or met with them, they cannot represent them!"

Bryant said he would not give up, and would have to reconsider his next strategy.

MURDER AND THEFT?

Sometimes we just cannot be sure of how accurate a report really is, and if so do the craft or 'beings' originate from alien or more human agencies?

In 1999, Glenn Schiller came out of the woodwork to support a Dr. Jonathon Reed who was not believed when he reported a similar incident in 1996. Glenn had only been ten years old when this occurred in 1951.

He was walking across a field with a friend when they noticed some birds circling over a patch of woods, about three hundred yards away. Usually that indicated something had died, and they went to investigate. On the way, they saw an object lying in the field. This 'craft' was on the ground, with one end flat, and the other elevated approximately two to three feet. Although the area was tall with weeds, there were no tracks or marks to indicate how it had got there, except perhaps from above. He had walked through that field nearly every day, and knew it hadn't been there before.

He carefully examined the object, and pounded on the sides, noticing it was cooler than the surrounding atmosphere. When he found a stick and tried to clear the tall grass and weeds from under the elevated side, he encountered some type of 'resistant' force in the air, which appeared to be emanating from the craft. He and his friend agreed they would show Glenn's father the object when he got home from work.

They left the object and continued on towards the woods, taking a trail through the middle of the trees. Below the circling birds, Glenn noticed what he first thought was a log;

"It was approximately the colour of a log. I then began to notice that it had legs, arms etc. I looked closer, and could see its mouth and its closed eyes. I saw that it was clothed in what I would now call a uniform-like outfit. The clothing was tight, or close to the skin, and in the area of its crotch...there was no indication or bulge that would normally define some form of sex gland. I would have guessed it to be a male, with that exception noted."

Glenn thought the creature was dead, and touched it on the chest, which felt hard and 'scale like'. It depressed in a normal manner, but appeared to be harder than expected, with an unusual thickness of the surface or 'skin';

"I did apply the same pressure a few more times, but with a stick. Then I leaned down, and with one of my fingers I opened one of its eyes. When I saw the vitality, the shine of the eye, I no longer thought that it was dead. I now thought that it might be sleeping...and backed off a couple of feet."

Glenn wondered if he might be in danger if the 'thing' woke up, and decided he should find a cage before examining it any further. He ran back across the field, and called out to his neighbour, Mr. Bembow, who always had 'unusual things' around his home. He asked for a strong cage, and as he was yelling out the description of the strange being, another neighbour, Mr. Theobald, heard the conversation.

"Mr, Theobald joined Mr. Bembow and they followed me back to the creature. I think Mr. Bembow's son, whose name was Billy, also joined us at that time.

"When we arrived back in the woods, the creature was still laying in the same position. They were trying to rationalise to me and themselves what they were looking at. At one point they thought that it was an animal...and I said; "animals don't wear clothes".

"...They were trying to rationalise the crispy and dark look of the skin, and said that it was an old dead person that had been there a long time. I said that I walked that trail nearly every day, and it had not been there before. I also pointed out that it was not even as tall as I was at ten years old."

Someone got the idea to cut the outfit to examine the rest of the body. They tried to cut it several times, but when they tried to cut from the neck area, they could only get through about three inches before the knife seemed 'dull', and they met some form of resistance. At times it would 'mend back together' again.

After a while they told Glenn to go home, as they were going to dispose of it, and he was too young to be there. He went back to the side of the road, and stood there with his sister, looking in the direction they had gone in with the creature;

"All of a sudden we heard a scream that was not like anything I had ever heard before. In the air, above the trees, in the direction they had gone, you could almost see the scream....There was a bubble like movement...a filmy clear bubble that filled the air and moved with the vibration of the horrible sound of the scream.

"When they returned, Billy Bembow said to me; "That thing wasn't dead. It gave them a hell of a time! Did you hear it scream? That thing was so fast, and it was strong."

When Mr. Bembow returned, he made the kids promise that they would forget about the incident, as if it never happened. They gave him their word, and then mentioned the strange craft, still lying in the field.

Glenn took them over to it, and after some investigation, they said it must be some form of construction equipment. They also encountered the area of 'resistance', and Mr. Theobald that this was not unusual, and he had heard of something like that being developed recently.

"One or two days passed. I came home from school one day, and Billy Bembow said to me; "You should have seen them. They tried to drill into that thing, then they tried to cut into it with a cutting torch. Nothing bothers that thing – they couldn't even scratch it."

A few days later, Glenn came home from school, and the object was gone. Further south than its original location, he found an area which looked as though it had been dug up. In the centre was a deep hole, and in it Glenn found a 'ball', about six or seven inches in diameter. It was very heavy, and looked like a crystal or diamond. When he got home, he went outside to wash the mud off it.

"Mr Theobald saw me and said; "What do you have there, Glenn?" He walked over and looked at it. It was unbelievable and shocking to me at the time, but he just reached down and took it. He said he knew who had lost it, and he was going to return it. This was in no way acceptable to me.

"I argued with him so loudly about it, that my mother heard us and came outside to see what the matter was. I accused him of stealing from me. My mother suggested strongly that I would not argue with him any longer, but would speak to my father about the incident when he returned from work."

Glenn's father did speak to Mr. Theobald, but Glenn never got his 'ball' back. In later years he became convinced that the disturbed area was an impact spot, and that the 'crystal or diamond ball' had a specific connection to the craft, and the strange being his neighbours had murdered.

In the 'good old days' the legal status of visiting aliens was subject to many differing viewpoints. In some American backwaters, local hillbillies would go out hunting them with shotguns, whilst in other Counties, the Sheriff would declare that was tantamount to murder.

In 1997, *'MUFON'* correspondent, Herbert Prouty, examined their legal status in some detail; *'The civil and criminal ramifications of killing an alien will depend on the facts and circumstances of how the alien was killed, and perhaps even on what type of alien was killed.'*

He suggested that the first consideration would be if the particular alien had 'human' or 'animal' status in relation to homicide or manslaughter statutes, which refer to the unlawful killing of a human being, and under what circumstances would it be excusable or justifiable?

The 'Nordic' type beings, who look similar to us, and display intelligence and humane characteristics, such as the ability to reason, and show compassion and sympathy for others, would most likely be deemed equal to our fellow citizens, and entitled to the protection of the law.

Reptilian, and other physically different visitors, may be in a different position, which has yet to be determined in a court of law. (Other than animals such as domesticated sheep and cattle, bred for meat, the killing of wild or many other animals is forbidden under environmental or cruelty laws.)

What about the Greys, who may be, as some believe, biological robots, devoid of any emotion? As Prouty points out, murder or manslaughter of foreign officials, official guests or internationally protected persons is prohibited by federal law. Are extraterrestrial entities ambassadors or officials of their planets and civilisations?

Since no government has officially recognised the existence of extraterrestrials, much less recognised them as a threat, or declared war against them, they cannot be placed in the category of 'enemy of the country'. Despite the accounts of assault, abductions, forcible medical procedures, killing and mutilation of livestock and violation of air space, each situation must be judged on its individual circumstances and merits.

Self defence is a justifiable excuse for killing another being, if one genuinely fears for his or her own safety, or in some cases to protect property from a trespasser, or damage such as cattle mutilations. Of course, the killing of an alien by the military or government agents, in the interests of 'national security', would never even be challenged.

Prouty also raised another interesting concept. Here on Earth, '*in case of a conflict, the higher law governs. For example, federal laws would generally govern over conflicting state laws, and some international laws would govern over national laws. It would seem logical that beings more intelligent than us have developed intergalactic laws and treaties, supreme over our laws, under which the slayer of an alien might be held responsible.*'

There were good reasons why the authorities did not want normal citizens shooting at what they believed to be 'aliens' and their craft.

In '*Aspects of UFOs and Aliens*', I wrote of a 1961 case from the U.S.A. In late November, four men, returning from a hunting trip, spotted what they thought was a landed aircraft, and later believed to be a UFO. After a fruitless representation to the local police, when the object had disappeared, they saw it again some 150 yards away from the road.

They crept towards it, and saw what appeared to be four human-type beings, wearing white coverall garments, standing around it. One of the hunters fired, hitting one of the occupants in the shoulder. He was helped up by a colleague, who looked over at the hunters, and yelled, in perfect English; "What the hell did you do that for?"

The hunters fled, realising they had probably made a terrible mistake!

AN ALIEN SPY?

There have always been disputes between researchers, especially as to whether extraterrestrial visitors are friendly, or a danger to our society.

In 1978, in Germany, Herr Woerner had run the 'UFO Studio' in Mayern, and Karl Veit the 'German Society of UFO Studies' in Weisdbaden. They had been good friends for years, co-operating on investigations and sharing information. In 1972 they had their first disagreement, when Karl Veit insisted the aliens were our friends, who only wanted to help us and prevent a devastating nuclear war.

Herr Woerner was adamant in his opposition; "*The visitors, far from wanting to avert an atomic war on earth, are simply waiting for one to start. Then, when most of the human population has been wiped out, they will move in and take over the world.*'

Later, Woerner, having heard the allegations of 'inhabitants of the inner earth', changed his stance; '*They do not come from space, they have bases deep in the earth...I presume you will now put an end to you previous activities, and cease to end as a mouthpiece for these Satanic powers.*'

When Karl Veit ignored him, Woerner took out a summons in the Frankfurt State Court, charging Veit with 'spying for extraterrestrial powers'.

On 22nd August, '*The Sunday Express*' quoted a court spokesman as saying; "*There is no question of throwing this case out as frivolous. It is most unusual, but Herr Woerner and Herr Veit are both serious men, and Herr Woerner clearly believes he has grounds for complaint.*

"*Our problem is that espionage cases are usually handled by the Federal Public Prosecutor, but he already has his hands full with cases concerning earthbound spies and terrorists. In any case, this is the first time any court, anywhere in the world, will have to deal with alleged space spying....I suppose, in this day and age, it had to come sometime!*"

WELCOME SPACELINGS!

Some citizens and 'off-beat' groups want to welcome, perhaps unwisely, any aliens who arrive on Earth.

On 3rd June 1967, St. Paul, in Canada, as part of the 'Canadian Centennial Projects', held the official opening of its 'St. Paul Flying Saucer Landing Pad'.

The original idea was conceived by William Treleavan of Dominion Foundries and Steel Co., Ontario, and Ken Reed from the International Harvester Co. in Calgary. The St. Paul Chamber of Commerce supported the idea, and accepted an offer from Car Quells Construction Co. to build it as their Centennial Project.

The project attracted a lot of local enthusiasm, with industrial, business and professional concerns giving practical help. The concrete-steel construction weighed over 130 tons, and the resultant oval-shaped 'pad', built on an 8ft high main column, was 30ft by 40ft in diameter.

It attracted the interest of, among others, *'Time Magazine'*, the *'Calgary Herald'*, and the *'BBC Television Services'*.

In an editorial, the *'Calgary Herald'* wrote in support of the project, and took a 'dig' at the 'debunkers' at the same time; *'Perhaps the reason for hesitancy on the part of pilots of flying saucers to land their craft on Earth has been uncertainty over whether they would be welcome. Nothing could be better designed to convince them that we earthlings would love to communicate with them, than this building of a welcome mat for them in the form of the saucer landing pad.'* Unable to resist a swipe at the sceptics, they added; *'In addition to the main pad for saucers, we suggest space should be provided, marked 'For Swamp Gas Only', so that all contingencies will be provided for!'*

The opening day was accompanied by a great deal of fanfare, with a Royal Canadian Air Force fly-past, helicopters bringing dignitaries and dropping miniature UFOs, the arrival of a realistic 'UFO' manned by suitably attired 'astronauts', and an auction of reserve land parcels on a sub-division on the planet Mars, with the proceeds going to the 'Retarded Children's Fund'. Local stores and restaurants joined in, and the native Indians performed smoke signals and dances to attract the Martians.

Paul Hellyer, Canada's then Minister of National Defence, cut the ribbon. He had a personal interest in ufology, and in dedicating the pad, in effect, to all Canadians, he said; *"It is with rather a curious sense of pride that I am dedicating the flying saucer pad. I say 'curious' because, as Minister of National Defence, I am fully aware that although most have been explained away, there have been some unidentified flying objects which have not been explained in terms of natural phenomena."*

But, this wasn't the first designated 'landing zone' in Canada. A month later, on 20th July 1967, Paul Hellyer told the *'Ottawa Journal'* what had, until then, been a 'Top Secret UFO Project'. Thirteen years earlier, the Canadian government had made available the Defence Research Board Experimental Station at Suffield, Alberta, as a landing site for Unidentified Flying Objects.

He stated that no extraterrestrial flying objects ever sought to land on this 1,000 square-mile restricted tract of land, over which no aircraft, defence or civilian, was allowed to fly without special permission. The idea behind the classified project was that if any UFO tried to make contact with Earth, it could land at the DRB station without being shot down by defence interceptors.

William Retoff wrote of another 'landing zone', which eventuated a few years later, in 1976, out of the 'United States Bicentennial'. Over 2,000 residents of Lake City, Pennsylvania, raised $6,000 to erect a 'flying disc terminal', following several sightings over their small community.

Mounted five feet above the terrain, on an isolated plot in the town park, just off Lake Erie, they fabricated a flat, seeded pad of earth. It was 100ft in diameter, and encircled by three concentric rings of red, white and blue lights. Just for good measure, a communications centre was added in case any radio messages were received.

Although it is not known if any extraterrestrials availed themselves of the facility, it attracted crowds of curious onlookers. The President of the local Chamber of Commerce, James Meeder, said; "I am sure we benefited from an economic standpoint, but I think we benefited more from the way the UFO project brought people together.

Some years earlier, commencing in 1973, a much more sophisticated 'landing area', in the 'hilly zone', northwest of Austin, Texas, was owned and operated by 'Project Starlight International', (PSI), an offshoot of the 'Association for the Understanding of Man'.

A 100ft circular area had a ring of 91 lights around the circumference, with a white-light 'flasher', capable of emitting code pulses, in the centre. Ray Standford, the project's director, was very proud of their $20,000 laser visual system, capable of visual communications with UFOs. In 1979, they added a 400 acre experimental district and a computer and radar tracking unit, with an optical equipment centre at their disposal. Although there had been several sightings over the facility, 'PSI' didn't say if any 'visitors' had landed.

During those heady days, the prospect of alien visitors, gave rise to many 'spiritual type', pseudo religions. In 1978, Wayne Aho, president of the 'New Age Foundation', announced they were dedicating a 14 acre tract of their land, on the lower region of Mt. Rainier, Washington, as a 'neutral zone' to entice aliens from space to land. He felt that the upsurge of UFO sightings was due to our development of nuclear weapons, and said he had 'requested the nation's armed forces to recognise and respect the neutrality of the New Age Zone'. (Good luck with that!)

"I WAS JUST HUNTING FOR UFOs"

In 1994, young Matthew Bevan from Wales, spent his nights at home, surfing on-line forums with nothing but his 'Commodore Amiga 1200'. It was still the days of expensive 'dial-up' internet, but he soon learned that by using a black market program, he could by-pass the phone company and use the net for free.

He found several bulletin boards discussing UFOs, and soon developed some cyberspace contacts who mentioned classified files on NASA and other top secret military sites.

Researcher, Ryan Sprague, noted that it didn't take Bevan long to master the art of hacking, and using the pseudonym 'Kuji', his first success was the 'Force Level Execution System', (FLEX), which was located at the Rome Laboratory at Griffiths Air Force Base, New York. He abandoned this particular exercise when he realised that with a little more effort he would have the potential to *singlehandedly launch missiles from the base.*

He confined his activities to searching for space related activities, and downloaded dozens of encrypted files from NASA's Goddard Space Flight Centre. These didn't really satisfy his quest for UFOs, so he turned his attention to the Wright Patterson Air Force Base in Ohio, where it was rumoured the wreckage of a crashed UFO was stored. Also he was looking for any records from 'Project Blue Book', purportedly conducted from that Base.

One of the systems' accounts wasn't even password protected, and soon he had access to emails between employees, discussing various projects, including diagrams of a prototype which seemed to use anti-gravity propulsion, similar to that theorised to be employed by UFOs.

He ended his covert activities at that stage, and thought no more of it until, in 1996, when several officers from Scotland Yard came to the office where he worked, and arrested him for hacking into the American facilities. He was running the risk of being charged with espionage, however whilst the police considered he was probably an 'X-Files idiot', they had to decide how to formally prosecute him.

In order to do this, the U.K. authorities needed specific details from the Americans as to exactly what information Bevan had stolen. Because the U.S. government were unwilling to reveal any secrets, the case against Bevan was dropped in 1997. Whilst he escaped with no more than 'a slap on the wrist', he was told that if he ever set foot on American soil, he would be arrested on the spot.

You would have thought that the Americans would have learned their lesson, and tightened up their cyber-security, but later, another British citizen, Garry McKinnon, was convicted of espionage in the U.S.A. He claimed that when he hacked into many of their government computers, he was just hunting for evidence of suppressed technology, and that UFOs actually existed; "I wanted to find out stuff the government wouldn't tell you about," he said.

His ingenuity was amazing. In 2001/2, he sat down, at his North London address, with just his home computer and a limited 56k modem. His computer programming experience came in useful, and he discovered that many U.S. top security systems were using an insecure 'Microsoft Windows' program that had no password protection at all;

"So I got commercially available off-the-shelf software, and used them to scan large military networks – anything that I thought might have possible links to UFO information."

Using the name 'Solo', he hacked into computers at the Pentagon, NASA and the Johnson Space Centre, as well as systems used by the U.S. Army, Navy and Air Force.

In a later interview with *'The Guardian'*, he made some astonishing claims; *"I knew that governments suppressed anti-gravity, UFO related technologies, free energy or what they call zero-point energy. This should not be kept hidden from the public when pensioners can't pay their fuel bills."*

He eventually was able to access the 'US Space Command' network, where he found evidence of an extraterrestrial mission; *"I found a lot of officers' names, under the heading 'Non-Terrestrial Officers'. What I think it means is not earth-based. I found a list of 'fleet-to-fleet transfers' and a list of ships' names.*

I looked them up. They weren't US Navy ships. What I saw made me believe they have some kind of spaceship, off-planet."

Furious U.S. officials claimed he caused $700,000 worth of damage, and even crippled vital defence systems shortly after the September 11 attacks. In March 2002, when arrested by British police, he defiantly stated that he was being made a scapegoat by U.S. authorities to deter other would-be hackers, rather than addressing their own security flaws. Regardless of this argument, he was extradited to the United States, where he was swiftly convicted and jailed.

HOAXES

Hoaxes, some of them for nefarious reasons, and very skilfully perpetrated, have always plagued serious researchers in their investigations.

Reuter's newsgroup published the following press release in its Latin press; *'Lima, August 7th 1965; Authorities in that capital had recently arrested a band of dangerous cat-burglars, led by an individual nick-named 'Pygmy'. They had been masquerading as 'Martians', and taking advantage of the current fantastic wave of flying saucer reports to Lima, they had fitted themselves out with 'space-suits', and had perpetrated a series of bold armed robberies and attacks against householders.'*

Investigators were far from happy or amused, when the following advert appeared in the *'Philadelphia Inquirer'* in November 1974;

'FOR SALE: SIMULATED SAUCER. Be the first in your block to create a real scare. Breaks down quickly and packs in ordinary station wagon for fast getaway. Glows in many colours and provides simulated radiation effect. Saucer creates radio and TV interference in 1.5km radius. Will not fly, and is not to be confused with CIA models. Set up saucer beside a road, and watch for fast results! Then be the first on the scene to 'investigate' the sighting and get fat interviews with newspapers and big time UFO researchers'.

Over the years, some mischievous pranksters just could not resist the urge to perpetrate a hoax on their fellow citizens. In 1970, Orson Wells was interviewed on the 'Dean Martin Show' regarding his infamous 'War of the Worlds' radio broadcast on 30th October 1938.

He had no idea at the time that it would cause such an uproar; *"Radio, at that time, before the tube and transistor, wasn't just a noise in somebody's pocket, it was a voice of 'Authority'. Too much so – and I thought it was time to 'take the mickey' out of some of its authority. Hence my broadcast, 'The War of the Worlds', which informed the public that Martians had landed in New Jersey, and were taking over the country."*

He noted that it was Halloween at the time; *"In my Middle Western childhood, that was the season for pranks; for soaping windows, for putting farmer Perkin's cow up in the belfry, - at least dressing up in a sheet and spooking the neighbours with a pumpkin head."* Not realising the consequences, he thought this was a time to say '*BOO*' to several million people over the network.

First, a musical program was interrupted by a 'news flash' that an unidentified object had landed on a farm near Groversville, Jersey, and police and state troopers were hurrying to the scene. This was followed by more of the musical broadcast, but not for long.

"Now, no news commentator was ever so convincing, as were our actors at their mythical posts throughout the nation, describing the real live disaster and horrendous arrival of Martian Invaders."

Another actor impersonated President Roosevelt, supposedly from Washington, who told the nation to; 'Remain united and not panic.' Soon after, bewildered police arrived at the studio, not sure whom to arrest; *'The phones were jammed in all networks for days, and you couldn't find a Network President for weeks.'*

People must have forgotten it was Halloween, and soon, apparently thousands of them took to the streets, some claiming they had seen, and even been attacked by the 'Martians'. Reserve Officers in the Marines, rushed to their headquarters to report for active duty, and personnel on the Naval Fleet, which had just arrived in New York Harbour, had their shore leave cancelled.

In New Jersey, astonished motor cycle police, who did not have access to a radio, saw speeding motorists, who would not pull over, all making for the hills. It took six weeks for some of them to be assured it was a hoax, and persuaded to come back.

Orson Welles finalised by saying; *"There is a theory that this is my doing – that my job was to soften you up – to sell you all the notion that creatures from outer space landing in our midst is just a hoax. That way, as more and more of these new UFOs make contact with our unsuspecting planet, there will still be a tendency to laugh.*

"Not everybody laughs at them, there are still a lot of well attested sightings by highly reliable witnesses. Now everybody doesn't laugh anymore, but most people do........Ladies and gentlemen, go on laughing, you'll be happier that way. Stay happy as long as you can, until the day our new masters choose to announce that the conquest of Earth is complete!"

The ramifications of this event were more far-reaching than anticipated, with the authorities using this hoax, and the furore which ensued, as their excuse for later withholding all UFO and extraterrestrial information from the public.

After this fiasco, you would have thought that radio stations would have realised that this kind of prank was very unwise. Not so 'Radio Quito', one of Ecuador's most popular radio stations. Investigator Scott Corrales wrote of the memorable night of 12th February 1949, when director Leonardo Páez decided to repeat the hoax.

At 7pm, a musical show was interrupted by an announcement that a 'flying object' had been seen over the Galapagos Islands, with another break in the music, soon after, to advise listeners that a flying saucer had landed in the Cotocollao district, on the outskirts of the nation's capital.

'We are again interrupting our programming to inform our listeners that we are at war. Strange lights are arriving and attacking northern Quito at Cotocollao. Spinning discs can be seen with strange hostile beams who are destroying it all. There is fire everywhere, as well as casualties. Ladies and gentlemen, we are at war!'

A team of skilled voice actors impersonated the mayor and government ministers, with added sound effects to convey the realism. Alleged phone calls from neighbouring areas claimed a 'cloud of toxic fumes' was spreading over the Andean foothills.

People flocked to their local churches, however the police and military, which had initially been mobilised, soon realised the truth. They quickly and quietly returned to their headquarters, not wanting the humiliation of having succumbed to a radio prank.

As soon as the citizens discovered they had been fooled, busloads of enraged people arrived at Radio Quito's building in the city. After throwing bricks and debris at the facade, they set fire to the lobby, with the flames taking hold on the first floor, where the *'El Comercio'* newspaper had its offices, along with stacks of current newsprint. Leoponardo and his actors had to escape from the studio by jumping to the roof of a neighbouring building, and not all of them survived.

In all, the riot had reputedly cost up to twenty lives, and $350,000 of damage. Leonardo Páez fled to Venezuela, where he lived until his death in the early 1990s.

Scott Corrales also noted that; *'Four years earlier, a radio station in Santiago de Chile had broadcast its own adaptation of 'La Guerra de los Mundos', ('War of the Worlds'), with similar reports. Rumour has it that a regional governor had even tried to mobilize his forces to fight the 'alien menace'.'*

John Maybury, a New Zealand radio host, also made a rather costly mistake in mid-1952. Years later, he told the *'Star Sports & Magazine'* how, for a couple of hours one morning, he faked a broadcast of pre-recorded fictitious eye witness reports of a UFO hovering over Hagley Park in Christchurch. A prominent local Anglican priest, with a lively sense of humour, had helped him with the scam, so it seemed a really great idea at the time. Unfortunately, it backfired.

He had got away with a few silly pranks in the past, and only two weeks earlier the Managing Director had told him to 'give radio a lift – inject more personality into your broadcasts!' John took him at his word. At 6am he had the fictitious UFO travelling across the countryside and hovering over the park. By 8.30am he had crashed the saucer and reported little green men running for the trees.

Thousands of people flocked to the park. Some came from twenty miles out of the city, causing one of the biggest traffic jams Christchurch had ever seen. The city was in an uproar, and the telephones 'went mad'. All the time John was sitting in his 3ZB radio studio, blithely broadcasting his ill-fated hoax.

Maybury was ordered off air, and banished to the radio station's programme department. He resigned, and didn't get another radio announcer job for another eighteen months.

Sometimes, hoaxes regrettably gain 'official' sanction. On 2nd April 1977, 'The Australian' newspaper thought it hilarious that Central Coast radio station, 2GO, had pulled off a spectacular 'April Fools' Day Joke.'

They constructed a fake spaceship, and sneaked it out onto the water, before announcing that a flying saucer had landed nearby. Residents left their beds, and drove to the scene. Police cordoned off the area, and CB operators broadcast the news interstate. Shire Councillors made statements, and unfortunately, *'the President of the local UFO organisation said he had seen it land'*. (Luckily, not me!)

'Mr. Bob Scott, the General Manager of 2GO, said; "The police and Emergency Services began checking it out after a while, but played along. When we called it out at 9am, there were a few red faces. The only ones who didn't laugh were the people from the UFO Club. They said we'd set them back 20 years, and the President was furious for being made a fool."

Twenty years later, when there was a genuine 'UFO flap' over the Central Coast, the media, who were dependent on us for information, were much more circumspect in their approach.

On 30th January 1981, the Victorian *'Geelong Advertiser'*, carried another story about a very successful hoax, perpetrated the previous day, by the local radio station's promotions manager, and the nearby movie drive-in.

The three metre high, silver fibreglass craft was donated for the stunt by a local firm, and placed overnight in a paddock near Moe, 139km east of Melbourne. The next morning, radio station 3UL, interrupted their broadcast five times, between 6am and 8.30am, to announce the landing of a spacecraft. Mr. Alistair Doherty, the General Manager, said; "I reported that the craft had landed in the paddock. I didn't say that it contained space-invaders – I let the peoples' imaginations work for themselves."

'Local police - who were in on the hoax – cordoned off the area, controlled the crowds flocking to the landing site, and sent urgent messages back to headquarters, requesting assistance dealing with the traffic and the extraterrestrial menace.'

After a couple of hours, astonished onlookers heard some sounds coming from the object. The conical top opened, and out came a 'Martian', in a pullover, holding a sign advertising a science fiction film being shown at the local drive-in.

Senior Sergeant, Bill Griffiths of Moe police commented; "The broadcasts were so realistic, that I had my superior officer jumping down the phone to find out how we were handling the situation."

My colleagues at VUFORS received three phone calls about 'the landing', but quickly recognised it as a prank. They, quite rightfully, commented; *'The main lesson to be gained by these experiences is that the officials will co-operate with the pranksters, which in this case was to gain a fast buck, but often refuse to do so when a serious case occurs.'*

In recent decades, companies have used 'ad-planes' to get out their message. Often they have an electronic message attached, usually controlled by an on-board computer. Often these flights are mistaken for a UFO, and although the pilots must keep a detailed flight-log, they sometimes get a giggle from the confusion they cause.

On the other hand, for many years bored university students have perpetrated often skilful, but usually harmless, hoaxes. They can cause problems to government agencies, and are certainly not welcomed by genuine investigators and researchers. Sometimes mature, responsible adults should have considered the consequences more carefully before practical joking!

On 6th September 1967, the *'Adelaide Advertiser'* wrote about a British university 'rag week' hoax that went further than intended.

Two student apprentices from the Royal Aircraft Establishment at Farnborough, manufactured some fake saucers, partly comprised of a fibreglass mould, mixed with aluminium powder, giving them a metallic appearance, which polished to a 'magnificent sheen'. The internal 'gadgets' were rigged to start 'bleeping' when the object was turned on its side.

Working in six teams, each of two students, they spread them out over various fields, in line, but in different localities, to give the impression that a 'flotilla' had landed there. One said; "We didn't mean to cause chaos – in fact we were rather surprised that it caused all this fuss!" But 'fuss' was what ensued.

The first 'saucer' was discovered by Wiltshire farmer, Richard Jenkins, in a field spread with fresh pig-muck. He telephoned the local police. P.C. Richard French, who initially took the call, thought it was a 'wind-up'; - "Are there any little green men, running around it?"

"No," Jennings replied, "or at least I 'aven't seen any, but it's ticking. You'd better come and have a look."

After the Chief Inspector, two Sergeants and several constables inspected the scene, they mumbled on about 'National Security', warned the press to stay away, and contacted the RAF Station at Colerne.

In 1968, my colleagues at *'Spacelink'* in the UK reported further on these events of the previous year; *'The RAF have had their leg pulled often enough before – but they still thought it worth sending Pilot Officer David Pepper and a driver. Probably, with his tongue in his cheek, Pilot Officer Pepper decided to hand it all over to the Army, and phoned the Bomb Disposal Unit at Tidswell, Wilts.*

'Southern Command immediately sent over its ammunition inspector, Capt. Fred Cantrell, with a corporal. Captain Cantrell made an on-the-spot decision to blow it up.

"Why blow it up?" I asked a witness. – "It's the Army," he said; "They always like blowing things up!"

The second saucer was found at 7.15am, by a newspaper delivery boy at Clevedon, ten miles from Bristol. He telephoned local police, and Constable Fred Pollard drove over to have a look. He didn't know how serious it all was, and picked up the strange object, and put it in his police car.

Back at the station, another Constable, Dennis Carter, thought it would be amusing to leave it on Sgt. John Durston's desk as a 'breakfast surprise'. As they turned it on its side, it let out a loud, ominous 'bleeping', and everybody fled.

Soon, the Police Inspector arrived to have a look, and called in Mr Greville Beale, from the Guided Weapons Department of the British Aircraft Corporation. While they were all gathered around, examining and photographing the strange object, the local garage owner, Michael Wilcox, interfered and dug a hole in the top.

'Out came a lot of smell, and a policeman jumped up and shouted; "It is a hoax!" By that time it was 5.30pm.'

The third saucer was discovered at 5.45am by a golf caddy at Bromley, Kent. *'Three policemen arrived, led by Inspector George Simmons, who let a sergeant and constable carry it back to Bromley Police Station.'*

They telephoned the Air Ministry, and followed their instructions, putting the object carefully down on the floor, and just watching. At 2pm, Detective Superintendent Ernest Barrett, from Scotland Yard's Forensic Division, took over. He called in his two explosive experts, who normally dealt with safe-blowings.

When, by nearly 5pm, they learned that the Air Ministry were not coming, Major Donald Henderson, one of the explosive experts, cut off the top with a hacksaw.

The U.S. Air Force took over Tullock Farm cornfield in Welford, near Newbury, when Saucer no. 4 was found near their base. Airmen were called in from RAF Abingdon, more U.S. servicemen joined in, and atomic scientists from Aldermaston were consulted about the bleeping object. Before they were advised it was a hoax, one scientist cut out a piece, and took it back to Aldermaston for testing.

The fifth object had been found at 8.30am near Ascot, Berkshire, and the local police picked it up in their van, and drove back to the police station. They had already heard about the kerfuffle at Newbury, and decided to put the 'saucer' in their backyard until they heard back from their colleagues, in case it really was a 'flying saucer'.

The sixth saucer was found at Queenborough, on the Isle of Sheppey, and proved to be the students' greatest success. The RAF flew a helicopter to one saucer, and airlifted it to its main research base. Air Ministry specialists rushed a portable X-ray machine to assist.

After the engineering experts had spent eleven hours, chiselling and hack-sawing their way into one disc, they found two car batteries, a British-made radio transmitter, and a six inch loudspeaker which was immersed in a gooey, smelly white liquid, which was later proved to be flour and water paste! Experts estimated that the components of each craft would have cost no more than twenty five pounds, apparently well within the means of mischievous students. They even had the audacity to demand their saucers back from the police, who refused, and made mention of the Director of Public Prosecutions, but were probably deterred from such action due to official embarrassment over the whole episode.

Once UFOs became a major and popular topic, hoaxes became more prevalent, usually perpetrated by the younger generation with time on their hands. They occurred all over the world.

In 1973, Tennessee railway workers found three helium-filled balloons, tied together in a package that included a tinfoil tail. No doubt they accounted for some of the sightings reported earlier.

A much more spectacular prank was carried off in the October of that year, when newspapers reported that a 'hullabaloo' broke out among 67,000 football fans at a Louisiana State University football game one Saturday night.

As it passed over the stadium, several thousand people started looking up at the bunch of lights, moving overhead, and shouted 'UFO!' It flew to the southwest, and was visible for over twenty minutes, with a police helicopter in hot pursuit.

All the local gendarmerie would say was that it was a solid, round, noiseless object, flat on the bottom, with a round transparent top; "We just did not know what it was. We are not allowed to give out any more information."

The next day, a newspaper cameraman, who used a telephoto lens to snap the object over the stadium, identified the object as a cellophane bag containing a candle that heated the air inside, carrying it aloft. Some experts doubted this explanation, as it was not affected by the helicopter's downdraft.

In Greenwood, Delaware, earlier that month, police had filed disorderly conduct charges against five firemen when they used a fire department generator to power orange lights covered by paper, and placed them in a wood, drawing 'thousands of spectators'.

Sometimes, those who should know better are guilty of this mischievous behaviour. British investigator, Jenny Randles, wrote of how, in 1989, the then young entrepreneur, Richard Branson, constructed a balloon, that looked like a classic flying saucer, piloted by a 'midget' in an alien silver suit.

His plan was to land it in central London as an 'April Fools' Day' prank, but unfortunately, that day the weather was not in his favour. The craft was blown off course, and landed early, in a field near a busy road.

The police responded to calls from a worried public, convinced they were witnessing a space invasion, only for the officers assigned to make 'first contact', left facing a stuntman. The cops edged backwards, and one later confessed that he'd never been so frightened in his career.

Jenny went on to note; *'Today, ironically, one of Sir Richard's own Virgin Atlantic Airbus 330's, carries the registration 'G-V UFO', as it plies the Atlantic route between Heathrow and the U.S. One wonders how many misperceptions this appropriately lettered jet has triggered?'*

Whilst authorities were clamping down on these practical jokers, some 'pranks', if they were pranks, were not quite so innocent.

As early as 1965, some 'hoaxes' had a more suspicious and sinister undertone. On 29th January 1965, Virginia newspapers in the USA, contained several articles articulating the danger of local hoaxes, which had 'gotten out of hand', and often resulted in armed residents going out to hunt aliens.

The next month, the *'Free Lance Star'* followed up with a debate as to the legality of shooting one of the 'little men'. The Attorney General, Robert Button, the local Sheriff, and Justice of the Peace John Goolrick articulated their points of view, and interpretation of the law. Apparently, one could not harm a 'person' without good cause, and Button had this to say;

"I do not know of anyone who has seen the little men sufficiently close to be able to specify whether or not they are 'persons'....Possibly some member of the Legislator from your area, if he has sufficient scientific knowledge to back up his beliefs, can have a definition added to our code as to whether these little men are 'persons'."

But were they all hoaxes? Were craft and their occupants landing in Virginia? One young amateur photographer claimed he had 'captured' a small alien on colour film. A fellow employee, at the local garage, claimed a government car had later come by and taken the young photographer to Washington.

In 1966, the Federal Aviation Authority, after disruptions to air traffic, brought in severe restrictions and fines for 'balloons', tethered or untethered. This followed a spate of teenage and student pranks in California, Michigan and Atlanta, one causing a fire in woodlands, which also threatened people's homes.

In the 1990s, hundreds of reports of 'orange lights' were received, and sometimes our own 'report' hot-line was flooded with calls. Most of these were common pranks, but in among these mysterious lights was something much more complex and interesting. In *'Contact Down Under'* I discuss the objects seen over Tom Price and other parts of Australia, that were definitely not pranks. In November 1996, similar orange lights to these were seen over Alice Springs, near the secretive base of Pine Gap. Investigating police found two military personnel, in plain clothes, in the process of launching another light, under a garbage type bag. Their van was full of the devices. What were the authorities trying to mask with their 'fake UFOs'?

This phenomena was not restricted to Australia. In New Zealand, in 2001, ever since the Kaikoura incident in 1978/9, these 'orange light' stunts had posed such a problem, that there were newspaper articles, (eg. *'The Timaru Herald'*, August 10th 2001), where the authorities explained the dangers these pranks posed, and how some perpetrators had already received suspended prison sentences and hefty fines. In Australia's Northern Territory, after these pranks caused the temporary closure of Darwin's main airport, their police also 'came out swinging'.

THE TEESDALE INHERITANCE

When 'A.F. Teesdale' passed away in the 1980's, he left a 'confession' that whilst serving as a soldier in World War I, he underwent a 'near-death' experience after a shell exploded near him. He alleged that he met a 'being', that called itself a 'sentinel' and gave him a curious object with instructions to hand it on to scientists. In a later encounter, the sentinel told him he would receive a second object.

Unfortunately, he was unable to interest anyone in these mysterious objects, so when he died, he apparently left the disposition of these objects to his trustees. They were to be given to a group seriously engaged in contacting and setting up relationships with extraterrestrials. In 1988, the alleged trustees placed an advert in a Paris magazine, in an attempt to locate a group that would satisfy the requirements of Teesdale's will.

Researcher, David Ritchie, wrote of the outcome; *'The inheritance was awarded to Claude Vorilhon, leader of the Raelians, a European movement devoted to contact with extraterrestrials. Vorilhon took possession of a cryogenic receptacle that presumably contained one or both of the objects.*

'Reportedly, a large sum of money was also awarded to Vorilhon's group, but the money was never delivered, and the firm handling the business turned out to be non-existent.'

Some hoaxes are unfortunately designed to be fraudulent money making schemes, rather than a 'bit of harmless fun', or the product of a disturbed mind.

This was the case with the 'Venus Project', devised in 1947 by con-men Karl Mekis and Franz Weber-Richter, both of whom had fled to South America following their dubious pasts.

'UFOIC Review' detailed how, from their base in Santiago, Karl and Franz set about convincing gullible people that the world was in imminent danger of being invaded by Venus. They hired some office staff, and established a 'World Republic of Venus', with Mekis appointed as 'Security Commissar'. All other appointments to this organisation, which would be running the world, on behalf of the Venusians, would be made upon payment of a hefty fee.

After manufacturing 'official documents', including Venusian passports, special passes and identity cards, they set about advertising across Europe for their victims. A typical advertisement read; *'Vacancy – Advisor for Economic Affairs in the World Republic of Venus Civil Service.'* They received an amazing number of replies, and Karl and Franz would mail off copies of the 'Constitution of the Republic of Venus', and other convincing propaganda, followed by a request for an 'Appointment Fee'.

One victim, Herr Freschner, a Bavarian inn-keeper and family man, was duped, and paid $100, (a lot of money in those days), for the appointment of 'Advisor for Economic Affairs (Food and Consumer Goods) in the World Republic of Venus Civil Service'. Other deceived people, purchased positions as local commissars, special administrators, clerks, secretaries and even as chauffeurs for top brass Venusian Generals.

When the Chilean police started to investigate, Karl and Franz quickly moved to Italy, and set up their base in Rome, advertising for more clerks and secretaries, at a reduced fee of $24. It went well for a while, however for some reason, in 1949, Karl decided to visit Austria, his country of origin, where he was arrested by police who had been tipped off by the Chilean authorities.

In a subsequent court case, it was alleged that the two fraudsters had netted $40,000 annually, and during the short time of their operation, conned a total of $120,000 out of their victims; *'The trial of the arch-grafter at times more resembled a scene from a musical comedy than one at the Palace of Justice. Even the learned judge was reduced to tears of laughter....Karl Mekis undeviatingly declared his innocence. In court, he warned the judge that, one day soon, when the Venusians invaded Earth, he, the judge, would be called to account for his actions and his attitude towards so important a member of the Republic's Government.'*

Whilst Mekis, who had been in jail for a year, served another four years of 'hard labour', Weber-Richter mysteriously disappeared. Nobody knew where he had gone, with some of his few remaining adherents suggesting that the Venusians had whisked him away!

In addition to pranks, advertising stunts and financial frauds, when discussing hoaxes, I cannot ignore the irresponsible and astounding articles, which are most probably totally fictitious, published in the more sensational tabloid magazines and newspapers to attract additional readers.

It had been occurring for decades, but it wasn't until 1992 that South African investigator, Cynthia Hind, decided to publicly 'call it out'. It brought the whole ufological community into disrepute, and wasted researchers' valuable time investigating the reports.

'There are several tabloids, in both the United States and Great Britain, which will take the kernel of a story and sensationalise it to the Nth degree.'

She noted that some incredible stories were, when checked out, based on truth, however, many appeared to be fabricated, and she quoted a couple of examples; *'According to the article, 'a top wildlife photographer, Brenda van der Hoerten', of South Africa, vanished without a trace while on an elephant photographing safari in Kenya in 1979.*

'Interviewed by a reporter from the paper, Brenda told how she had been abducted by aliens who whisked her off to Mars, where for twelve terrible years, she was treated like a caged monkey by beings who never spoke to her, kept her naked, ignored her cries and screams and pleading, regularly ran scanner-like devices over her body, and brought her the most disgusting, 'foul-tasting slop' to eat, composed of rotting vegetables and plants that looked as if they had been brought up from planet Earth.

'.... She forced herself to eat the slop, hoping that her captors would eventually tire of her and release her. After twelve years of poking prodding and observing her, they eventually did, returning her clothes and equipment and dropping her back in the exact spot where they had picked her up in 1979.

'After she was beamed down in the Kenyan wildlife reserve near Nairobi, where she had been on safari, she stumbled around in the bush, where she was found, bleeding and bruised, by park rangers. They took her to hospital for treatment.'

She made her way back to South Africa and Johannesburg, where she started a search for her husband and two children, of whom she could find no trace. In the meantime, she rented a room and took a menial job in order to support herself.

'Some of the ufologists who questioned her, believed she was telling the truth. Claude Richelier, a French ufologist, is quoted as saying that Brenda's facts

never varied after each questioning, and that hers was a fascinating story. She told him that after being seized, she had felt a tingly sensation all over her body, then suddenly found herself inside a strange metallic room, surrounded by the man-like beings.'

Apparently, Brenda had claimed that she was sure it was Mars she had been taken to, as when the craft came in to land, she recognised the terrain from photographs she had seen of the planet, and she was imprisoned in a cell-like room, with a clear bubble top. Her captors, who were always silent, had large football-shaped heads, big round eyes and no sign of ears or a mouth.

Claude, who wanted to conduct further investigations, urged her to return to Paris with him, but Brenda refused, preferring to live a normal life and continue her search for her family.

Cynthia Hind contacted an investigator in Johannesburg, and together they wrote to two leading newspapers, but received no reply. As of 1992, they were unsuccessful in locating Brenda, despite appeals to the public and members of their group.

(Perhaps researchers should just have treated the entire report with scepticism, but there were other incidents in the past, which Graham Birdsall later spoke about; *'In September 1962, farm animals, which included cows and pigs, mysteriously disappeared from a wide area of Barcelos in Brazil, which was experiencing a wave of UFO sightings at the time.*

'On the 1st September, plantation workers at Vila Conceicao watched Telemaco Xavier walking down the road when a glowing UFO suddenly appeared from nowhere, and three entities emerged. The three grabbed the screaming Telemaco back into their craft, which then took off. He was never seen again!')

Another case Cynthia cited was when; *'The Weekly World News', of July 12th 1988, reported that scientists had found a tribe in the jungle of Zaire who claimed to have come there from Mars in 1812. Of the original 25 'planetary travellers' three remained alive in 1988 when they were discovered, - they would then have been 176 years old!'*

Swedish scientist, Dr. Signe Winslof, who said his party had discovered these people while studying Zairean tribal cultures, claimed they had told him that their spacecraft was still hidden in the bush, near their settlement east of Kisangani.

'After initial distrust, the tribesmen showed them the rusted remains of 'a silver, crescent-shaped star-ship' in which they originally fled Mars to escape a virus that was wiping out their race. They had settled in the jungle, where their descendants now numbered fifty. The report said they were black, and totally human, save for their eyes, which were 'completely white'.

'The Swedish party said that though the tribe spoke a 'typical African dialect' among themselves, they used Swedish and English when conversing with the scientists. They would not talk about their ancestors' life on Mars, but although they still had maps of that planet and the Solar System, they were not prepared to reveal anything about their past.

'Dr. Winslof said the experts would return to the area later in 1988 and 'publish a full scientific report with photographs.'

Cynthia Hind disdainfully noted they were still waiting for this 'published report'!

Sometimes a researcher can be caught in a quandary. The most credible reports turn out to be a hoax, and the most ridiculous – genuine. I am just undecided in regards to the following incident, detailed by John la Fontaine in a 1981 *'Danish UFO Report'*.

John had been lecturing at a Danish exhibition, when he noticed a distinguished looking man, about sixty years old, who attended several times, and seemed very interested in the slides depicting 'humanoids'. Eventually, John spoke with him, and after gaining his confidence, was extremely interested when the elderly man said he had once spoken to an alien who looked similar to one of those on the slides.

Apparently, the witness whom I'll call 'Peter', was working, in July 1955, as a lumberjack in the Gulf of Bothnia, Vestra Nordland, Sweden. Early one morning, he and his fellow workers, heard a crashing noise as a cigar-shaped object flew haphazardly through the trees. It appeared to have silently hit the ground some 300 metres away, and only thirty to forty meters from the banks of a nearby river. Its impact was accompanied by a gigantic flash of brilliant light, and a 'vacuum wave' sucking everything towards the centre of the light.

Thinking it must have been a small plane, which had lost its wings, 'Peter' and his two colleagues stumbled as leaves went flying past them, but once they had recovered they made their way to the site of the 'crash'. They could see some timber scattered around a clearing, but not any wreckage. When they were about to leave, one of them spotted a lifeless body at the entrance to the forest, and assumed the craft must have crashed into the river, with the pilot being hurled out.

They all stared at the motionless figure lying on the ground. It was of small stature, about four feet tall, and around its body, like a halo, was a vibrating white light. One of the men tried to touch it, to see if it was still alive, and received an electric shock. The 'being' opened its eyes, and said in perfect Swedish; "Do not touch me – it will only bring you difficulties."

'Peter' said; *"He was no dwarf. He was very well-built, with broad shoulders and normal features. His skin was yellowish, like that of an Asian. His eyes were deep-socketed and black, without any white around. His face was badly bruised, with a couple of deep wounds on the chin and forehead. It did not bleed, but the skin watered around the wounds.*

"The top of his head was slightly downy and the hair almost white. The earlobes were one with the neck, and resembled a shark's fin. The lips were wrinkled, narrow and colourless. When he smiled reassuringly – which he did a lot – he revealed a row of small teeth in the upper as well as the lower part of his mouth......His canine teeth were as flat and broad as ours.....and his hands were small with five slender fingers without nails."

'Peter' said he was wearing a reddish, metallic uniform, which appeared to be 'glued' to his body, and extended down into his feet, which were in closed shoes. Around his waist he had a broad, silvery metal belt, with an unusually large buckle, which shone slightly in a light-blue shade, and turned dark blue later, when he was dead. In the middle of the buckle was a yellow 'UV' sign. His head and hands were free.

'Peter' sensed that this stranger could read his thoughts, as he answered questions not even spoken. At one stage he said; *"It is because of the clothing I can stay with you. Internally, I am destroyed."*

Peter then noticed his hand disappeared somewhere into his clothing, and he brought out a very small box, with several indentations, which he poked with a small 'pencil' attached to the box, before throwing it a few yards away.

"Don't touch it," he said smilingly. "It will tell my fellowmen what has happened, so they don't come looking for me. Where I come from, someone is waiting for me."

After the being seemed to be sleeping, 'Peter's' two colleagues left, but he stayed by his side, until he regained consciousness, and they continued their conversation. John la Fontaine was unable to get "Peter' to divulge everything that was said, and had to be content with these few snippets;

"The stranger came from a place in the vicinity of the constellation we call 'The Eagle'. Several races have visited us, some so far advanced that we could only see them when they 'materialised' or 'dematerialised' to visit a parallel universe in the orbit of Earth.....Some kept people on Earth under surveillance and had done so for thousands of years......Others took samples of the Earth, with a view to later settlements....Still others had contact with mankind, and had for centuries."

Just before the stranger died, he gave 'Peter' a folded bag, which he took out from under his uniform, and said; *"When I am dead, the light will disappear from my body, and with the help of the other two men, you shall put me in this bag, and carry me out into the river, where I shall disappear. Then you shall rinse yourself thoroughly in the water, so that you don't get ill."*

The being eventually died, and the brothers came back. He was quite heavy – 90 to 100 kilos – but with their help 'Peter' got his body into the bag, and carried it to the river. Once in the water, there was a lot of 'bubbling' around the bag, and after five minutes, nothing remained.

Sometimes, we will never know the truth or otherwise of accounts of the 'visitors' and their messages.

Jim and Coral Lorenzen, in their book, *'UFOs over the Americas',* told of a book, which had been found buried under the sand near Coro, Venezuela. It appeared to be a diary, written in both English and Russian, by an American doctor, and detailing his interaction and conversations with some 'extraterrestrial beings'.

Their spaceship had been forced, due to mechanical problems, to land nearby, and apparently, the physician, who lived in Coro, had assisted them by obtaining certain materials needed for repairs.

During the time he spent assisting them, although he never knew their planet of origin, the doctor learned much about their base of operation and methods of propulsion and travel. They also discussed some of Earth's geological history, and emphasised the dangers if we continued our use of nuclear weapons.

One interesting aspect was also contained in the Lorenzen's account; *'All beings that inhabit the galaxy came from the same origin, and there are no extreme anthropomorphic differences among the races. The first inhabitants from the galaxy to arrive on Earth were of a reddish skin, but could be classified as Caucasians.'*

CHAPTER SIXTEEN

PRIESTS AND CLERGYMEN

THEIR SIGHTINGS AND THOUGHTS

Back in the 'good old days', most reported 'contacts' were with mostly blond-haired, Caucasian 'visitors', who preached love and peace. Several cults and 'pseudo-religions' were subsequently formed, often led by self professed 'contactees'. Some investigators made reference to the 'Gods' who came from the skies in ancient times.

Soon, many 'cult' type religions evolved, often led by 'chosen ones', who claimed to be contactees. They often followed 'beings' such as 'Rael' and 'Ashtar', or George King, the self-styled leader of the Aetherius Society. I don't intend to devote much time to them here.

Some, including 'The Church of Jesus the Saucerian', were not quite as radical as many others. In 1964, Los Angeles leader, 'Bob Geyer' explained their beliefs to author Eric Norman;

"Briefly, Jesus was an exalted being from another world. He came to earth with a mission to teach humanity all the important truths. When he finished, he returned home. We believe in a supreme being – God. We believe the Bible is a spiritual record of the benevolence of astronauts from other worlds.

"We know the Bible contains many accounts of space landings during those times. The Exodus from Egypt was guided by a flying saucer. The prophet, Ezekiel, was a Biblical contactee who saw beings from other worlds. When the Bible mentions angels, they refer to our brothers from the stars. They are our brethren from space.

"They have watched over humanity since the beginning of time. This is probably how the phrase 'guardian angel' started. Our modern concept of an angel is formed in our Sunday Schools. Religious paintings portray them as celestial goody-two-shoes floating around the skies, flapping their wings. Angels didn't have wings. They were beings from other worlds, who arrived in spaceships or flying saucers. The medieval artists had to depict an angel that could fly. They slapped on the wings."

Eric asked Bob about the 'Satan' and his legion of 'demons'; *"They were also beings from other worlds. They came down from another planet. Once, Satan was a member of God's astronauts. He became too greedy and ambitious. He may have exploited the inhabitants of Earth, or other planets. He may have tricked people into slavery. Consider the stories of pacts with the Devil. That is an agreement for pure and simple slavery of the physical and spiritual body.'*

Most, but not all, conventional ministers of religion avoided the divisive topic of UFOs or visitors from space.

Not so, the Rev. E. M. Broomhead, who had this to say in the *'Sunday Mail'* on 5th January 1963; *'Well, here's 1963 – and with it comes the very pertinent question – Have you met the man from outer space? Be careful, this might be the year.*

'As the father of two sub-teenagers, I am as interested as you are. Will the first boyfriend come from next door, or from some far-off nebula? You can never tell. What with all the goings-on, (and especially the goings-off), at Cape Canaveral, it won't be terribly long before we're exchanging visits with the aliens on Mars, or slipping off to the lodge on Pluto, or judging a baby show on Saturn.

'Now, just a word of warning – sheer good taste demands that you don't flick an eyelid if your first interstellar caller has green skin, or a couple of extra heads, or even clothing as ugly as your own. And above all, greet him, or her, with a handshake, and not with a gun. That slight disparity as to the count of heads, or colour of skin, doesn't alter the fact; your man from outer space is probably wiser, kinder, purer and more brotherly than you.

'For the chances are pretty even that intelligent beings do live on other worlds, but there is only a remote chance that their worlds, like our own are 'fallen'. In other words, other planets didn't go 'bad', simply because ours did. All in all, then neither our persons or our morals are likely to be in danger when we meet that man from Mars.

'But they are likely to suffer from abominable damage from the man you meet each morning in the mirror. And he can be rendered wholesome only by Somebody you may have already come across; The Man from outer space, Who has already come.'

Fred Stone, the Australian researcher, and editor of the *'Australian Saucer Record'* commented that he had met the Reverend on several occasions, and congratulated him on his outspoken views on the subject.

Over seventy years earlier, during Lent, in April 1889, a slightly bemused French newspaper published verbatim excerpts of Dominican theologian, Abbott Monsabre's, address to the faithful at Notre Dame Cathedral in Paris.

Jesus Tencrio included some of his lecture in an article about this in a May 1970 edition of the Mexican City Daily, *'El Excelsior'*.

"It is true that God has done great things for mankind, but it is also true that God has shared His good things with, and has dominion over, others in addition to us. It is a point of faith, (understand this well), that there are other intelligent beings upon whom the Creator has also lavished his generosity. 'God', says St. Thomas, 'has created as many of them, for they are perfect.' Every number that can be imagined is insufficient if it is to describe their number."

Monsabre suggested that 'angels' lived in the universe, and that we on earth were part of a small minority of 'fallen angels'... *"that fell tragically from the heavens into the pit of ignominy and suffering, but the majority remained faithful.*

"And if you come down into the emptiness from heaven, where the angels enjoy nothing but eternal bliss, you will see in the emptiness thousands of spheres, larger and more beautiful than our mean world, and of course, you will wonder if these spheres are trackless wildernesses, uninhabited and without sound, created only for us to wonder at and provide surprises for astronomers, and perhaps you will say to the sages, who study the elements and the frameworks of heavenly bodies – "There must be living beings up there! Why shouldn't the stars be peopled with beings less perfect than the angels, but more perfect than we? There is space for other lives between the intuitive life of pure spirits and our complete rational life.

"......Perhaps because the Good Shepherd, being desirous of leading His entire flock to pastures of eternal joy, left the 99 sheep, that were following the right path, in space, and came to seek out the Earth, and the 100th sheep that was lost.....Why should not the inhabitants of all the spheres, scattered in space, who

were created by God as surely as we were, and who are covered by Jesus Christ, not be instructed in the Truth and Virtue of redemption by the angels that rule those worlds, or by the resurrected Jesus? Finally, why should God be prevented from reaching out to countless legions of the blissful in the deeps of space?

"Add to this the fact that creation, as we know it, cannot be the only creation that God has imagined. He is surrounded by eternity on all sides and possesses unlimited power to expand space indefinitely and multiply those beings. He is an infinite goodness that wants nothing more than to grow, be made known and make others happy. You cannot deny, if all of this is true, that it is impossible to count the number of beings that have been created."

In those 'good old days', several members of the clergy also witnessed inexplicable objects in the sky. On February 20th 1952, in Greenfield, Massachusetts, the Rev. Albert Baller, of the German Congregational Church, was looking out of a train window, when he saw three, perfectly circular, silver objects in a 'V' formation in the sky: *"They moved without vapour – or smoke trail, and at approximately the speed of a second hand on a watch."*

He said that when nearly over the train; - *"They stopped and hovered for perhaps ten seconds. Then I noted that the lead object was slowly reversing and appearing to pull into line with the other two between them. After this brief shift, there was another quick motion by all three, and they began to depart in a direction at right angles to their approach.*

"My astonishment increased as I saw them leave, because they went with such speed, that they dwindled to specks in not more than six seconds."

Researcher, Rowan Wilson, wrote of a similar incident that occurred later that year, on 22nd November 1952, in Bocaranga, Africa. Father Carlos Maria was going to see his dentist, and hitched a lift with a businessman going that way.

It was dusk when they spotted a large disc, low over the tree lined road. It disappeared, but later, when they stopped for fuel, he and seven other witnesses clearly saw four pale coloured discs, two above and two below, come to a standstill in the sky.

Father Carlos later recounted the incident; *"I had several opportunities of seeing them in motion, and had a strong idea that the lower pair only were revolving, just before moving, when they blazed up, as bright as the sun.*

"They seemed to arrange themselves in a group, which proceeded to describe circles, before returning to their starting point. When they stopped, the bright blaze died down to the original dull silver....We were watching them from 10pm to 10.20pm. After several minutes they then departed in an opposite direction to ours, gradually diminishing in luminosity until they were lost in the darkness of the night,"

On November 5th 1955, the pastor of the Grace Lutheran Church, in Cleveland, Ohio, Rev. Kenneth Hoffman, and his wife, were driving to the airport. Suddenly they saw a row of bright lights approaching in the sky. They stopped their car when the strange phenomena were about half a mile away, and realised that they were looking at a huge, oval craft, similar in appearance to two saucers, the uppermost inverted and resting on the edges of the lower one.

Eight large windows, emitting a bright white light, were around the perimeter. The object looked metallic, light grey in colour, with a diameter of about one hundred feet. As the Hoffmans started the car, and gradually edged down the highway, the strange craft moved slowly and silently towards the west, and was lost from view behind the tree-line.

It was only after they heard about other people's sightings, that they decided to report the event to 'NICAP'.

It is not known if Rev. R. Bennett offered any explanation to his congregation when three 'flying cigars' were seen over an open-air cinema, in Vuyyuru, India, on 27th April 1956.

It was about 8.30pm, and he was arranging his projectors, before showing some films to the waiting audience of over fifty people. Suddenly, what looked like three luminous cigar-shape forms, came down from the north. They appeared to be heading south, and flying in a triangular formation at an altitude of about 3,500ft.

They descended to 2,500ft, and just before reaching where the cinema audience were sitting, wheeled in a sharp arc, and still losing height, turned in an east-south-east direction. As they silently turned, the witnesses realised there were actually five craft in the formation, which soon disappeared into the night.

In June 1957, the Rev. George Tiley, Vicar of Powick, near Worcester in England, was surprisingly outspoken and set in his beliefs.

The *'Flying Saucer Review'* told of how he preached about space ships and space visitors from other worlds; *"The men who live on Venus and Mars are far in advance of us. They have learned to use everything constructively. They have outlawed war, disease and poverty. In a sense, they have begun to live the Golden Age. They are so far advanced they would rather be killed than kill."*

DR BARRY DOWNING

Barry Downing, who held a B.A. degree in physics, and a Ph.D in the philosophy of science and religion, became an assistant pastor at his Northminster Presbyterian Church, in Endwell, New York, in 1967, and published his groundbreaking, and controversial book, *'The Bible and Flying Saucers'*, the next year. In some ways, his views were similar to those of Bob Geyer. This did not prevent his elevation to senior pastor three years later.

He said; *"At the time, my senior pastor was very supportive, although a lot of eyebrows were raised. I understand that one family left the church because they were embarrassed by it, just as current members sometimes take a bit of kidding from those outside our church. Of course, I rarely say anything about UFOs from the pulpit."*

He said that because his book was not released until after he was ordained, the only way the Presbyterian Church hierarchy could have got rid of him was via a 'heresy' trial, which they were probably not willing to undertake. Further, he was very popular with his own parishioners, having instigated a children's ministry, and a program for senior citizens. He remained there for the rest of his ministry, unsure if any other congregation would accept his more 'radical' views.

His book equates biblical events, some theologians claimed were impossible myths, with the advanced science of extraterrestrial beings and flying saucers.

This eventuated out of his doctoral studies which focussed on the relationship between science and religion, and an ever growing 'God is dead' movement, which seemed to be gaining momentum.

Speaking at the 1988 'MUFON International Symposium', Downing said; *"Future evidence may indicate that from the beginning the U.S. Government was very worried about the theological implications of UFOs, and the psychological impact that 'UFO theology' might have on our culture. I would say that this concern is well justified.*

"It seems likely that the Soviet Union is well aware of the existence of UFOs, and that the possibility of an emerging 'UFO theology' was considered by both sides of the 'cold war'....Release of UFO information would have unpredictable religious and cultural responses in both America and Russia.'

Later, in 1990, he agreed with Jacques Vallee's viewpoint, that UFOs could well contribute to a new form of spiritual movement and religion. Downing wrote; *'Christian fundamentalists already claim that UFOs are in league with the devil. If the government came forth and identified 'the enemy' much of the religious and UFO communities would undoubtedly flock to their viewpoint.....'*

Later, at MUFON's 'International Symposium', he said; *"If our government leaders secretly consulted with a few modern theologians, and said to them, 'We know UFOs are real. Should we tell the people, or keep quiet?', I am sure the majority of clergy would say; 'Keep it quiet.'*

"Suffice to say that there is much at stake for Western religion in the UFO experience. If the government revealed the truth about UFOs, I am not sure what might be the social and religious-spiritual consequences for our society."

REV. LIONEL BROWNING

The *'Examiner'* newspaper was the first to take up this report. At 6.10pm on October 4th 1960, Anglican Minister, the Rev. Lionel Browning and his wife, who lived in Cressy, in the northern midlands of Tasmania, were looking out of the rectory window when they saw a dull, greyish colour, cigar-shaped object emerge from a rain squall.

It was about three or four miles away, and they thought it would have been about 300ft long, and travelling, below cloud level, at less than 50mph, in a northerly direction about 400ft above the ground. A rod jutted out of the bow end, and there were four vertical bands along the side, which seemed to have a dull surface, even though the setting sun was shining upon it.

He then explained what happened next; *"The ship travelled in a perfectly straight direction towards Western Junction. After about a minute of steady movement, the ship stopped mid-air. It hovered above the Panshanger Estate, about three miles away, and we watched the stationary object for about 30 seconds – fascinated.*

"Then out of the clouds, above and behind the ship, five or six small discs came shooting at speed. They came towards the ship like flat stones, skipping along the water. The small objects stationed themselves, besides their mother ship, within a half mile radius."

Browning said that these smaller, light grey craft looked like 'flying saucers', and were about 30ft in diameter, with a flat underside, rounded top, and no other distinguishing marks.

"After several seconds, the ship, accompanied by the saucers, reversed the way it came. It did not manoeuvre to return because the rod end was the last section of the ship to be covered in the rain cloud. It returned faster than the speed at which it had emerged, and was gone from sight after thirty seconds."

Whilst Browning had informed officials at Launceston airport, he only decided to release the information when he heard that there were other witnesses. Two hours after his sighting, residents were disturbed by a large explosion, followed by a rumbling and vibrations, which shook their houses. Some thought it may have been an earthquake. Civil Aviation authorities confirmed there were no aircraft in the vicinity at the time of Browning's and the other witness's reports.

Afterwards, the rectory was besieged with enquiries, to which he replied; *'I do not believe that the saucers come from another planet. Their movements seem to suggest that they were accustomed to the earth's atmospheric conditions and local terrain.'* He then supposedly added that in his opinion their source was Russia, however he later told the Rev. Cruttwell, that these words were 'put in his mouth' by a reporter who asked him if the craft were from Earth, where did he think they would have come from.

Later, in 1961, Rev. Browning, who was also a member of the Tasmanian Council of Churches, was not happy when Air Force investigators, in their 'Intelligence Report', stated that the sightings were – *'phenomena as a result of a moon rise associated with meteorological conditions at the time.'*

In the meantime, he had been contacted by a woman and her daughter, who at 4.30pm, ten days after his sighting, had seen a cigar-shaped object, flying about 300ft above the ground. Air Force investigators had spent considerable time with the mother and daughter, and finalised by telling them not talk about what they had seen.

The witnesses also added that the investigators told them of a similar strange sighting in the U.S. the previous year, when three jets were sent up to investigate and the strange craft disappeared, as if into thin air.

Rev. Browning said that the sighting, by the woman and daughter, backed up his story. He disputed the official findings, and accused the Air Force of 'whitewashing' the reports.

It was many years before the Rev. Bill Drooger, from the Oatlands Presbyterian Church in Tasmania, gained enough courage to send my colleague, Paul Norman, a written report of his sighting, which occurred five years after Rev. Browning's.

One evening, in 1965, Drooger had to visit the church's Sessions Clerk, four miles to the west of Oatlands on the road to Interlaken. At about 7pm, when he was halfway there, he saw something approaching in the sky.

'It would have been approximately between 4,000 to 5,000 feet high, and appeared to me to be a plane on fire. I had seen quite a few of those in Holland during the war, from 1940-1945. I stopped the car on the side of the road, because if the plane fell down, as I thought it would do, I might be able to render some help.'

He got out of the car, and realised that he could not hear any noise coming from the strange craft, which was unusual. Further, it was keeping a constant speed and altitude. He looked up, and could see the body of the 'plane' but not any wings.

'Then, six smaller objects, that looked like lighted arrow heads, shot out from the main object. Coming out at the same interval of about ten seconds, three of the objects came out from each side. The ones from the left hand side of the object continued on an angle of approximately 45° to the WNW, while those from the right hand side of the object shot out at the same 45° angle to the NNE.

'I did not see any alteration in the height or speed of all those six lighted arrowheads, or the lighted up body of the plane, which I realised at the time was not on fire but just lit up. It was an even glow of light, fairly bright. No lighted up windows could be seen as you would normally see on a plane.'

As soon as he arrived he told his Session Clerk, who advised him to report it to the police, which he did the next morning. A couple of days later, they told him there were no planes known to be in the area at that time. Drooger said; *'I did not check up any further for fear of being ridiculed.'*

One cannot help wondering if what the Reverends Browning and Drooger witnessed were extraterrestrial or our own early drone experiments? But, could this have been the case as early as 1949-1950? Researcher, Leonard Stringfield, told of an Ohio case involving many witnesses, including scientists, Catholic clergy, press and military.

In August 1949, the 'Norwood Church of Saints Peter and Paul' was hosting a carnival, and the Reverend Gregory Miller along with his brother, Father Cletus Miller, had purchased a surplus 8-million-candle-power searchlight for the occasion. As his military assistant, and congregation member, Sgt. Donald Berger, swept the bright beam across the sky, it unexpectedly illuminated an intensely glowing, stationary, giant, circular object hovering in the darkened heavens.

It was seen on more than one night, and filmed and photographed by Sgt. Leo Davidson of the Norwood Police Department. He commented that many witnesses saw two groups of five small objects, each with halos brighter than the searchlight beam, leaving the parent object. Some witnesses described them as being 'shaped like the apex of Indian arrow-heads'.

Physicist Dr. D. A. Wells, from the University of Cincinnati, calculated the main object to be at an altitude of ten miles, with a diameter of ten thousand feet. His colleague, astronomer Dr. Paul Herget, apparently told the *'Cincinnati*

Post' – "It's not a fake – We need an explanation to quash people's fears – It may be caused by the illumination of gas in the atmosphere!"

It wasn't until 1975, more than 25 years later, that Stringfield was approached by Paul Koch, who on October 23rd 1949, lived with his mother, only a block away from the church. That night, they were at the church, watching the small objects illuminated by the searchlight beam.

'Then, suddenly, his attention was turned to a military jeep arriving on the grounds. Two men in uniform jumped out, one a four-star general.

'The general went directly to the searchlight and ordered Sgt. Berger to switch off the light. Father Miller intervened. Hot words were exchanged. The general again ordered Berger to switch off the searchlight, put his hand on an unbuckled holster at his side, and said; "If you don't turn off the light, I'll shoot it out!"

Despite Father Miller's protests, Sgt. Berger obeyed his superior officer. *'The next Sunday, Father Miller's sermon condemned the military interference with his rights on church property.'*

It may also be significant that two of the best photographs, showing the parent craft and its 'brood', sent to *'Time'* magazine for inclusion in an article, were never returned, and the article not published.

FATHER GILL

In *'Contact Down Under'*, I wrote about several events in Papua/New Guinea, including those reported by Father Gill

In 1959, Rev. Gill was a freelance journalist, and for several years, a staff member of the Anglican Mission in the north-east coast of the Goodenough Bay area in Papua.

At 6.45pm. on 26th June, Father Gill was outside and noticed a bright white light in the northwest sky, which began silently descending towards him. He called out Eric Langford and Stephen Moi Gill, who confirmed it was similar to a light which had been seen the previous Sunday. Within ten minutes it was hovering about 350ft over the sea a very short distance away. They called more people out to have a look. The craft was solid, about 35ft in diameter, with a top deck measuring about 25ft across. It was a dull yellow to pale orange colour, and at first they could see a man-like figure moving around the flat top of the object.

Over the next few hours Father Gill and at least thirty-seven neighbours (medical assistants, school teachers, villagers and children), watched as up to four glowing figures at a time, came and went. They moved above the upper deck and were obviously busy 'doing something'. Although they were illuminated by the object itself, both the figures and the craft had a sparkling effect around them, like a child's sparkler. There was a gap separating the outline and the 'shimmering sparkle.'

A powerful blue beam shot straight into the air at an angle. It went on and then off several times – a few seconds on, and then off. Perhaps five or ten minutes later it was on for another few seconds. Then the craft hovered, went very high and disappeared behind a cloud.

On Saturday 27th June the visitors returned. At 6pm. Annie Borewa, a medical assistant, saw a large object in a similar position as the one the previous night. She ran down to Father Gill calling out; "It's back, it's back!" He immediately came out, soon to be followed by many more locals, and they all watched from a nearby open playing field.

On the Friday they had also seen four smaller discs in the sky, this night there were seven, and Father Gill felt they were definitely companion discs to the larger craft, although they never saw them going in or out of it; "They were quite easy to see – their outline was quite distinct. They were not the shape of the big one, and I should think quite a lot smaller, unless they were very, very high up, but they didn't appear to be.

"One disc was overhead, and as it slanted towards us, it clearly showed five panels on the side, they could have been windows, but they formed duller or brighter parts of the object. It was hard to distinguish on the others, but all of them had four legs – like two sets of bipods, and unlike the four balls on the object seen by Stephen the previous Sunday.

"We stood there as the larger craft descended over the playing field. We all thought it was going to land. We hoped it was going to land, and were in a state of anticipation. They came down, and then stopped. The figures were so near and so close, although we still couldn't discern very much of their appearance, I have calculated their height to be about 5 feet 8 inches.

"We spontaneously waved, and they waved back, which was a surprise. It occurred to me that although it was a form of acknowledgement, they copied us. When we used one hand, they waved with one hand; when with two hands they waved with two hands, and when I waved with my hand above my head, so did they – they copied us." – (This begs the question – were they sentient beings or robots?)

"We were still hoping it would land, so I got one of the boys to bring my torch. I began to flash things – dots and dashes, and things, and then we got the answer by movement. We couldn't see any figures on deck but the whole thing swung across the sky, like a pendulum, three or four times before coming back to its original position. I flashed a number of times, and every time it answered, until the man came back on deck and seemed to lose interest in us. Despite the interaction, at no time, during any incidents did we hear any noise from the craft or its occupants.

"They seemed to be adjusting something, and then this blue light came up again, and lasted for some time before it flashed off. The craft moved off across the sky, hovered and disappeared over the hill, only to come back then shoot thirty miles across the bay in less than a second.

"The third night, the 28th June, we only saw the larger craft very high up, and a few of the smaller discs around at a lower altitude. We saw no more after the Sunday. If I'd been rich enough to afford a camera, of course I would have taken photographs, but at least we had the signed statements of multiple witnesses."

Father Gill talked about a colleague, Reverend Norman Cruttwell, who lived thirty miles away across the bay at Menapi. He was miffed that he was the only European in the area who had not seen a UFO. He even went to bed each night with a portable telescope and camera – hoping to strike it lucky;

"In August 1959, his school – he's got a school over there with about 200 children in it, and a dozen Papuan teachers - that school is the only place on record in the area, in New Guinea, I think, that's had a daylight sighting. It was a great, big silver disc which sped, faster than a plane, over the school yard, at about 9 a.m. All the kids were lined up to go into the classrooms, so they, and all the teachers saw it. A couple of teachers and children ran to the house, but by the time the unfortunate Reverend raced out, it had gone."

In October 1959, Father Gill spoke at a meeting of the 'Victorian UFO Research Society', where when he described the events which occurred earlier that year, he commented; *"Although I am a believer in the possibility of people living on other planets, I would not commit myself to any particular theory – there are so many theories – that I would only emphasis that I am only an observer and recorder of certain events that happened in New Guinea during July and August this year.'*

Later, after his return to Australia, Father Gill became Social Studies and English Master at Essendon Grammar School in Melbourne, Victoria. During a visit to Queensland, he told a Brisbane *'Courier Mail'* reporter; *"I did not believe in flying saucers or unidentified flying objects beforehand. Now I believe in the existence of something out there, according to my own definition. I am still speculative about the origin of it."*

In 1980, Father Gill wrote an article for *'The Australian UFO Bulletin'*. In it he said; *'During the twenty-one years that have elapsed since the P.N.G. experience, science seems no closer to identifying the phenomenon or finding out the Flying Saucer's origin or its purpose.*

'Compilation of evidence and collection of anecdotes have together added little that is significant to knowledge or enlightenment. And so it has become easier to talk and write about UFOs than to devote a lifetime investigating them: easier to theorise on alien visitations or to deliberate upon the psychological condition of any who claim to have been confronted with Flying Saucers, than to probe for some tangible evidence for the reason for their existence.'

Reverend Cruttwell later went on to conduct investigations into unidentified objects over New Guinea, with many of the natives, puzzled, and often frightened, coming in from the jungle and describing 'boats in the sky'. He produced excellent reports for London and Brisbane societies.

Cruttwell, who was a firm defender of Father Gill, was furious when F. Lang, on behalf of the RAAF in Canberra, concluded that the object and entities, seen from the Mission, were 'known planets seen through fast moving cloud, or meteorological phenomena'.

Cruttwell noted that the evidence did not rest on Father Gill's word alone, there were at least 38 Papuan witnesses, several of whom were school teachers. *"Also"*, he said; *"unknown to Father Gill, on the 26th June, the very night of the first sighting, a trader named Ernest Evennett was staying at Giwa, on the other side of Goodenough Bay, about fifteen miles from Boiania. He was astounded to see an object, like a shooting star, come down to within 500ft of him, and reveal itself as an oval craft, with a band around it, and four portholes below the band. It hovered for four minutes just above him, and appeared so large that he could cover only half of it with his closed hand at arm's length. He could see no men, but it was obviously a manned aircraft of some sort. When it took off again, it made a curious triple sound, described as 'woomp –woomp – woomp'. It became brilliantly luminous with a green light, and shot away over the mountains. This sighting is an amazing independent corroboration that there were strange things over Goodenough Bay that night.*

"On the second night of the Boiania sightings, objects were also seen by the Government Officers at Baniara, A.D.O. Ronald Orwin and P.O. Robert Smith, and by the Roman Catholic Mission at Sideia. These objects were much further away, and appeared spherical in shape, but they further corroborate the existence of strange craft in the sky.

"The one seen at Baniara was accompanied by a small bronze disc, which seemed to hover at a fixed distance below the glowing spherical object, and moved in perfect sympathy with it, as if attached by an invisible wire. Then, when the main object suddenly dived, as if it was about to land, and became dazzlingly bright, the disc appeared to jump upwards to meet it, and vanished into it. Such an extraordinary phenomena is hardly likely to have been invented!"

He quoted other events in 1958 and 1959 and concluded; *"One thing is only clear, in my opinion. The many witnesses, government officials, doctors, traders, missionaries and intelligent Papuans cannot all have had hallucinations, many of them at the same time and in different places. There was something there! And the behaviour of these objects suggests that they were manned by intelligent, probably humanoid, beings, very like us, who for some reason of their own were making an intensive survey of this small area of South East Papua......*

"They do not appear to have had any hostile intent, indeed the waving to Father Gill seems to indicate definite friendliness. They have done no harm to anyone or anything, and have now, apparently, departed. Who are they? Where do they come from? Why did they concentrate on this remote backwater of our planet? And why, having come so close, did they not land? These are questions we cannot answer. We need more evidence."

Although a 'man of the cloth'. Cruttwell kept his research well within scientific confines. In 1961, he wrote an article, for Britain's *'Flying Saucer Review'* where he noted; *'My impression is that there are many types of UFOs visiting our planet, just as we have many different models of aircraft. Some of these types are now becoming recognisable as they have appeared a number of times in different places.'*

That same year, he wrote about *'UFOs and Religion'*, for *'Orbit'*, the Newsletter of the 'Tyneside UFO Society'. In it, he was dismayed at the 'spiritual type' UFO worshiping groups which had sprung up, and stressed the danger of mixing the subject and research with religion.

'Nature abhors a vacuum' – *this familiar cliché not only applies to physical science, but also man's spiritual condition. Cast out one devil, and seven more evil will enter. Destroy one religion, and another, less desirable, will take its place. In these days, when a false notion of science has caused many to throw aside the traditional faith of Christianity, it is not surprising that many are turning to all sorts of weird beliefs in order to try to fill their empty and lonely spiritual nature, and to quiet their fear of the future. The advent of the mysterious 'Flying Saucers' has been a godsend to them, and all sorts of different kinds of religious significance has been attached to them.*

'Some regard them as purely spiritual and ethereal apparitions, in spite of the fact that they have been photographed and tracked on radar. Others regard them as vehicles containing angelic beings, apostles, prophets, or even Our Lord himself; who are apparently living in space or on other planets, and are still confined to physical bodies which require machines for transportation.

'Others look on them as reincarnations, supermen, Lords of the Planets, messengers of God, people who lived on this Earth millions of years ago and were taken away in space ships, or the descendents of such people. There is a welter of fantastic ideas about them, based on little or no evidence, and seemingly inspired by the desire for something outside ourselves, something great, that we can cling to, as a drowning man clings to a raft....

'UFOs are not primarily a religious problem, except in as so far God is behind all phenomena. We have first to establish, scientifically, whether they exist – if so, whether they are terrestrial, interplanetary or even interstellar, and thirdly, who are their inhabitants? Only when we have solved these mysteries can we begin to assess their purpose and significance. It is only when we begin to have genuine communication with them, in an open and public manner, that we shall begin to understand.

'The question of their existence seems to be answered in the affirmative as the sightings continue to pour in, but the further questions are still far from being satisfactorily solved, and the reports of communication are most unconvincing and contradictory. It seems we should confine ourselves to one step at a time....

'However there is one aspect of the problem which is bound to affect our outlook on religion, and this is really a wider question altogether. If there is life on other planets in the universe, how does it affect our faith? I think that it is quite legitimate to consider this problem, as an increasing number of scientists are inclining to the belief that there is intelligent life elsewhere in the universe. The UFOs greatly reinforce this belief, however many people cannot accept this at all, and their scepticism, or 'will not to believe', is due to their fear of it.

'The belief in life on other worlds alters neither our faith in God, our belief in Christ, or our duty to live the Christian life. It has been held by many theologians from the time of St. Augustine, that when God wishes to reveal its meaning to us, He will. Up to now, it has not been necessary. Perhaps the day of that revelation is drawing near.'

REV. SEGUNDO REYNE

In 1967, the *'U.F.O.I.C. Newsletter'* quoted the Rev. Segundo Reyne, who was a Jesuit priest and internationally recognised astronomer in Argentina. Father

Reyne, who was the Director of the Adhara Observatory at San Miguel, Beunos Aires, said he had seen dozens of UFOs from the observatory, and some through a telescope. He had taken several photographs, one of which showed the typical oval form. He said his conviction about beings from outer space did not conflict with his religious beliefs;

'Unidentified Flying Objects do exist. They are craft manned by living beings from another world. These alien beings are currently studying the Earth and its inhabitants, and sooner or later, they will establish formal contact with mankind....From a theosophical point of view, the existence of these intelligent visitors, from beyond the Solar System, is not only just possible, but is probable and likely.

'We would be naive to believe that God's Grace has only been given to the inhabitants of Earth. I believe that God has created rational beings on other planets in the Universe, who have developed advance civilisations, explored space, found us and eventually will communicate with us.

'I don't just 'believe' in UFOs, I know that they exist, and the intelligent beings on board have been watching us for some time. Scientifically, it would be foolhardy to claim that no intelligent life could exist anywhere else in the Universe. In our galaxy alone, there are more than one million planets where life, as we know it, could be sustained and where rational beings could have developed fabulous civilisations – and remember, our galaxy is only one of millions in the Universe.'

Many years ago, a witness, who later became a close colleague of mine, had an encounter outside the seminary where he was staying. The priest immediately wanted to 'exorcise' the 'devil' who may have accosted him! What about the modern day church and theologians? It seems there has been a change in attitude.

Vatican priest, Monsignor Carrado Balducci, has always been outspoken about the UFO phenomenon. He elaborated on his beliefs in an interview with Paola Harris, which was documented in the Nov./Dec. 2000, *'UFO Magazine'*. He said; *"My true interest in ufology was born many years ago, and came from my research into demonology, parapsychology, and the paranormal in general."*

He noted that human testimonies are believed when determining miracles recognized by the church; - *"then logically, why do we not believe those who are reporting an extraordinary phenomenon?*

"...The manifestations of Satan must not be confused with those who say they have contact with ETs. They are two separate paranormal phenomena....Perhaps, with the UFO phenomenon, we are talking about beings like us, material and spiritual. Surely, there must be many more levels involved....they must be superior beings, because if we look at our civilisation and how we behave, we remain at the lower levels on the spiritual ladder.....It is absurd to believe that the only type of intelligent life is ours."

Paola went on to ask him about the third prophecy of Fatima, made in 1917, which the Vatican had said was regarding an assassination attempt on the Pope, and was seemingly absurd, considering the long period of secrecy. It was supposed to have been released in 1960!

In 1999, before the official pronouncement, Baldacci had said; *'This secret dealt with two subjects, a possible nuclear war, before the end of the millennium, with weapons more powerful than 'one thousand suns'. The Biblical text, he stressed, says that the 'survivors will envy the dead'.* This would only happen 'if humanity didn't change its current course'.

Baldacci said; *"So it is all conditional? I'm optimistic. We, as men, can change the inevitability of prophecy, or postpone the date and lessen the intensity of these events, minimizing the effect. It is always possible that the extraterrestrials could help us, but I believe that we should not wait for anyone. It has to be mankind to change and mature."*

In order to suppress all information on extraterrestrial beings and visitations, Governments often used the excuse that any such public knowledge would cause the collapse of society and traditional religions. That may not have been an accurate analysis.

In March 1965, the *'San Francisco Chronicle'* reported that; *'Representatives of six religions were asked, in a series of interviews last week by the 'North American Newspaper Alliance', what effect the discovery of intelligent life elsewhere in the universe would have on the traditional Judeo-Christian beliefs of western civilisation.*

'The question was not by any means intended to be frivolous – indeed, all six churchmen agreed that one day it may no longer be a merely diverting hypothesis, but a reality that must be engaged. And, possible or not, the idea always refocussed analysis of the churches' roles here-and-now and down-to-earth.'

Rev. Timothy Flynn, from the New York Catholic Archdiocese, felt that extraterrestrials would be unlikely to share our framework of belief, and rather than attempting any form of conversion, 'we should, in the spirit of brotherhood, maintain every human contact with humans of other planets'.

Mormon, Bishop Earl Tingey did not rule out missionary work in the outer limits of the universe, but stated; *"Life has all manner of forms. The Mormon concept of Truth is that which embraces serenity and peace. We would be most happy to find Truth wherever it exists, and from whatever form it is transmitted to us. What we have is for everyone, and we would not exclude anyone."*

New York Methodist Pastor, Richard Francis, rather than wanting to 'convert' the aliens, suggested that we may be converted to their faith instead; *"I might be converted if I believed that God, through these different people had brought us open revelation. The Bible teaches us that there are progressive revelations of God to man. I believe that God has not revealed all of Himself to us.....Maybe, as humans, we feel we have reached the highest form of life, but our potentialities have not."*

Russian Orthodox Priest, George Crabbe, thought that humans were superior. He declared that we should accept that soul-life exists all over the universe, however we should also accept that 'life on earth is the crown of creation.'

Christian Science spokesman, David Sleeper, expressed a similar point of view, noting that the discovery of extraterrestrial life,... *"may be a renaissance for all people when God's infinity is felt throughout the universe. We will have a refreshing consideration of metaphysical and spiritual causes for all our earthly concerns."*

Only a couple of decades after the Holocaust, Jewish Professor Abraham Heschel, was more outspoken; *"We live in a time of emergencies. It is an abuse of one's mind to dwell too much on interstellar fascinations. When my house is on fire, should I spend my time trying to think of how to redecorate it, or wondering how to put out the flames?"*

The problem of confronting grotesque creatures did not bother him; *"...since too many people I meet on earth are 5 percent human and 95 percent beast."* More angelic type beings would be acceptable... *"Here on earth we are more and more in danger of becoming an affluent society of spiritual idiots, commercial and soulless. If humans on other planets can show us that their own religions are based on decency, kindness, bother-to-brother love and respect, that is fine."*

The next year, the Canadian *'Toronto Daily Star'* conducted a similar survey. British Lord Soper, who was also a Methodist minister, (the Rev. Donald, Lord Soper), was very outspoken on most matters, often preaching from a soapbox in London's Hyde Park. He said his daughter, who was married to a Cambridge professor, had once seen a UFO.

After claiming that the British took the matter more seriously than the North Americans, who were 'less sophisticated', he noted that space beings could exist in forms totally alien to our concepts of living organisms. He hoped they would be friendly, and "not as retarded as we are!"

"...They must have their own incarnations of God. This fact would not invalidate at all the picture we have of God in Jesus Christ. Christ is the human photograph of God, but beings on other worlds must have their own appropriate photographs of the Eternal Spirit...They must have their own incarnation of God."

Presbyterian, Dr. Geddes MacGregor, shared a similar viewpoint; *"There is but one Christ, our Lord, but this does not exclude the possibility that there are millions of other divine incarnations throughout the innumerable galaxies."*

Anglican, Rev. Dean Johnson, from St. Peter's Episcopal Church, in Sycamore Illanois, said that in May 1963, he and his wife had seen an enormous circular craft, on the shores of Lake Michigan, which had descended to tree top level. For twenty minutes they, and many other witnesses, watched the silent craft which had two rows of windows, one lighted and one dark.

"What we saw in daylight, definitely was a craft, but it was definitely not of this earth. The only natural conclusion was that it came from space."

He also believed that; *"Christ was the incarnation or embodiment of God on Earth, - it is possible that these incarnations have appeared to other civilisations in space. For me, the reality of UFOs makes me realise that our relationship to God and the universe is much wider then we have thought."*

Some religious leaders believed the 'Ancient Aliens' theory, that Christ was an exalted being from another planet, who returned home in a flying saucer, but promised to come back to earth at some future date.

Rev. Helmut Wipprecht, of the United Church of Canada in Cobalt, said the biblical description on angels fits 'intelligent beings from space'; *"The star of Bethlehem probably was a spaceship, because stars do not stand still and hover over one place."*

In later years, after 'bug-eyed greys' with their unwelcome abductions were beginning to be reported, not all religious leaders thought that UFOs and their occupants were a good omen.

Father Seraphim Rose, an Eastern Orthodox Christian theologian, turned to religion after completing a degree at the University of California. He co-founded the St. Herman of Alaska Brotherhood, a monastic community in Platina, California, and at one stage, studied the UFO phenomena in the light of the teachings of the Orthodox Church.

In the 1970s he was quite outspoken in his belief that UFOs, especially cases involving close encounter experiences, were a manifestation of demonic activity. He said they were the signs of the coming of the 'Antichrist', his brief reign over Earth, and the second coming of Christ.

Researcher, David Ritchie, documented some of Father Rose's beliefs; *'Citing the suggestion that UFOs constitute a 'control system' for influencing human beliefs, Rose wrote that UFOs might serve to draw humankind away from traditional Christian faith and persuade the public instead to worship as divine a diabolical presence that announced its advent with spectacular and mysterious light shows in the skies.*

'Rose noted numerous and close similarities between UFO close-encounter phenomena and manifestations of demonic activity as described in the

experiences of Eastern Orthodox saints. Other modern observers of the UFO phenomenon have reached essentially the same conclusions as Rose did.'

In 1978, my colleague, Gordon Creighton, discussed an article which appeared in the British newspaper, the *'Sunday People'.* The Rev. Anthony Millican, Vicar of St. Christopher's Bristol; *'believes these demonic 'angels of light' emanate from a Parallel World in the unseen. – "Jesus warned that in the Last Days there would be 'in the sky terrors and great portents". – The Vicar maintains that the aim of the UFOs is to change the world in order for the Devil to take over.*

'Gordon Creighton said; "I tend to agree with him". He once thought they were extraterrestrial beings, but doesn't think so now; "Basically it could be a case of demons and angels. I believe there are good visitations and bad, mostly bad for the human race." – Creighton , who claims he had his first UFO sighting in China in 1941, adds; "Whatever the UFOs are, they are not beneficial to man."

In 1979, Jacques Vallee wrote in his book, *'Messengers of Deception'*, that UFOs;....*'are real...Their methods are those of deception: systematic manipulation of witnesses and contactees; covert use of various sects and cults; control of the channels through which the alleged 'space messages' can make an impact upon the public.'*

Many years later Victoria Alexander, conducted another survey of U.S. clergy regarding their religious responses to extraterrestrial life. Gone were the original innocent concepts of the 'Space Brothers'. By this time, contact with the benevolent 'Nordics' had mainly been replaced by more worrying accounts involving the 'Greys' and their disturbing practices, including the possible attempts at genetic manipulation.

The results were published in the September 1994 *'MUFON Journal'* and it appeared that, by then, whilst not necessarily endorsing the aliens, most would be able to incorporate their existence into their current dogma.

He noted the comments of Dr. Thomas Bullard in his paper; *'Comparative Analysis of UFO Abduction Reports'* (1987): - *'What we find is that the beings neither tolerate nor respect the faith of their captives. The abductors are not Christians, that conclusion at least seems clear from the meagre data available.'*

He also noted that, at the 1988 'MUFON International Symposium', Raymond Boeche had said; *"Along with this initial social destabilisation would come the political consequences. A widespread authority crisis could develop, with sharp criticism levelled at political, scientific and religious leaders. The alien culture would, in the minds of many, usurp or overshadow the figures of absolute authority, (Presidents, Popes, Premiers), which society has come to rely on to establish the 'rules of the game'. Removal of these clear-cut standards of authority could then lead to the next stage, societal anomy, (instability or lawlessness)."*

Alexander noted that given our own history, here on Earth, precedent would indicate a merging of religions, rather than the wholesale destruction of one religion by another; *'If people would prefer to join an alien religion, surely we would be able to grant the same tolerance we, as a nation, give to the Church of Satan, Santeria, or Christian serpent handling sects. These religious groups are not a threat to mainstream religions, and according to the Survey results, an alien religion wouldn't be either.....From the responses we can reasonably infer that it is assumed that faith in current beliefs would remain firmly established.'*

As the years went by, society became more accepting of the possibility of extraterrestrial life.

In 2008, Ted Peters reported, in the *'MUFON Journal'*, how he asked several contemporary theologians their opinion on intelligent extraterrestrial life. Catholic, Hans Küng, from the University of Tübingen, said; *"We must allow for living beings, intelligent – although quite different – living beings, also on other stars of the immense universe."* Jose Funes, Director of the Vatican Observatory, near Rome, added the following observation; *"How can we rule out that life may have developed elsewhere? Just as we consider earthly creatures as 'brothers' and 'sisters', why should we not talk about an 'extraterrestrial brother'? It would still be part of creation."*

(In 2001, Scott Corrales, from the 'Institute of Hispanic Ufology', had also translated the thoughts of Jesuit George Coyne, a previous Director of the Vatican Observatory, who reported directly to the Holy See; *'He is convinced of the existence of extraterrestrial life – and it would be 'madness' to think that humans are alone in the universe; – "The more we study the stars, the more we become aware of our own ignorance. Science does not undermine faith; rather it stimulates it."*

(While Coyne admitted not having any proof of extraterrestrial life, he said each day new data was being amassed. He insisted that there was not necessarily any conflict between the Biblical origin of the Cosmos, and the current ones, such as the 'Big Bang', being championed by science.)

Protestant theologians seem a little more conservative. Wolfhart Pannenberg, of the University of Munich, seemed more interested in the issue of the redemption of extraterrestrial creatures, however, British scientist- theologian, David Wilkinson, was a little more enthusiastic and speculative about the search for extraterrestrial intelligence. He said; *"At present, there is no strong evidence for extraterrestrial intelligence, yet as a scientist and Christian, I want to encourage the search......I believe the discovery of extraterrestrial intelligence would be exciting for the Christian, for it would open up even more of the glory and stunning creativity of the God revealed to us in Jesus."*

We must ask ourselves whether, in the 'good old days', any members of the clergy had direct contact with our more benign 'visitors from space'. It certainly seems possible.

Dan Wright, from 'MUFON' Michigan, reported on a 1967 case from Albion. In the late August of that year, 'Bill' Smith was driving his pick-up truck along a deserted road, when his engine suddenly stalled.

'He looked up through the top of the windshield to see a large domed saucer hovering over the vehicle. Telepathically, Smith is told to contact his priest, Father Gerald Boyer, and convey the message of their presence. The ship then departed, and Bill continued home.'

Minutes later, when in his front yard, Bill and his wife Marge, saw two red-orange fireballs, each about fifteen feet in diameter, hovering over their barn

250 feet away. They moved slowly and silently over the roof of their house, and disappeared above some swampy woods, 300 yards away.

Three months went by, and Bill had not yet spoken to Father Boyer. Perhaps the 'visitors' were trying to give him a nudge? On 24th November, he and Marge stared in astonishment as a much smaller fireball, about one foot in diameter, hovered over their house before accelerating away.

Bill went to see the priest, and told him of the events, and the message he was instructed to convey: - *'Father Boyer not only believed him, but claimed to be one of the extraterrestrials incarnate in human form!'*

After that, the priest visited the Smith home to watch for any return visits. On March 14th 1968, Father Boyer, along with the Smiths, and eight other witnesses, four of whom were nuns, watched as three fireballs approached. The nuns fled in terror.

'Two months later, on May 7th; *'Smith, Father Boyer, and a third witness observed a very large, bulbous cylinder in the sky, glowing amber and ejecting numerous auto-size discs that were also glowing amber.*

'That same evening, Smith witnessed the landing of one of the ejected discs. Several four-and-a-half-foot beings, clad in silver suits, descended a ramp, and once again telepathically communicated with him.'

They offered him a 'ride' in their craft, and seemed to respect his apprehension and refusal, telling him that he would receive subsequent messages to pass on to Father Boyer.

'Smith also claimed that a helicopter crew landed in his field around that time. When he went out to ask them what they were doing, he was told to "get out". Shortly thereafter, a plain-clothed gentleman, who identified himself as 'Maj. Holmes', came to his door asking questions about the encounters.'

In fact; *'during an eighteen month period in 1967/68 dozens of neighbours, friends, relatives and other visitors observed regular intrusions of glowing spheres over the Smith property.'*

Bill felt he had a duty to protect Father Boyer's involvement, and furthermore, after the helicopter incident, decided he did not trust the government. He refused to reveal anything to this mysterious 'Maj. Holmes'.

The Catholic Church has always, for several centuries, involved itself in scientific research, in an attempt to reconcile the differences between science and religion, not always an easy task. Currently, the 'Vatican Pontifical Academy of Sciences', which was established in 1936, maintains an interest and input into many subjects, including that of astronomy and extraterrestrials.

Over the years, it has included many prominent scientists, including, during the twentieth century, such well known names such as Stephen Hawking, Max Planck, Niels Bohr and Erwin Schrödinger.

Researcher Michael Mason recently wrote; *'It currently boasts more than 80 international academicians, many of them Nobel Laureates, and not all of them Catholics....Candidates are chosen on the basis of their scientific achievements and high moral standards.'*

In 1992, Pope John Paul II told the members that; *"The purpose of your academy is to precisely to discern and to make known, in the present state of science, and within its proper limits, what can be regarded as an acquired truth, or at least as enjoying such a degree of probability that it would be imprudent and unreasonable to reject it."*

Beside the Vatican Observatory itself, the Jesuits operate much more advanced facilities in Alaska, Arizona and Argentina. Rome is also home to the 'Regina Apostolorum Pontifical University', where there are many projects incorporating science and faith.

Perhaps one of the most astounding accounts comes from an article by Cristoforo Barbato, *'The Omega Secret'*, published in a 2007 *'Nexus'* magazine.

Barbato interviewed a Jesuit priest who claimed membership of the Vatican's Intelligence Agency – 'Sevizio Informazioni del Vaticana' the 'SIV'. The priest spoke of the 'Nordic' aliens, who, like us, had bodies and were 'flesh and bone', although they were very evolved from a technological and spiritual viewpoint.

He said that these beings had convinced Pope Pius XII to collaborate with them, as they wished to assist the Church of Rome in all its missions, especially in determining the character of social and political situations internationally; *'Thereafter, even Pope John Paul benefitted from the support of these beings, who had espoused the Christian cause, but he always preferred to keep it secret, speaking solely of 'angelic intervention'. Pope John XIII had inherited, in a manner of speaking, an agreement for collaboration between the Holy See and these beneficent aliens, of the Nordic race, as stipulated by his predecessor.'*

The Jesuit explained that John XIII had, on many occasions, expressed, to the leaders of the 'SIV', his fears of placing too much trust in these beings; *'That is why today we believe that one of the main reasons for convening the Second Vatican Ecumenical Council was the need to take the first step toward the renewal of the Church, in view of the possibility of imminent contact.'*

The Jesuit confirmed not only George Adamski's visit to the Pope in 1963, (see my book, *'The Alien Gene',*) but also that it was an unsuccessful attempt to attain a final agreement between the aliens and the dying Pontiff. Pope John had already decided that the Church not entertain any further direct contact with these aliens, even if they were positive. Further, he considered that it was unacceptable to reveal this relationship to the Christian populace; *'This meant, in essence, that the presumed positive activities of these aliens should be 'blessed' and not opposed, (or obstructed), but always kept distinct from and parallel to the Church.'*

In 1998, *'The Times'* published an article detailing the statements of Father Balducci from the Vatican. He expressed his beliefs that although extraterrestrials probably existed, and would be superior to us, that would not negate the teachings of Christ.

The Vatican astronomer, Dr. Christopher Corbally, had already been outspoken in 1997, when he urged mankind to become an integral part of a cosmic community, and told a science meeting in Seattle; *"We have always believed that God created all things. If he created life elsewhere, then fair enough."*

In 2001, it was reported that Italian astronaut, Umberto Guidoni, on board the space shuttle, 'Endeavour', wanted to read a message from the Pope. Just as the space shuttle was deployed alongside the International Space Station, to install a new cradle arm, Guidoni was forbidden to read the message, which would have been transmitted on a 'live' TV link. NASA later said that the message may have 'offended non-Catholic astronauts'.

In August 1969, perhaps 'United Press International' said it all when they published an article by religious writer Louis Cassels, which noted that; ... *'all those who believe the Earth to be unique in all creation as the abode of life, might find the discovery of alien life on other planets a most shattering experience if they have entered the space age with a stone age conception of God....There is really no need for any Christian or Jew to pin his religious faith to the precarious proposition that earth is the only place where the creative will of God has been expressed in the bringing forth of life.'*

FRED and PHYLLIS DICKESON

Perhaps one of the most touching accounts I have read was in a letter written on 6th July, 1955, by New Zealand researcher, Fred Dickeson, to George Adamski and Lucy McGinnis in the U.S.A.

Fred and Phyllis Dickeson were aerial photographers with the New Zealand Air Force during WW II, and soon after founded one of New Zealand's first UFO research groups.

Their family were devout Christians, and Fred had discussed with the church warden, who was a friend, his interest in the 'Space Brothers', their messages of peace and love, and a similar belief in God.

'A couple of Sundays ago I took our three children to the Family Service at St. Marys, and during the service the Archdeacon said, or rather told us a story of a little boy who said he did not know where God was. His mother told him that God could hear his prayers.

'He therefore tried to prove this by calling to God; "Can you hear me God?" As there was no answer, he called out louder. Still no reply, and his mother came up, wanting to know what the noise was. She still insisted that God could hear him, but the little boy said that God had bad manners because God did not answer him when he spoke to Him.

'He grew up, but still got no answer from God. One day he was out on his bike, and he came to a small church in the country. He went in, and all was silent. He knew if anywhere, God would be there. He called out again – still no answer.

'He went outside, and as it was a lovely summer day, he lay down and soon was asleep. Presently, he woke up and saw a man in a shiny suit coming toward him. He said to him; "My flying saucer has broken down. Have you a bit of string I can fix it with?"

'The boy had a piece of string, and the man fixed the dynamo in his saucer. The boy asked him if he knew where God was. He said he didn't know, but he knew a man on a planet who did know, so he took the boy for a ride in his flying saucer.

'Well, after a long way through space, they came to a planet and landed, and an old man greeted them. The boy asked him where God was, and he said that he was a silly boy because God was inside him, and that was why He could hear his prayers. Well, they had to get into the flying saucer again, and off they went towards Earth. Then the boy woke up in the sunshine.

'That, Mr. Adamski, was the story. You can imagine how my children reacted. I had quite a job to quieten them down, because when flying saucers were mentioned, their eyes glistened and one said, in a loud voice; "He said 'flying saucers', Daddy!"

'A number of people looked at me and smiled. It was rather strange, because as we go into church, we kneel down and pray a private prayer. Well, I did ask for guidance and help in this big job of getting the people interested in flying saucers, and then this story was in the service. It seems so strange. With all this ridicule we get, we do feel we are getting somewhere, but it is taking time.'

CHAPTER SEVENTEEN

THE PUZZLING CASES

THE GREEN 'FIREBALLS'

After the end of World War II, from the late 1940s to the early 1950s, an increasing amount of 'Green Fireballs' were reported over the U.S. skies, usually shooting across the atmosphere of New Mexico, where, at the time, the American nuclear facilities, missile bases and secret military installations were housed. Thousands of people reported them. (They were even seen over the Sizewell nuclear power stations in Sussex, England.)

These objects were not meteorites, which can burn up with a green glow as they crash through our atmosphere. Everybody was mystified, and some of the best experts were called upon to provide an explanation.

One explanation was only feasible for a minority of reports. Some SR-71 craft would make a fast dive, at a 30 degree angle, then pull out and accelerate skyward more than twice the speed of sound. This manoeuvre, called a 'Dipsy Doodle' could cause the exhaust to periodically glow green.

This certainly could not explain earlier events, one as far back as 1882, when a British astronomer reported that a 'great circular disc of greenish light' appeared from the east-north-east and moved smoothly and steadily across the sky.

Investigator, Ivan Sanderson, wrote of several other incidents which occurred during World War II. There had been some disturbing intelligence reports of these strange green objects, and it took an unexpected turn when a contingent of British troops was rushed to Jamaica after the fall of the Netherlands.

One evening they were marching, eight abreast, around an inland lagoon, when a glowing green sphere, about two feet in diameter, descended slowly out of the sky, bounced along the road ahead of the troops and went into a culvert. The officer-in-charge ordered his men to go after it, but the strange intruder shot out and raced back into the sky above.

Later, Sanderson was on a sailing ship, off the coast of Nicaragua, when he and the captain spotted, in the night sky, a very bright green, spherical object which seemed to be coming disconcertingly closer before it silently exploded. The object had displayed signs of intelligent control, so he immediately notified his superiors in London, and received the following coded reply;

'To: No. XXXX; From ----- Kindly desist, repeat desist, reporting green lights and other aerial phenomena, and proceed with assigned duties – There is a war going on you know!'

On December 5th 1948, eight separate 'fireballs' had been seen. The crew of a military C-47 plane were astonished when a brilliant green object climbed from below in the sky, then arched upwards and levelled off before streaking past.

One was also seen by a commercial airliner, a Pioneer Airlines DC-3, whose crew saw the object, which originally appeared to be a red-orange colour, and changed to green as it became bigger and brighter and neared the plane. The pilot, fearing a collision, forced the DC-3 into a tight, spiralling turn. After the object seemed to fly abreast of the airliner, it fell away, growing dimmer as it disappeared into the distance. As soon as they landed at Albuquerque airport, the crew were interrogated for nearly an hour by Air Force intelligence officers.

Three days later, two of the intelligence officers took off in a plane from Kirkland Air Force Base, and spotted a bright green 'fireball' 2,000 feet above them. It passed overhead, at some considerable speed, before seeming to drop rapidly and fade as it went into the distance.

Some witnesses were highly qualified people. During the summer of 1948, physicist Carl Mitchell, observed three green discs as they passed over Easton, Pennsylvania, one second apart.

In 1949, the U.S. Air Force established 'Project Twinkle', under Dr. Lincoln La Paz, to investigate these bright green intruders. Dr. La Paz was Director of the Institute of Meteorites and Head of the Department of Mathematics and Astronomy at the University of New Mexico. He had served as a consultant with the military at the New Mexico Proving Grounds, and also with the Air Force from 1943 to 1945.

There was great concern in the administration regarding this phenomenon, and initial conferences during 1949, included the FBI, the U.S. Air Force, and the U.S. Atomic Energy Commission.

Lincoln La Paz, who was a prominent pioneer in meteor studies, believed they were not meteors or fireballs, but intelligently controlled devices. Although a number of Los Alamos scientists agreed that they were not natural phenomena, and in spite of a couple of 'observation posts' being set up, nobody was able to positively identify their origin or purpose.

It seemed that whenever an observation/photographic post was set up in some of the most 'top secret' and sensitive areas where the 'fireballs' had been seen, they would suddenly be conspicuous by their absence. Due to their appearance near sensitive installations, La Paz had suggested that they may be of domestic origin, and secret U.S. missile tests. Although these may have been the origin of some sightings, a 1947 document, issued by the U.S. Air Force Intelligence Division noted that 'it was the considered opinion of some elements of the U.S. military, that 'Flying Saucers' and 'Flying Discs' represented 'interplanetary craft of some kind'.

Later, researcher Kevin Randle quoted a 'confidential' memo from the Air Force files; *'There is reasonable doubt in the minds of some of the project personnel that this, (green fireballs), is a natural phenomenon. As long as reasonable doubt exists, it is not wise to discontinue the observation. Dr. Whipple's suggestion that these may be moon reflections on small clouds cannot be discounted. It may be considered significant that fireballs have ceased abruptly as soon as a systematic watch was set up.'*

The project, which was understaffed and insufficiently funded, was not a success, and petered out when the military were forced to concentrate their resources on the Korean War. However, there was some criticism levelled at Dr. Elterman, who, at the end of 1951, recommended 'no further expenditure of time and effort be spent on the project', and suggested that most sightings were due to natural phenomena.

He had revealed a serious deficiency in the project. Even if there was photographic footage captured by the observation posts.... *'there were insufficient funds built into the contract to analyse the film.'* Researcher, Bruce Maccabee later commented; *'What sort of scientific project is that? Did they want it to succeed, or did they want it to fail?'* In his book, *'UFO-FBI'*, Maccabee also wrote; *'It was during the time of this project that one of these Askania phototheodolites got the proof of existence of flying saucers. It was also during this project that the proof was ignored or covered up.'*

During the next few years there was a diminishing number of sightings reported, and no fragments recovered. Although no definitive explanation as to their nature or origin was ever reached, Edward Ruppelt, from 'Project Blue Book', spoke to several scientists, who all agreed they were not a natural phenomenon. They believed that there was a giant UFO 'mother-ship', parked above the earth, which was shooting green 'probes' into the atmosphere.

Perhaps these strange objects were, as some suspected, a form of observation craft. 'MUFON' investigator, Jan Aldrich, wrote of a case which occurred in 1939 in Forth Worth, Texas. This was long before the concerns and investigations of the 1940s and 50s.

A woman was sleeping in a bed, out in her backyard. It was early autumn, perhaps rather hot inside, and a clear night with the moon shining down. Suddenly she heard a whirring noise – 'like an electric fan' – and propped herself up on her elbow to see what it was.

A strange object was coming directly toward her, from a height of twenty to thirty feet. It slowed, and descended to a height even with her bed. *'It appeared to be three feet long by ten feet high, greyish in colour, and with strata or veins running through it. It was shaped like an old time Mississippi steam boat. Surrounding it was a soft blue-green glow.'*

The object then moved to the foot of her bed, and suddenly zoomed off into the sky and disappeared.

In April 1950, several parts of America were witness to silent, livid green glowing discs. The Director of Civil Aviation at Laredo issued the following statement to the press; *'For several days discs have been seen on both sides of the Rio Bravo. Before crashing, this particular disc deliberately buzzed the field six or seven times, each time more slowly, finally diving into the field, to narrowly miss the largest hanger. Following the crash, airport personnel and firemen hurried to the scene of the wreck. The crashed disc measured only a couple of yards across.'*

Near the end of 1950, over the other side of the world, in Australia, UFO Research Queensland received a report from Paddington Fire Station. A spherical green orb was seen travelling from the north-east to the south-west over the Taylor Ranges.

Suddenly, it changed direction and moved to the south at 'terrific' speed. It gained height, and changed direction again, this time moving east at 'jet speed', and then seemed to change shape, and resembled a thin convex lens.

The witness said that although at times the rate of climb was on par with a meteor, who ever saw one ascending or changing direction?

Although 'Project Twinkle' was theoretically 'non functional', those mysterious green balls had apparently 'not got the message'.

In their book *'Mysteries of the Skies'*, researchers Gordon Lore and Harold Deneault told of an incident, investigated by NICAP, from the fall of 1952; *'Three airplane crews, flying fifteen minutes apart, sighted a huge green ball. Captains Charles Zammett, Robert Harris and William Hutchins of Pan American World Airways were flying about 600 miles south of New York, en route to Puerto Rico, when they saw ahead of them, an enormous green sphere that appeared to be stationary. It was extremely brilliant, and much larger than the moon's apparent size.*

'One pilot called to the other crews; - "Do you see that?"

"I'll say I see it. What the devil is it?" the reply came.

'Then the third crew broke in; "We see it too. Who could miss it!"

'For forty-five seconds they watched as the object hung motionless. Then the green globe shot off to the west at tremendous speed, moving away from them on a horizontal path until it disappeared.'

Even the Soviet Union, who obviously did not participate in 'Project Twinkle', also experienced these 'pesky' phenomena. In the spring of 1959 hundreds of flying saucers and UFOs were sighted, during a twenty-four hour period, over the town of Sverdolok, which was the headquarters for the Russian Tactical Missile Command. One Russian Air Force pilot fired upon a glowing green 'fireball' encountered during a flight over Sverdolok, but it easily evaded the rockets fired from the MIG fighter plane.

Scott Corrales noted two of many cases of these strange objects also appearing over Cuba and the Caribbean.

In 1953, Waldo Martinez, a Lieutenant in the Cuban army, was driving towards a Trinidad hospital, when the engine in his military jeep suddenly failed. A powerful green light flew past his vehicle, and landed 200 metres away. When the object's light dimmed, his vehicle regained power, and Martinez and his passengers were able to resume their journey. Later, a sixty feet diameter burned circle was discovered on the ground.

The title 'Fireball' was undoubtedly a misnomer, as many of these objects were solid craft, emitting a bright green light. On 30th July 1952, ground-staff at a Braintree airfield in Mass. U.S.A., witnessed a saucer, emitting a bluish-green light, as it circled, at high speed overhead. It was tracked by both GCI and plane radar. When a F-94 was sent up, the mysterious object soon outdistanced it.

Dr. Richard Haines wrote of an incident in early 1951, during the Korean War. Private Francis Wall was stationed with his army unit near the city of Chorwon. One night, whilst on manoeuvres with 25 other soldiers, a blue-green pulsating light approached. Later, Wall said he thought this must have been 'an alien spacecraft – like nothing I had ever seen'. He noticed that some ineffective artillery fire had been aimed at it, and as the object neared his platoon, the pulsating blue-green light became more intense. He immediately requested for, and received, permission to fire upon it. As he opened up with his M-1 rifle, he could hear his armour-piercing bullets hitting the object's apparent metallic surface.

The craft 'went wild', and was moving erratically from side to side. By the time the other soldiers unleashed a barrage of fire, it had restored its equilibrium. Wall later thought that until then, it had no hostile intent, and its defences were 'down'.

The object made a weird, deep noise, then emitted a ray of light, which swept across them in 'pulses'. The soldiers felt a burning, tingling sensation all over their bodies, and retreated to their bunker. The strange craft hovered overhead for some time, before shooting off, with incredible speed, at a 45 degree angle.

Within three days, all the men, some of whom were too weak to walk, had to be evacuated by ambulance. They had dysentery, and an extremely high white blood cell count, which puzzled the doctors. Since that time, Pte. Wall suffered periods of disorientation, severe headaches and memory loss. His weight dropped from 180 pounds to only 138 pounds. He was deemed to be disabled and retired from duty.

In 1997, the *'UFO Magazine'* told of how in 1953, Captain Allison, a R.A.F. pilot, and his radio operator, Heavers, were on a night flying exercise out of R.A.F. Coltishall in Norfolk, when they spotted a speeding cigar-shaped craft with internal green lights visible through its windows.

Three minutes later, another aircrew, flying 100 miles away, near their base at R.A.F. Maidstone, Kent, reported an identical sighting. It was calculated that the object's speed would have been about 2,000 m.p.h., well in excess of any aircraft in the U.K. at that time.

Across the English Channel, in Namur, Belgium, postman M. Muyldemans was driving along the road at 7.30 pm on 5th June 1955. He slowed down when he saw a low-flying green disc, which had three spheres underneath. He thought it was about to land, so he grabbed his camera before stopping his car and getting out.

Our postman was also a photographer, and he got three excellent shots – one whilst the object was stationary, one as it came lower, and a third as it climbed to speed away, at an estimated speed of 500km/hr. An expert who examined them calculated the object as being at least twelve metres in diameter, and a minimum 1,500 metres altitude on the last frame.

A clue as to the origin of some of these 'green fireballs' can be found in George Hunt Williamson's book, *'The Saucers Speak'*, where, in 1952, he and colleagues were secretly communicating with extraterrestrials by ham radio.

In one conversation, when they were conversing with their 'contacts', the visitors explained; *'...then there is the Mother-Ship that you call a cigar-shaped craft. These can be many miles in length, and send out the 'green fireballs' to explode, then photographs of the magnetic fault lines can be taken. You would be astonished if you knew what these fireballs really were. They are not the same as your remote controlled devices.'*

Certainly, in December 1948, several reports told of these soundless objects racing, in a straight course, over the U.S. Southwest and silently exploding, casting a brilliant green glow for hundreds of miles. Afterwards, not even a fragment of wreckage could be found. These mystifying objects were tracked at speeds up to 14,000 miles per hour.

However, incidents where these 'green fireballs' were seen to explode were not all that common. Major Donald Keyhoe (ret), a prominent researcher in his day, talked of one such case which occurred on the 2nd of November 1951.

'An American Airlines DC-4 had been flying from Los Angeles to Tulsa by way of Dallas. At 7.15am the airliner was cruising east of Abilene on Airway G-5. The altimeter read 4,500ft.

'Suddenly, a bright green object streaked past the airliner at the same altitude, and holding the same course. As nearly as the crew could judge, the projectile-shaped device was about the size of their plane. As it raced ahead, the pilots saw a white trail, which they took to be exhaust vapour.

'The DC-4 was cruising at 220 miles an hour, and it was only a matter of seconds before the strange green fireball had shot ahead. Then, to the crew's amazement, the strange missile exploded, shooting red balls of fire in all directions.

"It was like a Fourth of July roman candle," the First Officer said later.'

Whilst commercial airliner reports of these bright green objects were quite rare, they did occur, both in the air and on the ground.

Researcher Dan Farcas discussed an incident which occurred in 1968, when, on 17th August, a Romanian 'Tarom' Company airliner was flying from Constanta in Romania to Düsseldorf in Germany.

The plane was flying at 7,600 metres, near Oradea, close to the Hungarian border, when Captain Benjamin Gabrian spotted, about a kilometre away, an unexpected object travelling at high speed. He naturally took notice, because it was at an altitude of just under 8,000 metres, a little too close for comfort.

He and his colleagues, Alexandru Niculescu and Marian Constantinescu estimated the object, which emanated an extremely strong, greenish light, to have a diameter of about three metres. The strange craft, which was possibly matching their speed, soon accelerated and disappeared into the west.

Two and a half minutes later, presumably the same object was seen in Austrian airspace by the crew of a Hungarian 'Malev' plane. They said it was heading westward, at an altitude of 6,000 metres, and a calculated speed of 14,000 kilometres per hour, which Dan Farcas doubted any plane could achieve at that altitude.

Unlike his western counterparts, pilot Benjamin Gabrian was allowed to talk to the press. The next day, the Constanta newspaper, *'Dobrogea Noud'*, quoted him as saying; *"I think what we have seen is routinely described in the international media under the term 'UFO'. The chance we could watch it for 10 to 15 seconds is due to the fact that the object had apparently reduced its speed.....Perhaps because the alien crew was interested in our machine and what was in it?"*

In my book *'UFOs Now and Then'* I describe the 1954 appearance of a large, bright green, metal 'ball' over Antananarivo in Madagascar. It was witnessed by several hundred people, and as it flew low over the town, all the animals in the local zoo, normally not perturbed by passing aircraft, displayed 'violent fright reactions'.

Although General Fleurquin, Madagascar's Commander-in-Chief, organised a 'scientific commission' to *'conduct an investigation into these phenomena'*, investigators could find no record of this inquiry in the archives.

Further to the west, one March night, in 1958, a French Foreign Legionnaire was on guard duty, during the Algerian War, at a camp near Bouahmama. A whistling noise accompanied an enormous elliptical object, which descended from the sky and silently hovered about fifty metres away and only 35-40 metres above the terrain. It was surrounded by a pale green light, and an intense conical beam of emerald-green light, which lit up the ground, was emanating from underneath.

Instead of picking up the telephone, going to investigate, or even firing his rifle, the soldier just sat there, as if in a trance. For over 45 minutes, time felt 'distorted'. He felt 'happy' as he stared at 'the most beautiful, relaxing and fascinating colours he had ever seen'. It was only upon hearing another noise, and watching as the object gently rose, and flew off at tremendous speed, that he remembered the War.

He rushed to advise his senior officers, who instigated an immediate investigation. For a week, he was confined to a military hospital in Paris, where psychiatrists and neurologists determined he was in a good state of mental and physical health, and apparently not affected by his experience or wartime service.

At about 8.15pm on December 11th 1956, two young men had gone for a motorcycle ride on Blubberhouses Moor, in Yorkshire, between Bolton Abbey and Addingham.

Suddenly, they were amazed to see a bright green 'ball', about twenty feet in diameter, with green and yellow flames shooting out, hovering about 2,000ft overhead. It was so bright, it lit up the area even when the motorcycle lights were turned off.

After about two minutes it started to slowly descend, and they lost sight of it behind a 'fold in the hill'. Another witness, from Grassington, also reported seeing the object.

In November the following year, further to the north in Edinburgh, fourteen potato pickers were all in the back of an open truck, and on their way home. The *'Sunday Mail'* reported how a 'humming, green-glowing flying saucer' swept in from over the North Sea.

Mary Horne, one of the passengers, said; *"I swear on the Bible, it was no balloon. It swooped down, and kept about 60ft behind us, until it suddenly stopped. It then flew away, leaving two vapour trails."*

Apparently Edinburgh police treated the matter quite seriously.

In 1957, these 'green' craft and fireballs were still quite active. Across the Atlantic, in Portland, Oregon, the '*Oragonian*' published a report about a spectacular green fireball which, on the 1st August, streaked across the Portland sky, at an estimated speed of 1,200 mph, before heading to northern and central California.

It was first witnessed by the control tower operators at Washington's Seattle-Tacoma airport, before being sighted by thousands of people in the Pacific Northwest. Initially estimated at travelling at 1,200 mph, many described it as being more like a cigar-shaped craft, with port-hole like spots along the side. At one stage it apparently slowed, before 'launching forward at an even greater speed.' Some smaller, glowing, saucer-like craft were visible for a short while before disappearing.

It wasn't until 1963 that '*Saucer News*' reported that one night the following November, in 1957, Olden Moore , who was living in Lake Country, Ohio, was driving along Route 56 near Montville, when he spotted what he first thought was a 'shooting star' moving across the sky in front of him. Suddenly, it split into two pieces, with one travelling upwards, and the other getting bigger and brighter as it moved closer.

As it approached, its colour changed from white to bright green. Olden could now see it was about 200ft above a nearby field, and realised it wasn't a meteorite. It slowly settled to the ground, and a faint whirring sound could be heard.

The strange object was about 500ft away, and for fifteen minutes Olden stood beside his car, before deciding to get a little closer. He walked about halfway towards it, before thinking that, since no-one else was around, he would go home and get his wife to be a possible extra witness.

He had already noted that the strange craft was surrounded by a blue-green haze, and the colour was slowly pulsating alternating between bright and dim. The craft itself was approximately fifty feet in diameter, disc shaped, and about fifteen feet thick, with a cone on top, making its overall height between twenty to thirty feet. It had a mirrored surface, but he could not see any portholes or windows.

When he returned with his wife, the object had gone, but the next day Lake County officials investigated the scene. Civil Defence Director, Kenneth Locke and his offsider, Lt. Reineck, discovered ground traces and reported higher than normal radiation readings in that area.

Olden confided to researcher Clyde Fitch that a few months later, he had been flown to Washington and interviewed by three military officers, who treated him very well. After questioning him for some time, as was the case with several pilots in those days, he was shown some photographs. They projected some slides, and even a 'movie film', (taken from inside a military plane), onto a screen. They all showed various UFOs, and Olden was told that about 30% of the UFOs on which they had information, were the type with the pointed dome, such as the one he had seen.

Clyde Fitch also wrote that; *'After being shown these slides and motion pictures, Moore was asked to sign papers to the effect that he would not reveal the fact that he had been shown this evidence of the existence of UFOs. Moore told me that he asked where these objects are from. He was told by the military officials that they are not ours or Russia's, and that they must therefore be from another planet, coming into our atmosphere from outer space. He was also told that the public has not been informed about this because the military themselves do not yet have all the answers...'*

Normally, these strange aerial objects did no harm to anyone on the ground, but there were exceptions. In 1958 George Fawcett told of how Haskell Raper, of Mississippi, was driving home from work when he saw a large 'greenish' UFO, about fifteen feet long, and nine feet high, flashing a beam of light. It was on the ground, about fifteen feet away.

Suddenly his car started heating up, and he had to jump from it when his engine burst into flames. 'The UFO 'cranked-up', sounding like a diesel engine, and lifted off the ground at rapid speed, before disappearing. As it did, the car's gas tank exploded, and his vehicle was a 'total wreck.' State police and Air Force officials could find no rational explanation for the incident.

Major Donald Keyhoe told of an incident in about 1953, when a Transocean DC-3, with eight crew and fifty passengers, crashed off Wake Island, during a flight from Guam to Oakland. During the search for and recovery of the wreckage, several plane crews and search vessels reported seeing green lights or fireballs.

The plane had just been inspected, and was 'in perfect condition'. Later examination of the wreckage indicated that the plane had either dived into the water, at fast speed, or had just 'gone to pieces in the air'.

It wasn't just in the northern hemisphere that these 'green balls' were being seen. In 1996, I received a report from an elderly gentleman, Martin Kelly, who wanted to tell me about what he had seen in June 1957, whilst working in Campbelltown, Sydney, as a carpenter-builder.

It was just after lunch when he had climbed the frame of a house they were working on, and was passing rafters up to a fellow workman, Ray Winter. Suddenly, he saw a bright gleaming light appear from the left side of the Sun. It was small, 'about Moon size', but very bright; "I shouted to my mate – "what the hell is that?" He looked up and nearly fell off the roof.

"We watched, and as it moved away from the Sun, it showed itself as a larger round object, shiny-metallic in appearance, and of a greenish blue colour. It seemed to be falling through space at great speed, rather than being driven. It was twisting, like an aircraft doing 'barrel rolls', but then changed course at right-angles to its brief arc, and corkscrewed straight up, at enormous speed, and vanished as if nothing had happened!

"There was no noise, vapour trails or evidence of any exhaust activity. The sky was crystal clear that day, and we estimated that the object, perhaps the size of a 'Jumbo Jet', was at around 40,000 feet, travelling at anything around 1,800 to 2,000 miles per hour.

"Naturally, we were both shocked, incredulous and slightly un-nerved by what we had seen. There was no way it could have been a weather balloon, aircraft or any one of a dozen other possibilities that came to mind.

"We thought it rather significant that two aircraft appeared in our area shortly after we sighted the object. They circled at height for some time, and we felt fairly sure they had come from the direction of Bankstown Airport."

In 1957-58 the *'Nambour Chronicle'* in Queensland, published reports of strange green 'circles of light' hovering over the cane fields, and farmers subsequently finding circular, singed depressions in their crops.

Whilst the number of reports diminished over the years, nearly a decade later, at the beginning of 1966, another case occurred, this time back in Britain at Wilmslow, Cheshire. Police Constable Colin Perks' report is held at the Public Records' Office.

He was on patrol in the town centre at 4.10am on the morning of Friday, 7th January, when he heard a high pitched whine. He turned around, and saw a greenish-grey glow, about one hundred yards away, and 35 feet up in the sky.

It was an elliptical shaped craft, with a flat bottom, about seventy feet long, twenty feet or more wide, and fifteen feet in height. He said it had a sharp, distinctive, definite shape and was certainly made of a solid substance, although he could not detect any portholes or 'places of entrance'. What impressed him most was the 'eerie green glow', which seemed to be emanating from the exterior of the object.

It was originally motionless, with no sign of rotation, but after a few seconds, moved off sideways and disappeared at a very fast rate in an east-south-east direction. His subsequent report passed up the chain of command, and the next month he was interviewed by an Air Force officer, whose report was categorised as a 'Restricted Memorandum'.

Perks himself, was confined to desk duties for the next month, by which time the press had got hold of the story.

Back in the U.S.A., researcher Michael Hervey, along with his colleague Kolman Von Keviezky, detailed an event in July 1963, which created quite a lot of interest and concern. Multiple reports were received from both Delaware and Long Island, New York, and there was definitely more than one object traversing back and forth across the skies that night.

Morris County police received over a dozen calls about a flashing object, of greenish hue, in the western sky. Other police stations, who received numerous calls from Wayne County, reported that some witnesses said a bright green UFO was seen to soar into the air and then return near Hackettstown Mountain.

Police and newspaper reporters made several searches of various areas, but found nothing, and experts ruled out meteorites.

One witness said; *"There was not the slightest doubt in our minds – it was a UFO. It was a circular object that appeared like a fluorescent greenish light. It seemed to throw off white fire streaks from a tail as it disappeared behind cloud then reappeared"*

The Chilean government's official newspaper, *'La Nación'*, reported that on December 30th 1966, Chilean National Airline mechanics, Mauro Correa and Fernando Jiminez, who were stationed at Lima's international airport, witnessed another case of this strange phenomenon; *'Correa stated that the strange craft were flying at great altitude, but that he was able to see them and count them because the sky was very clear. He added that the objects were emitting an intense green light, and were spherical in shape.'*

Back in Australia, in 2003, where these strange green objects had also been seen, a woman told 'UFO Research Qld.' how thirty or forty years ago, possibly some time during the 1960s, she was driving alone from Albury, on the NSW border, towards Melbourne. It was a lonely stretch of road, and at about 9pm, she noticed a strange craft, seemingly 100 metres away on her left, and only at telegraph pole height. She looked closer, as she thought it appeared to be pacing her vehicle.

It was a large, lime-green cigar-shaped object, about the size of a small car, and she could see what looked like six people sitting inside. It was difficult to distinguish their features, but they were all dressed in some form of identical uniform.

She was quite frightened, as the object was matching her pace, slowing down and then speeding up as she tried to 'shake' her unwanted companion. Eventually, she reached the Diggers' Rest Hotel, where she stopped and went in to get a drink to settle her nerves. The strange craft had disappeared, and she did not tell her friends at the bar what had happened, as she felt they would just laugh. Neither did she tell her own family, fearing they would not believe her and question her sanity.

In 1967, Harry Cox, from *'People'* magazine told of Dr. Antonin Kukla, who, along with his companion Audrey Lawrence, was investigating rock formations twelve miles north of Pimbie Station, near Carnarvon, West Australia.

At about 7.40pm, on the night of 27th July, 1965 they noticed a green light, moving slowly across the sky. After moving behind a cloud, it, or a second bright, reddish-orange object reappeared, and, with a right-angle movement, dived straight towards their land cruiser's headlights.

As Kukla threw on his brake, the object, which had changed back to a green colour, and looked like a 'squashed football' or 'saucer', about three feet wide, stopped and hovered about fifteen away. There was complete silence as it gently rocked from side to side. Their dog, 'Snowy', who was usually the first out of the car, was crouched in the back seat, with her 'hackles up'.

They watched for about thirty minutes as the strange object slightly changed position, at one time appearing to be hovering on its edge. It was last seen drifting westward until it disappeared. It changed colour slightly, but the predominant hue was a pulsing green.

Later Kuckla and Audrey Lawrence spoke to Ron Butler, the owner of Mooka Station. He told them that the same night his entire camp had been lit up with a greenish glow when something passed over it.

Even the Japanese, to the north, were sighting these strange 'green' objects. On March 18th 1965, a Japanese Convair 240 airliner, with 28 passengers on board, was flying over Shikaku Island. At an altitude of about one mile, Captain Yashika Inaba and his co-pilot Tesu Umashima saw a circular object, about 50 feet in diameter, and emitting a green light, approaching their aircraft.

As it neared, all instruments in the cabin ceased to function, including the auto-pilot, and radio communications with the nearest airport were lost. The strange object followed the Covair for some time, before slowing down for about three minutes. Suddenly, it picked up speed, and continued tailing the aircraft, staying close to the left wing, for the next fifty miles. When they reached the city of Matsuyama, the UFO, which had also been sighted by another pilot, and from the ground, sped away as quickly as it had come.

Back in Britain, in November 1967, the *'Daily Express'* carried an article about Karl Farlow who had reported a strange encounter, just before midnight, on the A338 road near the New Forest. The lights and radio on his truck suddenly went out, although his diesel engine kept running.

When he pulled up to investigate, he suddenly saw a strange object, hovering over the road, no more than fifteen yards ahead of him. A white Jaguar car, coming from the opposite direction, seemed to lose both his lights and engine, and also came to a halt;

"It glowed the most beautiful green colour I have ever seen. It was like nothing on earth. I'm convinced I saw a flying saucer or some object from outer space! It hovered quite still for a couple of minutes, then made off at fantastic speed. I could clearly see a whitish coloured dome underneath. I sat in the cab petrified. I don't want ever to experience anything like that again. This was no hallucination."

After the craft departed, both vehicles operated normally. The Jaguar driver took off, and Karl rang the police. Constable Roy Nineham, who attended in his patrol car, later said; *"Mr. Farlow was very frightened. The most startling part was that his lights failed, and came on again when the object he saw disappeared."*

Further to the north-east in Sweden, another incident, between Kungälv and Marstrand, had occurred at 11pm on March 22nd 1967. Investigator Ake Jonsson detailed how Ann-Lis Danielsson was driving along the road when she noticed a green shimmer in the top right-hand corner of her windscreen.

She turned around to see what it was, and about 150 metres away, at an altitude of about 400 metres, a round disc-shaped object, about fifteen metres in diameter and emitting an intense greenish light, was hovering.

Although her car windows were closed, she could hear a powerful 'whirring' sound as the strange craft kept pace with her for several kilometres along the straight road. Suddenly, it changed direction, and headed away, disappearing into the west and in the direction of the sea.

In the September of that year, Canadian forestry worker, Russell Hill, who was stationed forty miles southwest of Calgary, was terrified on four occasions when strange green-glowing objects shot through the skies around his lookout cabin, before departing at tremendous speed.

One looked like two bowls clamped onto a saucer-like body, and pulsated with a throbbing hum to the extent that his radio and lights temporarily failed. It was about 75 feet in diameter, and he could see porthole-type indentations around the side, and another greenish light rotating inside the 'top'.

THE DRONES

Whilst drones are commonplace today, very few, if any, existed in 'The Good Old Days'. It is not known if there is any connection between the 'green balls' and drones, however one interesting case from a winter's night in 1953 comes to mind.

Tom Beck was just a lad when he and eight other friends, having been to the cinema, were making their way back to their small country boarding school, just outside Haslemere, in Surrey.

Suddenly, they saw a large, luminescent green, oval shaped object high in the sky overhead. They stared in astonishment when, after a minute or so, two rows of four, much smaller objects of exactly the same shape and colour, emerged from the same sides of the saucer. When they had lined up into two columns of four in each, they suddenly flew off, at an incredible speed, in different directions.

The main saucer remained stationary for about five minutes, and then the smaller objects returned, and re-entered the 'mother ship' at the same point from which they had emerged. The main saucer moved off very fast, however the excited twelve-year-olds' chased after it, and saw it stop once more, when it went through the same ritual, this time moving off for good after the eight little craft returned.

Pilotless craft, from tiny drones to much larger, sophisticated machines, have come into their own for over three decades. (Much longer in fact, if you consider satellites and other related technology.) They are used, unchecked, militarily and commercially, for everything from parcel deliveries, surveillance, and armed attacks. It often makes it nigh impossible to differentiate what is ours and what is not.

In the late nineties, the Australian Defence Force announced that, in a lead-up to Defence Exercise 'Crocodile 99', it would be testing a pilotless vertical take-off and landing craft over the Northern Territory. Their new toy, about 1.8m tall with a rotor diameter of four metres, could travel up to 200km from its ground control station. Its flight path could be pre-programmed or remote controlled.

Wing Commander Carrer said there were no other aircraft of its kind in use in Australia at that time. I wonder if that was exactly true. In October 1981, the Department of Defence wrote to investigator John Auchettl, following his questions about the Jindivik Drone.

They advised that during the mid 1970s it conducted operations at Woomera Rocket Range for both National and International projects. At the time of their correspondence, the drone was stationed at the NSW Jervis Bay Range Facility. It was operated by the Navy for use by the three Australian Armed Services, and was not being deployed or operated anywhere else in Australia. This information was also not entirely correct. Woomera Testing Ground was apparently using the 'Jindivik' as early as 1957.

Years before the Pentagon had unveiled a saucer-shaped pilotless reconnaissance plane, worth ten million dollars, which they claimed could 'detect a basketball on the ground from a height of 13,500 metres, even in poor weather'.

The *'Times'*, a New Zealand provincial newspaper, said that serious experimentation with drones, as electronic counter-surveillance craft, commenced in the 1960s. It has also been reported that, at that time, Lockheed Skunk Works had manufactured thirty-eight D21 unmanned drones, and in 1963 they were mated with a mother-ship aircraft for the first time, although the initial flight did not occur until December 1964. This would explain some, but not all, of the many reports of smaller objects leaving and returning to a larger craft. There were much earlier reports of exactly such an aerial system.

Investigator, Richard Hall, had undertaken a comprehensive survey of these early 'drones', and my friend and colleague, Paul Norman, discussed some of these incidents in the *'Australian UFO Bulletin'* in 1992.

'On numerous occasions, when a number of small objects is observed, there is a cigar-shaped object nearby. One of the earliest recordings of modern day 'satellite' cases occurred in the Summer of 1944, when three smaller discs were

seen to be detaching themselves from a parent, oval-shaped object over Grenada, Mississippi, U.S.A. They moved away in different directions.

'On July 23rd 1952, aircraft plant engineers watched a silver, elliptical object launch two smaller discs over Culver City, California. The discs circled the area then flew back to the parent ship which climbed straight up at high speed.'

On August 27th 1952, three witnesses in Denham, Buckinghamshire, England saw a large object eject several smaller objects. Later, two more flew out of the parent craft, and disappeared in different directions.

Later that year, on December 6th, the crew of a B-29 who had been on a training flight over the Gulf of Mexico, were returning to their base in Texas. They were at an altitude of 18,000ft when some unknown objects, flying at high speed, passed their plane. One object had been picked up on radar, then a second, followed by four more.

They were small and round, and lit by a blue-white light. The first two groups had flown past, but the third had slowed behind the bomber and paced it for about ten seconds before accelerating and shooting off.

Then an enormous object appeared on their radar screen. The smaller objects were seen to merge with it, after which the larger craft picked up speed and shot away at over 9,000 mph. The speed of the smaller UFOs had been estimated at 5,240 mph.

These strange craft seemed to be intelligently controlled; Paul Norman mentioned another case when a plane was flying from Birmingham, Alabama to Chattanooga, Tennessee during the autumn of 1951. The pilots saw five smaller objects flying out of a larger object. When they attempted to radio the sighting to Air Traffic Control, all the objects quickly disappeared.

On June 30th 1954, the crew and passengers of a BOAC airliner, flying from New York to London, saw a large cigar-shaped 'craft' flying with six smaller objects, three in front and three behind. As soon as an interceptor approached from Labrador, the small objects went back into the larger craft, which flew away at a fast speed.

'On September 22nd 1954, at Fontainebleau, France, a luminous ball emitted several smaller ball-like objects from its underside, which flew away in all

directions. As an airplane approached, the large object rose into the sky at high speed.'

French researcher, Aimé Michel, investigated several 1954 instances of these 'great cloud cigars' or 'mother-ships' and their small companions, in France; *'Moreover, every time the 'great cloud cigar' is seen motionless, the place where it was reported will appear on the map as a dispersing or collecting centre for small objects.'*

Charles Garrau, in *'Soucoupes Volantes'*, documented another sighting. In the early morning of 23rd August 1954, M. Miserey had returned home to Vernon, and was putting his car away, when he noticed the town was bathed in a pale light. Looking up he saw a huge cigar-shaped object, about 100 metres long, hovering vertically in the sky, about 300 metres above the north bank of the river.

A small disc-shaped object seemed to fall from the bottom, rocked, hovered, then brightened, headed in his direction, and disappeared at speed behind him. Three others followed soon after. A fifth object emerged, dropped a bit lower, then headed in the opposite direction.

The 'mother-ship' seemed to fade from view, but the witness later learned that the entire display had also been seen by two policemen in a patrol car and engineer M. Millet.

Another sighting was reported two years earlier, on 27th October 1952, from Galliac in France. About ten witnesses, including a Mayor, a school principal and a teacher saw a cylindrical-like object, hanging at a 45 degree angle over the town. A few minutes later, a large number of spherical objects appeared before and behind the cylinder.

Many other witnesses in the area also made reports, and said that up to sixteen small discs, with domes, moved in pairs in a rapid zigzag motion, and appeared to release a strange substance, which may have been what we later called 'angel hair'.

In September, near St-Prouant, a large object was seem 'sowing' a little metallic disc, and earlier, on August 19th, several witnesses in the Vernon area saw a 'huge vertical cigar, standing still and launching five small discs'.

These little 'drone' type craft were also being seen in Austria. Researcher, Gordon Creighton, translated a 1963 report from the *'Bulletin of the Austrian Interplanetary Society'*.

On July 28th, Alexander Santner and his wife were staying at his Saileralm Alpine herdsman's hut, near Klein-Reifling. They were mystified when, just after midnight, they saw, for nearly two hours, a globe-shaped object, which varied in brilliance and zigzagged and hovered over the Almkogel and Bodenwies regions.

Two weeks later, at about the same time, on 11th August, when Alexander had both his wife and fifteen-year-old son with him, they were woken by a commotion among the cattle. When they went out to investigate, they saw forty to fifty luminous globes, of various dimensions, flying in and out of the nearby Arzmäuer Caves.

The whole family stared in astonishment until, over three hours later, a very large flying object, with big torpedo-shape openings of various sizes, descended to a height of about 1,400 metres; *'They watched as it sailed to and fro between Almkogel and Bodenwies several times, giving off intermittent luminous flashes.*

'In the meantime, the small flying objects continued to pass in and out of the caves. Then the large object began to gather up the small ones, by turning so that one particular opening was in line with the small object. Then it approached it and drew the small object in through the opening.'

After a while, their view was interrupted by a bank of cloud, but they saw similar phenomena over the next few days. On 24th August, members of the Linz section of the 'AIS', together with the Santner family and other witnesses, observed a globular, yellowish-white pulsing light flying in a zigzag pattern over the area, as if making 'an investigation'. They watched it for about fifty minutes, and described it as being four times bigger than a star, with 'flickering peaks of light' on its outer edges. The magnetic needle of their compass oscillated wildly, and two excellent photographs were taken.

In September, experts examined the caves, but found nothing of significance.

In Australia, we were also receiving reports of these strange craft and their smaller companions.

In 1958, in the N.S.W. town of Goulburn, a shearer's wife looked out of her window one morning. It was just after daybreak, and she was surprised to see what she described as a 'clear shaped object' in the paddock, approximately half a mile away. It was about five hundred feet above the ground, and five or six smaller, silver disc-shaped objects flew up to it and disappeared inside. The larger craft then took off at great speed and disappeared.

Investigator Paul Norman also went to nearby Young in N.S.W. to interview five farmers. In May 1961, while they were marking lambs, a large round craft hovered overhead. Shortly after, four 'V-shaped' objects flew out, two in opposite directions. The large craft remained stationary for two hours, only flying away after the four smaller objects returned.

On August 22nd 1968, Captain Walter Gardin and Gordon Smith were flying from Adelaide to Perth, when some distance away they spotted a formation of objects – one large in the midst of five smaller ones. The large craft appeared to open up at the centre, allowing the smaller objects to travel back and forth.

Just after Gardin checked with Kalgoorlie Civil Aviation, to ensure there were no other aircraft in the area, he lost all communications until the entire formation seemed to 'join together' and speed off.

In 1972, the *'Macleay Argus'* in northern N.S.W. reported that when greengrocer Allan James had stopped his truck to check on the load, he spotted a large cigar-shaped object in the sky, which he watched for over ten minutes.

'It was 100 times bigger than a Boeing 707, and from each end came small objects – flying saucers which grouped into two arrowhead formations – one inside the other - before heading southeast. Mr. James said the small objects left the mother ship like fighters leaving an aircraft carrier. Once the flying saucers were out of sight, the large craft climbed at such speed that it had disappeared in seconds.'

In *'Contact Down Under'* I have noted several other similar incidents off the east coast of Australia.

A 1985 edition of the *'International UFO Reporter'*, contained an interesting article by Australian researcher Bill Chalker, who during an overseas trip, was able to interview a witness from a 1969 event, which took place on a Chilean Naval destroyer, in the Pacific Ocean, about 350 miles off the Chilean coast.

Just after midnight on 24th October, the radar operator detected an unidentified plane, travelling at over 12,000mph, in the southeast; *'Suddenly, the single contact became six 'targets....and one massive object and five small objects were approaching at high speed.'*

The larger craft, was much bigger than the 110 metres-long destroyer, looked like a big box with semi-circles scooped out in the side. The bluish, smaller objects, were egg-shaped, and no bigger than eight foot long and five to six feet wide.

When the main UFO was only 200 yards from the destroyer, the crew could hear a humming sound. The smaller objects pulled away, and flew in 'elliptical circles' between their 'host' and the destroyer. When the huge craft passed over the naval vessel, it lit up everything on and above the decks. They could see bright red lights moving back and forth under the UFO, and pulsing green or blue lights on the side.

At the same time, their power 'went out', and wasn't restored until after the intruder had moved 200 yards further on. The smaller objects continued flying around the ship, never coming any closer than 500 yards, and then joined their 'mother-ship' on the other side. The objects continued across the sky for at least two miles, before the sailors lost sight of them.

As soon as the ship reached port, the six witnesses were taken away, separated, and interviewed by two Chilean Naval officers, and four American naval attaches from the U.S. Embassy. They were held for two days, and repeatedly told; *"No, you didn't see it. You didn't see anything. You know nothing."*

One week later, Chalker's informant was transferred from his duties on the destroyer, and never saw the other witnesses again.

The Soviets were also less than happy that 'someone' or 'something' was spying on them. Researcher, Gabriel Green, wrote of an interesting incident which occurred over a missile base outside Rubinsk, about 140 kms north of Moscow, on 21st June 1961.

An alarm sounded when a bright metallic disc, about three hundred feet in diameter, became visible on radar, then hovered overhead. It was about twenty thousand metres up in the sky, and quickly released several smaller discs which raced down towards the base, and moved in tight flight formations, as if photographing or gathering intelligence.

The military suspected that it may be the Americans, and more religious personnel thought it was the 'devil'. The commander, knowing it was not Russian, ordered the soldiers to fire their missiles at it, however before they could reach their target, the rockets exploded mid-air.

The smaller discs hovered closer to the installation, which immediately lost power, from both its prime source and emergency generators. The giant saucer remained in place for another ten minutes before the smaller discs returned, and it moved away.

We have no way of knowing if these little craft were alien, one of our own, or an enemy's later 'drones' being covertly tested. In the Chilean case, given the estimated dimensions of the smaller craft, I wondered about another case from California, twenty-two years earlier.

In 1981, MUFON investigator, Paul Cerny, interviewed a witness who was only nineteen in the summer of 1947. When he was cutting hay, in a field in Salinas, California, the foreman from the farm next door told him, and a fellow worker, that a strange object was lying in their carrot patch. It had apparently 'come down' overnight, and the ranch owners had already informed the military.

The two young fellows, filled with curiosity, raced over to have a look; '....it was approximately nine feet in diameter, four feet high, and appeared to be made out of dull metal, resembling aluminium. The shape was double-discoid - that is like two soup bowls, edge to edge. There was a series of elongated or rectangular ports completely surrounding the edge or rim area. Nothing could be observed through these. There were no markings, insignia, numbers or any other I.D. on the craft. It seemed undamaged and unoccupied. No visible means of propulsion could be seen.'

For a while, they kept a reasonable distance, and then the witness ran up and kicked it, but there was no reaction. Shortly after, several military, with an Air Force truck, with a long flatbed arrived.

After being told to "get lost", and warned not to say anything to anybody, the two young lads watched from a distance as the strange craft was loaded up, covered with a tarp, and driven away, along with its military escort.

UNDER THE GROUND AND THE WATER

UNDER THE GROUND

Since the days of the caveman, humans have sought shelter in underground caverns, and this practice has continued into current times.

Our governments, all over the world, have constructed many huge underground facilities and bases, some that we are aware of, and others much more secretive. We now have huge 'tunnel boring' machines, which have also enabled projects such as the "Chunnel', the tunnel under the English Channel, and many other underground roads and railways. It only stands to reason that alien technologies would be more advanced than ours, and they would certainly be able to have hidden bases of their own under Earth's land and sea.

All over the world there a rumours of underground bases, which I am sure exist, but are they all a product of our own military, or more alien in nature? Maybe both. Researcher, Richard Sauder, following years of far-reaching investigations, has written extensively on this subject.

Even in Australia there are rumours and speculation. A female colleague told me that, when she was dating an ex-military fellow, they often went for drives in the NSW countryside. One day he pulled up, and told her to wait in the car while he went up to what appeared to be the entrance to a disused mine. She noticed there was a 'guard', who appeared to be military, at the entrance, however her boyfriend was allowed in. When he returned he would not tell her anything about the facility, or the purpose of his visit.

Rumours of UFOs entering and exiting the sides of cliffs or mountains have been received from all over the world.

In Qld. Australia, mysterious rumblings have been reported from the Glasshouse Mountains. Local police at Gordonvale, who checked into the reports, told of seeing an egg-shaped UFO suddenly appearing from a mountainside and performing 'impossible aerobatics'. Other residents had seen the same object emerging from a mountain after dark.

One said; "The mountainside was bathed in bright yellow light, and as it hovered in front of the mountain, we were amazed at the way it was spinning, with the lights changing colour. Then it seemed to shrink, and we both felt certain it was somehow going back into the hillside. Since that night I've seen two more strange objects that seemed to be swallowed into the mountain."

In 1996, when Bryan Dickeson and I were interviewing witnesses for our book *'The Gosford Files',* one witness told me he had seen a 'saucer' hovering in the gorge at the side of the Central Coast light industrial suburb of Somersby. He swore that it suddenly went into the side of the cliff and disappeared, as if going through some hidden entrance.

(Another witness also told me that there were some Egyptian –type hieroglyphs, similar to those found in nearby Kariong, inscribed on the cliffs in that gorge. Unfortunately, I was unable to find someone prepared to abseil down to take photographs.)

The next year, *'Nexus'* magazine published a letter from a reader who had been talking to a fellow student on his computer course. This man told him he was working at Somersby, and the details of their conversation were very interesting;

'When I enquired what his occupation was, I was told he couldn't tell me what organisation he worked for, except to say that it was a private organisation. From there on, it got more interesting.

'He told me it involved nuclear physics and 'new energy' sources, and that he was covered under the 'National Securities Act', (which unfortunately I know little about.) Supposedly he isn't able to use anything he has learned from this organisation, if he ever leaves. (Incidentally, he told me he earns a six figure salary, an inducement not to leave.) When I asked him if it involves our government, he told me it involved both our government and the United States Government.

'I jokingly said to him; "So the things Brian Wilshire, (a radio talk host), comes out with aren't so far-fetched after all?" He replied that fellow workers often come into work, saying that something else had been leaked onto the airwaves. He remarked that there were so many secret facilities in this country that people weren't aware of.

'This man didn't leave me with the impression that he was playing a joke on me...Whilst I would like to know if anyone has heard anything on the grapevine about this place.... I didn't press him with too many questions, because I feel that the less you ask people like this, the more you are likely to be told.'

In the 1990 book, *'Underground Alien Bases'*, there was a very lengthy report made, in 1961, by amateur spelunkers Arnold White, Rick Grayton and Don Lawrence. They recounted how they believed they had discovered an underground UFO base whilst exploring one of the many old iron mine-shafts located in Newfoundland, near the Quebec border in Canada.

In the past, there had been much local speculation about this particular facility, which was one of the deepest in the area. Miners reported hearing 'strange music' and 'mumbling voices' whilst underground, and lights and machinery became erratic or failed to work.

More ominous events caused the miners to hesitate to work there at all, and eventually the mine was condemned and closed down. This happened after one miner claimed when he went in, late one night, to check on some equipment, he was attacked by some 'little men' who seized his lantern, and 'shot' him with something that left him unconscious against the mine wall.

Although he physically survived the encounter, the next 'victim' was obviously not so lucky. A night watchman disappeared, and although his hat and lamp were found deep below, he was never located.

In March 1961 the team of spelunkers arrived at the mine entrance where two policemen denied them entry, and threatened to arrest them if they persisted. Early the next morning, at about 1.30am, they set out on a different route. Arnold and Don entered the mine while Rick remained outside as a 'lookout'.

Arnold commented that he was surprised that the mine had been condemned as it showed no signs of deterioration. He said; *'We had just completed our preliminary investigation when we heard someone, apparently deep within the mine, shout in a high pitched voice – 'Come'. We stopped dead in our tracks, and then walked in the general direction from where the voice seemed to originate. Then we heard someone or something running. We lit a flare, but saw nothing. The running sounds ceased abruptly, and we saw a faint blue light radiating from a far recess. Then we heard what we thought was the clank of a metal door closing.'*

They quickly found the area from where the blue light emanated, but could find no opening. After tapping the walls with a pick hammer, they heard hollow metal sounds in some places. They returned the next night with a battery-powered rock drill, and penetrated about three inches into the rock, when they struck metal. After eventually breaching this barrier, they saw the soft, blue shining light on the other side.

'Suddenly, we heard a low, humming noise and were startled to see the section of the wall we were working on, abruptly lift out of sight. It would be an understatement to say we were frightened. What lay before us was incomprehensible; a blue-lit corridor which appeared to be made of some sort of translucent, seamless, self-illuminating, blue-coloured metal or plastic.'

After initial hesitation, they entered the corridor, which was only five feet high, and after proceeding for fifty yards, decided to explore a second corridor leading off to the left. A hundred yards further on was a steep, spiralling stairway. After a twenty minute descent, they encountered further corridors, which were more brilliantly lit in a greenish shade.

After negotiating other passageways – *'We came next to a huge chamber which appeared to be some type of scientific laboratory and hydroponic garden. In one section were rows of giant exotic plants, and in another, some type of chemistry equipment. Lining the walls of this laboratory were arrays of multi-size TV screens, dials, gauges and other electronic equipment. Some of the screens were at least ten feet square.*

'In the centre section was a great mass of scintillating, varicoloured crystal: it had a rough, natural exterior and apparently performed some function, though unknown. The rest of the chamber contained many other strange devices and apparatus that none of us could identify. The entire ceiling was one great light.

'At the end of the chamber stood something that looked like a car-lift, with a disc-shaped metal object resting on it...It was circular in shape, about 35 feet in diameter, and four feet in thickness. Suddenly, Don exclaimed; "It's a flying saucer!"

When Rick tapped on it lightly with his hammer, an entire section of the tail seemed to dematerialise, revealing about half of the inner mechanism. Again, they could not find a single piece of equipment with which they were familiar, and they speculated that this was a remotely controlled device.

Whilst they were still inspecting the 'laboratory', the 'lift' descended two feet onto the floor, and the chamber lighting changed from a soft white to a deep red; *'In short order, the screen directly above and to the right of us, flashed on. Due to the unnatural lighting, we could not make out the image on the screen. Then we heard a voice, coming from the screen. It said in a high pitch; "You have been expected. You have been observed since first you entered our domain. You gaze upon the upper regions of our world. You are the first of your kind to be permitted this privilege. Let it be known this truth: we harbour you no ill will; we depend not on your superficial world for our sustenance or pleasure.*

'Those of your kind who make themselves the interpreters of our intentions are naught but the picayunish deceivers of your civilisation. Let it again be said, that we desire man no harm, and wish only to pursue our independent existence on this, our mutual planet. We shall not influence nor bring to you discord in any medium.

'We are not doers of evil. Our world spans the inner gulf of your globe. We have existed since before your time. Had we wished harm on you, we would also have been its receivers. We beg you a friendly farewell, and hope our message will be heeded, and find wide acceptance among those of your kind who find it necessary to concern themselves with our domain.'

The screen and image faded, the red lighting in the chamber became deeper, and the men felt dizzy and then passed out. When they regained consciousness, they were lying outside the entrance to the mine. They had still retained their personal effects, such as wallets, notebooks etc. but their safety hats, pick-hammers, chisels and Geiger counter had disappeared.

Let's not forget that both humans and aliens lie. Even if this is what our intrepid explorers were told, it may have been far from the truth as to what was really going on deep beneath that mine!

UNDER THE WATER

In 2001, Richard Sauder wrote; *'It is important to understand, that the technology exists for constructing manned, undersea bases hundreds, or even thousands of feet beneath the sea floor. The experience, the expertise, the machinery, the trained personnel and the financial means for constructing manned bases beneath the ocean floor have been in place for at least 35 years.*

'Bear in mind that the petroleum industry routinely and frequently carries out major industrial operations in deep water, well out to sea. It also routinely bores down into the deep rock beneath the ocean floor.'

This is nothing new, and even as long as fifty years ago, I was told of coal mines, constructed many years earlier, on the coast of New South Wales, Australia, which had tunnels going at least six miles, out under the ocean. Apparently there were also British coalmines which extended out under the North Sea and the Firth of Clyde, with depths of up to 1,800ft below the sea floor. Similarly, Canada, Chile, New Zealand, Japan and Taiwan also have 'submarine' coal mines.

Author, Kathleen McErlain, wrote; *'Richard Sauder explained the construction of an underwater base in his book, 'Underwater and Underground Bases', and he also demonstrated clear evidence that the U.S. Navy had been capable of building underwater bases, since the 1960's, to the depth of 12,000ft and distances offshore up to hundreds of miles.'*

However, despite the fact that we probably have secret underwater bases, to the best of my knowledge, we still do not have craft which can not only travel underwater, but also fly through the air – but somebody has! Many researchers have suggested that these occurrences may indicate that the 'visitors' also have bases under our lakes or oceans.

In the summer of 1945, there was some concern over an incident which occurred in the north-east Pacific. The U.S. Army transport ship, the '*Delarof*', was taking munitions and supplies to Alaska, when early one evening, the crew saw a large object emerging from the sea. It climbed straight up, and then curved into a level flight and silently circled the ship two or three times before disappearing to the south.

One of the other earlier cases occurred in 1950 when Argentinean, Romeo Suarez, had just started his epic 4,000 km trip, on foot, across the country. Investigator, Joseph Brill, wrote that a few days after his journey began, Suarez was walking through a coastal region, about 600 metres from the Atlantic Ocean.

It was about 11pm, and all was quiet, when suddenly there was a loud noise, which disturbed the sheep that had been sleeping in the field. A large, oval, luminous object emerged vertically from the sea, about 500 metres off shore, made a ninety degree turn, and shot through the air towards Argentine territory.

'Some fifteen days later, also at night, when he was between Rio Gallegos and the city of Santa Cruz, a similar phenomenon occurred. This time, although he could not determine the exact distance from the coast, four small luminous objects came up out of the Atlantic.

'They repeated the same manoeuvre as the previous object; that is they gained altitude vertically, and then in perfect formation approached the coastline and moved off towards the west, in the direction of the Andes Mountains.'

There were several reports of a similar phenomena occurring off the Atlantic coast in the following years. In August 1962, Vincente Bordoli, a truck driver from Buenos Aires, and his son, Hugo, told police that they had observed a strange, brilliant formation off the Atlantic coast. It had periodically entered the Gulf of San Matias before emerging and eventually climbing up into the sky and disappearing.

In 1964, a witness driving from Caleta Oliva to Comodora Rivadavia saw some strange objects descend into the sea. After stopping to watch, he resumed his journey, and a short time later saw more luminous objects emerge from the surface of the water. They circled around at a dizzy speed before climbing upwards and disappearing into the night sky.

In the summer of 1954, Capt. Boshoff on the Netherlands government ship the *'Groote Beer'*, eighty miles out of New York, was called to the bridge when an unknown object surfaced out of the sea. It was a flat, 'moon-like' disc, grey in colour, with what appeared to be lights around its edges.

Whilst they were still staring, unsure of what to do next, the craft rose up out of the water, and quickly shot up into the sky until it was lost from view.

On 1st September 1956, police at Porthcawl, Glamorgan, in Wales, saw a blood-red object, with a jagged black streak across its centre, rise from the sea. They described it as being 'a good deal larger than a full-size harvest moon', and the two officers of the law just stared in amazement as it headed out towards the Atlantic Ocean.

In January 1959, across the other side of the world, in South Australia, Peter, a former pilot, was walking along the Port Gawler beach with his wife and daughter.

Suddenly they saw a spherical object, rising, to a considerable height, out of the sea. It shone like silvery aluminium, and moved towards the young family who were staring in astonishment. Another craft flew in from the south, and stopped next to the strange sphere before moving south. Its companion, which had 'risen out of the depths', then took off at a speed estimated to be approximately 3,000 miles per hour.

Again in 1959, another one of these strange objects was active on the coast of Cuba. Researcher, Scott Corrales told of how, early one morning, Pablo Rodriguez and a friend were fishing in the sea near Havana; *'All of a sudden the waters near the fishing boat began to bubble intensely as a massive silvery disc emerged from the depths, hanging in mid-air, and dripping sea water, before taking off at great speed. As if that experience had not been shocking enough, Rodriguez claimed seeing 'some figures clad in black, like undersea fishermen', swimming only a few metres from his boat.'*

The same year, soldiers near Kolobrzeg in coastal Poland, were fearful when a triangular object, with 12ft sides, rose out of the Baltic Sea and circled their barracks, before speeding off and vanishing in the sky.

Scott Corrales also documented another 1959 report from researcher, Orestes Girbau, which detailed a sighting by a troop of boy scouts, and their leaders, who were hiking along the Cuban Bay of Mantazas on the morning of July 5th.

The silent, glowing, silver metallic object, which was also witnessed by two fishermen, was wingless and oval, or disc-shaped, and between 20 and 26 feet in diameter. It rose out of the sea, hovered over the water, then levelled off and rose straight up into the sky, at astonishing speed, vanishing within less than fifteen seconds.

On 2nd August 1965, the crew of the steamship *'Raduga'*, saw a sixty metre diameter sphere shoot out of the Red Sea and hover 150 metres above the water. Later reports said that some fishermen, in a motor boat, were much closer, and the turbulence in the water was such that one of them drowned. Investigators Paul Stonehill and Philip Mantle noted that a few months later three of the fishermen died. They wondered if it was due to their close exposure to the object.

On 4th August 1967, Dr Hugo Yepez was fishing in the Gulf north of Arrecife, Venezuela, when a 'circle in the sea' suddenly started violently bubbling. A large, flat disc rose up through it, and dripping with water, hovered just above the surface. It was greyish-blue in colour, and had a revolving section with a number of triangular, window-like structures. Suddenly, it moved upwards, in a curved path, and streaked out of sight.

Later that month, Ruben Norato was on the beach at Catia la Mar, Venezuela, when the water started churning and three huge, plate-like discs ascended and flew rapidly off into the distance.

That same year, a Peruvian witness was travelling from Cuzco to Urubama. At about 9pm, he was driving around the shore of a lake when his car engine suddenly stalled. After he got out and opened the bonnet, a sudden flash of light illuminated the whole area.

He turned to see a disc-shaped object emerge from, and hover about fifty metres above, the water. It had a metallic shine, and was about eight metres in diameter. He could see what looked like 'portholes', and on top was a 'kind of dome', which rotated.

After a few minutes, the strange craft speedily moved off, and climbing, passed over the road. Its dome was spinning more rapidly, sending out alternative red and green flashes.

There was a lot of speculation in South America. British researcher, Gordon Creighton, wrote; *'According to an 'Agence France-Press' dispatch of November 11th 1968, from Buenos Aires, published in Spanish newspapers that same month, a report had been received from Lima, capital of Peru, to the effect that the flying saucers, seen so frequently over South America, had a base in the depths of Lake Titicaca. People living near the shores of this large Andean lake, between Peru and Bolivia, had reported that saucers were constantly seen heading towards the lake and vanishing there.*

'The report went on to say that the presence, on the Bolivian side of the lake, of a French scientific expedition, led by the well-known underwater exploration expert, Commander Cousteau, had produced much speculation, and was adding strength to the rumours about a saucer base in the lake. In fact, many local inhabitants were convinced that this was what Commander Cousteau was there to investigate.'

This phenomenon was also occurring in Russia, although reports were few and far between. The Kamchatka Peninsula in the northeast of the country is close to the Arctic Circle, and its largest lake, Kronotsky, is situated in a depression surrounded by a chain of sixteen volcanoes.

In August 1970, a group of hydrologists were aboard a boat, conducting research on the lake. Suddenly, about a kilometre away, they noticed a dome of water rising, from which a grey-coloured, oval object, about forty to sixty metres in size, emerged.

It ascended to an altitude of a few hundred metres, and hovered, motionless, at an angle for a couple of minutes. The scientists suddenly discovered that the motor on their boat wouldn't work, but just as they started to row, the UFO sped off at speed, and their motor sprang back to life.

These unidentified aerial/aquatic objects were also seen entering the sea. In late February 1963, a British frigate, patrolling thirty to fifty miles off the Norwegian coast, spotted an unidentified object on radar. It was calculated as being a solid craft, 100-120ft across, and flying at 35,000ft. When jet planes were sent on an intercept course, before they could reach it, the object plummeted, at speed, into the water.

The ship's sonar tracked the object as it travelled under the water, but it soon evaded detection as it sped, in a zigzag course, onwards and downwards into deeper depths.

There are times when we just don't know the answers. 'MUFON Canada' reported that on 4th October 1967, several strange craft had been seen in the skies.

Just a little after 11pm that night, a perplexing event occurred at the small fishing village of Shag Harbour in Nova Scotia, Canada.

Locals watched for a few minutes as an aerial vehicle, with some unusual flashing orange lights, hovered over the ocean. When it suddenly plummeted into the water, everyone assumed it must be a plane crash. They could see the lights bobbing on the surface, and immediately contacted the police, (RCMP), to initiate a rescue mission.

The three police, who initially attended the scene, watched as the lights changed to yellow, and left a yellowish wake as they appeared to be drifting further from the shore. They all described it as being dome-shaped, about sixty feet long, and ten or so feet high. The Coast Guard was dispatched, and two policemen and a few local fishermen set off in small boats.

When they reached the area, the lights were no longer visible, but there was a lot of yellow foam, indicating that something may have submerged. After several hours of searching, no wreckage or survivors were found, however it was discovered that no known aircraft were in the area that night – so what had crashed?

The Canadian military sent out the HMCS *'Granby'*, with advanced equipment and trained Navy divers, and systematically searched the sea floor, but found nothing.

At the time, military personnel were ordered to remain silent, but many years later, investigators discovered that in fact the object had been tracked underwater for about twenty-five miles to a place called Government Point, where a small, but technically advanced military base managed a 'Magnetic Anomaly Detection System', used for detecting and tracking submarines in the North Atlantic.

Naval vessels were dispatched to salvage any remains, which were 80 to 100ft down, but before they could commence operations, another unidentified craft moved in and joined the first object on the ocean floor. The Navy, unsure of what to do, stood by on the surface above, and just observed.

Before they could take any action, they were called away to investigate the appearance of a Russian submarine in Canadian waters. During their absence, the two objects made their escape, travelling at great speed and accelerating underwater to the Gulf of Maine.

'The remaining Navy vessels pursued them toward the United States, but the objects continued to distance themselves from their trackers. To the astonishment of the pursuers, both of the objects broke through the surface, and shot skywards to vanish within seconds.'

In later years, witness Dan Willis gave the following testimony to the 'Disclosure Project'; *"My name is Dan Willis. I was in the United States Navy. I held a top secret crypto level-14 extra sensitive material handling security clearance.*

"I worked in the code room at the Naval communications station in San Francisco. In 1969, I received a priority message from a ship near Alaska, that was classified secret. The ship reported, emerging out of the ocean, near the port bow, a bright glowing, reddish/orange elliptical object, approximately 70ft in diameter. It emerged out of the water, shot into space, travelling at about 7,000 miles per hour. This was tracked on ship's radar and substantiated.

"Years later, I worked at the Naval electronics and engineering centre in San Diego for 13 years. A co-worker worked with NORAD. When he first started working at the facility he noticed objects on the screens that track everything out in space and in the air. Objects going off the scale, doing right-angle turns.

"When he enquired, his older supervisor advised him, quote: 'it was just a visit from one of our little friends.' That was a little unusual!"

Reports of 'Underwater UFOs' were few and far between, and I had been a serious researcher and investigator for over twenty years before I encountered my first case.

Carl Roberts was an artist/cartoonist/designer who worked on commissioned projects for the media and other professionals, including comic-book companies. He lived at Brooklyn, on the estuary of the Hawkesbury River, between Sydney and the New South Wales Central Coast. In October 1997, he quietly approached me at a UFO seminar, still obviously shaken by an experience two weeks earlier, but not wanting anyone else to hear what he had to report.

Carl was quite agitated, and spoke in a very excited manner. It took a while to calm him down and get the details in a logical, chronological manner. (On the plus side, due to his artistic abilities he was able to draw some very good pictures of the object):

"It was about 2.30 a.m., I had been working from home, and after several hours of concentration, went for a stroll along the water's edge, near Wobby Beach, to clear my mind. My peaceful evening stroll was suddenly disturbed by a huge, bubbling commotion out on the river. Water was spraying up to 25 feet into the sky. Inside this turbulence was a light, which made the foam look like a city fountain at night.

"Transfixed and speechless, I watched for about twenty minutes. Not knowing what it was, I wanted somebody else to turn up so I could say; 'Hey, look at that! What is that thing?' I left where I was sitting and climbed down onto the rocks at the edge of the water, to get a better look at it. The bubbling and light were about a hundred feet away, but too far out in the water to get a better view. At first I thought it was some form of underwater pipe leaking white light; it looked like an underwater spotlight.

"The light underwater began to circle, or rotate, like a glowing football swimming around in circles. I remember feeling glad that I had not run off to find another witness, or I would have missed this underwater movement. I felt I was watching something very special and rare, but hadn't considered a UFO or anything like that.

"It shot up, out of the water, and for about a minute, circled about one to two feet above the river. Whilst the water had stopped thrashing and spraying up, the surface still appeared to be boiling. As it circled it passed to within ten feet of where I was standing on the rocks. I could see it was bigger than what I had first thought, and shaped like a cylinder – big enough to hold two soccer balls, and it made a soft and menacing electrical buzz.

"It was circling faster and higher over the centre of the river. I thought to myself: 'Shit! I've seen my first UFO! Speedy little guy! Why is it getting brighter? What's that light shining off it?'

"It was then I spotted the 'real UFO', the 'Big Momma', hanging there some thirty metres above the water's surface. I could see this global hull. It was huge, as long as three or four cars, and solid metal. The outer rim was turning, not the whole thing, just the one part of its rim, which seemed to fit into the hull somehow, so that it could slowly revolve. It was silent – 'impossible' – and I could not make out any other markings or details. There were no portholes, aerials, lights, symbols, markings, wings, or jets. I wondered what was holding it up. The little guy buzzed with electricity or something, but this big one was totally silent. I got this strange sensation, as if there was some form of lens or force field between us.

"The smaller object was zooming around underneath it, lighting up its lower surfaces. That was how I first saw it. I became a little scared. Was it there all the time? Had it been watching me and my reaction? It still gives me the creeps!

"The fast little object shot into its centre, and was gone. And so was my source of light. The whole area blacked out and I realised that one little object had been lighting up everything. I couldn't see much in the dark, but I could hear the 'Mothership' leave. A huge whoosh and then a really ice cold wind blew all around me for a few minutes. I was scared.

"I sat in that spot for another half hour with the worst case of the shakes. I was amazed as to just how real it all was. I was sober, and couldn't put it out of my mind with an excuse of a dream or hallucination. I was not expecting it, and it was gone!"

CHAPTER EIGHTEEN

THE VISITORS' AND THEIR MESSAGES

After World War II, many people in this battle weary world were calling for peace. One interesting development came early from Hollywood, in the film *'The Day the Earth Stood Still'*. Researcher Robbie Graham, in an article published in the *'UFOLOGIST'* magazine in 2014, claims that investigator, Linda Moulton-Howe, said that in 1983, Air Force officers told her that the film was 'inspired by the CIA' and was 'one of the government tests of public reaction, (to an alien landing).'

Graham also noted that the scriptwriter, Edmund North, had previously been a Major in the Army Signal Corps, and that Darryl Zanuck, the producer, in a memo dated 10th August 1950, stressed that *'every effort should be made to compel the audience to completely accept this story as something that possibly happens in the not too distant future.'*

Apparently Zanuck was personally acquainted with the future CIA Director, Allen Dulles, and soon to be President, Dwight Eisenhower. There were some striking similarities in the details in the movie to those reported by early witnesses. The visitor, 'Klaatu', who looked totally human in appearance, was accompanied by a robot, 'Gort', who could emit a destructive 'beam'. His domed craft, which was taken and examined by the military, 'hummed' and was made of impenetrable metal. 'Klaatu' also infiltrates human society, easily walking undetected among us, until it is time for him to leave.

In the film, before 'Klaatu' departs Earth, he gives a speech which was comparable to the messages received by contactees; *"I am leaving soon, and you will forgive me if I speak bluntly. The universe grows smaller every day, and the threat of aggression by any group, anywhere, can no longer be tolerated. There must be security for all, and no-one is secure.....It is no concern of ours how you run your planet, but if you threaten to extend your violence, this Earth of yours will be reduced to a burned-out cinder.*

"Your choice is simple: join us and live in peace, or pursue your present course and face obliteration. We shall be waiting for your answer. The decision rests with you."

This is interesting, because the movie was released in 1951, long before George Adamski met his human-like 'visitor', Orthon, in the desert, and received messages not only about their concern regarding our use of nuclear weapons, but also the inequality between the rich and the poor on our planet. This created some concern with authorities, who considered his pronouncements to indicate communist tendencies.

In my book, *'The Days of the Space Brothers'*, I wrote in more detail about the early 1950s contactees George Adamski and Daniel Fry.

Adamski quoted his mentors as saying; *'Our main purpose in coming to you at this time is to warn you of the grave danger which threatens men of Earth today. In your first meeting with our Brother here, he indicated to you that the exploding of bombs on Earth was of interest to us. Even though the power and radiation from the test explosions has not yet gone out beyond your Earth's sphere of influence, these radiations are endangering the life of men on Earth.*

'A decomposition will set in, in time, that will fill your atmosphere with the deadly elements which your scientists and your military men have confined into what you term 'bombs'.

Adamski's contemporary, contactee Dan Fry, was also told something similar; *'...unless some ways and means are found to stimulate the growth of the spiritual and social sciences on your earth, a time will inevitably come when your emphasis on those matters which are material will cause your civilisation to collapse.'*

During 1955-56, Dan Fry founded his 'Understanding' group, and published regular newsletters, sent around the world, containing the 'visitors' messages.

In my book, *'The Days of the Space Brothers'*, I explain how George Adamski was led to his initial 1952 meeting with the extraterrestrial 'Orthon', by George Hunt Williamson, his wife and George and Betty Bailey, who had received a message from the 'visitors' whilst engaging in radio communications with them from radio shack behind the home of Lyman Streeter in Arizona.

These very secretive communications with extraterrestrials had been going on for some time, and Williamson reveals the details of some of these ongoing activities in his book. *'The Saucers Speak'.*

Williamson obviously had contacts of his own, however he was not so outspoken about them. He did, nevertheless, mention some contacts and messages, and repeated one of interest from August 1952;

"Your bombs will destroy universal balance. Your hydrogen bomb could make an asteroid belt out of you. This happened many years ago to the planet of the fifth orbit. We knew what they were doing, but we didn't interfere. We cannot stand by and see another waste.

"After they, (Maldek's) destruction, there were terrible disasters on Masar, (Mars). Great volcanic eruptions took place. Many of our people were destroyed. We would have been thrown out of the Solar System and lost if we had not quickly constructed two artificial satellites. Some of your scientists have noticed that Phobos and Diemos reflect too much light to be made of earthly substance. They are right. They, (the moons of Mars), are metallic in nature. They readjusted our unstable position and saved a planet.

"I am 'Zo', head of a Masar contact group. " We didn't interfere when the Asuras guided the misguided of Maldek,", said Zo, "but this time they are interfering. Serving 'God-the-Destroyer', the Asuras perform a necessary scavenging function in the Universe, but the Creator and his Agents can set limits to Free Will, otherwise the balance between God-the-Creator and God-the-Destroyer would be upset and evolution impeded, as in the case of Maldek".

Whilst this may seem to be 'gobble-de-gook' to many, it must be noted that New Zealand contactee, 'Mr. X', (see my book *'The Days of the Space Brothers'*), was also told that, by necessity, both good and evil exist in the Universe, and for some reason, not understood by me, must balance each other out.

By the beginning of the twentieth century, Nikola Tesla and Thomas Edison realised that if we were able to send messages into space, we should also be capable of receiving replies. Both claimed that they had received intelligent signals back from space, but in the form of a strange code, similar to that of our own 'Morse'.

By 1950, the 'American Radio Relay League' were conducting experiments of their own, and soon collaborated in the knowledge of the best transmitting frequencies and times, and the installation of better antennae, technology and equipment. Soon many were receiving 'Morse' type messages, and not long after, having also experimented with some forms of 'telepathy', were able to engage in 'oral' ham radio contact with persons whom they claimed were the occupants of a 'space ship, practically in our atmosphere'.

Although Hunt Williamson was aware of other ham operators in the U.S.A., including in Iowa and Virginia, making similar secretive contacts, I personally had been told of more, from around the world, including South Africa and New Zealand. All were very clandestine, fearing if their governments found out, they would lose their licenses or worse.

Many messages were received, a couple of which I found very pertinent, and similar to what was being told to most contactees; *'We have great powers, but we have not destroyed each other because we have followed the Infinite Father. You have not. Yes, you have many churches and seem to worship what you call God, but you worship by word, not by deed.*

'You say; "Peace is for the strong", but your Holy Book tells you; "The meek shall inherit the earth!" 'Thou shalt not kill"- yet you kill. One came and said to you; "Turn the other cheek" – but you do not. **Your government contacted us a few years ago. They would like to know our secrets, but they never will, no matter how hard they try.'**

In another transmission they said; *'Only technical advance has been made on Earth, and this is the wrong kind of achievement, for you are now engulfed in a darkness that has no equal!*

'Men of Earth have sought only the ways of the flesh. They have a form of spirituality, but deny the power and majesty of the Creator. The so-called educated man is a fool, the nations are bathed in the blood of myriads of young men, women and children. What will Earth do with her new powers? You are as children with a dangerous toy.

'We are out in the vastness, and we watch your industries where greed is born; your capitals where war is born; your laboratories where discoveries are made. We see the birth cradle and we see the early death shroud. There is something far more beautiful, more satisfying, than you have attained.

'We have been observing you for a long time now. We are your brothers. Have we not shown this to be true over and over again? If there is violence, it will be of your making, not ours! We know that among you there are those who desire

and seek the love and knowledge which alone makes man free. We have tasted of it, and it is good, it is sweet. Look up, people of Earth. Be of one mind and purpose. We are not unattainable, for we are here with you. We wait, we watch, we listen!'

In *'The Complete Book of UFOs'*, Jenny Randles and Peter Hough wrote about Richard Miller, a lesser known contactee, who, in 1954, also communicated with extraterrestrials on his short-wave ham radio. He too, was given instructions to go to a remote location, this time near Ann Arbor in Michigan, where, after fifteen minutes, a disc-shaped object landed nearby. A staircase descended;

"There, standing at the head of the stairway, was a young man dressed in a brown one-piece suit. He beckoned me to enter the ship, which I did. I was standing in a large circular hallway, which seemed to encircle the whole craft. Although nothing had yet been said, the young man radiated a kind of friendliness, which put me at ease."

Richard was taken to the control room, where he met Soltec, the craft's commander, who greeted him in perfect English; *'He explained that their planet, Centurus of the Alpha Centauri system, belonged to the 'Universal Confederation', a group of over 680 planets which earned the right to membership by their evolutionary progress.*

'..... Before Earth could become a member, mankind would have to awaken to higher spiritual values: "When love of your fellow man becomes established, then will the Sons of Light appear and the Kingdom of your God will reign on Earth." The 'Sons of Light', Miller was told, were what the Bible referred to as 'angels'.'

Richard was told many things during his subsequent meetings, and at one stage asked why they contacted ordinary people, and not our scientists and leaders; *'The extraterrestrials had contacted government heads and top scientists, but they had spurned the aliens, not wanting to give up their power base in the coming New Age; a cover-up had been agreed by the establishment. So Soltec and his friends sought to contact general members of the public, in the hope that they would spread the word and that the resultant pressure would force governments to change their policies.'*

Obviously Richard did not seek publicity, however; *'his contacts continued for over twenty years, all meticulously recorded in a library of writings and tape recordings.'*

In later years, researcher Gerard Aartsen, reflected upon the similar messages being received by other early contactees. He mentioned Dutch contactee, Adrian Beers, who reported that in 1965, the 'space people' said; *"Culture is the measure through which a society cares for the least fortunate man. The measure in which the sick, invalid, old or poor people are taken care of, in short, the measure of collective unselfishness.'*

When Adrian suggested that their technical assistance could help solve the world's problems, he was told; *"The last thing you need is technological information to increase the gap between your intellectual development and your almost non-existent social development. Carry on playing with your Mars probes for the moment, as half of your world's population lives in poverty and hunger. The only information you need lies in the field of societal standards."*

Gerard considered that whilst we had improved to a certain extent, little had changed, and there was still a disparity in the distribution of global wealth and opportunity; *'Western nations began the process of giving market forces free reign, by removing regulations and restrictions that protect citizens and consumers, and selling off national assets such as electricity networks, public transport, postal services, health care, housing and even water supplies to large corporations that now operate or trade them for profit....and use their greater freedom to secure their own interests at the expense of society by influencing not only public opinion, but also elections, the democratic process itself, and the judiciary.'*

There were, in the early days, cults and groups, headed by 'gurus', who claimed, as 'the chosen one', to be receiving messages from alien visitors. In so far as these 'gurus' meeting with the 'visitors', and being given 'messages', in a private letter to New Zealand's Fred Dickeson, dated 4th March 1956, George Adamski wrote; *'As for the message about which you requested information, 'Ashtar' is a spiritualistic character, without reality, according to the Brothers. Ashtar messages are coming from mediums, automatic writers and people who are sincere in desire, but without understanding, and who open themselves mentally in hope of contacting the Brothers. Such messages are sent to us from many parts of the world.*

'In every case you will find divisions such as; 'those who believe' or 'those who have raised their vibrations'. The Earth is called 'Shan' or 'Terra', which names the Brothers never use. Specific dates are given for dire events to take place, along with specific places in many cases. We have even received messages where 'Ashtar' has introduced Jesus Christ, George Washington, Patrick Henry etc. with praises for America, warnings about America's acts, warnings about Russia and other places, and many such things. The Brothers, who are living human beings, like you and I, never do such things, nor do they say such things.

'It is things like these that easily identify the real from the unreal. Do not be affected by them! Keep yourself on a basis of reality as you have been doing all along. You have been doing excellent work and you may be assured that the real visitors from other worlds are well aware of your work.

'You have been wanting to be met and assured by the Brothers. Do you know that you have not been? I am always sceptical of those who claim personal meetings with identification at the first contact, unless, of course, there is a space craft in the picture at the time. This has happened on many occasions, but according to those with whom I have had meetings, they do not reveal their identities unless the Earthman recognises them first by his own inner feeling. If this takes place, and it is right for them to identify themselves, they will respond with a mental thought. Otherwise, they might visit with you many hours, and many times, without identifying themselves. So it is up to you folks, each one, to be alert at all times, to your inner feelings, hunches, or whatever you may call them. There will not be anything conspicuously different in their personal appearances. And remember that over-anxiety creates a tenseness that can act as a barrier to your 'feeling' alertness.'

In *'The Days of the Space Brothers'* I also wrote of how, in later years, New Zealand's Mr X., was a new contact.

Apparently, in the 1960s, a new group of 'Space Brother' missionaries had arrived so that their predecessors could return to their home planet. They were not happy at how Adamski and other contactees had gained fame, publicity, and in many cases a cult following. In Adamski's case he had embellished the truth and made false claims.

In New Zealand, Fred and Phyllis Dickeson, who ran a research group with many members and overseas contacts, were once devoted followers of Adamski, but were now 'calling him out'. Perhaps this is why the 'Brothers' visited, and made contact with a middle-aged gentleman, who lived near them in Timaru, and had no interest in the subject.

Mr. X was told; *'We have been visitors to your earth for the past many thousands of years and have been described in different ways by those whose good chance it was to see us and we have appeared to and spoken with many persons who have been afraid to tell of their meeting with us because of the fear of being disbelieved; we do not blame them; we merely are sorry that society is such that it forces the isolated individual to keep silent. We know that many of those whom we have met would be very happy to tell about it if it were not for all this disbelief and suspicion. And so the world works against itself.'*

They then continued, and counteracted some of Adamski's more recent fanciful claims; *'It has been written that we, on isolated occasions, have taken certain earthlings for rides into outer space and to other planets in your system. This we have not done, and it is all mere sensationalism or literary window dressing because the plain truth is not exciting enough. Earthlings must gradually, and of their own free will, accustom themselves to our mode of travel. They cannot be just taken out there as easily as stepping into your conventional vehicles. Much rubbish has been written, and we are more than surprised that there were so many who have been tricked by it.'*

Once Mr X was convinced of the authenticity of his visitors, he obeyed their request that he never made his identity publicly known, and would pass their messages on to the Dickesons, who would publish them in their newsletter.

In a message to their followers in New Zealand, the Space Brothers said; *'...You can never know at what moment you may be in our company, as it was with the writer of this message, some years ago, when we first approached him. We do not make ourselves known to any individual unless we have a special reason, yet even you, as an individual may, at some time, sit right next to one of us.*

'There is no noticeable effect but one, when this happens to an 'Earthling', as he who is favoured will notice a feeling of elation while in our company, but will likely not know the reason for it. You will feel 'drawn' towards our 'Messenger' – the stranger at your side. You will find that you wish to speak with him and you will not be able to understand why. You may even suspect that he is one of us if you are so inclined, and you may even ask the direct question if the opportunity arises, but for our own safety, your question will be parried, and turned to other pleasantries, but we would not lie to you.

'....At the beginning of your year 1964, we inspired your writer to commit to paper some verses of poem which we believe could be included at this juncture as appropriate to what we have just been telling you, and so we request him to do that.'

'THAT FOR WHICH YOU SEEK'

*'In the misty forest where footsteps are
muffled by a misty carpet,
And shafts of sunlight stab the mouldy earth,
In the bush-clad valleys where snow-fed
streams give great rivers their birth.*

*'Tis there my friend where you will find
that for which you seek;
For this to you may sound quite odd,
As we reveal to you this Truth,
That there, you are nearest to God.*

*'He is less evident in bricks and mortar
of which most edifices are made,
For those reveal not his handiwork;
Although they are built to His glory,
Even therein the Devil may lurk.*

*'Go you then to the forest where the carpet
is thicker and yet more rugged,
Where tree trunks stand like people;
For therein you will find His glory
In a church without a steeple.*

'T'is around the mountain tops where clouds
kiss the lofty peaks,
T'was on one of such – Mount Sinai,
Where God first gave his law:
For in the heights and these quiet places,
Reigns He for evermore.'

'We inspired the writer with the above verses on your 21st January, in your year 1964, for the writer of his own volition could not make such an arrangement. We have given him other poems, but only since he was chosen by us to do our work some years ago.'

The Space Brothers regretted how our established religions had gained control over much of society; *'Fear and ignorance have wrought havoc in the past, yet you are learning slowly that fear of something is caused by ignorance of its nature.*

'Fear of the unknown, fear of the Creator, fear of the dark because you do not know what is behind it all, and this is all brought about through ignorance, and ignorance in its turn has produced fantastic religions. Many of us are even now living among you, and we know that you are still being advised to fear God; but why? We not only believe, but know, that all this will be swept away and that the Light will truly shine with understanding and Love of all things pure, well knowing that you will see the Creator as He really is. By all means have Faith, as without Faith you will be lost, but let your faith be well founded on Truth, for Truth must prevail, and it is Truth which we give to the world. You may well ask, "What is Truth?" For your answer you must trust us, for we love you all, and shall not lead you astray.

'We are scattered through many countries, enter your concert halls and chat at random with persons on your streets, and some of you are alert enough to know that there is something about us which marks us out as different to the average person. We encourage this interest, and recognise this alertness, for this is how we gain our contacts without being too deliberate.

'As in times of old, we are willing to visit any sincere seeker after Truth who is ready to clear a pathway for us through the wall of bias and superstition. We cannot come to anyone who is not willing to receive us, and even then, there

will be a long period of testing and probing before actual contact is made with he who is willing, and as before stated, the visits will be of the most private nature.

'We are doing this now in certain parts of your world, and each one is given his particular work to do. If he is already engaged in our work, then it is unnecessary for us to visit as we need all the time we can get in order to visit others who need us more. Bias and superstition in this matter are evil for which there is no place with us.

'In some cases firm friendships have resulted and blossomed into further meetings, which in turn, as in the writer's case, has developed into something more than firm friendship, as it is through the writer that you now learn more about our true nature.

'Even the writer himself will learn facts here which he never knew previously. We have met him on more than one occasion, and know that he is giving the Truth in the way we intend it. We have greeted him hand to hand, and all the time he has said little to others about it because of the same fear-ridicule. Now he gets his chance, which was all part of our promise to him some years ago.

'The writer has no definite evidence nor eyewitnesses to his meeting us; yet we gave him that evidence not long after the first meeting between us. We promised to show ourselves in the heavens on a certain night, and at a certain time and in a certain position. He has witnesses to confirm that we kept our appointment to the minute.'

Although Fred and Phyllis Dickeson, prominent New Zealand researchers, and leaders of the *'Scientific Approach to Cosmic Understanding'* group and newsletter, denied meeting Mr. X's Space Brother 'Friends', they once let it slip that they had in fact met them on three occasions, which the remainder of this message also seems to indicate.

*'**Your local Editor-Publisher** is highly esteemed by us, for he along with those nearest and dearest to him have remained faithful to our Cause. This we cannot and will not forget, and when the opportunity presents itself, we shall approach him personally and press his hand.*

'We have enjoyed every moment of our talk with all of you. Our time is now very short, and we have much to do and May Our God Be Your God Also. So

with love and Understanding in all our hearts, we say "God bless you all'. - 'We shall always be – Your Two Friends.'

Insofar as sharing their advanced technology with us, the 'Two Friends' were a little more reticent; *'Earthlings often wonder why we do not reveal scientific information to them, but let us see first what they do with all the scientific wonders which they have already acquired. Every could-be blessing Earthlings receive is assessed according to its destructive value and we have no wish to help them along these lines until they learn wisdom in the use of that which they already have. When you will have reached the point where you can be trusted, (and there is still no sign of that), then we shall gladly open up greater vistas to you.*

'We have no desire to help you take your evils with you and spread havoc among those of us who do not deserve it. The greatest could-be blessing ever so far acquired by you was used for evil purposes – we refer to the building material of which all things are made, yet further evil is at this time being plotted by nations – bigger and more powerful explosions are wanted, and we know that they are not wanted for constructive purposes.

'We know your weaknesses, and it would not matter what we revealed to you, you would value it according to its destructive force. Even if we gave you a plan of how to build our ships, we would be putting temptation in your way, thereby making our position unsafe, and why should we endanger our people? When you can prove worthy, we shall willingly help. We have no more to say on this question, as we have said all that can be said.'

Another respected New Zealand investigator/researcher, Vic Harris, desperately wanted, with little success, to have contact with the 'visitors'.

He had spoken with many Maori elders, and already knew of their history, which like that of many indigenous people around the world, mentioned beings coming from the sky. They spoke of a 'flying man' named Tama-rau, and the God 'Hau-ki-waho' apparently ascended into the heavens and returned to Earth, bringing with him much previously unknown knowledge.

He was described as wearing clothing that we would now recognise as being similar to a space suit, and did not really resemble a human being; *'He was said to have no nose, no forehead and no eyebrows...Nothing could be seen save the eyeholes, the opening of the mouth, and those of the ears and of the nostrils.'* Other legendary descriptions of 'Gods' suggest the landing of an object with a plexiglass type dome and four legs.

'Another myth concerned the great Polynesian voyager Toi, who was said to have deserted his first wife, Te Kura, when she bore a son to a God, Tama-i-waho, who descended to Earth and came from Hawaiki by means of flying through the air.'

Vic desperately wanted to understand more about the 'visitors' and their intentions, and both he and his wife learned meditation and other psychic practices in order to make contact. It seemed to be without success until one night, in 1978, after the 'two friends' had ceased communicating with Mr. X, he received what were to be his first and only clairaudient messages.

One said; *'It is pointless to explain where we come from, the point is we are: Many have seen our craft and some have seen our Bothers who pilot them. To tell Earthman that we come from one part of the galaxy or another is futile, for he will spend much time in arguing why there can or cannot be life in that particular part or state of the Universe, instead of getting on with what must be done at this immediate time...Putting himself in order on an individual basis, then as a whole. Man must realise that he and his brothers are all individual parts of an overall whole, and until some unison can be brought to play in his society, then chaos will continue to reign.'*

The full transcript of the messages received by Vic Harris can be found in my book *'The Days of the Space Brothers'*.

Contactee Orfeo Angelucci's book, *'The Secret of the Saucers' Story'* contained a similar message from the ETs he encountered; *'The aggressive men of Earth want our scientific advancements. For these they would shoot our crafts from the skies. But additional scientific knowledge we cannot give to Earth except as we are doing now in a manner perfectly in accord and harmony with cosmic law. Already, man's material knowledge has far outstripped the growth of brotherly love and spiritual understanding in his heart.*

'To add to the destructive phase of man's scientific knowledge is not permitted. We are working to turn that knowledge to constructive purposes on Earth. Also, we hope to give men a deeper knowledge and understanding of their true nature and a greater awareness of the evolutionary crisis facing them at present.'

In the early 1970s, following his landing and walk on the Moon in Apollo 14, astronaut Edgar Mitchell spoke out. When he announced the establishment of his 'Institute of Noetic Sciences' much of what he had to say echoed the messages our extraterrestrial visitors;

"Fellow Humans: I believe that civilization is in a critical state, and mankind is at an evolutionary crossroad. On one hand problems and conflicts have arisen which are global in scale and have brought society to a condition of escalating planetary crisis. On the other hand, man's potential for creative change, fulfilment, and benevolent control of his environment have never been greater.

"I believe that both problems and potentialities are ultimately a function of human consciousness, i.e., there will never be a better world until there are better people. The most effective and enduring way to resolve the problems and to realise the potentialities is through the enlightenment of individuals.

"I believe man's consciousness is the critical factor in the future we will build for ourselves, therefore: We need to know more about the mysteries of the ages.....what is human consciousness? How can it be developed? Does it survive physical death? .....More about the energies which provide life and activity in physical matter on our planet in order to discover new energy sources for our nation and the world." Whilst Mitchell did not admit to any contact with extraterrestrials, he was definitely expressing their sentiments.

When researcher, Richard Thieme asked him if extraterrestrials had assisted our first ventures to the Moon, Mitchell cryptically replied; *"If we could do what they can do, they wouldn't have sent me to the Moon in a 'tin lizzie'!"*

In a later interview with Steven Greer he said; *"Yes, there have been UFO visitations. There have been crashed craft. There have been material and bodies recovered. And there is some group of people somewhere that may or may not be associated with Government at this point, but certainly were at one time that have this knowledge. They have been attempting to conceal this knowledge or not permit it to be widely disseminated."*

At a conference in the USA in the 1990s, he had more to say, but non-the-less divulged nothing that could have been considered a state secret or an admission of a contact of his own; *"The American government, and governments throughout the world, have thousands of files of UFO sightings which cannot be explained. As a scientist, it is logical to me that at least some of these have been witness to alien craft...*

"The question of whether or not aliens are still visiting us is more complex. Such is our existing secret technology that what may look like an alien craft may well turn out to be a top-secret military plane. On the other hand, the craft may be an alien spaceship. Personally, however, I'd say yes, it's quite possible we are still being visited."

In 1973, the 'British Interplanetary Society' published the following letter in their magazine *'Spaceflight'* Vol. 16 No. 2. Whilst there is no way of verifying the authenticity of this report, it does reflect the alien opinions apparently being expressed to the contactees of the day. The following was apparently the transmission researchers 'picked up'; *'Earth creatures are now beginning to venture out into space. This activity must be viewed with concern, as these creatures are potentially dangerous. They have very imperfect understanding of and control over their emotions, and are consequently extremely unpredictable and unreliable.*

'In addition, they are very quarrelsome and exceptionally stupid. For instance, they have a money system which is based on, and indeed encourages some of their worst instincts, notably selfishness, greed and lust for power. The same system effectively and drastically slows down every effort these creatures make to improve their living conditions and increase their knowledge – this includes space research.

'Earth creatures seem incapable of working together on a large scale for the common good. On the contrary, there are endless stupid quarrels during which large numbers may be killed and maimed by their own species, often using exceptionally brutal and cruel methods.

'Efforts are being made to instil some measure of cosmic responsibility into these creatures, by telepathy and other means, but so far these efforts have met with little success, as the stupidity, ignorance and complacency of these creatures is almost beyond belief.

'Meanwhile, there is a grave danger that the species will become extinct, either owing to unwise exploitation of natural resources leading to deterioration of the environment, or to self-destructive wars. Although one regrets the disappearance of any species from the Universe, it has to be admitted that this particular species is at the moment one of Nature's less successful experiments.

'For the time being, efforts will continue to prepare this very backward species for cosmic co-operation. In view of the unpromising material, it must be some considerable time before any tangible results can be expected.' Message ends!

Following his passing in 1962, over the subsequent sixty years, many have forgotten about, or never heard of the Canadian, Wilbur Smith, or his contact and work with the 'Space Brothers', whom he called 'The Boys Topside'.

Wilbur Smith was a highly respected Canadian scientist and senior government official. He had been Chief of the Telecommunications and Electronics Branch of the Dept. of Transport, receiving many awards, and owning several patents. His reputation was one of complete sincerity and integrity.

In 1968, following criticism from some people who said nothing during his life, the 'Ottawa New Sciences Club' published a lengthy article, in his defence, in their newsletter, *'Topside'*. They were angry that detractors now claimed that Wilbur's contact with the space people and 'Topside' was merely 'spiritualism'.

My friend and colleague, U.S. investigator Rosemary Decker, who was, for a long time, MUFON's historian, and a 'closet' contactee herself, was good friends with and a supporter of Wilbur Smith. She confirmed to me that Wilbur himself did have direct contact with the 'Space Brothers', and also received information via other contactees.

Wilbur Smith was originally a sceptic, and primarily a scientist. In the 1950s, with the advent of increased UFO activity around the planet, he made an intensive study into the mystery, and as an indefatigable searcher for advanced scientific truths, finally became convinced of the reality of extraterrestrials visiting Earth in spacecraft of superior technology, capable of performing feats which defied our present knowledge of physics. This led him to eventual direct communication with the 'Space Brothers', and knowledge of their philosophy. He said; "There was the answer in all its grandeur!"

In their *'Topside'* article, Wilbur's supporters lauded his achievements: *'In July 1967, the Canadian government, (with what appeared to be a change in its UFO policy), released to the press, through one of its Cabinet Ministers, the Hon. Paul Hellyer, (at that time the Minister of Defence), details of a hitherto secret UFO project, namely the establishment of a UFO landing site at its Defence Research Board Experimental Station in Suffolk, Alberta, making mention of an earlier special scientific committee set up in Canada to investigate UFOs, of which Wilbur Smith was a member.*

'It was further stated that as part of 'Project Magnet', Wilbur Smith set up at Shirley's Bay Research Station near Ottawa, specially designed apparatus for the purpose of detecting UFOs passing overhead. We may add that evidence exists of the official closing down of the UFO side of 'Project Magnet', after which Wilbur Smith continued this work on a private basis, with permission to use government laboratory facilities, etc., on his own time at no cost to Treasury.' ('Project Magnet' was officially created in 1950, and terminated at the end of 1954.)

In 1953, Wilbur, who was first and foremost still a patriot, had unsuccessfully urged for the official continuation of 'Project Magnet. He wrote in a report; *'It appears then, that we are faced with a substantial probability of the real existence of extraterrestrial vehicles, regardless of whether they fit into our scheme of things.*

'Such vehicles of necessity must use a technology considerably in advance of what we have. It is therefore submitted that this next step in this investigation should be a substantial effort towards the acquisition of as much as possible of this technology which would, without a doubt, be of great value to us.'

Wilbur received information from the 'Space Brothers' both personally and through other contactees. *'Topside'* had quite a lot to say about this;

'As regards the scientific data Wilbur Smith obtained from his space friends, 'The Boys from Topside', he was able to test their genuineness and practical workability by protracted tests and experiments in the laboratory. In this

connection it should be pointed out, that since it is against the Cosmic Laws of the Space Brothers to drop unearned answers to scientific questions into the laps of Earth scientists, all that Wilbur received from them were certain guidelines or suggested avenues of research for him to explore. The actual work of finding the answers to scientific problems was left for him to fathom out.

'Always, the Space Brothers were helpful, quick to point out when he was on the wrong track, and offering further suggestions of approach to the solution of the problem, but never once did they spell out the complete answer. This would have been contrary to the Universal Law, that there is no value or merit to anything that is not achieved by personal effort.

'However, by diligent research and many experiments on a trial or error basis, Wilbur eventually proved much of the truth of the scientific data conveyed to him by the Space Brothers and unique inventions resulted. Some of these devices, thoroughly tested and proved accurate in results by Wilbur and his group, have regrettably remained unacceptable to Earth scientists because of their unorthodox origin, but the day may come when they will be used for the benefit of humanity.'

In 1958 Wilbur wrote; 'It soon became apparent that there was a very real and quite large gap between the alien science and the science in which I had been trained. Certain crucial experiments were suggested and carried out, and in each case the experiments confirmed the validity of the alien science.'

'Topside' went on to say; 'It may interest our readers to learn that the specially-selected contactee used by the Space Brothers to pass on purely scientific data for Wilbur Smith, invariably found this information completely unintelligible – but it proved most pertinent to, and was clearly understood by Wilbur.

'It is a strange fact, but since the passing of Wilbur Smith, this particular channel has never been used again, which would seem to indicate proof-positive of the genuineness of the contact. Conversely, the contactee channels supplying information on the Space Brothers' Philosophy remain open to us – proof that we still have a job to do. Our space friends are wonderfully logical!'

Wilbur once said; "The Space Brothers often work this way, using any sincere, receptive channel through whom to pass on valuable information. Any *dedicated UFO worker may be assured that his or her services, either consciously or unconsciously, are being effectively used by those of the space people concerned with the welfare of their Earth Brothers, as part of the Great Plan to enlighten mankind on Earth and prepare it for the wider horizons of the New Age.'*

Philip Human, from the South African group 'Contact', published a very enlightening article in their *'Skywatch'* newsletter in 1968.

He spoke their own work, research and contacts with these saucer occupants and those who live among us. He addressed the claims of people who have reported an interaction with these beings.

'Already there are scores of people who claim to have had a physical contact with space people, and some have even travelled in their craft. There are others who have had similar experiences, but for reasons of their own, have preferred to remain silent rather than to be silenced.

'Unfortunately, some of these claims were later proved to be untrue, as was the case with some 'genuine' flying saucer pictures which turned out to be fakes. But this still leaves us with the true contactee, and the genuine saucer photographs which compel us to continue investigating, sky-watching and consciously welcoming our visitors until contact is established.

'How I wish the whole world would accept them as friends and bid them welcome. They have told us repeatedly that they "come in peace". But this is how two saucer pilots feel at present about our planet and its people;

"If only the people of your planet would accept our friendship, all the knowledge we have gained would be yours. Your planet would never regret taking us as their friends. Your nations would learn to live in peace. Conditions on your planet would change. There would be no more poverty and no wars.

"How I wish we could come freely to your planet, but this is impossible. We cannot land where we choose to. We have to get permission from our high superiors, and they will not give permission until your planet has fully accepted us.

"WE COME ONLY IN PEACE! We do not wish to invade your planet. We only wish to bring happiness and peace and to teach you better ways of living. There are many other planets that have accepted this. Why are the Earth people so different?"

'Another one said: "I was patrolling your Solar System, and whilst gazing down on your beautiful planet, I wondered to myself why people of Earth were so different.

"When I once spent a period of time on your planet, I encountered many strange beliefs that you people have about people on other planets. The majority believe that the planet Earth is the only inhabited one in the heavens. But when the Almighty Creator created your planet, He also created other planets. He not only created life on all His creations, but He also gave them intelligence.

'But there are people who believe that inhabitants from other planets are deformed and hideous creatures who wish only to bring harm to your planet. Believe me, we have all been created in the same image and likeness. We all see, hear, speak and look the same. But the strangest belief of all is that space people are supposed to be spirits who do not exist in the flesh. They can walk through doors and walls, and cannot die.

"We all have a body of flesh and blood. We can die like anyone else! We feel sorrow and pain. We also feel happiness and joy. All the solar systems that my ancestors have visited, and all the solar systems that I have travelled to, all those people have flesh and blood. They all resemble our likeness. They do not exist in spirit form. They are all made the same – flesh and blood.

"If your people would accept us as their friends, our craft would come to your planet, division after division. Your skies would ring with the noise of our magnetic motors. Our knowledge would be yours, and all that we have gained over the many centuries would be given to you FREELY.

"Forgive me if I was preaching, but I have often wondered about your peoples and your planet. Let us hope that some day your planet will accept us as your friends and brothers!"

Philip Human finished his article with these words; *'Let us therefore not deviate from the course we have set ourselves: spread the news that flying saucers are real; that man on planet Earth is not an unique creature, that we have mighty friends, loving friends, who are willing to share their all if only we would accept their friendship instead of begrudging them an abode in our Father's house of 'many mansions'.*

These were the sentiments of many at the time, but our perceptions had changed by the end of the twentieth century, when the 'bug-eyed' greys with their bedroom abductions, and objectionable behaviour became more and more prevalent.

MUSIC

Many UFO advocates have not considered the effect musical notes can have upon us, physically, mentally and emotionally, however, it appears that our extraterrestrial visitors have also used this method to communicate with us.

In South Africa, in 1981, after housewife Connie Cook Smith stood transfixed by a bright white light, hovering outside her window, she said her head was full of music and words, which she did not fully understand. She felt, nevertheless, compelled to 'get the music down on paper'. Previously, she had no musical training at all, except for a few piano lessons as a child, and a stint in the percussion section of her school band. She bought a small electric keyboard, and began 'tinkering'.

Researcher, James Schmaltz, wrote; *'...the songs she produces are baffling to musicologists. David Watt, a senior writer for 'Rolling Stone' magazine was quoted as saying there is something 'otherworldly' about the songs, which utilize notes 'that seem to come from somewhere else, a few of which don't even translate to music paper'. "Technically, they don't even exist", stated Chicago record producer and music expert, Jim Van Petten.*

'.....It's not the words in the songs that are supposed to impart celestial information – in fact, a lot of songs have no lyrics at all – but rather the vibration of the pieces themselves.'

Connie, who claimed many visits from the spacemen, including a later manifestation of a being in her bathroom, whilst she was brushing her teeth, said; *"Playing their songs fills your mind with wordless instructions on how to be happier, less stressful, healthier and gentler. But, most of all, the music helps achieve what is supposedly the ultimate guide of humankind – to become fourth dimensional."*

Apparently, some medical practitioners took to playing her music to patients, and in one case, confirmed by her astonished doctor, one woman's tumours had turned from malignant to benign.

In my book, *'The Days of the Space Brothers'*, I discuss New Zealand contactee, 'Mr. X', and of how his extraterrestrial contacts imparted a musical talent into him. Previously he had no musical talent whatsoever.

Australian investigator, Fred Stone, who also claimed secret contact with the 'Space Brothers', visited Mr. X in 1964, and had this to say; *'Mr. X is a great musician and composer. He claimed the 'Space People' had inspired many of his compositions. Half way during the evening he said he felt moved to improve a piece of music – a simple composition which had just come floating through his mind. He went to the piano and began playing. Suddenly I felt myself also being moved, and as each note was played, I knew what was coming and began to hum the tune as though I had known it all the while. At the end I asked Mr. X if he knew the name of the tune, and he replied that - no he didn't know – what was it?*

'Without thinking I said 'Dedication'- there are verses to it. Play it again.' He returned to the piano, and as he replayed the theme, the verses came into the mind telepathically from the Space Brothers, who were unseen, yet present. This was witnessed by everyone present at the time.

'Surely this was evidence that we two men were being moved together in unison to be instruments of service. Maybe you may not be impressed by this account, or feel it was a proof of the genuineness of either party, but one had to be present to know what was felt and transpired in that room. We were not being moved by our own powers, but from those of a much higher source.'

Mr. X's 'music' has intrigued me. Perhaps he was unwittingly channelling it and passing on more information and inspirational contact from his two friends. Our bodies and cells react to sound – their vibrations and frequencies. Perhaps there were more messages being secretly transmitted within the pulse and harmonics of the notes.

Contactee George van Tassel and his family also sang popular songs, and sometimes hymns to their guests under the 'Giant Rock'. A couple who were visiting commented; "On one occasion they sang a certain song which Van had obtained directly from one of his space contacts. To us the music was very unusual, and the words were both simple and beautiful."

As an investigator, I have always found the claims of self-professed 'contactee', Howard Menger, to be very dubious. It is, however, interesting that he also claimed that although he could not play the piano, he was able to play music that the Space Brothers had taught him.

They explained that every note had a specific density and frequency which causes a sympathetic vibration when created at the correct frequency and in certain combinations. People's subconscious state would initially be affected when hearing the themes, and they would later react in their conscious state with increased understanding and brotherly love toward one another.

In my book, *'The Alien Gene'*, I discuss the events on Waiheke Island, which is just off the coast of New Zealand. In the 1970s some residents witnessed many visitations by, and had contact with, humanoid aliens who were working with scientists on a secret project. Patty, one of those involved, said that sometimes the 'visitors' would walk around, unrecognised, in the town. The project closed down later, and when the children reached adulthood, many left the island.

In 1999 Patty and her then partner, Mark, went back to visit her father, and they met up with all their childhood friends in the local pub, where Mark and Patty were singing in a band.

Their friend Gillian reminisced; "It was so strange, a lot of others were there, people we had gone to school with. It was like something had simultaneously drawn us all to come back at the same time. Many of our contemporaries were very musical, it was something in the notes and rhythm, and we all felt this tremendous bond and connection with each other."

Throughout history we have been aware of the hidden elements in sound and music. Acoustic phenomena – sound, pitch, rhythm, frequency, vibration, resonance – have all been known to produce an amazing effect and outcomes in unimaginable ways. In fact, these subliminal forces are far more powerful than most people realise.

The Egyptians, Greeks and Romans all incorporated music in their sacred rituals and ceremonies, as did the Sumerians before them. The Gregorian Chants of the Catholic Church were believed to impart spiritual blessings when sung in harmony during religious masses. The Tibetans use sound and vibration in their religious practices, including the art of levitation.

Two modern 'New Age' composers, Steve Halpern and Medwyn Goodall, both credit their music to 'higher sources'.

Steve Halpern said; "As my life and career have unfolded, I've had a number of experiences that suggest some of the insights I've received in vision, meditation and dreams had an extraterrestrial dimension."

Medwyn Goodall was also forthcoming; "I have four guides who assist me with my music. They act as a single entity. They do not communicate with me verbally, and there is nothing written down, we communicate through music.

"Today, I have a clearer picture of the guides. There are four entities who appear to be humanoid males. They pool their talents together and act as one. They have a spokesperson who I now know by name. He has long white hair, blue eyes and a youthful appearance.

"I have now come to understand that their work with me is to inter-weave light and high vibrational frequency into the very fabric of my music. The albums are light encoded and have the divine capacity to spiritually awaken people, to heal, to trigger dormant artistic talents and to ground light into Mother Earth.

"I have come to understand that other guides assist on a program which is very specific. If I wanted to produce a very ethnic album, a guide who has experience of that culture would join in the influencing of the music."

It has become obvious, due to the testimony of many people, that there are several ways in which extraterrestrials can communicate with us.

INDEX

www.ingramcontent.com/pod-product-compliance
Lightning Source LLC
Chambersburg PA
CBHW072037020426
42334CB00017B/1304